THE JERUSALEM TALMUD
FIRST ORDER: ZERAÏM
TRACTATES *PEAH* AND *DEMAY*

STUDIA JUDAICA

FORSCHUNGEN ZUR WISSENSCHAFT DES JUDENTUMS

HERAUSGEGEBEN VON
E. L. EHRLICH

BAND XIX

WALTER DE GRUYTER · BERLIN · NEW YORK
2000

THE JERUSALEM TALMUD
תלמוד ירושלמי

FIRST ORDER: ZERAÏM
סדר זרעים
TRACTATES *PEAH* AND *DEMAY*
מסכות פיאה ודמאי

EDITION, TRANSLATION, AND COMMENTARY

BY
HEINRICH W. GUGGENHEIMER

WALTER DE GRUYTER · BERLIN · NEW YORK
2000

ISBN 978-3-11-068133-8
e-ISBN (PDF) 978-3-11-081658-7

This volume is text- and page-identical with the hardback published in 2000.

Library of Congress Control Number: 2020942836

Bibliographic information published by the Deutsche Nationalbibliothek
The Deutsche Nationalbibliothek lists this publication in the
Deutsche Nationalbibliografie;
detailed bibliographic data are available on the Internet at http://dnb.dnb.de.

Printing and binding: CPI books GmbH, Leck

www.degruyter.com

Preface

The present volume is the second in a projected series of five volumes covering the entire first order of the Jerusalem Talmud. The principles of the edition regarding text, vocalization and commentary have been spelled out in detail in the Introduction to the first volume. The text is based on the *editio princeps* and, where that text is manifestly corrupt, on manuscript readings. There are no emendations. For ease of study, the text in the present edition has been subdivided into paragraphs and vocalized following the rules of Sephardic rabbinic Hebrew. The extensive commentary is not based on emendations. Biographical notes have been attached to the names of those personalities not already mentioned in the first volume.

Again I wish to thank my wife, Dr. Eva Guggenheimer, who acted as critic, style editor, proof reader, and expert on the Latin and Greek vocabulary. Her own notes on some possible Latin and Greek etymologies are identified by (E. G.).

Contents

Introduction to Tractate Peah	1
Peah Chapter 1, אלו דברים	
Halakhah 1	3
Halakhah 2	59
Halakhah 3	61
Halakhah 4-5	65
Halakhah 6	73
Peah Chapter 2, ואילו מפסיקין	
Halakhah 1	83
Halakhah 2	93
Halakhah 3	96
Halakhah 4	98
Halakhah 5	99
Halakhah 6	102
Halakhah 7	108
Peah Chapter 3, מלבנות	
Halakhah 1	115
Halakhah 2	120
Halakhah 3	123

Halakhah 4 128
Halakhah 5 130
Halakhah 6 133
Halakhah 7 136
Halakhah 8 138
Halakhah 9 146
Halakhah 10 155

Peah Chapter 4, הפיאה
Halakhah 1 158
Halakhah 2 163
Halakhah 3 171
Halakhah 4 175
Halakhah 5 176
Halakhah 6 180
Halakhah 7 190
Halakhah 8 182

Peah Chapter 5, גדיש
Halakhah 1 196
Halakhah 2 203
Halakhah 3 212
Halakhah 4 215
Halakhah 5 218
Halakhah 6 221
Halakhah 7 225

Peah Chapter 6, בית שמאי
Halakhah 1 227
Halakhah 2 233
Halakhah 3 240
Halakhah 4 248
Halakhah 5 251

Halakhah 6 253
Halakhah 7 254
Halakhah 8 256
Halakhah 9 259
Halakhah 10 261

Peah Chapter 7, כל זית
Halakhah 1 264
Halakhah 2 269
Halakhah 3 274
Halakhah 4 275
Halakhah 5 285
Halakhah 6 287
Halakhah 7 300
Halakhah 8 302

Peah Chapter 8, אלו דברים
Halakhah 1 309
Halakhah 2 312
Halakhah 3 315
Halakhah 4 317
Halakhah 5 317
Halakhah 6 322
Halakhah 7 325
Halakhah 8 330
Halakhah 9 336

Introduction to Tractate Demay 347

Demay Chapter 1, הקלים
Halakhah 1 351

Halakhah 2 364
Halakhah 3 373
Halakhah 4 392

Demay Chapter 2, אלו דברים
Halakhah 1 399
Halakhah 2 423
Halakhah 3 459
Halakhah 4 465
Halakhah 5 475
Halakhah 6 477

Demay Chapter 4, הלוקח פירות
Halakhah 1 479
Halakhah 2 481
Halakhah 3 486
Halakhah 4 490
Halakhah 5 491
Halakhah 6 496
Halakhah 7 501
Halakhah 8 503
Halakhah 9 506

Demay Chapter 5, הלקח מן הנחתום
Halakhah 1 508
Halakhah 2 514
Halakhah 3 523
Halakhah 4 526
Halakhah 5 528
Halakhah 6 530
Halakhah 7 532
Halakhah 8 534

Halakhah 9 535
Halakhah 10 545

Demay Chapter 6, המקבל
Halakhah 1 548
Halakhah 2 555
Halakhah 3 558
Halakhah 4 572
Halakhah 5 573
Halakhah 6 576
Halakhah 7 582
Halakhah 8-9 583
Halakhah 10 588
Halakhah 11 590
Halakhah 12 593

Demay Chapter 7, המזמין
Halakhah 1 600
Halakhah 2 607
Halakhah 3 610
Halakhah 4 611
Halakhah 5 613
Halakhah 6-7 622
Halakhah 8 622
Halakhah 9 629
Halakhah 10 633
Halakhah 11 635

Indices
Index of Biographical Notes 641
Index of Biblical Quotations 642
Index of Greek and Latin Words 643

Introduction to Tractate Peah

Peah, "corner," is the first tractate dealing specifically with agricultural laws, in particular with the obligatory gifts to the poor. The tractate derives its name from the first such obligation, *viz.*, not to harvest the last corner of one's field but to let the poor gather its produce. It is also the treatise in which the general obligation to give to charity is established (Halakhah 1:1), as well as the rules of organized and private charity which are detailed in Chapter 8. In Halakhah 1, the obligations of honoring father and mother, and that of using one's time, not only one's money, for charitable deeds are discussed at length. In addition, the doctrine of reward and punishment in this and the future worlds is developed in detail.

The obligation of *peah* is discussed in Chapters One to Three and the first part of Chapter Four. The definition of the minimum size of a field for *peah* leads to a digression, in Chapter Three, on the use of real estate in all kinds of contracts and documents.

The second obligation is to let the poor collect the gleanings of a harvest, as described in the story of Ruth. This is the theme of the second half of Chapter Four.

Next comes the right of the poor to collect sheaves forgotten on the field; connected with it is the definition of abandoned property, discussed in Chapters Five and Six.

Chapter Seven deals with the right of the poor to harvest single berries growing on vines and the gleanings of olives which technically is quite distinct from the right to gleanings of grain stalks. In addition, one discusses the produce of a vineyard in the fourth year after it was planted, when its fruit should be eaten as a thanksgiving.

Finally, Chapter Eight takes up the time frame in which the poor may collect their produce and, mainly, the general rules of the public welfare organization that every Jewish community is required to establish, including criteria of entitlement of the poor.

Commentaries consulted include all those contained in the Wilna editions of the Yerushalmi (mainly of R. Moshe Margalit, R. Solomon Cirillo, the Gaon of Wilna, and R. Jacob David from Słuck), the Mishnah (mainly Maimonides, R. Simson of Sens, and R. Isaac ben Malchisedek Simponti), and the Code of Maimonides (mainly R. Joseph Karo and R. David ibn Zimra). In addition, the editions and commentaries by R. Eliahu Fulda, R. Moshe Ḥabib, R. Zacharias Frankel, *Sefer Nir* by R. Meïr Marim of Kobrin, and *Tosefta Kifshutah* by R. Saul Lieberman were used constantly. All other sources used are indicated in the commentary.

אלו דברים פרק ראשון

(fol. 15a) **משנה א.** אֵילּוּ דְּבָרִים שֶׁאֵין לָהֶן שִׁיעוּר הַפֵּיאָה וְהַבִּכּוּרִים וְהָרֵאָיוֹן וּגְמִילוּת חֲסָדִים וְתַלְמוּד תּוֹרָה. אֵילּוּ דְּבָרִים שֶׁאָדָם אוֹכֵל פֵּירוֹתֵיהֶן בָּעוֹלָם הַזֶּה וְהַקֶּרֶן קַיֶּמֶת לוֹ לָעוֹלָם הַבָּא כִּיבּוּד אָב וָאֵם וּגְמִילוּת חֲסָדִים וַהֲבָאַת שָׁלוֹם בֵּין אָדָם לַחֲבֵירוֹ וְתַלְמוּד תּוֹרָה כְּנֶגֶד כּוּלָּן.

Mishnah 1: These are the matters that have no measure[1]: Peah[2], first fruits[3], appearance[4], works of kindness[5], and Torah study[6]. These are the matters whose product a person eats in this world and whose capital remains for him[7] in the future world: Honoring father and mother, works of kindness, making peace between people; the study of Torah is worth all of these.

1 These are obligations spelled out in the Torah, so one has to fulfill them; but the Torah did not specify either minimum or maximum obligation. However, there are rabbinic minima and sometimes maxima established for all obligations.

2 In harvesting a field, one is not permitted to harvest the last corner (פאה); that must be abandoned to be harvested by the poor (*Lev.* 19:9,23:22). There is no minimum mentioned in the Torah; the Talmud will discuss whether one may declare one's entire field as *Peah*.

3 There is an obligation to bring the first fruits of one's land to the Temple, *Lev.* 23:19, 34:26; *Neh.* 10:36. No amount has been specified. This obligation is the subject of tractate *Bikkurim.*

4 There is an obligation to appear in the Temple on the three holidays of pilgrimage (*Ex.* 23:17, 34:23-24, *Deut.* 16:16). It is forbidden to appear in the Temple emptyhanded (*Ex.* 23:15, 34:20, *Deut.* 16:16), i. e., without bringing a sacrifice. The Torah does not directly spell out the value of the sacrifice, but the verse in *Deuteronomy* requires it to

be "proportional to the blessing that the Eternal has bestowed on you." The Talmud will discuss which of the two obligations (appearance or sacrifice) is meant here.

5 Charity has two aspects: one is giving money and valuables to the needy; this has no explicit lower and upper limit, but it does have rabbinic limits in both directions. This, in addition to the laws of *Peah*, is one of the topics of the tractate. The other aspect is giving one's time to attend funerals, weddings, visiting the sick and mourners, to work for the public good, and similar deeds. That aspect has no limits, upper or lower, expressed anywhere.

6 It is written of the Torah (*Jos.* 1:8): "You should meditate upon it day and night." Hence, there is no upper limit. The obligation of Torah study can be fulfilled by the recitation of *Shema'*, but that recitation is also an independent obligation. Hence, Torah study *per se* has no lower limit.

7 As deeds which merit reward in the future life.

הלכה א: רִבִּי בִּנְיָמִין בַּר לֵוִי אָמַר רִבִּי יִצְחָק וְרִבִּי אִימִּי הֲווֹן יְתִיבִין מַקְשׁוֹי אֲמַר לָמָּה לֹא תַנֵּינָן תְּרוּמָה עִמְּהוֹן. אָמַר רִבִּי אִימִּי מִפְּנֵי הַמַּחְלוֹקֶת. אָמַר רִבִּי יוֹסֵי אָדָם עוֹשֶׂה כָל־שָׂדֵהוּ בִּיכּוּרִים וְאֵין אָדָם עוֹשֶׂה כָל־שָׂדֵהוּ תְּרוּמָה. הֲתִיבוּן הֲרֵי הוּא אוֹמֵר פֵּיאָה הֲרֵי אֵין אָדָם עוֹשֶׂה כָל־שָׂדֵהוּ פֵּיאָה וְתַנִּיתָהּ. אָמַר רִבִּי יוֹסֵי קְצִירַת שִׁיבּוֹלֶת הָרִאשׁוֹנָה דוֹמָה לְמֵירוּחוֹ עַד שֶׁלֹּא קָצַר שִׁיבּוֹלֶת הָרִאשׁוֹנָה לֹא נִתְחַייְבָה שָׂדֵהוּ פֵּיאָה. מִשֶּׁקָּצַר שִׁיבּוֹלֶת הָרִאשׁוֹנָה נִתְחַייְבָה כָל־שָׂדֵהוּ פֵּיאָה. בִּיקֵּשׁ לַעֲשׂוֹת כָּל־שָׂדֵהוּ פֵּיאָה עוֹשֶׂה. בְּרַם הָכָא עַד שֶׁלֹּא נִתְמָרֵחַ הַפְּרִי לֹא נִתְחַייֵב פִּרְיוֹ תְּרוּמָה. בִּיקֵּשׁ לַעֲשׂוֹת כָּל־פִּרְיוֹ תְּרוּמָה אֵינוֹ עוֹשֶׂה דְּתַנֵּינָן תַּמָּן הָאוֹמֵר כָּל־גּוֹרְנִי תְּרוּמָה וְכָל־עִיסָּתִי חַלָּה לֹא אָמַר כְּלוּם עַד שֶׁיְּשַׁייֵר מִקְצָת.

Halakha 1: Rebbi Benjamin ben Levi[7] said: Rebbi Isaac and Rebbi Immi[8] were sitting and asking: Why did they not state *terumah*[9] with these? Rebbi Immi said, because of the disagreement[10]. Rebbi Yose said[11], one may declare one's entire field first fruits but one may not declare one's entire field *terumah*. They objected: Look, it mentions *peah*, but nobody may make his entire field *peah*[12], but it was stated! Rebbi Yose said: The cutting of the first ear is compared to smoothing[13]. Before he cut the first ear, the field was not obligated for *peah*. After he cut the first ear, the entire field became obligated for *peah* and if he then wants to declare his entire field as *peah* he may do so[14]. But here, before he smoothed his grain heap, the heap was not obligated for *terumah*. When he wants to declare his entire heap as *terumah*, he may not do so since we have stated there (*Ḥallah* 1:9): "He who says: My whole threshing floor shall be *terumah* or my entire dough shall be *ḥallah*[15] did not say anything unless he reserves part of it[16]."

7 A Galilean Amora of the fourth generation, one of the teachers of R. Abun.

8 He is Rebbi Ammi.

9 The gift to the Cohen from the harvest, cf. *Berakhot*, Chapter 1, Note 3. There are two kinds of *terumah*. The first one, *terumah gedolah* "the great *terumah*" must be given to the Cohen as absolutely first gift after the completion of the harvest. Then a tithe of ten percent, *maäser*, must be given to the Levite who in turn has to give ten percent, one percent of the original, to the Cohen. The two *terumot* must be eaten in ritual purity by the priestly families; in contrast the tithe is a civil obligation and is profane food in the hands of the Levite. An infraction of the rules of purity for *terumah* is a deadly sin. One speaks here about *terumah gedolah* for the quantity of which the Torah does not give any rules; hence, one grain may be given for an entire silo full of grain. Today, this grain, being ritually impure, has to be burned.

10 In Mishnah *Terumot* 3:5 we find a disagreement between Tannaïm. Rebbi Eliezer is of the opinion that one may not give more than 10% of the crop as *terumah gedolah*. Rebbi Ismael gives 50% as upper limit, and Rebbis Aqiba and Tarphon permit one to give as much as one likes on condition that some profane food be left over. Hence, one cannot say that *terumah gedolah* has no upper limit from the Torah, at least not according to Rebbis Eliezer and Ismael.

11 Rebbi Yose (the fourth generation Amora) explains that even

according to Rebbis Aqiba and Tarphon, who are followed in practice, *terumah* has no place in the Mishnah.

12 Tosephta 1:1.

13 In harvesting grain, the last operation is smoothing the heap of grain (so that theft could be easily detected. In modern terms, the equivalent would be storing the grain in a silo.) *Terumah* is not due before the end of the harvesting process since it is an obligation only for food. The implication is that workers may eat from the kernels before the end of the harvesting process (cutting, threshing, winnowing, and storing); after that one may not eat from it before *terumot* are separated.

14 It is not "the entire field," only "the entire field that is obligated for *peah*;" hence, the Tosephta that forbids the entire field will permit the field minus one stalk.

15 *Ḥallah* is the obligatory gift to the Cohen from a (large enough) batch of bread dough, discussed in tractate *Ḥallah*. It has the status of *terumah*; hence, today is must be burned.

16 Even though the remainder may be a single grain; the difference to *peah* is in the theoretical basis, not the practical side.

שִׁיבּוֹלֶת הָרִאשׁוֹנָה מַהוּ שֶׁתְּהֵא חַייֶבֶת בְּפֵיאָה. אֵיפְשַׁר לוֹמַר הִיא חִייְבָה כָּל־שָׂדֵהוּ פֵּיאָה וְהִיא חַייֶבֶת בְּפֵיאָה. קָצַר שִׁיבּוֹלֶת הָרִאשׁוֹנָה וְנִשְׂרְפָה מַהוּ שֶׁיְּהֵא צָרִיךְ לִקְצוֹר פַּעַם שְׁנִיָּיה. נִשְׁמְעִינָהּ מִן הָדָא. קָצַר חֶצְיָהּ וּמָכַר חֶצְיָהּ וּמָכַר מַה שֶׁקָּצַר קָצַר חֶצְיָהּ וְהִקְדִּישׁ מַה שֶׁקָּצַר נוֹתֵן מִן הַמְשׁוּאָר עַל הַכֹּל. וְהֶקְדֵּשׁ לָאו כִּשְׂרוּף הוּא. הָדָא אָמְרָה קָצַר שִׁיבּוֹלֶת הָרִאשׁוֹנָה וְנִשְׂרְפָה אֵינוֹ צָרִיךְ לִקְצוֹר פַּעַם שְׁנִיָּיה.

Is the first ear obligated for *peah*? It is impossible to say that it obligated the entire field for *peah* and itself should be obligated for *peah*[17]. If he cut the first ear and it was burned, does he have to cut another one a second time[18]? Let us hear it from the following[19]: "If he cut half the field and sold the other half, or he sold what he had cut, if he cut half the field and dedicated[20] what he had cut, he gives from the leftover for everything." If it is dedicated is it not as if it was burned[21]? This says that if he cut the first ear and it was burned, he does not have to cut a second time[22].

17 As explained in the preceding paragraph.

18 If he wants to give his entire field to the poor as *peah*, must the ear he cut first be in existence at the moment of dedication?

19 A statement similar to this *baraita* is in Tosephta 1:9; the reference is to Mishnah 2:7: "If he cut half the field and sold the other half, the buyer gives *peah* for everything. If he cut half the field and dedicated the other half, the one who redeems it gives *peah* for everything." In both cases, the field is given or dedicated as is, with all obligations on the harvest, since *peah* must be given at the last corner to be harvested.

20 To the Temple, the proceeds to be used for the upkeep of the Temple. While the material is in the hands of the Temple authorities, any private use of it is forbidden.

21 Since no benefit whatsoever may be derived from it at this stage.

22 Because if he dedicated the first half and cut the second half for himself, he must give *peah* for the entire field from his part. If we replace the dedicated half by the burned ear, we have exactly the case that we are dealing with.

כִּילָּה אֶת שָׂדֵהוּ אַתְּ אָמַר חָזְרָה פֵּיאָה לָעֲמָרִין. מַהוּ שֶׁתַּחְזוֹר פֵּיאָה לִקְצִירַת שִׁיבּוֹלֶת הָרִאשׁוֹנָה. אָמַר רִבִּי יוֹסֵי נֵילַף פֵּיאַת עֲמָרִין מִפֵּיאַת קָמָה. מַה פֵּאַת קָמָה לֹא חָזְרָה קָמָה לִקְצִירַת שִׁיבּוֹלֶת הָרִאשׁוֹנָה. אַף פֵּיאַת עֲמָרִין לֹא תַחְזוֹר פֵּיאָה לִקְצִירַת שִׁיבּוֹלֶת הָרִאשׁוֹנָה.

If he finished the field[23], you say that *peah* devolves on the sheaves. Would *peah* turn back to the first ear[24]? Rebbi Yose said, let us learn *peah* of sheaves from *peah* of standing grain. Since *peah* from standing grain does not return to the first ear[25], *peah* of sheaves likewise should not return to the first ear.

23 He harvested the entire field without leaving *peah* for the poor. The reference is to Tosephta 1:5: "If he did not give from standing grain, he must give from sheaves. If he did not give from sheaves, he must give from stacks. If he did not give from stacks, he must give from the grain heap. If he did not give from the grain heap before it was smoothed, he must first give *terumah*

and tithes and only then *peah*." See also Mishnah 1:6, Halakha 7:2, 4:1; an extended version is in Babli *Baba qama* 94a.

24 That the first cut also may be *peah* from its sheaf if the entire field was cut.

25 As explained in the preceding paragraph, the first cut is not subject to the laws of *peah* at all since it enables the laws to be applied.

הַפֵּיאָה יֵשׁ לָהּ שֵׁיעוּר מִלְּמַטָּן וְאֵין לָהּ שֵׁיעוּר מִלְּמַעְלָן. הַבִּיכּוּרִים וְהָרֵאָיוֹן אֵין לָהֶם שֵׁיעוּר לֹא מִלְּמַעְלָן וְלֹא מִלְּמַטָּן. אִית תַּנֵּי תַּנָּא הַפֵּיאָה וְהַבִּיכּוּרִים וְהָרֵאָיוֹן אֵין לָהֶם שֵׁיעוּר לֹא לְמַעְלָן וְלֹא לְמַטָּן. מַה נְפִיק מִן בֵּינֵיהוֹן וְהֵן חַד מִן שִׁשִּׁים. מַן דָּמַר הַפֵּיאָה יֵשׁ לָהּ שֵׁיעוּר מִלְּמַטָּן וְאֵין לָהּ שֵׁיעוּר מִלְּמַעְלָן מַה שֶׁנָּתַן נָתַן חָזַר וְהוֹסִיף חַיָּיב בְּמַעֲשֵׂר עַד שָׁעָה שֶׁיַּשְׁלִים. מַן דָּמַר הַפֵּיאָה וְהַבִּיכּוּרִים וְהָרֵאָיוֹן אֵין לָהֶם שֵׁיעוּר לֹא מִלְּמַעְלָן וְלֹא מִלְּמַטָּן מַה שֶּׁנָּתַן כְּבָר נִפְטַר. חָזַר וְהוֹסִיף חַיָּיב בְּמַעְשְׂרוֹת.

Peah has a minimum measure but no maximum measure. First fruits and appearance have neither minimum nor maximum measures. There are those who state: *Peah*, first fruits and appearance have no measure, neither minimum nor maximum. What is the difference between them, is it not one in sixty[26]? According to him who says that *peah* has a minimum measure but no maximum measure: What he gave[27], he gave; if he had second thoughts and added to it, it is subject to tithes until he makes up for it[28]. According to him who says *peah*, first fruits and appearance sacrifices have no measure, neither minimum nor maximum: What he gave already freed from the obligation; if he has second thoughts and adds, that is subject to tithes[20].

26 Mishnah 2 states that the rabbinic minimum for *peah* is one sixtieth of the field, $1\frac{2}{3}$ percent. In both formulations it is agreed that *peah* has no minimum from the Torah but it has a minimum by rabbinic usage. The problem is the strength of that rabbinic usage.

27 When he harvested but left less than $1\frac{2}{3}$% of the harvest standing on the field. The standing grain certainly has the status of *peah* and, no longer being the property of the farmer, is not subject to the requirement of *terumah* and tithes. [The interpretation of R. Simson of Sens is that, while as Biblical commandment there is no lower limit to what he must give, by rabbinic decree any gift of less than $1\frac{2}{3}$% is not considered *peah* and is subject to the laws of tithes even though it is the property of the poor and not of the farmer.]

28 Any amount he adds which together with the standing *peah* does not add up to $1\frac{2}{3}$% of the yield of the entire field, is a voluntary gift, rather than *peah*, and has the status of grain given after threshing and smoothing the heap. The farmer is obliged to separate from it *terumah* and tithes. Only if he reaches the rabbinic threshhold of $1\frac{2}{3}$% [according to R. Simson of Sens, only if he gives all of $1\frac{2}{3}$% at one time] does the rule of *peah* apply again and the produce may be taken by the poor without further obligation.

29 In this opinion, the rabbinic measure of $1\frac{2}{3}$% is a guideline, not a rigid prescription. Hence, if he gave any *peah*, he has fulfilled the biblical precept and the field is freed from any further obligation in this respect. Nothing he gives afterwards can have the status of *peah*.

רִבִּי בֶּרֶכְיָה בְּעִי וְלָמָּה לֹא תַנֵּינָן עֲפַר סוֹטָה. וְלָמָּה לֹא תַנֵּינָן אֵפֶר פָּרָה. וְלָמָּה לֹא תַנֵּינָן רוֹק יְבָמָה. וְלָמָּה לֹא תַנֵּינָן דַּם צִיפּוֹר שֶׁל מְצוֹרָע. לֹא אֲתִינָן מַתְנִיתָא אֶלָּא דְּבָרִים שֶׁהוּא מוֹסִיף עֲלֵיהֶן וְיֵשׁ בַּעֲשִׂיָּיתָן מִצְוָה. וְאֵילּוּ אַף עַל פִּי שֶׁהוּא מוֹסִיף עֲלֵיהֶן אֵין בַּעֲשִׂיָּיתָן מִצְוָה.

Rebbi Berekhiah asked: Why did we not state the dust for the straying[30]? Why did we not state the ashes of the heifer[31]? Why did we not state the spittle of the sister-in-law[32]? Why did we not state the blood of the bird for the "leper"[33]? Our[34] Mishnah deals only with things to which he may add and adding is a worthy deed. As for those, even though he may add to them, doing so is no worthy deed.

30 The straying wife who was seen in a secret rendez-vous with another man. The jealous husband may bring his wife to the Temple where she has to drink water mixed with some dust from the Temple floor as an ordeal (*Num.* 5). There is no minimum amount of that dust prescribed.

31 The ashes of the red heifer must be strewn on the water with which people defiled by contact with a dead body could be purified for entrance to the Temple (*Num.* 19). Since these ashes are extremely valuable, using more than a minimum amount is a misdeed.

32 The childless widow who is not married by her brother-in-law becomes free to marry outside the family only by removing a shoe from the foot of the unwilling brother-in-law and spitting out before him (*Deut.* 25:9). The spittle falling to the earth must be seen by the court but no minimum is established.

33 The bird needed for the ritual cleansing of the "leper" (*Lev.* 14:1-7). The symptoms of the "leper" have no relation to what today is called leprosy.

34 In old French sources, R. Simson of Sens and Tosaphot *Ḥagigah* 7a, this is a statement of the Amora R. Yose mentioned in the previous paragraphs, contemporary of R. Berekhiah.

וְהָרֵיאָוֹן. מַתְנִיתִין בְּרֵאָיַית קָרְבָּן אֲבָל בְּרֵאָיַת פָּנִים יֵשׁ לָהּ שִׁיעוּר. וַאֲתְיָיא כַּיי דָּמַר רִבִּי יוֹחָנָן מָעָה כֶסֶף שְׁתֵּי כֶסֶף דְּבַר תּוֹרָה.

"Appearance"[35]. Our Mishnah[36] is about appearance with a sacrifice, but appearance in person has a measure. This agrees with what R. Joḥanan said: "One silver obolus and two silver coins are words of the Torah"[37].

35 Quote from the Mishnah that introduces a new subject.

36 R. Simson of Sens already noted that this is a scribal error and that the subsequent discussion shows that it is the value of the obligatory sacrifice which has a fixed minimum. Hence, one should read: "Our Mishnah is about appearance with a sacrifice but appearance in person has no measure."

37 Mishnah Ḥagigah 1:2 fixes the minimum amount to be spent on the two obligatory sacrifices as, respectively, one silver obolus and two silver coins. [The two sacrifices are the holocaust for the altar and a family

sacrifice of which only a small part was burned on the altar. The houses of Shammai and Hillel disagree on the distribution of these sums but not on the principle that the first has to be a silver obolus and the second two silver coins.] According to most commentators, the "silver coins" mentioned also are oboli [6 oboli equal one drachma (denar) and four drachmas equal one tetradrachma (סלע)]. In the Roman empire only the emperor could mint silver coins. The Eastern mint was at Tyre; hence, silver coins are also called Tyrian money. Before the inflation of the military anarchy, local coinage was of copper and worth one eighth of the corresponding silver coinage.

The following discussion will determine whether these minimal amounts have rabbinic or biblical status.

תַּנָּא רִבִּי יַסָּא קוֹמֵי רִבִּי יוֹחָנָן רֵאָיָה כָּל־שֶׁהוּא חֲכָמִים הֵן שֶׁאָמְרוּ מָעָה כֶסֶף שְׁתֵּי כֶסֶף. אָמַר לֵיהּ יֵשׁ כֵּן זוֹ. אָמַר רִבִּי יוֹנָה וְכָל־הַשִּׁיעוּרִין לֹא חֲכָמִים הֵן שֶׁנָּתְנוּ כְּזַיִת מִן הַמֵּת וּכְזַיִת מִן הַנְּבֵלָיה וְכַעֲדָשָׁה מִן הַשֶּׁרֶץ. לֹא אַתְייָא מִישְׁאוֹל אֶלָּא כְּהָדָא דְתַנֵּי רִבִּי הוֹשַׁעְיָא. לֹא יֵרָאוּ פָנַי רֵיקָם אֲפִילוּ כָּל־שֶׁהוּא. חֲכָמִים הֵן שֶׁאָמְרוּ מָעָה כֶסֶף שְׁתֵּי כֶסֶף. וְקַשְׁיָא מִן דּוֹ סְמַךְ לִדְבַר תּוֹרָה הוּא. (חֲכָמִים הֵן שֶׁנָּתְנוּ כְּזַיִת מִן הַמֵּת וּכְזַיִת מִן הַנְּבֵילָה וְכַעֲדָשָׁה מִן הַשֶּׁרֶץ) [הוּא אָמַר חֲכָמִים הֵן שֶׁאָמְרוּ מָעָה כֶסֶף שְׁתֵּי כֶסֶף.] אָמַר רִבִּי יוֹסֵי בֵּי רִבִּי בוּן רִבִּי יוֹחָנָן כְּדַעְתֵּיהּ דְּרִבִּי יוֹחָנָן אָמַר כָּל־הַשִּׁיעוּרִין הֲלָכָה לְמֹשֶׁה מִסִּינַי דּוֹ אָמַר (fol. 15b) מָעָה כֶסֶף שְׁתֵּי כֶסֶף דְּבַר תּוֹרָה. רִבִּי הוֹשַׁעְיָא כְּדַעְתֵּיהּ דְּרִבִּי הוֹשַׁעְיָא אָמַר הָאוֹכֵל אִיסּוּר בִּזְמַן הַזֶּה צָרִיךְ לִרְשׁוֹם עָלָיו אֵת הַשִּׁיעוּרִין שֶׁמָּא יַעֲמוֹד בֵּית דִּין אַחֵר וִישַׁנֶּה עָלָיו אֶת הַשִּׁיעוּרִין וִיהֵא יוֹדֵעַ מֵאֵי זֶה שִׁיעוּר אָכַל.

Rebbi Yasa stated before Rebbi Johanan: The appearance is with anything[38]; the sages only said: "One silver obolus, two silver coins." He said to him: Is there anything like[39] that? Rebbi Jonah said, are not all measures determined by the sages[40]? They said: "The volume of an olive from a corpse[41], the volume of an olive from a cadaver[42], the volume of a lentil from a dead reptile[43]." The question here is only what Rebbi Hoshaia stated: (*Ex.* 23:15, 34:20) "They should not be seen before Me empty-handed," with anything[44]; the sages only said: "A silver obolus, two silver coins." The difficulty is that this[45] is support for the opinion that [the rule] is based on words of the Torah. He said that only the sages instituted[46]: "One silver obolus, two silver coins." Rebbi Yose ben Rebbi Abun said: Rebbi Johanan follows his own opinion since Rebbi Johanan said that all measures[47] are practice taught by Moses at Sinai; he says that "one obolus and two silver coins are the word of the Torah." Rebbi Hoshaia follows his own opinion since Rebbi Hoshaia said: He who eats forbidden food in the present time has to note down the quantities[48]; maybe a new court will arise and change the measures for him; then he will know what measure he ate.

38 One may appear in the Temple with one sacrifice for the appearance and one for the family holiday; no minimal expenditure is required. The monetary minimum is purely a rabbinic one.

39 Yerushalmi כן is contracted from כְּעֵין "in the kind of."

40 There are many biblical precepts that are applied only to some minimal amount and volume. None of these are spelled out in the Torah; they are all rabbinic formulations.

41 All rules of defilement by parts of a corpse apply only if a minimum size of the volume of one olive is present. Hence, somebody in a house in which less than that volume of a corpse is present may go to the Temple without the purification procedure of the ashes of the red heifer even though going there in impurity is a strict biblical prohibition.

42 To bring a sin offering for having eaten from a cadaver needs this minimum amount; the same minimum applies to the impurity caused by touching or carrying pieces of the cadaver of an otherwise kosher animal.

43 The minimum volume from a carcass that causes the severe impurity incurred by touching dead reptiles.

44 No minimal amount required.

45 Two verses (and an additional one in *Deut.*) insist that one may not appear empty-handed; this must mean that a negligible amount is counted as nothing and, therefore, forbidden by the Torah.

46 The text in parentheses is the

one of the Venice print here; the text in brackets is from the word-by-word parallel in *Ḥagigah* 1:2 (fol. 76b). The translation is that of the *Ḥagigah* text which alone makes sense. It may be assumed that the copyist of the manuscript used for printing had before him a manuscript in which the entire sentence was only indicated by "etc." and the copyist chose the wrong statement to complete.

47 Including those stated by R. Jonah and all similar ones.

48 Since one is required to bring a sin-offering only if he ate more than the volume of an olive, he is forbidden to bring one if he ate less than that volume. Hence, the determination of that volume is essential. The statement of R. Hoshaia here is attributed to R. Eleazar, student and colleague of R. Johanan, in Babli *Yoma* 80a. There, the interpretation is that not the rule of "volume of an olive" might change but rather its interpretation. A. Y. Greenfield, in his article "The Connection Between the Measures of an Olive and an Egg," תחומין 14 (5754) 396-411 shows that modern interpretations of the "volume of an olive" vary on a scale of 1 to 30. Hence, once the Temple is rebuilt, an authoritative interpretation is needed even according to R. Joḥanan.

אָמְרֵי חָזַר בֵּיהּ רִבִּי יוֹחָנָן מִן הָדָא. רִבִּי יוֹנָה וְרִבִּי יוֹסֵי תְּרַוֵּיהוֹן אָמְרִין לֹא חָזַר בֵּיהּ וְעוֹד מִן הָדָא דְּאָמַר רִבִּי לָא בְשֵׁם רִבִּי אַמִּי אִיתְפַּלְּגוּן חִזְקִיָּה וְרִבִּי יוֹחָנָן. חִזְקִיָּה אָמַר אָדָם חוֹלֵק אֶת חוֹבָתוֹ לִשְׁתֵּי בְהֵמוֹת. רִבִּי יוֹחָנָן אוֹמֵר אֵין אָדָם חוֹלֵק אֶת חוֹבָתוֹ לִשְׁתֵּי בְהֵמוֹת. אֶלָּא צָרִיךְ שֶׁיְּהֵא בְיָדוֹ שְׁתֵּי כֶסֶף לְכָל אַחַת וְאַחַת.

They said, Rebbi Joḥanan changed his mind about this. Rebbis Jonah and Yose said, he did not change his mind; additionally, Rebbi La said in the name of Rebbi Ammi: Ḥizqiah and Rebbi Joḥanan disagreed. Ḥizqiah said, a man may split his obligation for two animals[49]. Rebbi Joḥanan said, nobody may split his obligation for two animals, but for each one he has to have two silver coins in his hand[50].

49 He has to spend an obolus and two silver coins on animals for his pilgrimage but, since this is a rabbinic ordinance, it does not matter if the

amount is split to pay for several animals.

50 Since it is the practice from the days of Moses to spend two silver coins for one sacrifice of the larger kind, this has the status of a biblical command and cannot be abrogated. Similarly, a full obolus must be spend on one animal of the smaller kind.

רִבִּי שִׁמְעוֹן בֶּן לָקִישׁ בְּשֵׁם חִזְקִיָּה אָדָם טוֹפֵל בְּהֵמָה לִבְהֵמָה. וְאֵין אָדָם טוֹפֵל מָעוֹת לְמָעָה. הֵיךְ עֲבִידָא הָיוּ לְפָנָיו עֶשֶׂר בְּהֵמוֹת וְהִקְרִיב חָמֵשׁ בְּיוֹם טוֹב הָרִאשׁוֹן וְהַמּוֹתָר מַהוּ שֶׁיִּדָּחֶה לְיוֹם טוֹב הָאַחֲרוֹן. רִבִּי קְרִיסְפָּא אָמַר אִיתְפַּלְּגוּן רִבִּי יוֹחָנָן וְרִבִּי שִׁמְעוֹן בֶּן לָקִישׁ. חַד אָמַר דּוֹחֶה וְחָרָנָא אָמַר אֵינוֹ דוֹחֶה וְלָא יָדְעִין מַה אָמַר דָּא וּמַה אָמַר דָּא. אָמַר רִבִּי זְעִירָא נְפָרֵשׁ מִילֵּיהוֹן דְּרַבָּנָן מִן מִילֵּיהוֹן דְּרִבִּי יוֹחָנָן דּוּ אָמַר אָדָם טוֹפֵל מָעוֹת לְמָעוֹת וְאֵין אָדָם טוֹפֵל בְּהֵמָה לִבְהֵמָה דּוּ אָמַר דּוֹחֶה. וְרִבִּי שִׁמְעוֹן בֶּן לָקִישׁ דּוּ אָמַר אָדָם טוֹפֵל בְּהֵמָה לִבְהֵמָה וְאֵין אָדָם טוֹפֵל מָעוֹת לְמָעָה הוּא דּוּ אָמַר אֵינוֹ דוֹחֶה. אָתָא שִׁמְעוֹן בַּר וָנָא בְּשֵׁם רִבִּי יוֹחָנָן לְעוֹלָם הוּא מוֹסִיף וְהוֹלֵךְ וְדוֹחֶה אֶת יוֹם טוֹב עַד שֶׁיֹּאמַר אֵין בְּדַעְתִּי לְהוֹסִיף.

Rebbi Simeon ben Laqish in the name of Ḥizqiah: A person adjoins an animal to an animal but no person may adjoin money to money[51]. What may be done[52]? There were before him ten animals, he sacrificed five of them on the first holiday. May the remainder push aside the last holiday[53]? Rebbi Crispus said, Rebbi Joḥanan and Rebbi Simeon ben Laqish have differing opinions. One said, they push; the other one said, they do not push. We do not know who said what. Rebbi Zeïra said, we may explain the words of the rabbis through the words of Rebbi Joḥanan, who[54] said: A person may adjoin coins to coins but not animals to an animal. He must say, they push[55]. But Rebbi Simeon ben Laqish said, a person adjoins an animal to an animal but no person may adjoin money to money. He must say, they do not push[56]. Simeon bar Abba came in the name of Rebbi Joḥanan: He adds[57] and pushes the holiday further until he says: I do not intend to add further.

51 The parallel is in Babli *Ḥagigah* 8a (and Yerushalmi *Ḥagigah* 1:2). In the Babli, it is explained that the obligation to spend an obolus and two silver coins must be satisfied by unencumbered money. Now four years out of seven there is a second tithe on agricultural produce of the Land of Israel. That second tithe is the property of the farmer but it must be consumed in Jerusalem; it also may be redeemed by money and the money taken to Jerusalem and there spent on food to be consumed in Jerusalem. In addition, the tenth newborn calf or lamb in a herd must be taken to Jerusalem and offered as a sacrifice (only some blood is sprinkled on the altar, the rest is to be eaten by the family of the rancher.) So one may assume that many people on their pilgrimage for the holiday have money and animals of the tithe that they want to eat in Jerusalem to absolve themselves at the same time of the obligations of pilgrimage and (second) tithe. According to Ḥizqiah, on the first day of the holiday one may bring small and cheap animals as obligatory sacrifices and then use the money or the animal of tithes for additional *ḥagigah* offerings but one may not add the money of second tithes to profane money to buy one large animal for any of the two obligations.

In the text, the corresponding statement by R. Joḥanan is missing, viz., that one may add money (if only the basic amount is profane) but not animals (since no animal worth less than two pieces of silver is acceptable as *ḥagigah).* The statement appears in *Ḥagigah.*

52 A rhetorical introduction to the main question, corresponding to: "They asked themselves" in the Babli.

53 If these animals retain the status of *ḥagigah*, they may be sacrificed on the last day of Pesaḥ or Sukkot which are also full holidays. If, however, they have only the status of sacrifices in fulfillment of a vow (since any dedication as sacrifice is a vow to bring the animal to the Temple), then they may be slaughtered only during the intermediate days of the holiday or after its conclusion, and they do not push aside holiday prohibitions.

54 Aramaic דו is a contraction of דְּהוּא.

55 Since each animal was bought with money dedicated for *ḥagigah*, they all have the status of *ḥagigah.*

56 Since one may not adjoin money, only the first animal was *ḥagigah*, the rest are not and cannot be used for holiday sacrifices.

57 Even during the intermediate

days of the holiday, when one's biblical obligation of appearing in the Temple with a sacrifice has already been satisfied, he can add money to the original money and still the animals bought will fall under the category of *ḥagigah*. But when he declares that it is enough, the next money spent will no longer buy *ḥagigah* sacrifices. This extension of R. Joḥanan's statement is not a logical consequence of his earlier one.

וּגְמִילוּת חֲסָדִים. הָדָא דְתֵימַר בְּגוּפוֹ. אֲבָל בְּמָמוֹנוֹ יֵשׁ לוֹ שִׁיעוּר. וַאֲתִייָא כַּיי דָּמַר רִבִּי שִׁמְעוֹן בֶּן לָקִישׁ בְּשֵׁם רִבִּי יְהוּדָה בֶּן חֲנִינָא נִמְנוּ בְאוּשָׁא שֶׁיְּהֵא אָדָם מַפְרִישׁ חוֹמֶשׁ מִנְּכָסָיו לְמִצְוֹת. עַד הֵיכָן רבן גַּמְלִיאֵל בֶּן אִינִינְיָא וְרִבִּי אַבָּא בַּר כָּהֲנָא חַד אָמַר עַד כְּדֵי תְרוּמָה וּתְרוּמַת מַעֲשֵׂר. וְחָרָנָא אָמַר כַּבֵּד אֶת יי מֵהוֹנֶךָ וּמֵרֵאשִׁית כָּל־תְּבוּאָתֶךָ. כְּמֵרֵאשִׁית כָּל־תְּבוּאָתֶךָ.

"Works of kindness.[58]" That means with his person[5]. But with his money it has a measure. This parallels what Rebbi Simeon bar Laqish said in the name of Rebbi Jehudah ben Ḥanina[59]: They voted at Usha[60] that a person may give a fifth of his property for good deeds. How far down? Rebbi Gamliel bar Ininia[61] and Rebbi Abba bar Cahana; one said corresponding to *terumah* and the *terumah* of the tithe[62], the other said (*Prov.* 3:9): "Honor the Eternal with your property and with the first of all your yield;" corresponding to the first of all your yield[63].

58 Quote from the Mishnah, introduction of the next subject.

59 An Israeli Amora of the first generation. All his known statements were transmitted by R. Simeon bar Laqish. [In the Babli, the Amora is Rebbi Ilaï, i. e., R. La who was mentioned earlier in this Halakha, a student of R. Simeon ben Laqish.]

60 Usha in lower Galilee was the place of residence of R. Jehudah bar Illaï who, through his good relations with the Roman authorities, obtained permission for the reconstitution of the Synhedrion. This decree must have been one of the first acts of the new Synhedrion; it is explained later that the formal decree was only a formalization or reaffirmation of earlier practice.

61 A Galilean Amora of the third generation, student of R. Mana I.

62 *Terumah gedolah* has to be given by estimate, not by measure (*Terumot* 1:7). A generous farmer will give one part in forty (2.5%), the average person one in fifty (2%), the stingy person one in sixty ($1\frac{2}{3}$%) (*Terumot* 4:3). The *terumah* of the tithe has to be given exactly as 1%. Hence, the minimal amount of charity one is obliged to give from his gross income varies between 2.67% and 3.5%, with 3% recommended.

63 *Terumah gedolah* is called "first of your grain and oil" in *Deut.* 18:4; in this opinion one is only required to spend for charity the 2% of his gross earnings equivalent to *terumah gedolah*.

רִבִּי גַמְלִיאֵל בֶּן אִינִינְיָא בְּעֵי קוֹמֵי רִבִּי מָנָא מַה חוֹמֶשׁ בְּכָל־שָׁנָה וְשָׁנָה. לְחָמֵשׁ שָׁנִים הוּא מַפְסִיד כּוּלָּא. אָמַר לֵיהּ בַּתְּחִילָּה לְקֶרֶן מִיכָּן וְאֵילַךְ לְשָׂכָר.

Rebbi Gamliel bar Ininia asked before Rebbi Mana: Does it mean one fifth every year? In five years he will have lost everything[64]! He said to him: The first time from the capital, from there on from net gain.

64 But, as Rashi explains in Babli *Ketubot* 50a, the entire rule was only enacted to make sure that nobody would bring on himself the need to accept welfare.

רַב הוּנָא אָמַר לְמִצְוֹת עַד שְׁלִישׁ. מַהוּ לְכָל־הַמִּצְוֹת עַד שְׁלִישׁ אוֹ לְמִצְוָה אַחַת. סָבְרִין מֵימַר לְכָל־הַמִּצְוֹת עַד שְׁלִישׁ. רִבִּי אָבוּן אָמַר אֲפִילוּ לְמִצְוָה אַחַת. רַב חָבִיבָא בְּשֵׁם רַבָּנִים דְּתַמָּן מַהוּ שְׁלִישׁ לְדָמִים. הֵיךְ עֲבִידָא לָקַח אָדָם מִצְוָה וְרָאָה אַחֶרֶת נָאָה הֵימֶנָּה עַד כַּמָּא מַטְרִיחִין עָלָיו עַד שְׁלִישׁ.

Rav Huna[65] said, for religious purposes up to a third. What does he mean, for all religious purposes or just for one purpose? They thought that this means, for all religious purposes up to one third[66]. Rebbi Abun said, even for one purpose only. Rav Ḥabiba[67] in the name of the rabbis from there: What means "up to a third?" For its cost! How is that done? A man buys a religious article and sees another one which is more beautiful, until when does one bother him? Up to one third[68].

65 In the parallel in the Babli (*Bava qama* 9a), the statements of Rav Huna and Rav Ḥabiba are both reported in the name of Rebbi Zeïra, student of Rav Huna.

66 For religious articles one may spend up to one third of one's net worth. In that interpretation, Rav Huna would exempt religious articles from the decree of Usha.

67 He must have been a Babylonian Amora of the third generation, a student of Rav Huna. The Rav Ḥabiba mentioned in the Babli belongs to the sixth generation, after the compilation of the Jerusalem Talmud and, therefore, he cannot be identical with the Rav Ḥabiba mentioned here.

68 Of the original cost. If one has a religious object, such as an *etrog* or *tefillin*, he should not spend for another one more than 133% of the cost of the object he already has. In this interpretation, the statement of Rav Huna has no relation to the decree of Usha.

תַּנֵּי רִבִּי יִשְׁמָעֵאל זֶה אֵלִי וְאַנְוֵהוּ וְכִי אֶיפְשַׁר לְאָדָם לְנַוּוֹת אֶת בּוֹרְאוֹ אֶלָּא אַנְוֶה לְפָנָיו בְּמִצְוֹת אֶעֱשֶׂה לְפָנָיו לוּלָב נָאֶה. סוּכָּה נָאָה. שׁוֹפָר נָאֶה צִיצִית נָאָה תְּפִילִין נָאִין. אַבָּא שָׁאוּל אוֹמֵר אֲדַמֶּה לוֹ. מַהוּ חַנּוּן וְרַחוּם. אַף אַתְּ תְּהֵא חַנּוּן וְרַחוּם.

Rebbi Ismael stated[69]: (*Ex.* 15:2) "This is my God and I will glorify Him!" Is it possible for a human to glorify his God? Rather I shall appear beautiful before Him with religious articles. I shall make before Him a beautiful *lulab*, a beautiful *sukkah*, a beautiful *shofar*, beautiful *ẓiẓit*, beautiful *tefillin*. Abba Shaul[70] said, I want to be like Him! Just as He is merciful and gracious, so you also should be merciful and gracious!

69 This is a side remark: why should one spend much money on religious articles? It is a short quote of a long statement in *Mekhilta deR. Ismael, Parshat Hashirah* 3 (6 authors mentioned), *Mekhilta deR. Simeon bar Iohai* pp. 78-79, shortened in *Massekhet Sopherim* 3:12, *Massekhet Sepher Torah* 3:10, in Babli sources *Sabbath* 133b, *Nazir* 2b, and, very much shortened, *Sukkah* 11b. In the latter sources, the name of R. Ismael is never mentioned.

70 A Tanna of the generation of students of R. Aqiba who collected the

traditions of prior generations; his collection is one of the sources of the Mishnah.

מַעֲשֶׂה בְּרִבִּי יְשֵׁבָב שֶׁעָמַד וְהֶחֱלִיק אֶת כָּל־נְכָסָיו לַעֲנִיִּים. שָׁלַח לוֹ רַבָּן גַּמְלִיאֵל וַהֲלֹא אָמְרוּ חוֹמֶשׁ מִנְּכָסָיו לְמִצְוֹת וְרַבָּן גַּמְלִיאֵל לֹא קוֹדֶם לְאוּשָׁא הָיָה. רִבִּי יוֹסֵי בֵּי רִבִּי בּוּן בְּשֵׁם רִבִּי לֵוִי כַּךְ הָיְתָה הֲלָכָה בְּיָדָם וּשְׁכָחוּהָ וְעָמְדוּ הַשְּׁנִיִּים וְהִסְכִּימוּ עַל דַּעַת הָרִאשׁוֹנִים. לְלַמֶּדְךָ שֶׁכָּל־דָּבָר שֶׁבֵּית דִּין נוֹתְנִין נַפְשָׁן עָלָיו סוֹף הוּא מִתְקַיֵּים. כְּמַה שֶׁנֶּאֱמַר לְמֹשֶׁה בְּסִינַי. וַאֲתִייָא כַּיי דָּמַר רִבִּי מָנָא כִּי לֹא דָבָר רֵק הוּא מִכֶּם. וְאִם הוּא רֵק מִכֶּם לָמָּה שֶׁאֵין אַתֶּם יְגֵיעִין בּוֹ. כִּי הוּא חַיֵּיכֶם. אֵימָתַי הוּא חַיֵּיכֶם בְּשָׁעָה שֶׁאַתֶּם יְגֵעִין בּוֹ.

It happened that Rebbi Yeshebab[71] went and let his entire property be distributed to the poor. Rabban Gamliel[72] sent to him: Did they not say one fifth of one's property for good deeds? And was not Rabban Gamliel before Usha[73]? Rebbi Yose ben Rebbi Abun, Rebbi Levi: That was the current practice, they forgot it[74], but the later ones got up and agreed to the opinion of the earlier ones, to teach you that everything the Court[75] insists on will come to be in the end, just as Moses was told on Sinai; as Rebbi Mana said (*Deut.* 32:47): "For it is not an empty word, from you," if it is empty it is from you because you do not exert yourself about it. "Because it is your life," when is it your life? At the time that you exert yourself!

71 A Tanna of the third generation, student of R. Joshua and colleague of R. Aqiba. He was one of the Ten Martyrs and was executed after the war of Bar Kokhba, at age 90, probably because he continued to teach in Judea.

72 In the parallel Babli, *Ketubot* 50a, it is R. Aqiba who objects and prevents him from executing his wishes.

73 Rabban Gamliel died before the war of Bar Kokhba but the assembly at Usha was long after that war. In addition, the language of Rabban Gamliel implies that "they", not "we", instituted the limitation; hence, it was

an old rule (but, as the text here shows, not one that was generally observed.)

74 The first two generations after the destruction of the Temple, at the least. The same statement by R. Yose ben R. Abun and R. Levi is quoted in *Ketubot* 8:11 (fol. 32c) on another practice.

75 The Synhedrion or any court whose authority is accepted by all of Israel.

רִבִּי תַּנְחוּמָא בְּשֵׁם רַב חוּנָא וּבְצַלְאֵל בֶּן אוּרִי בֶן חוּר לְמַטֵּה יְהוּדָה עָשָׂה אֵת כָּל־אֲשֶׁר צִוָּה אוֹתוֹ מֹשֶׁה אֵין כְּתִיב כַּאן אֶלָּא אֲשֶׁר צִוָּה יי אֶת מֹשֶׁה אֲפִילוּ דְּבָרִים שֶׁלֹּא שָׁמַע מִפִּי רַבּוֹ הִסְכִּימָה דַּעְתּוֹ כְּמַה שֶׁנֶּאֱמַר לְמֹשֶׁה מִסִּינַי. רִבִּי יוֹחָנָן בְּשֵׁם רִבִּי בְּנָיָיה כַּאֲשֶׁר צִוָּה יי אֶת מֹשֶׁה עַבְדּוֹ. וְכֵן צִוָּה מֹשֶׁה אֶת יְהוֹשֻׁעַ. וְכֵן עָשָׂה יְהוֹשֻׁעַ לֹא הֵסִיר דָּבָר מִכָּל־אֲשֶׁר צִוָּה אוֹתוֹ מֹשֶׁה אֵין כְּתִיב כַּאן אֶלָּא אֵת אֲשֶׁר צִוָּה יי אֶת מֹשֶׁה. אֲפִילוּ דְּבָרִים שֶׁלֹּא שָׁמַע מִפִּי רַבּוֹ הִסְכִּימָה דַּעְתּוֹ כְּמַה שֶׁנֶּאֱמַר לְמֹשֶׁה מִסִּינַי. רִבִּי יוֹחָנָן בְּשֵׁם רִבִּי בְּנָיָה רִבִּי חוּנָה בְּשֵׁם רִבִּי תּוֹרַת אֱמֶת הָיְתָה בְּפִיהוּ. אֲפִילוּ דְּבָרִים שֶׁשָּׁמַע מִפִּי רַבּוֹ. וְעַוְלָה לֹא נִמְצָא בִשְׂפָתָיו. אֲפִילוּ דְּבָרִים שֶׁלֹּא שָׁמַע מִפִּי רַבּוֹ.

Rebbi Tanḥuma[76] in the name of Rav Huna: It does not say (*Ex.* 38:22) "Bezalel ben Uri ben Ḥur of the tribe of Judah made everything Moses had commanded him," but "that the Eternal had commanded Moses." Even matters he did not hear from Moses he did by himself in the way it was said to Moses on Sinai. Rebbi Joḥanan in the name of Rebbi Benaiah[77] (*Jos.* 11:15): "As the Eternal had commanded His servant Moses, so Moses commanded Joshua, and so Joshua executed it." It does not say "he did not omit anything Moses had commanded him," but "everything the Eternal commanded Moses." Even matters he did not hear from his teacher, he did by himself in the way it was said to Moses on Sinai. Rebbi Joḥanan in the name of Rebbi Benaiah, Rebbi Ḥuna in the name of Rebbi[78]: (*Mal.* 2:6) "True teaching was in his mouth[79]," these[80] are the things he heard from his teacher, "injustice was not found on his lips," even in matters he did not hear from his teacher."

76 These homilies are inserted as examples of the previous statement that deep involvement with the words of the Torah leads to such a way of life that even in situations not covered by what one has learned, he will act as it was indicated to Moses on Mount Sinai.

77 A scholar of the generation of transition between Tannaïm and Amoraïm who, in the Babylonian form ר' בנאה, is quoted in halakhic *baraitot*. His homilies are transmitted mostly by R. Joḥanan.

78 In *Yalqut Shim'oni Prophets* #588, the reading is "R. Jehudah" instead of Rebbi (Jehudah the Prince.)

79 While the person described is called "Levi" by the prophet, the traditional interpretation is that the reference is to Aaron who learned Torah from Moses.

80 It seems that אפילו here and in the next clause is a scribal error by dittography from the earlier homilies and that one should read אלו. This is the reading of *Yalqut Shim'oni Prophets* #588. In the next clause this reading is also supported by the Rome manuscript of the Yerushalmi.

וְרַבָּנִין אָמְרִין כִּי יי יִהְיֶה בְכִסְלֶךָ וְשָׁמַר רַגְלְךָ מִלָּכֶד. אֲפִילוּ דְּבָרִים שֶׁאַתְּ כְּסִיל בָּהֶן וְשָׁמַר רַגְלְךָ מִלָּכֶד. רִבִּי דוֹסָא אָמַר מִן הַהוֹרָיָיה. וְרַבָּנָן אָמְרֵי מִן הָעֲבֵירָה. רִבִּי לֵוִי אָמַר מִן הַמַּזִּיקִין. אָמַר רִבִּי אַבָּא אִם נָתַתָּ מִכִּיסְךָ צְדָקָה הַקָּדוֹשׁ בָּרוּךְ הוּא מְשַׁמְּרְךָ מִן הַפִּיסִין וּמִן הַזִּימִיוֹת וּמִן הַגּוּלְגּוֹלִיּוֹת וּמִן הָאַרְנוֹנִיּוֹת.

And the rabbis say (*Prov.* 3:26): "For the Eternal will stand by your confidence and prevent your foot from being caught." Even in matters in which you are stupid, He will prevent your foot from being caught. Rebbi Dosa said, in religious decisions[81]. The rabbis say, in sin. Rebbi Levi said, from damaging spirits. Rebbi Abba said, if you gave charity from your wallet[82], the Holy One, praise to Him, will guard you from taxes[83], penalties[84], head taxes, and contributions[85].

81 The verse is one of a group praising the student of Torah. The explanation is based on identifying כסל "confidence" with כסל "stupidity". The different opinions define the object in which one's foot might otherwise be

caught. R. Dosa's opinion continues the statements of the earlier homilies that the true student of Torah will render the correct decision if confronted with a religious question for which he knows no precedent.

82 Replacing כסל "confidence, hope" by כיס "wallet." This opinion is mentioned last because it leads back to the main theme, the importance of charity and charitable works.

83 An Aramaic (Syriac) word, פסא, "piece, portion", here used in the sense of the amount apportioned by the local council among the different householders to pay the taxes imposed *en bloc* on the community by the government.

84 Greek ζημία.

85 Latin *annona*, obligations to deliver provisions, usually for the army.

מוֹנְבַז הַמֶּלֶךְ עָמַד וּבִזְבֵּז אֶת כָּל־נְכָסָיו לָעֲנִיִּים שָׁלְחוּ לוֹ קְרוֹבָיו וְאָמְרוּ לוֹ אֲבוֹתֶיךָ הוֹסִיפוּ עַל שֶׁלָּהֶן וְעַל שֶׁל אֲבוֹתֵיהֶן. וְאַתְּ בִּיזְבַּזְתָּה אֶת שֶׁלְּךָ וְאֶת שֶׁל אֲבוֹתֶיךָ. אָמַר לָהֶן כָּל־שֶׁכֵּן אֲבוֹתַי גָּנְזוּ בָאָרֶץ וַאֲנִי גָנַזְתִּי בַשָּׁמַיִם שֶׁנֶּאֱמַר אֱמֶת מֵאֶרֶץ תִּצְמָח וְצֶדֶק מִשָּׁמַיִם נִשְׁקָף. אֲבוֹתַי גָּנְזוּ אוֹצְרוֹת שֶׁאֵין עוֹשִׂין פֵּירוֹת. וַאֲנִי גָנַזְתִּי אוֹצְרוֹת שֶׁהֵן עוֹשִׂין פֵּירוֹת שֶׁנֶּאֱמַר אִמְרוּ צַדִּיק כִּי טוֹב כִּי פְרִי מַעַלְלֵיהֶם יֹאכֵלוּ. אֲבוֹתַי כָּנְסוּ בְמָקוֹם שֶׁהַיַּד שׁוֹלֶטֶת בּוֹ. וַאֲנִי כָנַסְתִּי בְּמָקוֹם שֶׁאֵין הַיַּד שׁוֹלֶטֶת בּוֹ שֶׁנֶּאֱמַר צֶדֶק וּמִשְׁפָּט מְכוֹן כִּסְאוֹ. אֲבוֹתַי כָּנְסוּ מָמוֹן. וַאֲנִי כָנַסְתִּי נְפָשׁוֹת שֶׁנֶּאֱמַר וְלוֹקֵחַ נְפָשׁוֹת חָכָם. אֲבוֹתַי כָּנְסוּ לַאֲחֵרִים. וַאֲנִי כָנַסְתִּי לְעַצְמִי שֶׁנֶּאֱמַר וּלְךָ תִּהְיֶה צְדָקָה. אֲבוֹתַי כָּנְסוּ בָעוֹלָם הַזֶּה. וַאֲנִי כָנַסְתִּי לְעוֹלָם הַבָּא שֶׁנֶּאֱמַר וּצְדָקָה תַּצִּיל מִמָּוֶת. וְלָא מִית אֶלָּא שֶׁלֹּא יָמוּת מִיתָה לֶעָתִיד לָבוֹא.

King Monobaz[86] distributed all his property to the poor. His relatives sent to him: Your forefathers added to what they had and to what their forefathers had, and you wasted yours and that of your forefathers. He said to them, that is correct! My forefathers locked it up in the earth, I locked it up in Heaven, as it is said (*Ps.* 85:12): "Truth will sprout from the earth, but charity[87] will gaze from Heaven." My fathers locked up treasures that bring no interest, but I locked up treasures that bring interest as it is said (*Is.* 3:10): "Say to the giver of charity that he did a good deed, that they will eat the fruits of their intentions." My forefathers collected in a place over which a (human) hand rules, but I collected in a place over which no hand rules, as it is said (*Ps.* 97:2): "Charity and truth are the foundations of His throne." My forefathers collected money but I collected souls, as it is said (*Prov.* 11:30): "He who acquires souls is wise[88]." My forefathers collected for others but I collected for myself, as it is said (*Deut.* 24:13): "Charity will be your property[89]." My forefathers collected in this world but I collected for the future world, as it is said (*Prov.* 10:2): "But charity will save from death." And does he not die[90]? But that he should not die an eternal death in the future world.

86 A king of Adiabene, in modern Kurdistan, who converted to Judaism together with his mother Helena during the last century of existence of the Second Temple. In the parallel sources, Tosephta *Peah* 4:18, Babli *Baba batra* 11a, it is spelled out that he spent his treasures on emergency relief during a famine. Hence, the story here does not contradict the rule, declared as much older than Usha, that one should not give away more than one fifth of one's property. It is rather an endorsement of deficit spending by the government during times of emergency.

87 In the entire paragraph, צדק "justice" is identified with צדקה "charity", and צדיק "the just" is taken to mean "giver of charity."

88 The entire verse reads: "The fruit of the giver of charity is a tree of life and he who buys souls is wise."

89 The plain sense of the clause is: It will be considered a good deed by you (before the Eternal, your God.)

90 The last three sentences are not in the (Babylonian) parallels, where the argument is based on *Is.* 58:8 (speaking about him who breaks his bread with the poor): "Your charity will walk before you, the glory of the Eternal will gather you in." The Aramaic sentence ולא מיית should not be corrected into Hebrew in order to remain in style with the rest of the paragraph.

צְדָקָה וּגְמִילוּת חֲסָדִים שׁוֹקֶלֶת כְּנֶגֶד כָּל־מִצְוֹתֶיהָ שֶׁל תּוֹרָה. שֶׁהַצְּדָקָה נוֹהֶגֶת בַּחַיִּים וּגְמִילוּת חֲסָדִים (fol. 15c) נוֹהֶגֶת בַּחַיִּים וּבַמֵּתִים. הַצְּדָקָה נוֹהֶגֶת לָעֲנִיִּים וּגְמִילוּת חֲסָדִים נוֹהֶגֶת לָעֲנִיִּים וְלָעֲשִׁירִים. הַצְּדָקָה נוֹהֶגֶת בְּמָמוֹנוֹ שֶׁל אָדָם וּגְמִילוּת חֲסָדִים נוֹהֶגֶת בֵּין בְּמָמוֹנוֹ בֵּין בְּגוּפוֹ. רִבִּי יוֹחָנָן בַּר מַרְיָא בְשֵׁם רִבִּי יוֹחָנָן אֵין אָנוּ יוֹדְעִין אֵי זֶה מֵהֶן חָבִיב אוֹ צְדָקָה אוֹ גְמִילוּת חֲסָדִים כְּשֶׁהוּא אוֹמֵר וְחֶסֶד יי מֵעוֹלָם וְעַד עוֹלָם עַל יְרֵאָיו וְצִדְקָתוֹ לִבְנֵי אָדָם. הָדָא אָמְרָא שֶׁגְּמִילוּת חֲסָדִים חֲבִיבָה יוֹתֵר מִן הַצְּדָקָה.

Charity and works of kindness[91] are as important as all commandments of the Torah. Charity applies to the living, works of kindness apply to the living and the dead. Charity applies to the poor, works of kindness apply to poor and rich. Charity is through a person's money, works of kindness through his money and his person. Rebbi Joḥanan bar Maria[92] in the name of Rebbi Joḥanan: We do not know what is more beloved, charity or works of kindness. Since it says (*Ps.* 103:17): "The kindness of the Eternal is from eternity to eternity on those who fear Him, and His charity towards men," that means that works of kindness are more beloved than charity.

91 This paragraph also appears in Babli *Sukkah* 39b, Tosephta *Peah* 4:19. In both sources the formulation is such that the rhetorical question of the next paragraph is answered before it may be asked.

92 A Galilean Amora of the fourth generation.

וְתַלְמוּד תּוֹרָה. שָׁאֲלוּ אֶת רִבִּי יְהוֹשֻׁעַ מַהוּ שֶׁיְּלַמֵּד אָדָם אֶת בְּנוֹ יְוָנִית. אָמַר לָהֶם יְלַמְּדֶנּוּ בְּשָׁעָה שֶׁאֵינָהּ לֹא יוֹם וְלֹא לַיְלָה דִּכְתִיב וְהָגִיתָ בּוֹ יוֹמָם וָלַיְלָה. מֵעַתָּה אָסוּר לְאָדָם לְלַמֵּד אֶת בְּנוֹ אוּמָנוּת בְּגִין דִּכְתִיב וְהָגִיתָ בּוֹ יוֹמָם וָלַיְלָה וְהָתַנֵּי רִבִּי יִשְׁמָעֵאל וּבָחַרְתָּ בַּחַיִּים זוֹ אוּמָנוּת. רִבִּי בָּא בְּרֵיהּ דְּרִבִּי חִיָּא בַּר וָוא רִבִּי חִיָּא בְשֵׁם רִבִּי יוֹחָנָן מִפְּנֵי הַמְּסוֹרוֹת. רִבִּי אַבָּהוּ בְשֵׁם רִבִּי יוֹחָנָן מוּתָּר לְאָדָם לְלַמֵּד אֶת בִּתּוֹ יְוָנִית מִפְּנֵי שֶׁהוּא תַכְשִׁיט לָהּ. שָׁמַע שִׁמְעוֹן בַּר

וְהָ אֲמַר בְּגִין דּוּ בְּעָא מַלְפָּא בְּנָתֵיהּ הוּא תְּלֵי לֵיהּ בְּרִבִּי יוֹחָנָן. יָבוֹא עָלַי אִם שְׁמַעְתִּיהָ מֵרִבִּי יוֹחָנָן.

And Torah study[93]. They asked Rebbi Joshua[94]: May a person teach Greek to his son? He said to them, he may teach him at an hour that is neither day nor night as it is written (*Jos.* 1:8): "You shall meditate about it day and night." If it is so, a man would be forbidden to teach a profession to his son since it is written: "You shall meditate about it day and night." But Rebbi Ismael stated (*Deut.* 30:19): "Choose life!" That refers to a profession[95]. Rebbi Abba, son of Rebbi Ḥiyya bar Abba, Rebbi Ḥiyya in the name of Rebbi Joḥanan: Because of informants[96]. Rebbi Abbahu in the name of Rebbi Joḥanan: A person may teach Greek to his daughter since it is an ornament for her. Simeon bar Abba heard that and said: Because he wants to teach his daughters, he attaches it to Rebbi Joḥanan. It should come over me[97] if I ever heard it from Rebbi Joḥanan.

93 Quote from the Mishnah.

94 This also appears in Yerushalmi *Soṭa* 9:9, the first sentence also in Tosephta *Avodah zarah* 1:20. In Babli *Menaḥot* 59b, not only are different persons involved but there the question is about Greek wisdom, not the Greek language.

95 Since only a profession will sustain a person; otherwise he will be forced to become a robber and commit capital crimes.

96 Greek-speaking Jews become intimate with Greek-speaking officials and will be hired as government officials. In the Babli, the verse in *Joshua* is explained not as a commandment but as a blessing, that Joshua will be able to meditate about Torah day and night.

97 A curse: if I now say that R. Joḥanan never said this but I really heard it from him and forgot. In the parallel *Sabbat* 6:1 (fol. 7c), Rebbi Abbahu retorts that a curse should come over him if he said that and did not hear it from Rebbi Joḥanan. [It seems that R. Joḥanan made that statement only in Caesarea, never in Tiberias.]

כִּיבּוּד אַב וָאֵם. רִבִּי אַבָּהוּ בְשֵׁם רִבִּי יוֹחָנָן שָׁאֲלוּ אֶת רִבִּי אֱלִיעֶזֶר עַד הֵיכָן הוּא כִּיבּוּד אַב וְאֵם. אָמַר לָהֶן וְלִי אַתֶּם שׁוֹאֲלִין לְכוּ וְשַׁאֲלוּ אֶת דָּמָה בֶּן נְתִינָה. דָּמָה בֶּן נְתִינָה רֹאשׁ פַּטֵרְבּוּלֵי הָיָה. פַּעַם אַחַת הָיְתָה אִמּוֹ מְסַטְּרָתוֹ בִּפְנֵי כָּל־בּוּלֵי שֶׁלּוֹ וְנָפַל קוֹרְדִּקוֹן שֶׁלָּהּ מִיָּדָהּ וְהוֹשִׁיט לָהּ שֶׁלֹּא תִצְטָעֵר. אָמַר רִבִּי חִזְקִיָּה גּוֹי אַשְׁקְלוֹנִי הָיָה וְרֹאשׁ פַּטֵרְבּוּלֵי הָיָה וְאֶבֶן שֶׁיָּשַׁב עָלֶיהָ אָבִיו לֹא יָשַׁב עָלֶיהָ מִיָּמָיו. וְכֵיוָן שֶׁמֵּת אָבִיו עָשָׂה אוֹתָהּ יִרְאָה שֶׁלּוֹ. פַּעַם אַחַת אָבְדָה יָשְׁפֶה שֶׁל בִּנְיָמִין. אָמְרוּ מַאן דְּאִית לֵיהּ טָבָא דִּכְוָותֵיהּ. אָמְרוּ אִית לְדָמָה בֶּן נְתִינָה. אָזְלוּן לְגַבֵּיהּ וּפָסְקוּ עִמֵּיהּ בְּמֵאָה דֵּינָר סְלִיק בְּעֵי מַיְיתָהּ לְהוּ וְאַשְׁכַּח אָבוּהּ דָּמִיךְ וְאִית דְּאָמְרִין מַפְתְּחָא דְתֵיבוּתָא הֲוָה יְתִיב גַּו אֶצְבְּעָתֵיהּ דְּאָבוֹי. וְאִית דְּמָרִין רִיגְלֵיהּ דְּאָבוּהּ הֲוַות פְּשִׁיטָא עַל תֵּיבוּתָא. נְחַת לְגַבּוֹן אֲמַר לָא יְכִילִית מַיְתוּתֵיהּ לְכוֹן. אָמְרוּ דִּילְמָא דּוּ בְּעֵי פְּרִיטִין טוּבָן אַסְקוּנֵיהּ לְמָאתַיִם אַסְקוּנֵיהּ לְאֶלֶף. כֵּיוָן דְּאִיתְעִיר אָבוּהּ מִן שִׁינְתֵיהּ סְלַק וְאַייתוּתֵיהּ לוֹן. בְּעוּ מַיְיתוּן לֵיהּ כִּפְסִיקוּ לֵיהּ אֲחַרָיְיָא לָא קְבִיל עָלוֹי. אֲמַר מַה אֲנָא מַזְבִּין לְכוֹן אִיקָרָא דְּאָבָהָתִי בִּפְרִיטִין אֵינִי נֶהֱנֶה מִכְּבוֹד אֲבוֹתַי כְּלוּם. מַה פָּרַע לוֹ הַקָּדוֹשׁ בָּרוּךְ הוּא שָׂכָר. אָמַר רִבִּי יוֹסֵי בֵּי רִבִּי בוּן בּוֹ בַלַּיְלָה יָלְדָה פָרָתוֹ פָּרָה אֲדוּמָּה. וְשָׁקְלוּ לוֹ יִשְׂרָאֵל מִשְׁקָלָהּ זָהָב וּנְטָלוּהָ. אָמַר רִבִּי שַׁבְּתַי כְּתִיב וּמִשְׁפָּט וְרֹב צְדָקָה לֹא יְעַנֶּה. אֵין הַקָּדוֹשׁ בָּרוּךְ הוּא מַשְׁהֵא מַתַּן שְׂכָרָן שֶׁל עוֹשֵׂי מִצְוֹת בַּגּוֹיִים.

"Honoring father and mother.[98]" Rebbi Abbahu in the name of Rebbi Johanan: They asked Rebbi Eliezer, how far does honoring father and mother go? He said to them, you are asking me? Go and ask Dama ben Netinah. Dama ben Netinah was the head of the city council[99]. Once his mother was slapping him in front of the entire council and a slipper[100] fell from her hand, and he handed it back to her so that she should feel no inconvenience. Rebbi Ḥizqiah said: He was a Gentile from Ascalon and the head of the city council. He never sat on the stone on which his father used to sit and when his father died, he worshipped the stone. Once the jaspis of Benjamin was lost[101]. They[102] inquired, who would have one of similar quality? They were informed that Dama ben Netinah did. They went to him and and agreed on 100 denars[103]. He went to the upper floor to bring it and found his father sleeping. Some say that the key to the chest was in his father's fingers; some say his father's foot was resting on the chest. He descended to them and told them: I could not bring it to you. They thought, maybe he wants wore money, and raised the price to two hundred, then to a thousand. When his father woke up from his sleep, he went up and brought it to them. They wanted to give him according to the amount mentioned last, but he refused. He said: Do I sell my father's honor for money? I will not have any advantage from honoring my father. What reward did the Holy One, praise to Him, give him? Rebbi Yose bar Abun said: The following night, his cow gave birth to a red heifer and Israel gave him its weight in gold and took it. Rebbi Sabbatai said (*Job* 37:23): "Justice and much charity He will not suppress." The Holy One, praise to Him, will not wait to give the reward for good deeds to the Gentiles[104].

98 Quote from the Mishnah to start a new section.

99 A mixed expression, ראש πατὴρ βουλῆς, "head, father of the Senate." Cf. the Hebrew אב בית דין "father of the court," used for the president of Jewish courts of law, and the Latin *pater senatus*. [The two stories here also appear in Yerushalmi *Qiddushin* 1:7 in slightly improved spelling (here the title is an unintelligible פטרכולי) and, in a shortened and less natural version, in Babli *Qiddushin* 31a/b.]

100 The *Arukh* explains the word as Italian *pappucce* "houseshoes". Rashi explains in *Yebamot* 102b: "Thin sandals one binds under thick shoes to protect them from water; they are called *underschuoch* in (Middle High) German." Also cf. Latin *chorda*, Greek χορδή "string, rope" (E. G.), see below, Note 105. [In a papyrus from Oxyrhynchus from Mishnaic times, κορδίκιον is mentioned as "an article of furniture".]

101 From the breast-plate of the High priest.

102 The Temple authorities.

103 In early Roman imperial money, when the coins were still honest, this amounted to 22 oz. of gold, an enormous sum since the buying power of gold was much larger than it is today. The amount mentioned in the Babli by authors living during the early military anarchy is 60'000 or 80'000 denar. According to the monetary reform of Diocletian, one Roman pound (12 ounces), 500 fine, would be 48'000 denar. At the end of the inflationary period, 100 early denar would therefore be the equivalent of 880'000 denar. Hence, the sums mentioned in the Babli are rather on the low side.

104 Since they do not believe in the Future World and, therefore, do not have part in it and must be rewarded in this word.

אִמּוֹ שֶׁל רִבִּי טַרְפוֹן יָרְדָה לְטַייֵל לְתוֹךְ חֲצֵרָהּ בְּשַׁבָּת. וְהָלַךְ רִבִּי טַרְפוֹן וְהִנִּיחַ שְׁתֵּי יָדָיו תַּחַת פַּרְסוֹתֶיהָ וְהָיְתָה מְהַלֶּכֶת עֲלֵיהֶן עַד שֶׁהִגִּיעָה לְמִיטָּתָהּ. פַּעַם אַחַת חָלָה וְנִכְנְסוּ חֲכָמִים לְבַקְּרוֹ אָמְרָה לָהֶן הִתְפַּלְּלוּ עַל טַרְפוֹן בְּנִי שֶׁהוּא נוֹהֵג בִּי כָּבוֹד יוֹתֵר מִדַּאי. אָמְרוּ לָהּ מַהוּ עֲבַד לֵיךְ וְתַנְיֵית לְהוֹן עוּבְדָּא אָמְרוּ לָהּ אֲפִילוּ עוֹשֶׂה כֵן אֶלֶף אֲלָפִים אַדַּיִין לַחֲצִי כָבוֹד שֶׁאָמְרָה תוֹרָה לֹא הִגִּיעַ.

Rebbi Tarphon's mother went to promenade in her backyard on the Sabbath[105]. Rebbi Tarphon went and put his two hands under her feet and she walked on them until she got to her couch. Once he fell ill and the sages came to visit him. She told them: Pray for my son Tarphon because he honors me too much. They asked her[106], what did he do for you? She told them what had happened. They said to her, even if he did this a million times, he did not yet reach even half of the honor that the Torah requires.

105 "And her shoe-string (or, her slippers) broke." This is missing here but appears in the parallel *Qiddushin* 1:7 (fol. 61b): נפסק קורדייקין שלה [A different story is in Babli *Qiddushin* 31b.] Since we cannot assume that an authority of the stature of R. Tarphon had no *eruv* made if one was needed for the backyard, one might ask why he could not bring a new pair of slippers to his mother. But if the word means "shoe-string", the reason would

be clear since repairing the slippers on the Sabbath by putting in a new string would be a desecration of the Sabbath.

106 Although she spoke to them in Hebrew, they answered in Aramaic; it seems that they did not expect a woman to be educated enough to converse in Hebrew. Her explanation must have been in Hebrew since their final answer was again in Hebrew.

אִמּוֹ שֶׁל רִבִּי יִשְׁמָעֵאל בָּאת וְקָבְלָה עָלָיו לְרַבּוֹתֵינוּ אָמַר לָהֶן גְּעוּרוּ בְּיִשְׁמָעֵאל בְּנִי שֶׁאֵינוֹ נוֹהֵג בִּי כָבוֹד. בְּאוֹתָהּ שָׁעָה נִתְכַּרְכְּמוּ פְּנֵיהֶן שֶׁל רַבּוֹתֵינוּ אָמְרוּ אֵיפְשַׁר לֵית רִבִּי יִשְׁמָעֵאל נוֹהֵג בִּכְבוֹד אֲבוֹתָיו. אָמְרוּ לָהּ מַה עֲבַד לֵיךְ. אָמְרָה כְּדוּ נְפַק מִבֵּית וַועֲדָה אֲנָא בְעָיָא מִשְׁזְגָא רִיגְלוֹי וּמִישְׁתֵּי מֵהֶן וְלָא שְׁבִיק לִי. אָמְרוּ לוֹ הוֹאִיל וְהוּא רְצוֹנָהּ הוּא כְבוֹדָהּ.

Rebbi Ismael's mother came and complained to our teachers about him. She said to them: Scold my son Ismael because he does not honor me! At that, the faces of our teachers became saffron colored[107]. They said, is it possible that Rebbi Ismael does not honor his parents? They said to her, what did he do to you? She said, when he[108] comes from the house of assembly, I want to wash his feet and drink from it[109], and he refuses. They said to him, since it is her wish it is her honor.

107 כַּרְכּוֹם "saffron," also used as yellow dye.

108 כְּדוּ = כְּשֶׁהוּא.

109 The water used for washing. It is clear that R. Ismael's mother was uneducated; she spoke Aramaic and did not know the rules of good taste. ("Water" is always a plural in Hebrew and Aramaic.)

אָמַר רִבִּי מָנָא יְאוּת אִילֵּין טְחוֹנָיָא אָמְרִין כָּל־בַּר נַשׁ וּבַר נַשׁ זְכוּתֵיהּ גַּו קוּפְּתֵהּ. אִימֵּיהּ דְּרִבִּי טַרְפוֹן אֲמַר לוֹן אָכִין וַאֲגִיבוּנָהּ אָכִין[110]. אִימֵּיהּ דְּרִבִּי יִשְׁמָעֵאל אֲמַר לוֹן אָכֵן וַאֲגִיבוּנָהּ אָכֵן. רִבִּי זְעִירָא הֲוָה מִצְטָעֵר וַאֲמַר הַלְוָאי הֲוָה לִי אַבָּא וְאִימָּא דְּאִיקְרִינְהוֹן דְּנִירַת גַּן עֵדֶן. כַּד שְׁמַע אִילֵּין תַּרְתֵּי אוּלְפָּנַיָּא אֲמַר בְּרִיךְ רַחְמָנָא דְּלֵית לִי לָא אַבָּא וְאִימָּא. לָא כְּרִבִּי טַרְפוֹן

יְכִילְנָא עֲבִיד וְלָא כְּרִבִּי יִשְׁמָעֵאל הֲוֵינָא מְקַבְּלָה עָלַי. אָמַר רִבִּי אָבוּן פָּטוּר אֲנִי מִכִּבּוּד אָב וְאֵם. אָמְרוּ כַּד עִבְּרָה לֵיהּ אִימֵּיהּ מִית אָבוֹי כַּד יְלָדֵיהּ מֵיתַת.

Rebbi Mana said: The millers are correct when they say that each and every person has in his chest that which is appropriate for him[111]. Rebbi Tarphon's mother said so and they answered her appropriately, Rebbi Ismael's mother said so and they answered her appropriately. Rebbi Zeïra was sorry and said, if only I had father or mother that I could honor them and inherit paradise[112]. When he heard these two instructions, he said: Praise to the All-Merciful that I have neither father nor mother. I could not have done as Rebbi Tarphon did and I could not accept what Rebbi Ismael accepted. Rebbi Abun said, I am free from honoring father and mother. They said, his father died when his mother was pregnant and she died in giving birth.

110 Reading of the parallel in *Qiddushin*. The Venice text has אביו instead of אכין; two easily made substitutions.

111 In moral matters, there are no universally valid standards, only individual circumstances.

112 In the second version of the Ten Commandments (*Deut*. 5:16), honoring father and mother is explicitly rewarded with the promise that "one will be well off" in the future world. Rebbi Zeïra's case is identical with R. Abun's.

יֵשׁ שֶׁהוּא מַאֲכִיל אֶת אָבִיו פְּטוּמוֹת וְיוֹרֵשׁ גֵּהִנָּם וְיֵשׁ שֶׁהוּא כוֹדְנוֹ בָּרֵחַיִם וְיוֹרֵשׁ גַּן עֵדֶן. כֵּיצַד מַאֲכִיל אֶת אָבִיו פְּטוּמוֹת וְיוֹרֵשׁ גֵּהִנָּם. חַד בַּר נַשׁ הֲוָה מַייכִיל לְאָבוֹי תַּרְנְגוֹלִין פְּטִימִין. חַד זְמַן אֲמַר לֵיהּ אָבוֹי בְּרִי אִילֵּין מְנָן לָךְ. אֲמַר לֵיהּ סַבָּא סַבָּא אֱכוֹל וַאֲדִישׁ דִּכְלָבַיָּא אָכְלִין וּמְדִישִׁין. נִמְצָא מַאֲכִיל אֶת אָבִיו פְּטוּמוֹת וְיוֹרֵשׁ גֵּהִנָּם. כֵּיצַד כּוֹדְנוֹ בָּרֵחַיִם וְיוֹרֵשׁ גַּן עֵדֶן. חַד בַּר נַשׁ הֲוָה אִיטְחִין בְּרֵיחָיָיא אֲתַת מִצְוָה[113] לַטֲחוֹנַיָּא. אֲמַר לֵיהּ אַבָּא עוֹל טְחוֹן תַּחְתַּי. אִין מָטַת מְבַזְּיָיא טַב לִי אֲנָא וְלָא אַתְּ. אִין מָטַת מִילְקִי טַב לִי אֲנָא וְלָא אַתְּ. נִמְצָא כּוֹדְנוֹ בָּרֵחַיִם וְיוֹרֵשׁ גַּן עֵדֶן.

Some person might serve his father fattened meat and inherit hell. Some person might bind his father to the grindstone and inherit paradise. How does one serve his father fattened meat and inherit hell? A person used to serve his father fattened chickens. One day, his father said to him: My son, from where do you get the money for these? He said to him: Old man, old man, eat and shut up just as dogs eat and are silent. It turns out that he serves his father fattened meat and inherits hell. How does one bind his father to the grindstone and inherits paradise? A person was a miller at a grindstone; there came a requisition for millers. He said: Father, go and grind in my stead. If it should come to pass that someone is degraded, it is better that it should happen to me rather than to you. If it should come to pass that someone is beaten, it is better that it should happen to me rather than to you. It turns out that he binds his father to the grindstone and inherits paradise.

113 This is the reading of the parallel in *Qiddushin*. The Venice text here has צמות "assembly". The requisition is from the government, probably for service with the army.

נֶאֱמַר אִישׁ אִמּוֹ וְאָבִיו תִּירָאוּ וְנֶאֱמַר אֶת יי אֱלֹהֶיךָ תִּירָא וְאוֹתוֹ תַעֲבוֹד. הֶקִּישׁ מוֹרָא אָב וְאֵם לְמוֹרָא שָׁמַיִם. נֶאֱמַר כַּבֵּד אֶת אָבִיךָ וְאֶת אִמֶּךָ וְנֶאֱמַר כַּבֵּד אֶת יי מֵהוֹנֶךָ. הֶקִּישׁ כִּיבּוּד אָב וְאֵם לְכִבוּד הַמָּקוֹם. נֶאֱמַר וּמְקַלֵּל אָבִיו וְאִמּוֹ מוֹת יוּמָת. וְנֶאֱמַר אִישׁ אִישׁ כִּי יְקַלֵּל אֱלֹהָיו וְנָשָׂא חֶטְאוֹ. הֶקִּישׁ קִלְלוֹת אָב וְאֵם לְקִלְלַת הַמָּקוֹם. אֲבָל אֵי אֶיפְשָׁר לוֹמַר מַכֶּה כְּלַפֵּי לְמַעְלָן. וְכֵן בְּדִין מִפְּנֵי שֶׁשְּׁלָשְׁתָּן שׁוּתָּפִין בּוֹ.

It[114] is said (*Lev.* 19:3): "Everybody must fear his mother and his father," and it is said (*Deut.* 6:13): "You must fear the Eternal, your God, and serve Him." This brackets the fear of father and mother with the fear of Heaven. It is said (*Ex.* 20:12): "Honor your father and your mother," and it is said (*Prov.* 3:9): "Honor the Eternal with your property." This brackets the honor of father and mother with the honor of the Omnipresent. Is is said (*Ex.* 21:17): "He who curses his father or his mother shall be put to death," and it is said (*Lev.* 24:19): "Everybody who curses his God must bear his sin." This brackets cursing father and mother with cursing the Omnipresent. It is impossible to speak about hitting relative to the Deity[115]. All this is logical since all three of them are partners in his creation[116].

114 The exact parallel is in *Sifra Qedoshim* 2-7; an almost identical quote is in Babli *Qidddushin* 30b.

115 It is written (*Ex.* 21:15): "He who hits his father or mother must be put to death." This law cannot have a parallel in relation to the Deity.

116 Since father and mother contribute the animal part of his being and God gives soul, spirit, and life (Babli *Niddah* 31a).

אֵי זֶהוּ מוֹרָא. לֹא יוֹשֵׁב בִּמְקוֹמוֹ וְלֹא מְדַבֵּר בִּמְקוֹמוֹ וְלֹא סוֹתֵר אֶת דְּבָרָיו. אֵי זֶהוּ כִיבּוּד. מַאֲכִיל וּמַשְׁקֶה מַלְבִּישׁ וּמַנְעִיל מַכְנִיס וּמוֹצִיא. מִן דְּמַאן הוּנָא בַּר חִייָא אָמַר מִשֶּׁל זָקֵן. וְאִית דְּבָעֵי מֵימַר מִשֶּׁלּוֹ. לֹא כֵן אָמַר רִבִּי אַבָּהוּ בְשֵׁם רִבִּי יוֹסֵי בֶּן חֲנִינָא מְנַיִין אֲפִילוּ אָמַר לוֹ אָבִיו הַשְׁלֵךְ אֶת הָאַרְנָק לַיָּם שֶׁיִּשְׁמַע לוֹ בְּהַהוּא דְּאִית לֵיהּ חוֹרִין וּבְעוֹשֶׂה הֲנָחַת רוּחַ שֶׁל אָבִיו.

What is fear[117]? He may not sit in his place and may not speak in his stead[118] nor contradict his words. What is honor? He feeds and gives him to drink, clothes him and puts on his shoes, leads him out and in[119]. From whose money? Huna bar Ḥiyya[120] said, from the old man's. Some want to say, from his own. Did not Rebbi Abbahu say in the name of Rebbi Yose bar Ḥanina: From where do we know that even if his father tells him to throw the wallet into the sea that he should obey him[121]? That is[122], if he has another one and if it helps to quiet his father's spirit.

117 *Sifra Qedoshim* 10, Babli *Qiddushin* 61b. What is classified here as "honor" is described in Tosephta *Qiddushin* 1:11 as "obligation of the son towards his parents."

118 If the father is present.

119 If the parent can no longer do these things.

120 A Babylonian Amora of the second/third generation, student of Rav Huna and Rav Jehudah, and son-in-law of Rav Jeremiah bar Abba. In the Babli, his statement is attributed to Rav Nathan bar Oshaia, a minor authority contemporary with Rav Huna bar Ḥiyya, and the statement that "some want to say" is attributed to Rav Jehudah. Even though Rav Jehudah is the much more important authority, his opinion is rejected in the Babli, in contrast to the Yerushalmi two paragraphs down.

121 In the Babli, this is one of the examples of Rebbi Eliezer about the seriousness of the obligation of honoring father and mother. The question is, why should the son be obliged to throw his own wallet (full of money) into the sea when he has to feed and clothe his parents from his own money? Hence, R. Abbahu must agree that the old parents must be cared for from their own money.

122 The proof from the statement of R. Abbahu is not conclusive. There are two conditions to be fulfilled in order that the son should follow his father's command: First, that the implications for the wealth of either parent or child are negligible and, second, that the act will have a positive influence on the mental health of the disturbed parent [otherwise, as the Babli points out explicitly, the son would infringe on the Biblical prohibition of wanton destruction and, as the verse *Lev.* 19:3 makes clear, one is not permitted to follow one's parents orders to commit a sin.]

אֶחָד הָאִישׁ וְאֶחָד הָאִשָּׁה. אֶלָּא שֶׁהָאִישׁ סְפֵיקָה בְיָדוֹ וְהָאִשָּׁה אֵין (fol. 15d) סְפֵיקָה בְיָדָהּ. מִפְּנֵי שֶׁיֵּשׁ רְשׁוּת לַאֲחֵרִים עָלֶיהָ. נִתְאַרְמְלָה אוֹ נִתְגָּרְשָׁה כְּמִי שֶׁהִיא סְפֵיקָה בְיָדָהּ הִיא.

Both men and women[123]. Only the man has the power in his hand, but the woman does not have the power in her own hand because others have disposition over her[124]. If she is widowed or divorced, the power is in her own hand.

123 Even though the verse *Lev.* 19:3 is formulated: "A man must fear his mother and his father," a woman is also obligated. It is then explained why the obligation of the man only is unconditional and spelled out.

124 She can only care for her parents with the consent of her husband who has the administration of her property.

מִילְתֵיהּ דְּרִבִּי חִייָא בַּר בָּא פְּלִיגִי דְּאָמַר רִבִּי חִייָא בַּר בָּא תַּנֵּי רִבִּי יוּדָן בַּר בְּרַתֵּיהּ דְּרִבִּי שִׁמְעוֹן בֶּן יוֹחַי דְּתַנֵּי רִבִּי שִׁמְעוֹן בֶּן יוֹחַי גָּדוֹל הוּא כִּיבּוּד אָב וָאֵם שֶׁהֶעֱדִיפוֹ הַקָּדוֹשׁ בָּרוּךְ הוּא יוֹתֵר מִכִּיבּוּדוֹ. נֶאֱמַר כַּבֵּד אֶת אָבִיךָ וְאֶת אִמֶּךָ וְנֶאֱמַר כַּבֵּד אֶת יי מֵהוֹנֶךָ. מִמָּה אַתְּ מְכַבְּדוֹ מִשֶּׁיְּחָנְנָךְ מַפְרִישׁ לֶקֶט שִׁכְחָה וּפֵיאָה מַפְרִישׁ תְּרוּמָה וּמַעֲשֵׂר רִאשׁוֹן וּמַעֲשֵׂר שֵׁנִי וּמַעֲשֵׂר עָנִי וְחַלָּה וְעוֹשֶׂה סוּכָּה וְלוּלָב וְשׁוֹפָר וּתְפִילִין וְצִיצִית וּמַאֲכִיל אֶת הָעֲנִיִּים וְאֶת הָרְעֵבִים וּמַשְׁקֶה אֶת הַצְּמֵאִים. אִם יֵשׁ לָךְ אַתְּ חַייָב בְּכָל־אֵילוּ. וְאִם אֵין לָךְ אֵין אַתְּ חַייָב בְּאַחַת מֵהֶן. אֲבָל כְּשֶׁהוּא בָּא אֵצֶל כִּיבּוּד אָב וְאֵם בֵּין שֶׁיֵּשׁ לָךְ הוֹן בֵּין שֶׁאֵין לָךְ הוֹן כַּבֵּד אֶת אָבִיךָ וְאֶת אִמֶּךָ וַאֲפִילוּ אַתְּ מְסַבֵּב עַל הַפְּתָחִים.

The words of Rebbi Ḥiyya bar Abba disagree[125], for Rebbi Ḥiyya bar Abba said that Rebbi Yudan, son of Rebbi Simeon bar Ioḥai's daughter[126], stated that Rebbi Simeon bar Ioḥai stated: Honoring father and mother is great because the Holy One, praise to Him, preferred it over His own honor. It is said (*Ex.* 20:12): "Honor your father and your mother," and it is said (*Prov.* 3:9): "Honor the Eternal with your property." When do you start to honor Him? When He was gracious to you! One gives gleanings, forgotten sheaves, and *peah*, one gives *terumah*, the First and Second Tithes[127] and the tithe for the poor, *ḥallah*, one makes a *sukkah, lulav,* and *shofar*, *tefillin* and *ẓiẓit*, one feeds the poor and hungry and gives to drink to the thirsty. If you have the wherewhithal, you are obliged for all of these; if you have nothing, you are not obliged even for one of them. But when it comes to honoring father and mother, whether you own property or you do not own property, you must honor father and mother, even if you are a beggar at people's doors[128].

125 The text of the first sentence is that of the parallel *Qiddušin* 1:7, fol. 61b. R. Ḥiyya bar Abba disagrees with the words of Huna bar Ḥiyya that all the children have to give to their parents is their time and attention but not their money.

126 He is not mentioned anywhere else in the Talmud.

127 The Second Tithe is not for the poor but for one's own family, to be eaten in Jerusalem. It is supposed that at any family festival one also lets the poor eat from the festive meal. The Second Tithe is due in years 1,2,4,5 of the *shemiṭṭah* cycle, the tithe for the poor in years 3,6.

128 Who takes charity instead of giving it.

רִבִּי אָחָא בְשֵׁם רִבִּי אַבָּא בַּר כֲּהָנָא כְּתִיב אוֹרַח חַיִּים פֶּן תְּפַלֵּס נָעוּ מַעְגְּלוֹתֶיהָ וְלֹא תֵדָע. טִילְטֵל הַקָּדוֹשׁ בָּרוּךְ הוּא מַתַּן שְׂכָרָן שֶׁל עוֹשֵׂי מִצְוֹת כְּדֵי שֶׁיְּהוּא עוֹשִׂין אוֹתָן בֶּאֱמוּנָה. רִבִּי אָחָא בְשֵׁם רִבִּי יִצְחָק כְּתִיב מִכָּל־מִשְׁמָר נְצוֹר לִבֶּךָ כִּי מִמֶּנּוּ תוֹצְאוֹת חַיִּים. מִכָּל־מַה שֶׁאָֽמְרוּ לָךְ בַּתּוֹרָה הִשָּׁמֵר שֶׁאֵין אַתְּ יוֹדֵעַ מֵאֵי זֶה מֵהֶן יוֹצֵא לָךְ חַיִּים. אָמַר רִבִּי אַבָּא בַּר כֲּהָנָא הִשְׁוָה הַכָּתוּב מִצְוָה קַלָּה שֶׁבְּקַלּוֹת לְמִצְוָה חֲמוּרָה שֶׁבַּחֲמוּרוֹת. מִצְוָה קַלָּה שֶׁבְּקַלּוֹת זֶה שִׁילּוּחַ הַקֵּן. מִצְוָה חֲמוּרָה שֶׁבַּחֲמוּרוֹת זֶה כִּיבּוּד אָב וָאֵם. וּבִשְׁתֵּיהֶן כְּתִיב וְהַאֲרַכְתָּ יָמִים. אָמַר רִבִּי אָבוּן אִם דָּבָר שֶׁהוּא פְּרִיעַת הַחוֹב כְּתִיב בּוֹ לְמַעַן יִיטַב לָךְ וּלְמַעַן יַאֲרִיכוּן יָמֶיךָ. דָּבָר שֶׁיֵּשׁ בּוֹ חִסָּרוֹן כִּיס וְסִיכּוּן נְפָשׁוֹת לֹא כָּל־שֶׁכֵּן. אָמַר רִבִּי לֵוִי וְהוּא דְרַבָּה מִינָהּ גָּדוֹל הוּא דָּבָר שֶׁהוּא בִּפְרִיעַת חוֹב מִדָּבָר שֶׁאֵינוֹ בִּפְרִיעַת חוֹב. תַּנֵּי רִבִּי שִׁמְעוֹן בֶּן יוֹחַי כְּשֵׁם שֶׁמַּתַּן שְׂכָרָן שָׁוֶה כָּךְ פּוּרְעָנוּתָן שָׁוֶה. מַה טַעַם עַיִן תִּלְעַג לְאָב וְתָבוּס לִיקְּהַת אֵם. עַיִן שֶׁהִלְעִיגָה עַל כִּיבּוּד אָב וָאֵם וּבִיזָּת עַל לֹא תִקַּח הָאֵם עַל הַבָּנִים יִקְּרוּהָ עוֹרְבֵי נַחַל יָבוֹא עוֹרֵב שֶׁהוּא אַכְזָרִי וְיִקְּרֶנָּה וְאַל יֶהֱנֶה מִמֶּנָּה. וְיֹאכְלוּהָ בְנֵי נֶשֶׁר. יָבוֹא נֶשֶׁר שֶׁהוּא רַחֲמָן וְיֹאכְלֶנָּה וְיֶהֱנֶה מִמֶּנָּה.

Rebbi Aḥa in the name of Rebbi Abba bar Cahana: It is written (*Prov.* 5:6): "She[129] does not smooth the way of life, her tracks deviate and you will not notice it." The Holy One, praise to Him, moved the rewards of those who fulfill the commandments (to the future world) so that they should act in faith. Rebbi Aḥa in the name of Rebbi Isaac: It is written (*Prov*. 4:23): "Observe carefully all which must be kept, for from it comes life," observe carefully all you were told in the Torah, for you do not know from which of them will life come to you. Rebbi Abba bar Cahana said, the verse equals the easiest commandment with the most difficult one. The easiest commandment is sending away the mother[130]. The most difficult one is honoring father and mother. For both of them it is written: "Your days will be lengthened." Rebbi Abun said, if for something that is repayment of debt[131] it is written (*Deut*. 5:16): "That you shall be well and that your days shall be lengthened," so much more something that involves monetary loss and personal danger[132]. Rebbi Levi said, this one is greater; repaying a debt is greater than fulfilling an obligation that does not involve repaying a debt. Rebbi Simeon ben Ioḥai stated: Just as their rewards are the same, so their punishments are identical. (*Prov*. 30:17) "The eye that scoffs at the father and despises to obey the mother," the eye that scoffs about honoring father and mother and despises the commandment not to take the mother with the chicks[133], "the river ravens should pick it out," the cruel raven[134] should come, pick it out, and not have any enjoyment from it, "the sons of the eagle should eat it," the merciful eagle should come and enjoy it.

129 The strange woman, symbolizing non-Jewish attitudes. The rewards of good deeds have been removed to the World to Come.

130 If one happens to find a bird's nest, one may take the eggs or the chicks but not the mother (*Deut*. 22:6-7).

131 Honoring father and mother for raising the child.

132 Sending away the mother is a potential loss; climbing a ladder to get the eggs or the chicks is a potential danger. [Rebbi Abun was in personal danger for refusing to worship the Roman emperor as a god; Yerushalmi *Berakhot* 5:1).]

133 In the verse it is written ליקחת

"referring to obeying;" in the Talmud text, this is shortened to לקחת and, apparently under the influence of the dialect of lower Galilee, which makes no difference between ה and ח, reads לקחת "to take." It must be noted that the writing of the letter *hē* as ה is a new development; in old texts its left leg touches the top but is displaced towards the right; it looks very much like ח.

134 Which is reputed not to feed its young (*Ps*. 147:9, cf. Babli *Ketubot* 49b).

רִבִּי יוֹנָתָן וְרִבִּי יַנַּאי הֲווֹ יְתִיבִין אֲתָא חַד בַּר נַשׁ וּנְשַׁק רִיגְלוֹי דְּרִבִּי יוֹנָתָן. אֲמַר לֵיהּ רִבִּי יַנַּיי מַה טִיבוּ הֲוָה שְׁלִים לָךְ מִן יוֹמוֹי אֲמַר לֵיהּ חַד זְמָן אֲתָא קְבַל לִי עַל בְּרֵיהּ דְּיְזוֹנִינֵיהּ וַאֲמְרִית זִיל צוֹר כְּנִישְׁתָּא עֲלוֹי וּבְזִיתֵיהּ. אֲמַר לֵיהּ וְלָמָּה לָא כְפִיתִינֵיהּ. אֲמַר לֵיהּ וְכוֹפִין לֵיהּ. אֲמַר לֵיהּ וַאֲדַיִין אַתְּ לְזוּ. חָזַר בֵּיהּ רִבִּי יוֹנָתָן וְקָבְעָהּ שְׁמוּעָה מִן שְׁמֵיהּ. אֲתָא רִבִּי יַעֲקֹב בַּר אָחָא רִבִּי שְׁמוּאֵל בַּר נַחְמָן בְּשֵׁם רִבִּי יוֹנָתָן שֶׁכּוֹפִין אֶת הַבֵּן לָזוּן אֶת הָאָב. אָמַר רִבִּי יוֹסֵי בֵּי רִבִּי בּוּן הַלְוַאי הֲווֹן כָּל־שְׁמוּעָתָא בְּרִירִין לִי כְּהָדָא שֶׁכּוֹפִין אֶת הַבֵּן לָזוּן אֶת הָאָב.

Rebbi Jonathan and Rebbi Yannai were sitting together[135]. There came a man and kissed Rebbi Jonathan's foot. Rebbi Yannai said to him: What kindness did he pay you back for from former days? He said to him: He once came and complained to me about his son that he should support him and I told him, go, assemble a congregation and humiliate him[136]. He said to him, why did you not force him[137]? He said to him, does one force him? He said to him, you still have questions about that? Rebbi Jonathan changed his opinion and fixed it as a tradition in his own name. The result is: Rebbi Jacob bar Aḥa, Rebbi Samuel bar Naḥman in the name of Rebbi Jonathan, one forces the son to feed his father. Rebbi Yose bar Abun said, if only all traditions were so clear to me as this one: One forces the son to feed his father.

135 In Babli *Ketubot* 49b/50a, a similar story is told about Rebbi Jonathan and Rebbi Ḥanina, but there one deals with a special situation that

does not imply anything for our case here.

136 Apply moral force to get him to support his penniless father.

137 By a decree of the Rabbinical court, following R. Simeon bar Iohai.

וּגְמִילוּת חֲסָדִים. דִּכְתִיב רוֹדֵף צְדָקָה וָחָסֶד יִמְצָא חַיִּים צְדָקָה וְכָבוֹד. כָּבוֹד בְּעוֹלָם הַזֶּה וְחַיִּים לָעוֹלָם הַבָּא. רִבִּי שְׁמוּאֵל בַּר רַב יִצְחָק הֲוָה נְסִיב שִׁיבֶּשְׁתֵּיהּ וַהֲוָה מְקַלֵּס קוֹמוֹי כַּלָּיָא. וַהֲוָה רִבִּי זְעִירָא חֲמִי לֵיהּ וּמִטְּמָר מִן קוֹמוֹי אֲמַר חֲמֵי לְהַדֵּין סַבָּא אֵיךְ הוּא מַבְהֵית לוֹן. וְכֵיוָן דִּדְמָךְ הֲוָה תְּלַת שָׁעִין קָלִין וּבְרָקִין בְּעָלְמָא. נַפְקַת בְּרַת קָלָא וְאָמְרָה דְּמָךְ רִבִּי שְׁמוּאֵל בַּר רַב יִצְחָק גְּמִיל חֲסָדַיָּא נַפְקוּן לְמִיגְמוֹל לֵיהּ חֶסֶד. נְחָתַת אֵישְׁתָּא מִן שְׁמַיָּא וְאִיתְעֲבִידַת כְּעֵין שִׁבְשָׁא דְּנוּר בֵּין עַרְסָא לְצִיבּוּרָא וַהֲווֹן בְּרִייָתָא אָמְרִין חִיוֵי דְּדֵין סַבָּא דְּקָמַת לֵיהּ שִׁבֶּשְׁתֵּיהּ.

"Works of kindness[138]." As it is written (*Prov.* 21:21): "He who pursues charitable donations and works of kindness will find life, justification, and honor." Honor in this world and life in the world to come. Rebbi Samuel bar Rav Isaac[139] used to take branches and danced while singing[140] before brides. Rebbi Zeïra saw him and hid himself before him; he said, look at that old man, how does he make us ashamed! But when he died there were three hours of thunder and lightning in the world. An echo came from Heaven and said: Rebbi Samuel bar Rav Isaac, the worker of charity, died, come out to do charity for him! Fire came down from Heaven that was formed like a fiery branch and separated between the bier and the people; the creatures were saying: Look, his branch stood up for the old man!

138 Quote from the Mishnah, to introduce the next theme.

139 The story is told at length in *Bereshit rabba* 59, and in a shortened version, which shows R. Zeïra in a better light, in Babli *Ketubot* 17a. The essence of the story is that personal effort, in particular for weddings and burials, will not go unrewarded.

140 From a root that appears in

Arabic as קלס "to dance while singing, singing harmoniously." He deviated from the standards of dignity upheld by rabbis.

וְהֲבָאַת שָׁלוֹם בֵּין אָדָם לַחֲבֵירוֹ. כְּתִיב סוּר מֵרָע וַעֲשֵׂה טוֹב בַּקֵּשׁ שָׁלוֹם וְרָדְפֵהוּ. בַּקְּשֵׁהוּ בִּמְקוֹמְךָ וְרָדְפֵיהוּ בְּמָקוֹם אַחֵר. אָמַר רִבִּי טַבְיוֹמָא נֶאֱמַר רְדִיפָה רְדִיפָה. מַה רְדִיפָה שֶׁנֶּאֱמַר לְהַלָּן כָּבוֹד בְּעוֹלָם הַזֶּה וְחַיִּים לָעוֹלָם הַבָּא.

"Making peace between people.[138]" It is written (*Ps.* 34:15): "Move away from evil and do good, look for peace and pursue it." Look for peace at your place, pursue it at another place. Rebbi Tavyome said: It says pursuing, pursuing[141]. Just as it was said there, honor in this world and life in the world to come.

141 Both the verse from Psalms here and the verse from Proverbs in the preceding paragraph use the root רדף "to pursue." Hence, one may assume that the meaning is the same in both cases.

וְתַלְמוּד תּוֹרָה. רִבִּי בֶּרֶכְיָה וְרִבִּי חִיָּיא דִּכְפַר תְּחוּמִין חַד אָמַר אֲפִילוּ כָּל־הָעוֹלָם כּוּלּוֹ אֵינוֹ שָׁוֶה אֲפִילוּ דָּבָר אֶחָד מִן הַתּוֹרָה. וְחַד אָמַר אֲפִילוּ כָּל־מִצְוֹתֶיהָ שֶׁל הַתּוֹרָה אֵינָן שָׁווֹת לְדָבָר אֶחָד מִן הַתּוֹרָה. רִבִּי תַּנְחוּמָא וְרִבִּי יוֹסֵי בֶּן זִמְרָא חַד אָמַר כְּהָדָא. וְחַד אָמַר כְּהָדָא. רִבִּי אַבָּא אָבוֹי דְּרִבִּי אַבָּא בַּר מָרִי בְּשֵׁם רִבִּי אָחָא כָּתוּב אֶחָד אוֹמֵר וְכָל־חֲפָצִים לֹא יִשְׁווּ בָהּ. וְכָתוּב אֶחָד אוֹמֵר וְכָל־חֲפָצֶיךָ לֹא יִשְׁווּ בָהּ. חֲפָצִים אֵילּוּ אֲבָנִים טוֹבוֹת וּמַרְגָּלִיּוֹת. חֲפָצֶיךָ אֵילּוּ דִּבְרֵי תוֹרָה. דִּכְתִיב כִּי בְאֵלֶּה חָפַצְתִּי נְאֻם יי.

"And Torah study.[138]" Rebbi Berekhiah and Rebbi Ḥiyya from Kefar Teḥumin[142]. One said that the entire world is not worth even one saying of the Torah. The other said that even all commandments of the Torah are not worth even one saying of the Torah[143]. Rebbi Tanḥuma and Rebbi Yose ben Zimra, one said like the first and one said like the second. Rebbi Abba, father of Rebbi Abba bar Mari[144], in the name of Rebbi Aḥa:

One verse says (*Prov.* 8:11) "all desirables do not equal it;" the other verse says (*Prov.* 3:15) "your desirables do not equal it." "Desirables" are gems and pearls, "your desirables" are the words of the Torah, for it is written (*Jer.* 9:23): "For these I desire - saying of the Eternal.[145]"

142 An Amora of the third generation, possibly from Capernaum. The statement here is the only one preserved from him (unless he is identical with R. Ḥama from Kefar Teḥumin, mentioned sometimes in Midrashim.)

143 He asserts that study is more important than doing, an attitude that is challenged below. [The contrary position is quoted without opposition in the Babli.]

144 At first glance, it seems impossible that Rebbi Abba should be the father of Rebbi Abba bar Mari. Now it is possible that one should read: "Rebbi Abba, father of Rebbi Abba Mari." It is also possible that Rebbi Abba bar Mari is the posthumous son of Rebbi Abba but did not want to be called Abba bar Abba to indicate by his name the unhappy circumstance of his birth; Mari would not be a personal name but a word meaning "my lord (father)."

145 The verse ends: "understanding and knowing Me," i. e., studying Torah. Even the words of the Torah are not equal to the commandments of the Torah and executing these is of higher value than study only, parallel to the position of the Babli.

אַרְטַבָן שְׁלַח לְרַבֵּינוּ הַקָּדוֹשׁ חַד מַרְגְּלִי טָבָא אַטִימֵיטוֹן. אֲמַר לֵיהּ שְׁלַח לִי מִילָּה דְטָבָה דִכְוָותָהּ. שְׁלַח לֵיהּ חַד מְזוּזָה. אֲמַר לֵיהּ אֲנָה שְׁלָחִית לָךְ מִילָּה דְלֵית לָהּ טִימֵי. וְאַתְּ שְׁלַחְתְּ לִי מִילָּה דְטָבָא חַד פוֹלָר. אֲמַר לֵיהּ חֲפָצֶיךָ וַחֲפָצַי לֹא יִשְׁווּ בָהּ. וְלֹא עוֹד אֶלָּא דְאַתְּ שְׁלַחְתְּ לִי מִילָּה דַאֲנָא מְנַטַּר לָהּ. וַאֲנָא שְׁלָחִית לָךְ מִילָּה דְאַתְּ דָּמָךְ לָךְ וְהִיא מְנַטְּרָא לָךְ דִּכְתִיב בְּהִתְהַלֶּכְךָ תַּנְחֶה אוֹתָךְ.

Artaban[146] sent a priceless[147] precious pearl to our holy teacher[148] and said to him: Send me a thing of equal value. He sent him a *mezuzah*. He said to him: I sent you a priceless thing and you send me something worth a *follis*[149]! He said to him, your possessions and mine together are not equal to it! Not only that, but you sent me something that I have to watch over and I sent you something that watches over you while you are sleeping, as it is written (*Prov.* 6:22): "I will make you rest when you are rambling."

146 Artaban III, the last ruler of the Parthian empire.

147 Greek ἀτίμητος, adj., "priceless"; τιμή "worth, price."

148 Rav, who has this title in several passages of the Yerushalmi.

149 Latin *follis*, Greek φόλλις, -εως, ὁ, in the late Roman empire a small copper coin ($^1/_{288}$ of a solidus or $^1/_{1728}$ of an ounce of gold), under the (much later) Byzantine emperor Anastasius equal to 40 units of the smallest coin called *nummus*. Originally, *follis* means "bellows", then "bag, small coin", later "money bag" representing a standard value. *Follis* as a coin appears only after Diocletian's currency reform. The use of the term reflects the time of the edition of the Yerushalmi, not the time of the actors in the story. (For a similar adaptation in a Babylonian source, cf. Note 102.)

רִבִּי מָנָא שָׁמַע כּוּלְהוֹן מִן הָדֵין קִרְיָא כִּי לֹא דָבָר רֵק הוּא מִכֶּם זֶה תַלְמוּד תּוֹרָה. כִּי הִיא חַיֵּיכֶם זֶה כִיבּוּד אָב וְאֵם. וּבַדָּבָר הַזֶּה תַּאֲרִיכוּ יָמִים זוּ גְמִילוּת חֲסָדִים. עַל הָאֲדָמָה זֶה הֲבָאַת שָׁלוֹם בֵּין אָדָם לַחֲבֵירוֹ.

Rebbi Mana understood all of them from this verse (*Deut.* 32:47): "Because it is not an empty word from you," that is the study of Torah, "because it is your life," that is honoring father and mother, "and by this you will have a long life," that are works of kindness, "on the earth," that is making peace between men.

וּכְנֶגְדָן אַרְבָּעָה דְּבָרִים שֶׁהֵן נִפְרָעִין מִן הָאָדָם בָּעוֹלָם הַזֶּה וְהַקֶּרֶן קַיֶּימֶת לוֹ לָעוֹלָם הַבָּא. וְאֵילוּ הֵן עֲבוֹדָה זָרָה וְגִילּוּי עֲרָיוֹת וּשְׁפִיכוּת דָּמִים. וְלָשׁוֹן הָרַע כְּנֶגֶד כּוּלָּן. עֲבוֹדָה זָרָה מְנַיִין. הִכָּרֵת תִּכָּרֵת הַנֶּפֶשׁ הַהִיא עֲוֹנָהּ בָהּ. מַה תַלְמוּד לוֹמַר עֲוֹנָהּ בָּהּ מְלַמֵּד שֶׁהַנֶּפֶשׁ נִכְרְתָה וַעֲוֹנָהּ עִמָּהּ. וּכְתִיב אָנָּא חָטָא הָעָם הַזֶּה

חֲטָאָה גְדוֹלָה וַיַּעֲשׂוּ לָהֶם אֱלֹהֵי זָהָב. גִּילּוּי עֲרָיוֹת מְנַיִין. וְאֵיךְ אֶעֱשֶׂה הָרָעָה הַגְּדוֹלָה הַזֹּאת וְחָטָאתִי לֵאלֹהִים. שְׁפִיכוּת דָּמִים מְנַיִין. וַיֹּאמֶר קַיִן אֶל יי גָּדוֹל עֲוֹנִי מִנְּשׂוֹא. כְּשֶׁהוּא בָּא אֵצֶל לְשׁוֹן הָרָע מַהוּ אוֹמֵר לֹא גָּדוֹל וְלֹא גְדוֹלָה וְלֹא הַגְּדוֹלָה אֶלָּא גְּדוֹלוֹת יַכְרֵת יי כָּל־שִׂפְתֵי חֲלָקוֹת לְשׁוֹן מְדַבֶּרֶת גְּדוֹלוֹת.

Correspondingly[150], there are four things that a person has to pay for in this world and the principal remains for him in the future world: Idolatry, incest and adultery, and murder. But slander is equivalent to all of these. Idolatry from where? (*Num.* 15:31) "This soul shall certainly be cut off, its sin is inside it." Why does the verse say "its sin is inside it?" This teaches that the soul is destroyed and its sin is still inside it. And it is written (*Ex.* 32:21): "Please, this people has committed a grave sin, they made for themselves golden gods.[151]" Incest and adultery from where? (*Gen.* 39:9) "How can I commit that grave evil and sin before God." Murder from where? (*Gen.* 4:13) "Cain said to the Eternal, my sin is grave, it cannot be removed." When he comes to calumny, it does not say in the singular "grave" or "the grave" but in the plural "grave" (*Ps.* 12:4): "May the Eternal cut off all slippery lips, all tongues speaking grave words[152]."

150 Tosephta *Peah* 1:2.

151 The first verse proves that the sin stays in the soul at death, the second verse is a paradigm that such a sin is called "grave;" the latter expression is then used to characterize the other deadly sins.

152 This is the introduction to a lengthy section on the sin of calumny.

כְּתִיב וַיָּבֵא יוֹסֵף אֶת דִּבָּתָם רָעָה אֶל אֲבִיהֶם. מַה אָמַר רִבִּי מֵאִיר וְרִבִּי יְהוּדָה וְרִבִּי שִׁמְעוֹן. רִבִּי מֵאִיר אָמַר חֲשׁוּדִין הֵן עַל אֵבֶר מִן הַחַי. רִבִּי יְהוּדָה אוֹמֵר מְזַלְזְלִין (fol. 16a) הֵן בִּבְנֵי הַשְּׁפָחוֹת וְנוֹהֲגִין בָּהֶן כַּעֲבָדִים. וְרִבִּי שִׁמְעוֹן אוֹמֵר נוֹתְנִין הֵן עֵינֵיהֶן בִּבְנוֹת הָאָרֶץ. אָמַר רִבִּי יוּדָה בֶּן פָּזִי פֶּלֶס וּמֹאזְנֵי מִשְׁפָּט לַיי מַעֲשֵׂהוּ כָּל־אַבְנֵי כִיס. מַה אָמַר חֲשׁוּדִין הֵן עַל אֵבֶר מִן הַחַי. אָמַר הַקָּדוֹשׁ

בָּרוּךְ הוּא כָּךְ אֲנִי מוֹכִיחַ עֲלֵיהֶן שֶׁהֵן שׁוֹחֲטִין וְאוֹכְלִין וַיִּשְׁחֲטוּ שְׂעִיר עִזִּים וַיִּטְבְּלוּ אֶת הַכֻּתֹּנֶת בַּדָּם. מַה אָמַר מְזַלְזְלִין הֵן בִּבְנֵי הַשְּׁפָחוֹת וְנוֹהֲגִין בָּהֶן כַּעֲבָדִים לְעֶבֶד נִמְכַּר יוֹסֵף. מַה אָמַר נוֹתְנִין עֵינֵיהֶן בִּבְנוֹת הָאָרֶץ. הָא דוּבָּא מִתְגָּרְיָא לָךְ. וַתִּשָּׂא אֵשֶׁת אֲדוֹנָיו אֶת עֵינֶיהָ אֶל יוֹסֵף וְגוֹמֵר.

In its written (*Gen*. 37:2): "And Joseph reported their evil slander to their father." What did he say? Rebbi Meir, Rebbi Jehudah, and Rebbi Simeon. Rebbi Meir said, they are suspected of eating flesh from a living animal[153]. Rebbi Jehudah said, they abuse the sons of the handmaidens and treat them like slaves. Rebbi Simeon said, they are infatuated with local girls[154]. Rebbi Judah ben Pazi said, (*Prov*. 16:11) "Balance and scales of justice are the Eternal's; all weight-stones are His work." What did he say, they are suspected of eating flesh from a living animal? The Holy One, praise to Him, said: So I testify for them that they first slaughter and then eat, (*Gen*. 37:31) "they slaughtered the he-goat and dipped the coat into the blood." What did he say, they abuse the sons of the handmaidens and treat them like slaves? (*Ps*. 105:17) "Joseph was sold as a slave." What did he say, they are infatuated with local girls? Lo, a she-bear will attack you, (*Gen*. 39:7) "his master's wife lifted her eyes to Joseph, etc."

153 This is forbidden for all mankind as one of the Seven Commandments to the Sons of Noah.

154 Canaanites whom they are forbidden to marry.

רִבִּי יַסָּא בְשֵׁם רִבִּי יוֹחָנָן זֶה שֶׁהוּא אוֹמֵר לָשׁוֹן הָרַע אֵינוֹ אוֹמֵר עַד שֶׁהוּא כוֹפֵר בְּעִיקָּר. וּמַה טַעֲמָא אֲשֶׁר אָמְרוּ לִלְשׁוֹנֵינוּ נַגְבִּיר שְׂפָתֵינוּ אִתָּנוּ מִי אָדוֹן לָנוּ. כָּל־הָעֲבֵירוֹת אָדָם חוֹטֵא בָאָרֶץ וְאֵילוּ חוֹטְאִין בַּשָּׁמַיִם וּבָאָרֶץ. מָה טַעֲמָא שַׁתּוּ בַשָּׁמַיִם פִּיהֶם וּלְשׁוֹנָם תִּיהֲלַךְ בָּאָרֶץ. אָמַר רִבִּי יִצְחָק בִּינוּ זֹאת שֹׁכְחֵי אֱלוֹהַּ פֶּן יִטְרוֹף וְאֵין מַצִּיל. אָמַר רִבִּי יְהוֹשֻׁעַ בֶּן לֵוִי תֵּשֵׁב בְּאָחִיךָ תְדַבֵּר בְּבֶן אִמְּךָ תִתֵּן דוֹפִי. מַה כְתִיב תַּמָּן וּלְרָשָׁע אָמַר אֱלֹהִים מַה לְּךָ לְסַפֵּר חֻקָּי וַתִּשָּׂא בְרִיתִי עֲלֵי פִיךָ.

Rebbi Yasa in the name of Rebbi Joḥanan: He who calumniates does not speak until he has disowned the principle[155]. What is the reason? (*Ps.* 12:5) "Who said, by our tongues we shall overcome, our lips are with us, who is master over us[156]?" All sins a person commits on earth, but this one they commit both in heaven and on earth. What is the reason? (*Ps.* 73:9) "They put their mouths in heaven and their tongue wanders about the earth." Rebbi Isaac said[157] (*Ps.* 50:22): "Understand that, those who are forgetting God, lest He will tear[158] and nobody may rescue." Rebbi Joshua ben Levi said (*Ps.* 50:20): "You sit, talk against your brother, you find fault with your mother's son." What is written there? (*Ps.* 50:16) "God said to the evildoer, what right do you have to speak about My laws, to keep My covenant in your mouth?"

155 The principle of the Jewish faith, that God is the Ultimate Judge.

156 This is a declaration of atheism.

157 It is difficult to see what the sermon of R. Isaac is. Probably, one should read: R. Isaac in the name of R. Joshua ben Levi said .... We also find elsewhere that R. Isaac quotes traditions of R. Joshua ben Levi. The essence of the latter's sermon is that the evildoer is defined as the calumniator and, by the last verse quoted, as such is forbidden to study Torah and to recite the *Shema'*; i. e., even if he did try to fulfill the basic intellectual commandments of Judaism it would be a sinful act on his part.

158 In the Biblical text: Lest I shall tear.

אַזְהָרָה לְלָשׁוֹן הָרַע מְנַיִין. וְנִשְׁמַרְתָּ מִכָּל־דָּבָר רָע. אָמַר רִבִּי לָא תַּנֵּי רִבִּי יִשְׁמָעֵאל לֹא תֵלֵךְ רָכִיל בְּעַמֶּךָ. זוּ רְכִילוּת לָשׁוֹן הָרַע. תַּנֵּי רִבִּי נְחֶמְיָה שֶׁלֹּא תְהֵא כְּרוֹכֵל הַזֶּה מַטְעִין דְּבָרָיו שֶׁל זֶה לְזֶה וּדְבָרָיו שֶׁל זֶה לְזֶה.

Where is a warning about calumny[159]? *(Deut.* 23:10) "Keep yourself from every evil word!" Rebbi La said that Rebbi Ismaël stated (*Lev.* 19:10): "Do not walk around as slanderer among your people," that is slandering, calumny. Rebbi Neḥemiah stated that you should not be like a trader who carries things from one person to another and vice versa.

159 Nothing can be forbidden that is not mentioned twice in the Pentateuch, once to state the prohibition and the second time to spell out the punishment for violating the commandment. [The same arguments, in the name of different Tannaïm, are in Babli *Ketubot* 46a. In *Sifry* on *Deut.* 23:10 (#254), "evil" is defined as a sin that brings exile on the people, and calumny is explicitly included.]

אָמַר רִבִּי חֲנִינָא בּוֹא וּרְאֵה כַּמָּה קָשֶׁה הוּא אֲבַק לָשׁוֹן הָרַע שֶׁדִּבְּרוּ הַכְּתוּבִים דִּבְרֵי בַּדַּאי בִּשְׁבִיל לְהַטִּיל שָׁלוֹם בֵּין אַבְרָהָם וְשָׂרָה. וַתִּצְחַק שָׂרָה בְּקִרְבָּהּ לֵאמוֹר אַחֲרֵי בְלוֹתִי הָיְתָה לִי עֶדְנָה וַאדֹנִי זָקֵן. וּלְאַבְרָהָם אֵינוֹ אוֹמֵר כֵּן אֶלָּא לָמָּה זֶּה צָחֲקָה שָׂרָה לֵאמוֹר הַאַף אֻמְנָם אֵלֵד וַאֲנִי זָקַנְתִּי. וַאדֹנִי זָקֵן אֵין כְּתִיב כָּאן אֶלָּא וַאֲנִי זָקַנְתִּי. אָמַר רַבָּן שִׁמְעוֹן בֶּן גַּמְלִיאֵל בּוֹא וּרְאֵה כַּמָּה קָשֶׁה הוּא אֲבַק לָשׁוֹן הָרַע שֶׁדִּבְּרוּ הַכְּתוּבִים דִּבְרֵי בַּדַּאי כְּדֵי לְהַטִּיל שָׁלוֹם בֵּין יוֹסֵף לְאֶחָיו. הַהוּא דִכְתִיב וַיְצַוּוּ אֶת יוֹסֵף לֵאמֹר אָבִיךָ צִוָּה לִפְנֵי מוֹתוֹ לֵאמֹר. כֹּה תֹאמְרוּ לְיוֹסֵף אָנָּא שָׂא נָא וגו׳. וְלָא אַשְׁכְּחָן דִּפְקַד כְּלוּם.

Rebbi Ḥanina said: Come and see, how hard is even a hint of calumny that the verses spoke untruth in order to make peace between Abraham and Sarah. (*Gen.* 18:12) "Sarah laughed to herself, saying: After having wilted I became dainty[160], but my master is old." To Abraham He does not say so, but rather (*Gen.* 18:13): "Why now did Sarah laugh, saying how can I give birth, being old?" It is not written "my master is old" but "I am old". Rabban Simeon ben Gamliel said[161]: Come and see, how hard is even a hint of calumny that the verses spoke untruth in order to make peace between Joseph and his brothers. That is what is written (*Gen.* 50:16-17): "They empowered [a messenger] to Joseph to say: Your father commanded before his death, saying: So you shall say to Joseph, please forgive etc." We do not find that he (Jacob) commanded anything.

160 Her wrinkles had disappeared and her period restarted.

161 The formulation in *Bereshit rabba* 100(9) is easier to understand: We have stated: Rabban Simeon ben Gamliel said, peace is great because even the tribes spoke untruth to obtain peace between themselves and Joseph.

רִבִּי שְׁמוּאֵל בַּר נַחְמָן בְּשֵׁם רִבִּי יוֹנָתָן מוּתָּר לוֹמַר לָשׁוֹן הָרַע עַל בַּעֲלֵי מַחְלוֹקֶת. וּמַה טַעַם וַאֲנִי אָבוֹא אַחֲרַיִךְ וּמִלֵּאתִי אֶת דְּבָרָיִךְ. רִבִּי זְעִירָא בְּעָא קוֹמֵי רִבִּי יַסָּא מִפְּנֵי מַה נֶהֱרַג אֲדוֹנִיָּה בֶּן חַגִּית מִפְּנֵי שֶׁתָּבַע אֶת אֲבִישַׁג הַשּׁוּנַמִּית. אָמַר לֵיהּ עֲיָלָה הָיוּ מְבַקְּשִׁין לְהַתִּיר דָּמָן שֶׁל בַּעֲלֵי מַחְלוֹקֶת.

Rebbi Samuel bar Naḥman in the name of Rebbi Jonathan: One may calumniate disruptive persons. What is the reason? (*1K*. 1:14) "I shall come after you and confirm your words.[162]" Rebbi Zeïra asked before Rebbi Yasa: Why was Adoniah ben Ḥaggit killed? Because he asked for Avishag of Shunem[163]? He said to him, they were looking for a pretext to proscribe the lives of disruptive persons.

162 While Bat Sheba told the truth, the intervention of Nathan is intended to cause trouble to Adoniah. Hence, the sin of calumny extends even to true statements unless their publication has some value for the public peace.

163 What was a problem for the Yerushalmi was none for the Babli, *Sanhedrin* 22b, where the Galilean Rebbi Jacob in the name of R. Joḥanan explains that Avishag, while she was not a concubine of David, had the legal status of one and, therefore, could not be married to anybody but a king.

בְּעוֹן קוֹמֵי רִבִּי יוֹחָנָן אֵי זֶהוּ לָשׁוֹן הָרַע הָאוֹמְרוֹ וְהַיּוֹדְעוֹ.

They asked before Rebbi Joḥanan: Who is guilty of calumny? He who says it and he who accepts it[164].

164 The person who accepts information which he recognizes as calumny without protesting is as guilty as the one who disseminates it.

חֲנוּתָא דְּכִיתְנָאֵי הֲוָה לוֹן צוֹמוּת וַהֲוָה תַּמָּן חַד מִיתְקְרֵי בַּר חוֹבֶץ וְלָא סְלִיק. אָמְרֵי מַה אֲנָן אָכְלִין יוֹמָא דֵין אֲמַר חַד חוֹבְצִין אֲמַר יֵיתֵי בַּר חֲבִיץ. אָמַר רִבִּי יוֹחָנָן זֶה אָמַר לָשׁוֹן הָרַע בְּהַצְנֵעַ. בּוּלֶווטַיָּה דְּצִיפּוֹרִין הֲוָה לְהוֹן צוֹמוּת וַהֲוָה תַּמָּן חַד מִיתְקְרֵי יוֹחָנָן וְלֹא סְלַק אֲמַר חַד לְחַד לֵית אֲנָן סָלְקִין מְבַקְּרָה לְרִבִּי יוֹחָנָן יוֹמָא דֵין. אָמְרִין יֵיתֵי יוֹחָנָן. אָמַר רִבִּי שִׁמְעוֹן בֶּן לָקִישׁ זֶה אָמַר לָשׁוֹן הָרַע בְּצֶדֶק.

The linen traders had an assembly[165]. There was one whose nickname was Bar Ḥovez̩ (son of the cheesemaker) who did not appear. They said: What are we going to eat today? One said: cheese, then the cheeser will come. Rebbi Joḥanan said, this one was calumniating in secret[166]. The city councilmen[167] of Sepphoris had an assembly. There was one by the name of Joḥanan who did not appear. One said to the other, let us visit Rebbi Joḥanan today. They said[168], Joḥanan will come[169]. Rebbi Simeon ben Laqish said, this one calumniated justly.

165 The root is צמת "to take, squeeze, together."

166 By making fun of a nickname.

167 Greek βουλευταί "councilmen".

168 This seems to be a scribal error since it follows from the next remark that a single person said so.

169 When he hears that he is given the title of Rebbi.

אָמַר רִבִּי אַבָּא בַּר כַּהֲנָא דּוֹרוֹ שֶׁל דָּוִד כּוּלָּן צַדִּיקִים הָיוּ וְעַל יְדֵי שֶׁהָיָה לָהֶן דֵּילָטוֹרִין הָיוּ יוֹצְאִין בַּמִּלְחָמָה וְהָיוּ נוֹפְלִין. הוּא שֶׁדָּוִד אָמַר נַפְשִׁי בְּתוֹךְ לְבָאִים אֶשְׁכְּבָה לוֹהֲטִים. נַפְשִׁי בְּתוֹךְ לְבָאִים זֶה אַבְנֵר וַעֲמָשָׂה שֶׁהָיוּ לְבָאִים בַּתּוֹרָה. אֶשְׁכְּבָה לוֹהֲטִים זֶה דוֹאֵג וַאֲחִיתוֹפֶל שֶׁהָיוּ לְהוּטִין אַחַר לָשׁוֹן הָרַע. בְּנֵי אָדָם שִׁינֵּיהֶם חֲנִית וְחִצִּים אֵלּוּ בַּעֲלֵי קְעִילָה. דִּכְתִיב הֲיַסְגִּרוּנִי בַּעֲלֵי קְעִילָה בְיָדוֹ הֲיֵרֵד שָׁאוּל. וּלְשׁוֹנָם חֶרֶב חַדָּה אֵילּוּ הַזִּיפִים בְּבוֹא הַזִּיפִים וַיֹּאמְרוּ לְשָׁאוּל. בְּאוֹתָהּ שָׁעָה אָמַר דָּוִד לִפְנֵי הַקָּדוֹשׁ בָּרוּךְ הוּא רִבּוֹן הָעוֹלָמִים מַה שְׁכִינָתְךָ לֵירֵד בָּאָרֶץ סַלֵּק שְׁכִינָתְךָ מִבֵּינֵיהוֹן. הַהוּא דִכְתִיב רוּמָה עַל שָׁמַיִם

אֱלֹהִים עַל כָּל־הָאָרֶץ כְּבוֹדֶךָ. אֲבָל דּוֹרוֹ שֶׁל אַחְאָב עוֹבְדֵי עֲבוֹדָה זָרָה הָיוּ וְעַל יְדֵי שֶׁלֹּא הָיָה לָהֶן דֵּילָטוֹרְיָא הָיוּ יוֹרְדִין לַמִּלְחָמָה וְנוֹצְחִין הוּא שֶׁעוֹבַדְיָהוּ אָמַר לְאֵלִיָּהוּ הֲלֹא הוּגַּד לַאדוֹנִי אֲשֶׁר עָשִׂיתִי בַּהֲרוֹג אִיזֶבֶל אֶת נְבִיאֵי יי וְגוֹמֵר וָאֲכַלְכְּלֵם לֶחֶם וָמָיִם. אִם לֶחֶם לָמָּה מַיִם וְאִם מַיִם לָמָּה לֶחֶם. אֶלָּא מְלַמֵּד שֶׁהָיוּ הַמַּיִם קָשִׁין לוֹ לְהָבִיא יוֹתֵר מִן הַלֶּחֶם. וְאֵלִיָּהוּ מַכְרִיז בְּרֹאשׁ הַכַּרְמֶל אֲנִי נוֹתַרְתִּי נָבִיא לְבַדִּי לַיי. וְכָל־עַמָּא יָדְעוּן וְלָא מְפַרְסְמִין לְמַלְכָּא.

Rebbi Abba bar Cahana said, the generation of David were all just[170] but because there were informers[171] among them they went to war and were falling. That is what David said (*Ps.* 57:9-10): "My soul, among lions I am lying down with blazing fires." "My soul, among lions," these are Abner and Amasah who were lions in Torah; "I am lying down with blazing fires;" these are Doeg and Aḥitophel who were eager for calumny. "The people, their teeth are spear and arrows," these are the owners of Qe'ilah, as it is written (*1Sam.* 23:11): "Will the owners of Qe'ilah deliver me in his hand, will Saul come?" "Their tongue is a sharp sword," these are the people of Ziph (*Ps.* 54:1): "When the people of Ziph came and told Saul." At that moment, David said before the Holy One, praised be He: Master of the Universe, why should Your glory descend among them? Remove Your glory from them! That is what is written (*Ps.* 57:6): "Rise over the Heavens, o God, higher than all earth Your glory!" The generation of Ahab were idolaters but since there was no informing among them they went to war and were victorious. That is what Obadiahu said to Elijah (*1K.* 18:13): "Certainly it was told to my lord what I did when Izebel slew all prophets of the Eternal etc., and I provided them with bread and water." [If bread, why does he have to mention water[172], and if water, why does he have to mention bread. This teaches you that it was more difficult for him to provide them with water than with bread.] But Elijah was standing on Mount Carmel and declaring (*1K.

18:22): "I remained alone as prophet for the Eternal," and everybody knew and nobody informed the king[173].

170 At least on the surface they were no idolaters.

171 Latin *delator* "informer," *delatio*, later form *delatura* "denunciation."

172 Since "bread" may mean "food".

173 That there were another hundred prophets hidden by Obadiahu.

וְלָמָּה קוֹרֵא אוֹתוֹ שְׁלִישִׁי שֶׁהוּא הוֹרֵג שְׁלֹשָׁה הָאוֹמְרוֹ וְהַמְקַבְּלוֹ וְזֶה שֶׁנֶּאֱמַר עָלָיו. וּבִימֵי שָׁאוּל נֶהֶרְגוּ אַרְבָּעָה דּוֹאֵג שֶׁאֲמָרוֹ שָׁאוּל שֶׁקִּיבְּלוֹ אֲחִימֶלֶךְ שֶׁנֶּאֱמַר עָלָיו וְאַבְנֵר. אַבְנֵר לָמָּה נֶהֱרַג. רִבִּי יְהוֹשֻׁעַ בֶּן לֵוִי וְרִבִּי שִׁמְעוֹן בֶּן לָקִישׁ וְרַבָּנִין. רִבִּי יְהוֹשֻׁעַ בֶּן לֵוִי אָמַר עַל שֶׁעָשָׂה דָמָן שֶׁל נְעָרִים שְׂחוֹק שֶׁנֶּאֱמַר יָקוּמוּ נָא וִישַׂחֲקוּ לְפָנֵינוּ וַיֹּאמֶר אַבְנֵר יָקוּמוּ. וְרֵישׁ לָקִישׁ עַל שֶׁהִקְדִּים שְׁמוֹ לִשְׁמוֹ שֶׁל דָּוִד הַהוּא דִכְתִיב וַיִּשְׁלַח אַבְנֵר מַלְאָכִים אֶל דָּוִד תַּחְתָּיו לֵאמֹר לְמִי הָאָרֶץ. כָּתַב מִן אַבְנֵר לְדָוִד. וְרַבָּנִין אָמְרִין עַל שֶׁלֹּא הִנִּיחַ לְשָׁאוּל לְהִתְפַּייֵס מִן דָּוִד. הַהוּא דִכְתִיב וְאָבִי רְאֵה גַּם רְאֵה אֶת כְּנַף מְעִילְךָ בְּיָדִי. אֲמַר לֵיהּ מַה אַתְּ בָּעֵי מִן גּוּלְגְּלוֹי הַדֵּין בְּסִירָה הוּעֲרַת. וְכֵיוָן שֶׁבָּאוּ לְמַעְגָּל אָמַר לֵיהּ הֲלֹא תַעֲנֶה אַבְנֵר. גַּבֵּי כָּנָף אָמְרַת בְּסִירָה הוּעֲרַת חֲנִית וְצַפַּחַת בְּסִירָה הוּעֲרוּ. וְיֵשׁ אוֹמְרִים עַל יְדֵי שֶׁהָיְתָה סְפֵיקָה בְיָדוֹ לִמְחוֹת בְּנוֹב עִיר הַכֹּהֲנִים וְלֹא מִיחָה.

Why is it called "triple[174]?" Because it kills three: The one who says it, the one who accepts it, and the one calumniated. And in the days of Saul, four were killed: Doeg who said it[175], Saul who accepted it, Aḥimelekh who was calumniated, and Abner. Why was Abner killed? Rebbi Joshua ben Levi, Rebbi Simeon ben Laqish, and the rabbis. Rebbi Joshua ben Levi said, because he made fun of the lives of his squires as it is said (*2Sam.* 2:14): "Let the squires get up and play before us, and Joab[176] said, let them get up." R. Simeon ben Laqish, because he prefaced his name before that of David; that is what is written (*2Sam.* 3:12) "Abner sent messengers to David the underling, saying: Whose is the land?" He wrote:

From Abner to David[177]. The rabbis say, because he did not let Shaul make peace with David. That is what is written (*1Sam.* 24:5): "My father, see, but see the corner of your coat in my hand!" He said to him, what do you want from the prattling[178] of this one, it was torn off by thorns[179]. But when they came to the circle, he said to him (*1Sam.* 26:14): "Can you answer, Abner?" About the corner, you said it was torn off by a thorn; were spear and pitcher cut off by a thorn? But some say, because he had it in his power to intervene for Nob, the city of priests, and he did not intervene.

174 In all Yerushalmi Targumim, calumny is called לִישָּׁן תְּלִיתָאִי "triple tongue." The same explanation is given in Babli *Arakhin* 15b.

175 That the priests of Nob had given David the holy bread.

176 The reading of the text, אבנר, not only contradicts the reading of the verse but makes no sense here since Abner was the instigator of the duel.

177 A letter addressed to the king would read: "To David from Abner." The supposed inversion is intended to show that Abner considered himself a king maker, not an executor of God's will as declared by Samuel.

178 It seems that Yerushalmi גלגל is the same as Babylonian לגלג.

179 Rabbinic feminine סירה is the same as Biblical masculine סיר "thorn."

חִצֵּי גִבּוֹר שְׁנוּנִים עִם גַּחֲלֵי רְתָמִים. כָּל־כְּלֵי זַיִין מַכִּין בִּמְקוֹמָן. וְזֶה מַכֶּה מֵרָחוֹק. כָּל־הַגְּחָלִים כָּבוּ מִבְּחוּץ כָּבוּ מִבִּפְנִים. וְאֵלּוּ אַף עַל פִּי שֶׁכָּבוּ מִבְּחוּץ לֹא כָּבוּ מִבִּפְנִים. מַעֲשֶׂה בְּאֶחָד שֶׁהִנִּיחַ גְּחָלִים בּוֹעֲרוֹת בְּחָג וּבָא וּמְצָאָן בּוֹעֲרוֹת בְּפֶסַח.

(*Ps.* 120:4) "The arrows of a hero are sharpened over hot broom coals." All weapons kill at their place but this kills[179] at a distance. All other charcoal that is extinguished on the outside, is also extinguished on the inside, but these, even though they are extinguished on the outside, are still burning on the inside. It happened to one that he put down burning charcoal on *Sukkot* and came and found them still burning on *Pesah*.

179 Arrow or calumny.

אָמַר רִבִּי שְׁמוּאֵל בַּר נַחְמָן אוֹמֵר לְנָחָשׁ מִפְּנֵי מַה אַתָּה מְהַלֵּךְ וּלְשׁוֹנְךָ שׁוֹתֵת. אָמַר לוֹן דּוּ גָרַם לִי. מַה הֲנָיָיה לָךְ שֶׁאַתְּ נוֹשֵׁךְ. אַרְיֵה טוֹרֵף וְאוֹכֵל זְאֵב טוֹרֵף וְאוֹכֵל אַתְּ מַה הֲנָיָיה לָךְ. אָמַר לָהֶן אִם יִשֹּׁךְ הַנָּחָשׁ בְּלִי לָחַשׁ. אִילוּלֵי אִיתְאַמַּר לִי מִן שְׁמַיָּא נְכִית לֹא הֲוֵינָא נְכִית. מִפְּנֵי מַה אַתָּה נוֹשֵׁךְ אֵבֶר אֶחָד וְכָל הָאֵיבָרִים מַרְגִּישִׁין. אָמַר לָהֶן וְלִי אַתֶּם שׁוֹאֲלִין אִמְרוּ לְבַעַל הַלָּשׁוֹן שֶׁהוּא אוֹמֵר כַּאן וְהוֹרֵג בְּרוֹמֵי. אוֹמֵר בְּרוֹמֵי וְהוֹרֵג בְּסוּרְיָה. וּמִפְּנֵי מַה אַתָּה מָצוּי בֵּין הַגְּדֵרוֹת. אָמַר לָהֶן אֲנִי פָּרַצְתִּי (fol. 16b) גְּדֵרוֹ שֶׁל עוֹלָם.

Rebbi Samuel ben Naḥman said: One says to the snake, why when you move does your tongue flow? It said to them, that[180] caused it for me[181]. What profit do you have from biting? A lion tears up and eats, a wolf tears up and eats; you, what profit do you have from biting[182]? It said to them (*Eccl.* 10:11): "If the snake would bite without a whisper," I would not bite unless it was said to me from heaven: bite! Why do you bite one limb and all limbs feel it? It said to them: Why do you ask me? Ask the master of the tongue[183] who speaks here and kills in Rome[184], speaks in Rome and kills in Syria. Why are you found among fences? It said to them, I broke the fence of the world[185].

180 דּוּ = דְּהוּא.

181 Because of my evil talk (and calumny about God) I was turned into a snake.

182 A human who is much too big to swallow.

183 The calumniator.

184 Hebrew spelling perhaps derived from Greek Ῥώμη, "Rome". The Latin locative *Romae*, "in Rome", since the word is preceded by בְּ, "in", is probably not meant. But redundant constructions involving foreign words are found in the Yerushalmi.

185 By being the first to commit adultery [cf. the author's *The Scholar's Haggadah* (Northvale 1995), pp. 308-309.]

הַזְּכוּת יֵשׁ לָהּ קֶרֶן וְיֵשׁ לָהּ פֵּירוֹת. עֲבֵירָה יֵשׁ לָהּ קֶרֶן וְאֵין לָהּ פֵּירוֹת. הַזְּכוּת יֵשׁ לָהּ קֶרֶן וְיֵשׁ לָהּ פֵּירוֹת שֶׁנֶּאֱמַר אִמְרוּ צַדִּיק כִּי טוֹב כִּי פְרִי מַעַלְלֵיהֶם יֹאכֵלוּ. עֲבֵירָה יֵשׁ לָהּ קֶרֶן וְאֵין לָהּ פֵּירוֹת שֶׁנֶּאֱמַר אוֹי לְרָשָׁע רָע כִּי גְמוּל יָדָיו יֵעָשֶׂה לּוֹ. מַה אֲנִי מְקַיֵּים וַיֹּאכְלוּ מִפְּרִי דַרְכָּם. אֶלָּא כָּל־עֲבֵירָה שֶׁעָשְׂת פֶּרִי יֵשׁ לָהּ פֶּרִי וּשְׁלֹּא עָשְׂת פֶּרִי אֵין לָהּ פֶּרִי.

Merit has capital[186] and yield[187]; sin has capital but no yield. Merit has capital and has yield, as it is said (*Is.* 3:10): "Tell the just that it is very well, that they will eat the fruit of their actions." Sin has capital but no yield, as it is said (*Is.* 3:11): "Woe to the bad criminal, the retribution for his actions will be come upon him." How can I confirm (*Prov.* 1:31): "They[188] will eat from the fruits of their way?" Every sin that produces fruit has yield[189], that which does not produce fruit has no yield.

186 It determines the reward in the world to come. (The entire paragraph is from Tosephta *Peah*, 1:2-3, also quoted Babli *Qiddušin* 40a).

187 The rewards in this world that are given without diminishing the rewards in the world to come.

188 Evildoers.

189 The adulterer who produces a bastard child will be punished for the child in this world while all the punishment for adultery is reserved for the future world.

מַחֲשָׁבָה טוֹבָה הַקָּדוֹשׁ בָּרוּךְ הוּא מְצָרְפָהּ לְמַעֲשֶׂה. מַחֲשָׁבָה רָעָה אֵין הַקָּדוֹשׁ בָּרוּךְ הוּא מְצָרְפָהּ לְמַעֲשֶׂה. מַחֲשָׁבָה טוֹבָה הַקָּדוֹשׁ בָּרוּךְ הוּא מְצָרְפָהּ לְמַעֲשֶׂה דִּכְתִיב אָז נִדְבְּרוּ יִרְאֵי יי אִישׁ אֶל רֵעֵהוּ. מַחֲשָׁבָה רָעָה אֵין הַקָּדוֹשׁ בָּרוּךְ הוּא מְצָרְפָהּ לְמַעֲשֶׂה אָוֶן אִם רָאִיתִי בְלִבִּי לֹא יִשְׁמַע יי. הָדָא דְתֵימָא בְּיִשְׂרָאֵל אֲבָל בַּגּוֹיִם חִילּוּפִין מַחֲשָׁבָה טוֹבָה אֵין הַקָּדוֹשׁ בָּרוּךְ הוּא מְצָרְפָהּ. מַחֲשָׁבָה רָעָה הַקָּדוֹשׁ בָּרוּךְ הוּא מְצָרְפָהּ. מַחֲשָׁבָה טוֹבָה אֵין הַקָּדוֹשׁ בָּרוּךְ הוּא מְצָרְפָהּ. דִּכְתִיב וְעַד מֶעָלֵי שִׁמְשָׁא הֲוָה מִשְׁתַּדַּר לְהַצָּלוּתֵיהּ. וְלָא כְתִיב לְשֵׁיזְבֵיהּ. מַחֲשָׁבָה רָעָה הַקָּדוֹשׁ בָּרוּךְ הוּא מְצָרְפָהּ. מִקָּטֶל מֵחֲמַס אָחִיךָ יַעֲקֹב. וְכִי הֲרָגוֹ. אֶלָּא מְלַמֵּד שֶׁחָשַׁב עָלָיו לְהוֹרְגוֹ וְהֶעֱלָה עָלָיו הַכָּתוּב כְּאִילּוּ הֲרָגוֹ.

The[190] Holy One, praise to Him, adds good intention to deeds; the Holy One, praise to Him, does not add bad intention to deeds. The Holy One, praise to Him, adds good intention to deeds as it is written (*Mal.* 3:16): "Then those who fear the Eternal will speak together, each man with his neighbor[191]." The Holy One, praise to Him, does not add bad intention to deeds (*Ps.* 66:12): "If I saw mischief in my heart, the Eternal would not listen." That refers to Israel, but for Gentiles it is the reverse; the Holy One, praise to Him, does not add good intention; bad intention the Holy One, praise to Him, does add. The Holy One, praise to Him, does not add good intention, as it is written (*Dan.* 6:15): "Until sundown he tried to rescue him;" it does not say "to save him[192]." The Holy One, praise to Him, adds bad intention: (*Obad.* 9-10) "From killing[193]. Because of the oppression of your brother Jacob." But did he kill him? This teaches that he thought about killing him and the verse counts it as if he had killed him.

190 The first clause of this paragraph is also in the Tosephta and Babli mentioned in Note 186. The second part is different both in the Babli and the Tosephta which both make a difference between good deeds that produced yield and those that did not. The Tosephta clearly represents the position of the Babli.

191 The proof is from the part of the verse not quoted: "The Eternal will be attentive and listen and write it into a book of remembrance before Him," simply for the good intention.

192 Even though the first part of the verse, not quoted here, declares that Darius tried to save Daniel from the lions' den.

193 In the masoretic text, the word belongs to the previous verse, stating that nobody from Mount Seïr will escape being killed. Here the word is taken as explanation of the following verse.

תַּנֵּי רִבִּי שִׁמְעוֹן בֶּן יוֹחַי הֲרֵי שֶׁהָיָה אָדָם צַדִּיק גָּמוּר כָּל־יָמָיו וּבְאַחֲרוֹנָה מָרַד אִיבֵּד זֶה כָּל־מַה שֶּׁעָשָׂה כָּל־יָמָיו מָה טַעַם וּבְשׁוּב צַדִּיק מִצִּדְקָתוֹ וְעָשָׂה עָוֶל.

רִבִּי שִׁמְעוֹן בֶּן לָקִישׁ אָמַר וּבְתוֹהֵא עַל הָרִאשׁוֹנוֹת. הֲרֵי שֶׁהָיָה אָדָם רָשָׁע גָּמוּר כָּל־יָמָיו וּבְסוֹף עָשָׂה תְשׁוּבָה הַקָּדוֹשׁ בָּרוּךְ הוּא מְקַבְּלוֹ מַה טַעַם וּבְשׁוּב רָשָׁע מֵרִשְׁעָתוֹ. אָמַר רִבִּי יוֹחָנָן וְלֹא עוֹד אֶלָּא כָּל־הָעֲבֵירוֹת שֶׁעָשָׂה הֵן נֶחֱשָׁבִין עָלָיו כִּזְכִיּוֹת מַה טַעַם מוֹר וַאֲהָלוֹת קְצִיעוֹת כָּל־בִּגְדוֹתֶיךָ. כָּל־בְּגִידוֹת שֶׁבָּגַדְתָּ בִּי הֲרֵי הֵן כְּמוֹר וַאֲהָלוֹת וּקְצִיעוֹת.

Rebbi Simeon ben Iohai stated: If a person was perfectly just all his days and at the end he rebelled, he lost all he worked for his entire life. What is the reason? (*Ez.* 33:18) "If a just person reverts from his justness and does mischief[194]." Rebbi Simeon ben Laqish said, if he wonders about his earlier deeds. If a person was perfectly evil all his days and at the end he repents, the Holy One, praise to Him, receives him. What is the reason? (*Ez.* 33:27) "If a sinner returns from his wickedness[195]." Rebbi Johanan said, not only that but all transgressions are counted as merits for him. What is the reason? (*Ps.* 45:9) "Myrrh, aloe, cassia, all your faithlessness[196]." All faithless acts in which you were faithless towards Me are like myrrh, aloe, and cassia.

194 His prior merit will not be counted.

195 His prior wickedness will not be counted.

196 In the context of the verse, the word means "your clothes." The Hebrew double root בגד "clothing - dealing treacherously" cannot be explained from cognate languages.

רוּבּוֹ זְכִיּוֹת וּמִיעוּטוֹ עֲבֵירוֹת נִפְרָעִין מִמֶּנּוּ מִיעוּט עֲבֵירוֹת קַלּוֹת שֶׁעָשָׂה בָּעוֹלָם הַזֶּה בִּשְׁבִיל לִיתֵּן לוֹ שְׂכָרוֹ מֻשְׁלָם לֶעָתִיד לָבוֹא. אֲבָל רוּבּוֹ עֲבֵירוֹת וּמִיעוּטוֹ זְכִיּוֹת. נוֹתְנִין לוֹ שְׂכַר מִצְוֹת קַלּוֹת שֶׁעָשָׂה בָּעוֹלָם הַזֶּה בִּשְׁבִיל לִיפָּרַע מִמֶּנּוּ מֻשְׁלָם לֶעָתִיד לָבוֹא. אֲבָל הַפּוֹרֵק עוֹל וְהַמֵּיפֵר בְּרִית וְהַמְגַלֶּה פָּנִים בַּתּוֹרָה אַף עַל פִּי שֶׁיֵּשׁ בְּיָדוֹ מַעֲשִׂים טוֹבִים נִפְרָעִין מִמֶּנּוּ בָּעוֹלָם הַזֶּה וְהַקֶּרֶן קַיֶּימֶת לוֹ לָעוֹלָם הַבָּא. עֲבוֹדָה זָרָה וְגִילּוּי עֲרָיוֹת. רִבִּי יוֹנָה וְרִבִּי יוֹסֵי חַד אָמַר בְּקַלּוֹת

וְחַד אָמַר בַּחֲמוּרוֹת. מַה הֲנָן קַייָמִין. אִם בְּאוֹתוֹ שֶׁעָשָׂה תְשׁוּבָה אֵין כָּל־דָּבָר עוֹמֵד בִּפְנֵי כָּל־בַּעֲלֵי תְשׁוּבָה. אֶלָּא כִּי אֲנָן קַייָמִין בְּאוֹתוֹ שֶׁלֹּא עָשָׂה תְשׁוּבָה וּמֵת בְּיִיסוּרִין.

From one who has mostly merit and a minority of sins they[197] collect in this world for the minority of light sins in order to give him his complete reward in the future. But to one who has mostly sins and a minority of merits they give the reward for light merits in this world in order to collect from him his complete punishment in the future world. But[198] from one who tears away the yoke, who breaks the covenant, and who finds aspects in the Torah, even though he has meritorious deeds to his credit, they exact payment in this world and the capital remains for him in the future world. Idolatry and incest and adultery, Rebbi Jonah and Rebbi Yose: One says, among the easy ones[199], and one says, among the hard ones. What are we talking about? If he repented, there is nothing that stands in the way of those who repent. But what we are talking about is one who did not repent but died in pain[200].

197 The Heavenly Court.

198 Similar but different statements in the name of R. Eliezer Hamodaï are in Mishnah *Avot* 3:11, *Avot dRebbi Natan A* 26. The meaning of the terms in this statement is explained in the next paragraph.

199 The easy sins are punished in this world, the hard ones in the World to Come.

200 The question is whether an idolater or adulterer who dies in pain has received his punishment or whether he has to expect his main punishment in the World to Come. The Babli, *Yoma* 86a, sides with the first opinion and reserves eternal punishment only for those who desecrate the Holy Name, i. e., bring disgrace upon the Jewish religion.

תַּמָּן תַּנֵּינָן אֵילּוּ שֶׁאֵין לָהֶן חֵלֶק לְעוֹלָם הַבָּא הָאוֹמֵר אֵין תְּחִייַת מֵתִים וְאֵין תּוֹרָה מִן הַשָּׁמַיִם וְאֶפִּיקוּרוֹס. רִבִּי עֲקִיבָה אוֹמֵר אַף הַקּוֹרֵא בִסְפָרִים

הַחִיצוֹנִים. וְהַלּוֹחֵשׁ עַל הַמַּכָּה וְאוֹמֵר כָּל־הַמַּחֲלָה אֲשֶׁר שַׂמְתִּי בְמִצְרַיִם לֹא אָשִׂים עָלֶיךָ כִּי אֲנִי ״ רוֹפְאֶךָ. אַבָּא שָׁאוּל אוֹמֵר אַף הָהוֹגֶה אֶת הַשֵּׁם בְּאוֹתִיּוֹתָיו. הוֹסִיפוּ עֲלֵיהֶן הַפּוֹרֵק עוֹל וְהַמֵּיפֵר בְּרִית וְהַמְגַלֶּה פָּנִים בַּתּוֹרָה אֵין לָהֶן חֵלֶק לְעוֹלָם הַבָּא. הַפּוֹרֵק עוֹל זֶה שֶׁהוּא אוֹמֵר יֵשׁ תּוֹרָה וְאֵינִי סוֹבְלָהּ. הַמֵּיפֵר בְּרִית זֶה שֶׁהוּא מוֹשֵׁךְ לוֹ עָרְלָה. הַמְגַלֶּה פָּנִים בַּתּוֹרָה זֶה שֶׁהוּא אוֹמֵר לֹא נִתְּנָה תוֹרָה מִן שָׁמַיִם. וְלֹא כְּבָר תַּנֵּיתָהּ הָאוֹמֵר אֵין תּוֹרָה מִן שָׁמַיִם. תַּנָּא רִבִּי חֲנַנְיָה עֶנְתּוֹנָיָא קוֹמֵי רִבִּי מָנָא זֶה שֶׁהוּא עוֹבֵר עַל דִּבְרֵי תוֹרָה בְּפַרְהֶסְיָא כְּגוֹן יְהוֹיָקִים מֶלֶךְ יְהוּדָה וַחֲבֵירָיו.

There (*Sanhedrin* 10:1) we have stated: The following have no part in the Future World: He who says there is no resurrection of the dead[201], that the Torah is not from Heaven, and the Epicurean[202]. Rebbi Aqiba says, also he who reads apocryphal books[203]. And he who recites magical spells over a wound and says (*Ex.* 15:26): "Any disease that I put upon Egypt I shall not put on you because I am the Eternal, your Healer.[204]" Abba Saul[205] says, also he who pronounces the Name[206] by its letters. They added him who tears away the yoke, him who breaks the Covenant, and him who finds aspects in the Torah to those who have no part in the Future World. He who breaks the yoke is one who says the Torah is obligatory but I cannot stand it. He who breaks the Covenant is one who pulls himself a prepuce. He who finds aspects in the Torah is one who says that the Torah was not given from Heaven. But did we not state separately: "He who says that the Torah is not from Heaven[207]?" Rebbi Ḥanania[208] Entanayah stated before Rebbi Mana: That is one who publicly transgresses the words of the Torah in the manner of Joiakim, king of Judah, and his circle.

201 However, in the Mishnah in *Sanhedrin*, the reading of the Yerushalmi is like the Babli, "He who says that there is no resurrection of the

dead from the Torah." The entire paragraph also appears in *Sanhedrin*.

202 Epicure was an avowed atheist; hence, in Jewish sources, an Epicurean is an atheist.

203 Books that pretend to Biblical status but have been excluded from the canon as spurious and pernicious.

204 Using the Torah for magic or exorcisms is equivalent to not believing in the Torah.

205 A Tanna of the third generation, younger than Rebbi Aqiba.

206 The Divine Name *YHWH* whose vocalization is a secret not following grammatical rules.

207 Has no part in the Future World.

208 In *Berakhot* and *Sanhedrin* he is called R. Ḥanina Entanayah.

רוּבּוֹ זְכִיּוֹת יוֹרֵשׁ גַּן עֵדֶן. רוּבּוֹ עֲבֵירוֹת יוֹרֵשׁ גֵּיהִנָּם. אָמַר רִבִּי יוֹסֵי בֶּן חֲנִינָא נוֹשֵׂא עֲוֹנוֹת אֵין כְּתִיב כַּאן אֶלָּא נוֹשֵׂא עָוֹן הַקָּדוֹשׁ בָּרוּךְ הוּא חוֹטֵף שְׁטָר אֶחָד מִן הָעֲבֵירוֹת וְהַזְּכִיּוֹת מַכְרִיעוֹת. אָמַר רִבִּי אֶלְעָזָר וּלְךָ יי חָסֶד כִּי אַתָּה תְשַׁלֵּם לְאִישׁ כְּמַעֲשֵׂהוּ. וְאִי לֵית לֵיהּ אַתְּ יְהִיב לֵיהּ מִן דִּידָךְ. הִיא דַעְתֵּיהּ דְּרִבִּי אֶלְעָזָר דְּרִבִּי אֶלְעָזָר אוֹמֵר וְרַב חֶסֶד מַטֶּה כְּלַפֵּי חֶסֶד.

He who has a preponderance of merit inherits paradise. He who has a preponderance of sins inherits hell. Rebbi Yose ben Ḥanina said: It does not say "He lifts sins," but rather (*Ex.* 34:7, *Michah* 7:18) "He lifts sin." The Holy One, praise to Him, seizes one document from the sins and the merits tilt[209]. Rebbi Eleazar said (*Ps.* 62:13): "Kindness is Yours, o Master, because You repay to everyone according to his deeds," and if he has none, You give him from Yours. That is the opinion of Rebbi Eleazar, because Rebbi Eleazar said[210] (*Ex.* 34:7): "And much kindness," He turns towards kindness.

209 The merits tilt the scales of justice to their side. This argument is given in cryptic brevity in Babli *Rosh Hashanah* 17a. The text follows the parallel in Sanhedrin 10:1 (in the Venice text, (נושה עון אין כתיב כאן)

210 In Babli *Rosh Hashanah* 17a, this is quoted in the name of the House of Hillel.

רִבִּי יִרְמְיָה אָמַר רִבִּי שְׁמוּאֵל בַּר רַב יִצְחָק בְּעֵי צְדָקָה תִּצֹּר תָּם־דָּרֶךְ וְרִשְׁעָה תְּסַלֵּף חַטָּאת. חַטָּאִים תְּרַדֵּף רָעָה וְאֶת צַדִּיקִים יְשַׁלֶּם טוֹב. אִם לַלֵּצִים הוּא יָלִיץ וְלַעֲנָוִים יִתֶּן חֵן. רַגְלֵי חֲסִידָיו יִשְׁמוֹר וּרְשָׁעִים בַּחֹשֶׁךְ יִדָּמוּ. כְּבוֹד חֲכָמִים יִנְחָלוּ וּכְסִילִים מֵרִים קָלוֹן. וּסְיָגִין סִייָגָה וְתַרְעִין תְּרִיעָה. רִבִּי יִרְמְיָה בְּשֵׁם רִבִּי שְׁמוּאֵל בַּר רַב יִצְחָק שׁוֹמֵר אָדָם אֶת עַצְמוֹ מִן הָעֲבֵירָה פַּעַם רִאשׁוֹנָה שְׁנִיָּיה וּשְׁלִישִׁית מִכַּן וָאֵילַךְ הַקָּדוֹשׁ בָּרוּךְ הוּא מְשַׁמְּרוֹ. מַה טַעַם כָּל־אֵלֶּה יִפְעַל אֵל פַּעֲמַיִם שָׁלֹשׁ עִם גָּבֶר. אָמַר רִבִּי זְעִירָא וּבִלְחוּד דְּלָא יְתִיב לֵיהּ מַה טַעַם וְהַחוּט הַמְשׁוּלָּשׁ לֹא לְעוֹלָם יִנָּתֵק אֵין כְּתִיב כַּאן אֶלָּא לֹא בִמְהֵרָה יִנָּתֵק. אֵין מִטְרַחַת עֲלוֹי מְפַסֵּק הוּא.

Rebbi Jeremiah said that Rebbi Samuel bar Rav Isaac asked: (*Pr*. 13:6) "Justice protects the one on the straight path but sin destroys the sinner." (*Pr*. 13:21) "Evil deeds will pursue sinners but He will reward the just." (*Pr*. 3:4) "While He makes scoffers targets of scoffing, He will bestow grace on the meek." (*1Sam*. 2:9) "He will watch over the feet of His pious, but evildoers will be silent in the darkness." (*Pr*. 3:35) "The wise will inherit honor, but shame will mark the stupid ones." Fences are made fences and doors doors[211]. Rebbi Jeremiah in the name of Rebbi Samuel bar Rav Isaac: If a person watches himself the first, second, and third times not to commit a sin, then in the future the Holy One, praise to Him, will watch over him. What is the reason? (*Job* 33:29) "All this God will do twice, three times, with a man." Rebbi Zeïra said, but only if the person does not revert[212]. What is the reason? It does not say "The triple thread will never snap" but rather (*Eccl*. 4:12) "The triple thread will not quickly snap." If you work on it, it will split.

211 A similar thought is expressed in Babli *Shabbat* 104a: "If somebody wants to live in sin, one opens for him the door [to sin] from Heaven; if he wants to live in purity, one helps him from Heaven."

212 Change his ways from good to bad.

רִבִּי חוּנָא בְשֵׁם רִבִּי אַבָּהוּ הַקָּדוֹשׁ אֵין לְפָנָיו שִׁכְחָה הָא בִשְׁבִיל יִשְׂרָאֵל נַעֲשָׂה שׁוֹכְחָן. מַה טַעַם נוֹשֵׂא עָווֹן כְּתִיב. וְכֵן דָּוִד אוֹמֵר נָשָׂאתָ עֲוֹן עַמֶּךָ כִּסִּיתָ כָל חַטֹּאתָם סֶלָה.

Rebbi Ḥuna said in the name of Rebbi Abbahu: There is no forgetting before the Holy One, but for Israel He becomes forgetful. What is the reason? It is written (*Ex.* 34:7, *Michah* 7:18) "He *forgets*[213] sin." And so David says (*Ps.* 85:3): "You *forgot* your people's sin, You covered up all their misdeeds, Selah."

213 Replacing נשׂא "to lift, carry" by נשה "to forget".

(fol. 15a) **משנה ב:** אֵין פּוֹחֲתִין לְפֵיאָה מִשִּׁשִּׁים. אַף עַל פִּי שֶׁאָמְרוּ אֵין לְפֵיאָה שִׁיעוּר הַכֹּל לְפִי גוֹדֶל הַשָּׂדֶה וּלְפִי הָעֲנִיִּים וּלְפִי הָעֲנָוָה.

Mishnah 2: One never gives *peah* less than one in sixty[214]. Even though they said that *peah* has no measure, everything is according to the size of the field, the poor, and the humility[215].

214 $1\frac{2}{3}\%$ of the yield of the field.

215 In the Rome manuscript הענבה "the size of the berries;" in the Munich manuscript of the Babli as well as the Code of Maimonides, הענייה "the answer" (of the field to the farmer's effort.) Both Maimonides and R. Simson explain that if one part of the field has a large yield and another part a meager one, one should not give all of *peah* from the meager part. The two readings imply that the religiosity of the farmer is no matter to consider here.

(fol. 16b) **הלכה ב:** תַּנֵּי אֵין אוֹמְרִים לוֹ הָבֵא גְמָלִים וּטְעוֹן. מַתְנִיתָא בְּיָתֵר מִכְּשִׁיעוּר. אֲבָל בִּכְשִׁיעוּר אוֹמְרִים לוֹ הָבֵא גְמָלִים וּטְעוֹן. שָׂדֵהוּ מְרוּבָּה וַעֲנִיִּים מוּעָטִין נוֹתֵן לְפִי שָׂדֵהוּ. שָׂדֵהוּ מְעוּטָּה וַעֲנִיִּים מְרוּבִּין נוֹתֵן לְפִי הָעֲנִיִּים. רִבִּי

שִׁמְעוֹן דָּרַשׁ שְׁנֵי דְבָרִים לְקֻלּוֹ שֶׁל בַּעַל הַבַּיִת. שָׂדֵהוּ מְרוּבָּה וַעֲנִיִּים מוּעָטִין נוֹתֵן לְפִי הָעֲנִיִּים. שָׂדֵהוּ מְעוּטָה וַעֲנִיִּים מְרוּבִּין נוֹתֵן לְפִי שָׂדֵהוּ. מַתְנִיתָא לֹא אָמַר כֵּן אֶלָּא הַכֹּל לְפִי גוֹדֶל הַשָּׂדֶה וּלְפִי הָעֲנִיִּים וּלְפִי הָעֲנָוָה.

Halakhah 2: It was stated: One does not say to him, bring camels and load up. The *baraita* speaks if he wants to give more than the measure[216], but if he gives according to the measure then one says to the poor to bring camels and load up. If his field is large and the poor few, he gives according to the field. His field is small and the poor many, he gives according to the poor. Rebbi Simeon explained two things to make it easy for the owner: If his field is large and the poor few, he gives according to the poor; if his field is small and the poor many, he gives according to the field. The Mishnah does not say so, but "everything is according to the size of the field, the poor, and the humility (yield).[217]"

216 The measure is the amount fixed by the rabbis, 1⅔%. If there is a large field and only one poor person one tells the poor to bring camels and load up the *peah*. The restriction on more than 1⅔% is introduced because *peah* is not subject to the laws of *terumah* and tithes; hence, what is given to the poor diminishes what is given to priests and Levites. On the other hand, one does not allow the farmer to get away with less than 1⅔% *peah*.

217 The implication is that the Mishnah, which is followed in practice, requires the farmer to give more than the minimum 1⅔% unless there is only one poor person and he would need a camel to remove the *peah*. This is also the interpretation of Maimonides (*Mattenot 'Aniïm* 1:16).

(fol. 15a) **משנה ג**: נוֹתְנִין פֵּיאָה מִתְּחִילַּת הַשָּׂדֶה וּמֵאֶמְצָעָהּ. רַבִּי שִׁמְעוֹן אוֹמֵר וּבִלְבַד שֶׁיִּתֵּן בַּסּוֹף כְּשִׁיעוּר. רַבִּי יְהוּדָה אוֹמֵר אִם שִׁייֵר קֶלַח אֶחָד סוֹמֵךְ לוֹ מִשּׁוּם פֵּיאָה וְאִם לָאו אֵינוֹ נוֹתֵן אֶלָּא מִשּׁוּם הֶבְקֵר.

Mishnah 3: One may give *peah* from the head of the field and from its middle[218]. Rebbi Simeon says, only on condition that he give the measure[219] at the end. Rebbi Jehudah says, if he left one stalk standing he adds to it[220] for *peah*; otherwise, he gives only as abandoned property[221].

218 At the start and during the actual harvest.

219 The rabbinically prescribed 1⅔%; the Halakhah will discuss how this *peah* is computed. In the Tosephta (1:6), quoted later (4:3), Rebbi Simeon explains his position that *peah* must be given at the end only, because not only is this the simple meaning of the verses speaking of the obligation of *peah* (that one may not *finish* cutting one's field) but also to exclude favoritism and give all poor the same chance by setting a reasonably fixed time-table when they may come and pluck the remaining stalks from the field.

Maimonides is of the opinion that R. Simeon makes the view of the *tanna* explicit, not that he disagrees with the first statement.

220 The Halakhah will explain what he may add as *peah*.

221 *Peah* is reserved for the poor (with the legal definition of the poor entitled to charitable gifts given in the last chapter); the House of Hillel rules that abandoned property is abandoned (and free from *terumah* and tithes) only if it is ownerless and abandoned to absolutely everybody. *Arukh* brings Aramaic expressions to show that the root בקר means "to be without master," in a human moral sense also "licentious."

(fol. 16b) **הלכה ג**: נוֹתְנִין פֵּיאָה מִתְּחִילַּת הַשָּׂדֶה וּמֵאֶמְצָעָהּ. רִבִּי יוֹסֵי בְּשֵׁם רִבִּי שִׁמְעוֹן בֶּן לָקִישׁ וּבְקֻצְרְכֶם מַה תַּלְמוּד לוֹמַר לִקְצוֹר אֶלָּא אֲפִילוּ יֵשׁ לוֹ כַּמָּה לִקְצוֹר. רִבִּי יוֹנָה בְּשֵׁם רִבִּי שִׁמְעוֹן בֶּן לָקִישׁ וּבְקֻצְרְכֶם מַה תַּלְמוּד לוֹמַר לִקְצוֹר אֶלָּא אַחַת בַּתְּחִילָּה וְאַחַת בַּסּוֹף. רִבִּי יוֹסֵי בְּשֵׁם רִבִּי יְהוֹשֻׁעַ בֶּן לֵוִי וּבְקֻצְרְכֶם מַה תַּלְמוּד לוֹמַר לִקְצוֹר אֶלָּא אַחַת לַגָּבוֹהַּ וְאַחַת לְהֶדְיוֹט. רִבִּי יוּדָן בְּעֵי כְּלוּם מָעוֹת הֶקְדֵּשׁ מִתְחַלְּלִין לֹא בְתָלוּשׁ שֶׁמָּא בִמְחוּבָּר. אָמַר רִבִּי חֲנִינָא שֶׁלֹּא תֹאמַר יֵעָשֶׂה קְצִיר הֶקְדֵּשׁ כִּקְצִיר הֶדְיוֹט.

Halakhah 3: "One may give *peah* from the head of the field and from its middle." Rebbi Yose in the name of Rebbi Simeon bar Laqish: (*Lev.* 19:9) "And at your harvesting," why does the verse have to say "to harvest"[222]? Even if he has still more to harvest[223]. Rebbi Jonah in the name of Rebbi Simeon bar Laqish: (*Lev.* 19:9) "And at your harvesting," why does the verse have to say "to harvest"? One for the beginning and one for the end[224]. Rebbi Yose in the name of Rebbi Joshua ben Levi: (*Lev.* 19:9) "And at your harvesting," why does the verse have to say "to harvest"? One for sacred property and one for private persons[225]. Rebbi Yudan asked, do not coins redeem sacred property only when it is cut; maybe when it is standing[226]? Rebbi Ḥaninah said, you should not say that harvest of sacred property should be treated like harvest of a private person[227].

222 The expression is considered redundant: "And on the occasion of your harvesting the harvest of your land, do not finish the corner of your field *during your harvesting* but abandon it for the poor and the stranger."

223 Hence, *peah* can be given at any time after the harvest has started. (It was already discussed in Halakha 1 that the very first stalk can never be *peah.*)

224 The disagreement seems to be that according to R. Jonah some *peah* must be given at the end (as explained by R. Simeon bar Iohai in the Mishnah) but that according to R. Yose all *peah* might be given earlier. According to R. Jonah, R. Simeon explains the first sentence; according to R. Yose, he disagrees with the first sentence.

225 R. Joshua ben Levi does not consider the second "to harvest" redundant but referring to a different kind of harvest.

הדיוט "private person", Greek ἰδιώτης.

226 While real estate donated to the Temple may be sold to private persons (and the proceeds used for the needs of the Temple), it is clear from many sources (e. g. Mishnah 4:5) that as long as the field is in the possession of the Temple, the rules of *peah* do not apply.

Hence, any *peah* taken would have to come from a field that was bought with the grain standing, not after harvest when the grain was already cut by the Temple staff and is exempt.

227 The argument of R. Joshua ben Levi differs from that of R. Simeon ben Laqish that the second "to harvest" adds something; it eliminates harvest that is not "yours" but public property. Hence, anybody who buys a field with its crop from the Temple is required to leave *peah*, but anybody who buys the field with its crop after it was cut by the personnel of the Temple has no obligation to give *peah* from his grain (Chapter 4, Mishnah 5).

רִאשׁוֹנָה מַהוּ. מִן מַה דְּתַנֵּי הֲרֵי זוֹ פֵּיאָה וְצָרִיךְ לִיתֵּן בְּסוֹף כְּשֵׁיעוּר הָדָא אָמְרָה (fol. 16c) קִדְּשָׁא מִשּׁוּם פֵּיאָה. מַהוּ כְּשֵׁיעוּר כָּל־שָׂדֵהוּ אוֹ כְּשֵׁיעוּר הַמִּשְׁתַּיֵּיר. אֵיפְשַׁר לוֹמַר קִדְּשָׁא מִשּׁוּם פֵּיאָה וְתֵימַר כְּשֵׁיעוּר כָּל־שָׂדֵהוּ אֶלָּא כְּשֵׁיעוּר הַמִּשְׁתַּיֵּיר.

What is the standing of the first batch[228]? Since we have stated[229] (*Tosephta* 1:5): "It is *peah* and he has to give the measure at the end." That means it becomes holy as *peah*. What means "the measure?" The measure of the entire field or the measure of the remainder? Is it possible to say, this lot becomes holy as *peah* and say, according to the measure of the entire field? Certainly the remaining measure!

228 According to Rebbi Simeon, who says that in any case one has to give *peah* in full measure at the end, does the amount given earlier have the status of *peah* or is it simply abandoned property, not reserved for the poor?

229 In the name of Rebbi Simeon himself. The implication is that the *peah* given at the end has to add up to $1\frac{2}{3}\%$ of the yield cut after the earlier *peah* was given.

רִבִּי חִייָא בְּשֵׁם רִבִּי יוֹחָנָן בִּמְחוּבָּר. רִבִּי יַסָּא בְשֵׁם רִבִּי יוֹחָנָן בְּתָלוּשׁ. מַה מִתְכַּוֵּן לִפְטוֹר אֶת שָׂדֵהוּ אוֹ לֹא. נִשְׁמְעִינָהּ מִן הָדָא. דְּאָמַר רִבִּי יַסָּא בְשֵׁם רִבִּי יוֹחָנָן לְעוֹלָם הוּא מוֹסִיף וְהוֹלֵךְ. מַה נָן קַייָמִין. אִם בְּמִתְכַּוֵּן לִפְטוֹר אֶת שָׂדֵהוּ כְּבָר נִפְטְרָה. אֶלָּא כִּי נָן קַייָמִין כְּשֶׁאֵינוֹ מִתְכַּוֵּן לִפְטוֹר אֶת שָׂדֵהוּ.

Rebbi Ḥiyya[230] in the name of Rebbi Joḥanan: when it is still standing[231]. Rebbi Yasa in the name of Rebbi Joḥanan: when it is cut. What is his intention[232], to free his field from the obligation or not? Let us hear from the following: Rebbi Yasa said in the name of Rebbi Joḥanan: He may always add. What are we talking about? If it is his intention to free his field from the obligation, it already has been freed[233]. So we must speak about the case where it is not his intention to free his field from the obligation[234]!

230 R. Ḥiyya bar Abba. This paragraph deals with the last part of the Mishnah, the statement of R. Jehudah that one may add to *peah* as long as at least one stalk remains uncut on the field (and the additional *peah* is not subject to the laws of *terumah* and tithes.) Cf. also Mishnah 6.

231 One may only add standing patches of grain, not cut grain. Rebbi Yasa is of the opinion that one even may designate grain already cut as *peah*.

232 Does R. Jehudah only say that one may add until one has given the required $1\frac{2}{3}\%$ of the yield (implying that if one starts out with less than $1\frac{2}{3}\%$ and then adds in one batch over that limit it is acceptable and even commendable) or does R. Jehudah apply the laws of *peah* even to produce given after the rabbinic threshold of $1\frac{2}{3}\%$ clearly has already been exceeded?

233 One could not say מוסיף והולך "he keeps adding" if he had to stop after reaching the threshold.

234 But the obligation was already fulfilled before he started to add.

(fol. 15a) **משנה ד**: כְּלָל אָמְרוּ בְּפֵיאָה כָּל־שֶׁהוּא אוֹכֶל וְנִשְׁמָר וְגִידּוּלָיו מִן הָאָרֶץ וּלְקִיטָתוֹ כְּאַחַת וּמַכְנִיסוֹ לְקִיּוּם חַיָּב בְּפֵיאָה. וְהַתְּבוּאָה וְהַקִּטְנִית בִּכְלָל זֶה.

משנה ה: וּבְאִילָן הָאוֹג וְהֶחָרוּבִין הָאֱגוֹזִים וְהַשְּׁקֵדִים הַגְּפָנִים וְהָרִימּוֹנִים הַזֵּיתִים וְהַתְּמָרִים חַיָּבִין בְּפֵיאָה.

Mishnah 4: They established a principle for *peah*: Everything that is food[235], is treated as private property[236], grows from the earth[237], is harvested at one time[238], and is stored[239], is subject to *peah*. Grain[240] and legumes[241] are included.

Mishnah 5: And among trees[242] sumac[243] and carob, walnut and almond, vine and pomegranate, olive and date palm are subject to *peah*.

235 But not industrial plants like flax, cotton, or indigo.

236 Not anything that is usually taken only from the commons.

237 Not mushrooms that grow on rotting wood, nor hydroponics.

238 Not produce that ripens slowly so that the same field or tree has to be harvested many times; as, for example, figs.

239 But not vegetables that are only sold green.

240 Since קציר means not only "harvest" but also "grain", the characteristics of crops subject to *peah* are derived from those of grain. "Grain" in the Talmud means only grain that may be leavened to make bread and in a leavened state is forbidden on Passover.

241 The talmudic definition of legumes covers all fruits other than grains which can be ground into a kind of flour: rice, millet, peas, beans, etc.

242 In the opinion of Maimonides, all *peah* of trees is a Biblical obligation. According to Rabbenu Simson, the only *peah* that is a Biblical obligation is that of grain, wine, and olives. Everything else is a rabbinical obligation.

243 Identification of Maimonides. The leaves of the sumac (*Rhus coriaria L.*) were used in tanning leather and as black dye but the fruits, very rich in citric and related acids, were eaten and used for the preparation of lemonade. Today, ground sumac seeds mixed with thyme are used as condiment (*sa'tar*). Hence, the fruits are subject to *peah* but not the leaves.

(fol. 16c) **הלכה ד-ה**: וּבְקֻצְרְכֶם אֵין לִי אֶלָּא קוֹצֵר. תּוֹלֵשׁ מְנַיִן תַּלמוּד לוֹמַר לִקְצוֹר. עוֹקֵר[246] מְנַיִן תַּלמוּד לוֹמַר קְצִירְךָ. אֵין לִי אֶלָּא תְבוּאָה. קִיטְנִית מְנַיִן תַּלמוּד לוֹמַר בְּאַרְצְכֶם. אִילָנוֹת מְנַיִן תַּלמוּד לוֹמַר שָׂדְךָ.

Halakha 4-5: (*Lev.* 19:9)[244] "And at your reaping,[245]" not only reaping; from where do we add plucking? The verse says "to harvest." From where do we add uprooting[246]? The verse says "your harvest." Not only grain, from where do we add legumes? The verse says "in your land." From where do we add trees, the verse says "your field[247]."

244 The derivation is given, with some variations, in *Sifra Kedoshim*, *Pereq* 1, Babli *Ḥullin* 137a, *Yalqut Shim'oni* #604.

245 The full verse reads: "At your reaping the harvest of your land, do not finish reaping the corner of your field, and do not pick up isolated stalks; do abandon them to the poor and the sojourner; I am the Eternal, your God."

246 This is the reading of the parallel sources and of S. Cirillo; the Venice print has "reaping", which certainly is incorrect.

247 An orchard in which the trees allow for plowing between them is called "a field of trees."

תַּנֵּי זוֹרְעִין זֵרָעִים וְזַרְעֵי אִילָן כְּאַחַת וְהַזּוֹרֵעַ מִן הַחַרְצַנִּים לוֹקֶה אַרְבָּעִים. אָמַר רִבִּי זְעִירָא כְּתִיב לֹא תִזְרַע כַּרְמְךָ כִּלְאַיִם. עִיקַּר כַּרְמְךָ לֹא תִזְרַע כִּלְאַיִם. רִבִּי יוּדָן קַפּוֹדְקִיָּא בְּעָא קוֹמֵי רִבִּי יוֹסֵי. תַּמָּן אָמְרִין אֵין[248] זַרְעֵי אִילָן קְרוּיִין זֵרָעִים וְכֹה אַתְּ אֲמַר זַרְעֵי אִילָן קְרוּיִין זֵרָעִים. אָמַר לֵיהּ תַּמָּן מִיעֵט הַכָּתוּב שֶׁאֵין דֶּרֶךְ בְּנֵי אָדָם לִהְיוֹת קוֹרִין אוֹתָן זֵרָעִים בְּרַם הָכָא רִיבָּה הַכָּתוּב עַל כָּל־זֶרַע זֵרוּעַ אֲשֶׁר יִזָּרֵעַ.

It was stated[249]: One may sow vegetable seeds and tree seeds together. But he who sows with grape kernels is whipped 40 times[250]. Rebbi Zeïra said, it is written (*Deut.* 22:9): "Do not sow your vineyard with two kinds;" the main produce[251] of your vineyard you should not sow with two kinds. Rebbi Yudan from Kappadokia asked before Rebbi Yose: There[252] they say that tree seeds are called seeds but here you say that tree seeds are not called seeds. He said to him: There[253] the verse excluded them since usually people do not call them "seeds," but here the verse added (*Lev.* 11:37) "any sown seed that may be sown."

248 This is the text in the parallel *Kilaim* 8:1; the word is missing in the manuscripts here.

249 Tosephta *Kilaïm* 1:15.

250 "40 times" means 39 times, the maximal punishment for the transgression of a Biblical prohibition (*Deut*. 25:3).

251 The main produce are grapes and the part used for sowing is grape seed.

252 In the rules of ritual impurity, e. g. Mishnah *Makhshirin* 1:2, all rules that apply to vegetables and grain also apply to tree fruits. "Here" refers to the rules of *kilaïm*. This shows that the main place of these paragraphs is in tractate *Kilaïm* (8:1).

253 In the answer, "there" and "here" should be switched; the first answer deals with *kilaïm* (and refers to the question dealt with there whether one transgresses the prohibition of sowing different kinds in a vineyard only if one sows there two kinds different from vines or only one.)

וְאִית דְּבָעֵי נִישְׁמְעִינָהּ מִן הָכָא כִּי תִבְצֹר כַּרְמְךָ מַה אַתְּ שְׁמַע מִינָהּ אָמַר רִבִּי יוֹנָה לֹא תְדַקְדֵּק כְּמַה דְּתֵימַר וְעוֹלֵל לָמוֹ. כִּי תַחְבֹּט זֵיתְךָ מַה אַתְּ שְׁמַע מִינָהּ אָמַר רִבִּי יוֹנָה לֹא תַקִּיפוּ פְּאַת רֹאשְׁכֶם. זַיִת מַה זַיִת וְכֶרֶם מְיוּחָדִין שֶׁלְּקִיטָתָן כְּאַחַת וּמַכְנִסָן לְקִיּוּם חַיָּבִין בְּפֵיאָה. אַף כָּל־דָּבָר שֶׁלְּקִיטָתוֹ כְּאַחַת וּמַכְנִסוֹ לְקִיּוּם חַיָּבִין. אִי מַה זַיִת וְכֶרֶם מְיוּחָדִין שֶׁהֵן חַיָּבִין בְּבִיכּוּרִין וְחַיָּבִין בְּפֵיאָה אַף כָּל־דָּבָר שֶׁהוּא חַיָּב בְּבִיכּוּרִין חַיָּב בְּפֵיאָה. תַּלְמוּד לוֹמַר קְצִירְךָ. אֲפִילוּ קְצִיר אוֹרֶז אֲפִילוּ קְצִיר דּוֹחַן.

Some would understand it from here: (*Deut*. 24:21) "When you harvest your vineyard." How do you understand this[254]? Rebbi Jonah said, do not be punctilious, as you say (*Lament*. 1:22) "to punish them repeatedly." (*Deut*. 24:21) "When you shake your olive tree." How do you understand this[255]? Rebbi Jonah said (*Lev*. 19:27): "Do not round off the *peah* of your head." Since olive and vineyard are special in that they are harvested at one time for storage, so also everything that is harvested at one time for storage is obligated[256]. But olive and vineyard are special in that they are subject to first fruits and subject to *peah*, so only that which is subject to first fruits should be subject to *peah*[257]. The verse says (*Lev.* 19:9): "Your harvest," even the harvest of rice and millet.

254 The entire verse reads: "If you harvest your vineyard, you should not go back to pluck the single berries; it should be for the convert, the orphan, and the widow." The definition of a single berry is given in Mishnah *Peah* 7:4. The question is about the meaning of the word עולל "to go over it a second time". The root עלל means "go over a second time, do anything a second time." In Arabic, علل means "to harvest fruits a second time". For example, עלילה means doing something following a well thought-out plan. Rebbi Jonah reads the verse in Lamentations as: "May all their evil come before You and may You *repeatedly* punish them, just as You *repeatedly* punished me for all my sins." One is not allowed to go over the vines a second time after one has harvested the bunched grapes; that is the equivalent of *peah* for vines. (מתעלל is usually translated "to abuse, to mistreat," it should be taken to mean "to mistreat repeatedly" with emphasis on the repetition of abuse.)

255 The verse reads: "If you shake your olive tree, do not investigate every branch afterwards; it should be for the convert, the orphan and the widow." The way of harvesting olives for pressing oil is to shake every branch, then the ripe olives will fall off and are collected under the tree in a cloth [translation of R. Saadiah Gaon]. The root פאר appears only here in the meaning "to glean"; usually it means "to appear in splendor". The first meaning reappears in the nouns פֻּארָה "crown of the tree", פֹּארוֹת "tree branch". Rebbi Jonah identifies first and second meanings, and reads: "Do not remove its splendor." Then he compares the splendor of the tree, פֻּארָה, to the splendor of one's head, the hair, that in the second verse also is called *peah*; hence it follows that the remaining olives on the tree have the status of *peah* and go under its rules. Accordingly, the rules of *peah* apply both for olive trees and vines.

256 By the principle בנין אב משני כתובים "principle established by two verses". If two necessary verses establish a common consequence, it will apply in general to all cases that are covered by their common antecedents (unless explicitly negated by another verse.) If the verses are partially overlapping in content, the principle is denied by some. The next paragraph will establish that there is

no overlap in content in the case under consideration.

257 This would exclude rice, peas, etc., which are explicitly included in the Mishnah (and would include figs).

יֹאמַר זַיִת וְלֹא יֹאמַר כֶּרֶם. שֶׁאִילּוּ נֶאֱמַר זַיִת וְלֹא נֶאֱמַר כֶּרֶם הָיִיתִי אוֹמֵר זַיִת שֶׁהוּא פָּטוּר מִן הַפֶּרֶט חַייָבִין בְּפֵיאָה כֶּרֶם שֶׁהוּא חַייָב בְּפֶרֶט לֹא יְהֵא חַייָב בְּפֵיאָה. הֲוֵי צוֹרֶךְ הוּא שֶׁיְּהֵא אוֹמֵר כֶּרֶם. אוֹ אִילּוּ נֶאֱמַר כֶּרֶם וְלֹא נֶאֱמַר זַיִת הָיִיתִי אוֹמֵר כֶּרֶם שֶׁהוּא חַייָב בְּפֶרֶט יְהֵא חַייָב בְּפֵיאָה זַיִת שֶׁהוּא פָּטוּר מִן הַפֶּרֶט יְהֵא פָּטוּר מִן הַפֵּיאָה. הֲוֵי צוֹרֶךְ הוּא שֶׁיְּהֵא אוֹמֵר זַיִת וְצוֹרֶךְ הוּא שֶׁיֹּאמַר כֶּרֶם.

It should mention the olive tree but not the vineyard. If it would mention olive tree but not vineyard, I would say that the olive tree, which is not subject to the rule of isolated berries[258], is subject to *peah*, but that vines, which are subject to the rule of isolated berries, are not subject to *peah*. Lo, the mention of the vineyard is needed. Or if it would mention vineyard but not olive tree, I would say that vines which are subject to the rule of isolated berries are subject to *peah*, but that the olive tree which is not subject to the rule of isolated berries is not subject to *peah*. Lo, the mention of the olive tree and of the vineyard is needed.

258 It is stated in *Lev*. 19:10: "Isolated berries of your vineyard (grape berries that do not grow in a bunch but sit directly on the branch and are not part of a row of such grape berries) you should not collect but abandon to the poor."

יָצָא זַיִת וְלִמֵּד עַל כָּל־הָאִילָנוֹת פֵּיאָה. יָצָא כֶּרֶם וְלִמֵּד עַל כָּל־הָאִילָנוֹת פֶּרֶט. וּכְשֵׁם שֶׁיָּצָא זַיִת וְלִמֵּד עַל הָאִילָנוֹת פֵּיאָה. כָּךְ יָצָא כֶּרֶם וְלִמֵּד עַל כָּל־הָאִילָנוֹת פֶּרֶט. אָמַר רִבִּי אָבִין דָּבָר שֶׁהוּא שָׁוֶה לִשְׁנֵיהֶן מְלַמֵּד. וְדָבָר (שֶׁהוּא) [שֶׁאֵינוֹ] שָׁוֶה בִשְׁנֵיהֶן אֵינוֹ מְלַמֵּד.

From[259] the olive tree one may infer *peah* for all trees. From the vineyard one should infer the rule of isolated berries for all trees. (Just as from the olive tree one infers *peah* for all trees so one should infer the rule of isolated berries for all trees from the vineyard.) Rebbi Abun said, any property that is common to both yields an inference but any property that is [not[260]] common to both yields no inference[261].

259 This is a second version of the proof that the two verses are really needed, that they are not "two parallel laws" which by their parallelism indicate that they express only these two cases and no general principle. The argument is: If the mention of *peah* for the olive tree alone would allow one to infer the duty of *peah* for all trees then from the verse in *Lev.* the duty of not collecting single fruits would apply to all trees. That is patent nonsense since most trees do not produce bunches of fruit but only isolated fruits. The sentence in parenthesis is dittography, or it may have been an attempt to explain the argument in a marginal note which subsequently entered the text.

260 Missing in the Venice print but clearly a scribal error already corrected by R. S. Cirillo.

261 Since it was established above that both verses are necessary, neither of them by itself would have a generally valid inference.

עַל דַּעְתֵּיהּ שֶׁל רִבִּי יִשְׁמָעֵאל נִיחָא דְּרִבִּי יִשְׁמָעֵאל דָּרַשׁ כָּל־דָּבָר שֶׁהוּא בִּכְלָל וְיָצָא לִידוֹן בְּדָבָר חָדָשׁ נֶעֱקַר מִן הַכְּלָל וַהֲרֵי הוּא בְּחִידּוּשׁוֹ צוֹרֶךְ הוּא שֶׁיֵּאָמֵר פֵּיאָה בְּכֶרֶם. עַל דַּעְתֵּיהּ דְּרַבָּנִין דְּאִינּוּן אָמְרִין הֲרֵי הוּא בִכְלָלוֹ וַהֲרֵי הוּא בְחִידּוּשׁוֹ. לְאֵי זֶה דָּבָר נֶאֱמַר פֵּיאָה בְּכֶרֶם. אָמַר רִבִּי אָבִין אִלָּא לֹא יָצָא אֶלָּא כֶּרֶם יְאוּת הֲוֵית מַקְשֵׁי. עַכְשָׁיו שֶׁיָּצָא כֶּרֶם וְזַיִת. אִילּוּ נֶאֱמַר זַיִת וְלֹא נֶאֱמַר כֶּרֶם הָיִיתִי אוֹמֵר זַיִת שֶׁהוּא פָּטוּר מִן הַפֶּרֶט חַיָּיב בְּפֵיאָה כֶּרֶם שֶׁהוּא חַיָּיב בְּפֶרֶט[265] יִפָּטֵר מִן הַפֵּיאָה.

It is fine according to the opinion of Rebbi Ismael. Since Rebbi Ismael established: Everything that was in a set and left the set to be applied to a new rule, is removed from the set and forms a new one[262]; it is necessary that *peah* should be mentioned for the vineyard. But for the rabbis[263] who say, it remains in its set and keeps its special status, why is *peah* mentioned for the vineyard? Rebbi Abin said, if only the vineyard were singled out, the question would be valid. But now that vineyard and olive tree are singled out[264], if it would mention olive tree but not vineyard, I would say that the olive tree, which is not subject to the rule of isolated berries[265], is subject to *peah*, but that vines, which are subject to the rule of isolated berries, are not subject to *peah*[266].

262 This is the formulation of the Yerushalmi. In the Babylonian version, (Introduction to *Sifra* and *Zebaḥim* 49a), the reading is: "Anything that was in a set and was taken out for an additional law, cannot be returned to its set except if the verse returns it explicitly." The example there is about different kinds of sacrifices (חטאת, אשם) which in some respect follow the same rules, while in other aspects they do not. Therefore, a special verse is needed for taking the two kinds together to imply that they form one set of sacrifices with common rules. Here, the rule of the single berry clearly separates the vine from all other trees. Hence, it is necessary that there be a separate verse to apply the rule of *peah* to vines.

263 These rabbis are not mentioned in the Babli.

264 For the rule of *peah*, which is not mentioned for any other tree.

265 Reading of the Rome manuscript. The Leyden manuscript and Venice print have "*peah*" by an obvious scribal error.

266 While this argument was brought earlier, the situation is slightly different here.

כְּמָה דְתֵימַר גַּבֵּי קָצִיר דָּבָר שֶׁלְּקִיטָתוֹ כְּאַחַת וְחַייָב בְּפֵיאָה וְאָמַר אַף בְּפוֹעֵל כָּךְ. אָמַר רִבִּי יוֹנָה שַׁנְייָה הוּא דִכְתִיב וְקָטַפְתָּ מְלִילוֹת בְּיָדֶךָ אֲפִילוּ מִדָּבָר שֶׁאֵינוֹ לְקִיּוּם.

Just[267] as you say for the harvest that its collection must be at one time in order to qualify for *peah*, should one say that the same is true for the laborer[268]? Rebbi Jonah said, there is a difference since it says (*Deut.* 23:26): "You may pluck rubbed ears," even of something that is not stored[269].

267 Here starts the discussion of the conditions imposed on produce that should be subject to *peah*.

268 The hired agricultural laborer, who is poor, may eat while harvesting or working in the field. May he eat only from fruits that qualify for *peah*, reserved for the poor?

269 Both conditions, that certain produce is harvested at one time, and that it usually is harvested for storage (or, in the case of wine and oil, is produced for storage), are necessary conditions for *peah*. Since rubbed ears are not stored, the verse makes a point to extend the right of the farmhand.

תַּנֵּי רִבִּי יוֹסֵי בֵּי רִבִּי יְהוּדָה אוֹמֵר רוּטְבֵי תְּמָרִים פְּטוּרִין מִן הַפֵּיאָה לְפִי שֶׁאֵין הָרִאשׁוֹן שֶׁבָּהֶן מַמְתִּין לָאַחֲרוֹן. יְאוּת אָמַר רִבִּי יוֹסֵי בֵּי רִבִּי יְהוּדָה. מַה טַעְמָא דְרַבָּנָן. אָמַר רִבִּי זְעִירָא מִפְּנֵי שֶׁכּוּלָּן צְרִיכִין שְׁאוֹר בַּת אַחַת.

It was stated (Tosephta *Peah* 1:7): "Rebbi Yose ben Rebbi Jehudah says[270], moist dates[271] are free from *peah* because the first among them does not wait for the last one." Rebbi Yose ben Rebbi Jehudah seems to say what is correct, what is the reason of the rabbis? Rebbi Zeïra said, because they all need moisture at the same time[272].

270 Since this is quoted in his name, it follows that it is not generally accepted like an anonymous statement.

271 Arabic רֻטַב, "moist and ripe dates." The author of *Kaphtor Waperaḥ* (Chapter 52, p. 706) notes that these dates are also called in Arabic בַּלַח , but that means "unripe dates", the verbal root בלח means "to be dry", the opposite of רטב.

272 Fruit becomes eligible for the rules of the gifts to the poor when it becomes fruit, and for dates that is the moment where moisture appears around the pit, so that it can be separated from the fruit. R. Zeïra asserts that, while these dates ripen outwardly at separate times, the ripening process starts at the same time for all of them and they could be

harvested and left to ripen in storage after the moisture first appears. Maimonides follows the rabbis in practice.

רִבִּי יִצְחָק בֶּן חֲקוֹלָה וְרִבִּי יְהוֹשֻׁעַ בֶּן לֵוִי תְּרֵוֵיהוֹן אָמְרִין קוֹלְקָס כְּיָרָק[273] לְמַעְשְׂרוֹת וְלִשְׁבִיעִית וּלְפֵיאָה וּלְבִיכּוּרִים וְלִנְדָרִים צְרִיכָא.

Rebbi Isaac ben Ḥaqolah and Rebbi Joshua ben Levi both say taro[274] is like a vegetable for tithes, the sabbatical year, *peah*, and first fruits. For vows it is questionable.

273 The text follows the parallel *Nedarim* 7:1; here: לירק.

R. Isaac ben Ḥaqolah is a contemporary of R. Joshua ben Levi. He was student of most of the Amoraïm of the first generation and teacher of many of the third.

274 Colocasia, Greek κολοκασία, Arabic קַלְקָאס. Its root is used to produce a kind of flour in Africa; hence, it is an intermediate between a vegetable and a legume. The only problem is that of vows (e. g., if a person makes a vow to abstain from vegetables), since in matters of vows one does not follow technical usage but the meaning in local dialects. Hence, there may be places where taro is commonly subsumed under vegetables and other places where it is not.

(fol. 15a) **משנה ו**: לְעוֹלָם הוּא נוֹתֵן מִשּׁוּם פֵּיאָה וּפָטוּר מִן הַמַּעְשְׂרוֹת עַד שֶׁיְּמָרֵחַ. וְנוֹטֵל מִן הַגּוֹרֶן וְזוֹרֵעַ וּפָטוּר מִן הַמַּעְשְׂרוֹת עַד שֶׁיְּמָרֵחַ. וּמַאֲכִיל לִבְהֵמָה לְחַיָּה וּלְעוֹפוֹת וּפָטוּר מִן הַמַּעְשְׂרוֹת עַד שֶׁיְּמָרֵחַ דִּבְרֵי רִבִּי עֲקִיבָה. כֹּהֵן וְלֵוִי שֶׁלָּקְחוּ אֶת הַגּוֹרֶן וְהַמַּעְשְׂרוֹת שֶׁלָּהֶן עַד שֶׁיְּמָרְחוּ. הַמַּקְדִּישׁ וּפוֹדֶה חַיָּיב בְּמַעְשְׂרוֹת עַד שֶׁיְּמָרֵחַ הַגִּזְבָּר.

Mishnah 6: Forever[275] he gives as *peah* and it is free from tithes until he smoothes. He may take from the threshing floor and sow and it is free from tithes until he smoothes[276]. And he feeds domestic animals, wild animals, and fowl and is free from tithes until he smoothes, the words of Rebbi Aqiba[277]. If a Cohen or a Levite bought all the grain of a threshing floor, the tithes belong to them until it was smoothed[278]. He who dedicates[279] to the Temple and then redeems is obligated for tithes unless it was smoothed by the Temple administrator[280].

275 A person who cuts his entire field without leaving *peah* has later to give *peah* to the poor. "Smoothing" is a technical term that designates the end of processing the grain harvest, when after threshing and cleaning from chaff, the grain is put into orderly heaps to be stored. The Mishnah states that the obligation of giving *peah* must be fulfilled as long as the relevant produce is in the hand of the farmer, but if it is given before smoothing then it is free from *terumah* and the two tithes. If *peah* is given later, the farmer has first to give *terumah* and tithes before he can discharge his obligation for *peah*. [In the Mishnah manuscripts there is a second sentence, that he who declares part of his crop as abandoned is freed from the relative *terumah* and tithes if it is abandoned before smoothing. This sentence is missing in the Yerushalmi and in the Munich manuscript of the Babli.]

The Halakhah takes the expression: "Forever he gives," as meaning that he can give under the rules of *peah* until he has smoothed the heap, even if he gave *peah* from grain standing on the field, and avoid the obligation of *terumah* and tithes for that amount. That seems to contradict our understanding of Mishnah 3.

276 Since seed grain is not food.

277 In the Mishnah manuscripts the sentence is anonymous; the previous one about seed grain is attributed to R. Aqiba. From the Halakhah later on (Note 287) it will be clear that the original Mishnah in the Yerushalmi also attributed only the statement about seed grain to R. Aqiba.

278 There is nothing in the Torah which states that a Cohen could not give his own *terumah* and tithes to himself. But the rabbis ordained that Cohen and Levite have to give their tithes away in order to create a level playing field, lest Cohen and Levite farmers could drive the others out of business since they have a built-in 10% advantage in costs over the non-Levitic farmer. In the opinion of Maimonides, the rule was established in order to

prevent the monopolizing of tithes by a few wealthy priests. However, if a priest bought produce before it was obligated for tithes, he may keep the tithe but not *terumah*.

279 His crop or his field.

280 Temple property is not subject to the laws of tithes. Hence, if the obligation of giving *terumah* and tithes arose in private property, it must be fulfilled; but if it arises in the property of the Temple, it does not apply even if the produce is later sold to private individuals.

(fol. 16c) **הלכה ו:** רִבִּי יוֹסֵי רִבִּי יַעֲקֹב בַּר זַבְדִּי בְּשֵׁם רִבִּי אַבָּהוּ רִבִּי נְחֶמְיָה בַּר עוּקְבָּן וּמָטֵי בָהּ בְּשֵׁם רִבִּי יוֹחָנָן הִפְרִישׁ בִּיכּוּרִים מִכְּרִי מְמוּרָח פָּטוּר מִתְּרוּמָה גְדוֹלָה. אָמַר רִבִּי חַגַּיי קוֹמֵי רִבִּי יוֹסֵי מַתְנִיתָא אָמְרָה כֵן לְעוֹלָם הוּא נוֹתֵן פֵּיאָה וּפָטוּר מִן הַמַּעְשְׂרוֹת עַד שֶׁיִּמְרַח. הָא אִם מֵירַח חַייָב מַה שֶׁאֵין כֵּן בִּתְרוּמָה. וְלֵימָא אַף בְּבִיכּוּרִים יְהֵא חַייָב אַף עַל פִּי שֶׁלֹּא מֵירַח. וְיֵידָא אֲמַר דָּא. וְלָמָּה נִקְרְאוּ שְׁמָן בִּיכּוּרִין שֶׁהֵן בִּיכּוּרִין לַכֹּל. וְכָל־הַקּוֹדֵם אֶת חֲבֵירוֹ חֲבֵירוֹ מִתְחַייֵב בּוֹ.

Rebbi Yose, Rebbi Jacob bar Zabdi in the name of Rebbi Abbahu, Rebbi Neḥemiah bar Uqban turned it in the name of Rebbi Joḥanan: If someone separated first fruits from a smoothed heap[281], it is free from the great *terumah*. Rebbi Ḥaggai said before Rebbi Yose: Does not the Mishnah say so: "Forever he gives *peah* and it is free from tithes until he smoothes." Hence, if he smoothed he is obligated, but this does not apply to *terumah*[282]? It should say that he also is obligated for first fruits even though he did not smooth yet[283]! But he[284] is the one who said this: "Why are they called firstlings? Because they are first before everything else." And anything which precedes something else, the latter is obligated for it[285].

281 Which now falls under the obligation of separating *terumah* and the first tithe. (While the first tithe is a civil obligation of the farmer towards the Levite, the *terumah* of the tithe is a religious obligation and it is a deadly

sin to eat from the produce as long as that *terumah* of the tithe is still not separated from the rest of the grain. The first *terumah* is called the *great terumah*.) It is now asserted that First Fruits, which are brought to the Temple and will be eaten there by the priests, are not subject to *terumah* even though *peah*, which is eaten by the poor, can no longer be separated from the heap before the farmer separates the two *terumot* from his grain.

282 Since the Mishnah speaks only of the obligation of tithes, not *terumah*.

283 This is the answer of R. Yose to R. Haggai, refuting his argument: If the Mishnah is supposed to mention every detail, it certainly should have mentioned First Fruits since they are really supposed to be designated when grain or fruits are still on field or tree. Hence, "tithes" is a catchword for all obligations and the Mishnah does not prove anything for the rule under discussion.

284 Rebbi Abbahu or Rebbi Joḥanan, whoever is the author of the statement about First Fruits, referred to the Mishnah *Terumot* 3:7: "From where do we know that First Fruits precede *terumah*? Each of them is called (in the Torah) *terumah* and *beginning*; but First Fruits should precede everything because they are first before everything."

285 This is a general principle which will be discussed at length in *Demai* 5:1. The fixed order of Biblical obligations is First Fruits (where applicable), *terumah*, First Tithe, Second Tithe. Hence, if somebody gave First Tithe before he gave *terumah*, he has to separate *terumah* from this First Tithe and he may not include *terumah* for the First Tithe in the *terumah* that he will give from the remaining grain, but *terumah* carries no obligation of tithe. As a consequence, First Fruits carry no obligation of *terumah* and even the fact that the heap now is under the obligation of *terumah* and tithes has no influence. This is the justification of R. Joḥanan/Abbahu.

מַתְנִיתָא דְּבֵית שַׁמַּיי הִיא דְּבֵית שַׁמַּיי אוֹמְרִים הֶבְקֵר עֲנִיִּים הֶבְקֵר.

Our Mishnah[286] is from the House of Shammai, since the House of Shammai say (Mishnah 6:1): "Property abandoned to the poor is ownerless property."

286 The Mishnah declares that "forever one may give as *peah*," meaning even after the prescribed $1\frac{2}{3}\%$ have been given. But earlier, it was agreed that once this amount is given, there is no more *peah* to be given separately. Hence, one must consider that the amount given before the heap was smoothed was given as property abandoned to the poor. Even for the House of Shammai, calling this *peah* strictly speaking would be a misnomer but, since for the House of Shammai property abandoned to the poor follows exactly all the rules of *peah*, it is free from all obligation of *terumah* and tithes; this is an admissible freedom in the use of language.

וַאֲתְיָא דְּרַבִּי עֲקִיבָה כַּחֲנוּיוֹת בְּנֵי חָנוּן דְּתַנָּא לָמָּה חָרְבוּ חֲנוּיוֹת בְּנֵי חָנוּן שָׁלֹשׁ שָׁנִים עַד שֶׁלֹּא חָרֵב בֵּית הַמִּקְדָּשׁ שֶׁהָיוּ מוֹצִיאִין אֶת הַפֵּירוֹת מִכְּלַל הַמַּעְשְׂרוֹת דְּהַוְויָן דָּֽרְשִׁין עַשֵּׂר תְּעַשֵּׂר פְּרָט לְלוֹקֵחַ. וְאָכַלְתָּ פְּרָט לְמוֹכֵר.

It turns out that Rebbi Aqiba[287] is like the stores of Bene Ḥanun as it has been stated[288]: Why were the stores of Bene Ḥanun destroyed three years before the destruction of the Temple? Because they eliminated produce from the duty of tithes since they were inferring (*Deut*. 14:22) "*You* should certainly give tithes[289]," that excludes the buyer, (*Deut*. 14:23) "*You* should eat," that excludes the vendor[290].

287 This refers to the part of the Mishnah in which R. Aqiba permits the use of grain for seeds and animal feed without the duty of tithing. While R. Aqiba disagrees with the practice of the Bene Ḥanun, he will agree that tithes are applicable only to produce used for human food.

288 *Sifra Deut*. #105, quoted in Babli *Bava Meẓia'* 88a where the name of the locality is corrupted to Bet Hini. It seems that these stores were located at or near the Mount of Olives and were destroyed at the start of the Roman siege of Jerusalem.

289 The verse reads: "*You* should certainly give tithes from all produce of *your* seed." Since the buyer did not sow, he is not included in the command. (As usual, only the first words of the verse are quoted; this never implies that the inference necessarily is from these words.)

290 This excludes the farmer who

sells his produce which then he cannot eat. The people of Bene Ḥanun were punished since the Jewish people under Ezra and Nehemiah had accepted the duty to give tithes and observe the laws of the Land in their rabbinic interpretation (*Shevi'it* 6:1, fol. 36b). Rebbi Aqiba will agree that according to all interpretations, produce that is not used as food is freed from the obligations.

אָמַר רִבִּי יוֹחָנָן קְנָס קָנְסוּ לָהֶן שֶׁלֹּא יְהוּ קוֹפְצִין לְגִיתּוֹת וּלְגָרְנוֹת.

Rebbi Joḥanan said, they fined them so that they should not run after wine presses and threshing floors[291].

291 This sentence refers to the statement of the Mishnah that a Cohen or a Levite, who had received or bought grain before it was made a staple in a smooth heap, has to give *terumah* to another Levite or Cohen, even though from the Torah there seems to be no reason to assume that the Cohen cannot eat his own *terumah*. The reason given is that we do not want Cohen or Levi to go and help with the harvest in order to exert moral pressure on the farmer to give *terumah* and tithes to him personally, since the Torah declares (*Num.* 5:10): "Everybody shall have control over his own Holy Things." The prohibition for a Cohen to exert pressure to force a non-Cohen to give him the required gifts is emphasized in Tosephta (*Demai* 5:20) and in both Talmudim stating that *terumah* and tithes may not be given to the Cohen or Levi as payment for helping in the harvest.

One does not really talk about fines here but about preemptive rules to avoid monopolization of priestly emoluments in the hands of a few individuals. The same reasoning applies to the Cohen butcher in the next paragraph.

טַבָּח כֹּהֵן חֲבֵרָיְיָא בְשֵׁם רִבִּי יְהוֹשֻׁעַ בֶּן לֵוִי פָּטַר לוֹ שַׁבָּת אַחַת. אָמַר רִבִּי יוֹסֵי אֲזָלִית לְדָרוֹמָה וְשָׁמְעִית רִבִּי חָנָן אָבוֹי דְּרִבִּי שִׁמְעוֹן בְּשֵׁם רִבִּי (שִׁמְעוֹן) בֶּן לֵוִי פָּטַר לוֹ שַׁבָּת אַחַת. רִבִּי יוּדָן מְדַמֵּי לָהּ לְהָדָא דְּרִבִּי יוֹחָנָן קְנָס קָנְסוּ בָּהֶן. אָמַר לֵיהּ רִבִּי יוֹסֵף וְאִם מִשֵּׁם קְנָס אֲפִילוּ שַׁבָּת אַחַת לֹא יִפְטוֹר לוֹ. חֶנְוָנִי כֹּהֵן רִבִּי יוּדָן אָמַר פּוֹטְרִין לוֹ שַׁבָּת אַחַת. רִבִּי יוֹסֵי אָמַר אֵין פּוֹטְרִין לוֹ שַׁבָּת אַחַת.

עַל דַּעְתֵּיהּ דְּרִבִּי יוֹסֵי מַה בֵּין חֶנְוָנִי מַה בֵּין טַבָּח. חֶנְוָנִי יָכוֹל לְהַעֲרִים טַבָּח אֵינוֹ יָכוֹל לְהַעֲרִים.

A butcher who is a Cohen[292]. The colleagues in the name of Rebbi Joshua ben Levi: One frees him for one week. Rebbi Yose said, I went to the South and I heard Rebbi Ḥanan, the father of Rebbi Simeon[293] in the name of Rebbi (Simeon) [Joshua] ben Levi: One frees him for one week. Rebbi Yudan compares it to the statement of Rebbi Joḥanan, they fined them. Rebbi Yose said to him, if it is because of a fine, even one week should not be free for him[294]. A grocer[295] who is a Cohen, Rebbi Yudan said, one frees him for one week. Rebbi Yose said, one does not free him for one week. According to Rebbi Yose, what is the difference between the grocer and the butcher? The grocer may cheat[296], the butcher cannot cheat.

292 Following *Deut* 18:3, the Cohen has to receive one front leg, the lower jaw, and the rennet bag from every slaughtered animal. Butcher here means a person who buys animals, slaughters them and then sells their meat. From the Torah, the Cohen might give the dues to himself. But as rabbinic decree this is allowed only during the first week after opening the store; all other parts destined for Cohanim he has to give away to other Cohanim.

293 Neither Rebbi Ḥanan nor Rebbi Simeon are known otherwise from rabbinic literature; probably the name is garbled and the next "R. Simeon" should be "R. Joshua" as indicated in the translation.

294 And nobody ever prohibited Cohanim from being butchers. [R. Joseph mentioned in the text is R. Yose, the colleague of R. Yudan.]

295 Who buys meat from a wholesale butcher to sell it in his retail store.

296 By mixing meat from a Cohen butcher with that from non-Cohen butchers he may make his customers believe that all meat is from a Cohen butcher and, therefore, is exempt from the gifts to the Cohen. But the butcher sells only meat that he slaughtered himself and, therefore, everybody

knows the amount of his obligation. Hence, since from the Torah he may take the gifts for himself, he may take them for one week.

תַּנֵּי לֹא נֶחֱלַק רִבִּי וְרִבִּי יְהוּדָה הַנָּשִׂיא עַל הַלּוֹקֵחַ פֵּירוֹת מְחוּבָּרִין מִן הַגּוֹי שֶׁהֵן חַיָּבִין בְּמַעְשְׂרוֹת וְעַל שֶׁל יִשְׂרָאֵל שֶׁנִּכְנַס תַּחְתָּיו. וְעַל הַלּוֹקֵחַ פֵּירוֹת תְּלוּשִׁין מִן הַגּוֹי שֶׁהֵן פְּטוּרוֹת מִן הַמַּעֲשֵׂר. עַל מַה נֶחְלְקוּ עַל הַלּוֹקֵחַ פֵּירוֹת תְּלוּשִׁין מֵחֲבֵרוֹ בִּשְׁנַת מַעֲשַׂר עָנִי. רִבִּי יְהוּדָה הַנָּשִׂיא אוֹמֵר אֶחָד עָנִי וְאֶחָד עָשִׁיר מוֹצִיאִין מִיָּדוֹ. וְרִבִּי אוֹמֵר עָשִׁיר מוֹצִיאִין מִיָּדוֹ. עָנִי אֵין מוֹצִיאִין מִיָּדוֹ. מַה טַעְמָא דְּרִבִּי יְהוּדָה הַנָּשִׂיא כְּשֵׁם שֶׁאֵין אָדָם זוֹכֶה בְּלֶקֶט שִׁכְחָה וּפֵיאָה שֶׁלּוֹ. כָּךְ לֹא יִזְכֶּה בְּמַעֲשַׂר עָנִי שֶׁלּוֹ. מַה טַעְמָא דְּרִבִּי. לֶקֶט שִׁכְחָה וּפֵיאָה אֵינָן טוֹבְלִין בְּמַעֲשַׂר עָנִי שֶׁהוּא טוֹבֵל. וּכְבָר נִטְבַּל עַד שֶׁהוּא בִּרְשׁוּתוֹ שֶׁל רִאשׁוֹן. מַה טַעְמָא דְּרִבִּי יְהוּדָה הַנָּשִׂיא מִשּׁוּם קְנָס. מַה טַעְמָא דְּרִבִּי עָשִׁיר יֵשׁ בְּיָדוֹ לִיקַּח. (fol. 16d) עָנִי אֵין בְּיָדוֹ לִיקַּח. שֶׁרִבִּי יְהוּדָה הַנָּשִׂיא אוֹמֵר מָצוּי הוּא לִלְווֹת וְרִבִּי אוֹמֵר אֵינוֹ מָצוּי לִלְווֹת.

It was stated[297]: Rebbi[298] and Rebbi Jehudah the Prince did not disagree about produce bought on the field from a Gentile that it is subject to tithes because the Jew takes his[299] place, nor about harvested produce bought from the Gentile that it is free from tithes. What did they disagree about? About him who buys harvested produce from his fellow in a year of tithes for the poor[300]. Rebbi Judah the Prince said, one takes it from him whether he be poor or rich. But Rebbi said, one takes it from the rich, one does not take it from the poor[301]. What is the reason of Rebbi Jehudah the Prince? Just as nobody has any rights on the single stalks, the forgotten sheaves, and the *peah* of his own field[302], so he should have no right to his tithe for the poor. What is the reason of Rebbi? Single stalks, the forgotten sheaves, and *peah* do not cause *ṭebel*[303], but the tithe for the poor creates *ṭebel*. It became *ṭebel* already in the possession of the first owner[304]! What is the reason of Rebbi

Jehudah the Prince? Because of a fine[305]! What is the reason of Rebbi? Only the rich person has the power to buy[306]; it is not in the power of the poor to buy. As Rebbi Jehudah the Prince says, he may take a loan; but Rebbi says that he will not be able to borrow.

297 Usually, "stated" refers to a tannaïtic statement. The statement here is amoraïc; it does not refer to any tannaïtic source.

298 The Patriarch R. Jehudah I, in the Babli usually called "R. Jehudah the Prince". R. Jehudah the Prince is the Patriarch R. Jehudah II, grandson of R. Jehudah I and Amora of the second generation. In the Babli, he usually is referred to as ר׳ יהודה נשיאה.

299 The Gentile's place. Since the harvest determines the obligations and the harvest was Jewish, the obligations of Jewish law fall on the harvest.

300 Second Tithe and tithe of the poor were defined in Note 127. The definition of "poor" for eligibility of tithe and public assistance will be given in the last chapter.

301 In contrast to the Cohen, the poor man who separates the tithe of the poor from the grain may then repossess it, not as owner but as poor person.

302 Mishnah 5:4. However, that Mishnah also denies the sharecropper the right to the tithe of the poor, hence the argument attributed to Rebbi Jehudah the Prince is redundant. While this is not stated explicitly, it is implicit in the fact that one looks for a second reason to sustain R. Jehudah's ruling.

303 *Ṭebel* is a technical term of unknown etymology which designates produce under obligation of *terumah* and tithes from which *terumah* has not been taken in both forms. To eat such produce is a deadly sin. It is stated in *Demai* 4:3 that eating produce under obligation for the tithe of the poor similarly is a deadly sin.

304 Since the obligation for the tithes of the poor is created by the act of harvesting, the corresponding amount is no longer a property of the farmer and cannot be sold; the buyer cannot acquire it even if he is poor! Hence, the argument attributed to Rebbi does not hold.

305 That poor people should not distort the market to the detriment of farmers because they get 10% more value for their money in buying grain than rich people.

306 There will be no distortion of markets because the poor neither have the money nor (as explained in the next sentence) can they find credit for such buys. [It might be that loans were more readily taken on in the time of R. Jehudah the Prince, in the inflationary environment of the military anarchy, than in the time of Rebbi, when currency and prices were stable under the Severan dynasty.]

ואילו מפסיקין פרק שני

משנה א. וְאֵילּוּ מַפְסִיקִין לְפֵיאָה הַנַּחַל וְהַשְּׁלוּלִית וְדֶרֶךְ הַיָּחִיד וְדֶרֶךְ הָרַבִּים וּשְׁבִיל הַיָּחִיד וּשְׁבִיל הָרַבִּים הַקָּבוּעַ בִּימוֹת הַחַמָּה וּבִימוֹת הַגְּשָׁמִים. הַבּוּר וְהַנִּיר וְזֶרַע הַקּוֹצֵר לְשַׁחַת מַפְסִיק דִּבְרֵי רִבִּי מֵאִיר. וַחֲכָמִים אוֹמְרִים אֵינוֹ מַפְסִיק אֶלָּא אִם כֵּן חָרַשׁ.

Mishnah 1: The following separate[1] regarding *peah*: The river[2], the water canal[3], a private road, a public road, a private path[4] or a public path open both summer and winter, a fallow field, a ploughed field[5] and [another kind of][6] seed. He who cuts[7] for animal feed makes a separation, the words of Rebbi Meïr; but the sages say it does not create a separation unless he ploughed.

1 One may not give one *peah* for two fields separated by one of the enumerated obstacles.

2 The Halakhah later makes it clear that one speaks of water even though the Biblical word נחל may also mean (dry) wady.

3 An aqueduct for drinking water or a water conduit that brings water from a river or lake to smaller irrigation canals. The irrigation canal that serves a field directly does not create an interruption.

4 A path has no minimal size, but it is required that it should be in use permanently, even in the rainy season when fields are newly seeded. Paths in use only as shortcuts on fields that have been harvested do not count. The Halakhah will discuss why public roads and paths have to be mentioned when private paths and roads already make an interruption. (In most Mishnah manuscripts, private paths are mentioned after public ones, so that the singular הקבוע applies only to private paths. The discussion will show that this is not the Yerushalmi tradition.) In the opinion of Maimonides, private roads are at least 4 cubits wide, public

roads at least 16 cubits, while paths are narrower. In this he adopts the definitions of the Babli. In the opinion of R. Abraham ben David, roads are used for travelling, paths for local agricultural use, independent of their width. This latter opinion agrees better with the discussions in the Yerushalmi.

5 A field that has been harvested and the stubbles ploughed under while on both sides of it grain is still standing. This creates two distinct fields for purposes of *peah*.

6 The word אחר translated in brackets is missing in the Mishnah in the Talmud and in one of the Tosephta manuscripts (1:8), but it appears in the separate Mishnah manuscripts and in *Sifra* Qedošim 2:1, and it is certainly understood here. Two wheat fields separated by a field of peas require two separate *peot*.

7 Unripe grain. R. Meïr considers grain grown for animal feed a kind different from grain grown for human consumption, probably because it is exempt from *peah*.

הלכה א: וְאֵילוּ מַפְסִיקִין לְפֵיאָה. שֶׁנֶּאֱמַר שָׂדְךָ. וּבִלְבַד שֶׁלֹּא יוֹצִיא מִשָּׂדֶה לַחֲבֶרְתָּהּ.

Halakhah 1: "The following separate regarding *peah*." Because it has been said (*Lev*. 19:9, 23:22): "Your field[8]," that he should not give from one field for another.

8 In the singular, cf. *Sifra* Qedošim 1:22.

וְאֵינוֹ מְחוּבָּר. וְאִין תֵּימַר מְחוּבָּר הוּא אֲפִילוּ שְׂדֵה הָאִילָן מַפְסִיק. דְּתַנֵּינָן תַּמָּן הַכֹּל מַפְסִיק לִזְרָעִים וְאֵינוֹ מַפְסִיק לְאִילָן אֶלָּא גֶּדֶר. הָא גֶּדֶר מְחוּבָּר וְאֵינוֹ מְחוּבָּר. אִין תֵּימַר מְחוּבָּר אֲפִילוּ שֶׂעָר כּוֹתֵשׁ לֹא מַפְסִיק דְּתַנֵּינָן שֶׂעָר כּוֹתֵשׁ אֵינוֹ מַפְסִיק אֶלָּא נוֹתֵן פֵּיאָה לַכֹּל. הָדָא אָמְרָה שֶׁאֵינוֹ מְחוּבָּר. אִין תֵּימַר מְחוּבָּר הוּא אֲפִילוּ מִצַּד אֶחָד מַפְסִיק דְּתַנֵּי אִם הָיָה שֶׂעָר כּוֹתֵשׁ מִיכָּן וּמִיכָּן אֵינוֹ מַפְסִיק. הָא מִצַּד אֶחָד מַפְסִיק.

It cannot be connected[9]. If you would say that it is connected, it should separate even a field of trees[10], but we have stated there (Mishnah 3):

"Everything separates for seeds but only a fence separates for trees." Hence, by a fence it is connected and not connected! If you say it is connected, even hair pressing down[11] does not separate, since we have stated: "Hair pressing down does not separate but he gives one *peah* for all!" That means that it is not connected. If you say it is connected then it should separate if it is one-sided, as we have stated[12]: "If the hair was pressing down from both sides it does not separate." Hence, from one side only it separates[13].

9 One now deals with the features that separate a field from its neighbor, such as a water canal. The problem is whether there must be a clean and total separation of two fields, or whether canals, ponds, fences, and paths separate even if they cover only parts of the boundary. The discussion centers on fences, because only for fences can we find contradictory tannaitic statements.

10 An orchard where trees are planted far enough apart that a plough drawn by a pair of oxen may pass between them.

11 This is the expression of the Mishnah. A fence is no interruption if on both sides there grow trees, their branches (the "hairs") are meshed together, and the lowest branches from both sides lie on the fence (which also may be a wall.)

12 In a *baraita*.

13 Hence, it is undecided whether the role of the fence as divider is undisputed (unless there are "hairs" from both sides, last argument) or whether it is not better than those of the Mishnah (first argument). It is not unusual that the Yerushalmi leaves questions of this kind undecided.

רִבִּי יוֹסֵי בְּשֵׁם רִבִּי יוֹסֵי בַּר חֲנִינָא הִפְרִישׁ פֵּיאָה מִשָּׂדֶה לַחֲבֶרְתָּהּ לֹא קָדְשָׁה.

Rebbi Yose in the name of Rebbi Yose bar Ḥanina: If someone gave *peah* from one field for another one[14], it does not acquire holiness[15].

14 The other field being separated from the first by one of the obstacles enumerated in the Mishnah.

15 It is not *peah* and, hence, subject to the laws of *terumah* and tithes.

רִבִּי זְעִירָא בְּעָא קוֹמֵי רִבִּי יָסָא נִתְכַּוֵון לְזַכּוֹת מִן הַמֵּצָר וּשְׁרַע מִינָּהּ. מוּחְלְפָא שִׁיטָּתֵיהּ דְּרִבִּי יָסָא דְּתַנֵּינָן תַּמָּן מוֹדִים חֲכָמִים לְרִבִּי עֲקִיבָה בְּזוֹרֵעַ שֶׁבֶת אוֹ חַרְדָּל בִּשְׁלֹשָׁה מְקוֹמוֹת. כֵּינִי מַתְנִיתָא שֶׁבֶת בִּשְׁלֹשָׁה מְקוֹמוֹת. חַרְדָּל בִּשְׁלֹשָׁה מְקוֹמוֹת. שְׁמוּאֵל אָמַר מִפְּנֵי שֶׁאֵין הָרִאשׁוֹן שֶׁבָּהֶן מַמְתִּין לָאַחֲרוֹן שֶׁבָּהֶן. רִבִּי יָסָא בְּשֵׁם רִבִּי יוֹחָנָן מִפְּנֵי שֶׁדַּרְכָּן לִיזָּרַע עֲרוּגוֹת עֲרוּגוֹת וְכֹה הוּא אָמַר אָכֵן. פְּשִׁיטָא לֵיהּ שֶׁהוּא מַפְסִיק. לֹא צִירְכָה וְלֹא קִידְּשָׁה מִשּׁוּם פֵּיאָה אִילָּא קִידְּשָׁה. תַּנֵּי רִבִּי אוֹשַׁעְיָא הִפְרִישׁ פֵּיאָה מִשָּׂדֶה לַחֲבֵרְתָּהּ לֹא קִידְּשָׁה. וּשְׁמַע מֵימַר אֲפִילוּ מֵיצָר.

Rebbi Zeïra asked before Rebbi Yasa: If he intended to let them acquire from the boundary strip[16]? He avoided answering him. The opinions of Rebbi Yasa are contradictory since we have stated there (Mishnah 3:2): "The sages agree with Rebbi Aqiba about someone who sowed dill or mustard in three places[17]." (The Mishnah means: dill in three places or mustard in three places.) Samuel said, because the first of them does not wait for the last[18]. Rebbi Yasa in the name of Rebbi Joḥanan: Because they are usually sown in separate beds[19]. And here he says so[20]? It is obvious for him that it separates[21]. What he could not decide is whether it does become sanctified as *peah* or maybe it does not become sanctified[22]! Rebbi Hoshaiah stated: If someone gave *peah* from one field for another one, it does not acquire holiness. One understands that this means even the boundary strip[23].

16 Every field is surrounded by a strip, mostly of grass, usually slightly elevated over the cultivated area. On this strip one may walk between fields and also deposit agricultural implements. Rebbi Zeïra asks what is the rule if some grain grew on the boundary strip and the owner of the field wants to fulfill his duty by abandoning this grain which cannot usually be harvested. Rebbi Yasa (Rebbi Assi in the Babli) avoided answering, perhaps because he did not know the answer.

There is a similar problem in *Baba Batra*, dealing with real estate left by a convert to Judaism who failed to start a Jewish family. Since by conversion the convert severed his ties to his former family, in the absence of a will his property becomes ownerless at his death and can be acquired by actual possession. Then the question is whether two adjacent fields can be acquired if one performs an act of possession (such as weeding) on one of them. In the Yerushalmi (*Baba Batra* 3:1, fol. 13d), R. Yasa states in the name of R. Joḥanan that if one weeded on one of two adjacent fields with the intention of thereby acquiring both fields but did not have the explicit intent to acquire the boundary strip also, he acquired only the field he weeded but no more. Then it is reported that R. Zeïra asked R. Yasa about somebody working on the boundary strip only (whether he would acquire both fields), and R. Yasa avoided answering. In the Babli (*Baba Batra* 55a), R. Assi states in the name of R. Joḥanan that boundary strip and *ḥaẓab* are dividers in respect to the property of a convert but not for *peah* whereas Ravin (Rebbi Abun) declares in the name of R. Joḥanan that it is not a divider for *peah*. For the Yerushalmi, R. Assi himself was not sure whether R. Joḥanan followed the opinion ascribed to himself in the Babli, or that ascribed to R. Abun.

17 The Mishnah deals with someone who spot-harvests his field, cutting at separate places and letting the rest grow for an extended period of time. Rebbi Aqiba requires that each time and at each place *peah* be given, but the sages require only one *peah* for the whole field, except for (expensive) spices.

18 Obviously, one plot is harvested at one time; otherwise, there would be no obligation for *peah*. Samuel asserts that spice plants can be harvested at greatly varying times.

19 Spices are never grown in large fields since they belong to intensive agriculture.

20 In fact, he refuses to say what he should say, *viz*., that the boundary strip is never sown intentionally and therefore cannot be counted as *peah*.

21 This is the opinion ascribed to R. Abun in the Babli.

22 Since *peah* is exempt from *terumah* and tithes, the status of the grain growing on the boundary strip remains in limbo.

23 Again supporting the opinion ascribed to R. Abun in the Babli. (In the Babli, Rabin is reputed to give the correct interpretations of sentences of R. Joḥanan.)

רִבִּי יוֹסֵי בֶּן חֲנִינָא אָמַר חֲצוּבוֹת מַפְסִיקִין לְפֵאָה. רַב חִסְדָּא בְּעֵי בָּהֶן חִילֵּק יְהוֹשֻׁעַ אֶת הָאָרֶץ. אֲתָא רִבִּי חֲנִינָא בְּשֵׁם רַב חִסְדָּא בָּהֶן תִּיחֵם יְהוֹשֻׁעַ אֶת הָאָרֶץ.

Rebbi Yose ben Ḥanina said, rue[24] separates for *peah*. Rav Ḥisda investigated whether they were used by Joshua to divide the Land. Rebbi Ḥanina asserted in the name of Rav Ḥisda: they were used by Joshua to fix the boundaries of the Land.

24 The identification of חצוב with rue or harmel (Arabic חֿיל) is from the Gaonic commentary to Mishnah *Kelim* 3:6. In modern Hebrew, following Loew and Ben Jehudah, the word denotes the sea onion, sea leek (*urginea*). It is more likely that bushes such as rue were used as boundary markers rather than bulbous plants whose dispersion by seeds is beyond control. (In Arabic, חֿצב is simply "greenery").

שְׁלוּלִית. כָּל־שֶׁהִיא מוֹשֶׁכֶת. נַחַל אַף עַל פִּי שֶׁאֵינוֹ מוֹשֵׁךְ.

A[25] water canal, whenever it is flowing. A river even though it does not flow[26].

25 Here starts the discussion of the terms used in the Mishnah.

26 The meaning seems to be that artificial water canals separate only if there is water flowing in them whereas natural waters separate both flowing and stagnant.

נִתְכַּוֵון דְּתַנֵּינָן דֶּרֶךְ הַיָּחִיד וְדֶרֶךְ הָרַבִּים מַה צוֹרְכָה אֲנָא מֵימַר לָךְ אֲפִילוּ דֶּרֶךְ הָרַבִּים אֵינוֹ מַפְסִיק לְאִילָן אֶלָּא גֶּדֶר. מִכֵּיוָן דְּתַנֵּינָן שְׁבִיל הַיָּחִיד שְׁבִיל הָרַבִּים מַה צוֹרְכָא לְהוֹצִיא אֶת הַקָּבוּעַ בִּימוֹת הַחַמָּה וְאֵינוֹ קָבוּעַ בִּימוֹת הַגְּשָׁמִים.

If[27] it is correct that we have stated "a private road," what is the need for "a public road?[28]" I tell you, even a public road does not separate for trees, only a fence does. Since we have stated "a private path," what is the need for "a public path?" To exclude one that is permanent in summer[29] but is not permanent in winter.

27 The Venice print has נחכוון מכיון which is redundant. All commentators delete the first word as unintelligible but the Rome manuscript shows that the second word has to be deleted and that there is a slight shift of emphasis from the first to the second question.

28 If a private road separates, the mention of a public road is redundant; it might be that there should be no mention of the private road. The answer is that for fields, the mention of public roads is redundant but that it is needed in Mishnah 3 where it is stated that all obstacles mentioned in Mishnah 1 are not separating for trees.

29 I. e., used regularly every summer through many years. Nevertheless, if it is not used during the plowing and planting period it does not count as separation.

רַב אָמַר בּוּר וְנִיר בֵּית רוֹבַע וְזֶרַע אַחֵר אֲפִילוּ כָּל־שֶׁהוּא. רִבִּי יוֹחָנָן אָמַר בּוּר וְנִיר וְזֶרַע אַחֵר כִּשְׁלוֹשָׁה תְלָמִים שֶׁל פְּתִיחַ. מַה וּפְלִיג. מַה דָּמַר רַב בְּחִיּוּב פֵּיאָה וּמַה דָּמַר רִבִּי יוֹחָנָן בִּפְטוֹר פֵּיאָה. וְהָתַנֵּי בּוּר וְנִיר חַיָּבִין בְּפֵיאָה. מִן מַה דָּמַר רַב מִשָּׂדֶה בֵּינוֹנִית. מִן מַה דָּמַר רִבִּי יוֹחָנָן בַּחֲמִישִּׁים עַל שְׁתַּיִם.

Rav said[30]: Fallow land and ploughed land of a *bet rova'*[31], other produce[32] even the tiniest amount. Rebbi Joḥanan said: Fallow land, ploughed land, and other produce at three preliminary furrows[33]. Do they disagree[34]? What Rav said[35] refers to produce subject to *peah*, what Rebbi Joḥanan said refers to produce not subject to *peah*[36]. But did we not state that fallow or ploughed land is subject to *peah*[37]? What Rav said refers to an average field, what Rebbi Joḥanan said refers to a plot 50 by 2[38].

30 Here starts the discussion of how large the interruption between two crops of the same kind must be so that two separate *peot* are due.

31 In general, surface area measurements are given in the Talmudim by the amount of seed grain needed for the area in cultivation. The measurements are standardized by the tradition that the courtyard of the Tabernacle, which was 50 by 100 cubits (*Ex.* 27:18), defined the area covered by two *seah*. One *seah* are six *qab*. Hence, the area covered by a

quarter *qab*, the *bet rova'*, is an area of 5000:48 = $104^1/_6$ square cubits. A cubit was at least 45 and at most 61 cm, probably 54.6 cm.

32 For example, if two fields of wheat are separated by a strip of barley.

33 Three wide parallel furrows. According to Rashi (*Is.* 28:24), in ploughing an uncultivated field one first ploughs wide and coarse "starter" furrows; for sowing one then ploughs narrow ones adapted to the particular seed. According to Maimonides (*Kilaim* 3:2), the coarse furrows serve to cover breaks in the soil which developed during the heat of summer. There is no practical difference between the two explanations. In any case, the total width of the three furrows cannot be larger than two cubits.

34 Is it necessary to assume that Rav and R. Joḥanan present different traditions? One tries to avoid disagreements over basic measurements as much as possible.

35 In matters of the separating produce only.

36 In the next paragraph it will be explained that, at least for Rebbis Meïr and Jehudah, plots subject to the obligation of *peah* are more powerful to interrupt between fields of the same kind than those not subject to it.

37 At least for the Sages who disagree with R. Meïr in the Mishnah. Since here Rav and R. Joḥanan give different measurements for identical situations, they seem to disagree.

38 If the entire field, in this example 100 square cubits, is smaller than a *bet rova'*, the rule of Rav becomes inapplicable and must be replaced by a smaller limit.

רִבִּי זְעִירָא בְשֵׁם רִבִּי אֶלְעָזָר רִבִּי מֵאִיר וְרִבִּי יְהוּדָה שְׁנֵיהֶם אָמְרוּ דָבָר אֶחָד. כְּמָה דְרִבִּי מֵאִיר אָמַר הַקּוֹצֵר לְשַׁחַת מַפְסִיק כֵּן רִבִּי יְהוּדָה אָמַר הַקּוֹצֵר לְשַׁחַת מַפְסִיק. כְּמָה דְרִבִּי יוּדָה אָמַר חִיּוּב בְּפֵיאָה מַפְסִיק כֵּן רִבִּי מֵאִיר אוֹמֵר חִיּוּב בְּפֵיאָה מַפְסִיק. וְהָא אַשְׁכְּחִנָן דְּרִבִּי מֵאִיר אוֹמֵר חִיּוּב בְּפֵיאָה מַפְסִיק כְּהָדָא דְתַנֵּי אֲכָלָהּ גּוּבַיי קִרְסְמוּהָ נְמָלִין אוֹ שֶׁבְּרָתָּה הָרוּחַ אוֹ בְהֵמָה פְּטוּרָה. הַכֹּל מוֹדִין אִם חָרַשׁ מַפְסִיק. אִם לֹא חָרַשׁ אֵינוֹ מַפְסִיק. מָנֵי הַכֹּל מוֹדִין לֹא רִבִּי מֵאִיר אָמַר מִשּׁוּם שֶׁהוּא פְּטוּר פֵּיאָה. אֲבָל אִם הָיָה חַיָּיב אֲפִילוּ לֹא חָרַשׁ מַפְסִיק. כַּיי דְתַנֵּינָן תַּמָּן אָמַר רִבִּי יוּדָן אֵימָתַי בִּזְמַן שֶׁהִתְחִיל עַד שֶׁלֹּא הֵבִיא

שְׁלִישׁ אֲבָל אִם הֵבִיא שְׁלִישׁ אָסוּר לִקְצוֹר. יִקְצוֹר חַיָּב בְּפֵיאָה. וְדָבָר שֶׁהוּא חִיּוּב פֵּיאָה מַפְסִיק.

Rebbi Zeïra in the name of Rebbi Eleazar: Both Rebbi Meïr[39] and Rebbi Jehudah[40] said the same. Just as Rebbi Meïr said that he who cuts for fodder separates, so Rebbi Jehudah will say that he who cuts for fodder separates. Just as Rebbi Jehudah said that an obligation for *peah* separates[41], so Rebbi Meïr will say that an obligation for *peah* separates. But we find that Rebbi Meïr says that an obligation for *peah* separates[42] since we have stated[43]: "If locusts ate it, ants undermined it, or a storm or animals broke it, it is free[44]; everybody agrees that if he ploughed[45] it separates, if he did not plough it does not interrupt[46]." Who is "everybody"? Does not Rebbi Meïr say, if it is free from *peah*[47], but if it were obligated it would interrupt even if he did not plough. Parallel to what we stated there[48]: "Rebbi Jehudah said, when? If he started before it was one-third ripe, but if it is one-third ripe one is forbidden to cut." If he cuts[49] he is obligated for *peah*. And anything that is obligated for *peah* separates[50].

39 In our Mishnah, referring to *peah*.

40 In Mishnah *Menaḥot* 10:8, dealing with the prohibition of using grain from the new harvest before the presentation of the *'omer* on the 16th of Nisan. We insist that they follow the same principle in both cases even though we have no statement of R. Jehudah on *peah* and no statement of R. Meïr about cutting green grain as animal fodder.

41 This statement is not obvious and has to be proven later.

42 From the Tosephta it will be deduced that everybody, including Rebbi Meïr, agrees that an independent obligation of *peah* between two fields separates the two fields into two entities from each of which one must give *peah*.

43 Tosephta *Peah* 1:8. A field on which grain grows but which is destroyed during growth is not subject

to the obligation of *peah*.

44 Cf. Mishnah 2:7.

45 If he ploughed under the empty stalks remaining after the disaster. "It" in this sentence refers to the ruined field.

46 If only part of the field was destroyed it is as if the entire field was sown but part of the seed grain did not germinate; it therefore remains one field.

47 Since it belongs to the same field and without the disaster there would not have been any separate obligation of *peah*, only separate ploughing will create two obligations. But if there were a separate obligation from the start, as in the example quoted next from R. Jehudah, then it seems that there are two obligations of *peah* created.

48 Mishnah *Menaḥot* 10:8. There is a Biblical prohibition on using new grain for human consumption before the 16th of Nisan (*Lev*. 23:14) and a rabbinical prohibition to harvest before that time. However, that rabbinical prohibition is waived either if it would cause monetary loss (as for fields in the region of Jericho that ripen very early) or if the grain is not used for humans. R. Simeon permits cutting for fodder anytime, R. Jehudah allows it only if the grain is less than one third ripe (since afterwards it is fit for human consumption as "green kernels").

49 After the grain is one-third ripened and the grain is potential human food. ("R. Yudan" here refers to R. Jehudah bar Illaï.)

50 If he harvested a strip of unripe grain in a field, he has to give *peah* from this strip. If that strip separated the remaining grain into two disjoint pieces, the two fields now are separately liable for *peah*.

רִבִּי זְעִירָא בְּעֵי כְּמָה דְּרִבִּי יְהוּדָה אָמַר הִתְחִיל עַד שֶׁלֹּא (fol. 17a) הֵבִיאָה שְׁלִישׁ וַאֲפִילוּ הֵבִיאָה שְׁלִישׁ פָּטוּר מִן הַלֶּקֶט וּמִן הַשִּׁכְחָה וּמִן הַפֵּיאָה. כֵּן רִבִּי מֵאִיר אָמַר הִתְחִיל עַד שֶׁלֹּא הֵבִיאָה שְׁלִישׁ וַאֲפִילוּ הֵבִיאָה שְׁלִישׁ פָּטוּר מִן הַלֶּקֶט וּמִן הַשִּׁכְחָה וּמִן הַפֵּיאָה.

Rebbi Zeïra questioned: Just as Rebbi Jehudah said, if he started before it was one-third ripe, even if he continued after it was one-third ripe he will be freed from collecting, forgotten sheaves, and *peah*[51], would Rebbi Meïr say that if he started before it was one-third ripe, even if he continued after it is one-third ripe he will be freed from collecting, forgotten sheaves, and *peah*[52]?

51 R. Jehudah, in the Mishnah just quoted, only asks that one has to start cutting for fodder as long as the grain is not yet fit for human consumption, but not that one has to stop at one-third ripeness; it is clear that subsequent cutting for fodder does not turn the fodder into human food and, therefore, the farmer is free from the obligations of letting the poor collect the single stalks not bound in sheaves (*Lev*. 19:9, *Ruth* 2) and leaving sheaves forgotten on the field (*Deut*. 24:19), and *peah*.

52 There is no logical necessity which would force R. Meïr to agree that wheat with edible green kernels does not constitute human food. The question is not answered since no other sources are available.

(fol. 16d) **משנה ב**. אַמַּת הַמַּיִם שֶׁאֵינָהּ יְכוֹלָה לְהִיקָּצֵר כְּאַחַת רִבִּי יְהוּדָה אוֹמֵר מַפְסֶקֶת וְכָל־הֶהָרִים אֲשֶׁר בַּמַּעְדֵּר יֵעָדֵרוּן אַף עַל פִּי שֶׁאֵין הַבָּקָר יָכוֹל לַעֲבוֹר בְּכֵלָיו הוּא נוֹתֵן פֵּיאָה אַחַת לַכֹּל.

Mishnah 2: An irrigation canal that cannot be harvested together[53], Rebbi Jehudah says it separates. For all hills subject to weeding[54], even if cattle can not pass by with their implements, he gives one *peah* for everything.

53 One cannot cut with one movement of a scythe on both banks of the irrigation canal. The exact description will be given in the Halakhah.

54 The language is from *Is*. 7:25. It means as long as the obstacle can be used agriculturally, even if it cannot be worked with ploughs or other implements drawn by animals, it does not separate for *peah* even if such a ridge separates a field into two parts as far as mechanical farming is concerned.

הלכה ב: הֲוֹון בְּעֵי מֵימַר וְלָא פְלִיגִין. אַשְׁכְּחַת תַּנֵּי אַמַּת הַמַּיִם(fol. 17a) הַקְּבוּעָה הֲרֵי זוֹ מַפְסֶקֶת.

Halakhah 2: They wanted to say that there is no disagreement[55]. It was found stated: "A permanent irrigation canal separates[56]"

55 The Mishnah does not mention any opinion differing from R. Jehudah. One might therefore think that it expresses a commonly held opinion even though in that case the Mishnah should have been anonymous.

56 The Mishnah is defective. The parallel in *Sifra, Qedošim* 3:2 reads: "A permanent irrigation canal separates. Rebbi Jehudah says, if (it) [both banks of the canal] cannot be harvested together, it separates. For all hills subject to weeding, even if cattle cannot pass by with implements, he gives one *peah* for everything." Hence, the majority of the Sages agree that a permanently installed irrigation canal separates for *peah* even if both banks can be cut at the same time; R. Jehudah's opinion is in the minority.

הֲוֹון בְּעֵי מֵימַר מַן מַה דְּאָמַר רִבִּי יוּדָה בְּעוֹמֵד מִצַּד אֶחָד וְאֵינוֹ יָכוֹל לִקְצוֹר מִצַּד הַשֵּׁנִי אֲבָל אִם הָיָה עוֹמֵד בְּאֶמְצַע וְקוֹצֵר מִיכַּן וּמִיכַּן אֵינוֹ מַפְסִיק. אַשְׁכְּחַ תַּנֵּי וּפְלִיג הָיָה עוֹמֵד בְּאֶמְצַע וְקוֹצֵר מִיכַּן וּמִיכַּן מַפְסִיק מִצַּד אֶחָד אֵינוֹ מַפְסִיק.

They wanted to say: What Rebbi Jehudah talks about is one who stands on one bank and cannot cut on the other bank, but if he stands in the middle[57] and cuts on both banks it does not separate. It was found stated[58] in disagreement: "If he was standing in the middle and harvesting on both banks, it separates; on one bank it does not separate."

57 In the water of the irrigation canal.

58 *Tosephta Peah* 1:8: "An irrigation canal that cannot be harvested together, R. Jehudah says if he has to stand in the middle in order to harvest on both banks, it separates, otherwise, it does not separate." The text before the Yerushalmi must have been similar.

חִייָא בַּר אָדָא בְשֵׁם רִבִּי שִׁמְעוֹן בֶּן לָקִישׁ הָיָה שָׁם סֶלַע עַל פְּנֵי כָל־שָׂדֵהוּ אִם עוֹקֵר הוּא אֶת הַמַּחֲרֵישָׁה מִצַּד זֶה וְנוֹתְנוֹ מִצַּד זֶה מַפְסִיק. מִצַּד אַחֵר אֵינוֹ מַפְסִיק. וְהָתַנֵּי מַדְרֵגוֹת שֶׁהֵן גְּבוֹהוֹת עֲשָׂרָה טְפָחִים נוֹתֵן פֵּיאָה מִכָּל־אֶחָד וְאֶחָד. פָּחוֹת מִיכֵּן נוֹתֵן מֵאֶחָד עַל הַכֹּל. וּפָחוֹת מִיכֵּן אֵינוֹ עוֹקֵר אֶת הַמַּחֲרֵישָׁה מִצַּד זֶה וְנוֹתְנוֹ מִצַּד זֶה. אֲפִילוּ פָּחוֹת מִיכֵּן עוֹקֵר הוּא. לָא אֲתִינָן מִיתְנֵי עֲשָׂרָה אֶלָּא בְגִין סוֹפָהּ שֶׁאִים הָיוּ רָאשֵׁי מַדְרֵיגוֹת מְעוּרָבִין שֶׁהוּא נוֹתֵן מֵאֶחָד עַל הַכֹּל.

Ḥiyya bar Ada in the name of Rebbi Simeon ben Laqish: If there was a rock along the length of his entire field[59], if he has to lift the plough from one side and transport it to the other side, it separates, from the other side[60] it does not separate. But did we not state[61]: "For terraces which are each ten hand-breadths[62] higher than the other[63], he must give *peah* for each one separately. Less than that he gives one *peah* for all of them." But for less than that[64], does he not have to lift the plough from one (terrace) and transport it to the other? Even for less than that he has to lift it. We had to state "ten" only because of the concluding statement: "If the heads of the terraces are connected, he gives one *peah* for all[65]."

59 Bare rock, not a place for weeding or other agricultural work, not covered by the Mishnah. Here starts the discussion of the second sentence of the Mishnah.

60 If he can slide the plough over the rock so that it does not lose contact with the ground.

61 Tosephta *Peah* 1:9, together with the quote at the end of the paragraph, forms one sentence there.

62 One cubit equals six hand-breadths. Ten handbreadths are about one yard difference from one terrace to the next.

63 On a terraced hillside, if the agricultural machines have to be lifted up from one terrace to the next, they are distinct fields for *peah*.

64 A terrace wall less than three feet high.

65 If on one side there is an incline which connects the different terraces, all counts as one field. One might

think that the statement is unnecessary since we already know that anything which can be ploughed together requires one *peah* for all and the incline makes possible the ploughing without lifting the plough. However, in general we say that a height of 10 handbreadths creates a new domain. For example, regarding the laws of Sabbath, "public domain" in which one may not carry extends only up to a height of 10 handbreadths from the ground. One might have thought that a level difference of 10 handbreadths also creates a new domain for *peah*, but this is not the case.

(fol. 16d) **משנה ג.** הַכֹּל מַפְסִיק לִזְרָעִים וְאֵינוֹ מַפְסִיק לְאִילָן אֶלָּא גֶּדֶר. וְאִם הָיָה שֵׂעָר כּוֹתֵשׁ אֵינוֹ מַפְסִיק אֶלָּא נוֹתֵן פֵּיאָה לַכֹּל.

Mishnah 3: Everything separates for seeds but only a fence separates for trees. But if hair was pressing down it does not separate and he gives one *peah* for all[66].

66 This was explained at the beginning of Halakhah 1, notes 12-13.

(fol. 17a) **הלכה ג**: הַכֹּל מַפְסִיק לִזְרָעִים. מַה כּוֹתֵשׁ וְעוֹלֶה כְּמַכְתֵּשׁ אוֹ כּוֹתֵשׁ עַל גַּבֵּי גֶדֶר. מִן מַה סְעָר כּוֹתֵשׁ אֵין הַגֶּדֶר כּוֹתֵשׁ. הָדָא אָמְרָה כּוֹתֵשׁ עַל גַּבֵּי גֶדֶר.

Halakhah 3: "Everything separates for seeds[67]." What is pressing down[68]? It rises while pressing as in a mortar[69] or must it press down on the fence? From the text "hair was pressing down," the fence does not press[70]. That means it presses down on the fence.

67 Quote from the Mishnah. However, the discussion is purely about the second sentence in the Mishnah.

68 What is the meaning of the condition that two orchards separated by a fence are subject only to one obligation of *peah* if the leaves of trees of one orchard come down and lie across the fence to the other orchard? Does it mean that the leaves actually

have to press on the fence or may they be in the air and just press down one branch on the other?

69 Rabbenu Simson in his commentary to *Kilaim* 5:3 quotes the text here as כעלי במכתש "like a pestle in the mortar," and explains, on the basis of the same language in *Kilaim*, that the branches have to press hard on the stone fence so as to create a dusty surface on the fence. Better is the interpretation of the uncorrected text, preferred by R. Moses Margalit, that the branches on both sides may be enmeshed but be higher than the fence, since the pestle is higher except for the short moments when it touches the bottom of the mortar.

70 While the "hair" must lie on the fence, it need not act on it. There is no eroding pressure needed on the stone fence.

רִבִּי מָנָא אָמַר זִמְנִין דִּתְהֵוֵי בָהּ בְּתוֹךְ אַרְבַּע אַמּוֹת וְזִמְנִין דִּתְהֵוֵי בָהּ בְּתוֹךְ עֲשָׂרָה טְפָחִים בִּנְטוּעִין מֵטַע עֶשֶׂר לְבֵית סְאָה. מַה אַתְּ שְׁמַע מִינָּהּ וְהוּא שֶׁיְּהוּ בְּתוֹךְ אַרְבַּע אַמּוֹת לְגֶדֶר וְהֵן שֶׁיְּהוּ בְּתוֹךְ עֲשָׂרָה טְפָחִים בֵּין נוֹף לְנוֹף בִּנְטוּעִין מֵטַע עֶשֶׂר לְבֵית סְאָה.

Rebbi Mana said: Sometimes they need to be inside four cubits and sometimes they need to be inside ten handbreadths if they are planted ten to a *bet se'ah*. How do you understand this? They[71] need to be within four cubits of the fence; the crowns have to be within ten handbreadths of one another[72] if they are planted ten to a *bet se'ah*[73].

71 The trees have to be planted close to the fence so that the stem of the tree whose branches lie on the fence is not farther than four cubits from the fence.

72 In the entire orchard, the crown of any tree must have the crown of another tree within 10 handbreadths (1⅔ cubits) distance.

73 If the trees are planted in a regular pattern, each tree gets an area of 250 square cubits, or 15.82 cubits square. This means that the crown of each fruit tree should reach a diameter of slightly over 14.2 cubits.

Ten trees to a *bet se'ah* are characteristic for a tree nursery (Mishnah *Sheviït* 1:7); adult trees form an orchard if a minimum of three trees are planted on a *bet se'ah* (Mishnah

Sheviït 1:2). Since Maimonides does not quote the rules of R. Mana in his code, he seems to consider them non-operative since trees that actually bear fruit are no longer in a tree nursery.

(fol. 16d) **משנה ד.** וְלֶחָרוּבִין כָּל־הָרוֹאִין זֶה אֶת זֶה. אָמַר רַבָּן גַּמְלִיאֵל נוֹהֲגִין הָיוּ בְּבֵית אַבָּא נוֹתְנִין פֵּיאָה אַחַת לַזֵּיתִים שֶׁהָיוּ לָהֶן בְּכָל הָרוּחַ וְלֶחָרוּבִין כָּל־הָרוֹאִין זֶה אֶת זֶה. רִבִּי אֶלְעָזָר בֵּי רִבִּי צָדוֹק אוֹמֵר מִשְּׁמוֹ אַף לֶחָרוּבִין שֶׁהָיוּ לָהֶם בְּכָל־הָעִיר.

Mishnah 4[74]: But for carob trees all that see one another[75]. Rabban Gamliel[76] said, in my father's house they used to give one *peah* for the olive trees they had in every direction[77] and for all carobs that saw one another. Rebbi Eleazar ben Rebbi Ẓadoq said in the former's name: also for all carob trees they had in the entire town.

74 This Mishnah is the continuation of the preceding one.

75 According to Maimonides, all the carob trees a man can see standing next to one of them. According to R. Abraham ben David, all the carob trees a man can see while standing on top of one of them. According to the second opinion, fences are never a problem for carob trees.

76 Rabban Gamliel of Jabneh, speaking of the family of Hillel.

77 Four *peot* for all olive trees in all four main directions.

(fol. 17a) **הלכה ד:** וְלֶחָרוּבִין כָּל־הָרוֹאִין. מִי מְכַוֵּין לָהֶן אֶת הָרוּחוֹת. הָעִיר מְכַוֶּנֶת לָהֶן אֶת הָרוּחוֹת. אָמַר רִבִּי יוֹסֵי בֵּי רִבִּי בּוּן שֶׁל בֵּית רִבִּי הָיוּ לָהֶן אַרְבָּעָה בַּדִּים לְאַרְבָּעָה רוּחוֹת הָעִיר וְהֵן נוֹתְנִין לְכָל־בַּד וּבַד לְפִי רוּחוֹ.

Halakhah 4: "But for carob trees all that see." What defines the directions for them? The town defines the directions for them[78]. Rebbi Yose ben Rebbi Abun said, the family of Rebbi had four oil presses in the four directions of the town and their used to give for each oil press according to its direction[79].

78 E, S, W, N are defined standing in the center of town. Chapter 5 of Mishnah *Erubin* explains that each town has to put up markers at the end of the Sabbath territory (2000 cubits from the last house of town) in the four cardinal directions.

79 The prescribed percentage of the olives processed in each of the oil presses.

הָיוּ שָׁם שְׁלֹשָׁה אִילָנוֹת הָרִאשׁוֹנִים רוֹאִין אֶת הָאֶמְצָעִיִּים וְהָאֶמְצָעִיִּים רוֹאִין אֶת הָרִאשׁוֹנִים וְאֵין הָרִאשׁוֹנִים רוֹאִין זֶה אֶת זֶה מַפְרִישׁ מִן הָרָאשִׁים עַל הָאֶמְצָעִיִּים וּמִן הָאֶמְצָעִיִּים עַל הָרָאשִׁים וְאֵינוֹ מַפְרִישׁ מִן הָרָאשִׁים עַל הָרָאשִׁים.

If there were three[80] (groups of) trees, the outer[81] ones see the middle ones, the middle ones see the outer ones, but the outer ones do not see one another, then one may give from the outer ones for the middle ones and from the middle ones for the outer ones but one may not give from the outer ones for the outer ones.

80 R. Simson of Sens reads: 30. This would explain the plural used for the three groups of trees.

81 While all sources have here הראשונים "the first ones", it is clear from the context that הראשים "the extremities" are meant.

(fol. 15d) **משנה ה**: הַזּוֹרֵעַ אֶת שָׂדֵהוּ מִין אֶחָד אַף עַל פִּי שֶׁהוּא עוֹשֶׂה שְׁתֵּי גְרָנוֹת נוֹתֵן פֵּיאָה אַחַת. זוֹרְעָהּ שְׁנֵי מִינִין אַף עַל פִּי שֶׁהוּא עוֹשֶׂה גוֹרֶן אַחַת נוֹתֵן שְׁתֵּי פֵיאוֹת. הַזּוֹרֵעַ אֶת שָׂדֵהוּ שְׁנֵי מִינֵי חִטִּים עֲשָׂאָן גוֹרֶן אַחַת עוֹשֶׂה גוֹרֶן אַחַת נוֹתֵן פֵּיאָה אַחַת. שְׁתֵּי גְרָנוֹת נוֹתֵן שְׁתֵּי פֵיאוֹת.

Mishnah 5: He who sows one species on his field gives one *peah* even though he works[82] at two different threshing floors. If he sows two species, he gives two *peot* even though he threshes them together[83]. He who sows two different kinds of wheat on his field gives one *peah* if he processes them together[84], two *peot* if he threshes them separately.

82 Literally: He makes two threshing floors. Not only the act of threshing is involved, but also the collection of threshed grain into orderly heaps. The best translation is: processing (grain on the stalk into a commercial commodity.)

83 And puts them together in the same heap.

84 That means that he treats them as one kind of wheat.

(fol. 16a) **הלכה ה**: קָצַר חֵצִי אַגִּידוֹ וְחֵצִי שְׁמוּתִית לַעֲשׂוֹתָן גּוֹרֶן אֶחָד וְנִמְלַךְ וַעֲשָׂאָן שְׁתֵּי גְּרָנוֹת אֵינוֹ מַפְרִישׁ מִן הָאַגִּדוֹ עַל הַשְּׁמוּתִית לֹא בַּתְּחִילָּה וְלֹא בְּסוֹף. קָצַר חֵצִי הָאַגִּדוֹ וְחֵצִי הַשְּׁמוּתִית לַעֲשׂוֹתָן שְׁתֵּי גְּרָנוֹת וְנִמְלַךְ וַעֲשָׂאָן גּוֹרֶן אַחַת מַפְרִישׁ עַל הָאַגִּדוֹ שֶׁבְּסוֹף עַל הַשְּׁמוּתִית שֶׁבְּסוֹף. מִן הָאַגִּדוֹ שֶׁבַּתְּחִילָּה עַל הַשְּׁמוּתִית שֶׁבַּתְּחִילָּה. מַפְרִישׁ מִן הָאַגִּדוֹ עַל הָאַגִּדוֹ בְּשֶׁכִּילָּה אֶת שָׂדֵהוּ. אֲבָל אִם לֹא כִילָּה אֶת שָׂדֵהוּ אֲפִילוּ מִן הָאַגִּדוֹ עַל הָאַגִּדוֹ אֵינוֹ מַפְרִישׁ. קָצַר חֲצִי אַגִּדוֹ וְכָל־הַשְּׁמוּתִית לַעֲשׂוֹתָן גּוֹרֶן אַחַת וְנִמְלַךְ וַעֲשָׂאָן שְׁתֵּי גְּרָנוֹת מַפְרִישׁ מִן הָאַגִּדוֹ עַל הָאַגִּדוֹ וְכָל־הַשְּׁמוּתִית שֶׁשָּׁם נִפְטְרָה.

Halakhah 5: If he cut half the fine wheat[85] and half the coarse wheat[86] to process them together and then he changed his mind and processed them separately he cannot give from the fine wheat for the coarse either the first time[87] or at the end[88]. If he cut half the fine wheat and half the coarse wheat to process them separately and then he changed his mind and processed them together, he may give from the fine wheat at the end for the coarse wheat at the end, from the fine wheat the first time for the coarse wheat the first time[89]. He gives from fine wheat for fine wheat if he finished harvesting his field, but if he did not finish harvesting, he may not give even from fine wheat for fine wheat[90]. If he cut half the fine wheat and all the coarse wheat to process them together and he changed his mind and processed them separately[91] then he gives from the fine wheat for the fine wheat and all the coarse wheat is exempted[93].

85 The reading of the Venice print here is איגדו, that of the Rome manuscript אגידו. This kind of wheat is usually spelled אגרו, אגורי, אגרי; this is R. Simson's spelling here. The spelling with *r* is probably correct. The term corresponds to Syriac איגורי דחיטתא "fine quality wheat" (Payne-Smith vol. I, col. 137). The entire exposition deals only with the case of a field sown with two kinds of wheat, as in the Mishnah.

86 Everywhere else, this kind of wheat is called שחמתית. The elision of *ḥ* shows that these rules were formulated in the region between Haifa and Beth She'an where ח was identified with ה. The root of the word is שחם "to be darkish" (Arabic سخم، سحم; cf. also شخم "spoiled"). This is the coarser kind of wheat.

87 When he cuts half of the field, since we require that the poor have a clear sign when *peah* will be given and that is at the end of the total harvest.

88 Since actions count more than intentions.

89 Here also the action cancels the prior intention. He may not give from the coarse wheat for the fine since that would be stealing from the poor. He may give from the fine wheat for the coarse since he gives to the poor more than they would be entitled to.

90 As explained before, all *peah* has to be given at the end.

91 Not the fine and the coarse kinds separately but the first and the second harvests separately. In that case, since *peah* has to be given at the end, there is only fine wheat to be given (for the entire field) and the farmer is not obligated to separate *peah* from the coarse wheat kernels in his heap. {The emendations proposed by the commentators are unconvincing.}

92 Not really exempted, but the farmer does not have to give from the brown wheat, as explained in the previous note.

(fol. 16d) **משנה ו**: מַעֲשֶׂה כְּשֶׁזָּרַע רִבִּי שִׁמְעוֹן אִישׁ הַמִּצְפָּה לִפְנֵי רַבָּן גַּמְלִיאֵל וְעָלוּ לְלִשְׁכַּת הַגָּזִית וְשָׁאֲלוּ. אָמַר נָחוּם הַלִּיבְלָר מְקוּבָּל אֲנִי מֵרִבִּי מִייַשָּׁא שֶׁקִּיבֵּל מֵאַבָּא שֶׁקִּיבֵּל מִן הַזּוּגוֹת שֶׁקִּיבְּלוּ מִן הַנְּבִיאִים הֲלָכָה לְמֹשֶׁה מִסִּינַי בְּזוֹרֵעַ אֶת שָׂדֵהוּ שְׁנֵי מִינֵי חִיטִּים אִם עֲשָׂאָן גּוֹרֶן אַחַת נוֹתֵן פֵּיאָה אַחַת שְׁתֵּי גְרָנוֹת נוֹתֵן שְׁתֵּי פֵּיאוֹת.

Mishnah 6: It happened that Rebbi Simeon from Mizpah[93] sowed before Rabban Gamliel; they ascended to the stone hall[94] and asked. Naḥum the scribe[95] said: I have the tradition from Rebbi Miasha, who received it from my father, who received it from the pairs[96], who received if from the prophets[97], a practice going back to Moses on Sinai, that he who sows two different kinds of wheat on his field gives one *peah* if he stores them together, two *peot* if he stores them separately.

93 A Mishnah collector in the times of Rabban Gamliel I; one of a very small number of scholars who lived during Second Temple times who is always mentioned with the title "Rebbi." {It is possible that before the destruction of the Temple, "Rebbi" did not designate a rabbi but a collector of legal statements.} Mizpah probably is today's Nebi Samwil, N. W. of Jerusalem.

94 The hall on the Temple Mount whose walls were formed by hewn stone and in which the high court held its sessions.

95 Cf. Latin *libellaris*, "of books." He was the clerk of Rabban Gamliel I's court.

96 The pairs of authorities, chiefs and deputy chiefs of the high court in Jerusalem, who are mentioned in the first chapter of *Pirqe Avot*.

97 Ḥaggai, Zachariah, Malachi, who by tradition are counted as members of the "Great Assembly."

(fol. 17a) **הלכה ו**: אָמַר רִבִּי זְעִירָא בְּשֵׁם רִבִּי יוֹחָנָן אִם בָּאָת הֲלָכָה תַּחַת יָדֶיךָ וְאֵין אַתְּ יוֹדֵעַ מַה טִיבָהּ אַל תַּפְלִיגֶינָּה לְדָבָר אַחֵר שֶׁהֲרֵי כַּמָּה הֲלָכוֹת נֶאֶמְרוּ לְמֹשֶׁה בְּסִינַי וְכוּלְּהֹן מְשׁוּקָּעוֹת בַּמִּשְׁנָה. אָמַר רִבִּי אָבִין וְיֵאוּת הִיא שְׁנֵי מִינֵי חִיטִּים אִילוּלֵי שֶׁבָּא נָחוּם וּפֵירֵשׁ לָנוּ יוֹדְעִין הָיִינוּ.

Halakhah 6: Rebbi[98] Zeïra said in the name of Rebbi Joḥanan: If you come to notice a practice of which you do not know the reason, do not push it aside as something alien since many practices were shown to Moses on Sinai and all of them were absorbed into the Mishnah. Rebbi Abin said, that is correct! If Naḥum had not come and explained it to us about the two kinds of wheat, could we have known[99]?

98 The entire following discussion on oral tradition is also in *Taäniot* 1:8.

99 That the rule of two kinds of wheat in one field is a practice revealed to Moses.

רִבִּי זְעִירָא בְשֵׁם רִבִּי אֶלְעָזָר אֶכְתָּוב לוֹ רוּבֵּי תוֹרָתִי. וְכִי רוּבָּהּ שֶׁל תוֹרָה נִכְתְּבָה אֶלָּא מְרוּבִּין הֵן הַדְּבָרִים הַנִּדְרָשִׁין מִן הַכְּתָב מִן הַדְּבָרִים הַנִּדְרָשִׁין מִן הַפֶּה. וְכֵינִי. אֶלָּא כֵינִי חֲבִיבִין הֵן הַדְּבָרִים הַנִּדְרָשִׁין מִן הַפֶּה מִן הַדְּבָרִים הַנִּדְרָשִׁין מִן הַכְּתָב.

Rebbi Zeïra in the name of Rebbi Eleazar: (*Hos.* 8:12) "I[100] wrote down for him most of My teaching."[101] But was most of the Torah written down? Rather, more things are derived from what is written than what is (only) oral tradition. Is that so? But so it is: Things derived from what is transmitted orally are preferred over those written.

100 Words of God.

101 In the Babli (*Giṭṭin* 60b), this is the definite statement of R. Eleazar. The later statement of R. Samuel bar Naḥman is attributed in the Babli to R. Joḥanan, and R. Zeïra follows the latter's argument.

רִבִּי יוּדָה בֶּן פָּזִי אוֹמֵר אֶכְתָּוב לוֹ רוּבֵּי תוֹרָתִי אֵלּוּ הַתּוֹכָחוֹת. אֲפִילוּ כֵן לֹא כְּמוֹ זָר נֶחְשָׁבוּ.

Rebbi Judah ben Pazi says: "I wrote down for him most of My teaching," these are the admonitions[102]. Nevertheless, is it not that (*Hos.* 8:12) "they were considered foreign".

102 *Lev*. 26:14-46, *Deut*. 28:15-69.

אָמַר רִבִּי אָבִין אִילוּלֵי כָתַבְתִּי לָךְ רוּבֵּי תוֹרָתִי לֹא כְמוֹ זָר נֶחְשָׁבוּ. מַה בֵּינָן לָאוּמוֹת. אֵלּוּ מוֹצִיאִין סִפְרֵיהֶן וְאֵלּוּ מוֹצִיאִין סִפְרֵיהֶן. אֵלּוּ מוֹצִיאִין דִּפְתְּרֵיהֶן וְאֵלּוּ מוֹצִיאִין דִּפְתְּרֵיהֶן.

Rebbi Avin said: If I had written down for you most of my teaching, would it not be considered Gentile? What is the difference between us and the Gentiles? These produce their books and those produce their books. These produce their parchments[103] and those produce their parchments.

103 Greek διφθέρα, ἡ, "leather prepared for writing." The argument is: If there were no oral Torah Jewish law would not differ from any Gentile law. Babli *Giṭṭin* 60b briefly alludes to this argument.

רִבִּי חַגַּיי בְּשֵׁם רִבִּי שְׁמוּאֵל בַּר נַחְמָן נֶאֶמְרוּ דְּבָרִים בְּפֶה וְנֶאֶמְרוּ דְּבָרִים בִּכְתָב וְאֵין אָנוּ יוֹדְעִין אֵי זֶה מֵהֶן חָבִיב. אֶלָּא מִן מַה דִּכְתִיב כִּי עַל פִּי הַדְּבָרִים הָאֵלֶּה כָּרַתִּי אִתְּךָ בְּרִית וְאֶת יִשְׂרָאֵל הָדָא אָמְרָה אוֹתָן שֶׁבְּפֶה חֲבִיבִין.

Rebbi Ḥaggai in the name of Rebbi Samuel bar Naḥmani: Things have been said orally and things have been said in writing, and we do not know which ones are preferred. From what is written (*Ex*. 34:27): "By the mouth of these words I concluded a covenant with you and Israel[104];" it follows that the oral traditions are preferred[105].

104 This argument is somewhat specious since the full verse reads: "The Eternal said to Moses, write down these words for yourself, because by the mouth of these words I concluded a covenant with you and Israel." In Babli *Giṭṭin* 60b, R. Simeon ben Laqish explains the verse as part of the covenant and states that written verses may not be recited by heart and oral traditions not written down.

105 A similar argument in the name of R. Johanan is reported in Babli *Giṭṭin* 60b.

רִבִּי יוֹחָנָן וְרִבִּי יוּדָן בֵּי רִבִּי שִׁמְעוֹן חַד אָמַר אִם שִׁימַּרְתָּ מַה שֶׁבְּפֶה וְשִׁימַּרְתָּ מַה שֶׁבִּכְתָב אֲנִי כוֹרֵת אִתְּךָ בְּרִית וְאִם לָאו אֵינִי כוֹרֵת אִתְּךָ בְּרִית. וְחָרָנָה אָמַר אִם שִׁימַּרְתָּ מַה שֶׁבְּפֶה וְקִייַּמְתָּ מַה שֶׁבִּכְתָב אַתָּה מְקַבֵּל שָׂכָר וְאִם לָאו אֵינְךָ מְקַבֵּל שָׂכָר.

Rebbi Joḥanan and Rebbi Yudan bar Rebbi Simeon[106]. One said that if you kept what is oral tradition and kept what is written I will conclude a covenant with you, otherwise I shall not conclude a covenant with you. The other one said, if you watched all that is oral tradition and kept all that is written you will receive your reward, otherwise you will not receive any reward.

106 He is Rebbi Jehudah bar Simon. The verse this homily refers to is the one quoted in the preceding paragraph.

רִבִּי יְהוֹשֻׁעַ בֶּן לֵוִי אָמַר עֲלֵיהֶם וַעֲלֵיהֶם כָּל כְּכָל דְּבָרִים הַדְּבָרִים מִקְרָא מִשְׁנָה תַּלְמוּד וַאֲגָדָה. אֲפִילוּ מַה שֶׁתַּלְמִיד וָתִיק עָתִיד לְהוֹרוֹת לִפְנֵי רַבּוֹ כְּבָר נֶאֱמַר לְמֹשֶׁה בְּסִינַי. מַה טַעַם יֵשׁ דָּבָר שֶׁיֹּאמַר רְאֵה זֶה חָדָשׁ הוּא. מֵשִׁיבוֹ חֲבֵירוֹ וְאוֹמֵר לוֹ כְּבָר הָיָה לְעֹלָמִים.

Rebbi Joshua ben Levi said[107]: On them, and on them; all, like all; words, the words; Bible, Mishnah, Talmud, and Aggadah. Even what a competent[108] student will discover[109] before his teacher was said to Moses on Sinai. What is the reason? (*Eccl.* 1:10) "There is something about which one would say, look, this is new!" His colleague will answer, "it already has been forever."

107 The reference is to *Deut.* 9:10: "The Eternal gave to me the two stone tablets, written by the Divine Finger, *and* on them *like* all *the* words that the Eternal spoke to you on the mountain at the day of assembly." The three italicized expressions are all unnecessary for the understanding of

the sentence; these are interpreted as referring to the three divisions of oral law contained in the complete Torah. (The same derivation is found in *Megillah* fol. 74d, and in very shortened form with different emphasis in Babli *Megillah* 19b.)

108 Arabic وثيق "strong, safe, secure, dependable, reliable". The interpretations of the untrained and incompetent are worthless.

109 Since a student may not rule, or teach, before his teacher, the root of the word להורות must be "to become pregnant," in this case, with an idea.

רִבִּי זְעִירָא בְּשֵׁם שְׁמוּאֵל אֵין לְמֵדִין לֹא מִן הַהֲלָכוֹת וְלֹא מִן הַהַגָּדוֹת וְלֹא מִן הַתּוֹסָפוֹת אֶלָּא מִן הַתַּלְמוּד. תַּנֵּי רִבִּי חֲלַפְתָּא בֶּן שָׁאוּל הִיא שְׁנֵי מִינֵי חִטִּין הִיא שְׁנֵי מִנֵי שְׂעוֹרִין. אָמַר רִבִּי זְעִירָא כָּךְ הָיְתָה הֲלָכָה בְּיָדָם וּשְׁכָחוּהָ הִיא שְׁנֵי מִינֵי חִטִּין הִיא שְׁנֵי מִנֵי שְׂעוֹרִים. וְהָתַנֵּינָן הַמְּחֲלִיק בְּצָלִין לַחִין לַשּׁוּק וּמְקַיֵּים יְבֵישִׁין לַגּוֹרֶן אִית לָךְ מֵימַר שׁוּק וְגוֹרֶן כָּךְ הָיְתָה הֲלָכָה בְּיָדָן וּשְׁכָחוּהָ.

Rebbi Zeïra in the name of Samuel: One makes inferences neither from practices[110], nor from homiletics[111], nor from extraneous sources[112], but only from study[113]. Rebbi Ḥalaphta ben Shaul stated: The case of two kinds of wheat is the same as the case of two kinds of barley[114]. Rebbi Zeïra said, that was part of the original practice and it was forgotten: The case of two kinds of wheat is the same as the case of two kinds of barley. But did we not state (*Mishnah* 3:3): "He who strips moist onions for the market and stores dry ones[115];" can you say about market and storage that this was of the original practice and was forgotten?

110 Rules of practice declared in the Mishnah; these may be overridden by arguments in the Talmud. The interpretation of this paragraph follows R. Samuel ben Meïr (Rashbam) to Babli *Baba batra* 130b, *s. v.* עד.

111 Homiletics, whether incorporated in the Talmud or given in separate *midrashim*. Unfortunately, since the sixteenth century this principle has been violated by Kabbalists in favor of practices mentioned in *Zohar*.

112 Rashbam reads תוספתות instead

of תוספות, but that may be a scribal error. The "additional sources" are tannaïtic materials not given in the Mishnah, either as single traditions or as part of a collection.

113 From the Talmud which fixes the reasons for each ruling, or from a decision made in the Talmud that practice follows the opinion of such-and-such.

114 If R. Ḥalaphta ben Shaul makes the inference that the rules for barley are identical with those for wheat, does he not violate Samuel's statement that one does not draw inferences from stated practices but only from an argument about the underlying principles?

115 He has to give *peah* two times; this rule cannot be deduced from the stated practice regarding two kinds of wheat since one deals here with only one kind of onion. Since this Mishnah cannot be a consequence of the original *Halakhah*, neither may one assert that the ruling of R. Ḥalaphta ben Shaul was part of the original *Halakhah*. Hence, neither the statement of R. Halaphta nor the Mishnah are exempt from logical scrutiny on the basis of accepted general principles.

רִבִּי חֲנַנְיָה בְשֵׁם שְׁמוּאֵל אֵין לְמֵדִין מִן הָהוֹרָייָה. הַכֹּל מוֹדִין שֶׁאֵין לְמֵדִין מִן הַמַּעֲשֶׂה. אֲמַר לֵיהּ רִבִּי מָנָא הָדָא דְתֵימַר בְּהַהוּא דְלָא סְבַר בְּרַם בְּהַהוּא דִסְבַר עֲבַד. אֲמַר לֵיהּ בֵּין סְבַר בֵּין לָא סְבַר בְּהוּא דִפְלִיגָא. בְּרַם בְּהוּא דְלָא פְלִיגָא בֵּין סְבַר בֵּין לָא סְבַר.

Rebbi Ḥananiah in the name of Samuel: One makes no inferences from a ruling[116]. Everybody agrees that one makes no inferences from an action[117]. Rebbi Mana said to him, that means somebody who does not understand[118], but he who understands may act. He said to him, whether one understands or one does not understand, if there is a disagreement[119]. But if there is no disagreement, whether one understands or one does not understand[120].

116 If a rabbi was asked about a practical problem and he gave a certain decision, a third party may make no practical applications of that decision unless he understands the reasoning behind the decision and

agrees with it.

117 If one saw a rabbinic authority act in a certain way, one may not act in the same way or make inferences from this action unless one knows both the background of and the reasoning for the particular action.

118 The reasoning of the rabbinic authority.

119 If in the Mishnah or another source there is mention of a disagreement between rabbis about the correct course, action is permitted only if there is an explicit understanding of and agreement with the reasoning behind the ruling.

120 In this case, one may act on the decision or imitate the action of a competent rabbinic authority even without a detailed inquiry into the arguments leading to decision or action.

(fol. 16d) **משנה ז**: שָׂדֶה שֶׁקְּצָרוּהָ גוֹיִים שֶׁקְּצָרוּהָ לִיסְטִים. קִרְסְמוּהָ נְמָלִין שֶׁבִּרְתָּהּ הָרוּחַ אוֹ בְהֵמָה פְטוּרָה. קָצַר חֶצְיָיהּ וְקָצְרוּ לִיסְטִים חֶצְיָיהּ פְּטוּרָה שֶׁחוֹבַת הַקָּצִיר בְּקָמָה. קָצְרוּ לִיסְטִים חֶצְיָיהּ וְקָצַר חֶצְיָיהּ נוֹתֵן פֵּיאָה מִמָּה שֶׁקָּצַר. קָצַר חֶצְיָיהּ וּמָכַר חֶצְיָיהּ הַלּוֹקֵחַ נוֹתֵן פֵּיאָה לַכֹּל. קָצַר חֶצְיָיהּ וְהִקְדִּישׁ חֶצְיָיהּ הַפּוֹדֶה מִיַּד הַגִּזְבָּר הוּא נוֹתֵן פֵּיאָה לַכֹּל.

Mishnah 7: A field harvested by Gentiles[121] or robbers[122], undermined by ants, ruined by a storm or animals, is free[123]. If he harvested half of it and robbers harvested the other half, it is free since the obligation of produce is when it is standing[124]. If robbers cut half of it and he harvested the other half, he must give *peah* from what he cut. If he harvested half and sold half, the buyer gives *peah* for everything[125]. If he cut half and dedicated half[128], he who redeemed it from the treasurer gives *peah* for everything.

121 Illegally, or that they bought the crop from the Jewish farmer while the grain was still standing.

122 Greek ληστής; in Galilean

dialect, final *m* for *s* is certainly a scribal error. Since Gentiles who rob are mentioned first, the robber here is a Jew.

123 Since the farmer gets nothing of the yield, he has no obligation to give from another field for the lost crop.

124 The obligation of *peah* arises at the end of the harvest, when some grain is still standing. Since at that moment the grain is in the hands of the robbers, no obligation is incurred by the owner of the field.

125 Since the obligation of *peah* did arise from his cutting. However, he may ask to deduct the value of the seller's *peah*, 1⅔% of the seller's harvest, from the selling price.

126 To the Temple. In this case, the obligation again is on the one who finishes the harvest but, since the farmer has no monetary advantage of it, the buyer has no regress for the value given for the *peah* of the first half.

(fol. 17a) **הלכה ז:** מַתְנִיתָא בְּשֶׁקְּצָרוּהָ לְעַצְמָן אֲבָל אִם קְצָרוּהָ לְיִשְׂרָאֵל חַיֶּיבֶת. וְתַנֵּי כֵן אֵין שׂוֹכְרִין פּוֹעֲלִין גּוֹיִים מִפְּנֵי שֶׁאֵינָן בְּקִיאִין בְּלֶקֶט.

Halakhah 7: The Mishnah[127], if they cut for themselves, but if they cut for a Jew it is obligated. And we have formulated regarding this[128]: One does not hire Gentile workers because they do not know about gleanings.

127 Dealing with the first case, if the field was harvested by Gentiles.

128 (Tosephta *Peah* 3:1). The Mishnah does not have to mention that the Gentiles harvest for themselves and not for the Jew, since for the grain harvest one may not hire Gentile workers who would pick up the single stalks not bound in sheaves.

מַתְנִיתָא בְּשֶׁקְּצָרוּהָ לְאָבְדָהּ. אֲבָל אִם קְצָרוּהָ שֶׁלֹּא לְאָבְדָהּ חַיֶּיבֶת. אָמַר רִבִּי הוֹשַׁעְיָא בַּר שַׁמַּי וַאֲפִילוּ תֵימָא כְּשֶׁקְּצָרוּהָ שֶׁלֹּא לְאָבְדָהּ פְּטוּרָה מֵאַחַר שֶׁהַפֵּיאָה נִיתֶּנֶת בִּמְחוּבָּר (fol. 17b) לְקַרְקַע וְאֵין קַרְקַע נִגְזָל.

The Mishnah[129], if they cut to destroy it. But if they do not cut to destroy it, it is obligated[130]. Rebbi Hoshaia ben Shammai[131] said, even if you say that they do not cut to destroy it, it is free since *peah* is given from standing produce and real estate cannot be robbed[132].

129 Dealing with the second case, if the field was harvested by Jewish robbers.

130 Since the robbers, while they are Jewish, are not expected to follow Jewish law and give *peah* from what they are cutting, the farmer has to give *peah* from any grain that he manages to obtain from the field. This might apply in particular to the next case, discussed in the next paragraph, when he harvested the first half of the field, in which case the language of the Mishnah may be read to mean that the farmer is totally freed from his obligation.

131 A fifth generation Galilean Amora from Caesarea Philippi (קצרין), a colleague of R. Mana II.

132 This is a principle repeated many times in both Talmudim, cf. *Kilaim* 7:5, Babli *Sukkah* 30b. The reason is that ownership of real estate is always documented; hence, real estate taken by force in a time of anarchy can always be recovered in court when the rule of law is reestablished.

According to R. S. Cirillo, since the robbers are not owners of the field, they are not owners of the grain as long as it stands. It is true that they become owners of the grain as soon as they cut it; the legal owner then has a claim for damages against them but not a claim to the actual grain. Hence, when the robbers cut the grain, there is no obligation of *peah* incurred by the farmer since neither he nor his employees are doing the harvesting. There also is no obligation on the robbers since the grain comes into their possession only after it is cut and the obligation of *peah* is already a past event. As a consequence, the field is cut without anybody incurring the obligation of *peah*.

מִפְּנֵי שֶׁהוּא מַפְרִישׁ מִן הַקָּצִיר עַל הַקָּמָה וּמִן הַקָּמָה עַל הַקָּצִיר וְאֵינוֹ מַפְרִישׁ מִן הַקָּצִיר לֹא עַל הַקָּצִיר וְלֹא עַל הַקָּמָה. פְּעָמִים שֶׁהוּא מַפְרִישׁ מִן הַקָּצִיר עַל הַקָּמָה. הֵיךְ עֲבִידָא כִּילָּא אֶת שָׂדֵהוּ וְשִׁיֵּיר בָּהּ כְּדֵי פֵּיאָה כֵּיוָן שֶׁקָּצַר שִׁיבּוֹלֶת הָרִאשׁוֹנָה חָזְרָה פֵּיאָה לָעוֹמָרִין מַפְרִישׁ מִן הַקָּצִיר. וְלֹא סוֹף דָּבָר שֶׁכִּילָּא אֶת שָׂדֵהוּ. אֶלָּא אֲפִילוּ כְשֶׁקָּצַר וְאָמַר מִיכָּן וְהֵילָךְ אֲנִי מַפְרִישׁ פֵּיאָה. כֵּיוָן שֶׁקָּצַר שִׁיבּוֹלֶת הָרִאשׁוֹנָה חָזְרָה פֵּיאָה לָעוֹמָרִין מַפְרִישׁ מִן הַקָּצִיר עַל הַקָּמָה.

Because[133] he separates[134] from cut grain for standing grain and from standing grain for cut grain but he does not[135] separate from cut grain for either cut or standing grain. Sometimes he has to separate from cut grain for standing grain. How can this be? If he finished his field and left something standing on it for *peah*, at the moment he cuts the first stalk from this, *peah* returns to the sheaves; he has to give from cut grain[136]. Not only if he finished his field but even if he cut some and said: "From here and further on I give for *peah*," at the moment he cuts the first stalk from this, *peah* returns to the sheaves and he separates from cut grain for standing grain.

133 The Mishnah must deal separately with the cases of robbers cutting the entire field or only part of the field because the obligation of *peah*, once incurred, may be discharged also from cut grain as explained in Mishnah and Halakhah 1:6.

134 Meaning that he sets aside as *peah* for the poor.

135 If everything is done correctly.

136 Since he stole from the poor by his action, some obligation is transferred to the grain already harvested as explained in Mishnah 1:6.

הַמּוֹכֵר מַהוּ שֶׁיִּזְכֶּה בְּפֵיאָה שֶׁהִיא מַתֶּרֶת אֶת הָעוֹמָרִין. נִשְׁמְעִינָהּ מִן הָדָא. אָמַר רִבִּי יְהוּדָה אֵימָתַי בִּזְמָן שֶׁקִּיבְּלָהּ מִמֶּנּוּ לְמֶחֱצָה לִשְׁלִישׁ וְלִרְבִיעַ. מַה בֵּינָהּ לְקַדְמִיתָא אֶלָּא לִכְשֶׁתִּקְצֹר שְׁלִישׁ תְּהֵא שֶׁלָּךְ. אָמַר רִבִּי בּוּן בַּר חִייָא הָדָא אָמְרָה שֶׁהַמּוֹכֵר זָכָה בְּפֵיאָה שֶׁהִיא מַתֶּרֶת אֶת הָעוֹמָרִין. אָמַר רִבִּי יוֹסֵי תַּמָּן לֹא נִתְחַיְּיבָה שָׂדֵהוּ בִרְשׁוּתוֹ בְּרַם הָכָא נִתְחַייְבָה שָׂדֵהוּ בִרְשׁוּתוֹ. אִילּוּ קָצַר חֲצִי שָׂדֵהוּ וּמָכַר מַה שֶּׁקָּצַר הַלּוֹקֵחַ מוּתָּר בְּלֶקֶט וּבְשִׁכְחָה וּבְפֵיאָה יְאוּת. הַלּוֹקֵחַ מַהוּ שֶׁיִּזְכֶּה בְּפֵיאָה שֶׁהִיא מַתֶּרֶת אֶת הָעוֹמָרִין שֶׁל מוֹכֵר בִּפְלוּגְתָּא דְּרִבִּי וּדְרִבִּי יְהוּדָה הַנָּשִׂיא.

May the seller get the *peah* which permits the sheaves[137]? Let us hear it from the following (Mishnah 5:4): "[138]Rebbi Jehudah said: When is this, if he received it for a half, a third, or a quarter." What is the difference between this and the first case[139]? It must be, "if you cut it, a third will be yours[140]." Rebbi Abin bar Ḥiyya said, this implies that the seller may get the *peah* which permits the sheaves[141]. Rebbi Yose[142] said, there the obligation of the field did not come during his ownership, but here the obligation of the field started during his ownership. It is correct that if he cut half of the field and sold what he cut, the buyer[143] is allowed gleanings, forgotten sheaves, and *peah*. May the buyer get the *peah* which permits the sheaves of the seller[144]? That is the disagreement of Rebbi and Rebbi Jehudah the Prince.

137 This refers to the case when the farmer cuts half the harvest and then sells the field with the remaining crop. If the seller is legally below the poverty line, may he take from the *peah* the buyer is obligated to give also for the grain he himself cut? The problem is that nobody is permitted to take his own *peah*.

138 The Mishnah deals with the case of the sharecropper who is not permitted to take from the *peah* of the field he is working on. Then Rebbi Jehudah explains (nobody dissenting) that this is only true for the sharecropper who has leased the field and has property rights to 50%, 33%, or 25% of the crop. But if the landlord acts as the owner of the field at all times and the sharecropper has no property rights to the crop except that he will receive 50%, 33%, or 25% of the harvest after it is harvested, then the *peah* was never his and, being poor, he may go and collect from the *peah* with the rest of the poor.

139 Of the usual sharecropper.

140 Only after the harvest is completed does the sharecropper have a claim.

141 Since at the moment of the actual obligation of *peah* the field is already sold, the *peah* was never the seller's and he may take his part among the other poor who come to collect.

142 He shows that the argument of R. Abin bar Ḥiyya is faulty. While the actual obligation of *peah* arises during the buyer's harvest, the potential obligation started with the seller's harvest. Hence, the seller should be barred from taking his part of the *peah*. In contrast, the sharecropper who is given ownership only of a part

of the harvest, not of the standing grain, has nothing at all to do with the obligation of *peah*.

143 Since he is poor and never acquired any ownership of the real estate, he may take everything a poor person is entitled to. This sentence is R. Yose's analysis of the correct parallel to the Mishnah of the sharecropper.

144 If the buyer is legally poor, may he take for himself the *peah* that he will give for the seller's harvest? The answer might be yes, unless we are afraid of unfair competition. This is the essence of the last argument in the quarrel between Rebbi and Rebbi Jehudah II the Prince as explained at the end of Halakhah 1:6.

רִבִּי פִּינְחָס בְּעִי קְצִירוּת חוּצָה לָאָרֶץ מַהוּ שֶׁתְּהֵא חַייֶבֶת בְּפֵיאָה. שֶׁלֹּא תֹאמַר הַהֶקְדֵּשׁ פָּטוּר וְחוּצָה לָאָרֶץ פָּטוּר. אִי מַה הֶקְדֵּשׁ חַייָב אַף חוּצָה לָאָרֶץ חַייָב. אַשְׁכַּח תַּנֵּי קְצִיר אַרְצְכֶם וְלֹא קְצִיר חוּצָה לָאָרֶץ.

Rebbi Phineas asked[145]: Can a harvest outside of the Land become subject to *peah*? Could you not say that a dedicated crop is exempt and (a crop) outside the Land is exempt; just as a dedicated crop may become obligated[146], so from outside the Land it may become obligated? He found it stated: (*Lev.* 19:9, 23:22) "When you harvest the harvest of your Land," and not the harvest outside of the Land[147].

145 Here starts the discussion of the last case of the Mishnah, if part of the field was dedicated to the upkeep of the Temple.

146 As explained in the Mishnah, if the field is sold by the Temple officials with the crop still standing.

147 Under any circumstance.

קָצַר הַגִּיזְבָּר חֲצִי חֶצְייָהּ וְלֹא הִסְפִּיק לִקְצוֹר אֶת הַשְּׁאָר עַד שֶׁפָּדָה אֶת כּוּלָּהּ מַפְרִישׁ מִן הַקָּצִיר עַל הַקָּצִיר. וְכָל־מַה שֶׁנִּקְצָר בִּרְשׁוּת הַהֶקְדֵּשׁ כְּבָר נִפְטָר.

If the treasurer cut half of the half but did not finish to harvest the rest before somebody redeemed everything, he gives from the harvest for what was harvested[148] but all that was harvested in the possession of the Temple is already exempted.

148 As explained in the Mishnah, the buyer has to give *peah* also for the harvest of the original owner. However, since the verse speaks to individuals, "when you cut the harvest of *your* land", the obligation is only on private individuals. It does not apply to the Temple which is the collective property of all of Israel.

מלבנות פרק שלישי

(fol. 17b) **משנה א**: מַלְבְּנוֹת הַתְּבוּאָה שֶׁבֵּין הַזֵּיתִים. בֵּית שַׁמַּאי אוֹמְרִין פֵּיאָה מִכָּל אֶחָד וְאֶחָד. בֵּית הִלֵּל אוֹמְרִין מֵאַחַת עַל הַכֹּל. מוֹדִין שֶׁאִים הָיוּ רָאשֵׁי הַשּׁוּרוֹת מְעוּרָבִין שֶׁהוּא נוֹתֵן פֵּיאָה מֵאַחַת עַל הַכֹּל.

Mishnah 1: Rectangles[1] of grain between olive trees[2]: The House of Shammai say, *peah* from each single one, the House of Hillel say, from one for all of them. They agree[3] that one gives one *peah* for all of them if the edges of the rows are touching.

1 This is the interpretation of Maimonides. R. Simson of Sens prefers to derive מלבן from לבן, "white"; a "white field" by definition is one of grain or legumes. [Then "a *white* field of grain" would be redundant.] Since מַלְבֵּן is a masculine word with a feminine plural, the gender of the numeral "one" in the Mishnah is undetermined and different manuscripts and prints vary between אחד, אחת, usually not in a consistent manner.

2 The Halakhah will explain that the disagreement is only for a standard field; there is no disagreement on fields planted wider or narrower than the standard.

3 The House of Shammai accept the position of the House of Hillel.

הלכה א: אֲנָן תַּנֵּינָן שֶׁבֵּין הַזֵּיתִים. תְּנָיֵי דְּבֵית רִבִּי שֶׁבֵּין הָאִילָנוֹת. מַתְנִיתִין צְרִיכָה לְדְבֵית רִבִּי וּדְבֵית רִבִּי צְרִיכָן לְמַתְנִיתִן. אִילּוּ תַּנֵּינָן אֲנָן וְלָא תַּנּוֹן דְּבֵית רִבִּי הֲוֵינָן אָמְרִין לֹא אֲמַרְנָהּ אֶלָּא שֶׁבֵּין הַזֵּיתִים דָּבָר שֶׁהוּא חַיָּיב בְּפֵיאָה. אֲבָל דָּבָר שֶׁהוּא פְּטוֹר פֵּיאָה אַף בֵּית שַׁמַּאי מוֹדִין שֶׁהוּא נוֹתֵן פֵּיאָה מֵאֶחָד עַל הַכֹּל. הֲוֵי צוֹרְכָה לְמַתְנִיתָה דְּרִבִּי. אוֹ אִלּוּ תְּנָיֵי דְּבֵית רִבִּי וְלָא תַנֵּינָן אֲנָן הֲוֵינָן

אֲמְרִין לֹא אָמְרוּ אֶלָּא שֶׁבֵּין הָאִילָנוֹת דָּבָר שֶׁהוּא פְּטוֹר פֵּיאָה. אֲבָל דָּבָר שֶׁהוּא חַיָּב בְּפֵיאָה אַף בֵּית הִלֵּל מוֹדֵיי שֶׁהוּא נוֹתֵן פֵּיאָה מִכָּל־אֶחָד וְאֶחָד. הֲוֵי צוּרְכָה לְמַתְנִיתִן וְצוּרְכָה לְמַתְנִיתָה דְּבֵי רַבִּי.

Halakha 1: We have stated: "between olive trees." In the House of Rebbi they stated "between fruit trees.[4]" Our Mishnah needs the one of the House of Rebbi and that of the House of Rebbi needs our Mishnah. If we had stated, but not the House of Rebbi, we would say that it said only "between olive trees", which in themselves are subject to *peah*, but for those which are free from the obligation of *peah*[5] even the House of Shammai will agree that he gives one *peah* for all of them. Hence, our Mishnah needs that of Rebbi. Or if there were the declaration of the House of Rebbi but we had not stated ours, we would say that it refers only to those which are between trees free from the obligation of *peah*, but for trees which in themselves are subject to *peah* even the House of Hillel will agree that he gives *peah* from each single one. Hence, both our Mishnah and the *baraita* of the House of Rebbi are needed.

4 Even though Rebbi edited the generally accepted Mishnah, either later generations changed the wording or, more likely, Rebbi insisted in his Yeshivah that in addition to the official Mishnah one would retain a more general version.

5 Since only the trees enumerated in Mishnah 1:5 are subject to *peah*, a general statement "fruit trees" includes (as a majority) those that are not subject to *peah*.

מַה נָן קַיָּמִין. אִי בִּמְרוּוָחִין אַף בֵּית שַׁמַּאי מוֹדֵיי שֶׁהוּא נוֹתֵן פֵּיאָה מֵאֶחָד עַל הַכֹּל. אִי בִּרְצוּפִין אַף בֵּית הִלֵּל מוֹדוּ שֶׁהוּא נוֹתֵן פֵּיאָה מִכָּל־אֶחָד וְאֶחָד. אֶלָּא כִּי נָן קַיָּמִין בִּנְטוּעִין מַטַּע עֶשֶׂר לְבֵית סְאָה. בֵּית שַׁמַּאי עָבְדִין לוֹן כִּמְרוּוָחִין. וּבֵית הִלֵּל עָבְדִין לוֹן כִּרְצוּפִין.

What are we dealing with? [6]If they are widely spaced, even the House of Shammai will agree that he gives one *peah* for all of them[7]. If they are densely planted, the House of Hillel will agree that he gives *peah* from each single one[8]. But we deal with the case of 10 plants on a *bet se'ah*[9]. The House of Shammai compare it to widely spaced[10], the House of Hillel compare it to densely planted ones[12].

6 This text is self-contradictory; it is the confluence of two contradictory texts. The text of Maimonides (*Hilkhot Mattenot Aniïm* 3:9) seems to have been: "If they are widely spaced, also the House of Hillel will agree that he gives one *peah* for all of them. If they are densely planted, the House of Shammai will agree that he gives *peah* from each single one. But we deal with the case of 10 plants on a *bet se'ah*. The House of Shammai compare it to widely spaced, the House of Hillel compare it to densely planted," inverting the roles of Shammai and Hillel in the first clause. But the version of R. Abraham ben David (*loc. cit.*) is: "If they are widely spaced, also the House of Shammai will agree that he gives one *peah* for all of them. If they are densely planted, the House of Hillel will agree that he gives *peah* from each single one. But we deal with the case of 10 plants on a *bet se'ah*. The House of Shammai compare it to densely planted ones, the House of Hillel compare it to widely spaced," inverting the statements in the second clause. There is no direct manuscript evidence of any Yerushalmi manuscript for one reading over the other.

7 Following R. Abraham ben David, the House of Shammai will agree that there are too few trees to make a difference; it is one field with some holes.

8 Since there are few open places large enough to allow wheat to be sown (which by the laws of *kilaim* must be well separated from the trees); hence, each patch is a separate field.

9 See Chapter 2, Notes 31,73.

10 This follows the text of Maimonides who argues that with widely spaced trees the owner could have sown one field. The fact that he chose to make separate rectangles proves that he wants to treat them as

separate fields. (Maimonides translates מלבן by "rectangle.")

11 By the nature of the field the farmer must sow in separate patches, but to him it is one field.

מַה טַעְמָא דְבֵית שַׁמַּאי. שֶׁאֵין דֶּרֶךְ בְּנֵי אָדָם לִהְיוֹת מַכְנִיסִין זְרָעִים בֵּין הָאִילָנוֹת. אַתְיָא דְבֵית שַׁמַּאי כְּרִבִּי יוֹסֵי. כְּמָה דְרִבִּי יוֹסֵי אָמַר אֵין דֶּרֶךְ בְּנֵי אָדָם לִהְיוֹת מַכְנִיסִין בְּצָלִים בֵּין הַיֶּרֶק. כֵּן בֵּית שַׁמַּאי אוֹמְרִים אֵין דֶּרֶךְ בְּנֵי אָדָם (fol. 17c) לִהְיוֹת מַכְנִיסִין זְרָעִים בֵּין הָאִילָנוֹת. מִסְתַּבְּרָא דְבֵית שַׁמַּאי יוֹדוּן לְרִבִּי יוֹסֵי. רִבִּי יוֹסֵי לֹא יוֹדֶה לְבֵית שַׁמַּאי. בֵּית שַׁמַּאי יוֹדוּן לְרִבִּי יוֹסֵי שֶׁכֵּן אֵין דֶּרֶךְ בְּנֵי אָדָם לִהְיוֹת מַכְנִיסִין בְּצָלִים בֵּין הַיֶּרֶק. רִבִּי יוֹסֵי לֹא יוֹדֶה לְבֵית שַׁמַּאי שֶׁכֵּן דֶּרֶךְ בְּנֵי אָדָם לִהְיוֹת מַכְנִיסִין זְרָעִים בֵּין הָאִילָנוֹת.

What is the reason of the House of Shammai? People do not usually introduce seeds between trees[12]. Does it turn out that the House of Shammai are like Rebbi Yose[13]? Just as Rebbi Yose said that people do not usually introduce onions between vegetables[14], so the House of Shammai say that people do not usually introduce seeds between trees! It is reasonable to say that the House of Shammai will agree with Rebbi Yose but Rebbi Yose will not agree with the House of Shammai[15]. The House of Shammai will agree with Rebbi Yose that people do not usually introduce onions between vegetables. Rebbi Yose will not agree with the House of Shammai because people usually introduce seeds between trees.

12 Hence, each spot sown is a separate field. R. David ben Zimra, in his commentary to Maimonides, points out that this argument supports Maimonides's reading in the preceding paragraph. "Seeds" usually refers to grain.

13 Since Rebbi Yose (ben Ḥalaphta) was the leading authority of his generation in the tradition of the House of Hillel, this would be remarkable indeed.

14 This refers to the second part of Mishnah 4 in this chapter:

"Rectangular beds of onions planted among other vegetables, R. Yose says: *Peah* from each bed, but the Sages say: From one bed for all of them." According to R. Yose, onions are detrimental to other vegetables growing near them.

15 In a poor country, the land between trees is much too valuable to be left lying fallow. Hence, everybody will sow between the trees if at all possible.

הָיָה שָׁם גֶּדֶר כְּמָן דְּהוּא אִילָן. הָיוּ שְׁנַיִם.

If there was a fence there, it is like a tree[16]. How about two[17]?

16 If each tree has 250 square cubits around it, one follows the House of Hillel's opinion in the Mishnah.

17 If there are two fences, do the House of Hillel still allow one *peah* for all? The question is asked but not answered [which for practical purposes is a negative answer.]

עַד כְּדוֹן בִּמְעוּרָבִין מִכָּן וּמִכָּן. הֲרֵי מְעוּרָבִין מִצַּד אֶחָד אוֹ בִשְׁלֹשָׁה תְלָמִים שֶׁל פַּתִּיחַ אוֹ אֲפִילוּ כָל־שֶׁהוּא.

So far[18] if they are combined from one side and the other. If they were combined only on one side, either by three coarse furrows[19] or at any place?

18 This refers to the last clause of the Mishnah, that one gives only one *peah* if the beds grown from seeds are connected at more than one place.

19 See Chapter 2, Note 33. Is it necessary that the beds touch in the width of three coarse furrows or is any contact acceptable? The answer here again is not given, which means for practical purposes that it is negative.

(fol. 17b) **משנה ב**: הַמְנַמֵּר אֶת שָׂדֵהוּ וְשִׁייֵר קְלָחִים לַחִים רִבִּי עֲקִיבָה אוֹמֵר פֵּיאָה מִכָּל אֶחָד וְאֶחָד. וַחֲכָמִים אוֹמְרִים מֵאֶחָד עַל הַכֹּל. מוֹדִין חֲכָמִים לְרִבִּי עֲקִיבָה בְּזוֹרֵעַ שֶׁבֶת אוֹ חַרְדָּל בִּשְׁלֹשָׁה מְקוֹמוֹת שֶׁהוּא נוֹתֵן פֵּיאָה מִכָּל־אֶחָד וְאֶחָד.

Mishnah 2: If someone harvests his field in spots and leaves moist stalks, Rebbi Aqiba says, *peah* from each spot, but the Sages say, from one for all of them. The Sages agree with Rebbi Aqiba that he who sows dill or mustard at three different places gives *peah* from each spot[20].

20 This is explained in Chapter 2, Notes 17-19.

(fol. 17c) **הלכה ב**: הַמְנַמֵּר שָׂדֵהוּ כו'. כְּהָדֵין נִימְרָה. מָקוֹם הַזִּבְלִין עוֹלִין תְּחִילָּה נִמְרָה[21] קְרִיי לָהּ.

Halakhah 2: "He who harvests his field in spots," etc. Like a spotted field[22]; the place where fertilizer makes plants grow early is called "spotted."

21 Reading of R. Shelomo Cirillo. The Venice print and manuscripts have בּמרידה; Z. Frankel corrects the last, unintelligible, word to נמרירה. That change is also implied by the commentary of R. Moshe Margalit. R. Eliahu Fulda does not comment on the passage.

22 The leopard is נמר in Hebrew; the Mishnah means: He who makes his field look like a leopard. The Talmud notes that a field which is fertilized unevenly and, hence, whose growth is spotty, is called in agricultural terminology נימרה "leopard-like." It is not clear whether we talk only of a field that is growing at different rates at different points (and, therefore, cannot be harvested at one time) or also of a field that looks normal but whose owner harvests in spots so that it looks "leopard like" at harvest time.

עַד כְּדוֹן כְּשֶׁהָיָה יָבֵשׁ מִכָּן וּמִכָּן וְלַח בְּאֶמְצַע. הָיָה לַח מִכָּן וּמִכָּן וְיָבֵשׁ בְּאֶמְצַע.

So far if it was dry on both sides and moist in the middle[23]. How about being moist on both sides and dry in the middle[24]?

23 Since grain usually is harvested when dry, in the case contemplated the farmer will legitimately harvest the dry sides and leave the green patch in the middle for a later harvest. In this case, R. Aqiba will consider the separate dry patches as separate fields since they can be harvested separately without difficulty.

24 In this case, access to the ripe grain is difficult and one may wonder whether R. Aqiba will insist that the cutting is a separate harvest. The question is not resolved (since practice follows the majority of the "Sages", including most of R. Aqiba's own surviving students, about whom see the Introduction to tractate *Berakhot*.)

רִבִּי בָּא רִבִּי חִיָּא בְשֵׁם רִבִּי יוֹחָנָן אַתְיָא דְרִבִּי מֵאִיר כְּשִׁיטַּת רִבִּי עֲקִיבָה רַבּוֹ. כְּמוֹ דְרִבִּי עֲקִיבָה אוֹמֵר לַח וְיָבֵשׁ שְׁנֵי מִינִין הֵן כֵּן רִבִּי מֵאִיר אוֹמֵר לַח וְיָבֵשׁ שְׁנֵי מִינִין. אָמְרֵי חֲבֵרַיָּא קוֹמֵי רִבִּי יוֹסֵי וְלָמָּה לֵיהּ כְּרִבִּי עֲקִיבָה אֲפִילוּ כְּרַבָּנִין דְּתַנֵּינָן תַּמָּן הַמְחַלִּיק בְּצָלִין לַחִין[25] לְשׁוּק וּמְקַיֵּים יְבֵשִׁין לְגוֹרֶן אָמַר רִבִּי יוֹסֵי שְׁמָעִינָן שׁוּק וְגוֹרֶן שְׁנֵי מִינִין. לַח וְיָבֵשׁ שְׁנֵי מִינִין.

Rebbi Abba, Rebbi Ḥiyya[26] in the name of Rebbi Joḥanan: "Rebbi Meïr follows the argument of his teacher Rebbi Aqiba. Just as Rebbi Aqiba says that moist and dry are two different kinds, so Rebbi Meïr[27] says that moist and dry are two different kinds." The colleagues said before Rebbi Yose: Why should he argue like Rebbi Aqiba? He could argue even like the Rabbis since we have stated there (*Mishnah* 3:3): "He who rips out[28] moist onions for the market and keeps dry ones for storage[29]!" Rebbi Yose answered: We understand that market and storage make two kinds, are moist and dry two kinds[30]?

25 Language of the Mishnah and the Rome manuscript.

26 The tradents are R. Abba bar R. Ḥiyya bar Abba and his father.

27 Who in Mishnah 2:1 asserted that if somebody cuts part of his grain green for fodder and part of it dry for grain he has to give *peah* twice.

28 See the lexical explanation in the next Mishnah.

29 He has to give *peah* twice.

30 Hence, R. Meïr agrees with R. Aqiba, not with the other Sages.

שְׁנֵי מִינִין חֶצְיוֹ לַח וְחֶצְיוֹ יָבֵשׁ אוּף רִבִּי עֲקִיבָה מוֹדֶה. וְהָתַנֵּינָן מוֹדִין חֲכָמִים לְרִבִּי עֲקִיבָה בְּזוֹרֵעַ שֶׁבֶת אוֹ חַרְדָּל בִּשְׁלֹשֶׁת מְקוֹמוֹת. כֵּינִי שֶׁבֶת בִּשְׁלֹשָׁה מְקוֹמוֹת חַרְדָּל בִּשְׁלֹשָׁה מְקוֹמוֹת. שְׁמוּאֵל אָמַר מִפְּנֵי שֶׁאֵין הָרִאשׁוֹן שֶׁבָּהֶן מַמְתִּין לָאַחֲרוֹן שֶׁבָּהֶן. רִבִּי יָסָא בְּשֵׁם רִבִּי יוֹחָנָן מִפְּנֵי שֶׁדַּרְכָּן לִיזָּרַע עֲרוּגוֹת עֲרוּגוֹת. עַל דַּעְתֵּיהּ דִּשְׁמוּאֵל מַפְרִישׁ מִכָּל־קֶלַח וְקֶלַח. עַל דַּעְתֵּיהּ דְּרִבִּי יוֹחָנָן מַפְרִישׁ מִכָּל־עֲרוּגָה וַעֲרוּגָה.

Two kinds, half moist and half dry, even Rebbi Aqiba will agree[31]. But did we not state[32]: "The Sages agree with Rebbi Aqiba that he who sows dill and mustard at three different places[33] . . ." It is so[34]: Either dill at three places or mustard at three places[35]. Samuel says, because the first one does not wait for the last one[36]. Rebbi Yasa in the name of Rebbi Joḥanan: Because they usually are being sown bed by bed[37]. According to Samuel, he has to give from each stalk[38]; according to Rebbi Joḥanan he has to give from each bed.

31 If a connected part of the field is already dry and ready for harvesting, even R. Aqiba will agree that then the harvest is the start of the harvest of the entire field and only one *peah* is due. This argument cannot apply to spot cutting.

32 Mishnah 3:2

33 He gives *peah* for each part separately.

34 The Yerushalmi expression כיני is discussed at length in J. N. Epstein, *Mavo lenosaḥ hammišnah*, 2nd ed., Jerusalem 1964, pp. 441-508.

35 Even though both the Mishnah and its quote in the Halakhah read "or", it seems that the argument refers to the reading "dill *and* mustard" found in the Parma and one of the Genizah manuscripts of the Mishnah. It is explained that any one kind of spice triggers the special rule of *peah* for spice beds.

36 Dill and mustard are special in that they cannot be harvested at one time. If they did not fall under the general category of legumes there would be no obligation of *peah* at all. Hence, Samuel restricts the meaning of the Mishnah to dill and mustard only; these kinds are mentioned for themselves and not as paradigms.

37 Spices are grown in small quantities. Hence, each bed is a separate field. For R. Johanan, dill and mustard are given as paradigms; the rule of the Mishnah applies to all spices.

38 This is almost impossible and implies a rejection of Samuel's argument.

(fol. 17b) **משנה ג**: הַמַּחֲלִיק בְּצָלִים לַחִין לְשׁוּק וּמְקַיֵּים יְבֵשִׁין לְגוֹרֶן נוֹתֵן פֵּיאָה לְאֵלּוּ לְעַצְמָן וּלְאֵלּוּ לְעַצְמָן וְכֵן בָּאֲפוּנִים וְכֵן בְּכֶרֶם. הַמֵּידָל נוֹתֵן מִן הַמְּשׁוּאָר עַל מַה שֶּׁשִּׁייֵר. וְהַמַּחֲלִיק מֵאַחַת יָד נוֹתֵן מִן הַמְּשׁוּאָר עַל הַכֹּל.

Mishnah 3: He who rips out[39] moist onions for the market and keeps dry ones for storage gives *peah* for each batch separately; the same applies to peas[40] and vineyards[41]. He who thins out gives *peah* for what is left[42]. He who rips out with one hand[43] gives from the remainder for everything.

39 This translation is tentative; according to Maimonides it simply means "cuts", based on *Is*. 41:7. According to R. Simson of Sens, it means either "leaves a bald spot" where the onions have been taken out or it means "splits" his field into two parts; it is possible that the expression is

intentionally ambiguous. [In Mishnah *Arakhin* 1:3, the word means "to finish, to play the final coda."] In Arabic, חלק means "to shave"; this supports the first interpretation of R. Simson, also supported by Mishnah *Ševiït* 4:4 which explains that "thinning" means taking out single plants but "ripping out" means pulling at least three together, leaving a bald spot.

40 Peas grown for meal. Those grown to be eaten as vegetable are not subject to the laws of *peah* (Mishnah *Peah* 1:4).

41 Table grapes are considered different from grapes used either for wine making or for raisins.

42 Since thinning is necessary for the better growth of many kinds, the plants taken out in thinning are not considered harvested.

43 The meaning of this expression is not clear. According to Maimonides, it means "taking from one side only". According to Rabbenu Simson, it means "taking from one kind only". The sentence may refer to the start of the Mishnah: If somebody harvests young onions to sell them green with their leaves, he has to give *peah* from these green onions. But if he rips out only a few at a time with one hand, at the end, at the time of the harvest of the fully ripe onions for storage, he gives *peah* also for the volume of those green ones that he took occasionally.

(fol. 17c) **הלכה ג**: תַּנֵּי הַמֵּרוֹג חַייָב בִּתְחִילָּתוֹ וְחַייָב בְּסוֹפוֹ. וְאֵיי דֵינוֹ מֵירוֹג. אָמַר רִבִּי יִרְמְיָה כְּהָדָא דְתַנֵּינָן הַמְּחַלִּיק בְּצָלִים לַחִים[44] לְשׁוּק וּמְקַייֵם יְבֵשִׁין לְגוֹרֶן. אָמַר רִבִּי יוֹסֵי הַדֵּין קִיצְחָה כַּד אַתְּ זְרַע לֵיהּ עֲבִיד בְּצֶל דַּקִּיק. כַּד אַתְּ שְׁתַל לֵיהּ עֲבִיד בְּצַל רָב. דִּי לָא כֵן מַה נָן אָמְרִין הוֹאִיל וְהוּא לִזְרִיעָה יְהֵא פָּטוּר מִן הַפֵּיאָה. וְחִיטִּין לֹא לִזְרִיעָה הֵן. חִטִּין רוּבָּן לַאֲכִילָה וְזֶה רוּבּוֹ לִזְרִיעָה. עַל דַּעְתֵּיהּ דְּרִבִּי יִרְמְיָה יֶרֶק חַייָב בְּפֵיאָה. מִינוֹ מַכְנִיסוֹ לְקִיּוּם. מַה עֲבַד לָהּ רִבִּי יוֹסֵי. גָּמוּר הוּא וְאֵינוֹ מְחוּסָּר אֶלָּא לְיַבֵּשׁ.

Halakha 3: It is stated[45]: "In patches[46] it is obligated at the beginning and at the end." What is "in patches?" Rebbi Jeremiah said, just as we have stated: "He who rips out moist onions for the market and keeps dry ones for storage." Rebbi Yose[47] said, for example nigella: If one sows it, it produces thin bulbs; if one plants seedlings, it produces large bulbs. For if it were not so, we would say because it is for sowing[48] it should be freed from *peah*. But are wheat grains not also for sowing? Wheat is mostly for eating, that one[49] is mostly for sowing. According to Rebbi Jeremiah, are vegetables subject to *peah*[50]? Its kind is collected for storage. How does Rebbi Yose deal with it[51]? It is finished and needs only to dry out.

44 Reading of the Rome manuscript only.

45 Tosephta *Peah* 1:9.

46 The text of the Tosephta reads: He who harvests in "patches." According to S. Lieberman (*Tosefta kifšutah Peah* p. 131), אורגא is the Syriac translation of ברוד "having white spots." Z. Frankel refers the word here to Aramaic מרג "escape control", which does not make sense. J. Levy refers to Arabic מַרַגַ "to be, to get into disorder", to which one may add מַרג "pasture".

47 R. Yose (the Amora) disagrees with R. Jeremiah and asserts that green onions are not in themselves subject to *peah*; only if part of the field is left to produce onions for storage does the obligation of *peah* fall on the entire field.

48 In the first phase, when the plot is sown with *nigella* seed, all will be taken out for replanting. Hence, by Mishnah 1:4, it should not be subject to *peah*. However, since the seeds of the strong plant will be stored as spice, it is subject to *peah* in every harvest.

49 Sown *nigella* does not produce usable spice.

50 Since by equating Mishnah and Tosephta he declares an obligation of *peah* for green onions even if the field does not produce any onions for storage. This contradicts Mishnah 1:4.

51 The problem of green onions.

תַּנֵּי לֶקֶט קְצִירְךָ וְלֹא לֶקֶט קִיטּוּף. רִבִּי זְעִירָא רִבִּי חִייָא בְּשֵׁם רִבִּי יוֹחָנָן הַמְלַקֵּט שִׁבֳּלִין לְעִיסָּתוֹ אֲפִילוּ כָּל־שֶׁהוּא פָּטוּר מִן הַפֵּיאָה. רִבִּי אֶלְעָזָר אוֹמֵר אֲפִילוּ בְמַגָּל. אָמַר רִבִּי יוֹסֵי וְהוּא שֶׁשִּׁייֵר. וְהָתַנֵּי הָיוּ לוֹ חָמֵשׁ גְּפָנִים וְהוּא

בּוֹצְרָן וּמַכְנִיסָן לְתוֹךְ בֵּיתוֹ פָּטוּר מִן הַפֶּרֶט וּמִן הָעָרְלָה וּמִן הָרְבָעִי וְחַיָּיב בְּעוֹלְלוֹת. אָמַר רִבִּי יוּדָן כָּאן בִּגְמוּרוֹת כָּאן בְּשֶׁאֵינָן גְּמוּרוֹת. אָמַר רִבִּי יוֹסֵי וַאֲפִילוּ תֵימָא כָּאן וְכָאן בִּגְמוּרוֹת. כָּאן וְכָאן בְּשֶׁאֵינָן גְּמוּרוֹת. תַּמָּן כְּשֶׁבִּיקֵּשׁ לְאוֹכְלָן עֲנָבִים. בְּרַם הָכָא כְּשֶׁבִּיקֵּשׁ לַעֲשׂוֹתָן יַיִן עוֹשֶׂה. הָדָא יַלְפָא מִן הַהִיא וְהַהִיא יַלְפָא מִן הָדָא. הָדָא יַלְפָה מִן הַהִיא שֶׁאִים בִּיקֵּשׁ לְאוֹכְלָן מְלִילוֹת וַאֲפִילוּ לֹא שִׁייֵר. וְהַהִיא יַלְפָא מִן הָדָא שֶׁאִים בִּיקֵּשׁ לִשְׁתּוֹתָן יַיִן וְהוּא שֶׁשִּׁייֵר.

It was stated: (*Lev.* 19:9) "The gathering of your harvest," not the gathering of your plucking[52]. Rebbi Zeïra, Rebbi Ḥiyya in the name of Rebbi Joḥanan: He who collects[52] ears for his dough in any quantity[53] is free from *peah*. Rebbi Eleazar says, even with a sickle[54]. Rebbi Yose[55] said, only if he left some standing. Did we not state (Tosephta *Peah* 1:10): "If he had five vines and he harvested them and brought them into his house[56], he is free from fallen berries[57], from *orlah*, from the *fourth year*[58], but he is obligated for gleanings[59]. Rebbi Yudan said, one for those which are fully ripe[60], one for those which are not fully ripe[61]. Rebbi Yose[42] said, you may even say that both deal with the case that they are fully ripe, or both deal with the case that they are not fully ripe. There[63] if he wanted to eat them as grapes, here[64] if he wanted to make them into wine, he may do so. This is informed from that and that is informed from this. This is informed from that, if he wants to eat them[65] as rubbed ears [he may do so] even if he did not leave a remainder. That is informed from this, if he wants to drink them as wine[66] [he may do so] only if he left a remainder.

52 By hand.

53 In the Babli this expression would mean "a minimal quantity." In the Yerushalmi it means "a quantity of indeterminate size."

54 It is not a harvest unless some is

collected for storage, not if everything is used for immediate consumption.

55 The Amora who in the Yerushalmi is known usually as R. Yasa and in the Babli as R. Assi.

56 Not to the winepress to make wine or to his roof to make raisins.

57 Berries fallen from the grape bunches during harvest, which may not be taken by the harvesters but must be left for the poor.

58 *Orlah* is the yield of the first three years of a newly planted tree that is forbidden for all use; the yield of the fourth year must be eaten in Jerusalem (or it may be redeemed and the money brought to Jerusalem) if there is a Temple. These obligations do not depend on the harvest; hence, they cannot belong to the text. Even though this text is found in both manuscripts of the Yerushalmi, it is not in the Tosephta where the reading is: he is free from fallen berries, forgotten sheaves, and *peah*. This is also the text implied by both Maimonides and R. Abraham ben David (הלכות מתנות עניים 4:27) and the mention of *peah* is implied by the discussion here. The corruption must have crept into a manuscript from which both the Leyden and the Rome manuscripts are derived.

The Tosephta does not mention a remainder; this seems to contradict R. Yasa.

59 Single berries which do not grow either in a bunch or in a row. They may not be harvested and must be left for the poor. Since they belong to the poor from the moment of their formation, the manner of harvesting is irrelevant.

60 Then any collecting is harvesting and a remnant is necessary so that the obligation of *peah* may be fulfilled.

61 Then *peah* is not due.

62 Ben Zabida, the late Amora.

63 Without remainder.

64 A remainder is required for wine grapes.

65 Ears of grain. Eaten as a snack directly from the field.

66 Even if the grapes are squeezed by hand to produce grape juice in the house.

הַמֵּידָל נוֹתֵן מִן הַמְשׁוּאָר עַל מַה שֶׁשִּׁייֵר. תַּנֵּי אָמַר רִבִּי יוּדָה בְּמַה דְּבָרִים אֲמוּרִים בְּמֵידַל לְשׁוּק אֲבָל בְּמֵידַל לְבֵית נוֹתֵן מִן הַמְשׁוּאָר עַל הַכֹּל. אָמַר רִבִּי

זְעִירָא הָדָא דְתֵימָא בְּשֶׁעִיבָּה עַל מְנָת לְהַדֵּל. אֲבָל אִם עִיבָּה עַל מְנָת שֶׁלֹּא לְהַדֵּל לֹא סוֹף דָּבָר לְבֵיתוֹ אֶלָּא אֲפִילוּ לְשׁוּק נוֹתֵן מִן הַמְּשׁוּאָר עַל הַכֹּל.

"He who thins out gives *peah* for what is left[67]." It was stated (Tosephta *Peah* 1:10): Rebbi Jehudah said: When has this been said? If he thins for sale[68], but if he thins for his own use he gives from the remnant for everything[69]. Rebbi Zeïra said, that means[70], if he sowed thickly in order to thin later. But if he sowed thickly without intention to thin later, not only if he uses it for himself but even for the market he gives from the remnant for everything.

67 Quote from the Mishnah.

68 The plants taken in thinning, even if they are marketable as produce, are certainly only vegetable that in its kind is never stored and, hence, is free from the obligation of *peah*. Nobody requires *peah* for thinnings that are discarded.

69 Because this is the use of the produce of the field for which it was planted.

70 That he does not have to give *peah* for marketable thinnings if they are marketed.

(fol. 17b) **משנה ד**: הָאִימָּהוֹת שֶׁל בְּצָלִים חַייָבוֹת בְּפֵיאָה. רִבִּי יוֹסֵי פּוֹטֵר. מַלְבְּנוֹת הַבְּצָלִים שֶׁבֵּין הַיֶּרֶק רִבִּי יוֹסֵי אוֹמֵר פֵּיאָה מִכָּל־אֶחָד וְאֶחָד. וַחֲכָמִים אוֹמְרִים מֵאֶחָד עַל הַכֹּל.

Mother onions[71] are subject to *peah*, Rebbi Yose frees. Rectangles of onions among vegetables, Rebbi Yose says *peah* from each single one, but the Sages say from one for everything[72].

71 The Halakhah will try to explain this expression.

72 For this controversy, see Halakhah 2.

(fol. 17c) **הלכה ד**: רַב אָמַר פורגרה וּשְׁמוּאֵל אָמַר צוּמְחָתָא.

Halakha 4: Rav says *pvrgrh*[71], Samuel says sproutings[72].

71 The word and its meaning are not clear; this is the opinion of I. Löw in his *Flora der Juden*, II p. 127. The explanations by Levy/Fleischer, Kohout, Kraus are all thoroughly unsatisfactory. R. Moses Margalit and Jastrow consider the word to be a *Pilpel* form of פרג which appears in three ways in Yerushalmi sources, first and second as parallels to Arabic פרג "to open, enlarge," (in the Yerushalmi as "blossom",) פרג "to make happy", third as parallel to Syriac פרג "keep apart, exchange." It is difficult to find the desired meaning here, also the form is not that of a Semitic reduplication. R. Simson reads פורגדה which Schwab takes to mean *paragauda* (Latin, "lace border of a garment", Greek παραγαύδης, -ου, ὁ "garment with purple border") and wants to find in this the meaning given to the word by Fleischer: "The tiny onions sometimes growing around a large bulb which are not marketable and, therefore, are left in the ground at harvest time." This explanation may be correct even if the etymology is unknown.

72 Spontaneous growth of remainders of bulbs and roots in the ground after the harvest.

רִבִּי יַעֲקֹב בַּר בּוּן בְּשֵׁם רִבִּי חֲנִינָא לֹא אָמַר רִבִּי יוֹסֵי אֶלָּא מִשּׁוּם הֶבְקֵר. רִבִּי בּוּן בַּר חִייָא בְּעֵי קוֹמֵי רִבִּי מָנָא וְהֶבְקֵר חַיָּיב בְּפֵיאָה. אָמַר לָהֶן בְּזָכָה בָהֶן אַחַת אַחַת. וְהָתַנֵּי אַף עַל פִּי שֶׁאֵינָן מִתְקַיְּימוֹת לוֹ בִּמְרוּבָּה מִתְקַיְּימוֹת בְּמוּעָט. הֲוֵי לֵית טַעֲמָא דְלָא מִשּׁוּם מַכְנִיסוֹ לְקִיּוּם.

Rebbi Jacob bar Abun[73] in the name of Rebbi Ḥanina: Rebbi Yose said only because of ownerless property[74]. Rebbi Abun bar Ḥiyya asked before Rebbi Mana: Is abandoned property obligated for *peah*? He said to them: When he reacquired them one by one[75]. But did we not state: Even though one with a large harvest will not store the mother-onions, one with only a small harvest will. Hence, the reason[76] is only that he collects them for storing[77].

73 A third generation Amora, student of R. Yose ben R. Ḥanina.

74 Since these "mother onions" are worthless according to both definitions, anybody may pick them up. Abandoned property is not subject to *peah* since it cannot be called produce of *your* field.

75 If the owner reasserted his right to these onions after they sprouted new growth they are not abandoned property.

76 Of the Sages.

77 The difference between Rebbi Yose and the Sages is a difference of opinion on matters of agricultural practice rather than on the theory of abandoned property.

(fol. 17b) **משנה ה**: הָאַחִים שֶׁחָלְקוּ נוֹתְנִין שְׁתֵּי פֵיאוֹת. חָזְרוּ וְנִשְׁתַּתְּפוּ נוֹתְנִין פֵּיאָה אַחַת. שְׁנַיִם שֶׁלָּקְחוּ אֶת הָאִילָן נוֹתְנִין פֵּיאָה אַחַת. לָקַח זֶה צְפוֹנוֹ וְזֶה דְרוֹמוֹ זֶה נוֹתֵן פֵּיאָה לְעַצְמוֹ וְזֶה נוֹתֵן פֵּיאָה לְעַצְמוֹ.

Mishnah 5: Brothers who split[78] give two *peot*. When they later form a cooperative, they give one *peah*[79]. Two people who together bought a tree give one *peah*. If one bought the North side and the other the South side, each gives *peah* for himself[80].

78 The inheritance. [Since an unspecified plural has a minimum of 2 but no maximum, such a plural in legal texts always means "2". The text should read: Two brothers who divided up an inheritance give two *peot*.]

79 The Babylonian Talmud (*Ḥulin* 135b) notes that *Lev.* 19:9 reads: "When you (plural) harvest the harvest of your (plural) land, do not finish to cut the corner of your (singular) field." This is taken to mean that *peah* is due from the owner, individual or collective [but not, as pointed out by *Sifra Qedošim* 1(11), if not all shareholders in the collective are Jews.]

80 Even though the care for the tree must necessarily be a common endeavor, only the property relationship matters.

(fol. 17c) **הלכה ה**: קָצַר חֲצִי שָׂדֶה בְשׁוּתְפּוּת וְחָלְקוּ אֵינוֹ מַפְרִישׁ מִשֶּׁלּוֹ לֹא בִתְחִילָּה וְלֹא בְסוֹף. חָזְרוּ וְחָלְקוּ וְנִשְׁתַּתְּפוּ וְקָצְרוּ חֲצִי שָׂדֶה בְשׁוּתְפּוּת וְחָלְקוּ מַפְרִישׁ שֶׁבְּסוֹף עַל חֲבֵירוֹ שֶׁבְּסוֹף. אֲבָל לֹא מִשֶּׁלּוֹ שֶׁבִּתְחִילָּה עַל חֲבֵירוֹ שֶׁבִּתְחִילָּה.

Halakha 5: [81]If he harvested half a field in company [with his brother] and then they split up, he[82] does not give from his own part either for the initial harvest or for the final one. When they changed their minds and after splitting formed a company and harvested half a field, and then separated again, he can give from his part at the end for his partner's part at the end[83], but not from his part at the start for his partner's part at the start[84].

81 In the Venice print, this sentence belongs to the previous Halakhah. It is the consensus of all commentators that it belongs to Halakhah 5.

82 According to Maimonides (*Mattenot Aniïm* 2:16), the entire sentence speaks about a man who took the harvested grain as his part and left the standing grain to his brother. He does not have to give *peah* for his part since the obligation rests on the standing grain and, if his brother would have cut the rest of the field without leaving *peah*, he cannot be asked to contribute to the *peah* that now has to be given from cut grain since he had no ownership rights at the time the last grain was cut.

83 Since his part is simply his part in the company proceeds, all he gives originally was company property.

84 When each of them was a separate owner of half a field, since giving *peah* cannot cross ownership lines.

אָמַר רִבִּי יוֹחָנָן קָצַר חֲצִי שָׂדֶה וְקָצַר חֲצִי חֶצְיָיהּ וְלֹא הִסְפִּיק לִקְצוֹר אֶת הַשְּׁאָר עַד שֶׁקָּצַר כּוּלָּהּ מַפְרִישׁ מִן הָרִאשׁוֹן עַל הָאֶמְצָעִיִין וּמִן הָאֶמְצָעִיִין עַל הָרִאשׁוֹן. וְאֵינוֹ מַפְרִישׁ מִן הָרִאשׁוֹן עַל הָרִאשׁוֹן. אָמַר רִבִּי יְהוֹשֻׁעַ בֶּן לֵוִי הָיְתָה לוֹ שָׂדֶה

אַחַת חֶצְיָיהּ הֵבִיאָה שְׁלִישׁ וְחֶצְיָיהּ לֹא הֵבִיאָה שְׁלִישׁ וְלֹא הִסְפִּיק לִקְצוֹר חֲצִי חֶצְיָיהּ עַד שֶׁהֵבִיאָה כוּלָּהּ שְׁלִישׁ מַפְרִישׁ מִן הָרִאשׁוֹן עַל הָאֶמְצָעִיִים וּמִן הָאֶמְצָעִיִים עַל הָרִאשׁוֹן וְאֵינוֹ מַפְרִישׁ מִן הָרִאשׁוֹן עַל הָרִאשׁוֹן.

Rebbi Joḥanan said: If he wanted to cut half of his field and actually cut[85] half of this half, but when he came to cut the other half he finished off his entire field, then he may give from the first cut on the intermediate ones[86] and from the intermediate ones on the first but not from the first[87] on the first[88]. Rebbi Joshua ben Levi said: If he had a field where half of it was one third ripe[89], the other half was not yet one third ripe, and by the time he finished harvesting half of the first half, the entire field also was one third ripe, he gives from the first cut on the intermediate ones and from the intermediate ones on the first[90] but not from the first on the first.

85 As explained in Halakhah 1:1, the obligation of *peah* starts with the first cut. But since at that point he intended only to cut half of his field, the second part has to be considered a separate field and, therefore, the obligation falls only on the first part of the field.

86 I. e., the remainder of the first part that was not harvested the first time.

87 The first cutting of the first part of the field.

88 The first cutting of the second part of the field, that now represents a new field.

89 Grain that is less than one third ripe is not grain in any commercial sense. Once it is one-third ripe it may be used either for animal feed or for human consumption as *Grünkern*. If he now has the intention of harvesting his field when it is one-third ripe, it is as if the field were divided into two fields. The explanation of this sentence is then completely parallel to that of the preceding statement of R. Joḥanan.

90 Maimonides (*Mattenot Aniïm* 2:17) reads: "And from the intermediate ones on the first and the last". He seems to argue that the first split was by nature, not by the farmer's

design; a change in nature changes the status and at the time of the second harvest the field was counted as one again. But the first cut of the first part cannot be used to free those parts of the field that were not yet a crop at the time of cutting. Since R. Abraham ben David does not disagree, both must have read "and the last" in the text of the Yerushalmi.

(fol. 17b) **משנה ו**: הַמּוֹכֵר קִלְחֵי אִילָן בְּתוֹךְ שָׂדֵהוּ נוֹתֵן פֵּיאָה מִכָּל אֶחָד וְאֶחָד. אָמַר רִבִּי יְהוּדָה אֵימָתַי בִּזְמָן שֶׁלֹּא שִׁייֵר בַּעַל הַשָּׂדֶה אֲבָל אִם שִׁייֵר שָׂדֵהוּ הוּא נוֹתֵן פֵּיאָה לַכֹּל.

Mishnah 6: He who sells tree trunks[91] in his field gives *peah* from each single one. Rebbi Jehudah says, when? If the owner of the field did not retain anything, but if he retained his field, he gives *peah* for all of them[92].

91 According to Maimonides (*Mattenot Aniïm* 3:18), the rule applies to any sale, not only of trees or tree roots, but even of standing grain.

92 See the first and last notes to the next paragraph.

(fol. 17c) **הלכה ו**: עַד כְּדוֹן כְּשֶׁהִתְחִיל לִקְצוֹר וַאֲפִילוּ לֹא הִתְחִיל לִקְצוֹר. נִשְׁמְעִינָהּ מִן הָדָא לָקַח גֵּז צֹאנוֹ שֶׁל חֲבֵירוֹ אִם שִׁייֵר הַמּוֹכֵר חַייָב וְאִם לָאו הַלּוֹקֵחַ חַייָב. רִבִּי יִרְמְיָה בְשֵׁם רִבִּי יוֹחָנָן דְּרִבִּי יְהוּדָה הִיא. שַׁנְייָא הִיא תַּמָּן בֵּין שֶׁהִתְחִיל לִגְזוֹז בֵּין שֶׁלֹּא הִתְחִיל לִגְזוֹז. וְכֹא לָא שַׁנְייָא בֵּין שֶׁהִתְחִיל לִקְצוֹר בֵּין שֶׁלֹּא הִתְחִיל לִקְצוֹר.

Halakha 6: So far when he started harvesting beforehand[93]; even if he did not start to harvest? Let us understand it from the following (Mishnah *Ḥulin* 11:2): "If he bought the shearings[94] of another man's sheep, if the seller retained anything, the seller is liable[95], otherwise the buyer is liable." Rebbi Jeremiah in the name of Rebbi Joḥanan: This is Rebbi Jehudah's[96]. Is there a difference? There, both if he started to shear or if he did not start to shear[97], and here there will be no difference whether he started harvesting beforehand or did not start beforehand[98].

93 If the seller started harvesting, the first cut establishes the obligation of *peah* (see Halakhah 1:1). Hence, the obligation of the seller can be satisfied only if he disposes of the entire field. The discussion centers on R. Jehudah's clarification.

94 I. e., the right to shear the sheep at a specified time in the future.

95 To give the first shearings to a Cohen, *Deut.* 18:4.

96 Although nobody seems to object to R. Jehudah's clarification, the Yerushalmi does not accept the thesis of the Babli that all statements of R. Jehudah starting with "when?" are undisputed practice. In any case, it looks as if the underlying principle was the same.

97 Will the seller be liable as long as he retains any wool for himself.

98 In the Babli (*Ḥulin* 138a), both Rav Ḥisda and Rava agree that *peah* is due only if the harvest started since it says (*Lev.* 19:9): "When you harvest the harvest of your land." But the obligation of giving the first wool to the Cohen exists independent of the act of shearing. Hence, the Babli negates the conclusion of the Yerushalmi here.

מַה טַעֲמָא דְּרִבִּי יוּדָה. מִשּׁוּם דְּחוֹבַת קְצִיר בְּקָמָה אוֹ מִשּׁוּם דַּהֲוֵי כְּמוֹכֵר לוֹ חוּץ מֵחוֹבָתוֹ. נִשְׁמְעִינָהּ מִן הָדָא לָקַח גֵּז צֹאן חֲבֵירוֹ אִם שִׁייֵר הַמּוֹכֵר הַמּוֹכֵר חַיָּב וְאִם לָאו הַלּוֹקֵחַ חַיָּב. רִבִּי יִרְמְיָה בְּשֵׁם רִבִּי יוֹחָנָן דְּרִבִּי יְהוּדָה הִיא. אִית לָךְ לְמֵימַר תַּמָּן שֶׁחוֹבַת קְצִיר בְּקָמָה לֹא מִשּׁוּם דְּמוֹכְרוֹ לוֹ חוּץ מֵחוֹבָתוֹ. וְכֹה בְּמוֹכְרוֹ חוּץ מֵחוֹבָתוֹ.

What is the reason of Rebbi Jehudah? Because the obligation of the harvest falls on the standing grain? Or because he sold to him, excluding his obligation[99]? Let us understand it from the following: "If he bought the shearings of another man's sheep, if the seller retained anything, the seller is liable, otherwise the buyer is liable." Rebbi Jeremiah in the name of Rebbi Johanan: This is Rebbi Jehudah's. Could you say there that the obligation of the harvest falls on the standing grain[100]? No, it is because he sold to him, excluding his obligation! And here also it is because he sold to him, excluding his obligation[101].

99 Unless explicitly stated, the buyer does not acquire the obligations attached to the property bought. Hence, the seller is assumed to have adjusted the asking price so that it covers the cost of *peah* for the harvest sold.

100 In contrast to *peah*, where the verse requires that the farmer refrain from cutting the last corner of his field, the obligation to give from the fleece to the Cohen is formulated in terms of shearing; the obligation does not exist as long as the wool is still on the sheep's back.

101 Otherwise, R. Johanan would be in error asserting the identity of the principles underlying the Mishnah here and in *Hulin*.

מַה נְפַק מִבֵּינֵיהוֹן. עָבַר הַלּוֹקֵחַ וְהִפְרִישׁ. אִין תֵּימַר מִשּׁוּם שֶׁחוֹבַת קְצִיר בְּקָמָה הִפְרִישׁ הִפְרִישׁ. וְאִין תֵּימַר מִשּׁוּם כְּמוֹכֵר לוֹ חוּץ מֵחוֹבָתוֹ הִפְרִישׁ וְנוֹטֵל מִמֶּנּוּ דָמִים. נִשְׂרַף חֶלְקוֹ שֶׁל מוֹכֵר אִין תֵּימַר מִשּׁוּם שֶׁחוֹבַת קְצִיר בְּקָמָה נִשְׂרַף נִשְׂרַף. וְאִין תֵּימַר מִשּׁוּם כְּמוֹכֵר לוֹ חוּץ מֵחוֹבָתוֹ נִשְׂרַף נוֹטֵל מִמֶּנּוּ דָמִים.

What is the difference between them[102]? If the buyer transgressed and separated *peah*. If you say, it is because the obligation of the harvest falls on the standing grain, what he gave he gave[103]. But if you say that because he sold to him, excluding his obligation, he gave and may collect money from him[104]. If the part of the seller burned, if it is because the obligation of the harvest falls on the standing grain, if it is burned it is burned[105]. But if you say that because he sold to him, excluding his obligation, if it is burned he[106] may collect money from him.

102 What are the practical differences that make it necessary for us to decide between the two possible explanations for R. Jehudah's statement?

103 Since *peah* may be given at the start, the middle, and the end of the harvest, it is legal *peah* but does not concern the seller.

104 The buyer may collect from the seller. Since the buyer has fulfilled the obligation of *peah* for his part, if he informs the seller that the latter may reduce the amount he has to give, the buyer may ask for indemnity for the reduction of the seller's obligation.

105 And the buyer must give *peah* from his part since the seller cannot do it for him.

106 The buyer, who bought unincumbered harvest and now has to give *peah* from what he bought, has regress on the seller for the amount of produce which goes into *peah*.

(fol. 17b) **משנה ז**: רִבִּי אֱלִיעֶזֶר אוֹמֵר קַרְקַע בֵּית רוֹבַע חַיָּיב בְּפֵיאָה. רִבִּי יְהוֹשֻׁעַ אוֹמֵר בְּעוֹשֶׂה סְאָתַיִם. רִבִּי טַרְפוֹן אוֹמֵר שִׁשָּׁה עַל שִׁשָּׁה טְפָחִים. רִבִּי יְהוֹשֻׁעַ בֶּן בְּתֵירָה אוֹמֵר כְּדֵי לִקְצוֹר וּלְשַׁנּוֹת וַהֲלָכָה כִדְבָרָיו.

Mishnah 7: Rebbi Eliezer says, a plot of a *bet rova'*[107] is obligated for *peah*. Rebbi Joshua says, if its yield is two *seah*[108]. Rebbi Ṭarphon says, six by six hand-breadths[109]. Rebbi Joshua[110] ben Bathyra said, if it is enough to cut and cut a second time[111]; practice follows his words.

107 See Chapter 2, Note 31.

108 He makes the obligation depend not on the size of the plot but the volume of the yield. Hence, the minimal size would vary with the type of grain grown. One *seah* = 6 *qab* = 24 *log*. One *log* is probably 533 cm^3. This makes the *seah* equal to .452 cubic feet (12.8 dm^3) and two *seah* about .9 cubic feet (25.6 dm^3).

109 One square cubit.

110 This Tanna is not known from any other source. Some Mishnah manuscripts have "R. Jehudah ben

Bathyra", referring to a Tanna of the third generation from Nisibis (*Neẓivin*) on the upper Tigris, today Urfa in Turkey. However, enough manuscripts from different sources have "R. Joshua" to suggest that the name should not be changed.

111 The first use of sickle or scythe starts the harvest; the amount left for the second cut then can be *peah*; see the discussion at the start of Halakha 1:1.

(fol. 17c) **הלכה ז**: מַה טַעֲמָא דְּרִבִּי אֱלִיעֶזֶר נֶאֱמַר כָּאן שָׂדְךָ וְנֶאֱמַר בְּכִלְאַיִם שָׂדְךָ מַה שָׂדְךָ שֶׁנֶּאֱמַר לְהַלָּן בֵּית רוֹבַע אַף כָּאן בֵּית רוֹבַע. מַה טַעֲמָא דְּרִבִּי יְהוֹשֻׁעַ נֶאֱמַר כָּאן שָׂדְךָ וְנֶאֱמַר לְהַלָּן וְשָׁכַחְתָּ עוֹמֶר בַּשָּׂדֶה מַה שָּׂדֶה שֶׁנֶּאֱמַר לְהַלָּן שְׁתַּיִם אַף כָּאן שְׁתַּיִם. מַה טַעֲמָא (fol. 17d) דְּרִבִּי טַרְפוֹן שִׁשָּׁה עַל שִׁשָּׁה מֵעֲרוּגָה. רִבִּי יְהוֹשֻׁעַ בֶּן בְּתֵירָה אָמַר כְּדֵי לִקְצוֹר וּלְשַׁנּוֹת וַהֲלָכָה כִדְבָרָיו. מָה קְצִירָה כְּדֶרֶךְ הַקּוֹצְרִים אוֹ אֲפִילוּ כָּל־שֶׁהוּא מִן מַה דִּכְתִיב אֲשֶׁר לֹא מִלֵּא כַפּוֹ קוֹצֵר וְחִצְנוֹ מְעַמֵּר. הָדָא אָמְרָה קְצִירָה כְּדֶרֶךְ הַקּוֹצְרִים.

Halakha 7: What is the reason of Rebbi Eliezer? It says here "your field[112]" and it says about *kilaim* "your field[113]". Just as "your field" mentioned there[114] means a *bet rova'*, so here it means *bet rova'*. What is the reason of Rebbi Joshua? It says here "your field" and it says further on (*Deut*. 24:19): "You might forget a sheaf on the field." Just as the field mentioned there means two[115], so here also two. What is the reason of Rebbi Ṭarphon? Six by six from a vegetable patch[116]. "Rebbi Joshua ben Bathyra says, if it is enough to cut and cut a second time, and practice follows his words." Does "harvesting" mean following the technique of harvesters, or is it any amount[117]? Since it is written (*Ps*. 132:7): "The harvester did not fill his palm with it, nor the binder of sheaves his bosom," that means that one follows the technique of harvesters.

112 *Lev*. 19:9, 23:22, speaking of *peah*.

113 *Lev*. 19:19: "Your field you shall not sow with two different kinds." It is assumed that a word in the Books of Moses never changes its meaning.

114 Mishnah *Kilaim* 2:10 states that two fields of different crops become forbidden if planted too closely one to the other but only if they are the minimum size of *bet rova'*.

115 Mishnah 6:5 states that a forgotten sheaf is for the poor only if it is less in volume than two *seah*. Similarly, Mishnah 6:6 states that a forgotten part of the field is not for the poor if its yield is at least 2 *seah*. Rebbi Joshua seems to argue that anything that is not a field for the definition of *leqeṭ* (collecting grain forgotten be the farmer) and *šikḥah* (collecting forgotten sheaves) cannot be a field for the definition of *peah* since all three obligations always go together.

116 In Mishnah *Kilaim* 3:1, the standard vegetable patch for intensive cultivation is defined as being one square cubit. R. Eliezer either is of the opinion that no vegetables are grown for storage or that onions grown for storage are such a rare case that one may take grain fields as the standard for everything. R. Ṭarphon seems to think that the smallest plot used to grow any plant for storage is the standard for all crops.

117 R. Joshua ben Bathyra argues that the verse: "When you harvest the harvest of your land," means all kinds of harvest and that therefore any plot which can be harvested is subject to *peah*. The question is only whether the harvest has to be professional or whether simple plucking is enough. The verse from Psalms is taken to mean that only a cut that will fill at least the hollow of one's hand qualifies for "harvesting." This argument is the base of the first discussion in Halakhah 1:1.

(fol. 17b) **משנה ח**: רִבִּי עֲקִיבָה אוֹמֵר קַרְקַע כָּל־שֶׁהוּא חַיֶּיבֶת בְּפֵיאָה וּבְבִיכּוּרִים וְלִכְתּוֹב עָלֶיהָ פְּרוֹזְבּוֹל וְלִקְנוֹת עִמָּהּ נְכָסִים שֶׁאֵין לָהֶן אַחֲרָיוּת בְּכֶסֶף וּבִשְׁטָר וּבַחֲזָקָה.

Mishnah 8: Rebbi Aqiba says: Any real estate[118] is subject to *peah* and first fruits[9], to write a *prozbol*[119] based on it, and to acquire simultaneously non-guaranteed property[121] with money or contract or possession[122].

118 Even if its area is a fraction of a square inch.

119 If it is used for agriculture.

120 Greek προσβολή, ἡ, "falling upon, application." As a legal term, "in an auction, document recording the knocking down of a lot to a purchaser" (L. & S.). Only in the Babli does the word appear with ס instead of ז ; the etymology proposed would require *s* and not *z* but this may be a matter of local dialect.

Prozbol was instituted by Hillel as a way to circumvent the annulment of debts in the Seventh Year in cases when that annulment would only be a rabbinic ordinance. Since only debts due to real persons are annulled by the Seventh Year, the creditor may deliver the debt to the court to be collected. Since the court is not a real person, the debt is not subject to annulment. The document may be written only as lien on real estate. The details of *prozbol* are given in tractate *Giṭṭin*.

121 Real estate is always sold with a title guarantee unless explicitly disclaimed. If the buyer loses the land he bought, either for lack of a valid title or because of a foreclosure of a pre-existing mortgage, he has regress on all other real estate owned by the seller. [The technical term אחריות "warranty" is אַחֲרָיוּת , corresponding to Latin *alienatio* "transfer of property to another person."]

122 Movable property can be acquired only by some act of taking possession, either actual or symbolic. This is necessary in order to determine the exact moment when responsibility for the article is transferred, to avoid situations in which the seller takes the money and then claims that the article was lost in an accident, leaving the buyer without any chance to prove that it was lost when the responsibility was the seller's. However, since buying real estate is a stronger form of contract, a contract or understanding to buy real estate can be extended to include movables. In that case, the moment of transfer of property rights to the real estate is determining also for the

movables. The ways of acquiring real estate are either a contract witnessed by two witnesses, or payment of cash in front of witnesses, or a court ruling confirming squatters' rights. The general theory of these matters is discussed in tractate *Qiddušin*; the exact and restrictive definition of enforceable squatters' rights is one of the topics of tractate *Baba Batra*.

(fol. 17d) **הלכה ח**: רִבִּי אִימִּי בְּשֵׁם רִבִּי שִׁמְעוֹן בֶּן לָקִישׁ בְּעֵי הַגַּע עַצְמָךְ שֶׁהָיָה שָׁם שִׁיבּוֹלֶת אַחַת עַד שֶׁלֹּא קָצַר אֵין כָּאן חִיּוּב מִשֶּׁקָּצַר אֵין כָּאן שִׁיּוּר. רִבִּי חֲנַנְיָה בְּשֵׁם רִבִּי פִּינְחָס תִּיפְתָּר כְּשֶׁהָיָה שָׁם קֶלַח אֶחָד וּבוֹ חָמֵשׁ שִׁבּוֹלִים.

Halakha 8: Rebbi Immi[123] asked in the name of Rebbi Simeon ben Laqish: Think of it, if there were only one ear! Before he cut, there was no obligation; after he cut, there will be nothing left![124] Rebbi Ḥananiah in the name of Rebbi Phineas: Explain it if there was one stalk with five ears!

123 He is Rebbi Ammi, cf. *Berakhot*, pp. 76, 85.

124 The question refers to the rule of Rebbi Aqiba, that even the tiniest amount of real estate carries an obligation of *peah*. If the plot is only big enough for one plant, there can never be an obligation since this would fall on the harvest, not on the bare earth. Hence, R. Aqiba also should be giving a minimal size of the plot which might carry an obligation of *peah*. The answer is that there might be a plant with multiple ears which is not cut but an ear of which is plucked. Then something is left on which the obligation might fall and R. Aqiba is justified. (Cf. the second paragraph in Halakhah 1:1.)

רִבִּי מָנָא בְּעֵי וְלֵיתְנָן אֲמַר קָמָה כָּל־שֶׁהִיא חַייֶבֶת בְּפֵיאָה אֶלָּא בְּגִין דְּתַנָּא בִּיכּוּרִים תַּנָּא קַרְקַע.

Rebbi Mana asked: Why does he not say: "Any crop is subject to *peah*?[125]" But because he has to enunciate first fruits he formulates it as "real estate."

125 This is a continuation of the previous question. If *peah* is not a tax on the soil but on plants which grow on it, should not the principle be formulated in terms of the crop? The answer is that then one would need two separate sentences, one for *peah* and one for first fruits since only fruits of "your land" may be brought (*Bikkurim* 1:2). Since the Mishnah was transmitted orally, that would make memorization much more difficult; a slight deviation from purely logical organization is therefore justified. The ease of memorization is a recognized principle in the formulation of Tannaïtic material.

תַּנֵּי וְהָרֵיאָיוֹן. רִבִּי יוֹסֵי בְשֵׁם רִבִּי יוֹחָנָן מִי שֶׁאֵין לוֹ קַרְקַע פָּטוּר מִן הָרֵיאָיוֹן. רִבִּי מָנָא בְּעֵי וְלָמָּה לָנָן אָמְרִין מִי שֶׁאֵין לוֹ קַרְקַע פָּטוּר מִן הַוִּידּוּי דִּכְתִיב מִן הָאֲדָמָה אֲשֶׁר נָתַתָּ לָנוּ. רִבִּי יוֹסֵי בֵּי רִבִּי בּוּן בְּשֵׁם רִבִּי יוֹחָנָן אָמַר שְׁמוּעָתָה כֵּן מִי שֶׁאֵין לוֹ קַרְקַע פָּטוּר מִן הַוִּידּוּי דִּכְתִיב מִן הָאֲדָמָה אֲשֶׁר נָתַתָּ לָנוּ.

It was stated: "And the appearance[126]." Rebbi Yose in the name of Rebbi Joḥanan: He who owns no real estate is freed from the appearance. Rebbi Mana asked: And why do we not say: He who has no real estate is freed from the declaration[127], since it is written (*Deut.* 26:15): "From the land that You gave us.[128]" Rebbi Yose ben Rebbi Abun[129] taught a tradition in the name of Rebbi Joḥanan: "He who has no real estate is freed from the declaration, since it is written: From the land that You gave us."

126 In the Temple, see Mishnah 1:1, note 4.

127 From Rashi and R. Samuel ben Meïr (Rashbam) in Babli *Qiddušin* 26a and *Baba Batra* 150b it is clear that in old Mishnah texts, the reading was that any real estate obligates its owner "for *peah*, first fruits, and declaration." They negate the last term since they read it as referring to the declaration to be made in the Temple that the tithes of the last three years were given as required. Since tithes are due also from a tenant farmer or a

sharecropper and, in case the farmer did not give tithes, even from the buyer of grain, and, in addition, the text does not require "tithes from your land," there is no place for this clause in the Mishnah. The reference in *Deut*. 26:15 is to את האדמה אשר נתת לנו.

Nachmanides quotes an explanation that the "declaration" is the one required for first fruits (*Deut*. 26:3-10); he is followed by Meïri and R. Yom Tov ben Abraham Al-Išbili. The reference would be to *Deut*. 26:10: מן האדמה אשר נתת לי. There is no verse האדמה אשר נתת לנו.

128 The text is slightly misquoted; it should read: "And the Land that You gave us."

129 What R. Mana put forward as a possibility is a tradition for R. Yose bar Abun.

רִבִּי יוֹסֵי בְשֵׁם רִבִּי יְהוֹשֻׁעַ בֶּן לֵוִי מִי שֶׁאֵין לוֹ קַרְקַע פָּטוּר מִן הָרְאָיָה שֶׁנֶּאֱמַר לֹא יַחְמוֹד אִישׁ אֶת אַרְצְךָ. מַעֲשֶׂה בְּאֶחָד שֶׁהִנִּיחַ אֶת כְּרִיוֹ וּבָא וּמָצָא אֲרָיוֹת סוֹבְבִין אוֹתוֹ. מַעֲשֶׂה בְּאֶחָד שֶׁהִנִּיחַ בַּיִת שֶׁל תַּרְנְגוֹלִין וּבָא וּמָצָא חֲתוּלוֹת מְקוּרָעִין לִפְנֵיהֶן. חַד בַּר נַשׁ שְׁבִיק בֵּיתֵיהּ פְּתִיחַ וַאֲתָה וְאַשְׁכַּח חֲכִינָה כְּרִיכָה עַל קֻרְקְסוֹי. רִבִּי פִּינְחָס מִשְׁתָּעֵי הָדֵין עוּבְדָּא. תְּרֵין אַחִין בְּאַשְׁקְלוֹן הֲווֹ לָהוֹ מְגוּרִין נוּכְרָאִין אָמְרֵי כְדוֹן אִילֵּין יְהוּדָאֵי סָלְקִין לִירוּשָׁלֵם אֲנָן נָסְבִין כָּל־מַה דְּאִית לְהוֹן. מִן מַה דְּסָלְקִין זִימֵּן לָהֶן הַקָּדוֹשׁ בָּרוּךְ הוּא מַלְאָכִים נִכְנָסִין וְיוֹצְאִין בִּדְמוּתָן. מִן דְּנַחְתּוּן שָׁלְחוּן לוֹן מִקְמָן אֲמַר לוֹן אָן הֲוִיתוּן אֲמַר לוֹן בִּירוּשָׁלֵם. אֲמַר לוֹן מַאן שְׁבַקְתּוּן בְּגוֹ בֵּיתָא אָמְרוּ וְלָא בַּר נַשׁ. אֲמַר בְּרִיךְ הָאוּ אֱלָהֵהוֹן דִּיהוּדָאֵי דְּלָא שְׁבָקוֹן וְלָא שְׁבִיק לְהוֹן.

Rebbi Yose in the name of Rebbi Joshua ben Levi: He who has no real estate is free from the appearance since it is said (*Ex*. 34:24): "Nobody will illegally desire your land[130]." It happened that one person left his grain heap[131]; when he returned, he found lions surrounding it. It happened that one left a chicken coop; when he returned, he found torn cats before it. One man left his house open; when he came, he found a snake rolled up on its tail[132]. Rebbi Phineas told the following story: Two brothers in

Askalon had Gentile neighbors. These said, if those Jews go up to Jerusalem, we will take all they have. When they went up, the Holy One, praise to Him, alotted to them two angels who came and went in their likeness. When they returned, they sent them[133] valuable presents. They said to them: where have you been? They said to them, in Jerusalem. They said to them: Whom did you leave in your house? They said, nobody. They said: Praised be the God of the Jews Who did not let us act and did not abandon them!

130 "When you go up to appear before the Eternal, your God, three times in the year."

131 Unprotected.

132 Greek κέρκος, ἡ "tail of an animal" (Explanation of De Rossi.)

133 In the entire story from here on, the singular is frequently used for the plural. This happens in several Yerushalmi passages.

מְנַיִין לִנְכָסִים שֶׁאֵין לָהֶן אַחֲרָיוּת שֶׁהֵם נִקְנִים עִם נְכָסִים שֶׁיֵּשׁ לָהֶם אַחֲרָיוּת בְּכֶסֶף וּבִשְׁטָר וּבַחֲזָקָה. רִבִּי יוֹסֵי בְּשֵׁם חִזְקִיָּה רִבִּי יוֹנָה רִבִּי חֲנִינָא תִּירְתָּיָיה בְּשֵׁם חִזְקִיָּה כְּתִיב וַיִּתֵּן לָהֶם אֲבִיהֶם מַתָּנוֹת רַבּוֹת לְכֶסֶף וּלְזָהָב וּלְמִגְדָּנוֹת עִם עָרִים בְּצוּרוֹת[134] בִּיהוּדָה. עַד כְּדוֹן כְּשֶׁהָיָה קַרְקָעוֹת עִם הַמְּטַלְטְלִין בְּמָקוֹם אֶחָד. הָיוּ קַרְקָעוֹת בְּמָקוֹם אֶחָד וּמְטַלְטְלִין בְּמָקוֹם אַחֵר. אָמַר רִבִּי בּוּן בַּר חִיָּיא נִשְׁמְעִינָהּ מִן הָדָא אָמַר לָהֶן רִבִּי אֱלִיעֶזֶר מַעֲשֶׂה בִּמְדוֹנִי אֶחָד שֶׁהָיָה בִּירוּשָׁלַ͏ִם וְהָיוּ לוֹ מְטַלְטְלִין הַרְבֵּה וּבִיקֵּשׁ לְחַלְּקָן לִיתְּנָן בְּמַתָּנָה אָמְרוּ לוֹ אֵין אַתְּ יָכוֹל אֶלָּא אִם כֵּן קָנִיתָ קַרְקַע. מֶה עָשָׂה הָלַךְ וְקָנָה סֶלַע אֶחָד בְּצַד יְרוּשָׁלַ͏ִם וְאָמַר חֶצְיָיהּ צְפוֹנִי אֲנִי נוֹתֵן לִפְלוֹנִי עִם מֵאָה חָבִיּוֹת שֶׁל יַיִן. חֶצְיָיהּ דְּרוֹמִי אֲנִי נוֹתֵן לִפְלוֹנִי עִם מֵאָה חָבִיּוֹת שֶׁל שֶׁמֶן. וּבָא מַעֲשֶׂה לִפְנֵי חֲכָמִים וְקִיְּמוּ אֶת דְּבָרָיו. אָמַר רִבִּי חֲנַנְיָה קוֹמֵי רִבִּי מָנָא וְלָאו שְׁכִיב מְרַע הוּא. לְפִי שֶׁבְּכָל־מָקוֹם אֵין אָדָם מְזַכֶּה אֶלָּא בִּכְתָב. וְכָאן אֲפִילוּ בִדְבָרִים. לְפִי שֶׁבְּכָל־מָקוֹם אֵין אָדָם מְזַכֶּה עַד שֶׁיְּהוּ קַרְקָעוֹת וּמְטַלְטְלִין בְּמָקוֹם אֶחָד. וְכָאן

אֲפִילוּ קַרְקָעוֹת בְּמָקוֹם אֶחָד וּמְטַלְטְלִין בְּמָקוֹם אַחֵר. אֲמַר לֵיהּ לָא רִבִּי אֱלִיעֶזֶר שַׁנְיָיא הִיא שְׁכִיב מְרַע דְּרִבִּי אֱלִיעֶזֶר כְּבָרִיא דְּרַבָּנָן.

From where that non-guaranteed property[135] may be acquired with guaranteed property[136], by money, document, or possession? Rebbi Yose[137] in the name of Ḥizqiah; Rebbi Jonah, Rebbi Ḥanina Tortaya in the name of Ḥizqiah, it is written (*2Chr*. 21:3): "Their father gave them many gifts, silver and gold and delicacies, with fortified cities in Jehudah[138]." So far real estate and movables were at the same place. If real estate was at one place and movables elsewhere? Rebbi Abin bar Ḥiyya said, let us hear from the following: Rebbi Eliezer[139] said to them, it happened that a man from Madon[140] was in Jerusalem, rich in movables. He wanted to distribute them, to give them as gifts. They said to him, you cannot do that[141] except if you acquire real estate. What did he do? He went and bought a rock[142] near Jerusalem and said: The Northern part I give to X with a hundred amphoras of wine, the Southern part I give to Y with a hundred amphoras of oil. The matter came before the Sages and they upheld his words[143].

Rebbi Ḥananiah said before Rebbi Mana: But was he not bedridden[144]? For in general a person might give property rights only in writing, and here even orally. In general, a person might give only if real estate and movables are at the same place, but here the real estate even was at one place and the movables elsewhere. He said to him: But is there a difference for Rebbi Eliezer? The sick person for Rebbi Eliezer is like the healthy person for the rabbis[145].

134 In the Bible text: מצורות.

135 Movables, which cannot have a title guarantee.

136 Real estate.

137 He is Rebbi Yasa, Assi. The entire paragraph is paralleled in Babli *Qiddušin* 26a-27a; there, the verse is simply quoted by Ḥizqiah himself.

138 The language implies that the gift of valuables was contingent on the gift of cities.

139 Reading in the Yerushalmi and *Baba Batra* 9:9, Babli *Baba Batra* 156b, and in Tosephta *Baba Batra* 10:12. The corresponding Mishnah, *Baba Batra* 9:9 reads R. Eliezer in the Yerushalmi and also in the Munich manuscript of the Babli, as well as in the Venice and Lublin prints. It was changed to R. Eleazar (ben Shamua) in modern prints of the Babli, following the reading at one place in Babli *Qiddušin*, on the authority of Rabbenu Tam (Tosaphot *Baba Batra* 156a) for stylistic reasons. However, the overwhelming majority of manuscript sources must have priority over arguments concerning style.

140 A town in Galilee, on the heights overlooking the sea of Galilee, mentioned *Joshua* 11:1. The man was in Jerusalem, fell ill, and wanted to distribute his property to people in his home town, other than the legal heirs.

141 Transfer movable property as gift without the recipients taking possession at least symbolically.

142 A cheap piece of land without practical use. (In one interpretation in the Babli *Baba Batra*, he bought land the size of a *sela'*, i. e., a tetradrachma, a silver coin about the size of a quarter. A pun may be intended, since Hebrew סלע also means "rock".)

143 It seems that the legal heirs went to court to annul the distribution. Since the amphoras could not be placed on the rock, it is clear that real estate and movables were at different places.

144 Many rules of transfer and wills are waved for seriously sick persons to assure them that their orders will be obeyed. The first example given by R. Ḥanania is generally accepted; the second one is then offered as interpretation of this Tosephta, that acquisition of movables remote from the land transferred might be valid only for bedridden persons.

145 In Mishnah *Baba Batra* 9:9, R. Eliezer (Bavli in some versions R. Eleazar) explicitly states that bedridden persons are not exempt from the stringent rules of transfer; he does not allow oral bequests.

תַּמָּן תַּנֵּינָן קַרְקַע כָּל־שֶׁהוּא חַיָּב בְּפֵיאָה וּבְבִיכּוּרִים. קַרְקַע כָּל־שֶׁהוּא מַהוּ טָב. אָמַר רִבִּי מַתַּנְיָה תִּיפְתָּר שֶׁהָיָה שָׁם מָקוֹם שִׁיבּוֹלֶת אַחַת וּמַרְגָּלִית טְמוּנָה בוֹ.

There, we have stated[146]: "Any real estate is subject to *peah* and first fruits." What is the use of "any" real estate[147]? Rebbi Mattaniah said, explain it if it had space for one stalk but a pearl was hidden in it.

146 In fact, it has been stated here. The main place of this and the preceding paragraph is *Baba Batra* 9:9, where "there", i. e., *Peah*, makes sense.

147 The question presupposes that one may not acquire movables elsewhere with the contract for real property. The Yerushalmi accepts the answer given in the previous paragraph that only R. Eliezer allows acquisition of remote movables with real estate. The Babli (*Qiddušin* 26b) asks the same question after quoting R. Eliezer; the answer given here by R. Mattaniah is there ascribed to Rav Ashi, a late Amora. But the Babli adds another lengthy discussion whose explicit outcome is that movables anywhere can be acquired with a contract for real estate. This is a difference in practice between Yerushalmi and Babli.

(fol. 17b) **משנה ט**: הַכּוֹתֵב נְכָסָיו שְׁכִיב מְרַע שִׁייֵר קַרְקַע כָּל־שֶׁהוּא מַתָּנָתוֹ קַייֶמֶת. לֹא שִׁייֵר קַרְקַע כָּל־שֶׁהוּא אֵין מַתָּנָתוֹ קַייֶמֶת. הַכּוֹתֵב נְכָסָיו לְבָנָיו וְכָתַב לְאִשְׁתּוֹ קַרְקַע כָּל־שֶׁהוּא אִבְּדָה כְתוּבָּתָהּ. רִבִּי יוֹסֵי אוֹמֵר אִם קִבְּלָה עָלֶיהָ אַף עַל פִּי שֶׁלֹּא כָתַב לָהּ אִבְּדָה כְתוּבָּתָהּ.

Mishnah 9: If someone signs over his properties[148] when bedridden and reserved for himself any real estate, his gift is permanent[149]; if he did not reserve any real estate for himself, his gift is not permanent[150]. If he signs over his properties to his sons and signs over some real estate for his wife, she lost her *ketubah*[151]. Rebbi Yose[152] says, if she accepted it, even if it was not in a written document, she lost her *ketubah*.

148 In a gift document.

149 Since he reserved property, the document is a gift and not a will, on condition that it was executed under all conditions of a valid gift.

150 If he did not reserve anything for himself, it is clear that he did not expect to survive. If he survives nevertheless, the entire document becomes void.

151 The *ketubah* is a mortgage on the husband's entire property, to be paid to the wife at the termination of the marriage, after divorce or after the husband's death. It represents the financial obligation of the husband to his wife; without such an obligation, any sexual relations between man and wife are considered illicit. The value of the obligation was fixed at 200 *zuz* (800 silver denars) for a virgin and 100 *zuz* (400 silver denars) for a previously married woman. A measure of the intended value of these sums is found in Mishnah 8:8,9, viz., that anyone with 200 *zuz* investment capital or 50 *zuz* business capital is living above the poverty line and barred from receiving charity.

The Halakhah explains the circumstances under which the wife may agree to be co-heir to the sons. The Mishnah appears in the context of the power of contracts involving real estate; the first part belongs to the matters treated in *Baba Batra* and *Giṭṭin*, the second part to *Ketubot*.

152 The Tanna, ben Ḥalaphta.

(fol. 17d) **הלכה ט**: אֵי זֶהוּ שְׁכִיב מְרַע כָּל־שֶׁלֹּא קָפַץ עָלָיו הַחוֹלִי. דֶּרֶךְ הָאָרֶץ הַקְּרוֹבִים נִכְנָסִין אֶצְלוֹ מִיַּד. וְהָרְחוֹקִים נִכְנָסִין אֶצְלוֹ לְאַחַר שְׁלֹשָׁה יָמִים. אִם קָפַץ עָלָיו הַחוֹלִי אֵלּוּ וְאֵלּוּ נִכְנָסִין אֶצְלוֹ מִיַּד. דִּלְמָה רִבִּי חוּנָא רִבִּי פִּינְחָס רִבִּי חִזְקִיָּה סָלְקוּן מְבַקְּרָא לְרִבִּי יוֹסֵי בָּתַר תְּלָתָא יוֹמִין. אָמַר לוֹן בִּי[153] בְּעִיתוּן מְקַיִּימָה מַתְנִיתָא.

Halakha 9: Who is bedridden? Anyone who did not get sick suddenly[154]. It is customary for the relatives to visit him immediately; unrelated persons visit him after three days. If he falls ill suddenly, everybody visits him immediately. A clarification: Rebbi Ḥuna, Rebbi Phineas, and Rebbi Ḥizqiah went to visit Rebbi Yose after three days. He said to them: Do you want to sustain the *baraita* in my case[155]?

153 Reading of R. S. Cirillo. The Leyden ms. and Venice print have כִּי.

154 But if he gets sick suddenly, he is called מְסוּכָּן "critical".

155 To act as if you were unrelated, while you are as dear to me as any relative.

שִׁייֵר קַרְקַע כָּל־שֶׁהוּא מַתְּנָתוֹ קַייֶמֶת וַאֲפִילוּ לֹא הִבְרִיא. לֹא שִׁייֵר קַרְקַע כָּל־שֶׁהוּא אֵין מַתְּנָתוֹ קַייֶמֶת וְהוּא שֶׁהִבְרִיא.

"If he reserved any real estate for himself, his gift is permanent," even if he did not recover[156]. "If he did not reserve any real estate for himself, his gift is not permanent" if he did recover[157].

156 Since he reserved property for himself, he did not think that he would die and the transaction is a valid gift.

157 He gave everything away because he thought that he would die and his action amounts to a will which is not valid as long as the testator is alive. Since the gift was not made in due form but under the special rule for sick people, it becomes invalid automatically when the testator recovers.

רִבִּי בָּא רַב הוּנָא בְּשֵׁם רַב עָשׂוּ דִבְרֵי שְׁכִיב מְרַע כְּבָרִיא שֶׁכָּתַב וְנָתַן וְהוּא שֶׁמֵּת מֵאוֹתוֹ הַחוֹלִי. הָא אִם הִבְרִיא לֹא. וּבִמְסַיֵּים וּבְאָמַר תְּנוּ שָׂדֶה פְּלוֹנִי לִפְלוֹנִי. אָמַר תְּנוּ חֲצִי שָׂדֶה פְּלוֹנִי לִפְלוֹנִי וַחֲצִי שָׂדֶה פְּלוֹנִי לִפְלוֹנִי כְּמִי שֶׁמְּסַיֵּים אוֹ עַד שֶׁיֹּאמַר חֶצְיָהּ בַּצָּפוֹן וְחֶצְיָהּ בַּדָּרוֹם.

Rebbi Abba, Rav Huna in the name of Rav[158]: They[159] declared oral instructions by a bedridden person equal to written and delivered ones[160] by a healthy person, on condition that he had died from that particular sickness and that he describes the property and says, give field X to Y[161]. If he says, half of the field to X and half to Y, is that designated? Or only if he says: the Northern half, the Southern half[162]?

158 In *Baba Batra* 9:6, this is a statement of R. Joḥanan in the name of R. Yannai, given as justification for the rules in the preceding paragraph.

159 The rabbis, originators of the rule.

160 A gift document becomes valid only on acceptance by the recipient or his representative.

161 If the instructions are ambiguous or leave the implementation to a third party, they do not invalidate the claims of the legal heirs.

162 In the interpretation of Maimonides (*Zekhiah umattanah* 3:5), the Babli in *Ketubot* 109b and *Giṭṭin* 8b accepts "half a field" as complete description which makes the gift valid and collectible. Since the Yerushalmi does not resolve the question, the law remains in doubt and, by the rule that the claimant has to prove his claim, the gift is not collectible.

רִבִּי בִּינָא בְשֵׁם רִבִּי יִרְמְיָה שִׁייֵר מְטַלְטְלִין לֹא עָשָׂה כְלוּם. אֲתָא חֲמִי שִׁייֵר קַרְקַע כָּל־שֶׁהוּא יֵשׁ לוֹ מִחְיָיה. שִׁייֵר אֲבָנִים טוֹבוֹת וּמַרְגָּלִיּוֹת אֵין לוֹ מִחְיָה. אָמַר רִבִּי יוֹסֵי יוֹדֵעַ הוּא הָאִישׁ הַזֶּה שֶׁשְּׁכִיב מְרַע מְזַכֶּה אֲפִילוּ בִדְבָרִים לְאֵי זֶה דָבָר כָּתַב בָּהֶן קִנְיָן כְּדֵי לַעֲשׂוֹת מַתְּנַת בָּרִיא.

Rebbi Avina in the name of Rebbi Jeremiah[163]: If he reserved movables, he did not do anything[164]. Come and look: If he reserved any real estate, he has something to live on[165]; if he reserved gems and pearls, does he have nothing to live on? Rebbi Yose said, this man knows that the gift of a bedridden person transfers property rights even verbally[166]. Why did he write it with an obligation of acquisition, in order to give it the status of a gift by a healthy person.

163 In the parallel *Baba Batra* 9:6, the reading is: R. Jeremiah in the name of Rav.

164 Since the Mishnah formulates that only a reservation of real estate validates the gift.

165 Presumably, the reservation clause means that he reserves enough to live on if he recovers. Nobody can live on the proceeds from real estate the size of a *sela*, but he can live comfortably as a dealer in gems and pearls. Hence, the exclusion of movables by R. Joḥanan does not seem to make sense.

166 Rebbi Yose notes that the Mishnah and the commentary of R. Jeremiah refer to a written gift of a bedridden person. Since it is unnecessary in this case to write a document, the fact that the document was written confers on it the status of a gift by a healthy person. The reservation clause is purely formal and the argument about livelyhood is irrelevant.

שִׁייֵר עֲבָדִים תַּנָּא רִבִּי יוֹדָן בַּר פָּזִי דְּבַר דְּלָיָא וְלָא יָדְעִין מַה תַּנָּא.

If he reserved slaves[167], about that R. Judan bar Pazi from Bar Delaiah stated something, but we do not know what he stated.

167 In certain respects, slaves are treated like real estate, but in others like movables. In the Babli (*Baba Batra* 150a) they are defined as movable real estate. In the Babli also it seems that the exclusion of slaves has no legal consequence.

כָּתַב לָזֶה וְחָזַר וְכָתַב לָזֶה. רַב אָמַר אֵינוֹ יָכוֹל לַחְזוֹר בּוֹ. רַב אַבָּא בַּר חוּנָא וְרִבִּי יוֹחָנָן אָמַר יָכוֹל לַחְזוֹר בּוֹ. הֵיךְ עֲבִידָא הָיָה רַבּוֹ הָרִאשׁוֹן וְהַשֵּׁנִי כֹּהֵן וְהַשְּׁלִישִׁי יִשְׂרָאֵל עַל דַּעְתֵּיהּ דְּרַב אֵין יָכוֹל לוֹכַל בִּתְרוּמָה עַל דַּעְתֵּיהּ דְּרַב אַבָּא בַּר חוּנָא אָמַר רִבִּי יוֹחָנָן יָכוֹל הוּא לוֹכַל בִּתְרוּמָה. הַכֹּל מוֹדִין שֶׁאִים הָיָה רַבּוֹ הָרִאשׁוֹן יִשְׂרָאֵל אֵינוֹ אוֹכֵל בִּתְרוּמָה שֶׁמָּא יַבְרִיא.

If he wrote for one and changed his mind and wrote for another[168], Rav says he cannot change his mind, Rav Abba bar Ḥuna and Rebbi

Johanan say he may change his mind. What does it mean[169]? If his first and second masters were Cohanim and the third[170] an Israel, in the opinion of Rav he may[171] not eat *terumah*[172], in the opinion of Rav Abba bar Huna in the name of R. Johanan he may eat *terumah*[173]. Everybody agrees that if his first master was an Israel[174], he may not eat *terumah;* maybe the giver will recuperate.

168 A bedridden person who gave property away by a written document in which no real estate was reserved. Then he wrote a second document to supersede the first one. If all had been oral, there is no doubt that a later will would annul the prior one. If the document was simply written and nobody performed an act of acquisition, it seems that even for the Yerushalmi the document is not valid (this is the explicit position of the Babli *Baba Batra* 152b). Hence, somebody must have received the document for the beneficiary. According to Rav, this makes the gift absolute as explained by R. Yose earlier. According to R. Johanan (in the Babli, Samuel), since in any case the deed will automaticaly be rescinded if the donor recuperates, the document is not executable as long as the donor lives and, hence, it is rescindable by him.

169 If the ownership of a slave is transferred in the gift document.

170 The first master is the donor, the second master is the beneficiary of the second gift, and the third master the beneficiary of the first gift.

171 This is the text of all manuscripts, including R. S. Cirillo. All commentators declare the text to be faulty and switch "may" and "may not" between Rav and Rebbi Johanan; however, this seems to be inadmissible.

172 A slave is a family member; hence, the slave of a Cohen may eat *terumah* (in ritual purity), the slave of a Jewish non-Cohen (Israel, including Levites) may not eat *terumah*. In the opinion of Rav, the Israel is the master if the donor dies and, since a gift is retroactive as explained in the second paragraph following, the slave is disqualified from the moment of the symbolic act of acquisition of the first document.

173 Since both the donor and the legal recipient are Cohanim, the question of ownership is irrelevant.

174 And both recipients are Cohanim.

רִבִּי יוֹסֵי בֵּי רִבִּי בּוּן בְּשֵׁם רַב חוּנָא מַתְנִיתִין מְסַייְעָה לְרַב אַבָּא בַּר חוּנָא וְרִבִּי יוֹחָנָן בָּרִיא שֶׁכָּתַב דְּיָיתֵיקֵי וּשְׁכִיב מְרַע שֶׁכָּתַב מַתָּנָה חוֹזֵר בּוֹ. בָּרִיא שֶׁכָּתַב דְּיָיתֵיקֵי חוֹזֵר בּוֹ וְלֹא עוֹד הוּא בָּרִיא וְדִכְווָתָהּ שְׁכִיב מְרַע שֶׁכָּתַב מַתָּנָה חוֹזֵר בּוֹ וְלֹא עוֹדֵהוּ שְׁכִיב מְרַע.

Rebbi Yose ben Rebbi Abun in the name of Rav Ḥuna, a *baraita* supports Rav Abba bar Ḥuna and Rebbi Joḥanan: "[175]A healthy person who wrote a will[176] and a bedridden one who wrote a gift document[177] may change their minds." A healthy person who wrote a will may change his mind, even as long as he is healthy. Similarly, a bedridden person who wrote a gift document may change his mind, even while he still is bedridden.

175 The Tosephta (*Baba Batra* 8:9) has quite a different (Babylonian) version: A healthy person who wrote a will (in the abridged form only permitted to bedridden persons), a bedridden one who wrote a gift document (in the language prescribed for healthy people), even though he let somebody acquire for the recipient, they did not do anything (their documents are invalid). But if somebody wrote as agent for another person (who is sick and afraid of his family) a gift document and let it be acquired, his action is valid.

176 Greek διαθήκη "will, testament".

177 In the language of a healthy person's gift that becomes valid on acceptance.

אֵי זוֹ הִיא דְּיָיתֵיקֵי. תְּהֵא לִי לִהְיוֹת וְלַעֲמוֹד. וְאִם מֵתִי יִנָּתְנוּ נְכָסַי לִפְלוֹנִי. אֵי זוֹ הִיא מַתָּנָה. כָּל־נְכָסַי נְתוּנִין לִפְלוֹנִי מַתָּנָה מֵעַכְשָׁיו וְשֶׁתְּהֵא כָתוּב בּוֹ מֵהַיּוֹם.

What is a will? "It should be granted to me to live[178] and get up from bed, but if I should die, my properties should be given to X." What is a gift? "All my properties are given as a gift to X from now on," or it must be written: "as of today[179]."

178 This is the reading of the Venice print and Leyden manuscript, and in all quotes of this passage by medieval authors. The Rome manuscript has לחיות "to live"; this is the reading preferred by S. Lieberman. The Babli (*Baba Batra* 155b) has למיקם "to get up". In any case, it is a wish that the testator should live and, in that case, the will should cease to be in force.

179 Since no gift document can enter into force after the death of its author. In the case of the will, it does not come into force, but there is an obligation on the heirs to fulfill the wishes of the dead. The language "from today" changes even a will into a gift.

אַחְתֵּיה דְּרִבִּי גּוּרִין כְּתָבַת נִכְסֵי לְאַחֲוָה וּסְלַק אַחוֹי רַבָּא פִּייְסָהּ וּכְתָבַת לֵיהּ. אֲתָא עוּבְדָּא קוֹמוֹי רִבִּי אִימִּי אָמַר כֵּן אָמַר רִבִּי יוֹחָנָן חוֹזֵר בּוֹ. אָמַר רִבִּי זְעִירָא לֹא מוֹדֵי רִבִּי יוֹחָנָן שֶׁאִם הָיָה כָּתוּב בָּהּ מֵהַיּוֹם שֶׁאֵינוֹ יָכוֹל לַחְזוֹר בּוֹ. אֲתָא רִבִּי אַבָּהוּ בְּשֵׁם רִבִּי יוֹחָנָן אֵינוֹ יָכוֹל לַחְזוֹר בּוֹ. אֲתָא רִבִּי לָא בְּשֵׁם רִבִּי יוֹחָנָן אֵינוֹ יָכוֹל לַחְזוֹר בּוֹ. וְאַנְהַר רִבִּי אִימִּי וְחָזַר עוּבְדָּא.

The sister of Rebbi Gurin[180] wrote her possessions over to her brother[181]. His older brother came, made peace with her, and she wrote her possessions over to him. The case came before Rebbi Immi. He said: So says Rebbi Joḥanan, one may change his mind. Rebbi Zeïra said, but does Rebbi Joḥanan not agree that if it was written "from today" one may not change his mind[181]? Rebbi Abbahu came in the name of Rebbi Joḥanan, one may not change his mind. Rebbi Illaï came in the name of Rebbi Joḥanan, one may not change his mind. Then Rebbi Immi remembered, and the judgement was reversed.

180 An Amora of the fourth generation, student of R. Yose bar Ḥanina and R. Simeon ben Laqish. His brother's name was Menaḥem.

181 It follows from the discussion of the case that the document contained the clause that it was valid "from today" even if it had a statement that it would become executable only after the testator's death. The gift to the elder brother was written in the same terms.

רַב אָמַר בִּמְזַכֶּה עַל יָדֶיהָ. וּשְׁמוּאֵל אָמַר בִּמְחַלֵּק לְפָנֶיהָ. רִבִּי יוֹסֵי בֶּן חֲנִינָא אָמַר מִקּוּלֵּי (fol. 18a) כְּתוּבָּה שָׁנוּ כָּן. וְכֵן תַּנֵּי בַּר קַפָּרָא מִקּוּלֵּי כְּתוּבָּה שָׁנוּ. אָמַר רִבִּי בָּא טַעְמָא דְּרִבִּי יוֹסֵי בֶּן חֲנִינָא לֹא סוֹף דָּבָר בִּכְתוּבָּתָהּ מָנֶה וּמָאתַיִם אֶלָּא אֲפִילוּ כְּתוּבָּה שֶׁל אֶלֶף דֵּינָר מִקּוּלֵּי כְּתוּבָּה שָׁנוּ.

Rav said[182], if he lets them acquire through her[183]. Samuel says, if he distributes in her presence[184]. Rebbi Yose ben Ḥanina said, they stated here a relaxation of the laws of *ketubah*[185], and so stated bar Qappara that a relaxation of the laws of *ketubah* is proclaimed here[186]. Rebbi Abba said, the reason of Rebbi Yose ben Ḥanina is that it applies not only to a *ketubah* of a mina[187] or two hundred[188], but even regarding a *ketubah* of one thousand gold denars they proclaimed a relaxation of the laws of *ketubah*[189].

182 This refers to the last part of the Mishnah and explains the circumstances under which the *ketubah* may be replaced by part of the inheritance.

183 If the wife is the person through whose acceptance the entire document becomes valid. Then it must be assumed that she agreed to its terms.

184 And she does not object.

185 In the Babli (*Baba Batra* 132 ab), R. Yose ben Ḥanina, while still calling it a relaxation of the rules of *ketubah*, offers a third possibility: If the husband offered the real estate as settlement of the *ketubah* and she accepted. This is not accepted in the Yerushalmi, probably to avoid the possibility that the husband exerts undue pressure on his wife in a purely

private transaction.

186 Both according to Rav or to Samuel. The relaxation is explained by Rebbi Abba.

187 100 *zuz*, the minimal *ketubah* of a previously married woman. Cf. Greek μνᾶ, ἡ, Latin *mina*, "sum or weight of 100 *drachmae*", derived from Hebrew/Syriac/Accadic מנה.

188 200 *zuz*, the minimal *ketubah* of a virgin.

189 The value of a regular *ketubah* of 200 *zuz* is easily satisfied by real estate. But for a thousand gold denars, representing a few million $ buying power in today's money, it is not likely that the full value will be covered by agricultural real estate.

(fol. 17b) **משנה י**: הַכּוֹתֵב נְכָסָיו לְעַבְדּוֹ יָצָא בֶּן חוֹרִין. שִׁיֵּר קַרְקַע כָּל־שֶׁהוּא לֹא יָצָא בֶּן חוֹרִין. רִבִּי שִׁמְעוֹן אוֹמֵר לְעוֹלָם הוּא בֶּן חוֹרִין עַד שֶׁיֹּאמַר הֲרֵי כָּל־נְכָסַי נְתוּנִין לְאִישׁ פְּלוֹנִי עַבְדִּי חוּץ מֵאֶחָד מֵרִיבּוֹא שֶׁבָּהֶן.

Mishnah 10: He who writes over his properties to his slave makes him free[190]. If he reserved any real estate, he does not make him free[191]. Rebbi Simeon says, the slave always becomes free unless the master says, all my properties are given to my slave X except one tenthousandth of them[192].

190 Since the slave is also property, he acquires himself and, therefore, becomes his own master. The gift document is at the same time the document of manumission.

191 Since he reserved something, in the interpretation of Maimonides (following the Babli, *Giṭṭin* 9a) the document does not refer exclusively to the slave and, therefore, is not a document of manumission. Since the master is now dead, nobody else can be forced to write a document of manumission for the slave. R. Simson's interpretation is that he writes the deed only to make sure that the slave take care to preserve the estate but he will have reserved the slave himself

for his heirs.

192 Since he did not spell out what is reserved, the slave himself may be reserved. But if he spelled out what is reserved, that is reserved and nothing else.

(fol. 18a) **הלכה י**: רִבִּי יָסָא בְשֵׁם רִבִּי לְעָזָר שִׁייֵר מְטַלְטְלִין לֹא עָשָׂה כְלוּם. אֲנִי אוֹמֵר גּוּפוֹ שִׁייֵר.

Halakha 10: Rebbi Yasa (Assi) in the name of Rebbi Eleazar: If he reserved some movables, he did not do anything[193]. I say that he reserved the slave's person.

193 Following both interpretations of the Mishnah, the situation is identical to the one where real estate was reserved and the document is invalid.

וּכְשֶׁבָּא מַעֲשֶׂה לִפְנֵי רִבִּי יוֹסֵי אָמַר שְׂפָתַיִם יִשָּׁק מֵשִׁיב דְּבָרִים נְכוֹחִים.

[194]When the case came before Rebbi Yose, he said (*Prov.* 24:26): "He who answers correctly should be kissed on his lips."

194 This refers to the opinion of R. Simeon who corrects the wrong attitude of the first teacher of the Mishnah. It is taken from Tosephta *Peah* 1:13: "He who writes over his properties to his slave makes him free. If he reserved any real estate, he does not make him free. Rebbi Simeon says, if he said all my properties are given to my slave X except one tenthousandth of them, then he did not say anything; but [if he said all] except the hamlet X or the field Y then the slave acquired the property and acquired his freedom. When these words were said before Rebbi Yose, he said: : "He who answers correctly should be kissed on his lips." R. Simson has in addition: "Even if the estate contains only this hamlet or that field," meaning that the slave acquires himself (his freedom) even if he acquires no other property from the estate of his dead master. This is the interpretation of all medieval authorities.

Since R. Yose is the most authoritative of the teachers of his generation, his support of R. Simeon's position makes that the valid practice, against the anonymous majority opinion of the Mishnah.

הפיאה פרק רביעי

(fol. 18a) **משנה א**: הַפֵּיאָה נִיתֶּנֶת בִּמְחוּבָּר לַקַּרְקַע. בְּדָלִית וּבְדֶקֶל בַּעַל הַבַּיִת מוֹרִיד וּמְחַלֵּק לָעֲנִיִּים. רִבִּי שִׁמְעוֹן אוֹמֵר אַף בְּחִילְקֵי אֱגוֹזִים. אֲפִילוּ תִּשְׁעִים וְתִשְׁעָה עֲנִיִּים אוֹמְרִין לְחַלֵּק וְאֶחָד אוֹמֵר לָבוֹז לְזֶה שׁוֹמְעִין שֶׁאָמַר כַּהֲלָכָה. וּבְדָלִית וּבְדֶקֶל אֵינוֹ כֵן אֲפִילוּ תִּשְׁעִים וְתִשְׁעָה אוֹמְרִין לָבוֹז וְאֶחָד אוֹמֵר לְחַלֵּק לְזֶה שׁוֹמְעִין שֶׁאָמַר כַּהֲלָכָה.

Mishnah 1: *Peah* is given connected to the ground[1]. From a climbing vine[2] and a date palm, the owner brings it down and divides it up among the poor. Rebbi Simeon says, also for smooth[3] nut trees. Even if 99 poor people say to distribute and one says to grab[4], one listens to him whose request is in keeping with practice. But for a climbing vine and a date palm it is not so; even if 99 say to grab and one says to distribute, one listens to him whose request is in keeping with practice.

1 Unharvested.

2 Climbing on a high pole or tree so that the grapes cannot be reached from the ground.

3 This is the reading of the Leyden manuscript and the Yerushalmi print. Some Mishnah manuscripts have חֲלַקֵי, meaning the same, and some חֲלוּקֵי "distributed". The majority seems to follow the reading "smooth", which according to *Tiferet Israel* means trees without branches to hold on to, which cannot safely be harvested without a ladder.

4 Harvest from standing crop.

הלכה א: לֹא תְכַלֶּה פְּאַת שָׂדְךָ בְּקֻצְרֶךָ. מִיכָּן שֶׁהַפֵּיאָה נִיתֶּנֶת בִּמְחוּבָּר לְקַרְקַע. יָכוֹל אֲפִילוּ בְּדָלִית וּבְדֶקֶל תַּלְמוּד לוֹמַר קְצִיר מַה קְצִיר מְיוּחָד שֶׁהַקָּטוֹן מוֹשֵׁל בּוֹ כַּגָּדוֹל יָצְאוּ הַדָּלִית וְהַדֶּקֶל שֶׁאֵין הַקָּטוֹן מוֹשֵׁל בּוֹ כַּגָּדוֹל.

Halakhah 1: (*Lev.* 23:22) "Do not finish off the corner of your field during your harvest." This shows that *peah* is given standing on the ground. One might think this also includes climbing vine and date palms, but the verse says "harvest." Harvest is special in that a small person can do it as well as a tall person; this excludes climbing vine and date palm where a small person cannot do it as well as a tall person[5].

5 This tannaïtic statement is not found in any of the parallel collections.

אִית דְּבָעֵי מַשְׁמְעִינָהּ מִן הָדָא תַּעֲזוֹב הַנַּח לִפְנֵיהֶן תְּבוּאָה בְּקַשָּׁהּ. תִּלְתָּן בְּעָמִיר תְּמָרִים בְּמִכְבֵּדוֹת. יָכוֹל בְּדָלִית וּבְדֶקֶל כֵּן תַּלְמוּד לוֹמַר אוֹתָם. מַה רָאִיתָ לְרַבּוֹת אֶת אֵלּוֹ וּלְהוֹצִיא אֶת אֵלּוּ. אַחַר שֶׁרִיבָּה הַכָּתוּב מִיעֵט. מַרְבֶּה אֲנִי אֶת אֵלּוֹ שֶׁאֵינָן שֶׁל סַכָּנָה וּמוֹצִיא אֲנִי אֶת אֵלּוֹ שֶׁהֵן שֶׁל סַכָּנָה.

Some[6] want to understand it from the verse (*Lev.* 19:10, 23:22) "abandon[7]," put before them grain in its straw, fenugreek in bundles, dates in brooms[8]. I might think that this also includes climbing vine and date palms, but the verse says "them[9]." What argument do you have to include these and to exclude those? After the verse included, it excluded. I include those that are not dangerous and exclude those that are dangerous[10].

6 *Sifra Qedošim* 2(5-7).

7 *Lev.* 19:10: "Do not glean in your vineyard, neither collect single berries, *abandon them* for the poor and the stranger; I am the Eternal, your God." *Lev.* 23:22: "When you are harvesting the harvest of your land, do not finish off the corner of your field during your harvest, neither collect the gleanings of your harvest, *abandon*

them for the poor and the stranger; I am the Eternal, your God." The implication is that *peah* has to be given before any further processing.

8 Dates grow in bunches that sit on the trunk; if the bunch is cut at the trunk and the dates are taken, the remainder may be used as a broom.

9 Only those items that are described by the term "harvest".

10 "Connected" here means "still hanging on the tree." Then the plucking cannot be described as "harvest". Since this derivation by inclusion and exclusion follows the method of R. Ismael, the preceding paragraph must represent the opinion of R. Aqiba.

אִין תֵּימַר מְחוּבָּר הוּא קוֹרֵא שֵׁם פֵּיאָה לְמַעְלָן. אִין תֵּימַר שֶׁאֵינוֹ מְחוּבָּר קוֹרֵא שֵׁם פֵּיאָה לְמַטָּן. אִין תֵּימַר קוֹרֵא שֵׁם פֵּיאָה לְמַעְלָן הוֹצָאָה מִשֶּׁל עֲנִיִּים אִין תֵּימַר קוֹרֵא שֵׁם פֵּיאָה לְמַטָּן הוֹצָאָה מִשֶּׁל בַּעַל הַבַּיִת. וַאֲפִילוּ תֵּימַר קוֹרֵא שֵׁם פֵּיאָה לְמַעְלָן הִטְרִיחוּ עַל בַּעַל הַבַּיִת שֶׁתְּהֵא הוֹצָאָה שֶׁלּוֹ מִפְּנֵי הַסַּכָּנָה.

Is it not connected[11]? He calls it by the name *peah* when it is on the tree[12]. If you say not from standing produce, he calls it by the name *peah* when it is taken down. If you say he calls it by the name *peah* when it is on the tree, the removal is charged to the poor. If you say he calls it by the name *peah* when it is taken down, the removal is the obligation of the owner. But even if you say that he calls it by the name *peah* when it is on the tree, they[13] charge the owner with taking it down because of the danger.

11 The fruits still are connected to the tree. This paragraph discusses whether climbing vines and dates are an exception to the rule that *peah* has to be given for the standing crop, or whether it is only a technicality requiring the owner to harvest the *peah* himself. The answer is that there is no exception; it may well be that the name *peah* has to be given when the fruits are still hanging on the tree, but this does not change the fact that the owner must pay for taking them down.

12 Since produce is not exempt

from tithes and may not be taken by the poor until the farmer has designated it as such, giving it the name "*peah*".

13 The religious authorities of earlier times.

תַּנֵּי בְשֵׁם רִבִּי מֵאִיר כָּל־הָאִילָנוֹת סַכָּנָה. רִבִּי מֵאִיר לֹא דָרַשׁ קָצִיר וְרַבָּנָן דָּרְשֵׁי קָצִיר. כָּל־עַמָּא דָּרְשֵׁי קָצִיר אֶלָּא רִבִּי מֵאִיר אָמַר כָּל־הָאִילָנוֹת סַכָּנָה. וְרַבָּנָן אָמְרֵי אֵין סַכָּנָה אֶלָּא הַדָּלִית וְהַדֶּקֶל בִּלְבָד. רִבִּי חֲנַנְיָה בְשֵׁם רִבִּי שִׁמְעוֹן בֶּן לָקִישׁ מַעֲשֶׂה שֶׁמֵּתוּ חֲמִשָּׁה אַחִים בַּחֲמִשָּׁה חֲלִיקֵי אֱגוֹזִים.

It was stated in the name of Rebbi Meïr[14]: All trees are dangerous. Does Rebbi Meïr not infer from "harvest" while the rabbis likewise infer from "harvest[15]?" Everybody infers from "harvest", except that Rebbi Meïr says that all trees are dangerous and the rabbis say only the climbing vine and the date palm are dangerous. Rebbi Ḥananiah in the name of Rebbi Simeon ben Laqish: It has happened that five brothers died climbing five smooth nut trees[16].

14 Reading of the Rome and Cirillo manuscripts. The Venice print has "Rebbi Immi"; that reading is impossible since Rebbi Immi was an Amora, not a Tanna, and the statement is a tannaïtic one. The further discussion is in the name of R. Meïr even in the Venice text.

15 The inference drawn in the first paragraph of this Halakhah from *Lev.* 23:22.

16 Accordingly, practice must follow Rebbi Meïr and Rebbi Simeon against the Mishnah. However, Maimonides follows the Mishnah both in his commentary and in his Code.

בַּעַל הַבַּיִת שֶׁקָּרָא שֵׁם פֵּיאָה וְכִילָּה קוֹרֵא אֲנִי עָלָיו לֹא תְכַלֶּה פְּאַת שָׂדְךָ בְּקֻצְרֶךָ. לֹא קָרָא שֵׁם פֵּיאָה וְכִילָּה קוֹרֵא אֲנִי עָלָיו לֹא תְכַלֶּה פְּאַת שָׂדְךָ בְּקֻצְרֶךָ.

If the owner called it *peah*[17] and nevertheless finished harvesting the entire field, I read for him: "Do not finish off the corner of your field during your harvest.[18]" If he did not call it *peah* and finished harvesting the entire field, I read for him: "Do not finish off the corner of your field during your harvest."

17 The last part of the grain on his field; this makes it legally the property of the poor. Then he proceeded to cut it.

18 Again, the entire verse is to be understood, including the second part: "Leave it for the poor and the stranger." Even though he has transgressed the first part of the injunction, he still is obligated for the second part, viz., to leave the cut *peah* to the poor by abandoning it on the field.

הִתְנוּ[19] בֵּינֵיהֶן אֲפִילוּ כֵן אֵין שׁוֹמְעִין לוֹ.

If they agreed among themselves[20], even so one does not listen to him.

19 Reading of R. Simson of Sens and R. Solomon Cirillo. The Venice print has "התנן", which is certainly incorrect.

20 The poor demanding that either the farmer should divide the produce instead of them harvesting it, or declaring that they want to climb the tree when he would be obligated to get the *peah* and give it to them. Since the Mishnah says that if 99 want to differ from the rule and one wants to comply with it (even if he acts out of selfishness because he would be able to grab more than the others), it follows that if all of them agree the agreement is valid. The Halakha notes that one does not listen to *him*, i. e., if the farmer is part of the agreement (and presumably its originator, but in any case a person of overriding influence over the poor) then the agreement is void. [This is the explanation of R. Simson of Sens. It seems that Maimonides reads הִתְנוּ בֵּינֵיהֶן שׁוֹמְעִין לָהֶן or a similar text, since in his Code (*Mattenot Aniïm* 2:16,17) he repeats twice that agreements among the poor about the manner of distribution are valid.]

בַּעַל הַבַּיִת יְחַלֵּק בְּיָדוֹ שֶׁלֹּא יִרְאֶה עָנִי מוֹדַעְתּוֹ וְיַשְׁלִיךְ לְפָנָיו. רִבִּי שְׁמוּאֵל בַּר אֶבוּדָמָא בְּעִי כִּילָּה אֶת שָׂדֵהוּ אַתְּ אֲמַר חָזְרָה פֵּיאָה לָעוֹמָרִין. אֲפִילוּ כֵן בַּעַל הַבַּיִת מְחַלֵּק בְּיָדוֹ שֶׁלֹּא יִרְאֶה עָנִי מוֹדַעְתּוֹ וְיַשְׁלִיךְ לְפָנָיו.

The owner has to distribute by hand to avoid that he would see a poor person of his acquaintance and throw it before him[21]. Rebbi Samuel bar Eudaimon questioned[22]: If he finished harvesting his field, you say that *peah* returned to the sheaves. Even so, does the owner have to distribute by hand to avoid that he would see a poor person of his acquaintance and throw it before him?

21 The Mishnah notes that the owner of the tree must divide *peah*; this means that he cannot simply take the fruits down and let the poor take them. Since we have the general rule of "abandon", any exception needs a justification.

22 He asks whether the obligation to distribute only applies to those fruits which never fall under the category of "grabbing" or whether it extends to all cases where the farmer has to bring the produce before the poor, as in the case of grain already bound in sheaves. The question remains unanswered.

מִשְׁנָה ב: נָטַל מִקְצַת הַפֵּיאָה וְזָרַק עַל הַשְּׁאָר אֵין לוֹ בָּהּ כְּלוּם. נָפַל לוֹ עָלֶיהָ וּפֵירֵס טַלִּיתוֹ עָלֶיהָ מַעֲבִירִין אוֹתוֹ מִמֶּנָּהּ וְכֵן בְּלֶקֶט וְכֵן בְּעוֹמֶר הַשִּׁכְחָה.

Mishnah 2: If he[23] took some of the *peah* and threw it on the rest[24], he has nothing of it[25]. If he fell on it or spread his talith on it, one removes him from it[26]. The same is valid for gleanings and the forgotten sheaf.

23 A poor man entitled to collect *peah*.

24 In order to claim possession. Since *peah* has the legal status of abandoned property, the slightest action of acquisition should be valid.

25 As punishment, since all poor should have equal access to any produce left by the farmer. According to R. Simson of Sens, the Mishnah means that he retains what he already had but his action is invalid as acquisition.

26 For the reasons given above.

חלכה ב: תַּנֵּי בְשֵׁם רִבִּי מֵאִיר קוֹנְסִין בּוֹ וּמוֹצִיאִין מִמֶּנּוּ אֶת הַתָּלוּשׁ וְאֶת הַמְּחוּבָּר. עַד כְּדוֹן מֵזִיד אֲפִילוּ שׁוֹגֵג וַאֲפִילוּ כְּרִיכוֹת.

Halakhah 2: It was stated in the name of Rebbi Meïr: "One punishes him and takes away from him both the cut and the standing produce.[27]" That refers to intentional misconduct; does it apply even to action in error or even to small sheaves[28]?

27 Tosephta *Peah* 2:1 reads: "If he took some of the *peah* and threw it on the rest, he has no claim to it. Rebbi Meïr says, one punishes him and takes away from him both the cut and the standing produce." This proves that the language of the Mishnah, the first sentence of the Tosephta, implies that he does not lose the *peah* he previously collected. Maimonides, who in his commentary to the Mishnah writes that he loses that *peah* also, explains the Halakhah, not the Mishnah.

28 If the poor collector already had made a small sheaf of his *peah*. The question is not answered; for practical purposes, it is answered in the negative.

רַבִּי שִׁמְעוֹן בֶּן לָקִישׁ בְּשֵׁם אַבָּא כֹּהֵן בַּר דָּלָיָא אָדָם זוֹכֶה בִּמְצִיאָה בְּתוֹךְ אַרְבַּע אַמּוֹת שֶׁלּוֹ[29] מַה טַעַם וְהִנֵּה בְעָנְיִי הֲכִינוֹתִי לְבֵית יי זָהָב כִּכָּרִים מֵאָה אֶלֶף וְכֶסֶף אֶלֶף אֲלָפִים כִּכָּרִים וְלַנְּחוֹשֶׁת וְלַבַּרְזֶל אֵין מִשְׁקָל כִּי לָרוֹב הָיָה וְעֵצִים וַאֲבָנִים הֲכִינוֹתִי וַעֲלֵיהֶם תּוֹסִיף.

Rebbi Simeon ben Laqish in the name of Abba Cohen Bar Dalaia[30]: A person acquires a find within four cubits of himself[31]. What is the reason?

(*1Chr.* 22:14) "Look, in my poverty[32] I prepared for the House of the Eternal 100'000 *kikkar*[33] of gold, 1'000'000 *kikkar* of silver, bronze and iron unweighed because it was so much, I prepared wood and stones, and you[34] should add to them."

29 Text of the Rome ms. here and the Venice print in the parallel *Giṭṭin* 8:3, fol. 49c. Venice print here: אדם זוכה לחבירו במציאה. The verse reads ואני בעניי

30 A Tanna of the first generations: Abba, a priest of the course of Dalaiahu, the 23rd of the 24 priestly divisions.

31 If somebody sees an abandoned object and intends to acquire it, it becomes his property when he is closer than 4 cubits to it, and nobody has the right to run past him and grab it. Since the Mishnah obviously declares that principle inoperative with regard to *peah*, there seems to be a contradiction between two rabbinic principles. The Babli (*Baba Meẓi'a* 10a/b) resolves the problem by restricting the principle of Abba Cohen to the public domain; it does not apply to private property such as a field. The Yerushalmi disagrees; since *peah* is abandoned property, as proved in the preceding Halakhah, it must be assumed that the ground on which *peah* grows is temporarily also abandoned to the poor.

The expression "himself" will be given special importance in the following discussion.

32 How can anybody (King David) who has the means of dedicating such enormous wealth, call himself "poor"? The explanation is that the wealth never actually came into his possession but that he dedicated it as soon as it became his property by intent and proximity.

33 One *kikkar* equals 3'000 *sheqel*, and, since the *sheqel* in the Talmud is defined as 2 drachmas, the *kikkar* is equal to the Greek talent of 6'000 drachmas. The 14 g silver *sheqalim* from the Jewish revolt were "sacred *sheqalim*" of double weight, or four civil denars. Honest silver denars or drachmae from the early principate weigh about 3.5 g. Taking civil *sheqalim*, one *kikkar* would be about 21 kg and David would have prepared 2 metric tons of gold and 20 metric tons of silver for the Temple.

34 Solomon.

רִבִּי יוֹנָה אָמַר רַב הוֹשַׁעְיָה בְּעֵי מַה נָן קַייָמִין אִם בְּתוֹךְ אַרְבַּע אַמּוֹת עָשִׁיר הוּא. אִם בְּחוּץ לְאַרְבַּע אַמּוֹת וְיֵשׁ אָדָם מַקְדִּישׁ דָּבָר שֶׁאֵינוֹ שֶׁלּוֹ. וְקִייַמְנוּהָ בְּמַקְדִּישׁ רִאשׁוֹן רִאשׁוֹן.

Rebbi Jonah said that Rebbi Hoshaiah asked: What are we talking about? If this was within four cubits from him, he was rich[35]. If it was outside of four cubits, may anybody dedicate anything that is not his[36]? We confirmed it[37] if he dedicated it piece by piece.

35 After he dedicated all he had, he was poor. But if one has the means to dedicate billions, he cannot say that he is in poverty at the act of dedication.

36 If A says to B that he dedicated a piece of B's property for charity or religious purposes, his words are null and void and have neither legal nor religious implications.

37 The argument in the previous paragraph is still valid if David never came to possess a single piece of gold or silver worth more than 200 *zuz*; then he could assemble all this wealth for the Temple without ever ceasing to be legally poor.

אָמַר רִבִּי אָבִין מַהוּ בְּעוֹנְיִי שֶׁאֵין (fol. 18b) עֲשִׁירוּת לִפְנֵי מִי שֶׁאָמַר וְהָיָה הָעוֹלָם. דָּבָר אַחֵר בְּעוֹנְיִי בְּעִינּוּי שֶׁהָיָה מִתְעַנֶּה וּמַקְדִּישׁ סְעוּדָתוֹ לַשָּׁמַיִם.

Rebbi Abun said, what means "in my poverty?" That there is no wealth before Him Who commanded and the world came into existence[38]! Another explanation: בְּעוֹנְיִי "in my deprivation[39]," because he fasted and donated the price of his meal to Heaven.

38 The expression "in my poverty" is homiletic and carries no legal meaning; the verse is inapplicable to our situation and the statement about the four cubits is a rabbinical institution without Biblical foundation.

39 The other uses of עוני in the Bible show that this is the usual meaning of the word. This also excludes the verse from being used as proof in our context.

הָתִיב רִבִּי יַעֲקֹב בַּר אִידִי קוֹמֵי[40] רִבִּי שִׁמְעוֹן בֶּן לָקִישׁ וְהָתַנֵּינָן רָאָה אֶת הַמְּצִיאָה וְנָפַל לוֹ עָלֶיהָ וּבָא אַחֵר וְהֶחֱזִיק בָּהּ זֶה שֶׁהֶחֱזִיק בָּהּ זָכָה בָהּ. אָמַר לֵיהּ תִּיפְתָּר בְּשֶׁלֹּא אָמַר יִזְכּוּ לִי אַרְבַּע אַמּוֹת שֶׁלִּי. וְהָתַנִּי נָפַל לוֹ עָלֶיהָ וּפֵירֵס טַלִּיתוֹ עָלֶיהָ מַעֲבִירִין אוֹתוֹ מִמֶּנָּה. אָמַר לֵיהּ עוֹד הִיא בְּשֶׁלֹּא אָמַר יִזְכּוּ לִי אַרְבַּע אַמּוֹת שֶׁלִּי. וְהָתַנִּי רִבִּי חִיָּא שְׁנַיִם שֶׁהָיוּ מִתְכַּתְּשִׁין עַל הָעוֹמֶר וּבָא עָנִי אַחֵר וַחֲטָפוֹ מִלִּפְנֵיהֶן זָכָה בָהּ. אָמַר לֵיהּ עוֹד הִיא בְּשֶׁלֹּא אָמַר יִזְכּוּ לִי אַרְבַּע אַמּוֹת שֶׁלִּי.

Rebbi Jacob bar Idi objected before Rebbi Simeon ben Laqish. Did we not state: (Mishnah *Baba Meẓi'a* 1:4) "If somebody saw a find and fell on it, when another person came and grabbed it, he who grabbed it had the rights to it?" He answered him: Explain it if the first one did not say that his four cubits should acquire it for him[41]. But did we not state[42]: "If he fell on it or spread his talith on it, one removes him from it?" He said to him, that is the same, if he did not say that his four cubits should acquire it for him. But did not Rebbi Ḥiyya state[43]: (Tosephta *Peah* 2:2) "If two[44] were pushing[45] one another because of a sheaf and another poor person came and grabbed it from before them, he is entitled to it. He said to him, it is the same, he[46] did not say that his four cubits should acquire it for him.

40 Reading of the parallel in *Baba Meẓi'a*. The Venice print has here בשם which makes no sense since this is clearly a report of a dialogue.

41 The Babli (*Baba Meẓi'a* 10b) explains that deeds speak louder than words and that by falling on the object the finder showed that he did not wish to acquire it by simple speech. In that case, it can be acquired only by grabbing, i. e., holding on to it and moving it. The Yerushalmi does not go so far; it only requires that an object should be within four cubits of the finder and that the latter should clearly express his intention of acquiring the

object. Afterwards, he can do as he wishes.

42 In our Mishnah.

43 In our Tosephta, the statement is anonymous. The tradition that the Tosephta is originally from the school of Rebbi Ḥiyya seems to be an old Yerushalmi one.

44 In the Tosephta: "Two poor persons."

45 Since כתש means "to hew to pieces", probably the translation should be: "Thrash one another." In any case, they quarrel by physical force rather than words; it may be assumed that neither of them intended to acquire the forgotten sheaf by speech.

46 Neither of the first two quarellers.

אָמַר רִבִּי יָסָא אָמַר רִבִּי יוֹחָנָן זוֹ בְגִיטִּין מַה שֶׁאֵין כֵּן בְּמַתָּנָה. רוּבָּהּ דְּרִבִּי יוֹחָנָן וְרוּבָּהּ דְּרִבִּי שִׁמְעוֹן בֶּן לָקִישׁ. רוּבָּהּ דְּרִבִּי יוֹחָנָן מַה אִם מְצִיאָה שֶׁאֵינוֹ זוֹכֶה בָּהּ מִדַּעַת אַחֵר הֲרֵי הוּא זוֹכֶה בָּהּ בְּתוֹךְ אַרְבַּע אַמּוֹת. מַתָּנָה שֶׁהוּא זוֹכֶה בָּהּ מִדַּעַת אַחֵר לֹא כָּל־שֶׁכֵּן. רוּבָּהּ דְּרִבִּי שִׁמְעוֹן בֶּן לָקִישׁ מַה אִם מַתָּנָה שֶׁאֵינוֹ זוֹכֶה בָּהּ בְּתוֹךְ אַרְבַּע אַמּוֹת הֲרֵי הוּא זוֹכֶה בָּהּ מִדַּעַת אַחֵר. מְצִיאָה שֶׁהוּא זוֹכֶה בָּהּ בְּתוֹךְ אַרְבַּע אַמּוֹת לֹא כָּל־שֶׁכֵּן.

Rebbi Yasa said in the name of Rebbi Joḥanan[47]: That refers to divorce documents, but it does not apply to a gift. Rebbi Joḥanan adds something[48], Rebbi Simeon ben Laqish adds something. Rebbi Joḥanan adds something. Since a find which cannot be acquired by the knowledge of another person[49] can be acquired within four cubits, should this rule not apply *a fortiori*[50] to a gift that is acquired by the knowledge of another person[51]? Rebbi Simeon ben Laqish adds something. Since a gift which cannot be acquired within four cubits[52] can be acquired by the knowledge of another person, should this not *a fortiori* apply to a find[53]?

47 The entire discussion belongs to the parallel in *Giṭṭin* 8:3 (fol. 49c), where it is stated in Mishnah 2 that a divorce document, of which it is

written (*Deut.* 24:1): "He wrote her a divorce document and delivered it into her hands," can be delivered by the husband's throwing the document close to her (within four cubits) in the public domain, with the wife's knowledge. Then Mishnah 3 adds: "The same rule applies to marriage and the settlement of debts," meaning that if a woman agrees to marry a certain man and the groom, while declaring that the wedding gift is given for the purpose of marriage, instead of delivering it into the bride's hand throws it close to her in the public domain in front of two witnesses, the marriage is valid. Similarly, if the creditor asks the debtor to throw to him the amount owed, if the debtor did that and it landed within the creditor's four cubits in the public domain, the debtor has discharged all his obligations. On this, Rebbi Joḥanan comments that a gift can be acquired only by actual possession, not by four cubits in the public domain.

48 His statement about gifts is far from trivial.

49 If two persons walk together, one sees a find and tells the second one to take it up for him, and the second one lifts it up with the intention of acting as the first person's agent, the first one acquired it (Mishnah *Baba Meẓi'a* 1:3). However, in that case the find must actually be taken up; the four cubits of the agent and his declaration are invalid. If the second person decides to take the find for himself, the four cubits and his declaration of intent of acquisition are valid and the find is his.

50 Hence, his statement excluding gifts is necessary.

51 Without the donor's intent of giving the gift, there is no gift and, hence, none can be acquired. [However, if A says to B: acquire the gift for C, the action of B is valid for C since one may let another person profit without the latter's knowledge (explanation of R. Moses ben Ḥabib)].

52 R. Simeon ben Laqish's premise is R. Joḥanan's conclusion and vice-versa. If the arguments were made by one person, they would be self-contradictory; for the position of two people they are acceptable.

53 Hence, the statement of R. Simeon ben Laqish in the name of Abba Cohen, that four cubits acquire for a person, is necessary insofar as it means acquisition for himself and not for another individual.

הָתִיב רִבִּי זְעִירָא קוֹמֵי רִבִּי יָסָא וְהָתַנֵּינָן וְכֵן לְעִנְיַן הַקִּידוּשִׁין. אָמַר לֵיהּ הִיא גִּיטִּין הִיא קִידּוּשִׁין. וְהָתַנֵּינָן וְכֵן לְעִנְיַן הַחוֹב. אָמַר לֵיהּ שֶׁכֵּן אִם אָמַר לֵיהּ זוֹרְקֵהוּ לַיָּם וִיהֵא מָחוּל לָךְ מָחוּל לוֹ. מֵעַתָּה אֲפִילוּ קָרוֹב לְלוֶֹה זָכָה הַלּוֶֹה. וְתַנֵּינָן קָרוֹב לַלּוֶֹה הַלּוֶֹה חַייָב שֶׁכֵּן אִם אָמַר לַיהּ זוֹרְקֵהוּ עַד שֶׁיִּכָּנֵס לִרְשׁוּתִי וַעֲדַיִן לֹא נִכְנַס בִּרְשׁוּתוֹ. אָמַר רִבִּי אַבָּהוּ כָּל־אִילֵּין הֲתוּבָתָה דַּהֲוָה רִבִּי זְעִירָא מָתִיב קוֹמֵי רִבִּי יָסָא. וְרִבִּי שִׁמְעוֹן בֶּן לָקִישׁ מוֹתִיב קוֹמֵי רִבִּי יוֹחָנָן מְקַבֵּל מִינֵיהּ פָּתַר לֵיהּ בְּאִילֵּין פִּיתְרָיָא.

Rebbi Zeïra objected before Rebbi Yasa: But did we not state[54]: The same applies to marriage? He answered him, divorce documents and marriage contracts have the same rules[55]. But did we not state: The same applies to debt? He said to him, because if he[56] said to him: Throw it into the sea and your debt will be forgiven, it would be forgiven. But if that is true, even if it fell down close to the debtor, the debtor should have the benefit! But we have stated[57], if it falls down close to the debtor, the debtor is still obligated. For he said to him, throw it so that it will enter my domain, and it did not yet enter his domain[58]. Rebbi Abbahu said, all those objections that Rebbi Zeïra raised before Rebbi Yasa, Rebbi Simeon ben Laqish raised before Rebbi Joḥanan. Did he accept them from him? He solved them with those same solutions.

54 Mishnah *Giṭṭin* 8:3.

55 The statement of R. Joḥanan about exclusion of gifts could as well have been formulated for marriage contracts.

56 The creditor tells the debtor to throw the repayment into the sea. If the debtor follows instructions, he has discharged his obligations.

57 In the same Mishnah, speaking of the debtor throwing the money to the creditor. Nothing of four cubits was mentioned in the first explanation.

58 If the money fell outside the creditor's four cubits in the public domain, the debt is not discharged since the condition was not satisfied. However, if the creditor stands on the

seashore and the money falls close to him into the sea, the debtor has discharged his obligation. The problem raised in the return question is considered to be different and receives a different answer.

(fol. 18a) **משנה ג**: פֵּיאָה אֵין קוֹצְרִין אוֹתָהּ בְּמַגָּלוֹת וְאֵין עוֹקְרִין אוֹתָהּ בְּקַרְדּוּמוֹת כְּדֵי שֶׁלֹּא יַכּוּ אִישׁ אֶת רֵעֵהוּ. שָׁלוֹשׁ אוֹבָעְיוֹת בַּיּוֹם בְּשַׁחַר וּבַחֲצוֹת וּבְמִנְחָה. רַבָּן גַּמְלִיאֵל אוֹמֵר לֹא אָמְרוּ אֶלָּא שֶׁלֹּא יִפְחֲתוּ. וְרִבִּי עֲקִיבָה אוֹמֵר לֹא אָמְרוּ אֶלָּא שֶׁלֹּא יוֹסִיפוּ. שֶׁל בֵּית נָמֵר הָיוּ מַלְקִיטִין עַל הַחֶבֶל וְנוֹתְנִין פֵּיאָה מִכָּל־אוֹמֶן וְאוֹמֶן.

Mishnah 3: One does not harvest *peah* with sickles and one does not uproot it with axes so that they should not injure one another. Three investigation periods[59] are there during the day, in the morning, at noontime, and in the evening. Rabban Gamliel says, they decreed this only to say that one may not do less. Rebbi Aqiba says, they decreed this only to say that one may not do more[60]. In Bet Namer[61] they insisted on collecting[62] along a rope and were giving *peah* from every strip[63].

59 Periods when the poor will go to the fields to see where they may collect *peah*. According to the interpretation of Maimonides (*Mattenot Aniïm* 2:17), the poor are not permitted to collect at other times. The root of the word is בעי "to question". (The Halakhah reads אבעיות). The Halakhah will clarify the meaning of the three periods.

60 The farmer is not allowed to declare *peah* at any other time, when not all poor have the opportunity to be present.

61 Identified with Biblical Bet Nimrah (*Num.* 32:2) on the Jordanian side of the Jordan, a *tell* called *Nymreïn*.

62 The *hiph'il* form, given by the overwhelming majority of manuscript

sources, is a causative: The farmer made his farmhands cut the grain along ropes stretched lengthwise along the field. In this way, the entire end-strip of the field became *peah*, given piecemeal during the harvest.

63 Greek ὄγμος, Byzantine pronunciation *oymos*, "furrow in plowing, swathe in reaping," also ὤγμος, "strip of cultivated land."

(fol. 18b) **הלכה ג**: מַהוּ אֹבָעִיּוֹת אָמַר רִבִּי בּוֹן דְּתֵימַר אֵיךְ נֶחְפְּשׂוּ עֵשָׂיו נִבְעוּ מַצְפּוּנָיו.

Halakha 3: What are **אֹבָעִיּוֹת**? Rebbi Abun said, just as you say (*Ob.* 6): "How was Esau searched out, his hidden places investigated[64]."

64 The root **בעה** in Obadiah has a meaning close to Rabbinic Aramaic **בעי**.

בְּשַׁחַר וּבְחַצּוֹת וּבְמִנְחָה. בְּשַׁחַר מִפְּנֵי הַמֵּנִיקוֹת. וּבְחַצּוֹת מִפְּנֵי הַתִּינוֹקוֹת. וּבְמִנְחָה מִפְּנֵי הַנְּמוּשׁוֹת.

"In the morning, at noontime, and in the evening." In the morning because of nursing women. At noontime because of the children. In the evening, because of the decrepit[65].

65 The old people; from the root **משש** "to totter."

רַבָּן גַּמְלִיאֵל[66] אוֹמֵר לֹא אָמְרוּ אֶלָּא שֶׁלֹּא יְפַחֲתוּ וְאִם רָצָה לְהוֹסִיף מוֹסִיף. וְרִבִּי עֲקִיבָה אוֹמֵר לֹא אָמְרוּ אֶלָּא שֶׁלֹּא יוֹסִיפוּ. הָא אִם רָצָה לִפְחוֹת אֵינוֹ פוֹחֵת.

"Rabban Gamliel says, they decreed this only to say that one may not do less;" if he wants to add, he may add. "Rebbi Aqiba says, they decreed this only to say that one may not do more;" does this mean that if he wants to give less frequently he may not do so?

66 Reading of the Rome manuscript, quote from the Mishnah. Venice: רבן שמעון בן גמליאל.

שֶׁל בֵּית נָמֵר הָיוּ מַלְקִיטִין אוֹתָהּ עִם הַחֶבֶל וְנוֹתְנִין פֵּיאָה מִכָּל אוּמָן וְאוּמָן. תַּנֵּי אַבָּא שָׁאוּל אוֹמֵר מַזְכִּירִין אוֹתָן לִגְנַאי וּמַזְכִּירִין אוֹתָן לְשֶׁבַח. מַזְכִּירִין אוֹתָן לִגְנַאי שֶׁהָיוּ נוֹתְנִין פֵּיאָה אֶחָד מִמֵּאָה. וּמַזְכִּירִין אוֹתָן לְשֶׁבַח שֶׁהָיוּ מַלְקִיטִין עַל הַחֶבֶל וְנוֹתְנִין פֵּיאָה מִכָּל אוּמָן וְאוּמָן.

"Those of Bet Namer insisted on collecting along a rope and were giving *peah* from every strip." It was stated: Abba Shaul says, one mentions them disapprovingly and one mentions them approvingly. One mentions them disapprovingly because they only gave *peah* of one percent[67]. And one mentions them approvingly because they insisted on collecting along a rope and were giving *peah* from every strip.

67 And not $1\frac{2}{3}\%$ as required by rabbinical ordinance.

תַּנֵּי בְּשֵׁם רִבִּי שִׁמְעוֹן מִפְּנֵי חֲמִשָּׁה דְבָרִים לֹא יִתֵּן אָדָם פֵּיאָה אֶלָּא בְסוֹף שָׂדֵהוּ. מִפְּנֵי גֶּזֶל עֲנִיִּים. וּמִפְּנֵי בִיטּוּל עֲנִיִּים. וּמִפְּנֵי הָרַמָּאִין. וּמִפְּנֵי מַרְאִית הָעַיִן. וּמִשּׁוּם שֶׁאָמְרָה תוֹרָה לֹא תְכַלֶּה פְּאַת שָׂדְךָ. מִפְּנֵי גֶּזֶל עֲנִיִּים כֵּיצַד שֶׁלֹּא יִרְאֶה אָדָם הַשָּׁעָה פְנוּיָה[68] וְיֹאמַר לִקְרוֹבוֹ עָנִי בֹּא וְטוֹל לָךְ אֶת הַפֵּיאָה. מִפְּנֵי בִיטּוּל עֲנִיִּים כֵּיצַד שֶׁלֹּא יְהוּ עֲנִיִּים יוֹשְׁבִין וּמְשַׁמְּרִין כָּל־הַיּוֹם וְאוֹמְרִים עַכְשָׁיו הוּא נוֹתֵן פֵּיאָה עַכְשָׁיו הוּא נוֹתֵן פֵּיאָה אֶלָּא יֵלְכוּ וִילַקְּטוּ בְשָׂדֶה אַחֶרֶת וְיָבוֹאוּ בִשְׁעַת הַכִּילּוּי. מִפְּנֵי הָרַמָּאִין כֵּיצַד שֶׁלֹּא יֹאמַר כְּבָר נָתַתִּי וִיהֵא בוֹרֵר אֶת הַיָּפֶה וּמוֹצִיא אֶת הָרָע. מִפְּנֵי מַרְאִית הָעַיִן כֵּיצַד שֶׁלֹּא יְהוּ הָעוֹבְרִים וְהַשָּׁבִים אוֹמְרִים רְאוּ הֵיאַךְ קָצַר אִישׁ פְּלוֹנִי שָׂדֵהוּ וְלֹא הִנִּיחַ פֵּיאָה לָעֲנִיִּים. וּמִשּׁוּם שֶׁאָמְרָה תוֹרָה לֹא תְכַלֶּה פְּאַת שָׂדְךָ.

It was stated[69] in the name of Rebbi Simeon: For five reasons one should give *peah* only at the end of one's field, because of robbing the poor, because of idling the poor, because of cheats, because of bad impression, and because the Torah said (*Lev.* 19:9): "Do not finish off the corner of your field." Because of robbing the poor, that no man should see a free hour and say to his poor relative: Come, and take this *peah* for yourself. Because of idling the poor, that the poor should not sit around, watch the entire day, and say: Now he is giving *peah*, now he is giving *peah*, but rather they should go, collect on another field, and come at the moment of finishing. Because of the cheats, that one should not say: I already gave, and then he chooses the good and brings out the bad[70]. Because of bad impression, that the passers-by should not say: Look, this man harvested his field and did not leave *peah* for the poor. And because the Torah said: "Do not finish off the corner of your field."

68 Reading of the Rome ms., *Sifra Qedošim* 1:10, and the Babylonian Talmud (*Šabbat* 23a). Venice: קנויה.

69 There are parallels in Tosephta *Peah* 1:6, *Sifra Qedošim* 1:10, Babli *Šabbat* 23a. In all these parallels, there are four reasons given, meaning that R. Simeon explains the reason of the Biblical law. In the Babli, R. Simeon is reputed to deduce laws from the reasoning behind Biblical precepts; the Yerushalmi does not seem to accept this but gives reasons separate from the verse. (The Tosephta in our hands is essentially a Babylonian compilation; *Sifra* is Palestinian material edited in Babylonia.) It is clear that R. Simeon supports here his argument in Mishnah 1:3 that *peah must* be given at the end, because of Biblical precept and rabbinical ordinance.

70 We are not concerned here with people who willingly transgress the ordinances of the Torah. Rather, we speak about so-called pious people who find ways to minimize their obligations. In this case, the farmer harvests the entire field without giving *peah*. Then he is obligated to give *peah* from the cut grain but here he has the possibility to select stalks with small kernels for the poor, whereas he has no such control if he refrains from cutting the last corner.

(fol. 18a) **משנה ד**: נָכְרִי שֶׁקָּצַר אֶת שָׂדֵהוּ וְאַחַר כָּךְ נִתְגַּייֵר פָּטוּר מִן הַלֶּקֶט וּמִן הַשִּׁכְחָה וּמִן הַפֵּיאָה. רִבִּי יְהוּדָה מְחַיֵּיב בְּשִׁכְחָה שֶׁאֵין הַשִּׁכְחָה אֶלָּא בִשְׁעַת הָעִימּוּר.

Mishnah 4: A Non-Jew who harvested his field and later converted is free from gleanings, forgotten sheaves, and *peah*[71]. Rebbi Jehudah obligates him for forgotten sheaves because that applies only at the time of binding the sheaves[72].

71 For *peah* and gleanings it is written: "At *your* harvesting," and for the forgotten sheaf it says: "If *you* harvest *your* harvest," and at the time of the harvest he still was an outsider.

72 To refrain from going back to collect a forgotten sheaf cannot apply as long as there are no sheaves. Hence, if the man converts between cutting the grain and binding the sheaves, the obligation comes to him as a Jew and he is bound by it.

(fol. 18b) **הלכה ד**: יְאוּת אָמַר רִבִּי יְהוּדָה מַה טַעֲמָא דְרַבָּנָן. רִבִּי יוֹסֵי בְּשֵׁם רַב רִבִּי חִזְקִיָּה רַב יְהוּדָה בְּשֵׁם שְׁמוּאֵל כְּתִיב וְשָׁכַחְתָּ עוֹמֶר בַּשָּׂדֶה וְשָׁכַחְתָּ קָמָה אֶת שֶׁיֵּשׁ לוֹ שִׁכְחַת קָמָה יֵשׁ לוֹ שִׁכְחַת עֳמָרִין. וְאֶת שֶׁאֵין לוֹ שִׁכְחַת קָמָה אֵין לוֹ שִׁכְחַת עֳמָרִין.

Halakha 4: Rebbi Jehudah said it well, what is the reason of the Rabbis? Rebbi Yose in the name of Rav, Rebbi Ḥizqiah, Rav Jehudah in the name of Samuel: It is written (*Deut*. 24:19): "If you forget a sheaf on the field." If you forget the standing grain[73]. What applies to forgetting while it is standing also applies to forgetting sheaves, but what does not apply to forgetting while it is standing , does not apply to forgetting sheaves.

73 The verse reads: "If *you* cut *your* harvest on *your* field and then you forget a sheaf on the field, do not return to collect it." The obligation

attaches not to sheafmaking but to harvesting. The *Sifri Debarim* 282 reads: "'Your harvest,' except if it was cut by Gentiles. From that they said: A Non-Jew who harvested his field and later converted is free from gleanings, forgotten sheaves and *peah*. Rebbi Jehudah obliges him for forgotten sheaves because that applies only at the time of binding the sheaves."

יִשְׂרָאֵל וְגוֹי שֶׁהָיוּ שׁוּתָּפִין בְּקָמָה חֶלְקוֹ שֶׁל יִשְׂרָאֵל חַייָב וְחֶלְקוֹ שֶׁל גּוֹי פָּטוּר. רִבִּי חִזְקִיָּה בְּשֵׁם רַב יִרְמְיָה בִּמְחוּלֶּקֶת[74].

If a Jew and a Gentile were partners in the standing grain, the part of the Jew is obligated but the part of the Gentile is free. Rebbi Ḥizqiah in the name of Rav Jeremiah: If it was divided up[75].

74 Reading of the Rome manuscript. The Venice print has: במחלוקת "in disagreement."

75 The parallel in Tosephta *Peah* 2:9 reads: "If a Jew and a Gentile were partners in the standing grain, the part of the Jew is obligated but the part of the Gentile is free. Rebbi Ismael said: If a Jew and a Gentile were partners in standing grain, it is free from *peah*. When is that? Only if the Gentile has veto power; if the Gentile has no veto power then it is obligated for *peah*." This means that if the Jew may harvest his part without getting the Gentile's permission, it is not a partnership as far as harvest is concerned but only a partnership for the growing period; accordingly, it is totally the Jew's harvest and is obligated. The Yerushalmi seems to apply the expression "when is that?" and the following to the beginning statement, not to the opinion of Rebbi Ismael.

(fol. 18a) **משנה ה**: הִקְדִּישׁ קָמָה וּפָדָה קָמָה חַייָב. עֳמָרִין וּפָדָה עֳמָרִין חַייָב. קָמָה וּפָדָה עֳמָרִין פְּטוּרָה שֶׁבִּשְׁעַת חוֹבָתָהּ הָיְתָה פְטוּרָה. וּכְיוֹצֵא בוֹ הַמַּקְדִּישׁ פֵּירוֹתָיו עַד שֶׁלֹּא בָאוּ לְעוֹנַת הַמַּעְשְׂרוֹת וּפְדָאָן חַייָבִין וּמִשֶּׁבָּאוּ לְעוֹנַת

הַמַּעְשְׂרוֹת וּפְדָאָן חַיָּבִין[76]. הִקְדִּישָׁן עַד שֶׁלֹּא נִגְמְרוּ וּגְמָרָן הַגִּזְבָּר וְאַחַר כָּךְ פְּדָאָן פְּטוּרִין שֶׁבִּשְׁעַת חוֹבָתָן הָיוּ פְּטוּרִין.

Mishnah 5: If somebody dedicated[77] standing produce and redeemed it standing, it is obligated[78]; in sheaves and redeemed in sheaves, it is obligated; standing and redeemed in sheaves it is free since at the time of obligation[79] it was free. Parallel to this, if somebody dedicated his produce before the time of tithes[80] and redeemed it, it is obligated; after the time of tithes, it is obligated. But if he dedicated it before it was finished, the treasurer finished it[81], and then the owner redeemed it, it is free since at the time of obligation it was free.

76 This is the text of the Leyden manuscript before correction and of the Rome manuscript. But the corrected text of the Leyden manuscript and the Venice print reads פטורין. However, the parallel in the Mishnah *Ḥallah* 3:3 in all sources reads חייבין. According to the text the two parts of the Mishnah are completely parallel. According to the Venice print, the two statements "but after the time of tithes" and "and the treasurer finished it" are identical and one of them is redundant.

77 As a monetary gift to the Temple. The Temple is the common property of all of Israel, hence the specific term "*your* (personal) harvest" is not applicable and produce harvested by the Temple administration is free from all obligations. The Temple did acquire real estate and other valuables only for redemption or sale, to be converted into currency.

78 Since at harvest time it is in private hands. The same applies in the next case; produce already obligated does not lose the obligation by dedication.

79 I. e., at harvest time.

80 This will be explained in the Halakhah.

81 Or, depending on the case, it grew to become obligated while in the hand of the Temple treasurer.

(fol. 18b) **הלכה ה:** וְלָמָּה תַּנִּיתָהּ תְּרֵין זִימְנִין. רִבִּי יוֹנָה רִבִּי חִייָא רִבִּי יְהוֹשֻׁעַ בֶּן לֵוִי בְּשֵׁם בַּר פְּדָיָה אַחַת לְמֵרוּחַ וְאַחַת לִשְׁלִישׁ. רִבִּי יוֹסֵי אָמַר רִבִּי בָּא וַחֲבֵרַיָּא. חֲבֵרַיָּא אָמְרֵי אַחַת לְמֵרוּחַ וְאַחַת לִשְׁלִישׁ. רִבִּי בָּא מְפָרֵשׁ בְּחַלָּה לְמֵירוּחַ. וּבְפֵיאָה בִשְׁלִישׁ.

Halakhah 5: And why is it stated twice[82]? Rebbi Jonah, Rebbi Ḥiyya[83], Rebbi Joshua ben Levi in the name of Bar Pedaiah[84]: One for smoothing[85], one for one third[86]. Rebbi Yose said, Rebbi Abba and the colleagues. The colleagues say, one for smoothing, one for one third[87]. Rebbi Abba explains: At *Ḥallah* for smoothing[88], at *Peah* for one third.

82 The statement about tithes appears both here and in Mishnah *Ḥallah* 3:3. The entire discussion also appears there in Halakhah 3.

83 Rebbi Ḥiyya bar Abba.

84 Rebbi Jehudah bar Pedaiah, Amora of the first generation in Galilee, nephew of Bar Qappara and teacher of R. Joshua ben Levi (and also R. Joḥanan).

85 The total obligation for heave and tithes starts only at the end of the harvest, when the grain is put into orderly heaps whose surface is smoothed (so that theft can easily be detected.) In modern terms, it would mean that the grain is stored in a silo.

86 Grain that is one-third ripe may be used as food, *Grünkern*. From this moment on, grain kernels may be eaten on the spot without giving heave and tithes, but they may not be used for household purposes without first separating the dues for Cohen and Levite.

87 But they do not know which refers to what.

88 Since *ḥallah* is the heave of bread dough (in a sizeable amount), it does not qualify for "eating on the spot" but must refer to the finished harvest.

מַתְנִיתִין דְּרִבִּי עֲקִיבָה דְּרִבִּי עֲקִיבָה אָמַר אַחַר שְׁלִישׁ הָרִאשׁוֹן אַתְּ מְהַלֵּךְ. וְאִיתְפַּלְּגוּן שָׂדֶה שֶׁהֶבִיאָה שְׁלִישׁ לִפְנֵי גּוֹי וּלְקָחָהּ מִמֶּנּוּ יִשְׂרָאֵל רִבִּי עֲקִיבָה אוֹמֵר פָּטוּר וַחֲכָמִים אוֹמְרִין בְּתוֹסֶפֶת חַייָב. מַיי כְדוֹן. תִּיפְתָּר כְּרִבִּי עֲקִיבָה (בְּמֵירוּחַ) [בְּמַחְלוֹקֶת][89]. וּכְדִיבְרֵי הַכֹּל בְּקוֹצֵר מִיַּד.

Our Mishnah is from Rebbi Aqiba since Rebbi Aqiba said that you go after the first third. And they differed: A field that was one-third ripened in the possession of a Gentile, and a Jew bought it after that time, Rebbi Aqiba said it is free[90], but the Sages say he is obligated for the additional growth[91]. How is that? Explain it for Rebbi Aqiba (after smoothing[92]) [in a disagreement[93]], or according to everybody if he harvested immediately[94].

89 במרוח is the text of the Venice print here, במחלוקת the text of all sources in *Ḥallah* 3:3.

90 The produce was in the hands of the Gentile at the time of the start of the obligation; so there is no obligation.

91 In the Babli, *Ḥullin* 137a, *Giṭṭin* 77a, the positions of R. Aqiba and the Sages are inverted.

92 In *Maäserot* 5:4, the same statement is quoted and there it is said in the name of R. Eleazar that even the Sages obligate only for the Second Tithe or the tithe of the poor. These two alternative obligations are attached only to smoothed, stored grain; their obligation does not start with grain that is only one-third ripe.

93 That our Mishnah really follows the opinion of R. Aqiba, which, therefore, becomes the operative practice. [Since the Babli switches the names in the statement, it is the position of the Babli that our Mishnah represents the majority opinion of the Sages.]

94 And there is no additional growth during the ownership of the Jew.

(fol. 18a) **משנה ו**: מִי שֶׁלִּיקֵּט פֵּיאָה וְאָמַר הֲרֵי זוּ לְאִישׁ פְּלוֹנִי עָנִי רִבִּי לְעָזָר אוֹמֵר זָכָה לוֹ. וַחֲכָמִים אוֹמְרִים יִתְּנֶנָּהּ לְעָנִי הַנִּמְצָא רִאשׁוֹן. הַלֶּקֶט וְהַשִּׁכְחָה וְהַפֵּיאָה שֶׁל נָכְרִי חַייָב בְּמַעֲשֵׂר אֶלָּא אִם כֵּן הִבְקִיר.

Mishnah 6: He[96] who collected *peah* and said: "This is for X, the poor man," Rebbi Eliezer says, he made him acquire it; but the Sages say, he should give it to the first poor person he meets. Gleanings, forgotten sheaves, and *peah* of a Non-Jew[97] are obligated for tithes, except if the Non-Jew declared it to be abandoned property.

96 The owner of the field.

97 From the language of the Mishnah it is not clear whether this is from a field (in the Land of Israel) belonging to a Non-Jew, or whether these are gleanings from the field of a Jew collected by a Non-Jew and given to a poor Jew. The first possibility is preferred by the Yerushalmi, the second by the Babli (*Giṭṭin* 47a). Regularly collected *peah*, gleanings, and forgotten sheaves are exempt from heave and tithes.

(fol. 18b) **הלכה ו**: רִבִּי יְהוֹשֻׁעַ בֶּן לֵוִי אוֹמֵר בְּבַעַל הַבַּיִת עָשִׁיר נֶחְלְקוּ. אֲבָל בְּבַעַל הַבַּיִת עָנִי מֵאַחַר שֶׁהוּא רָאוּי לִיטּוֹל זָכָה.

Halakhah 6: Rebbi Joshua ben Levi says: They disagree about a rich owner[98]. But a poor owner, since he has the right to take it[99], the other person acquired it.

98 Since he may not take *peah* for himself, he may not take it for others. The Babli (*Baba Meẓi'a* 9b) explains that R. Eliezer disagrees: since everybody can make himself poor by giving away all his property, he is a potential receiver of charity and may collect, but he may not keep it as long as he is not poor.

99 For himself; he may acquire it legally even according to the Sages. That the poor farmer may not keep his own *peah* is a rabbinic institution that does not influence the status of the *peah* taken by any poor person.

אָמַר רִבִּי זְעִירָא רִבִּי לָעְזָר לַחֲבֵירוֹ וְרִבִּי יוֹחָנָן וְרִבִּי יְהוֹשֻׁעַ בֶּן לֵוִי שֶׁלְּשְׁתָּן אָמְרוּ דָּבָר אֶחָד. רִבִּי לָעְזָר דְּאָמַר רִבִּי זְעִירָא בְשֵׁם רִבִּי לָעְזָר אָדָם זָכָה לַחֲבֵירוֹ בִמְצִיאָה. רִבִּי יוֹחָנָן דְּתַנֵּינָן תַּמָּן מְצִיאַת בְּנוֹ וּבִתּוֹ הַקְּטַנִּים עַבְדּוֹ וְשִׁפְחָתוֹ הַכְּנַעֲנִים מְצִיאַת אִשְׁתּוֹ הֲרֵי אֵלּוּ שֶׁלּוֹ. מְצִיאַת בְּנוֹ וּבִתּוֹ הַגְּדוֹלִים וְעַבְדּוֹ וְשִׁפְחָתוֹ הָעִבְרִים מְצִיאַת אִשְׁתּוֹ שֶׁגֵּירְשָׁהּ אַף עַל פִּי שֶׁלֹּא נָתַן לָהּ כְּתוּבָּתָהּ הֲרֵי אֵלּוּ שֶׁלָּהֶן. אָמַר רִבִּי יוֹחָנָן בְּשֶׁאֵינָן טְפוּלִין. אֲבָל אִם הָיוּ טְפוּלִין לַאֲבִיהֶן מְצִיאָתָן שֶׁלּוֹ. רִבִּי יְהוֹשֻׁעַ בֶּן לֵוִי דְּרִבִּי יְהוֹשֻׁעַ בֶּן לֵוִי אָמַר בְּבַעַל הַבַּיִת עָשִׁיר נֶחְלְקוּ. אֲבָל בְּבַעַל הַבַּיִת עָנִי מֵאַחַר שֶׁהוּא רָאוּי לִיטוֹל זָכָה.

Rebbi Zeïra said: Rebbi Eleazar[100] (about one's friend), Rebbi Joḥanan, and Rebbi Joshua ben Levi said the same thing. Rebbi Eleazar, as Rebbi Zeïra said in the name of Rebbi Eleazar: A man may acquire a find for his friend[101]. Rebbi Joḥanan, as we have stated there (Mishnah Baba Meẓiah 1:5): "The finds of his minor sons and daughters[102], of his Gentile slaves and slave girls, and of his wife[103], belong to him. The finds of his adult sons and daughters[104], of his Jewish slaves and slave girls[105], and of his divorced wife in case that he had not yet paid her *ketubah*[106], belong to them. Rebbi Joḥanan said, if they[107] are not dependents. But if they are dependent on their father, their finds belong to him. Rebbi Joshua ben Levi, as Rebbi Joshua ben Levi said: They disagree about a rich owner. But if the owner is poor, since he has the right to take it, the other person acquired it.

100 The Amora.

101 If a man finds abandoned or lost property, he may pick it up to acquire it for another person. This essentially is giving a gift of something that is not his property since it was not his property while it was lying in the street, and he picked it up with the intention of not acquiring it himself. It is enough that he could have picked it up for himself to empower him to give it directly to the beneficiary. This is

the exact parallel to the poor farmer collecting *peah*, not to give later to somebody else, but so that the other should be the immediate owner of every collected stalk. [Later in this Halakhah and in the Babli (*Baba Meẓi'a* 10a), this appears as a statement of R. Joḥanan. Since a statement X in the name of Y usually means that X did not hear the statement directly from Y, it is to be assumed that R. Zeïra heard the statement of R. Eleazar in the yeshivah of R. Joḥanan.]

102 They have no independent legal status but can act for their father. The same holds for slaves and their master.

103 It is a rabbinic ordinance that the wife's finds and earnings belong to the husband, in exchange for his obligation to totally support his wife. If the wife is an earner, that clause may be abrogated by mutual consent.

104 Who are legal persons in their own right.

105 They are not really slaves but indentured servants for at most 6 years and do not lose their legal status. (The institution of Jewish slavery ended with the deportation of the first of the 10 tribes, since it was valid only as long as the distribution of land under Joshua was in force.)

106 Cf. Chapter 3, Note 151. As long as the *ketubah* is not paid, the ex-husband has to support his ex-wife, but her earnings and finds are hers to keep.

107 The adult children. If they live in the father's house and are supported by him, their earnings go to the father. Hence, if they find something, it is automatically assumed that they acquire the found property for their father.

תַּנֵּי הַשּׂוֹכֵר אֶת הַפּוֹעֵל לַעֲשׂוֹת עִמּוֹ בְּכָל־מְלָאכָה מְצִיאָה שֶׁל בַּעַל הַבַּיִת. רִבִּי שִׁמְעוֹן בֶּן לָקִישׁ בְּעֵי רָצָה לַחְזוֹר חוֹזֵר בּוֹ. וְאַתְּ אָמַר מְצִיאָה שֶׁל בַּעַל הַבַּיִת. רִבִּי יַעֲקֹב בַּר אָחָא אָמַר רִבִּי יָסָא מַקְשֵׁי מַה צוּרְכָה לְהַהִיא דְאָמַר רִבִּי שִׁמְעוֹן בֶּן לָקִישׁ וְלָא נָן שְׁמִיעַ דָּמַר רִבִּי יַעֲקֹב בַּר אָחָא אִיתְפַּלְגוּן רִבִּי יוֹחָנָן וְרִבִּי שִׁמְעוֹן בֶּן לָקִישׁ. רִבִּי יוֹחָנָן אָמַר אָדָם זוֹכֶה לַחֲבֵירוֹ בִּמְצִיאָה. וְרִבִּי שִׁמְעוֹן בֶּן לָקִישׁ אָמַר אֵין אָדָם זוֹכֶה לַחֲבֵירוֹ בִּמְצִיאָה.

It was stated: If one hires a worker to do all kinds of work[108] for him, the worker's findings belong to his employer. Rebbi Simeon ben Laqish asked: If he wants to quit, he may quit[109]; and you say that the find belongs to the employer[110]? Rebbi Jacob bar Aḥa[111] said that Rebbi Yasa asked, why do we need that of Rebbi Simeon ben Laqish, did we not understand that Rebbi Jacob bar Aḥa said that Rebbi Joḥanan and Rebbi Simeon ben Laqish disagree? Rebbi Joḥanan said, a man may acquire a find for his friend. But Rebbi Simeon ben Laqish said, a man cannot acquire a find for his friend[112].

108 The duties are not specified. If the worker is hired for a specific kind of work, e. g., for ploughing, the find belongs to the worker (Babli *Baba Meẓi'a* 10a, 12b, 118a).

109 In the Yerushalmi, this is a statement of R. Joḥanan (*Baba Meẓi'a* 6:2); there Rav is of the opinion that in a hiring contract both parties may dissolve the relationship without notice (but the party that changes the contract is liable for damages arising for the other party.) In the Babli (*Baba Meẓi'a* 10a), Rav states that a worker can quit without notice since it is written (*Lev.* 25:42): "(The Children of Israel) are My slaves," and not slaves of slaves. Hence, any contract that restricts the ability of the worker to leave his place of work is invalid.

110 If the findings are worth more than the daily wages, the finder could simply quit his job before picking up the find and then the employer would have no rights.

111 Since R. Jacob bar Aḥa quotes himself in our text, his name here seems to be a scribal error.

112 R. Simeon ben Laqish has no need for his objection since, for him, the question does not arise at all. In the Babli (*loc. cit.*), the objection to R. Joḥanan's rule is raised and answered, that as long as the journeyman does not quit, all he does that day is to the employer's benefit.

רִבִּי רְדִיפָה אִיתְפַּלְּגוּן רִבִּי יוֹנָה וְרִבִּי יוֹסֵי. חַד אָמַר הָרָאוּי לִיטּוֹל זָכָה. וְחַד אָמַר הָרָאוּי לִיתֵּן זָכָה. מָן דָּמַר הָרָאוּי לִיטּוֹל כָּל־שֶׁכֵּן לִיתֵּן. מָן דָּמַר הָרָאוּי לִיתֵּן הָא לִיטּוֹל לֹא.

Rebbi Redifa[113]: Rebbi Jonah and Rebbi Yose disagree. One says, he who may take may acquire[114]; the other says, he who may give may acquire[115]. He who says "he who may take" certainly includes him who may give. He who says "he who may give," excludes him who may take.

113 An Amora of the last generation of Galilean Amoraïm who collected sayings of the Sages of the preceding generation.

114 He who may take for himself may acquire for another person without first taking possession himself.

115 He who may distribute property may acquire for a third person directly since he could acquire and then give it away.

מַתְנִיתָא פְלִיגָא (fol. 18c) עַל מָן דְּאָמַר הָרָאוּי לִיטּוֹל זָכָה דְּתַנֵּינָן תֵּן גֵּט זֶה לְאִשְׁתִּי שֶׁכֵּן רָאוּי לְקַבֵּל גֵּט בִּתּוֹ. וּשְׁטָר שִׁחְרוּר זֶה לְעַבְדִּי שֶׁכֵּן רָאוּי לְקַבֵּל שְׁטָר שִׁחְרוּרוֹ. וְתַנֵּינָן הִתְקַבֵּל גֵּט זֶה לְאִשְׁתִּי אוֹ הוֹלֵךְ גֵּט זֶה לְאִשְׁתִּי אִם רָצָא לְהַחֲזִיר לֹא יַחֲזִיר. וְהָעֶבֶד רָאוּי הוּא לְהוֹלִיךְ אֶת הַגֵּט. פָּתַר לָהּ לִצְדָדִין.

A Mishnah disagrees with him who says that he who may take may acquire, since we have stated[116]: "Give this divorce document to my wife . . .," because he may receive the divorce document of his minor daughter[117]. "And the document of manumission to my slave . . .," since he may receive his own document of manumission[118]. But did we not state[119]: "Receive this divorce document for my wife or bring this divorce document to my wife; if he wants to change his mind . . . he may not do so." Is a slave empowered to bring a divorce document? Explain it by different cases[117].

116 *Gittin* 1:6. This paragraph is elliptic and almost incomprehensible. The Mishnah reads: "If someone says, give this divorce document to my wife or this document of manumission to my slave, and then wants to change his

mind in either case, he may do so in the opinion of R. Meïr. But the Sages say, in the case of a wife, but not in the manumission of slaves since one may favor a person without his knowledge." Since the divorce is considered bad for the wife, it can become valid only with her knowledge. R. Meïr thinks that manumission also may be bad for the slave who will have to accept all duties of a free Jew; the Sages consider manumission always to be good. With the wife's knowledge, however, the emissary, a man, can acquire the divorce document for her. But as a man, he is not in a position ever to receive a divorce document.

117 The minor daughter who was formally betrothed (קידושין) but not yet actually married, can become free to marry another man only by divorce. The bill of divorce must be accepted by her father, or by herself on the instruction of the father, since she becomes of age only by actual marriage. Hence, a man, while he cannot receive the document in question, is in theory able to receive some bills of divorce.

118 We have to assume that the emissary is a fellow slave who could receive his own manumission.

119 Mishnah *Giṭṭin* 6:1: "If someone says: Receive this divorce document for my wife, or convey this divorce document to my wife, and wants to change his mind, he may do so. If the woman said: Receive the divorce document for me, if he {the husband} wants to change his mind {after handing over the document}, he may not do so {since the transaction was done with the wife's knowledge.}" That is the case if the emissary of the wife is a free man; she is divorced the moment the document comes into her emissary's hand. But since a slave has no "hand" in the legal sense, how can this Mishnah be reconciled with the one quoted first?

120 Only the case of the bill of manumission in the first Mishnah presupposes a slave as intermediary. In all other cases, an adult free Jew is the emissary.

הָא מַתְנִיתָא פְלִיגָא עַל מָן דְּאָמַר הָרָאוּי לִיטּוֹל[121] זָכָה דְּתַנֵּינָן תַּמָּן עִישּׂוּר אֶחָד שֶׁאֲנִי עָתִיד לִימוֹד נָתוּן לַעֲקִיבָה בֶּן יוֹסֵף שֶׁיִּזְכֶּה בוֹ לָעֲנִיִּים וּמְקוֹמוֹ מוּשְׂכָּר לוֹ. וְרִבִּי עֲקִיבָה רָאוּי הוּא לִיטּוֹל. פָּתַר לָהּ עַד שֶׁלֹּא הֶעֱשִׁיר. וַאֲפִילוּ תֵימָא מִשֶּׁהֶעֱשִׁיר תִּיפְתָּר כְּשֶׁהָיָה פַּרְנָס וְיַד פַּרְנָס כְּיַד עָנִי.

The following Mishnah disagrees with him who says that he who may take may acquire, since we have stated there[122]: "One tithe that I will measure in the future is given to Aqiba ben Joseph that he should let the poor acquire it, and its place is rented to him." But is Rebbi Aqiba entitled to take? Explain it, before he got rich[123]. And even if you say, after he became rich[124], when he was an administrator[125], and the hand of the administrator is equal to the hand of the poor.

121 Reading of Rome and R. Solomon Cirillo manuscripts. Venice print and Leyden ms.: ליתן.

122 *Maäser Šeni* 5:9. The Mishnah discusses the case of a man who was away on a trip at the time (Passover Eve) when the tithes must be given. Rabban Gamliel, Rebbi Joshua, Rebbi Aqiba, and Rebbi Eleazar ben Azariah were travelling on a ship on that day (probably to or from Rome on official business) when Rabban Gamliel designated the first tithe to Rebbi Joshua, a Levite, and the tithe of the poor to Rebbi Aqiba. In order not to transgress the Biblical command of distributing the tithes, Rebbi Aqiba must have been able to let the poor acquire their tithe while on the ship.

123 When he was a student, his wife supported him because she wanted him to become a scholar. But because he was poor, his very rich father-in-law disowned them.

124 This is the more likely scenario because in this setting he already was one of the most prominent rabbis.

125 Of the public charity funds. Cf. Greek πρόνοος, ον adj., "careful, prudent"; also late form προνοητής, οῦ, ὁ, "supervisor, administrator" (E. G.).

מִילְתֵיהּ דְּרִבִּי יְהוֹשֻׁעַ בֶּן לֵוִי הָרָאוּי לִיטּוֹל זָכָה. דְּרִבִּי יְהוֹשֻׁעַ בֶּן לֵוִי אָמַר בְּבַעַל הַבַּיִת עָשִׁיר מַחְלוֹקֶת. אֲבָל בְּבַעַל הַבַּיִת עָנִי מִתּוֹךְ שֶׁרָאוּי לִיטּוֹל זָכָה.

The word of Rebbi Joshua ben Levi is that he who may take may acquire, since Rebbi Joshua ben Levi said: They disagree about a rich owner. But in the case of a poor owner, since he has the right to take it, the other person acquired it.

רַבִּי חִזְקִיָּה רַבִּי יִרְמְיָה[126] בְּשֵׁם רַבִּי יוֹחָנָן כְּמָאן דְּאָמַר יֵשׁ קִנְיָין לְגוֹי בְּאֶרֶץ יִשְׂרָאֵל לְפוֹטְרוֹ מִן הַמַּעְשְׂרוֹת. בְּרַם כְּמָאן דְּאָמַר אֵין קִנְיָין לְגוֹי בְּאֶרֶץ יִשְׂרָאֵל לְפוֹטְרוֹ מִן הַמַּעְשְׂרוֹת אֲפִילוּ הִבְקִירוֹ חַיָּיב. רַבִּי יוֹסֵי בְּשֵׁם רַבִּי יוֹחָנָן כְּמָאן דְּאָמַר אֵין קִנְיָין לְגוֹי בְּאֶרֶץ יִשְׂרָאֵל לְפוֹטְרוֹ מִן הַמַּעְשְׂרוֹת. בְּרַם כְּמָאן דְּאָמַר יֵשׁ קִנְיָין לְגוֹי בְּאֶרֶץ יִשְׂרָאֵל לְפוֹטְרוֹ מִן הַמַּעְשְׂרוֹת קַל הֵיקִילוּ חֲכָמִים בְּלִיקוּטִין.

Rebbi Ḥizqiah, Rebbi Jeremiah, in the name of Rebbi Joḥanan[127]: [128]According to him[129] who says that a Gentile may acquire real estate in the Land of Israel to free it from tithes[130]. But according to him who says that a Gentile may not acquire real estate in the Land of Israel to free it from tithes, even if he declared it abandoned property it is obligated[131]. Rebbi Yose in the name of Rebbi Joḥanan[132]: [128]According to him who says that a Gentile may not acquire real estate in the Land of Israel to free it from tithes[133]. But according to him who says that a Gentile may acquire real estate in the Land of Israel to free it from tithes, the Sages decreed special leniency for gleanings[134].

126 Reading of the Rome manuscript. Since all other occurrences show that R. Ḥizqiah was R. Jeremiah's student, the reading here of the Venice print/Leyden ms. "R. Jeremiah, R. Ḥizqiah" must be a scribal error. In the next paragraph, the Venice print also has the reading given here.

127 Here starts the discussion of the last part of the Mishnah: Gleanings, forgotten sheaves, and *peah* of a Gentile are obligated for tithes, except if the Gentile declared it to be abandoned property.

128 Add: "The Mishnah is only understandable . . ."

129 The opinions of R. Jehudah and R. Simeon in *Demaï* 3:4, 5:9. The opposite opinion in *Demaï* 5:9 (fol. 24d), *Kilaïm* 7:4 (fol. 30d) and in the Babli, *Giṭṭin* 47a, is attributed to R. Meïr. The Yerushalmi clearly accepts the opinion of RR. Jedudah and Simeon. Cf. also *Demay*, Chapter 5, Note 102.

130 It is explained in *Demaï* (*loc. cit.*) and elsewhere that the Biblical duties of heave and tithes ceased with the Babylonian exile. The returnees from Babylonia took these duties upon themselves and future generations in a solemn covenant with God (*Neh.* 10:1) in those regions (Judea, the Southern Plains, Galilee, and Golan Heights) settled by the returnees; hence the problem is not one of Biblical precepts but of the meaning of this covenant. According to the position taken here, the obligation of *peah*, gleanings, and forgotten sheaves is a later Rabbinic obligation on the land as far as Jews are concerned (*Demaï* 3:4, fol. 23d). Since the Gentile has no obligation to give to the poor, he cannot designate anything under these names. But since he is the owner, he may legally abandon the produce just as a Jew might abandon it.

131 According to R. Meïr, the obligation is on the Land, not on the owner. If the agricultural real estate is owned by a Gentile, the obligation obviously cannot be enforced since the Gentile has no obligation to abide by the covenant. However, if the produce is then bought by a Jew, it will be a deadly sin for him to consume anything from it before he has given the heave and, at least, the priest's part of the tithe. The only exception is abandoned property (by Mishnah 6:1, this must be abandoned to any taker, not just the poor.) Now, *peah*, gleanings, and forgotten sheaves also are free of heave and tithes but these can be given only by persons obligated to give. Hence, *peah*, gleanings, and forgotten sheaves designated by Gentiles do not have the legal status of *peah*, gleanings, and forgotten sheaves, and are not exempt; neither does abandoning the property help since nothing the Gentile does can possibly influence the duties upon the produce.

132 Note that "in the name of" always implies an indirect transmission of statements; it might be that R. Jeremiah deals only with the statement about abandoned property and R. Yose with that about *peah*, gleanings, and forgotten sheaves.

133 The obligation of *peah*, gleanings, and forgotten sheaves is on the Land and is activated as soon as the produce comes into Jewish hands. R. Yose is of the opinion that the Gentile owner still may legally abandon the produce.

134 If the Gentile designated some produce as *peah*, or left gleanings on the field, he clearly abandoned this to

the poor. The general rule is that abandoned property must be abandoned to rich and poor alike (Mishnah 6:1), but in the case before us the rabbis made an exception; it is the leniency mentioned here. This is part of Nehemiah's covenant; such a leniency would be impossible for a Biblical obligation.

רִבִּי לָעְזָר שָׁאַל וְאֵין לוֹ קִנְייַן נְכָסִים. לָא עַל הָדָא אִיתְאֲמָרַת אֶלָּא עַל הָדָא. רִבִּי חִזְקִיָּה רִבִּי יִרְמְיָה בְּשֵׁם רִבִּי יוֹחָנָן כְּמָאן דְּאָמַר יֵשׁ קִנְייָן לְגוֹי בְּאֶרֶץ יִשְׂרָאֵל לְפוֹטְרוֹ מִן הַמַּעְשְׂרוֹת. בְּרַם כְּמָאן דְּאָמַר אֵין קִנְייָן לְגוֹי בְּאֶרֶץ יִשְׂרָאֵל לְפוֹטְרוֹ מִן הַמַּעְשְׂרוֹת עֲלֵיהּ רִבִּי לָעְזָר שְׁאִיל וְאֵין לוֹ קִנְייַן נְכָסִים. רִבִּי חֲנִינָא בְּשֵׁם רִבִּי פִּינְחָס אַף קַדְמִיָיתָא עַל דְּרִבִּי יוֹסֵי מַקְשֵׁי דְּרִבִּי יוֹסֵי בְּשֵׁם רִבִּי יוֹחָנָן כְּמָאן דְּאָמַר אֵין קִנְייָן לְגוֹי בְּאֶרֶץ יִשְׂרָאֵל לְפוֹטְרוֹ מִן הַמַּעְשְׂרוֹת. בְּרַם כְּמָאן דְּאָמַר יֵשׁ קִנְייָן לְגוֹי בְּאֶרֶץ יִשְׂרָאֵל לְפוֹטְרוֹ מִן הַמַּעְשְׂרוֹת עֲלֵיהּ רִבִּי לָעְזָר שָׁאַל וְאֵין לוֹ קִנְייַן נְכָסִים.

Rebbi Eleazar[135] asked, does he not acquire movables? Not on the last statement this was asked, but on the following: Rebbi Ḥizqiah, Rebbi Jeremiah, in the name of Rebbi Joḥanan: According to him who says that a Gentile may acquire real estate in the Land of Israel to free it from tithes. But according to him who says that a Gentile may not acquire real estate in the Land of Israel to free it from tithes, on this Rebbi Eleazar asked, does he not acquire movables[136]? Rebbi Ḥanina in the name of Rebbi Phineas, also on the preceding one, on that of Rebbi Yose he asked: Rebbi Yose in the name of Rebbi Joḥanan: According to him who says that a Gentile may not acquire real estate in the Land of Israel to free it from tithes. But according to him who says that a Gentile may acquire real estate in the Land of Israel to free it from tithes, on this Rebbi Eleazar asked, does he not acquire movables[137]?

135 As student and colleague of R. Joḥanan, he certainly cannot quarrel with Rebbis Ḥizqiah and Ḥanina, but he must question R. Joḥanan directly. In the first version, one accepts only the statement of R. Ḥizqiah as authoritative; in the second version, one accepts both statements of R. Joḥanan as genuine but referring to different parts of the Mishnah, as explained above.

136 It cannot be said that even abandoned property is subject to tithes since everybody agrees that the yield of the Land legally belongs to the Gentile owner and his declaration of abandoned property is unquestionably valid in Jewish law.

137 Since the produce belongs to the Gentile according to everybody (*Demaï* 5:9), even for R. Meïr, and certainly for RR. Jehudah and Simeon, there cannot be an obligation for heave and tithes on any *peah*, against the statement in the Mishnah. Since the question is not answered, R. Eleazar's position is accepted.

(fol. 18a) **משנה ז**: אֵי זֶהוּ לֶקֶט הַנּוֹשֵׁר בִּשְׁעַת הַקְּצִירָה. הָיָה קוֹצֵר קָצַר מְלֹא יָדָיו תָּלַשׁ מְלֹא קוּמְצוֹ. הִכָּהוּ קוֹץ וְנָפַל לָאָרֶץ הֲרֵי זֶה שֶׁל בַּעַל הַבַּיִת. תּוֹךְ הַיָּד וְתוֹךְ הַמַּגָּל לָעֲנִיִּים. אַחַר הַיָּד וְאַחַר הַמַּגָּל לְבַעַל הַבַּיִת. רֹאשׁ הַיָּד וְרֹאשׁ הַמַּגָּל רִבִּי יִשְׁמָעֵאל אוֹמֵר לָעֲנִיִּים. רִבִּי עֲקִיבָה אוֹמֵר לְבַעַל הַבַּיִת.

Mishnah 7[138]: What are gleanings? That which falls down at harvest time. If in harvesting he cut what his hands grabbed, or he uprooted a handful, when he was stung by a thorn and it fell to the ground, this belongs to the owner[139]. From inside the hand and/or[140] inside the sickle it belongs to the poor[141]. From the back of his hand or the back of the sickle, it belongs to the owner. From fingertips and the tip of the sickle, Rebbi Ismael says, to the poor, Rebby Aqiba says, to the owner.

138 From here to Mishnah 5:6 follow the rules of gleanings.

139 Anything falling down in an accident is not "gleanings from your harvest." This reason is given in an extended version of the text of the Mishnah in *Sifra Qedošim* 2:5. The somewhat awkward wording היה קוצר קצר is also used there; it cannot be emended away.

140 Whether to translate "and" or "or" is discussed in the Halakhah.

141 Since this falls down in the course of a professional harvest. From the back of hand or sickle it is accidental. From the tip it is a matter of opinion.

(fol. 18c) **הלכה ז**: תַּנֵּי לֶקֶט קְצִירְךָ לֹא כָל־הַקּוֹצֵר בְּיָדוֹ. וְדִכְוָותֵיהּ פֶּרֶט כַּרְמְךָ לֹא כָל־הַפּוֹרֵט בְּיָדוֹ.

Halakha 7: It was stated: The gleanings of your harvest, not what anybody harvests with his bare hands[142]. And equally, the dropped berries of your vineyard, and not what drops from hand-picking[143].

142 See Chapter 3, Halakhah 3: The gathering of your harvest, not the gathering of your plucking.

143 If single berries are plucked rather than whole bunches cut off with a knife.

רַב כַּהֲנָא וְרַב תַּחְלִיפָא. חַד אָמַר תּוֹךְ הַיָּד וְתוֹךְ הַמַּגָּל. וְחָרָנָה אָמַר תּוֹךְ הַיָּד וַאֲפִילוּ לְאַחַר הַמַּגָּל.

Rav Cahana and Rav Taḥlifa[144]. One said, both from inside the hand and inside the sickle; the other one said, from inside the hand, even if it is from behind the sickle.

144 This probably should be *Rebbi* Taḥlifa, a colleague of Rav Cahana (II) in the yeshivah of Rebbi Joḥanan.

(fol. 18a) **משנה ח**: חוֹרְרֵי הַנְּמָלִים שֶׁבְּתוֹךְ הַקָּמָה הֲרֵי זֶה שֶׁל בַּעַל הַבַּיִת. וְשֶׁל אַחַר הַקּוֹצְרִים הָעֶלְיוֹנִים לָעֲנִיִּים וְהַתַּחְתּוֹנִים לְבַעַל הַבַּיִת. רִבִּי מֵאִיר אוֹמֵר הַכֹּל לָעֲנִיִּים שֶׁסָּפֵק לֶקֶט לֶקֶט.

Mishnah 8: Antholes inside the standing produce belong to the owner[145]. In those appearing after the harvesters left, the tops are for the poor[146] and the bottoms for the owner. Rebbi Meïr says, everything is for the poor because gleanings in doubt[147] are gleanings.

145 I. e., the kernels taken by the ants and stored in their holes.

146 The kernels which can be seen from the outside should have been picked up at harvest time; those for which the hole has to be dug out are out of the reach of the poor and, hence, belong to the owner.

147 Since the lower lying grains become visible when the upper layer is taken, the boundary between upper and lower grains is not fixable and, hence, cannot legally exist.

(fol. 18c) **הלכה ח**: רִבִּי יְהוּדָה בְּשֵׁם רִבִּי שְׁמוּאֵל הָעֶלְיוֹנִים לָעֲנִיִּים בִּלְבָנִים וְהַתַּחְתּוֹנִים לְבַעַל הַבַּיִת בִּירוֹקִין. רִבִּי מֵאִיר אוֹמֵר הַכֹּל לָעֲנִיִּים שֶׁסָּפֵק לֶקֶט לֶקֶט שֶׁאִי אֶפְשַׁר לְגוֹרֶן לָצֵאת בְּלֹא יְרוֹקִין.

Halakha 8: Rebbi Jehudah in the name of Rebbi Samuel[148]: The tops are for the poor, viz., white ones[149]. The bottom ones are for the owner, viz., green ones. Rebbi Meïr says, everything is for the poor because gleanings in doubt are gleanings, since no threshing will end without some green ones[150].

148 It probably should read: Rav Jehudah in the name of Samuel. It is very unlikely that the reference should be to the fourth generation Rebbi Jehudah (Yudan) and the third generation Rebbi Samuel, student of Rebbi Abbahu.

149 Completely dry kernels belong to the poor if they were not picked up before the surrounding grain was

harvested. Green kernels were taken by the ants before the harvest and, therefore, are not possibly gleanings that fell down during harvest time. Hence, "top" and "bottom" do not have to be taken literally.

150 Accordingly, all green kernels lying on the ground also belong to the poor. Rebbi Meïr considers an event as legally possible even if the probability of the event is much smaller than 50%; the statement "that it is impossible" is not to be taken too literally.

אָמַר רִבִּי יוֹחָנָן[151] דְּרִבִּי יְהוּדָה בֶּן חַגְרָא הִיא. דְּתַנֵּי גֵּר שֶׁנִּתְגַּייֵר וְהָיְתָה לוֹ קָמָה נִקְצֶרֶת עַד שֶׁלֹּא נִתְגַּייֵר פָּטוּר מִשֶּׁנִּתְגַּייֵר חַייָב. וְאִם סָפֵק פָּטוּר. רִבִּי יְהוּדָה בֶּן חַגְרָא מְחַייֵב. רִבִּי שִׁמְעוֹן בֶּן לָקִישׁ אָמַר דִּבְרֵי הַכֹּל הִיא יִשְׂרָאֵל שֶׁעִיקָּרוֹ חַייָב סְפֵיקוֹ חַייָב וְגוֹי שֶׁעִיקָּרוֹ פָּטוּר סְפֵיקוֹ פָּטוּר. אָמַר רִבִּי יוֹחָנָן כָּךְ הָיָה רִבִּי מֵאִיר מֵשִׁיב אֶת רִבִּי יְהוּדָה בֶּן חַגְרָא אֵין אַתְּ מוֹדֶה לִי שֶׁסָּפֵק לֶקֶט לֶקֶט. רִבִּי שִׁמְעוֹן בֶּן לָקִישׁ כָּךְ הָיָה מֵשִׁיב רִבִּי מֵאִיר אֶת הַחֲכָמִים אֵין אַתֶּם מוֹדִים לִי שֶׁסָּפֵק לֶקֶט לֶקֶט.

Rebbi Johanan said: It is by Rebbi Jehudah ben Hagra[152], as it was stated: "A Gentile who converted but had cut grain before he converted is free[153]; after he converted, he is obligated. If it is in doubt, he is free. Rebbi Jehudah ben Hagra obligates him[154]." Rebbi Simeon ben Laqish said, it[155] agrees with everybody: A Jew, who is obligated in principle, is also obligated in doubtful cases; a Gentile, who is not obligated in principle, is not obligated in doubt. Rebbi Johanan said: So did Rebbi Meïr argue with Rebbi Jehudah ben Hagra, do you not agree with me that gleanings in doubt are gleanings[156]? Rebbi Simeon ben Laqish: So did Rebbi Meïr argue with the Sages, do you not agree with me that gleanings in doubt are gleanings[157]?

151 Reading of the Rome ms.; the Venice print has "R. Jehudah"; no R. Jehudah is ever mentioned as opponent of R. Simeon ben Laqish.

152 In the parallel in Babli *Ḥulin* 134a, he appears as R. Jehudah bar Agra (from Kefar Acco), a Tanna of the fourth generation. There in *Ḥulin*, R. Jehudah ben Agra explicitly formulates that *peah*, gleanings, and forgotten sheaves in case of doubt belong to the poor, confirming the interpretation of R. Joḥanan.

153 From the obligation of gleanings, even if he converted before the grain was bound into sheaves. The poor may collect gleanings only after the cut grain is bound into sheaves.

154 If he is Jewish at the moment the field is ready to be searched by the poor, he cannot collect gleanings after his conversion.

155 Even Rebbi Meïr will agree with the Sages against R. Jehudah ben Ḥagra since our question is not one of doubt but of principle.

156 And you obligate the convert because of a legal doubt, viz., whether the obligation of leaving the gleanings is incurred at the moment of cutting, in which case there would be no obligation, or at the moment the field is abandoned to the poor, in which case the convert is obligated.

157 But the case of R. Jehudah ben Ḥagra is not comparable to that of the Mishnah.

וּמְנַיִין שֶׁסָּפֵק לֶקֶט לֶקֶט. רִבִּי שְׁמוּאֵל בַּר נַחְמָן בְּשֵׁם רִבִּי יוֹנָתָן עָנִי וְעָשִׁיר הַצְדִּיקוּהוּ בְּמַתְּנוֹתָיו. רִבִּי שִׁמְעוֹן בֶּן לָקִישׁ בְּשֵׁם בַּר קַפָּרָא לֹא תַטֶּה מִשְׁפַּט אֶבְיוֹנְךָ בְּרִיבוֹ. בְּרִיבוֹ אֵין אַתְּ מַטֵּהוּ. אֲבָל מַטֵּהוּ אַתְּ בְּמַתְּנוֹתָיו. אָמַר רִבִּי יוֹחָנָן וְכֹה זֹכֶה הוּא מַה שֶּׁשִּׁינָּה לָנוּ רִבִּי תַּעֲזוֹב הַנַּח לִפְנֵיהֶן מִשֶּׁלָּךְ. אָמַר רִבִּי לָא כְּתִיב לַגֵּר לַיָּתוֹם וְלָאַלְמָנָה יִהְיֶה בֵּין מִדִּידָךְ בֵּין מִדִּידֵיהּ הַב לֵיהּ.

From where that gleanings in doubt are gleanings? Rebbi Samuel ben Naḥman in the name of Rebbi Jonathan: "Poor and rich, justify him[158]" in his gifts. Rebbi Simeon ben Laqish in the name of Bar Qappara: (*Ex.* 23:6) "Do not bend the lawsuit of your destitute." In his lawsuit, you may not bend[159], but you may bend for him in his gifts[160]. Rebbi Joḥanan said, he[161] acquires in this case, as Rebbi instructed us (*Lev.* 19:10, 23:22): "abandon," put something before him of your own[162]. Rebbi La said, it is written (*Deut.* 24:19-21): "It shall be the sojourner's, the orphan's, and the widow's;" give him both from yours and from his!

158 There is no such verse in Scripture. The consensus of the commentators is that it should read: (*Ps.* 82:3) "Do justice for the poor and needy." One does justice in also giving him the gifts that are in doubt.

159 The judge may not say: His opponent has deep pockets; let me rule for the poor; then he will need no public assistance.

160 To rule for him also in doubtful cases.

161 The poor acquires as his right, not as a possibility as in the previous argument.

162 The term "abandon" first refers to the gifts that belong to the poor as of right; the second mention in the same verse refers to the doubtful cases when one has to renounce his rights; a similar argument is found in *Sifra Qedošim* 2:7. The same applies for the triple expression quoted by R. La. It is clear from here that Practice has to follow R. Meïr; this is also the decision of Maimonides (*Mattenot Aniïm* 4:9).

גדיש פרק חמישי

(fol. 18c) **משנה א**: גָּדִישׁ שֶׁלֹּא לוּקַט תַּחְתָּיו כָּל־הַנּוֹגְעוֹת בָּאָרֶץ הֲרֵי הוּא שֶׁל עֲנִיִּים. הָרוּחַ שֶׁפִּיזְּרָה אֶת הָעֳמָרִין אוֹמְדִין אוֹתָהּ כַּמָּה לֶקֶט הִיא רְאוּיָה לַעֲשׂוֹת וְנוֹתֵן לָעֲנִיִּים. רַבָּן שִׁמְעוֹן בֶּן גַּמְלִיאֵל אוֹמֵר נוֹתֵן לָעֲנִיִּים נְפָלָה.

Mishnah 1: For a grain stack under which gleanings were not collected, all ears that touch the ground are for the poor[1]. If the wind dispersed any sheaves[2], one estimates what amount of gleanings that would have yielded, and he gives that to the poor. Rabban Simeon ben Gamliel says, he gives to the poor the average fall[3].

1 Since gleanings cannot be taken from under the stack, the farmer robbed the poor by not letting them search before he used that space. He is punished by an extreme application of the principle that "gleanings in doubt belong to the poor."

2 In this case, the farmer has the obvious right to rake the dispersed stalks together. But thereby he also takes the gleanings for the poor and has to make up for this.

3 Which has been determined once and for all and is explained in the Halakhah.

(fol. 18d) **הלכה א**: הָכָא אַתְּ אָמַר אוֹמְדִין אוֹתָהּ כַּמָּה לֶקֶט רְאוּיָה לַעֲשׂוֹת וְנוֹתֵן לָעֲנִיִּים. וְכָה אַתְּ אָמַר כָּל־הַנּוֹגְעוֹת בָּאָרֶץ הֲרֵי הוּא שֶׁל עֲנִיִּים. רַבִּי אַבָּהוּ בְשֵׁם רַבִּי יוֹחָנָן קְנַס קָנְסוּ בוֹ שֶׁגָּדַשׁ עַל גַּבֵּי לֵיקֶטָן שֶׁל עֲנִיִּים. עַד כְּדוֹן מֵזִיד אֲפִילוּ שׁוֹגֵג אֲפִילוּ כְּרִיכוֹת אֲפִילוּ חִטִּים עַל גַּבֵּי שְׂעוֹרִין אֲפִילוּ גָּדְשׁוּ אֲחֵרִים חוּץ מִדַּעְתּוֹ וַאֲפִילוּ קָרָא לָעֲנִיִּים וְלֹא בָאוּ.

Halakhah 1: Here you say that "one estimates what amount of gleanings that would have yielded, and he gives that to the poor." But there, you say "all ears that touch the ground are for the poor." Rebbi Abbahu in the name of Rebbi Johanan: They fined him because he put the stack on the gleanings of the poor. That is for intentional transgression; it is also for unintentional error, for sheaves, for a wheat stack on top of barley, even if it was stacked by others without his knowledge, even if he called the poor and they did not come[4].

4 The translation follows the interpretation of Maimonides (*Mattenot Aniїm* 4:7), that this is a declarative sentence, a rule promulgated by the Court without exceptions. One might also read the sentence as a question: are these also for the poor? Since the question is not answered, the practical answer would be in the negative.

רִבִּי אִימִּי בְּשֵׁם רִבִּי שִׁמְעוֹן בֶּן לָקִישׁ דְּבֵית שַׁמַּאי הִיא דְּבֵית שַׁמַּאי אוֹמְרִין הֶבְקֵר לָעֲנִיִּים הֶבְקֵר. אָמַר לֵיהּ רִבִּי יָסָא שָׁמַעְנוּ שֶׁהוּא פָּטוּר מִמַּעְשְׂרוֹת שֶׁהֶבְקֵר בֵּית דִּין הֶבְקֵר. כְּתִיב וְכָל־אֲשֶׁר לֹא יָבֹא לִשְׁלֹשֶׁת הַיָּמִים כַּעֲצַת הַשָּׂרִים וְהַזְּקֵנִים יָחֳרַם כָּל־רְכוּשׁוֹ. מְנַיִין שֶׁהוּא פָּטוּר מִן הַמַּעְשְׂרוֹת. רִבִּי יוֹנָתָן בְּרֵיהּ דְּרִבִּי יִצְחָק בַּר אָחָא שָׁמַע לָהּ מִן הָדָא אֵין מְעַבְּרִין אֶת הַשָּׁנָה לֹא בִשְׁבִיעִית וְלֹא בְמוֹצָאֵי שְׁבִיעִית וְאִם עִבְּרוּהָ הֲרֵי זוֹ מְעוּבֶּרֶת. בְּחֹדֶשׁ אֶחָד שֶׁהוּא מוֹסִיף לֹא פָטוּר הוּא מִמַּעְשְׂרוֹת. עַד כְּדוֹן בִּשְׁבִיעִית. מוֹצָאֵי שְׁבִיעִית מְנַיִין. אָמַר רִבִּי אָבוּן שֶׁלֹּא לְרַבּוֹת בְּאִיסּוּר חָדָשׁ.

Rebbi Immi in the name of Rebbi Simeon ben Laqish: This is from the House of Shammai, since the House of Shammai say that property abandoned to the poor is abandoned[5]. Rebbi Yasa said to him: We understand that it is free from tithes because property abandoned by a court order is abandoned[6]. It is written (*Ezra* 10:8): "Anybody who will not come within three days conforming to the decree of the rulers and the elders, all his property shall be devoted to destruction[7]." From where that it[8] is free from tithes? Rebbi Johanan, the son of Rebbi Isaac bar Aḥa[9] understood it from the following[10]: One intercalates[12] years neither in the Sabbatical year, nor in the year following the Sabbatical; but if they did intercalate it is intercalated. The one month he adds, is it not free from tithes[13]? That refers to the Sabbatical year. What about the year after the Sabbatical? Rebbi Abun said, not to prolong the prohibition of new grain[14].

5 As explained in the next Mishnah, we require that the poor be given produce ready for immediate use. While harvested grain becomes subject to heave and tithes only after being gathered into orderly heaps, a farmer who really wants to create problems gives tithes from unthreshed grain. Hence, there already is a potential obligation on the produce after harvesting and the grain which is given in lieu of gleanings should be subject to heave and tithes. On the other hand, abandoned property is not "your harvest," and as such is free from heave and tithes. In Chapter 6, the House of Shammai rule that property abandoned only to the poor, such as *peah* and gleanings and grain given in lieu of *peah* and gleanings, is considered legally abandoned. The House of Hillel disagree and restrict the notion of abandoned property to things abandoned to everybody, rich and poor alike. Since the Mishnah does not require heave and tithes to be given for grain given in lieu of gleanings, it seems to disagree with the House of Hillel who determine our practice.

6 The grain given in lieu of gleanings is given by a decree of the High Court, not by personal choice. Hence, it is legally abandoned.

7 If the decree of the Court did not make the property abandoned, its destruction would have to be considered theft. Since Ezra was a teacher of the Law, his rulings have to be accepted.

From here on to Note 24, the text also appears in *Šeqalim* 1:2.

8 Property abandoned by decree

of court.

9 According to the interpretation of A. Zacut (*Sefer Yoḥasin*) of an unclear note in Babli *Pesaḥim* 114a, R. Isaac bar Aḥa is quoted as "R. Isaac" without a patronymic.

11 A different text, identical in meaning, appears in Tosephta *Sanhedrin* 2:9 and Babli *Sanhedrin* 12a.

12 Since the Jewish year is both lunar and solar, but 12 lunar months are only approximately 254 days, in 19 years there have to be seven intercalary years of 13 months. For details see the author's *Seder Olam* (Jason Aronson, Northvale NJ, 1998).

13 Since the spontaneous growth of the Seventh Year may be taken by everybody, it is not "your harvest" and, hence, free from heave and tithes even if taken by the owner of the land. If the Supreme Court declared the year intercalary against the rules, it is nevertheless a valid 13 months year and all produce is legally abandoned property.

14 New grain may be eaten only after the *Omer* sacrifice on the 16th of Nisan. An intercalation of a month, which always falls in early spring, unnecessarily postpones the harvest of new grain.

רִבִּי זְעִירָא בְשֵׁם רִבִּי אַבָּהוּ הָדָא דְתֵימַר עַד שֶׁלֹּא הִתִּיר רִבִּי לְהָבִיא יָרָק מְחוּצָה לָאָרֶץ לָאָרֶץ. אֲבָל מִשֶּׁהִתִּיר רִבִּי לְהָבִיא יָרָק מְחוּצָה לָאָרֶץ הִיא שְׁבִיעִית הִיא שְׁנֵי שָׁבוּעַ. תַּנֵּי אֵין מְעַבְּרִין אֶת הַשָּׁנָה לֹא בִשְׁבִיעִית אֶלָּא בִשְׁאָר שְׁנֵי שָׁבוּעַ וְאִם עִבְּרוּהָ הֲרֵי זוֹ מְעוּבֶּרֶת. אָמַר רִבִּי מָנָא הָדָא דְתֵימַר בָּרִאשׁוֹנָה שֶׁהָיוּ הַשָּׁנִים כְּסִדְרָן. אֲבָל עַכְשָׁיו שֶׁאֵין הַשָּׁנִים כְּסִדְרָן הִיא שְׁבִיעִית הִיא שְׁנֵי שָׁבוּעַ.

[15]Rebbi Zeïra in the name of Rebbi Abbahu: That is only before Rebbi permitted the importation of vegetables from outside the Land[16]. But after Rebbi permitted the importation of vegetables from outside the Land, the Sabbatical year is as any other year[17]. It was stated: One does not intercalate in the Sabbatical Year but only in other years of a Sabbatical period, but if they did intercalate it is intercalated. Rebbi Mana said, that refers to earlier times when years were in order[18], but now that years are not in order[19], the Sabbatical year is like any other year.

15 This paragraph is an aside, taken from *Šebiït* 6:4, also *Nedarim* 6:13. It explains why our calendar today does not take the Sabbatical year into consideration when determining intercalary months in the 19 year cycle. (Since 19 and 7 are relatively prime, the Sabbatical rules would force seven different calendars to be made!)

16 The soil outside the Land of Israel is unclean (cf. *Amos* 7:17). In former times Jews did not use vegetables from outside the Land since it might have particles of soil still clinging to it. But after the last remnants of the ashes of the red heifer disappeared, these laws became inoperative and it was possible for everybody, even the most scrupulous, to eat imported vegetables. This has to be dated to the times of Rebbi (Jehudah the Prince); cf. commentary to Mishnah *Berakhot* 1:1.

17 Since there is enough food for everybody.

18 Taxes were paid on income, which means that in Sabbatical years the farmer did not have to pay taxes.

19 Now that the government levies taxes on arable land without regard to the actual yield, the farmer has to grow crops on his land even in the Sabbatical year on the authority of R. Mana (*Šebiït* 4:2).

תַּנֵּי שֶׁל בֵּית רַבָּן גַּמְלִיאֵל עִבְּרוּהָ בְמוֹצָאֵי שְׁבִיעִית מִיָּד[20] אָמַר רִבִּי אָבִין מִן הָדָא לֵית אַתְּ שְׁמַע מִינָּהּ כְּלוּם שָׁמוֹר אֶת חֹדֶשׁ הָאָבִיב. שָׁמְרֵהוּ עַד שֶׁיָּבוֹא בְחִידּוּשׁוֹ.

It was stated: The house of Rabban Gamliel intercalated immediately after the end of the Sabbatical year[21]. Rebbi Avin said, from this[22] you do not infer anything. (*Deut.* 16:1) "Watch the spring month." Watch it that it should come in its renewal.

20 Reading of the parallel in *Šeqalim* 1:2, in the Venice print מד.

21 This means that after the destruction of the Temple, the restriction of the year after the Sabbatical was no longer observed.

22 All the previous arguments which prove that the action of the court can free produce from the Biblical obligations of heave and tithes

are not relevant since there is a Biblical obligation to manipulate the calendar so that Passover should fall in the month of the Spring equinox. Hence, the obligation to intercalate is biblical and not rabbinic.

וַיי דָא אֲמַר דָא גָדִישׁ שֶׁלֹּא לוּקַט תַּחְתָּיו. רִבִּי מָנָא בְּשֵׁם רִבִּי שִׁמְעוֹן בֶּן לָקִישׁ דְּבֵית שַׁמַּאי. אָמַר לֵיהּ רִבִּי יָסָא שָׁמַעְנוּ דִבְרֵי הַכֹּל הִיא מִשּׁוּם קְנָס. וּכְבֵית הִלֵּל עֲנִיִּים מְעַשְּׂרִים וְאוֹכְלִין.

What text implies this[23]? "For a grain stack under which gleanings were not collected, . . . " Rebbi Mana in the name of Rebbi Simeon ben Laqish: This is from the House of Shammai. Rebbi Yasa said to him: We understand that according to everybody, this is a fine[24]. Following the House of Hillel, the poor give tithes and eat.

23 Which Mishnah text implies that property decreed ownerless by the court is legally abandoned property.

In *Šeqalim* 1:2, the author of the objection is R. Immi. This is the better text since R. Yasa was a colleague of R. Immi, much earlier than R. Mana.

24 As R. Johanan had said, this is a fine imposed on the farmer and has no connection with the duties imposed on produce. The Mishnah does not say that all ears which touch the ground are gleanings, but that all ears which touch the ground must be abandoned to the poor. Hence, they are not gleanings and are exempt from heave and tithes only for the House of Shammai. (Maimonides follows the earlier opinion of R. Yasa that it is produce abandoned by court order and free from heave and tithes.)

רִבִּי זְעִירָא רִבִּי אַבָּהוּ בְּשֵׁם רִבִּי יוֹחָנָן אַרְבַּעַת קַבִּין לְכוֹר. רִבִּי זְעִירָא בְּעִי קוֹמֵי רִבִּי אַבָּהוּ אַרְבַּעַת קַבִּין לְכוֹר אוֹ לְבֵית כּוֹר. אָמַר לֵיהּ לְבֵית כּוֹר. תַּמָּן תַּנֵּינָן מַה קִיצְבָה כְּרִי אֶלָּה אִם כֵּן יֵשׁ בָּהּ כְּדֵי נִיפְלָה. אָמַר רִבִּי אַבָּהוּ בְּנוֹפֵל לָהּ כְּדֵי לְזוֹרְעָהּ וְכֹא הוּא אָמַר הָכֵן.

[25]Rebbi Zeïra, Rebbi Abbahu in the name of Rebbi Joḥanan: Four *kab* per *kor*[26]. Rebbi Zeïra asked before Rebbi Abbahu: Four *qab* per *kor* or per *bet kor*[27]? He said to him, per *bet kor*. There[28], we have stated: "What is the definition of a heap? Rather, if it is enough to let it fall[29]. Rebbi Abbahu said, enough to let it fall as seed[30]." And here, he says so!

25 Here starts the discussion of the opinion of Rabban Simeon ben Gamliel, that the gleanings of the poor are given as a fixed percentage of the harvest.

26 In the Babli, *Baba Meẓi'a* 105b, this is also given by R. Abbahu; the reading (of an otherwise unattested) "R. Abuh" in the current editions of the Babli is a late printer's error according to *Diqduqe Soferim Baba Meẓi'a* p. 155. A *kor* is 30 *seah* or 180 *qab*.

27 Do you mean 4 *qab* in volume for any *kor* in volume, 1 in 45, or 4 *qab* (about 4.5 U. S. pints) for a field of area 1 *bet kor* = 30 *bet seah* = 30×2500 square cubits = 75'000 square cubits (570.25 acres)? The first option is unlikely because that would make gleanings 2.2% of the harvest, much more than the larger *peah*. Since an ear of grain can be expected to yield at least 15 grains, the second option would mean gleanings of 4 *qab* for at least 2'700 *qab* harvested.

28 Mishnah *Baba Meẓi'a* 9:5: "He who received a field as a sharecropper, and it failed to grow, nevertheless is required to tend it as long as the yield will be sufficient to form one heap. Rebbi Jehudah says: What is the definition of a heap? Rather, if it is enough to drop it." Rashi explains there, "enough to use it as seed." R. Jehudah complains that "heap" cannot be a legal definition [even though R. Abbahu in the Babli, R. Joshua ben Levi in the Yerushalmi (*Baba Meẓi'a* 9:5, fol. 12a), define it as a mound in which a shovel stays upright.]

29 This is the same expression as the one used here by Rabban Simeon ben Gamliel. The Babli *Baba Meẓi'a* 105b declares, again in the name of R. Joḥanan, that this means four *qab* per *bet kor*.

30 I. e., the field produces at least as much grain as was used for sowing. This is also R. Abbahu's definition in *Baba Meẓi'a*; it is much more than the נפלה defined here. How may R. Abbahu give two different definitions for the same legal expression? The question is

not answered. Maybe this is the reason why Maimonides, in his Code, does not follow Rabban Simeon ben Gamliel, even though his opinions are almost always the practice to be followed.

(fol. 18c) **משנה ב:** שִׁיבּוֹלֶת שֶׁבְּקָצִיר וְרֹאשָׁהּ מַגִּיעַ לַקָּמָה אִם נִקְצֶרֶת עִם הַקָּמָה הֲרֵי הִיא שֶׁל בַּעַל הַבַּיִת וְאִם לָאו הֲרֵי הִיא שֶׁל עֲנִיִּים. שִׁיבּוֹלֶת שֶׁל לֶקֶט שֶׁנִּתְעָרְבָה בְגָדִישׁ מְעַשֵּׂר שִׁיבּוֹלֶת וְנוֹתֵן לוֹ. אָמַר רַבִּי אֱלִיעֶזֶר וְכִי הֵיאַךְ הֶעָנִי הַזֶּה מַחֲלִיף דָּבָר שֶׁלֹּא בָא לִרְשׁוּתוֹ אֶלָּא מְזַכֶּה אֶת הֶעָנִי בְּכָל־הַגָּדִישׁ וּמְעַשֵּׂר שִׁיבּוֹלֶת אַחַת וְנוֹתֵן לוֹ.

Mishnah 2[31]: A single ear on the field to be harvested and its head reaches to the grain that is still standing, if it can be cut together with standing grain, it belongs to the owner, otherwise it is for the poor[32]. An ear of gleanings that was mixed up in a stack of grain, he gives tithes for one ear and gives it to him[33]. Rebbi Eliezer said, how can the poor man exchange something that never was in his possession[34]? But he has to give the poor rights to the entire stack[35]; then he gives tithes for one ear and gives it to him.

31 Here start the laws of forgotten sheaves and other forgotten harvests.

32 If it can not be cut in one movement of the sickle together with some stalks of grain still standing in bunches, it is like a forgotten sheaf and one may not return to take it.

33 Since the farmer is required to give to the poor something that may be consumed right away, after it is mixed up in the stack it cannot be given away until at least the heave of the tithe has been given. Hence, one ear has to be given to the Cohen as heave, the other one to the poor in lieu of gleanings. In this sentence, "he" is the farmer and

"him" refers to the poor.

34 The procedure of the first Tanna does not work, since the poor man does not receive gleanings but grain in lieu of gleanings. But since the gleanings never were in the poor man's possession, the poor person has no right to exchange his gleanings for the stalk which the owner gives to him and if the owner later uses that ear of gleanings in his stack he still robs the poor.

35 This is known as "a gift on condition that it must be returned," which legally is a gift as long as it is with the recipient. In our case, the poor has to get possession of the stack only long enough to accept any other stalk in lieu of the gleaning he should be given; then the stack reverts to the owner and now the latter may give the heave of the tithe to the Cohen and a stalk to the poor.

(fol. 18d) **הלכה ב**: אֵי זוּ הִיא קָמָה שֶׁהִיא מַצֶּלֶת אֶת הַקָּמָה. אָמַר רִבִּי יוֹחָנָן כְּהָדָא דְתַנֵּינָן שִׁבּוֹלֶת שֶׁבְּקָצִיר וְרֹאשָׁהּ מַגִּיעַ לְקָמָה. אָמַר רִבִּי יוֹסֵי וְהוּא שֶׁיְּהֵא הַקָּצִיר סוֹבְבָהּ וְהוּא שֶׁיְּהֵא רֹאשָׁהּ מַגִּיעַ לַקָּמָה וְהוּא שֶׁתְּהֵא יְכוֹלָה לְהִיקָּצֵר אִם הַקָּמָה. הָיְתָה יְכוֹלָה לְהִיקָּצֵר אִם הַקָּמָה וְאֵין הַקָּמָה יְכוֹלָה לְהִיקָּצֵר עִמָּהּ נִיצּוֹלֶת. הָיוּ שְׁתַּיִם הַפְּנִימִית יְכוֹלָה לְהִיקָּצֵר עִם הַקָּמָה הַחִיצוֹנָה וְאֵין הַחִיצוֹנָה יְכוֹלָה לְהִיקָּצֵר עִם הַקָּמָה הַפְּנִימִית נִיצּוֹלֶת וּמַצֶּלֶת.

Halakhah 2: What is standing grain that saves standing grain[36]? Rebbi Johanan said, the same as we have stated: a single ear on the field to be harvested and its head reaches to the standing grain. Rebbi Yose said, only if the harvested field surrounds it[37], and only if its head reaches the standing grain, and only if it can be cut together with standing grain. If it can be cut together with standing grain but standing grain cannot be cut with it[38], it is saved. If there were two, the inner one can be cut together with the outermost standing grain, but the outer one cannot be cut with the standing grain; the inner one is saved and saves[39].

36 In Mishnah 6:7 it is stated that standing grain saves other standing grain which the farmer forgot to cut. The question is, how far away may an entire uncut patch be from the main uncut field that it should not be forgotten? The answer is the same as in our Mishnah, that the head of one of the stalks of the forgotten patch may be bent, without breaking the stem, to touch the as yet uncut part of the field.

37 Otherwise, it never can be counted as forgotten. In contrast to the next two conditions which restrict the case in which it is not forgotten, this one restricts the possible applications of the rules of forgotten produce.

38 If the angle of the sickle with the ground is too large when the harvester stands close to the unharvested grain, the harvester cannot start cutting the single stalk and reach the standing patch with one sweep of the sickle.

39 It saves the outer one if the outer one could be cut together with the inner one and the inner one could be cut together with standing grain. Hence, the notion of being saved is transitive for any row of stalks that could be cut in pairs.

אָמַר רִבִּי הוֹשַׁעְיָא רוֹמֵס הָיִיתִי זֵיתִים עִם רִבִּי חִייָא הַגָּדוֹל וְאָמַר לִי כָּל־זַיִת שֶׁאַתְּ יָכוֹל לִפְשׁוֹט יָדְךָ וְלִיטְלוֹ אֵינוֹ שִׁכְחָה. אָמַר רִבִּי יוֹחָנָן כֵּיוָן שֶׁעָבַר עָלָיו וּשְׁכָחוֹ הֲרֵי זֶה שִׁכְחָה. מַתְנִיתָא פְלִיגָא עַל רִבִּי הוֹשַׁעְיָא שִׁבּוֹלֶת שֶׁל קָצִיר וְרֹאשָׁהּ מַגִּיעַ לַקָּמָה. שִׁבּוֹלֶת שֶׁבְּקָצִיר אֵינוֹ יָכוֹל לִפְשׁוֹט יָדוֹ וְלִיטְלָהּ. רִבִּי לָא בְשֵׁם רִבִּי הוֹשַׁעְיָא בְּאוּמָן הַשֵּׁנִי אָמְרוּ.

Rebbi Hoshaia said, when I was mashing olives with the great Rebbi Ḥiyya, he said to me: Any olive that you can reach when stretching out your hand is not forgotten[40]. Rebbi Joḥanan said, if he passed it over and forgot it, it is forgotten[41]. The Mishnah disagrees with Rebbi Hoshaia: A single ear on the field to be harvested and its head reaches to the grain. Can you not stretch out your hand and take a single ear on the harvested field[42]? Rebbi Illai in the name of Rebbi Hoshaia: They said that about the second row[43].

40 After shaking the olive tree you may go around over all branches you worked on and take the olives still on the tree. It is only when you move your ladder that the remainder becomes property of the poor.

41 If in his mind he is finished with one branch, he may not return to it.

42 The condition that the ear must touch the standing stalks is certainly much more restrictive than that a harvester, standing in front of the grain, cannot pluck by hand on the other side.

43 The Mishnah speaks of a stalk left over from cutting the first row. If in harvesting the second row one returns to the place of that ear, it is as when in plucking leftover olives one returns to a harvested spot after moving the ladder and then even R. Ḥiyya agrees that this is forgotten property.

דָּבָר שֶׁהוּא רָאוּי לְהַצִּיל[44] וּשְׁכָחוֹ מַהוּ שֶׁיֵּעָשֶׂה שִׁכְחָה. נִישְׁמְעִינָהּ מִן הָדָא עִימֵּר אֶת הָרִאשׁוֹן וְאֶת הַשֵּׁנִי וְאֶת הַשְּׁלִישִׁי וְשָׁכַח אֶת הָרְבִיעִי. אִית תְּנָיֵי תַּנֵּי אִם נָטַל אֶת הַחֲמִישִׁי הֲרֵי זוּ שִׁכְחָה. וְאִית תְּנָיֵי תַּנֵּי אִם שָׁהָא לִיטּוֹל הַחֲמִישִׁי הֲרֵי זוּ שִׁכְחָה. אָמַר רִבִּי בּוּן בַּר חִיָּיא מָאן דְּאָמַר נָטַל אֶת הַחֲמִישִׁי בְּשֶׁיֵּשׁ שָׁם שִׁישִּׁי. מָאן דְּאָמַר אִם שָׁהָא לִיטּוֹל אֶת הַחֲמִישִׁי בְּשֶׁאֵין שָׁם שִׁישִּׁי. אִם עַד שֶׁלֹּא נָטַל אֶת הַחֲמִישִׁי לֹא נִרְאֶה לוֹ הָרְבִיעִית לִידוֹן כְּשׁוּרָה. הָדָא אָמְרָה דָּבָר שֶׁהוּא רָאוּי לְהַצִּיל וּשְׁכָחוֹ הֲרֵי הוּא שִׁכְחָה.

Can something that is apt to be saved but was forgotten become legally forgotten? Let us hear from the following: "When he removed[45] the first, second, and third sheaves[46] but forgot[47] the fourth, some state: If he took away the fifth one, it (the fourth) becomes legally forgotten, but some state: If he waited long enough that he could have taken away the fifth one, it becomes legally forgotten." Rebbi Avin bar Ḥiyya said, he who says, "if he removed the fifth one," (speaks of the case) where there is a sixth one[48], but he who says, "if he waited long enough that he could have removed the fifth one," (speaks of the case) where there is no sixth one[49]. Before he took away the fifth one, would not the fourth one be apt to be considered starting a row[50]? That means that something that is apt to be saved but was forgotten can become legally forgotten.

44 The vocalization of this word is tentative. Z. Frankel notes that probably this is one of the many scribal mix-ups of י for ו and one should read a *nif'al* לְהִצּוֹל; this form is translated.

45 עימר as a verbal form "removing the sheaf" is defined by Rashi in *Šabbat* 127a. R. S. Lieberman points out that this parallels Biblical דִּשֵּׁן "removed the ashes", from the noun דשן "ashes."

46 He not only bound them but he also removed them to a storage place or threshing floor. This statement puts the standard row of sheaves at three sheaves. Hence, the full second row would be sheaves 4,5,6.

47 To remove the fourth after it was bound.

48 Because sheaves in a row are saved by the next sheaf just as stalks in a row are saved by the next stalk. Hence, the fourth can become legally forgotten only if the fifth, which saves it from being legally forgotten, is removed.

49 Since there is no row of three sheaves, they will be taken to be removed individually and not as a row. It suffices that the fifth could have been finished and removed.

50 If there are six sheaves, the fourth does not become legally abandoned until the sheaf which saves it is removed.

דָּבָר שֶׁהוּא[51] רָאוּי לְהַצִּיל וּשְׁכָחוֹ מַהוּ שֶׁיֵּעָשֶׂה שִׁכְחָה. נִישְׁמְעִינָהּ מִן הָדָא סְאָה תְבוּאָה עֲקוּרָה וּסְאָה שֶׁאֵינָהּ עֲקוּרָה וְתַצִּיל עֲקוּרָה אֶת שֶׁאֵינָהּ עֲקוּרָה. הָדָא אָמְרָה דָּבָר שֶׁהוּא רָאוּי לְהַצִּיל וְשָׁכַח הֲרֵי הוּא שִׁכְחָה. אָמַר רִבִּי יוֹנָה תִּיפְתָּר בְּקוֹצֵר שׁוּרָה וּמְעַמֵּר שׁוּרָה וּכְבָר שָׁכַח אֶת הַקָּמָה עַד שֶׁלֹּא יִשְׁכַּח אֶת הָעוֹמָרִין.

Can something that is apt to save but was forgotten become legally forgotten? Let us hear from the following[52]: "One *seah* of cut grain and one *seah* of uncut grain." Here the cut grain should save the uncut grain[53]. That means that something that is apt to save, but was forgotten, can become legally forgotten. Rebbi Jonah[54] said, explain it if he was cutting and removing the sheaves row by row[55]. He already forgot the standing grain before he might forget the sheaves.

51 Reading of the Rome manuscript. The Venice print has שאינו which is contradicted by the last sentence of the paragraph.

52 Mishnah 6:6 reads: "Standing grain in the volume on two *seah* (about .9 cubic feet) cannot be legally forgotten." Then Mishnah 6:8 adds: "One *seah* of cut grain and one *seah* of uncut grain do not combine." That means, both of them may become legally forgotten.

53 If they are contiguous and would combine. In Halakhah 6:8 it is pointed out that Mishnah 6:8 seems to follow the ruling of Rabban Gamliel in Mishnah 6:5 that sheaves which add up to a volume of 2 *seah* are exempt from the law of forgotten sheaves. Then there is no reason why cut and uncut grain should not be combined.

54 In Halakhah 6:8, "Rebbi Jonathan." The reading here is the more likely one since Rebbi Jonathan is a very early Amora.

55 The field contains much more than two rows of a *seah* each. Hence, the two do not have to be adjacent in space or time and the Mishnah has no implication for our question.

כֵּיצַד הוּא עוֹשֶׂה. מֵבִיא שְׁתֵּי שִׁבּוֹלִים וְאוֹמֵר אִם לֶקֶט הִיא הֲרֵי זֶה יָפֶה וְאִם לָאו הֲרֵי מַעְשְׂרוֹתֶיהָ קְבוּעִין בְּזוּ וְנוֹתֵן לוֹ אֶת הָרִאשׁוֹנָה וְחָשׁ לוֹמַר שֶׁמָּא אוֹתָהּ שֶׁקָּבַע בָּהּ מַעְשְׂרוֹת לֶקֶט הוּא. אָמַר רִבִּי יוֹנָה מֵבִיא שְׁתֵּי שִׁבּוֹלִים וְאוֹמֵר אִם לֶקֶט הוּא זֶה הֲרֵי יָפֶה וְאִם לָאו הֲרֵי מַעְשְׂרוֹתֶיהָ קְבוּעִין בְּזוּ וְנוֹתֵן לוֹ אֶת אַחַת מֵהֶן.

How does he do it[56]? He brings two ears and says: If this one is gleanings, all is fine; but if not, then its tithes are contained in the other one, and he gives him[57] the first one. Do we not have to worry that the one used to contain tithes in it was gleanings? Rebbi Jonah said, he brings two ears and says: If this one is gleanings, all is fine; but if not, then its tithes are contained in the other one, and he gives him one of them[58].

56 Here starts the discussion of the second sentence of the Mishnah, the requirement that the farmer give tithes before he delivers the replacement for the gleanings to the poor. The problem is that heave and tithes can be given only from produce subject to the laws of heave and tithes. Gleanings are exempt from these laws and, therefore, cannot be used as either heave or tithes.

57 The poor person. The other one is given to the priest.

58 He must treat the two ears equally and make the declaration twice. He then is restricted to give the ear only to a poor person who may eat tithes, i. e., a Levite or a Cohen. The other ear is then to be given as tithes, not necesarily to a poor person. [Interpretation of this elliptic statement given by R. David ben Zimra to Maimonides, *Mattenot Aniïm* 4:10.]

רִבִּי אַבָּהוּ בְּשֵׁם רִבִּי שִׁמְעוֹן בֶּן לָקִישׁ דְּרִבִּי יוֹסֵי הִיא דְּתַנֵּינָן תַּמָּן שֶׁרִבִּי יוֹסֵי אוֹמֵר כָּל־שֶׁחִילוּפָיו בְּיַד כֹּהֵן פָּטוּר מִן הַמַּתָּנוֹת. וְרִבִּי מֵאִיר מְחַייֵב. אָמַר רִבִּי בָּא דִּבְרֵי רִבִּי יוֹסֵי צָרִיךְ לְזַכּוֹתוֹ לְכֹהֵן. אָמַר רִבִּי יוֹסֵי הָדָא דְּרִבִּי בָּא פְּלִיגָא עַל דְּרִבִּי שִׁמְעוֹן בֶּן לָקִישׁ דְּתַנֵּינָן תַּמָּן אֶלָּא מְזַכֶּה אֶת הֶעָנִי בְּגָדִישׁ וּמְעַשֵּׂר שִׁיבּוֹלֶת אַחַת וְנוֹתֵן לוֹ. אָמַר רִבִּי בָּא דִּבְרֵי רִבִּי יוֹסֵי צָרִיךְ לְזַכּוֹתוֹ לְכֹהֵן הוֹי לֵית הִיא דְּרִבִּי יוֹסֵי. אָמַר רִבִּי מָנָא כָּל־גַּרְמָהּ אָמַר דְּהִיא דְּרִבִּי יוֹסֵי. תְּנָייָא קוֹמָייָא סָבְרֵי מֵימַר אֵינוֹ מְזַכֶּה אֶת הֶעָנִי בְּכָל־הַגָּדִישׁ אֶלָּא שִׁבּוֹלֶת אַחַת. הַתְּנָייָא אַחֲרָייָא סָבְרֵי מֵימַר מְזַכֶּה אֶת הֶעָנִי בְּכָל־הַגָּדִישׁ. וְהַתְּנָייָא קוֹמָייָא סְבַר מֵימַר כְּזַכֶּה מִימִינוֹ לִשְׂמֹאלוֹ וְאֵינָהּ זְכִייָה. וְהַתְּנָייָא אַחֲרָייָא סְבַר מֵימַר אֵינוֹ מְזַכֶּה מִימִינוֹ לִשְׂמֹאלוֹ וּזְכִייָה הִיא.

Rebbi Abbahu[59] in the name of Rebbi Simeon ben Laqish, this follows Rebbi Yose[60], as we have stated there[61]: "For Rebbi Yose says that everything whose replacement is in the hand of the Cohen is freed from the obligatory gifts, but Rebbi Meïr obligates him." Rebbi Abba said, the words of Rebbi Yose imply that he has to empower the priest[62]. Rebbi Yose[63] said, the statement of Rebbi Abba contradicts Rebbi Simeon bar

Laqish since we have stated here: "He has to give the poor rights to the entire stack; then he gives tithes for one ear and gives to him." Rebbi Abba said, the words of Rebbi Yose imply that he has to empower the priest, hence[64] this is not from the words of Rebbi Yose. Rebbi Mana said, the Mishnah itself testifies that it is by Rebbi Yose[65]. The first Tanna wants to say that he transfers as property to the poor not the entire stack but only one ear. The other Tanna wants to say that he transfers the entire stack as property to the poor. The first Tanna wants to say that this[66] is like the transfer of property from one's right hand to his left hand; it is no transfer. The other Tanna wants to say that it is not transferring property from one's right hand to his left hand; it is transfer[67].

59 Here we discuss the last part of the Mishnah, the disagreement between the Sages and R. Eliezer on whether it is possible to transfer property of a single ear or whether it is necessary first to give the entire stack to the poor.

60 Bar Ḥalaphta, the Tanna.

61 The Mishnah *Bekhorot* 2:6 deals with a sheep whose first lambs are male twins of which it is unknown which one was the firstborn. It is then decreed that one of them be given to the Cohen, and the other one (who might be the firstborn and, if without blemish, should be brought as sacrifice) should graze until it develops a bodily defect and then can be eaten. The first Tanna (representing R. Meïr) insists that the second animal is subject to the rule of obligatory gifts to the Cohen as profane meat. Rebbi Yose disagrees, and in a *baraita* (also Babli *Bekhorot* 18a) explains that every animal whose exchange is in the hand of the Cohen is freed from the rule of obligatory gifts. The Babli explains, in an apparent disagreement with the interpretation of the Yerushalmi, that this is not a general principle but it underlines the special status of the second animal which, as a potential sacrifice, may not be shorn or used for work.

62 It is not enough to designate an ear as tithes; it must actually be delivered into the hand of the Cohen.

63 The later Amora.

64 This is the Amora Rebbi Yose's inference.

65 Everybody agrees that transfer of property must take place, but not necessarily delivery; the Tanna R. Yose requires only transfer of property rights.

66 The symbolic transfer of the entire stack to the poor as a "gift on condition that it be returned" is considered a subterfuge without legal validity.

67 And is legally valid.

וְהָתַנֵּי רִבִּי זְעִירָא רִבִּי אַבָּהוּ בְּשֵׁם רִבִּי יוֹחָנָן מְחִלְפָא שִׁיטָתֵיהּ דְּרִבִּי לִיעֶזֶר תַּמָּן הוּא זָכָה לוֹ. וְכֹא הוּא אָמַר הָכֵין. (fol. 19a) בְּשִׁיטָתָךְ הֱשִׁיבֵהוּ בְּשִׁיטָתוֹ דְּאַתְּ אָמַר עַל יְדֵי הַחִילוּפִין. הֵיאַךְ הֶעָנִי הַזֶּה מַחֲלִיף דָּבָר שֶׁלֹּא בָא לִרְשׁוּתוֹ אֶלָּא מְזַכֶּה אֶת הֶעָנִי בְּכָל־הַגָּדִישׁ וּמְעַשֵּׂר שִׁיבּוֹלֶת וְנוֹתֵן לוֹ.

Rebbi Zeïra stated[68]: Rebbi Abbahu in the name of R. Joḥanan: The reasoning of Rebbi Eliezer is inverted! There[69] he makes him acquire, and here he says thus? He answered "according to your reasoning[70]," in your reasoning that you say it is by exchange[71]. "How can the poor man exchange something that never was in his possession? But he has to give the poor man rights to the entire stack; then he gives tithes for one ear and gives to him."

68 These three words are not in the text of R. Simson of Sens and not in that of R. Solomon Cirillo. The text of R. Simson is certainly smoothed in the sense of standard Hebrew grammar; the text of R. S. Cirillo may be smoothed.

69 In chapter 4, Mishnah 6, Rebbi Eliezer declares that any person can collect for a poor one, so that the second one is the immediate owner and the collector never has ownership. How can this be squared with the statement of R. Eliezer in the current Mishnah?

70 A standard expression in both Talmudim. Rebbi Eliezer points out a logical flaw in the reasoning of his opponents; the objection is irrelevant for himself, by Mishnah 4:6.

71 Since the Sages oppose R.

Eliezer in Mishnah 4:6, holding that the non-poor X can never acquire gifts to the poor for the poor Y, how can the owner transfer ownership in gleanings by exchange? R. Eliezer's procedure with the formal gift is needed only for his opponents in 4:6; for himself he will rule that the owner may acquire the gleanings for the poor recipient.

(fol. 18c) **משנה ג**: אֵין מְגַלְגְּלִין בְּטוֹפֵיחַ דִּבְרֵי רִבִּי מֵאִיר. וַחֲכָמִים מַתִּירִין מִפְּנֵי שֶׁאֵיפְשָׁר. בַּעַל הַבַּיִת שֶׁהָיָה עוֹבֵר מִמָּקוֹם לְמָקוֹם וְצָרִיךְ לִיטּוֹל לֶקֶט שִׁכְחָה וּפֵיאָה וּמַעְשַׂר עָנִי וּכְשֶׁיַּחְזוֹר לְבֵיתוֹ יְשַׁלֵּם דִּבְרֵי רִבִּי אֱלִיעֶזֶר. וַחֲכָמִים אוֹמְרִים עָנִי הָיָה בְאוֹתָהּ שָׁעָה.

Mishnah 3: One does not use a waterwheel with buckets[72], the words of Rebbi Meïr. But the Sages do permit it, because it is impossible[73]. A householder wandering from one place to another who was in need of taking gleanings, forgotten sheaves, *peah*, and tithes of the poor[74] should repay them once he comes home, the words of Rebbi Eliezer[75]. But the Sages say, he was poor at that moment[76].

72 After the harvest, before the poor had cleaned out vineyard (or field), to avoid hurting the vines (or to prepare the field for the next season.)

73 To do otherwise, since the vineyard would dry up. [This translation follows תוספתא כפשוטה p. 155; it is not much different from the explanation of *Arukh* (s. v. טפח) in the name of R. Daniel Gaon.]

74 Since his money had run out.

75 Taking into account his property at his place of residence, at no time was he eligible for public assistance.

76 Having no money with him and unable to get credit.

(fol. 19a) **הלכה ג**: תַּנֵּי הַמְּרַבֵּץ שָׂדֵהוּ עַד שֶׁלֹּא יָרַד עָנִי לְתוֹכָהּ אִם הֶיזֵּיקוֹ מְרוּבָּה עַל שֶׁל עָנִי מוּתָּר. וְאִם הֶזֵּיק עָנִי מְרוּבָּה עַל שֶׁלּוֹ אָסוּר. רִבִּי יְהוּדָה אוֹמֵר בֵּין כָּךְ וּבֵין כָּךְ מֵנִיחָן עַל הַגֶּדֶר וְהֶעָנִי בָּא וְנוֹטֵל אֶת שֶׁלּוֹ.

Halakhah 3: It was stated[77]: He who waters his field before a poor person had entered it, if his potential loss is greater than the poor man's, it is permitted, but if the poor man's loss is greater than his, it is prohibited. Rebbi Jehudah says, in both cases he deposits them on the fence and the poor man comes and takes what is his.

77 Tosephta *Peah* 2:20. There, the reading is: "R. Jehudah says, he collects (the part of the poor) and deposits it on the fence."

מְחְלְפָא שִׁיטָּתֵיהּ דְּרִבִּי יְהוּדָה. תַּמָּן הוּא אוֹמֵר כְּשֵׁם שֶׁהוּא מֵידָל בְּשֶׁלּוֹ כָּךְ הוּא מֵידָל בְּשֶׁל עֲנִיִּים. וְכָא הוּא אָמַר הָכֵין. תַּמָּן הֵן גָּרְמוּ לְעַצְמָן וְלֹא בָאוּ. בְּרַם הָכָא הֲרֵי בָּאוּ.

The reasoning of Rebbi Jehudah is inverted: There[78], he says that just as he prunes for himself, so he prunes for the poor; but here he says thus[79]! There, they caused it for themselves since they did not come[80], but here they came.

78 Mishnah 7:5: "If somebody is pruning vines, just as he is pruning his, he may prune the poor's, the words of Rebbi Jehudah. Rebbi Meïr says, he is empowered to do it on his own vines, but not on the poor's." One prunes new shoots of vines at the start of the growing season; at that moment, the poor have rights only to the grapes growing singly, not in bunches, directly on the branch.

79 He collects and puts the poor's part aside.

80 Nobody is wasting time to pluck budding single grape berries. In Halakhah 7:5, there is an another answer given: Since by pruning one makes the vine grow more grape bunches, the poor's part also will be increased in the future.

מְחְלְפָא שִׁיטָּתֵיהוֹן דְּרַבָּנִין. תַּמָּן אָמְרִין אִם הֶזֵּיקוֹ מְרוּבֶּה עַל שֶׁל עָנִי. וְכָא אִינּוּן אָמְרִין הָכֵין. תַּמָּן אֶפְשַׁר בְּרַם הָכָא אֵיפְשָׁר.

The reasoning of the rabbis is inverted: There[81], they say if his potential loss is greater than the poor's, and here they say thus[82]! There, it is possible[83], but here it is impossible.

81 In Mishnah 7:5, R. Meïr, who disagrees with R. Jehudah, is identified with the anonymous opponent of Rebbi Jehudah in the Tosephta quoted at the start of this Halakhah.

82 In our Mishnah, they permit using the water wheel to mechanically water the vineyard.

83 To prune only after the poor collected their share.

וְהָא רִבִּי מֵאִיר אָמַר אֵין מְגַלְגְּלִין וְשָׁמִין שֶׁל בַּעַל הַבַּיִת בְּהֶפְסֵדוֹ. וְהָא רַבָּנִין אָמְרִין מְגַלְגְּלִין וְשָׁמִין לָעֲנִיִּים בְּהֶפְסֵידָן. וּלְמִי הוּא מְשַׁלֵּם. אָמַר רִבִּי יוֹנָה לַעֲנִיֵּי אוֹתָהּ הָעִיר דְּלָא כֵן מַה נָן אָמְרִין. אָמַר רִבִּי חִיָּיא בַּר אָדָא לְמִידַּת הַדִּין נִצְרְכָה.

Now Rebbi Meïr says, one does not use the water wheel, and one estimates the loss to the owner. Now the rabbis say, one uses the water wheel and estimates the loss to the poor[84]. To whom does he pay? Rebbi Jonah said, to the poor of his place, because otherwise, what could we say[85]? Rebbi Ḥiyya bar Ada said, it is needed for the measure of justice[86].

84 So why does R. Meïr insist on not watering, if all accounts can be satisfied with money?

85 There is no individual claimant; hence, there would be no payment unless the head of the local charity institution brings action in the name of all local, potentially empowered, poor.

86 Even the administrator of charity could not bring action unless specifically empowered to do so. It is therefore not superfluous to restrict the potential claimants to those represented by the administrator of charity.

(fol. 18c) **משנה ד**: הַמַּחֲלִיף עִם הָעֲנִיִּים בְּשֶׁלּוֹ פָּטוּר וּבְשֶׁל עֲנִיִּים חַיָּב. שְׁנַיִם שֶׁקִּבְּלוּ שָׂדֶה בְּאָרִיסוּת זֶה נוֹתֵן לְזֶה חֶלְקוֹ וּמַעֲשַׂר עָנִי וְזֶה נוֹתֵן לְזֶה חֶלְקוֹ וּמַעֲשַׂר עָנִי. הַמְקַבֵּל שָׂדֶה לִקְצוֹר אָסוּר בְּלֶקֶט וּבְשִׁכְחָה וּבְפֵיאָה וּבְמַעֲשַׂר עָנִי. אָמַר רִבִּי יְהוּדָה אֵימָתַי בִּזְמָן שֶׁקִּבְּלָהּ מִמֶּנָּה לְמֶחֱצָה לִשְׁלִישׁ וְלִרְבִיעַ אֲבָל אִם אָמַר לוֹ שְׁלִישׁ מַה שֶׁאַתָּה קוֹצֵר שֶׁלָּךְ מוּתָּר בְּלֶקֶט וּבְשִׁכְחָה וּבְפֵיאָה וְאָסוּר בְּמַעֲשַׂר עָנִי.

Mishnah 4: If he[87] switches with the poor, what he receives is exempt but what the poor get is obligated. If two persons received a field as sharecroppers[88], one gives his part and his tithes of the poor to the other one[89], and vice-versa. He who receives a field to harvest is barred from its gleanings, forgotten sheaves, and *peah*. Rebbi Jehudah said, when is this so[90]? When he received it for one-half, one third, or one quarter[91]; but if he told him, one third of what you will harvest will be yours[92], he may take gleanings, forgotten sheaves, and *peah* but not the tithes of the poor.

87 If the farmer takes from the poor their gleanings or *peah* in exchange for grain from his storage, what he takes is not subject to tithes, since gleanings and *peah* are exempt, but what the poor take is subject to heave and tithes.

88 That means, both are poor. [The meaning of the word אריס is "cultivator of the soil", from Arabic اريس, designating a tenant farmer. In both Talmudim, the designation is restricted to sharecroppers.]

89 Nobody may take tithes of the poor, gleanings, etc., from his own harvest even if he is poor. Since the sharecropper has a proprietary interest in the growing plants, he may not take any of the gifts to the poor. But if two poor people work two sides of one field, each one is entitled to all the gifts to the poor accruing from the other's half.

90 The Babli postulates that everywhere R. Jehudah is mentioned with the question אימתי, he does not

disagree with the anonymous text of the Mishnah but gives it a restrictive definition. The Yerushalmi seems to agree with this.

91 The standard terms of a sharecropper's contract.

92 In this case, the sharecropper has no property claim to the standing grain; the harvest is the landowner's and the sharecropper may take the gifts to the poor from this crop. However, tithes of the poor, like any other tithes, are an obligation on the threshed grains and there the sharecropper is already an owner and the tithes of the poor are prohibited to him.

(fol. 19a) **הלכה ד**: תַּנֵּי אַב וּבְנוֹ אִישׁ וּקְרוֹבוֹ שְׁנֵי אַחִין שְׁנֵי שׁוּתָּפִין פּוֹדִין זֶה לָזֶה מַעֲשֵׂר שֵׁנִי וְנוֹתְנִין זֶה לָזֶה מַעֲשַׂר עָנִי. אָמַר רִבִּי יוּדָן תָּבוֹא מְאֵירָה לְמִי שֶׁהוּא נוֹתֵן לְאָבִיו מַעֲשַׂר עָנִי. אָמַר מְנַיִין שֶׁאִים הָיוּ שְׁנֵיהֶן עֲנִיִּים.

Halakhah 4: It is stated[93]: A father and his son[94], a man and his relative, two brothers, two associates redeem Second Tithe[95] for one another and give tithe of the poor to one another[96]. Rebbi Jehudah said, a curse should come upon him who gives tithe of the poor to his father[97]. He said, why? If they were both poor[98]!

93 Tosephta *Maäser Šeni* 4:7 in a slightly different wording. A third version, in which the answer to R. Jehudah is missing, is given in Babli *Qiddushin* 32a.

94 The grownup son who earns his own money.

95 Cf. Chapter 1, Note 127. In the times of the Temple, if the accumulated amount of Second Tithe was too large, the produce could be redeemed and the money taken to Jerusalem to be spent on similar food (*Deut.* 14:25). After the destruction of the Temple, Second Tithe has to be redeemed for a symbolic amount since the redemption money then has to be destroyed. However, it is spelled out in the last chapter of *Leviticus* that a person who redeems any of his dedications has to add another 25% to the redemption sum. A redemption by a third party is not subject to this surtax. It is therefore in everybody's

interest to let a third party redeem Second Tithes.

96 If they qualify as poor.

97 Even if his father can no longer work and has no savings, the son should not treat him as receiver of charity.

98 If the son himself qualifies for public assistance as a poor person, it is acceptable that he give the tithe of the poor of his plot to his father.

מַה בֵינָהּ לְקַדְמִיתָא אֶלָּא לִכְשֶׁתִּקְצוֹר שְׁלִישׁ הֲרֵי הִיא שֶׁלָּךְ. אָמַר רִבִּי חִייָא בַּר רִבִּי בּוּן הָדָא אֶמְרָה שֶׁהַמּוֹכֵר זַכַּיי בְּפֵיאָה שֶׁהִיא מַתֶּרֶת אֶת הָעוֹמָרִים. אָמַר רִבִּי יוֹסֵי בֵּי רִבִּי בּוּן תַּמָּן נִתְחַייְבָה שָׂדֵהוּ בִרְשׁוּתוֹ בְּרַם הָכָא לֹא נִתְחַייְבָה שָׂדֵהוּ בִרְשׁוּתוֹ.

What[99] is the difference between this and the first case[100]? It must be "if you cut it, a third will be yours[101]." Rebbi Abin bar Ḥiyya said, that implies that the seller may get the *peah* which permits the sheaves[102]. Rebbi Yose ben Rebbi Abun[103] said, there the obligation of the field did come during his ownership, but here the obligation of the field did not come during his ownership.

99 This paragraph is almost identical with one in Chapter 2, Halakha 7, with references to "here" and "there" switched as required. The name of the tradent has been switched from the correct "Abin bar Ḥiyya" to a non-existent "Ḥiyya bar Abin". The discussion is about the ruling by R. Jehudah that the sharecropper may take the gifts to the poor if his share is only produce which is already cut.

100 Of the usual sharecropper who has rights to the growing plants.

101 Only after the harvest is completed does the sharecropper get rights.

102 In the situation of Mishnah 2:7, at the moment of the actual obligation of *peah* the field is already sold, the *peah* was never the seller's and he may take from it if he is poor.

103 He shows that the argument of R. Abin bar Ḥiyya is faulty. While the actual obligation of *peah* arises during the buyer's harvest, the potential obligation started with the seller's harvest. Hence, the seller should be barred from taking his part of the

peah. In contrast, the sharecropper who is given ownership only of a part of the harvest, not of the standing grain, has nothing at all to do with the obligation of *peah*.

אָמַר רִבִּי אַבָּהוּ בַּר נַגָּרִי שַׁנְיָיא הִיא בְּלֶקֶט שִׁכְחָה וּפֵיאָה שֶׁהֵן בַּעֲזִיבָה.

Rebbi Abbahu bar Naggari[104] said, there is a difference for gleanings, forgotten sheaves, and *peah* because they have to be abandoned.

104 An Amora whose time and place cannot be determined. His reasoning parallels R. Yose's: Gleanings etc. have to be abandoned on the field and it was not the share-cropper's field. But tithes, including the tithe of the poor, have to be given after threshing, and in that poor and rich are in the same situation.

(fol. 18c) **משנה ה**: הַמּוֹכֵר שָׂדֵהוּ הַמּוֹכֵר מוּתָּר וְהַלּוֹקֵחַ אָסוּר. לֹא יִשְׂכּוֹר אָדָם אֶת הַפּוֹעֵל עַל מְנָת שֶׁיְּלַקֵּט בְּנוֹ אַחֲרָיו. וּמִי שֶׁאֵינוֹ מֵנִיחַ אֶת הָעֲנִיִּים לְלַקֵּט אוֹ שֶׁהוּא מֵנִיחַ אֶת אֶחָד וְאֶת אֶחָד לָאו אוֹ שֶׁהוּא מְסַייֵעַ אֶת אֶחָד מֵהֶן הֲרֵי זֶה גוֹזֵל אֶת הָעֲנִיִּים. עַל זֶה נֶאֱמַר אַל תַּסֵּג גְּבוּל עוֹלָם.

Mishnah 5: If someone sells his field, the seller is permitted[105] but the buyer is barred. Nobody should hire a worker on condition that his son may collect gleanings after him[106]. He who does not let the poor collect gleanings, or who lets one person collect but not the other, or helps one of them, robs the poor. On him it was said (*Prov*. 22:28, 23:10): "Do not displace an eternal boundary[107]."

105 If he is poor at harvest time.

106 And for this pay him smaller wages, since he is paying his debts with the money of the poor.

107 The implication is from the second part of the verse: "Nor intrude on the land of orphans." On *Prov.* 22:28, Rashi comments: "Do not displace an eternal boundary," do not change established usage; our teachers said: He who puts a basket under the vine at harvest time so that the single berries fall into it, on him it is said, do not displace an eternal boundary. On *Prov.* 24:10, Rashi writes, "Nor intrude on the land of orphans," the gleanings, forgotten sheaves, and *peah* which belong to them.

(fol. 19a) **הלכה ה**: מַתְנִיתָא בְּשֶׁמָּכַר לוֹ שָׂדֵהוּ וְקָמָיָהּ. אֲבָל מָכַר[108] לוֹ קָמָה וְשִׁייֵר לוֹ שָׂדֶה אֵצֶל זֶה אֲנִי קוֹרֵא שָׂדְךָ וְאֵצֶל זֶה אֲנִי קוֹרֵא קְצִירְךָ.

Halakhah 5: Our Mishnah is about someone who sold the field with the standing crop. But if someone sold the standing crop and retained the field for himself, for him I read "your field", for the other one I read "your harvest.[109]"

108 Reading of R. Simson of Sens. In the Leyden manuscript and Venice print, אם אמר.

109 Since *Deut.* 24:19 reads: "When you are harvesting your harvest on your field," both the owner of the field and the owner of the harvest are forbidden to take of the gleanings and *peah.*

אִם עוֹשֶׂה כֵן הֲרֵי זֶה גוֹזֵל אֶת הָעֲנִיִּים. בַּעַל הַבַּיִת שֶׁעוֹשֶׂה כֵן גוֹזֵל הָעֲנִיִּים. פּוֹעֵל שֶׁעָשָׂה כֵן הֲרֵי זֶה גוֹזֵל לְבַעַל הַבַּיִת וְלָעֲנִיִּים וְעַל זֶה נֶאֱמַר אַל תַּסֵּג גְּבוּל עוֹלָם.

"By doing so, he robs the poor." The owner who does that robs the poor[110]. The worker who does that robs the owner[111] and the poor, and about him it was said: "Do not displace an eternal boundary."

110 Either by not giving at all or by limiting the chances of the disfavored.

111 He robs the owner of the merit, either leading him into sin by offering to work for lower wages on condition that his son get all gleanings and *peah*, or, if the owner does not know that he lets his son take everything, by not letting him fulfil the Biblical commandments. The Babli (*Baba Meẓi'a* 12a) disagrees and postulates as standard labor practice that the worker's minor son may collect gleanings after his father. The Babli must restrict the meaning of the Mishnah to the case that the worker agrees to take wages smaller than customary.

רַב יִרְמְיָה וְרַב יוֹסֵף חַד אָמַר אֵלּוּ עוֹלֵי מִצְרַיִם. וְחָרָנָא אָמַר אֵלּוּ שֶׁיָּרְדוּ מִנִּכְסֵיהֶן. לְסַמְיָא צְווֹחִין סַגְיָא נְהוֹרָיָא. אָמַר רִבִּי יִצְחָק וַעֲנִיִּים מְרוּדִים תָּבִיא בָיִת. אָמַר רִבִּי אָבִין אִם עָשִׂיתָ כֵּן מַעֲלֶה אֲנִי עָלֶיךָ כְּאִלּוּ הֵבֵאתָ בִּיכּוּרִים לְבֵית הַמִּקְדָּשׁ. נֶאֱמַר כָּאן תָּבִיא. וְנֶאֱמַר לְהַלָּן רֵאשִׁית בִּכּוּרֵי אַדְמָתְךָ תָּבִיא בֵּית יי אֱלֹהֶיךָ וגו'.

Rav Jeremiah and Rav Joseph[112], one said these are the ones who came up from Egypt, the other said these are the ones who lost their property; a blind man is called "plenty of light.[113]" Rebbi Isaac said, (*Is*. 58:7) "degraded poor you shall bring to your house[114]." Rebbi Abin said, if you do this[115], I will credit it to you as if you had presented First Fruits in the Temple. It says here, "you shall bring," and it says there (*Ex*. 23:19): "The first fruits of your land you shall bring to the Eternal's Temple[116]."

112 This homily is based on a reading in the Mishnah, not אַל תַּסֵּג גְּבוּל עוֹלָם but אַל תַּסֵּג גְּבוּל עוֹלִים "do not displace the boundary of the rising." This reading is attested to by Maimonides in his Commentary and is found in most Mishnah manuscripts of Babylonian type. One might assume that the scribes of most of the Mishnah manuscripts of Yerushalmi type were more versed in Biblical verses and copied from memory rather than from the text before them. As explained before, the part important for the

Mishnah is the second part of the verse. Here, by a change of vocalization, one author wants to give a better parallel to "orphan" than "eternal".

113 Those coming down in the world are called "rising".

114 He objects to the previous homily since a verse explicitly called the poor "degraded."

115 To bring the poor into your house. This homily no longer is connected to the Mishnah.

116 See the commentary of I. A. Rabin to *Mekhilta Mišpatim* 20 (p. 335) that there is a clear disagreement between Babylonian and Galilean Amoraïm in the interpretation of "to bring" in this verse, and the interpretation given here is Babylonian.

(fol. 18c) **מִשְׁנָה ו**: הָעוֹמֶר שֶׁשְּׁכָחוּהוּ פוֹעֲלִים וְלֹא שְׁכָחוֹ בַּעַל הַבַּיִת שְׁכָחוֹ בַּעַל הַבַּיִת וְלֹא שְׁכָחוּהוּ פוֹעֲלִים עָמְדוּ הָעֲנִיִּים בְּפָנָיו אוֹ שֶׁחִיפּוּהוּ בְקַשׁ הֲרֵי זֶה אֵינוֹ שִׁכְחָה.

Mishnah 6: A sheaf forgotten by the workers but not by the owner, by the owner but not by the workers, or the poor stood before it or covered it with straw[117], is not a forgotten sheaf.

117 Anything the poor hide in any way when the sheaves are loaded to be brought to the barn.

(fol. 19a) **הלכה ו**: הָעוֹמֶר שֶׁשְּׁכָחוּהוּ פוֹעֲלִין וְלֹא שְׁכָחוֹ בַּעַל הַבַּיִת אֵינוֹ שִׁכְחָה דִּכְתִיב קְצִירְךָ וְשָׁכַחְתָּ. שְׁכָחוֹ בַּעַל הַבַּיִת וְלֹא שְׁכָחוּהוּ פוֹעֲלִים אֵינוֹ שִׁכְחָה דִּכְתִיב כִּי תִקְצוֹר וְשָׁכַחְתָּ. רִבִּי שִׁמְעוֹן בֶּן יְהוּדָה אוֹמֵר מִשּׁוּם רִבִּי שִׁמְעוֹן אֲפִילוּ חַמָּרִין שֶׁהֵן עוֹבְרִין בַּדֶּרֶךְ וְרָאוּ עוֹמֶר אֶחָד שֶׁשְּׁכָחוּהָ פוֹעֲלִים וְלֹא שְׁכָחוֹ בַּעַל הַבַּיִת אֵינוֹ שִׁכְחָה עַד שֶׁיִּשְׁכְּחוּהוּ כָּל־אָדָם.

Halakhah 6: A sheaf forgotten by the workers but not by the owner is not a forgotten sheaf since it is written (*Deut.* 24:19): "When you harvest and you forget[118]." If the owner forgot but the workers did not, it is not a forgotten sheaf since it is written: "When you are harvesting and you forget." Rebbi Simeon ben Jehudah[119] says in the name of Rebbi Simeon: Even if donkey drivers[120] passing by on the road saw a sheaf forgotten by the workers but not by the owner[121], it is not a forgotten sheaf unless everybody forgot it.

118 The verse reads: "When you are harvesting your harvest on your field and forget a sheaf on the field, you may not return to take it." Since "harvesting a harvest" is redundant language, it is split into two. "Your harvest" refers to the owner, "harvesting" refers to the farmhands who do the actual work. Both have to forget. (This implies that the owner must have known of the sheaf.)

119 A fifth generation Tanna, from Kefar Acco, student of R. Simeon (bar Iohai). His statement also appears in Tosephta *Peah* 3:1.

120 In the Tosephta and the original scribe (who usually is better than the corrector) of the Leyden manuscript: "others".

121 The language is difficult but is attested to by the Yerushalmi manuscripts and R. Simson of Sens. According to R. Saul Lieberman, it means that the owner never knew of the sheaf and he was not on the field during harvest. In our Tosephta manuscripts, "and not by the owner" is missing. R. Moshe Margalit writes that in his Tosephta manuscript, "by the workers" also is missing; there is only a reference to "them" who forgot. From the text of Maimonides (*Mattenot Aniïm* 5:1) it seems that he read: "was forgotten by the workers and by the owner."

הָיָה עוֹמֵד בָּעִיר וְאוֹמֵר יוֹדֵעַ אֲנִי שֶׁהַפּוֹעֲלִין שְׁכֵיחִין עוֹמְרִין שֶׁבְּמָקוֹם פְּלוֹנִי וּשְׁכָחוּהוּ אֵינוֹ שִׁכְחָה. הָיָה עוֹמֵד בַּשָּׂדֶה וְאוֹמֵר יוֹדֵעַ אֲנִי שֶׁהַפּוֹעֲלִין שְׁכֵיחִין

עוֹמְרִין שֶׁבְּמָקוֹם פְּלוֹנִי הֲרֵי זוֹ שִׁכְחָה שֶׁנֶּאֱמַר בַּשָּׂדֶה וְשָׁכַחְתָּ וְלֹא בָעִיר וְשָׁכַחְתָּ. רִבִּי זְעִירָא בְשֵׁם שְׁמוּאֵל אַף לְעִנְיַן מְצִיאָה כֵן. מַה נָן קַייָמִין אִם בְּיָכוֹל לִיגַּע בָּהֶן בְּתוֹךְ הָעִיר אֲפִילוּ בְּתוֹךְ שָׂדֵהוּ[122]. רִבִּי אַבָּא בַּר כַּהֲנָא רִבִּי יָסָא בְשֵׁם רִבִּי יוֹחָנָן וְהוּא שֶׁיָּכוֹל לִיגַּע בָּהֶן אֲפִילוּ בְּתוֹךְ שָׂדֵהוּ.

If he stood in town and said: I know that the workers are forgetting sheaves at place X; if they forgot it is not a forgotten sheaf[123]. If he stood on the field and said: I know that the workers are forgetting sheaves at place X; [if they forgot] it is a forgotten sheaf, since it says (*Deut.* 24:19): "On your field and you forget a sheaf." On the field you forget, but in town you do not forget. Rebbi Zeïra in the name of Samuel[124]: The same holds in regard to found objects[125]. Where are we holding? If he may touch it, in the city, even inside his field[126]. Rebbi Abba bar Cahana, Rebbi Yasa in the name of Rebbi Joḥanan: Only if he can touch them, even inside his field.

122 Reading of the Leyden (first hand) and Rome manuscripts. The corrected Leyden ms. and the Venice print have: מַה לִי בְּתוֹךְ הָעִיר מַה לִי בְּתוֹךְ שָׂדֵהוּ.

123 Tosephta *Peah* 3:1, reading of the Vienna manuscript. The Erfurt manuscript and printed editions have "this is a forgotten sheaf;" this is the Babylonian version (*Baba Meẓi'a* 11a). The parallel in the Babli in every case adopts a position opposite to that taken by the Yerushalmi. The explanation given here follows the analysis in *Tosephta Kifshutah* 1, p. 159-160.

124 In the Rome manuscript, "Rebbi Zeïra, Rav Jehudah in the name of Samuel." Since Rav Jehudah was Samuel's student and R. Zeïra's teacher, the formula of indirect quote "in the name of" there is superfluous. The Babli (*Baba Meẓi'a* 11a) has: "Rav Jehudah said, Samuel said," as direct transmission.

125 This refers to the Mishnah *Baba Meẓi'a* 1:4: "If he saw them running after a lost object, a deer with broken bones, pigeon chicks not yet able to fly, and he said: My field should acquire this for me, it acquires for him" (on

condition that the field be either fenced in or that something is growing which makes it inaccessible to the public.) In the case of sheaves, if he is not standing on the field and wants the field to acquire the sheaf, it is valid. However, if he stands in or near the field, the field cannot acquire for him since the sheaf is his and nobody can acquire anything he already owns. Hence, if he stands in his field and claims that sheaf but later forgets it, the earlier remembrance will not help him since, in that case, the field will not acquire for him. In our case he must be able to go and reach the slowly moving animals before they leave his field.

126 Does he acquire only if the deer is so severely injured that he still will find it inside his field when he goes there from town? In the name of R. Johanan, the answer given confirms the questioner's opinion.

הָיָה כּוּלּוֹ מְחוּפֶּה בְקַשׁ. נִשְׁמְעִינָהּ מִן הָדָא וְכֵן הַסּוּמָא שֶׁשָּׁכַח יֵשׁ לוֹ שִׁכְחָה. וְסוּמָא לֹא כְּמִי שֶׁכּוּלּוֹ בְקַשׁ מְחוּפֶּה הוּא. רִבִּי יוֹנָה אָמַר בְּזוֹכֵר אֶת הַקַּשִּׁים. אֲתָא דְּרִבִּי יוֹנָה כְּרִבִּי זְעִירָא כְּמַה דְּרִבִּי זְעִירָא אָמַר בְּזוֹכֵר אֶת הָעֶלְיוֹן כֵּן רִבִּי יוֹנָה אָמַר בְּזוֹכֵר אֶת הַקַּשִּׁים.

If it was completely covered by straw[127]? Let us hear from the following: "The blind[128] who forgot makes a forgotten sheaf." Is a blind person not like a sheaf completely covered by straw? Rebbi Jonah said, if he remembered the straw[129]. Rebbi Jonah's position is parallel to Rebbi Zeïra's; just as Rebbi Zeïra said[130], if he remembers the upper one, so Rebbi Jonah said, if he remembered the straw.

127 Not intentionally covered by the poor, but a sheaf lying covered under straw, which nobody noticed when the sheaves were taken in.

128 If the farmer is blind, his disability does not change the laws.

129 Since he will come back to collect the straw, he must stumble upon the sheaf. The sheaf is not forgotten since he will be returning to it.

130 Chapter 6, Halakhah 3, speaking about two sheaves to be taken by one of the workers and forgotten by the farmer. The farmer personally lifted

the upper one; by lifting he acquired it permanently. The lower one was covered and, therefore, cannot be a forgotten sheaf. Rebbi Zeïra explains that the lower, covered sheaf is forgotten unless the farmer remembered the upper, already acquired one.

(fol. 18c) **משנה ז**: הַמְעַמֵּר לְכוֹבָעוֹת וּלְכוּמָסוֹת לַחֲרָרָה וּלְעוֹמָרִין אֵין לוֹ שִׁכְחָה. מִמֶּנּוּ לְגוֹרֶן יֵשׁ לוֹ שִׁכְחָה. הַמְעַמֵּר לְגָדִישׁ יֵשׁ לוֹ שִׁכְחָה מִמֶּנּוּ וּלְגוֹרֶן אֵין לוֹ שִׁכְחָה. זֶה הַכְּלָל כָּל־הַמְעַמֵּר לְמָקוֹם שֶׁהוּא גְּמַר מְלָכָה יֵשׁ לוֹ (fol. 18d) שִׁכְחָה מִמֶּנּוּ וּלְגוֹרֶן אֵין לוֹ שִׁכְחָה. לְמָקוֹם שֶׁאֵינוֹ גְּמַר מְלָכָה אֵין לוֹ שִׁכְחָה. מִמֶּנּוּ לְגוֹרֶן יֵשׁ לוֹ שִׁכְחָה.

Mishnah 7: He[131] who makes sheaves as helmets[132], round bundles[133], wheels[134], and small sheaves[135] is not subject to the law of forgotten sheaves. If he takes them from there to the threshing-floor, the rules on forgotten sheaves apply. If he makes sheaves for a stack, it is subject to the rules on forgotten sheaves. If he takes them from there to the threshing-floor, the rules on forgotten sheaves do not apply. This is the principle: Everybody who makes sheaves for a place that is the end of his work[136] is subject to the rule on forgotten sheaves, from there to the threshing-floor is not subject to the rule on forgotten sheaves[137]. To a place that is not the end of his work it is not subject to the rule on forgotten sheaves, from there to the threshing-floor[138] is subject to the rule on forgotten sheaves.

131 Translation and interpretation follows in the main Maimonides in his Commentary on the Mishnah. "He" is the farmer, the owner of the crop.

132 As explained in the Halakhah, sheaves bound together at the top, just under the ears, looking like hats.

133 Bound together at the bottom. Loew accepts a derivation parallel to Arabic كمز "collecting and making round bundles with one's hands."

134 Grain bundles in the shape of wheels.

135 Needed to make stacks, not to be taken directly to the threshing floor.

136 As harvester; from there a new phase of the work starts.

137 That transport is no longer part of the harvest.

138 The end of the harvest.

(fol. 19a) **הלכה ז:** רִבִּי יוֹנָה אָמַר מִן לְעֵיל. כְּמָה דְתֵימַר וְכוֹבַע נְחוֹשֶׁת עַל רֹאשׁוֹ. לְכוּמָסוֹת. רִבִּי אֲבִינָא אָמַר מִן לְרַע כְּמָה דְתֵימַר הֲלֹא הוּא כָּמוּס עִמָּדִי. לַחֲרָרָה. גַּלְגַּל. לְעוֹמָרִין. אָמַר רִבִּי יוֹחָנָן כִּי תִקְצוֹר קְצִירְךָ בְשָׂדֶךָ וְשָׁכַחְתָּ עוֹמֶר בַּשָּׂדֶה. מַה קָצִיר שֶׁאֵין אַחֲרָיו קָצִיר. אַף עוֹמֶר שֶׁאֵין אַחֲרָיו עוֹמֶר.

Halakhah 7: Rebbi Jonah says, from the top, as you say (*1Sam*. 17:5): "A brass helmet on his head." Round bundles, Rebbi Avinah said, from the bottom, as you say (*Deut*. 32:34): "It is hidden with me." [139]חֲרָרָה a wheel. Small sheaves, Rebbi Joḥanan said (*Deut*. 24:19): "When you will be harvesting the harvest of your field and you forget a sheaf on the field," just as harvest has no other harvest after it[140], so too a sheaf, which has no other sheaf-making after it.

139 With the different meanings of the Hebrew/Aramaic root חרר, this could mean 1) something burned (a charcoal-broiled cake), 2) a round mass, 3) a hole, 4) freedom. Hence, it is necessary to spell out that meaning 2) is meant.

140 On the same field. This would imply that he who cuts part of his field green either for fodder or for *Grünkern*, is not subject to the law of the forgotten sheaf.

בית שמאי פרק ששי

(fol. 19a) **משנה א**: בֵּית שַׁמַּאי אוֹמְרִין הֶבְקֵר לָעֲנִיִּים הֶבְקֵר. וּבֵית הִלֵּל אוֹמְרִין אֵינוֹ הֶבְקֵר עַד שֶׁיַּבְקִיר אַף לָעֲשִׁירִים כִּשְׁמִיטָּה. כָּל־עוֹמְרֵי הַשָּׂדֶה שֶׁל קַב קַב וְאֶחָד שֶׁל אַרְבַּעַת קַבִּין וְשָׁכְחוּ בוֹ. בֵּית שַׁמַּאי אוֹמֵר אֵינוֹ שִׁכְחָה וּבֵית הִלֵּל אוֹמְרִין שִׁכְחָה.

Mishnah 1: The House of Shammai say, property abandoned to the poor is abandoned[1], but the House of Hillel say, it is not abandoned unless it is abandoned also to the rich, as in a Sabbatical year[2]. If all sheaves of a field are of one *qab* each, except one which is of four *qab* and they forgot about that one, the House of Shammai say, it cannot be a forgotten sheaf[3], but the House of Hillel say, it can be a forgotten sheaf.

1 It is free from any obligation of heave and tithes.

2 I. e., what grows on the fields in a Sabbatical year without being planted or sown, which is exempt from heave and tithes.

3 Because it may be unbundled into several sheaves and, therefore, is not a final sheaf as required by the preceding Mishnah.

(fol. 19b) **הלכה א**: רִבִּי חִיָּיא בְשֵׁם רִבִּי יוֹחָנָן טַעֲמֵייְהוּ דְּבֵית שַׁמַּאי לֶעָנִי וְלַגֵּר מַה תַלְמוּד לוֹמַר תַּעֲזוֹב אוֹתָם יֵשׁ לָךְ עֲזִיבָה אַחֶרֶת כְּזוֹ. מַה זוֹ לָעֲנִיִּים וְלֹא לָעֲשִׁירִם. אַף מַה שֶׁנֶּאֱמַר בְּמָקוֹם אַחֵר לָעֲנִיִּים וְלֹא לָעֲשִׁירִם.

Halakhah 1: Rebbi Ḥiyya[4] in the name of Rebbi Joḥanan: The reason of the House of Shammai (*Lev.* 19:10, 23:22)[5] "for the poor and the sojourner." Why does the verse say, "relinquish them"? There is another relinquishing like this one. Just as this one is for the poor and not the rich, also what is spoken of elsewhere[6] is for the poor and not for the rich.

4 Rebbi Ḥiyya bar Abba.

5 "Do not go over your vineyard a second time, nor pick up the single berries of your vineyard; to the poor and the sojourner relinquish them." Why does it say "relinquish," and not "give"?

6 Any meaning of עזב must conform with this paradigm.

אָמַר רִבִּי שִׁמְעוֹן בֶּן לָקִישׁ טַעֲמֵיהוֹ דְּבֵית הִלֵּל תִּשְׁמְטֶנָּה וּמַה תַלְמוּד לוֹמַר וּנְטַשְׁתָּהּ יֵשׁ לְךָ נְטִישָׁה אֲחֶרֶת כְּזוֹ. מַה זוֹ בֵּין לָעֲנִיִּים בֵּין לָעֲשִׁירִם. אַף מַה שֶׁנֶּאֱמַר בְּמָקוֹם אַחֵר בֵּין לָעֲנִיִּים בֵּין לָעֲשִׁירִם.

Rebbi Simeon ben Laqish said, the reason of the House of Hillel, (*Ex.* 23:11)[7] "let drop," why does the verse say, "and abandon it"? There is another abandoning like this one. Just as this one is for poor and rich alike, also what is spoken of elsewhere[8] is for poor and rich alike.

7 Speaking of the produce of the Sabbatical year.

8 Any meaning of נטש must conform with this paradigm.

מַה מְקַיְימִין בֵּית הִלֵּל טַעֲמֵיהוֹן דְּבֵית שַׁמַּאי. תַּעֲזוֹב אוֹתָם מִיעוּט זוֹ לָעֲנִיִּים וְלֹא לָעֲשִׁירִם. אֲבָל מַה שֶׁנֶּאֱמַר בְּמָקוֹם אַחֵר בֵּין לָעֲנִיִּים בֵּין לָעֲשִׁירִם. מַה מְקַיְימִין בֵּית שַׁמַּאי טַעֲמֵיהוֹן דְּבֵית הִלֵּל. תִּשְׁמְטֶנָּה וּנְטַשְׁתָּהּ נְטִישָׁה מִיעוּט זֶה בֵּין לָעֲנִיִּים בֵּין לָעֲשִׁירִם. אֲבָל מַה שֶׁנֶּאֱמַר בְּמָקוֹם אַחֵר לָעֲנִיִּים אֲבָל לֹא לָעֲשִׁירִם. אָמַר רִבִּי אָבִין מַתְנִיתָא מְסַיְּיעָא לְרִבִּי שִׁמְעוֹן בֶּן לָקִישׁ עַד שֶׁיַּבְקִיר אַף לָעֲשִׁירִים כִּשְׁמִיטָּה.

How[9] do the House of Hillel deal with the reason of the House of Shammai? "Relinquish *them*" is a restriction, *these* are for the poor, not for the rich, but what is spoken of elsewhere[10] is for poor and rich alike.

How do the House of Shammai deal with the reason of the House of Hillel? "Let it drop and abandon *it*" is a restriction, this abandoning is for poor and rich alike, but what is spoken of elsewhere[11] is for the poor but not for the rich. Rebbi Avin said, the Mishnah supports Rebbi Simeon ben Laqish[12]: "Abandoned also to the rich, as in the Sabbatical year."

9 As in most Talmudic discussions, if themes 1 - 2 are introduced in order, they will be discussed as 2 - 1. The verse whose interpretation is ascribed to the House of Shammai is also the base of R. Johanan's interpretation for the House of Hillel.

10 Where עזב is used, it does not have to conform to the paradigm.

11 Where נטש is used, it does not have to conform to the paradigm.

12 Since the House of Shammai disappeared soon after the destruction of the Temple and R. Johanan and R. Simeon ben Laqish lived almost 200 years later, their deductions are intellectual exercises which moreover have been shown here to be contradictory, as the same principles applied to two different verses lead to contradictory results. But R. Simeon ben Laqish's argument very likely is historically true.

הֶבְקֵר לִבְהֵמָה אֲבָל לֹא לְאָדָם לְגוֹיִם אֲבָל לֹא לְיִשְׂרָאֵל. לָעֲשִׁירִם אֲבָל לֹא לָעֲנִיִּים דִּבְרֵי הַכֹּל אֵין הֶבְקֵרוֹ הֶבְקֵר. לְאָדָם אֲבָל לֹא לִבְהֵמָה. לְיִשְׂרָאֵל אֲבָל לֹא לְגוֹיִם. לַעֲנִיֵּי אוֹתָהּ הָעִיר אֲבָל לֹא לַעֲנִיֵּי עִיר אַחֶרֶת. פְּלוּגְתָא דְּרִבִּי יוֹחָנָן וּדְרִבִּי שִׁמְעוֹן בֶּן לָקִישׁ. עַל דַּעְתֵּיהּ דְּרִבִּי יוֹחָנָן הֶבְקֵרוֹ הֶבְקֵר. עַל דַּעְתֵּיהּ דְּרִבִּי שִׁמְעוֹן בֶּן לָקִישׁ אֵין הֶבְקֵרוֹ הֶבְקֵר. אָמַר רִבִּי לָא בְּפֵירוּשׁ פְּלִיגִין רִבִּי יוֹחָנָן אָמַר הֶבְקֵרוֹ הֶבְקֵר. רִבִּי שִׁמְעוֹן בֶּן לָקִישׁ אָמַר אֵין הֶבְקֵרוֹ הֶבְקֵר.

Property abandoned to animals but not to humans, to Gentiles but not to Jews, to rich but not to poor, everybody agrees that it does not have the status of abandoned property[13]. For humans but not for animals, for Jews but not for Gentiles, for the poor of one town but not for the poor of any other town[14] is a disagreement between Rebbi Johanan and Rebbi Simeon ben Laqish. In the opinion of Rebbi Johanan, this abandoning is legal abandoning[15]. In the opinion of Rebbi Simeon ben Laqish, this abandoning is not legal abandoning[16]. Rebbi Lia said, they disagree explicitly: Rebbi Johanan said, this abandoning is legal abandoning. Rebbi Simeon ben Laqish said, this abandoning is not legal abandoning.

13 And is subject to the laws of heave and tithes.

14 This shows that the entire discussion is about the opinion of the House of Shammai. However, in Tosephta *Peah* 3:1 it is stated that "the House of Shammai agree with the House of Hillel that if he abandoned property for humans but not for animals, for Jews but not for Gentiles, it is legally abandoned." This, then, must be taken as the Babylonian position.

15 In his opinion, restrictive abandoning is permitted.

16 Since he deduces the rules from the Sabbatical year, and there animals and the stranger are explicitly mentioned as beneficiaries.

אָמַר רִבִּי אָבִין בַּר חִייָא הָדָא דְאָמְרָה הֶבְקֵר לָעֲנִיִּים וְזָכוּ בָהֶן עֲשִׁירִין תַּפְלִיגְתָא דְרִבִּי מֵאִיר וְרִבִּי יוֹסֵי. עַל דַּעְתֵּיהּ דְּרִבִּי מֵאִיר דּוּ אָמַר כֵּיוָן שֶׁאָדָם מַבְקִיר דָּבָר מֵרְשׁוּתוֹ הֶבְקֵרוֹ הֶבְקֵר. עַל דַּעְתֵּיהּ דְּרִבִּי יוֹסֵי דּוּ אָמַר אֵין דָּבָר יוֹצֵא מִתַּחַת יְדֵי הַבְּעָלִים אֶלָּא בִּזְכִייָה אֵין הֶבְקֵרוֹ הֶבְקֵר.

Rebbi Abin bar Hiyya said, that which was said, if it was abandoned to the poor but grabbed by the rich is a difference between Rebbi Meïr and Rebbi Yose[17]. According to Rebbi Meïr, who asserts that [it is legally abandoned] as soon as a person abandons anything from his property, [in our case] it is legally abandoned[18]. According to Rebbi Yose, who says that nothing may leave the hands of its owners except if it is taken up [by another person, in our case] it is not legally abandoned[19].

17 The main source is *Nedarim*, Babli 43a ff., Yerushalmi 4:10. The Mishnah speaks of a person A who made a vow not to use anything belonging to another person B. According to R. Meïr, B may abandon some property which A may take, but according to R. Yose, the abandoned property still belongs to B (who is also responsible for any damage caused by or on this property) until someone picked it up; hence, A may not take up the abandoned property.

18 The rich person, while acting in an improper way, nevertheless acquired the abandoned article.

19 Since under the terms of the abandonment, the rich person will not acquire it even if he picks it up.

עַד[20] כְּדוֹן בְּשֶׁהִבְקִירָהּ לִזְמַן מְרוּבָּה. אֲבָל הִבְקִירָהּ לִזְמַן מוּעָט. נִישְׁמְעִינָהּ מִן הָדָא הִבְקִיר אֶת שָׂדֵהוּ שְׁנַיִם וּשְׁלֹשָׁה יָמִים חוֹזֵר בּוֹ. תַּנֵּי רִבִּי שִׁמְעוֹן דימא[21] קוֹמֵי רִבִּי זְעִירָא אֲפִילוּ לְאַחַר שְׁלֹשָׁה חוֹזֵר בּוֹ. אָמַר לֵיהּ מִכֵּיוָן דְּאַתְּ אָמַר אֲפִילוּ לְאַחַר שְׁלֹשָׁה יָמִים הִיא לְאַחַר שְׁלֹשָׁה הִיא לְאַחַר כַּמָּה. לִישָׁן מַתְנִיתָא מְסַייֵעַ לְרִבִּי זְעִירָא בַּמֶּה דְּבָרִים אֲמוּרִים כְּשֶׁהִבְקִיר סְתָם. אֲבָל אִם אָמַר שָׂדִי מוּבְקֶרֶת יוֹם אֶחָד שַׁבָּת אַחַת חֹדֶשׁ אֶחָד שָׁנָה אַחַת שָׁבוּעַ אֶחָד אִם עַד שֶׁלֹּא זָכָה בֵּין הוּא בֵּין אַחֵר הוּא[22] יָכוֹל לַחֲזוֹר בּוֹ. אֲבָל מִשֶּׁזָּכָה בֵּין הוּא בֵּין אַחֵר אֵינוֹ יָכוֹל לַחֲזוֹר בּוֹ. הָדָא אָמְרָה הוּא זְמַן מְרוּבָּה הוּא זְמַן מוּעָט. הָדָא אָמְרָה לֹא חָשׁוּ עַל הַעֲרָמָה. הָדָא אָמְרָה שֶׁאָדָם מַבְקִיר וְחוֹזֵר וְזוֹכֶה. הָדָא פְשִׁיטָא שְׁאִילְתֵּיהּ דְּרִבִּי זְעִירָא. דְּרִבִּי זְעִירָא אָמַר הוּא זְמַן מְרוּבָּה הוּא זְמַן מוּעָט.

So far[23], if he abandoned it for a longer period of time. But if he abandoned only for a short time? Let us hear from the following[24]: "If he abandoned his field, he may cancel his action during two or three days[25]." Rebbi Simeon Dima stated before Rebbi Zeïra: Even after three he may cancel his action. He said to him, since you say after three days, is it the same after three or after many? The language of a *baraitha* supports Rebbi Zeïra: "About when is this said[26]? If he abandoned in an unspecified way. But if he said: My field shall be abandoned one day, one week, one month, one year, a sabbatical period, as long as nobody took it over, either he or another person, he may cancel. But after somebody acquired it, either he or somebody else, he cannot cancel." This means that short or long periods are the same. It also means that they were not worried about dishonesty[27]. That obviously answers Rebbi Zeïra's question, since Rebbi Zeira had said, are short and long times the same?

20 This paragraph is also in *Nedarim* 4:10 where the text is somewhat better preserved.

21 In *Nedarim* דַּייְנָא. In the Rome manuscript ר' יימא. Since he is not mentioned again, the correct name cannot be established.

22 This is the text in *Nedarim*. In *Peah*, אינו, a scribal error as seen from the next sentence.

23 These two words belong to *Nedarim*, not here. The question is, whether a person may abandon real property on condition that it automatically revert to the previous owner unless picked up by another person in a certain interval of time. In order to avoid declarations of abandonment simply for the purpose of evading heave, tithes, and taxes, restrictions might have been placed by the Rabbinic Court on the right of reversal.

24 The two passages in quotation marks are from a text close to Tosephta *Ma'serot* 3:11; see also Babli *Nedarim* 43b-44a.

25 But after that, the renunciation becomes absolute.

26 That after two days the act becomes irrevocable.

27 Since the probability that nobody else took the property is very small.

מַה נָן קַייָמִין. אִם מִשּׁוּם דָּבָר מְסוּייָם דַּיּוֹ שְׁנַיִם. אִם מִשּׁוּם שׁוּרָה דַּייוֹ שְׁלֹשָׁה. חַד בַּר בֵּי רַב אָמַר הָדָא[28] דְּרִבִּי יוֹחָנָן קוֹמֵי רִבִּי שִׁמְעוֹן בֶּן לָקִישׁ כָּל־שֶׁהוּא יָכוֹל לְחוֹלְקוֹ וְלַעֲשׂוֹתוֹ שׁוּרָה כְּבֵית שַׁמַּאי. רִבִּי יוֹנָה וְהוּא בָּעֵי שֵׁיעוּרָא כָּל־עוֹמְרֵי הַשָּׂדֶה שֶׁל קַב קַב וְאֶחָד שֶׁל אַרְבַּעַת קַבִּין וּשְׁכָחוּ כָּל־עוֹמְרֵי הַשָּׂדֶה שֶׁל שְׁנֵי קַבִּין וְאֶחָד שֶׁל שְׁמוֹנַת קַבִּין.

What are we discussing[29]? If it should be recognizable, two would be enough. If for a row[30], three would be enough. One scholar quoted this statement by Rebbi Joḥanan before Rebbi Simeon ben Laqish: Anything he can split and make into a row following the House of Shammai[31]. Rebbi Jonah: That goes by proportionality; "if all sheaves of a field are of one *qab* each, except one which is of four *qab* and they forgot about that one," if all sheaves of a field are of two *qab* each, except one which is of eight *qab*.

28 Reading of R. S. Cirillo. The Venice print has a garbled: חד בא רבי אמר חדא

29 This deals with the last part of the Mishnah, quoted by R. Jonah, that an outsize sheaf left on the field is not "forgotten" for the House of Shammai.

30 This refers to Mishnah 4, which states that two sheaves constitute forgotten sheaves, but three sheaves do not. On this, the Halakhah specifies that the three sheaves must form a row in order to escape the law of forgotten sheaves.

31 At the end of Mishnah 4, the House of Shammai is quoted as giving three sheaves to the poor, four sheaves to the farmer.

(fol. 19a) **משנה ב**: הָעוֹמֶר שֶׁהוּא סָמוּךְ לְגָפָא וּלְגָדִישׁ וּלְבָקָר וּלְכֵלִים וּשְׁכָחוֹ בֵּית שַׁמַּאי אוֹמְרִים אֵינוֹ שִׁכְחָה. וּבֵית הִלֵּל אוֹמְרִים שִׁכְחָה.

Mishnah 2: A sheaf that was near a closure[32], a stack, cattle[33], or vessels, if it was forgotten, the House of Shammai say, it is not a forgotten sheaf, but the House of Hillel say, it is a forgotten sheaf.

32 Where an opening in a fence was closed with wood or other materials. This is the concurrent explanation of Rashi (*Baba Meẓi'a*

25b), Rabbenu Ḥananel (*loc. cit.*), and Maimonides (Commentary on the Mishnah) and, therefore, Geonic tradition. Ben Jehudah derives the word from the root גוף, גפף "to close an opening." For example, מגופה is a clay block with which the top of an amphora containing wine or olive oil is sealed. The deviating explanation of R. Simson of Sens, "a stone fence made without mortar," is preferred by modern Talmudic dictionaries. Schwab translates: "fence of pales," close to the Modern Hebrew acception: "fence made of a weave of reeds or rods."

33 Cattle rather than horses were used to draw agricultural implements.

(fol. 19b) **הלכה ב**: וְקַשְׁיָא עַל דְּבֵית שַׁמַּאי בְּגָפָא וּבְגָדִישׁ דָּבָר שֶׁהוּא מְסוּיָּם וְאִינּוּן אָמְרֵי אֵינָן שִׁכְחָה. וְקַשְׁיָא עַל דְּבֵית הִלֵּל בְּבָקָר וּבְכֵלִים דָּבָר שֶׁאֵינוֹ מְסוּיָּם וְאִינּוּן אָמְרִין הוּא שִׁכְחָה.

Halakhah 2: It is difficult about the House of Shammai; closure and stack are definite things, and they say it is not a forgotten sheaf. It is difficult about the House of Hillel; cattle and vessels are not definite things, and they say it is a forgotten sheaf[34].

34 The background of the question is not clear. It is stated in the paragraph after the next that in one interpretation the Mishnah deals only with the case that the sheaf was already taken up to be brought to the threshing floor but then was deposited somewhere and forgotten. It is stated as a general principle of the House of Shammai that the farmer already acquired final possession of the sheaf by taking it up. The House of Hillel is of the opinion that the Biblical ordinance of the forgotten sheaf overrides everything until the grain is removed from the fields. The operating term in this respect is (*Deut.* 24:19) "and *you* will forget," i. e., it must be you who forgets. We have to assume that the House of Shammai in principle also will agree to such an interpretation. Then we would say that it is difficult to forget something deposited near a landmark; hence, if it is forgotten, the House of Shammai are not justified not to declare it a

forgotten sheaf. On the other hand, if the sheaf was deposited near movable objects and is not easily found again, the House of Hillel should have accepted the action of prior acquisition. (Interpretation of *Tosafot Yom Tov* on the Mishnah.)

But the position of this set of questions before the interpretation of the Mishnah seems to indicate that the question is asked in a general way, rather than about a sheaf which was already taken up. Therefore, most commentators, from R. Simson to R. Z. Frankel, prefer to change the text and switch the names of Hillel and Shammai. There is no textual basis for this. The best interpretation of the text as it stands is the one of R. Moshe Margalit, who explains as follows: "It is difficult about the House of Shammai; (*if their reason is that*) closure and stack are definite things (*location not easily forgotten*), and they say (*even for cattle and vessels, which are easily moved*) it is not a forgotten sheaf! It is difficult about the House of Hillel, (*if their reason is that*) cattle and vessels are not stationary, and they say (*even for closure and stack*) it is a forgotten sheaf!"

בִּמְקוֹמוֹ הוּא עוֹמֵד בְּצַד הַגַּת אוֹ בְצַד פִּירְצָה מַתְנִיתָא דְבֵית שַׁמַּאי דְּבֵית שַׁמַּאי אָמְרִין אֵינוֹ שִׁכְחָה. אָמַר רִבִּי יוֹסֵי דִּבְרֵי הַכֹּל הִיא. תַּמָּן דָּבָר מְחוּבָּר בְּצַד דָּבָר מְחוּבָּר בְּרַם הָכָא דָבָר תָּלוּשׁ בְּצַד דָּבָר מְחוּבָּר.

"By its place, if it was standing beside the wine press or beside a breach in the fence[35]." This Mishnah follows the House of Shammai, since the House of Shammai say, it is not a forgotten sheaf[36]. Rebbi Yose said, it is everybody's opinion. There a stationary object[37] is beside a stationary one, but here a movable object[38] is beside a stationary one.

35 This is a quote from Mishnah 7:1: "Every olive tree which has a special name on the field, for example 'a dripping olive tree' at harvest time, if it was forgotten, is not subject to the law of the forgotten sheaf. How is this said? By its name, its yield, or its place. . . . By its place, if it was standing beside the wine press or beside a breach in the fence."

36 If the sheaf was forgotten near a well-defined breach in the fence. This would imply that practice has to follow the House of Shammai, against the general rule to follow the House of Hillel.

37 The olive tree.

38 The sheaf, which according to the House of Hillel is considered forgotten in the legal sense.

אָמַר רִבִּי אִילְעַאי שָׁאַלְתִּי אֶת רִבִּי יְהוֹשֻׁעַ בְּאֵילוּ עוֹמָרִין חֲלוּקִין בֵּית שַׁמַּאי וּבֵית הִלֵּל אָמַר לִי[39] הַתּוֹרָה הַזֹּאת עוֹמֶר הַסָּמוּךְ לְגָפָה וּלְגָדִישׁ וּלְבָקָר וּלְכֵלִים וּשְׁכָחוֹ בֵּית שַׁמַּאי אוֹמְרִים שִׁכְחָה. וּבֵית הִלֵּל אוֹמְרִים אֵינוֹ שִׁכְחָה. וּכְשֶׁבָּאתִי אֵצֶל רִבִּי אֱלִיעֶזֶר אָמַר לִי לֹא נֶחְלְקוּ בֵּית שַׁמַּאי וּבֵית הִלֵּל עַל הָעוֹמֶר שֶׁהוּא סָמוּךְ לְגָפָה וּלְגָדִישׁ וּלְבָקָר וְלַכֵּלִים וּשְׁכָחוֹ שֶׁהוּא שִׁכְחָה. וְעַל מַה נֶחְלְקוּ עַל הָעוֹמֶר שֶׁנְּטָלוֹ וּנְתָנוֹ בְּצַד הַגָּפָה בְּצַד הַגָּדִישׁ בְּצַד הַבָּקָר בְּצַד הַכֵּלִים וּשְׁכָחוֹ שֶׁבֵּית שַׁמַּאי אוֹמְרִים אֵינוֹ שִׁכְחָה מִפְּנֵי שֶׁזָּכָה בוֹ. וּבֵית הִלֵּל אוֹמְרִים שִׁכְחָה. וּכְשֶׁבָּאתִי וְהִרְצֵיתִי אֶת הַדְּבָרִים לִפְנֵי רִבִּי לָעְזָר בֶּן עֲזַרְיָה אָמַר לִי הַבְּרִית (fol. 19c) הֵן הַדְּבָרִים שֶׁנֶּאֶמְרוּ לוֹ לְמֹשֶׁה בְּחוֹרֵב.

[40]Rebbi Ilaï[41] said: I asked Rebbi Joshua, about which sheaves do the Houses of Shammai and Hillel disagree? He said to me, this is the teaching: The sheaf which was near a closure, a stack, cattle, or vessels, if it was forgotten, the House of Shammai say it is a forgotten sheaf, but the House of Hillel say it is not a forgotten sheaf[42]. But when I came to Rebbi Eliezer, he told me that the Houses of Shammai and Hillel did not disagree that a sheaf near a closure, a stack, cattle, or vessels, if it was forgotten, was a forgotten sheaf. What did they disagree about? About a sheaf he took up[43] and put beside a closure, beside a stack, beside cattle, beside vessels, and forgot about it; in that case the House of Shammai say it is not a forgotten sheaf because he already acquired rights to it. But the House of Hillel say it is a forgotten sheaf. And when I came and lectured about these things before Rebbi Eleazar ben Azariah, he said to me, by the Covenant[44], these are the words that had been spoken to Moses on Horeb.

39 Reading of the Tosephta. The Venice print has אומר ליה.

40 With some minor deviations, this is Tosephta *Peah* 3:2.

41 A Tanna of the third generation, student mostly of R. Eliezer, but also of the other great leaders of the second generation. Through his son, Rebbi Jehudah, the teachings of Rebbi Eliezer became so influential in the Mishnah.

42 I. e., the Mishnah deals with the status of these sheaves under various circumstances. The text here switches the positions of the Houses of Hillel and Shammai. In the Tosephta, the rest of the sentence starting with "the House of Shammai say," is missing. Hence, either R. Joshua disagrees with the Mishnah which is formulated in the tradition of R. Eliezer, or there is a scribal error. While in general, the opinion of R. Joshua prevails against that of R. Eliezer, here R. Eliezer's opinion is endorsed in the strongest terms by R. Eleazar ben Azariah and should determine practice (Maimonides *Mattenot Aniïm* 5:3).

43 And removed the sheaf away from the original field; since the owner cannot acquire his own property on his own field, he must have moved on the public road at least for a few steps. Then the only question is whether the commandment of the forgotten sheaf overrides the acquisition.

44 An oath formula.

תַּמָּן תַּנֵּינָן הָאִשָּׁה שֶׁנָּפְלוּ לָהּ נְכָסִים עַד שֶׁלֹּא תִתְאָרֵס מוֹדִים בֵּית שַׁמַּאי וּבֵית הִלֵּל שֶׁהִיא מוֹכֶרֶת וְנוֹתֶנֶת וְקַיָּים. נָפְלוּ לָהּ מִשֶּׁנִּתְאָרְסָה בֵּית שַׁמַּאי אוֹמְרִים תִּימְכּוֹר וּבֵית הִלֵּל אוֹמְרִים לֹא תִמְכּוֹר. רִבִּי פִינְחָס בְּעָא קוֹמֵי רִבִּי יוֹסֵי וְלָמָּה לֹא תַנֵּינָתָהּ מִקּוּלֵּי בֵית שַׁמַּאי וּמֵחוּמְרֵי בֵית הִלֵּל. אֲמַר לֵיהּ לָא אֲתִינָן מַתְנִיָּתָא אֶלָּא דָּבָר שֶׁהוּא חוֹמֶר מִשְּׁנֵי צְדָדִין וְקַל מִשְּׁנֵי צְדָדִין. בְּרַם הָכָא חוֹמֶר הוּא מִצַּד אֶחָד וְקַל מִצַּד אֶחָד. וְהָתַנֵּינָן בֵּית שַׁמַּאי אוֹמְרִין הֶבְקֵר לָעֲנִיִּים הֶבְקֵר הֲרֵי הוּא קַל לָעֲנִיִּים וְחוֹמֶר הוּא לְבַעַל הַבַּיִת וְתַנִּיתָהּ. קַל הוּא לָעֲנִיִּים וְאֵינוֹ חוֹמֶר לְבַעַל הַבַּיִת שֶׁמִּדַּעְתּוֹ הוּבְקְרוּ. אָמַר לֵיהּ וְהָתַנֵּינָן עוֹמֶר שֶׁהוּא סָמוּךְ לְגָפָה וּלְגָדִישׁ וּלְבָקָר וְלְכֵלִים וּשְׁכָחוֹ הוּא קַל לְבַעַל הַבַּיִת וְחוֹמֶר הוּא לָעֲנִיִּים וְתַנִּיתָהּ. אָמַר לֵיהּ קַל הוּא לְבַעַל הַבַּיִת וְאֵינוֹ חוֹמֶר לָעֲנִיִּים שֶׁאַדַּיִין לֹא זָכוּ בָהֶן וֶאֱמוֹר אוּף הָכָא קַל הוּא לָאִשָּׁה וְאֵינוֹ חוֹמֶר לְבַעַל הַבַּיִת שֶׁאַדַּיִין לֹא זָכָה בָהּ. אָמַר לֵיהּ מִכֵּיוָן שֶׁקִּדְּשָׁהּ לִזְכוּתָהּ וְלִזְכוּתוֹ נָפְלוּ.

There[45] we have stated: "A woman who inherited property before she was betrothed[46], the Houses of Shammai and Hillel both are of the opinion that she may sell or give away and her actions are valid. If she inherited after she was betrothed, the House of Shammai say, she may sell, but the House of Hillel say, she may not sell[47]." Rebbi Phineas asked before Rebbi Yose, why did we not state it with the leniencies of the House of Shammai and the stringencies of the House of Hillel[48]? He said to him, the Mishnaiot come only for circumstances that are either stringent on both sides or lenient on both sides. But here it is a stringency on one side[49] and a leniency on the other side. But did we not state: "The House of Shammai say, property abandoned to the poor is abandoned?" Is this not lenient for the poor and stringent for the householder, and it was stated! It is lenient for the poor[50] and not stringent for the householder, since it was abandoned by his intent. He said to him, did we not state: "The sheaf that was near a closure, a stack, cattle, or vessels, if it was forgotten," is this not lenient for the householder and stringent for the poor, and it was stated! He said to him, it is lenient for the householder but not stringent for the poor, because they did not acquire it yet. You may also say here[51], it is lenient for the woman and not stringent for the husband since he did not yet acquire property rights to it. He[52] said to him, since he became betrothed to her, the inheritance fell to both of them.

45 *Ketubot* 8:1; there this paragraph and the next one appear.

46 A Jewish marriage is performed in two stages. The first, *qiddushin*, which for lack of a better English equivalent was translated as "betrothed," requires the groom to hand over to the bride an object of value (today, a gold ring) and to declare before two witnesses that the woman is

betrothed to him. From that moment on they are married as far as penal law is concerned. In antiquity, the propective bride (who probably was in her early teens) did not prepare any trousseau. Hence, after *qiddushin* she was given adequate time to prepare and then was married to live with her husband in a second public ceremony, *nissuïn*, the execution of the *ketubah* document, in which the groom mortgages all his possessions and earnings for the upkeep of his wife and the care of his children, followed by the public recitation of seven benedictions (in the presence of 10 adult males). From that moment on, the couple is required to live in intimacy. Today, the two ceremonies are separated only by the reading of the *ketubah* and, sometimes, by a rabbi's sermon. The period between *qiddushin* and *nissuïn* is one in which the groom is married, but as he is forbidden marital relations with his wife, as yet has no financial responsibility. After *nissuïn*, since the wife has a claim on his property enforceable in court, he receives administration of her estate.

47 Since the husband will have a monetary interest in the property after *nissuïn*.

48 In the fourth chapter of *Iddiut*, the few cases in which the House of Shammai are more lenient than that of Hillel are enumerated. The first two Mishnaiot of the present chapter are included in that list, the one from *Ketubot* is not.

49 On the wife, who is restricted in her actions. The law is lenient for the husband, who gets veto power over the actions of his wife before he mortgages all his property to her.

50 In that non-poor persons may not acquire it.

51 In the case of *Ketubot*.

52 Rebbi Yose.

אָמַר רִבִּי יוּדָה אָמְרוּ לִפְנֵי רַבָּן גַּמְלִיאֵל הוֹאִיל וְהָאֲרוּסָה אִשְׁתּוֹ וְהַנְּשׂוּאָה אִשְׁתּוֹ מַה זּוֹ מִכְרָהּ בָּטֵל אַף זוֹ מִכְרָהּ בָּטֵל. אָמַר לָהֶן בַּחֲדָשִׁים אָנוּ בוֹשִׁין אֶלָּא שֶׁאַתֶּם מְגַלְגְּלִין עִמָּנוּ הַיְשָׁנִים. אֵילּוּ הֵן הַחֲדָשִׁים מִשֶּׁנִּשְּׂאֵת. וְאֵלּוּ הֵן הַיְשָׁנִים עַד שֶׁלֹּא נִשְּׂאֵת וְנִשְּׂאֵת.

Rebbi Jehudah said[53], they argued before Rabban Gamliel: Because betrothed she is his wife and married she is his wife; just as the sale by the latter is void, the sale by the former also should be void. He said to them, we are ashamed of the new ones[54], now you want to roll old ones over us[55]! The new ones, after *nissuïn*; the old ones before *nissuïn,* when she was married in the second ceremony.

53 This paragraph belongs only to *Ketubot*; it was copied with the preceding paragraph.

54 To require the husband's consent to any financial or business transaction by his wife.

55 Extending the husband's rights to *qiddushin*.

(fol. 19a) **משנה ג**: רָאשֵׁי הַשּׁוּרוֹת עוֹמֶר שֶׁכְּנֶגְדּוֹ מוֹכִיחַ. הָעוֹמֶר שֶׁהֶחֱזִיק בּוֹ לְהוֹלִיכוֹ אֶל הָעִיר וְשָׁכַח מוֹדִים שֶׁאֵינוֹ שִׁכְחָה. אֵלּוּ הֵן רָאשֵׁי הַשּׁוּרוֹת שְׁנַיִם שֶׁהִתְחִילוּ בְּאֶמְצַע הַשּׁוּרָה זֶה פָּנָה לְצָפוֹן וְזֶה פָּנָה לְדָרוֹם וְשָׁכְחוּ לִפְנֵיהֶן וּלְאַחֲרֵיהֶן. שֶׁלִּפְנֵיהֶן שִׁכְחָה וְשֶׁל אַחֲרֵיהֶן אֵינוֹ שִׁכְחָה. הַיָּחִיד שֶׁהִתְחִיל מֵרֹאשׁ הַשּׁוּרָה וְשָׁכַח לְפָנָיו וּלְאַחֲרָיו. שֶׁלְּפָנָיו אֵינוֹ שִׁכְחָה וְשֶׁלְּאַחֲרָיו שִׁכְחָה. שֶׁהוּא בְּבַל תָּשׁוּב. זֶה הַכְּלָל כָּל־שֶׁהוּא בְּבַל תָּשׁוּב שִׁכְחָה וְכָל־שֶׁאֵינוֹ בְּבַל תָּשׁוּב אֵינוֹ שִׁכְחָה.

Mishnah 3: Heads of rows[56], the sheaf next to it proves[57], and a sheaf that was taken up to be brought to town[58] and then was forgotten, they all agree that they never are forgotten sheaves. The following describe heads of rows: Two who started in the middle of the row, one turned North and the other turned South, and they forgot before them or after them. The one before them is a forgotten sheaf[59], the one after them is not a forgotten sheaf. A single person who started at the head of a row and forgot before and after himself. The one before him is not a forgotten sheaf[60], but the one after him is a forgotten sheaf because it falls under (*Deut.* 24:19) "do not return to take it." This is the principle: Anything that falls under "do not return to take it," is a forgotten sheaf, but anything that does not fall under "do not return to take it," is not a forgotten sheaf.

56 When sheaves are arranged in rows, the first sheaf in each row is always exempt from the law of forgotten sheaves since either one starts from it or one ends at it; in neither case could one return to it.

57 If sheaves were arranged in parallel rows, and the sheaves were then removed by rows in one direction. If a sheaf from one was left standing but in the orthogonal direction there was a sheaf standing next to it, the standing sheaf now belongs to a row in the other direction; it is not forgotten until it is isolated in all directions from the rest of the sheaves still on the field. (By Mishnah 4, two isolated sheaves may be "forgotten", a group of three is not.)

58 The House of Hillel agree with that of Shammai that as soon as the sheaf is taken up to be removed from growing areas, the laws of the forgotten stalk no longer apply.

59 Any sheaf that at the start of the collection was in front of one of the workers, if forgotten, is subject to the law of forgotten sheaves. But if a sheaf was between the two, in the back of both of them, it is not forgotten since it never was considered, and it remains the head of an East-West row.

60 If he leaves sheaves before him but does not jump over one, these belong to East-West rows and do not have the status of being forgotten.

(fol. 19c) **הלכה ג:** מְנַיִין לְרָאשֵׁי שׁוּרוֹת. אָמַר רִבִּי יוֹנָה כְּתִיב כִּי תִקְצוֹר קְצִירְךָ בְשָׂדֶךָ וְשָׁכַחְתָּ מַה שֶׁאַתָּה קוֹצֵר אַתָּה שׁוֹכֵחַ. עַד כְּדוֹן רָאשֵׁי שׁוּרוֹת קָמָה. סוֹף שׁוּרוֹת קָמָה אָמַר רִבִּי יוֹנָה לֹא תָשׁוּב לְקַחְתּוֹ. מִמְּקוֹמוֹ שֶׁבָּאָת לֹא תָשׁוּב לְקַחְתּוֹ. עַד כְּדוֹן רָאשֵׁי שׁוּרוֹת עוֹמָרִין. סוֹף שׁוּרוֹת עוֹמָרִין. אָמַר רִבִּי יוֹנָה נֵילַף רֹאשׁ שׁוּרוֹת עוֹמָרִין מֵרֹאשׁ שׁוּרוֹת קָמָה וְסוֹף שׁוּרוֹת קָמָה מִסּוֹף שׁוּרוֹת עוֹמָרִין.

Halakhah 3: From where about heads of rows[61]? Rebbi Jonah said, it is written (*Deut*. 24:19): "When you are harvesting your harvest on your field and you forget," what you harvest you can forget[62]. That refers to the start of rows of standing grain. End of rows of standing grain? Rebbi Jonah said, "do not return to take it." From the place you came from you should not return to take it[63]. So far, about starts of rows of sheaves, ends of rows of sheaves? Rebbi Jonah said, we learn starts of rows of sheaves from starts of rows of standing grain and ends of rows of standing grain from ends of rows of sheaves[64].

61 That they are exempt from the laws of forgotten sheaves.

62 But you cannot forget what you only start to harvest. Hence, uncut stalks at the start of a row to be cut are not for the poor.

63 At the end of the row one goes to the next row; since one is at the end of the field he cannot retrace his steps to the end of the row.

64 The verse speaks of the forgotten sheaf but is formulated in terms of harvesting standing grain. Just as forgotten standing stalks at beginning and end of rows are not for the poor, neither are sheaves at beginning and end of rows.

הָעוֹמֶר שֶׁכְּנֶגְדּוֹ מוֹכִיחַ. כֵּיצַד הָיוּ לוֹ עֶשֶׂר שׁוּרוֹת שֶׁל עֲשָׂרָה עֲשָׂרָה עוֹמָרִין עִימֵּר אֶחָד מֵהֶן בִּצָפוֹן וְדָרוֹם וְשָׁכַח אֶחָד מֵהֶן אֵינוֹ שִׁכְחָה מִפְּנֵי שֶׁהוּא נִידּוֹן מִזְרַח וּמַעֲרָב. עִימֵּר מִזְרַח וּמַעֲרָב וּשְׁכָחוֹ מַהוּ שֶׁיֵּעָשֶׂה שִׁכְחָה. נִישְׁמְעִינָהּ מִן הָדָא עִימֵּר אֶת הָרִאשׁוֹן וְאֶת הַשֵּׁנִי וְאֶת הַשְּׁלִישִׁי וְשָׁכַח אֶת הָרְבִיעִי. אִית תַּנָּיֵי תַּנֵּי אִם נָטַל אֶת הַחֲמִישִׁי הֲרֵי הוּא שִׁכְחָה. וְאִית תַּנָּיֵי תַּנֵּי אִם שֶׁהָא לִיטּוֹל אֶת הַחֲמִישִׁי הֲרֵי הוּא שִׁכְחָה. אָמַר רִבִּי בּוּן בַּר חִיָּיא מָאן דְּאָמַר נוֹטֵל אֶת הַחֲמִישִׁי בְּשֶׁיֵּשׁ שָׁם שִׁישִּׁי. מָאן דְּאָמַר אִם שֶׁהָא לִיטּוֹל אֶת הַחֲמִישִׁי בְּשֶׁאֵין שָׁם שִׁישִּׁי. אִם עַד שֶׁלֹּא נָטַל אֶת הַחֲמִישִׁי לֹא כְּבָר נִרְאֶה אֶת הָרְבִיעִי לִידּוֹן כְּשׁוּרָה. אִם אָמַר שִׁכְחָה וְהָכָא שִׁכְחָה.

"The sheaf next to it proves[65]." How is that? (Tosephta *Peah* 3:4): "If he had ten rows of ten sheaves each and he removed one row of them in a North-South direction; when he forgot one of them it is not forgotten because it is considered East-West[66]." When he then removed the sheaves East-West and forgot one of them, let us hear from the following[67]: When he removed the first, second, and third sheaves[68] but forgot[69] the fourth, some state: If he removed the fifth, it becomes legally forgotten, but some state: If he waited long enough that he could have removed the fifth, it becomes legally forgotten. Rebbi Avin bar Ḥiyya said, he who says, "if he removed the fifth" if there is a sixth[70], but he who says, "if he waited long enough that he could have removed the fifth" if there is no sixth[71]. Before he took away the fifth, would not the fourth be apt to be considered starting a row[72]? If this is named "forgotten," then also in our case[73] it is "forgotten."

65 Quote from the Mishnah.

66 It is connected to the part of the field not yet worked over in the orthogonal direction.

67 Word-by-word parallel to Chapter 5, Halakhah 2.

68 He not only bound them but he also removed them to a storage place or threshing floor. This statement assumes that a standard row of sheaves are three sheaves. Hence, the full second row would be sheaves 4,5,6.

69 To remove the fourth after it was bound.

70 Because sheaves in a row are saved by the next sheaf just as stalks in a row are saved by the next stalk. Hence, the fourth can become legally forgotten only if the fifth, which saves it from being legally forgotten, is removed.

71 Since there is no row of three sheaves, they will be taken to be removed individually and not as a row. Hence, it is enough that the fifth could have been finished and removed.

72 If there are six sheaves, the fourth does not become legally abandoned until the sheaf which saves it is removed.

73 Of sheaves first taken N-S, then E-W.

הָיָה עוֹמֶר אֶחָד גָּדוֹל עִימֵּר צַד הַחִיצוֹן בְּצַד הַפְּנִימִי נִידּוֹן כְּשׁוּרָה. עִימֵּר צַד הַפְּנִימִי בְּצַד הַחִיצוֹן מַהוּ שֶׁיִּדּוֹן כְּשׁוּרָה. עִימֵּר צַד הָעֶלְיוֹן בְּצַד הַתַּחְתּוֹן נִידּוֹן כְּשׁוּרָה. עִימֵּר הַתַּחְתּוֹן בְּצַד הָעֶלְיוֹן מַהוּ שֶׁיִּדּוֹן כְּשׁוּרָה.

If there was an oversize sheaf[74] and he removed a sheaf from the outside next to the inside, it is considered a row[75]. If he removed from the inside next to the outside, may it be considered a row[76]? If he removed from the top beside the bottom it is considered a row[77]. If he removed from the bottom beside the top, is it considered a row?

74 And he decided to split it into regular size sheaves.

75 If only part of the sheaf is removed, that part must be bound in a separate sheaf. We must assume that there is another sheaf standing nearby, so that there are three sheaves standing close together which form a row for the House of Hillel (Mishnah 4), or that the farmer splits his oversized sheaf into three, working from the outside in (which is the natural thing to do.)

76 We still have a minimum of three sheaves (see preceding Note) but since the farmer works from the inside out he is going back and, by R. Jonah's argument at the start of the Halakhah, the sheaf formed by the outside stalks should not be protected as "head of row."

77 That means, he takes off the top stalks to form a separate sheaf, the bottom part taking the place of the original oversized sheaf. This certainly is legitimate. However, if the farmer contrives a way to pull the lower stalks out of the sheaf, the question is as before, whether any of the resulting sheaves can be protected as heads of a row. These purely theoretical questions are not answered.

רַב כַּד נְחַת לְתַמָּן אָמַר אֲנָא הוּא בֶּן עַזַּאי דְּהָכָא. אֲתָא חַד סָב שְׁאַל לֵיהּ שְׁנֵי הֲרוּגִים זֶה עַל גַּבֵּי זֶה סְבַר רַב שֶׁהֵן עוֹרְפִין. אֲמַר לֵיהּ אֵין עוֹרְפִין. אֲמַר לֵיהּ לָמָּה. אֲמַר לֵיהּ הַתַּחְתּוֹן מִשּׁוּם טָמוּן וְהָעֶלְיוֹן מִשּׁוּם צָף. כַּד סְלַק לְהָכָא אֲתָא לְגַבֵּי רִבִּי אֲמַר לֵיהּ יְאוּת אֲמַר לָךְ כִּי יִמָּצֵא וְלֹא כִּי יִמָּצְאוּ.

When Rav descended there[78], he declared: I am this place's Ben Azai[79]. There came an old man and asked him, two slain people, one on top of the other[80]? Rav was of the opinion that one breaks the neck. He told him, one does not break the neck. He asked him, why? He said to him, not the lower one for he is hidden[81], not the upper one because he floats. When he ascended here, he came to Rebbi, who told him: He told you correctly, "if he is found," and not "if they are found."

78 "There" always means Babylonia; going to Babylonia is "descending," going to the Land of Israel is "ascending." The story appears in the same context in Babli *Sotah* 45a, the actor being Abbaie, three generations after Rav; the Yerushalmi version is also in *Sota* 9:2.

79 Ben Azai, one of the most outstanding students of Rebbi Aqiba, was a walking encyclopedia and used to stroll through the markets of Tiberias, ready to immediately answer any question of Jewish learning. He died during mystical studies before he could marry R. Aqiba's daughter. In the Talmudim, several sages are reported to have tried to imitate Ben Azai but all of them were quickly confronted with a question for which they gave the wrong answer or did not know any answer at all. The story is inserted here because a few paragraphs down hidden sheaves will be discussed.

80 This refers to *Deut*. 21:1-9, about the purification ceremony when a person is found murdered and the murderer is not found. Then a calf's neck is broken in a ravine not used for agriculture.

81 The relevant verse is *Deut*. 21:1: "If a corpse is found on the land the Eternal, your God, gives to you . . . ." The lower body is not "found"; he is only discovered when the other body is removed. The upper body is not found *on the land*.

רִבִּי יְהוּדָה בִּרְבִּי אָמַר הָיָה שָׁם אַמַּת הַמַּיִם עַל פְּנֵי כָל־הַשָּׂדֶה אִם עִיקֵּר אֶת הַמַּחֲרֵישָׁה מִצַּד זֶה וְנִיתְּנָהּ בְּצַד זֶה אֵינוֹ נִידּוֹן כְּשׁוּרָה. וְאִם לָאו נִידּוֹן כְּשׁוּרָה. קָצַר חֲצִי שׁוּרָה וּבָא לְמָחָר נִידּוֹן כְּשׁוּרָה. יָשַׁב לֶאֱכוֹל יָשַׁב לִישָׁן קָרָא לוֹ חֲבֵירוֹ חֲשֵׁיכָה.

The great Rebbi Jehudah[82] said: If a water canal crossed the entire field, if he has to lift the plough on one side and put it on the other side, it is not considered one row, otherwise it is considered one row[83]. If he cut half a row and came back the next day it is considered a row[84], when he sat down to eat, when he sat down to sleep, when his friend called him, when it got dark.

82 He probably is Jehudah bar Ḥiyya, son of the great R. Ḥiyya and twin brother of Ḥizqiah.

83 If the irrigation canal is so shallow that the farmer can plough right across, the rows on both sides form just one row together. But if the plough has to be lifted and carried to the other side, then even if the furrow on one side is the exact continuation of the one on the other side, there are legally two rows and four ends that are protected from the law of forgotten sheaves.

84 As in the following examples, anytime the harvest or the work on the sheaves was interrupted, the new start is counted as head of row and exempt from becoming "forgotten."

עוֹמֶר שֶׁנְּטָלוֹ וְהוֹלִיכוֹ לָעִיר וּנְתָנוֹ עַל גַּבֵּי חֲבֵירוֹ וְשָׁכַח אֶת שְׁנֵיהֶן הַתַּחְתּוֹן שִׁכְחָה וְהָעֶלְיוֹן אֵינוֹ שִׁכְחָה. רִבִּי שִׁמְעוֹן אוֹמֵר שְׁנֵיהֶן אֵינָן שִׁכְחָה הַתַּחְתּוֹן מִפְּנֵי שֶׁהוּא מְכוּסֶּה וְהָעֶלְיוֹן מִפְּנֵי שֶׁזָּכָה בוֹ. רִבִּי זְעִירָא אָמַר בְּזוֹכֵר. אֲתִיָא דְּרִבִּי זְעִירָא כְּרִבִּי יוֹנָה. דְּרִבִּי יוֹנָה אָמַר בְּזוֹכֵר אֶת הַקַּשִּׁין כֵּן רִבִּי זְעִירָא אָמַר בְּזוֹכֵר אֶת הָעֶלְיוֹן.

"[85]A sheaf he took to bring to town, put it on another one, and forgot about both, the lower one is a forgotten sheaf but the upper one is not a forgotten sheaf. Rebbi Simeon[86] said, neither of them is a forgotten sheaf; not the lower one because it is covered[87] and not the upper one because he already had acquired it." Rebbi Zeïra said, if he remembers[88]. Rebbi Zeïra parallels Rebbi Jonah, just as Rebbi Jonah said[89], if he remembers the straws, so Rebbi Zeïra said, if he remembers the upper one.

85 An almost identical text is Tosephta *Peah* 3:3. R. Eliahu Fulda explains that חבירו refers to a friend of the farmer; he and his friend both carry a sheaf. This is impossible since one speaks about "upper and lower" sheaf. The other commentators, from Rashi on the Babli to R. S. Lieberman on the Tosephta, do not note the incongruity of having the farmer taking up one sheaf and forgetting two. One has to explain that חבירו is another sheaf; now two are lying on top of one another. {This is good Hebrew style, cf. *Ex.* 26:3 where gobelins are "sisters".} When the upper one is taken up, it is acquired. The lower one then lies uncovered in the field and its status is the subject of the disagreement in the Tosephta. (Problem noted by E. G.)

86 In the Babli, *Sotah* 45b, this is quoted in the name of R. Simeon ben Jehudah who earlier in 5:6 quoted the tradition of R. Simeon (bar Iohai.)

87 R. Simeon follows the opinion of R. Jehudah in Mishnah 9 that covered sheaves do not fall under the law of forgotten sheaves.

88 If he somehow later remembers the upper one, it is his by prior acquisition as spelled out in the Mishnah. If he never remembers the upper one, then the lower one is not covered by anything different from itself and, therefore, cannot legally qualify as hidden.

89 Chapter 5, Halakhah 6, speaking about a sheaf covered under straw which is not forgotten as long as the farmer has the intention of collecting the straw since then the sheaf will automatically be discovered.

שָׂדֶה שֶׁעוֹמָרֶיהָ מְעוּרְבָּבִין וְשָׁכַח אֶחָד מֵהֶן אֵינוֹ שִׁכְחָה עַד שֶׁיִּטּוֹל אֶת סְבִיבָיו.

(Tosephta *Peah* 3:4) "A field whose sheaves are mixed up, if one was forgotten it is not a forgotten sheaf until he removes all around it[90]."

90 The principle of the Mishnah is applied here to a field whose sheaves are not in orderly rows. Nevertheless, a sheaf is not legally forgotten unless it is completely isolated.

(fol. 19a) **משנה ד**: שְׁנֵי עֳמָרִין שִׁכְחָה וּשְׁלֹשָׁה אֵינָן שִׁכְחָה. שְׁנֵי צִיבּוּרֵי זֵיתִים וְהֶחָרוּבִין שִׁכְחָה וּשְׁלֹשָׁה אֵינָן שִׁכְחָה. שְׁנֵי הוּצְנֵי פִשְׁתָּן שִׁכְחָה וּשְׁלֹשָׁה אֵינָן שִׁכְחָה. שְׁנֵי גַרְגּרִים פֶּרֶט וּשְׁלֹשָׁה אֵינָן פֶּרֶט. שְׁנֵי שִׁבֳּלִים לֶקֶט וְשָׁלֹשׁ אֵינָן לֶקֶט כְּדִבְרֵי בֵית הִלֵּל. וְעַל כּוּלָּם בֵּית שַׁמַּאי אוֹמְרִין שְׁלֹשָׁה לָעֲנִיִּים וְאַרְבָּעָה לְבַעַל הַבָּיִת.

Mishnah 4: Two sheaves may qualify as forgotten sheaves, three may not. Two heaps of olives or carob may qualify as "forgotten sheaves", three may not. Two plants[91] of hemp may qualify as "forgotten sheaves", three may not. Two berries may qualify as dropped berries[92], three may not. Two stalks may be gleanings, three may not, following the House of Hillel. About all of these, the House of Shammai say three are for the poor and four for the proprietor.

91 Definition of Maimonides and R. Simson, cf. Arabic חוץ "palm leaves." R. Isaac ben Malchisedek Simponti translates by Italian *manelle* "sheaves."

92 Refers to *Lev*. 19:10: "The dropped berries in your vineyard you shall not collect; abandon them to the poor and the stranger."

(fol. 19c) **הלכה ד**: רִבִּי בּוּן בַּר חִיָּא עֲשָׂאָן כְּמִין גַּם.

Halakhah 4: Rebbi Abun bar Ḥiyya in the name of Rebbi Joḥanan: If he made them like a Gamma (Γ)[93].

93 The sentence combines the Mishnah and the end of the previous Halakhah: A sheaf is not forgotten unless it became isolated from the others. Then how can two sheaves become forgotten sheaves? If they stood like the ends of a Γ separated by a missing sheaf at the angle.

לֹא אָמַר אֶלָּא צִיבּוּרִין הָא זֵיתִים לֹא. מַה בֵּין הַצִּיבּוּרִין מַה בֵּין הַזֵּיתִים. צִיבּוּרִין גְּמַר מְלָאכָה. זֵיתִים אֵינָן גְּמַר מְלָאכָה.

He said[94] only "heaps", not olives. What is the difference between heaps and olives? Heaps are the end of the harvest[95], single olives are not the end of the harvest.

94 The Mishnah speaks of "heaps of olives," not single olives.

95 Hence, by Mishnah 5:7, the law of forgotten sheaves applies. Once the olives are put in orderly heaps, the work of the harvest is finished and that of the oil press starts.

אָמַר רִבִּי הוֹשַׁעְיָא רוֹמֵס הָיִיתִי זֵיתִים עִם רִבִּי חִייָא הַגָּדוֹל וְאָמַר לִי כָּל־זַיִת שֶׁאַתְּ יָכוֹל לִפְשׁוֹט יָדֶךָ וְלִיטְלוֹ אֵינוֹ שִׁכְחָה. אָמַר רִבִּי יוֹחָנָן כֵּיוָן שֶׁעָבַר עָלָיו וּשְׁכָחוֹ הֲרֵי זֶה שִׁכְחָה.

Rebbi Hoshaia said[96], when I was mashing olives with the great Rebbi Ḥiyya, he said to me: Any olive you can reach when stretching out your hand is not forgotten. Rebbi Joḥanan said, if he passed it over and forgot it, it is forgotten.

96 For comment, see Chapter 5, Halakhah 2, Note 40.

רִבִּי לָעְזָר בְּשֵׁם רִבִּי חִייָא רַבָּה חֲצִי אֶשְׁכּוֹל פֶּרֶט. תַּנֵּי רִבִּי חִייָא חֲצִי אֶשְׁכּוֹל אוֹ אֶשְׁכּוֹל שָׁלֵם פֶּרֶט. וְהָתַנֵּי שְׁנֵי גַרְגְּרִים פֶּרֶט. רִבִּי אִימִּי בְּשֵׁם רִבִּי חִייָא בְּקוֹצֵר וּמֵנִיחַ תַּחַת הַגֶּפֶן.

Rebbi Eleazar in the name of the great Rebbi Ḥiyya: Half a bunch of grapes are dropped berries. Rebbi Ḥiyya stated: Half a bunch of grapes or an entire bunch are dropped berries. But did we not state: "Two berries are dropped berries?" Rebbi Immi in the name of Rebbi Ḥiyya: If he cuts and deposits them under the vine[97].

97 Where the grapes become dusty and cannot be put in the basket to be transported either to the wine press or to market.

הָיוּ עֲשׂוּיִן כְּמִין סִינְפוֹן. מְנַחֵם בְּשֵׁם רִבִּי יוֹנָתָן וְהוּא שֶׁיְּהֵא חוֹתְכָן בְּשָׁוֶה.

If they are made like a shepherd's flute[98]? Menaḥem[99] in the name of Rebbi Jonathan: Only if he cuts them equally[100].

98 Greek σίφων, -ωνος, ὁ, "pipe, water spout; a musical instrument" (I. Löw), same as Biblical (pl.) סופניא (*Dan.* 3:10); Gesenius and Lysowski explain as bagpipe. A shepherd's flute made from reeds of different lengths glued together; the question is whether a plant (probably hemp) that grows different stalks of different lengths from one root is counted as one (and is under the law of forgotten sheaves) or as several (and is not).

99 A Galilean Amora of the third generation. His time may be determined from the fact that he quotes R. Ammi and is mentioned as teacher of R. Ḥaggai.

100 They may be counted as separate plants if they are cut equally near the ground. But stalks cut together count as one.

אָמַר רִבִּי אָבִין טַעֲמַיְהוּ דְּבֵית שַׁמַּאי לַגֵּר לַיָּתוֹם וְלָאַלְמָנָה יִהְיֶה. טַעֲמַיְהוּ דְּבֵית הִלֵּל לֶעָנִי וְלַגֵּר. אָמַר רִבִּי מָנָא שְׁנֵיהֶן מִקְרָא אֶחָד דָּרְשׁוּ לַגֵּר לַיָּתוֹם וְלָאַלְמָנָה יִהְיֶה. בֵּית שַׁמַּאי אוֹמְרִין לָעֲנִיִּים וּבֵית הִלֵּל אוֹמְרִין לְבַעַל הַבַּיִת.

Rebbi Abin said, the reason of the House of Shammai (*Deut.* 24:19,20,21): "It shall belong to the stranger, the orphan, and the widow[101]." The reason of the House of Hillel (*Lev.* 19:10): "For the poor and the stranger." Rebbi Mana said, both of them explained the same verse, "it shall belong to the stranger, the orphan, and the widow." The House of Shammai say, for the poor[102], and the House of Hillel say, for the proprietor[103].

101 Since there are three categories mentioned, each of them should have the possibility to get a separate piece.

102 All three, as given by R. Abin.

103 Since there is only one connective "and", only two belong

together. However, there are three categories of people entitled to collect gleanings and leftovers.

(fol. 19a) **משנה ה**: הָעוֹמֶר שֶׁיֵּשׁ בּוֹ סְאָתַיִם וּשְׁכָחוֹ אֵינוֹ שִׁכְחָה. שְׁנֵי עֳמָרִים וּבָהֶן סְאָתַיִם רַבָּן גַּמְלִיאֵל אוֹמֵר לְבַעַל הַבַּיִת. וַחֲכָמִים אוֹמְרִים לָעֲנִיִּים. אָמַר רַבָּן גַּמְלִיאֵל וְכִי מֵרוֹב הָעֳמָרִים יוֹפִי כֹחַ שֶׁל בַּעַל הַבַּיִת אוֹ הוֹרַע כֹּחַ שֶׁל בַּעַל הַבַּיִת. אָמְרוּ לוֹ יוֹפִי כֹחַ. (fol. 19b) אָמַר לָהֶן מַה אִם בִּזְמַן שֶׁהוּא עוֹמֶר אֶחָד וּבוֹ סְאָתַיִם וּשְׁכָחוֹ אֵינוֹ שִׁכְחָה. שְׁנֵי עֳמָרִין וּבָהֶן סְאָתַיִם אֵינוֹ דִין שֶׁלֹּא יְהוּ שִׁכְחָה. אָמְרוּ לוֹ אִם אָמְרוּ בְּעוֹמֶר אֶחָד שֶׁהוּא כְגָדִישׁ. תֹּאמַר בִּשְׁנֵי עוֹמָרִין שֶׁהֵן כִּכְרִיכוֹת.

Mishnah 5: A sheaf containing two *seah*[104] that was forgotten is not a "forgotten sheaf." Two sheaves that together are two *seah*, Rabban Gamliel says, they are for the proprietor, but the Sages say, they are for the poor. Rabban Gamliel said to them: Does large size of the sheaves increase or decrease the power of the proprietor? They said to him, it increases it. He said to them: Since a sheaf containing two *seah* that was forgotten is not "forgotten sheaf," it is only logical that two sheaves that together are two *seah* should not be "forgotten sheaf" either. They said to him, if they said that about one sheaf that is like a stack[105], do you want to say the same about two sheaves that are like bundles?

104 25.6 liter, about .9 cu. ft., cf. *Berakhot*, Chapter 3, Note 164. Halakhah 6 spells out that the grain kernels alone, without the straw, are meant.

105 Exempt from the laws of "forgotten sheaves," Mishnah 6:2. This applies to sheaves as large as a stack.

(fol. 19c) **הלכה ה**: אָמַר רִבִּי לָעְזָר כְּתִיב כִּי תִקְצוֹר קְצִירְךָ בְשָׂדֶךָ וְשָׁכַחְתָּ עוֹמֶר בַּשָּׂדֶה. עוֹמֶר שֶׁאַתְּ יָכוֹל לִפְשׁוֹט יֶדְךָ וְלִיטְלוֹ. אִית תַּנָּיֵי תַּנֵּי וְשָׁכַחְתָּ עוֹמֶר וְלֹא גָדִישׁ.

Halakhah 5: Rebbi Eleazar said, it is written (*Deut.* 24:19): "When you are harvesting your harvest on your field and you forget a sheaf on the field," a sheaf to which you may stretch out your hand and take it[106]. Some Tannaïm stated[107]: "And you forget a sheaf," but not a stack.

106 But not one where you need both hands.

107 *Sifry Deut.* 283.

הֵיךְ עֲבִידָא שָׁכַח עוֹמֶר אֶחָד בְּצִידּוֹ אִין תַּעֲבְדִינָהּ עוֹמֶר דִּבְרֵי הַכֹּל שִׁכְחָה. וְאִין תַּעֲבְדִינָהּ גָּדִישׁ מַחְלוֹקֶת שַׁמַּאי וְהִלֵּל. שָׁכַח שְׁנֵי עוֹמָרִין בְּצִדּוֹ אִין תַּעֲבְדִינָהּ עוֹמֶר מַחְלוֹקֶת בֵּית שַׁמַּאי וְהִלֵּל אִין תַּעֲבְדִינֵיהּ גָּדִישׁ אֵינוֹ נִידּוֹן כְּשׁוּרָה.

How does it work out[108]? If he forgot one sheaf next to it, if you make it a sheaf, everybody agrees that it is "forgotten sheaf.[109]" If you make it a stack, a difference between Shammai and Hillel[110]. If he forgot two sheaves, if you make it sheaves, a difference between the Houses of Shammai and Hillel[111]; if you make it a stack it will not be considered a row[112].

108 What is the practical difference between R. Eleazar who treats the oversized sheaf as sheaf and the Tanna who treats it as a stack?

109 Then you have two sheaves which for everybody are subject to "forgotten sheaves."

110 This should read: the Houses of Shammai and Hillel. The House of Shammai in Mishnah 6:2 freed the sheaf next to a stack from "forgotten sheaves;" the House of Hillel did not.

111 For the House of Hillel, one has three sheaves and it is an exempted row; for the House of Shammai one would need four.

112 Then one only has two sheaves which even for the House of Hillel are not a row.

(fol. 19b) **משנה ו**: קָמָה שֶׁיֵּשׁ בָּהּ סָאתַיִם וּשְׁכָחָהּ אֵינָהּ שִׁכְחָה. אֵין בָּהּ סָאתַיִם אֲבָל אִם רְאוּיָה לַעֲשׂוֹת סָאתַיִם אֲפִילוּ הִיא שֶׁל טוֹפַח רוֹאִין אוֹתָהּ כְּאִילוּ הִיא עֲנָבָה שֶׁל שְׂעוֹרִים.

Mishnah 6: Standing produce of two *seah* which was forgotten is not "forgotten sheaf." If it does not have two *seah* but it might bring two *seah*, even if it were oats[113] it is considered like barley grains.

113 Arabic קוּרְטְמָאן "oats", with short kernels (Translation of Maimonides). Arukh translates טופח by Arabic גֻּלְבָּאן peas. Barley grains are three to an inch. The field would not be under the laws of "forgetting" if it would yield .9 cu. ft. if all grains were the size of barley grains (in the shell, hairs attached.)

(fol. 19c) **הלכה ו**: אָמַר רִבִּי יוֹנָה כִּי תִקְצוֹר קְצִירְךָ בְשָׂדֶךָ וְשָׁכַחְתָּ עוֹמֶר בַּשָּׂדֶה. עוֹמֶר שֶׁיֵּשׁ בּוֹ סָאתַיִם וּשְׁכָחוֹ אֵינָהּ שִׁכְחָה. קָמָה שֶׁיֵּשׁ בָּהּ סָאתַיִם וּשְׁכָחָהּ אֵינָהּ שִׁכְחָה. אָמַר רִבִּי יוֹסֵי וּבִלְבַד שִׁבֳּלִין. הָיוּ דַקּוֹת רוֹאִין אוֹתָן כְּאִילוּ הֵן אֲרוּכוֹת. שְׁדוּפוֹת רוֹאִין אוֹתָן כְּאִילוּ הֵן מְלֵיאוֹת.

Halakhah 6: Rebbi Jonah said (*Deut*. 24:19): "When you are harvesting your harvest on your field and you forget a sheaf on the *field*," a sheaf containing two *seah* that was forgotten is not "forgotten sheaf." Standing produce[114] containing two *seah* that was forgotten is not "forgotten sheaf." Rebbi Yose said, considering only the ears[115]. If they were thin, one looks at them as if they were long, if they were scorched, one looks at them as if they were full.

114 The *field* of the verse.

115 But not the straw.

(fol. 19b) **משנה ז**: קָמָה מַצֶּלֶת אֶת הָעוֹמֶר וְאֶת הַקָּמָה. וְהָעוֹמֶר אֵינוֹ מַצִּיל לֹא אֶת הָעוֹמֶר וְלֹא אֶת הַקָּמָה. אֵי זוּ הִיא קָמָה שֶׁהִיא מַצֶּלֶת אֶת הָעוֹמֶר כֹּל שֶׁאֵינָהּ שִׁכְחָה אֲפִילוּ קֶלַח אֶחָד.

Mishnah 7: Standing produce saves sheaves and standing produce[116]. But a sheaf[117] saves neither sheaves nor standing produce. What is standing produce that saves sheaves? Everything that is not forgotten, even if it is only one stalk.

116 Standing produce which was not forgotten protects produce nearby that was forgotten from becoming legally "forgotten." "Nearby" was defined earlier as close so that the ears of one may touch the other.

117 A sheaf which either is not forgotten or which itself is exempt from the laws of the "forgotten sheaf."

(fol. 19c) **הלכה ז**: אָמַר רִבִּי אִילָא[118] כְּתִיב כִּי תִקְצוֹר קְצִירְךָ בְשָׂדֶךָ וְשָׁכַחְתָּ עוֹמֶר בַּשָּׂדֶה. עוֹמֶר שֶׁסְּבִיבוֹתָיו (fol. 19d) קָצִיר וְלֹא עוֹמֶר שֶׁסְּבִיבוֹתָיו קָמָה. וְלָמָּה עוֹמֶר שֶׁסְּבִיבוֹתָיו עוֹמָרִין וְלֹא עוֹמֶר שֶׁסְּבִיבוֹתָיו קָמָה עוֹמֶר שֶׁסְּבִיבוֹתָיו עוֹמָרִין מַה שֶּׁתַּחְתָּיו שָׂדֶה. עוֹמֶר שֶׁסְּבִיבוֹתָיו קָמָה מַה שֶּׁתַּחְתָּיו קַשִּׁין.

Halakhah 7: Rebbi Illa said, it is written (*Deut*. 24:19): "When you are harvesting your harvest on your field and you forget a sheaf on the *field*," a sheaf surrounded by harvest and not a sheaf surrounded by standing produce. And why a sheaf surrounded by harvest and not a sheaf surrounded by standing produce? Under a sheaf surrounded by harvest is the field[119], under a sheaf surrounded by standing produce is straw.

118 Or Lia, La, Illaï. This is the reading of R. S. Cirillo's manuscript; the name is missing in the other sources. (It cannot be Rebbi Jehudah the Prince since it is introduced by אמר, not by תנא, as noted by R. Z. Frankel.)

119 Since the harvest is not finished.

אֶת שֶׁל שְׂעוֹרִין דִּבְרֵי רִבִּי. וַחֲכָמִים אוֹמְרִים אֵינָהּ מַצֶּלֶת אֶלָּא שֶׁלּוֹ אֵינָהּ מַצֶּלֶת אֶלָּא מִמִּינָהּ.

It was stated[120]: "The standing produce of his neighbor saves his own[121], the standing produce of a Gentile saves that of a Jew, the standing wheat saves barley, the words of Rebbi. But the Sages say, only his own produce saves and only its own kind."

120 Tosephta *Peah* 3:5; there (and in the manuscript of R. S. Cirillo) the name of the first Tanna is R. Meïr.

121 If his forgotten patch of produce is close to the neighbor's field that was not yet harvested.

תַּנֵּי רַבָּן שִׁמְעוֹן בֶּן גַּמְלִיאֵל כְּשֵׁם שֶׁהַקָּמָה מַצֶּלֶת אֶת הָעוֹמֶר כָּךְ הָעוֹמֶר מַצִּיל אֶת הַקָּמָה. וְדִין הוּא וּמַה אִם הַקָּמָה שֶׁיִּפֶּה בָהּ כֹּחַ הֶעָנִי וּשְׁכָחָהּ הֲרֵי הִיא מַצֶּלֶת. עוֹמֶר שֶׁהוּרַע בּוֹ כֹּחַ הֶעָנִי אֵינוֹ דִין שֶׁיַּצִּיל. אָמַר לוֹ רִבִּי וּמַה אִם קָמָה שֶׁיִּפֶּה כֹּחַ הֶעָנִי בָהּ וּשְׁכָחָהּ הֲרֵי הִיא מַצֶּלֶת. עוֹמֶר שֶׁהוּרַע כֹּחַ הֶעָנִי בּוֹ וּשְׁכָחוֹ אֵין דִּין שֶׁיַּצִּיל. מִדִּבְרֵי שְׁנֵיהֶן נִלְמַד מַצִּילִין עוֹמֶר מֵעוֹמֶר וְאֵין מַצִּילִין קָמָה מִקָּמָה.

Rabban Simeon ben Gamliel stated[122]: Just as standing produce saves the sheaf, so the sheaf saves the standing produce. This is logical: If standing produce, on which the power of the poor is enhanced[123], saves if any of it was forgotten, it is only logical that the sheaf should save, since on it the power of the poor is reduced[124]. Rebbi[125] answered him: If standing produce, on which the power of the poor is enhanced, saves if any of it[126] was forgotten, is it logical that the sheaf, on which the power of the poor is reduced, if any of it was forgotten should save[127]? From the words of both of them we infer that sheaf is saved by sheaf[128], but standing produce is not saved by standing produce[129].

122 Tosephta *Peah* 3:6. In the edition of R. S. Lieberman, the punctuation and interpretation of the abbreviation are incorrect. The text of the Tosephta is garbled and the good text of the Yerushalmi was misunderstood by R. Simson and the other commentators.

123 Since he has the right to *peah*, gleanings, and forgotten sheaves.

124 It is reduced to the forgotten sheaf.

125 The son of Rabban Simeon ben Gamliel.

126 The sheaf, on which the power of the poor is weak.

127 The standing produce, to which the claim of the poor is much stronger!

128 If both sheaves are close together. For Rabban Simeon ben Gamliel it follows from his logical argument, for Rebbi it follows since the claim of the poor to the sheaf is reduced.

129 For neither of them is there an argument that anything should save standing produce to which the claim of the poor is enhanced.

הָא אִם שָׁכַח שִׁכְחָה. תִּיפְתָּר בְּשֶׁשָּׁכַח אֶת הַקָּמָה תְּחִילָּה.

Hence[130], if he forgot, is it "forgotten sheaf"? Explain it if he forgot the standing produce first.

130 This paragraph is part of the next Halakhah in the manuscripts and first prints. But it belongs here, as discussion of whether "even if it is only one stalk" means that if a single stalk is forgotten, nothing is saved. The answer is that it is enough if one stalk was not forgotten.

(fol. 19b) **משנה ח**: סְאָה תְּבוּאָה עֲקוּרָה וּסְאָה שֶׁאֵינוֹ עֲקוּרָה וְכֵן בְּאִילָן הַשּׁוּם וְהַבְּצָלִים אֵינָן מִצְטָרְפִין. רִבִּי יוֹסֵי אוֹמֵר אִם בָּאַת רְשׁוּת לְעָנִי בְּאֶמְצַע אֵין מִצְטָרְפִין וְאִם לָאו הֲרֵי אֵלּוּ מִצְטָרְפִין.

Mishnah 8: A *seah* of uprooted grain and a *seah* of not uprooted grain[131], also trees[132], garlic and onions do not combine[133]. Rebbi Yose says, if a poor man's right comes in the middle[134], they do not combine, otherwise they do combine.

131 They do not combine to form the two *seah* that exempt from the laws of forgotten sheaves.

132 Harvested and hanging fruits do not combine.

133 They belong to the same family but different species.

134 If at any time after the cutting of the first part the poor had the right to collect *peah*, gleanings, or forgotten sheaves, the two parts cannot be combined. In vineyards, the poor have the right to collect the single berries that grow on the vines. But for other trees, the poor have no rights until the end of the harvest; for R. Yose, harvested and hanging fruits of other trees combine.

(fol. 19d) **הלכה ח**: הָא אִם שְׁתֵּיהֶן עֲקוּרוֹת לְבַעַל הַבַּיִת. מַתְנִיתָא כְּרַבָּן גַּמְלִיאֵל.

Halakhah 8: Hence, if all[135] is cut it is for the proprietor. Our Mishnah follows Rabban Gamliel[136].

135 Adding up to two *seah*.

136 Who asserted in Mishnah 5 that sheaves which together add up to 2 *seah* do not fall under the law of the forgotten sheaf. Since the Mishnah is formulated as anonymous statement, practice has to follow Rabban Gamliel.

וְתַצִּיל עֲקוּרָה שֶׁאֵינָהּ עֲקוּרָה. הָדָא אָמְרָה דָּבָר שֶׁהוּא רָאוּי לְהַצִּיל וּשְׁכָחוֹ הֲרֵי הוּא שִׁכְחָה. אָמַר רִבִּי יוֹנָתָן תִּיפְתָּר בְּקוֹצֵר שׁוּרָה וּמְעַמֵּר שׁוּרָה וּכְבָר שָׁכַח אֶת הַקָּמָה עַד שֶׁלֹּא שָׁכַח אֶת הָעוֹמָרִין.

Then[137] the cut grain should save the uncut grain. This means that something that is apt to save, but was forgotten, can become legally forgotten. Rebbi Jonathan[138] said, explain it if he was cutting and removing the sheaves row by row. He already forgot the standing grain before he might forget the sheaves[139].

137 If we follow Rabban Gamliel. The same text, with a different thrust, is found Chapter 5, Halakhah 2.

138 There, R. Jonah.

139 And Rabban Gamliel will not have the two combined if they are separated in space and time.

מַה עַד שֶׁתָּבוֹא מַמָּשׁ אוֹ אֲפִילוּ נִרְאֵית לְהָבִיא. נִישְׁמְעִינָהּ מִן הָדָא [140]כְּגוֹן תְּבוּאָה וְכֶרֶם. וְכֶרֶם לֹא עַל אֲתָר הוּא. הָדָא אָמְרָה אֲפִילוּ נִרְאֵית לָבוֹא.

Does it mean that it really comes, or only that it is able to come[141]? Let us hear from the following[142]: "For example grain and vineyard." And is the vineyard on the spot[143]? That means, even if it is able to come[144]!

140 Readings of R. Simson and the Cirillo manuscript. In the Venice print and Leyden manuscript: בגין תבואה שבכרם.

141 Does it mean that Rebbi Yose excludes combining only if the poor actually could exercise their rights, or even if there is only a theoretical possibility.

142 Tosephta *Peah* 3:5: "According to R. Yose, Ḥananiah, the nephew of R. Joshua, said that whenever a poor man's right comes in between, for example grain and vineyard, they do not combine. Whenever a poor man's right does not come in between, for example fruits of trees, they do combine."

143 It is true that there is no manual grain harvest without gleanings; the poor always have the right to enter after cutting and binding of the sheaves. But there are vines which do not produce single berries; in a vineyard, the right of the poor is conditional.

144 It includes all vineyards and mechanical harvesting.

(fol. 19b) **משנה ט**: תְּבוּאָה שֶׁנִּיתְּנָה לְשַׁחַת אוֹ לַאֲלוּמָה וְכֵן בְּאִיגּוּדֵי הַשּׁוּם וַאֲגוּדַּת הַשּׁוּם וְהַבְּצָלִים אֵין לָהֶן שִׁכְחָה וְכָל־הַטְּמוּנִין בָּאָרֶץ כְּגוֹן הַלּוּף וְהַשּׁוּם וְהַבְּצָלִים. רִבִּי יְהוּדָה אוֹמֵר אֵין לָהֶן שִׁכְחָה. וַחֲכָמִים אוֹמְרִים יֵשׁ לָהֶן שִׁכְחָה.

Mishnah 9: Grain cut for animal feed[145] or to bind sheaves, and similarly garlic used to bind[146] as well as bundles of garlic and onions[147] are not subject to "forgotten sheaves." Anything hidden in the ground[148], such as *luf*[149], garlic, and onions, Rebbi Jehudah says, they are not subject to "forgotten sheaves", but the Sages say, they are subject to "forgotten sheaves."

145 Cut as fodder (in contrast to grain cut for human consumption but used as fodder) means that it was cut green. In the same way, grain cut to bind sheaves must still have flexible stalks; it cannot be dry and does not qualify as "harvest."

146 Garlic leaves used to bind bundles of garlic or onions.

147 Onions and garlic are bound or plaited in small bundles for later use but these are then bound together in large bunches for transport. The small bundles are not made for transport to storage and by Mishnah 5:7 do not fall under the law of the forgotten sheaf.

148 Plants whose edible part, or main part, is the one hidden in the ground.

149 In classical Arabic, לוף means serpentary, snake weed, *Arum Dracunculus L.*, a plant with a large bulb. This is the identification given by Arukh, based on a Gaonic source. Maimonides (Commentary on the Mishnah) declares it "doubtless to be a kind of onion." Rashi (*Shabbat* 126b) declares it to be a kind of legume. The determination by Arukh must be accepted. (In modern Arabic, לוף *liffa* is *Luffa cylindrica Roem*, dishcloth gourd, which is inedible.)

(fol. 19d) **הלכה ט**: אָמַר רִבִּי יוֹנָה לֹא סוֹף דָּבָר נוֹתְנָהּ אֶלָּא אֲפִילוּ נוֹטְלָהּ עַל מְנָת לִיתְּנָהּ.

Halakhah 9: Rebbi Jonah said[150], not only if he gave it but even if he took it with the intention of giving it.

150 At the moment the decision is made to use certain produce as fodder, not for human consumption, it becomes exempt from the law of the forgotten sheaf.

תַּמָּן תַּנֵּינָן הַמַּדְלִיק אֶת הַגָּדִישׁ וְהָיוּ בוֹ כֵלִים רִבִּי יְהוּדָה אוֹמֵר מְשַׁלֵּם כָּל־מַה שֶּׁבְּתוֹכוֹ. וַחֲכָמִים אוֹמְרִים אֵינוֹ מְשַׁלֵּם אֶלָּא גְּדִישׁ חִיטִּין אוֹ גְּדִישׁ שְׂעוֹרִין. מַחְלְפָה שִׁיטָּתֵיהּ דְּרִבִּי יְהוּדָה תַּמָּן הוּא אוֹמֵר לְרַבּוֹת אֶת הַטָּמוּן. וְכָא הוּא אָמַר פְּרָט לְטָמוּן. תַּמָּן וְנֶאֱכַל הַגָּדִישׁ אוֹ הַקָּמָה. מְמַשְׁמַע שֶׁנֶּאֱמַר קָמָה אֵין אָנוּ יוֹדְעִין שֶׁהַגָּדִישׁ בִּכְלָל. וּמַה תַּלְמוּד לוֹמַר גָּדִישׁ לְרַבּוֹת אֶת הַטָּמוּן. וְהָכָא שָׂדְךָ בְּגָלוּי פְּרָט לְטָמוּן. מַחְלְפָה שִׁיטָּתָן דְּרַבָּנִין תַּמָּן אִינּוּן אָמְרִין פְּרָט לְטָמוּן. וְכָא אִינּוּן אָמְרִין לְרַבּוֹת אֶת הַטָּמוּן. תַּמָּן אוֹ הַקָּמָה אוֹ הַשָּׂדֶה. מַה שָּׂדְךָ בְגָלוּי אַף כָּל־דָּבָר שֶׁהוּא גָלוּי. בְּרַם הָכָא שָׂדְךָ בְּגָלוּי פְּרָט לְטָמוּן. קְצִירְךָ בְּגָלוּי פְּרָט לְטָמוּן. וַהֲוֵי מִיעוּט אַחַר מִיעוּט וְאֵין מִיעוּט אַחַר מִיעוּט לְרַבּוֹת הַטָּמוּן.

There[151] we have stated: "If someone sets fire to a stack in which were hidden vessels, Rebbi Jehudah says, he pays for all that was in it. But the Sages say, he only pays for a stack of wheat or barley[152]." The argument of Rebbi Jehudah is inverted; there he says to include the hidden things, but here he says to exclude the hidden things. There (*Ex*. 22:5) "and a[153] stack or standing grain was consumed." I understand that since it says "standing grain" it includes a stack. Why does the verse add "a stack?" In order to include the hidden things. But here (*Deut*. 24:10) "your field," in the open, to exclude anything hidden. The argument of the rabbis is inverted; there they say to exclude the hidden things, but here they say to include the hidden things. There, "or standing grain or a field," just as a field is in the open, so all must be in the open. But here, "your field," in the open, to exclude that which is hidden; "your harvest," in the open, to exclude that which is hidden. That is a restriction after a restriction and every restriction after a restriction is only[154] to add the hidden things.

151 The discussion is paralleled in *Baba Qama* 6:5 in a different formulation.

152 Both Babli and Yerushalmi are agreed that the Mishnah refers only to a man who lights a legal fire on his own field and it burns out of control. But an arsonist has to pay for everything under any circumstance. The Babli (*Baba Qama* 61b) states that the Sages agree that whoever started the fire is responsible for agricultural implements usually hidden in stacks. Hence, in the opinion of the Babli but not the Yerushalmi, the Sages free him only from the responsibility for unexpected losses.

153 This is the Biblical text, not "the stack" as given here. "If fire gets out of control and a stack, or the standing grain, or the field is consumed, the person who caused the fire should certainly pay."

154 There is an אלא missing in the text or the אין is superfluous (*Yebamot* 12:1). The principle that a restriction after a restriction is an extension is universally accepted in both Talmudim; in *Horaiot* 1:1 it is generalized to the statement that any sequence of restrictions of an even number of elements is an extension; for an odd number of elements it is a restriction.

(fol. 19b) **משנה י**: הַקּוֹצֵר בַּלַּיְלָה וְהַמְעַמֵּר וְהַסּוּמָא יֵשׁ לוֹ שִׁכְחָה. וְאִם הָיָה מִתְכַּוֵּן לִיטּוֹל אֶת הַגַּס הַגַּס אֵין לוֹ שִׁכְחָה. אִם אָמַר הֲרֵי אֲנִי קוֹצֵר עַל מְנָת מַה שֶּׁאֲנִי שׁוֹכֵחַ אֲנִי לוֹקֵחַ יֵשׁ לוֹ שִׁכְחָה.

Mishnah 10: He who harvests at night or removes the stacks, or a blind person[155], are subject to the law of forgotten sheaves. But if he[156] intended only to take the large pieces, he is not subject to the law of forgotten sheaves. If he said: "I harvest on the understanding that I shall take what I might forget," he is subject to the law of forgotten sheaves.

155 All of whom are likely to miss some standing produce or some sheaves.

156 The one who harvested or removed the sheaves at night, and the blind (Maimonides *Mattenot Aniïm* 5:8).

(fol. 19d) **הלכה י:** כֵּינִי מַתְנִיתָא הַקּוֹצֵר בַּלַּיְלָה וְהַמְעַמֵּר בַּלַּיְלָה וְהַסּוּמָא בֵּין בַּיּוֹם בֵּין בַּלַּיְלָה.

Halakhah 10: So is the Mishnah: He who harvests at night or removes the stacks at night, or a blind person day or night.

אָמַר רִבִּי יוֹנָה לֹא סוֹף דָּבָר גַּסִּין אֶלָּא דַקִּין וְכִי מֵאַחַר שֶׁדַּרְכּוֹ לִבְחוֹן בְּגַסִּין אֲפִילוּ דַקִּין אֵין לָהֶן שִׁכְחָה.

Rebbi Jonah said[157], not only for the large pieces, but also for the thin pieces. Since he is going to check for the large ones, the thin ones likewise are not subject to the law of forgotten sheaves.

157 He refers to the second sentence in the Mishnah.

אָמַר הֲרֵינִי קוֹצֵר עַל מְנָת מַה שֶּׁאֲנִי שֹׁכֵחַ אֲנִי לוֹקֵחַ יֵשׁ לוֹ שִׁכְחָה שֶׁהִתְנָה עַל מַה שֶּׁכָּתוּב בַּתּוֹרָה וְכָל־הַמַּתְנֶה עַל מַה שֶּׁכָּתוּב בַּתּוֹרָה תְּנָאוֹ בָטֵל.

If he said: "I harvest on the undertanding that I shall take what I might forget," he is subject to the law of forgotten sheaves, since he made a condition[158] against what is written in the Torah, and if anybody makes a condition against what is written in the Torah, his condition is invalid[159].

158 Not a condition in the legal sense, since a legal condition needs a positive and a negative and he cannot say, "if I cannot take everything then what I harvest shall not be harvested." Probably, "condition" should be read as "understanding."

159 Except in the matter of civil contracts.

כל זית פרק שביעי

(fol. 19d) **משנה א**: כָּל־זַיִת שֶׁיֵּשׁ לוֹ שֵׁם בַּשָּׂדֶה אֲפִילוּ כְּזַיִת הַנְּטוּפָה בְשַׁעְתּוֹ וּשְׁכָחוֹ אֵינוֹ שִׁכְחָה. בַּמֶּה דְבָרִים אֲמוּרִים בִּשְׁמוֹ וּבְמַעֲשָׂיו וּבִמְקוֹמוֹ. בִּשְׁמוֹ שֶׁהָיָה שֶׁפְּכָנִי אוֹ בֵּישָׁנִי. בְּמַעֲשָׂיו שֶׁהוּא עוֹשֶׂה הַרְבֵּה. בִּמְקוֹמוֹ שֶׁהוּא עוֹמֵד בְּצַד הַגַּת אוֹ בְצַד הַפִּרְצָה. וּשְׁאָר כָּל־הַזֵּיתִים שְׁנַיִם שִׁכְחָה שְׁלֹשָׁה אֵינָן שִׁכְחָה. רַבִּי יוֹסֵי אוֹמֵר אֵין שִׁכְחָה לַזֵּיתִים.

Mishnah 1: Every olive tree that has a special name on the field, for example "a dripping olive tree[1]" in its time, if it was forgotten, is not subject to the law of the forgotten sheaf. When does this apply? For its name, its production, and its place. By its name, if it was dripping[2] or from Beth Shean. By its production, if it produced much. By its place, if it stood next to the wine-press or near a hole in the wall. For all other olive trees, two are subject to the law of the forgotten sheaf, three are not. Rebbi Yose says, there is no law of the forgotten sheaf for olive trees.

1 Maimonides identifies this as "from Beth Netofa (in Galilee);" then it should be vocalized נְטוֹפָה . But the form נְטִיפָה in the Halakhah requires נְטוּפָה here. The addition "in its time" can only mean that the olives start dripping even on the tree, at the end of the growing season, for a short time every year.

2 Literally, "pouring" or "from a town Shipkoun".

(fol. 20a) **הלכה א**: אָמַר רִבִּי לָא כְּתִיב וְשָׁכַחְתָּ עוֹמֶר בַּשָּׂדֶה עוֹמֶר שֶׁאַתְּ שׁוֹכְחוֹ לְעוֹלָם יָצָא זֶה שֶׁאַתְּ זוֹכְרוֹ לְאַחַר זְמָן.

Halakhah 1: Rebbi La said, it is written (*Deut*. 24:19): "You will forget a sheaf on the field," a sheaf you forget forever; this excludes one you certainly will remember after some time[3].

3 Because it has a specific name or property.

רִבִּי יִרְמְיָה בְּעִי הָיָה מְסוּיָּים בְּדַעְתּוֹ כְּמִי שֶׁהוּא מְסוּיָּים. הָיָה עוֹמֵד בְּצֵל הַדֶּקֶל הַדֶּקֶל מְסַיְּימוֹ הָיוּ שְׁנֵיהֶן נְטוּפָה זֶה מְסַיֵּים אֶת זֶה וְזֶה מְסַיֵּים אֶת זֶה. הָיְתָה כָל־שָׂדֵהוּ נְטוּפָה נִישְׁמְעִינָהּ מִן הָדָא רִבִּי יוֹסֵי אוֹמֵר אֵין שִׁכְחָה לַזֵּיתִים. אָמַר רִבִּי שִׁמְעוֹן בַּר יָקִים לֹא אָמַר רִבִּי יוֹסֵי אֶלָּא בָרִאשׁוֹנָה שֶׁלֹּא הָיוּ הַזֵּיתִים מְצוּיִין שֶׁבָּא אַדְרִייָנוּס הָרָשָׁע וְהֶחֱרִיב אֶת כָּל־הָאָרֶץ. אֲבָל עַכְשָׁיו שֶׁהַזֵּיתִים מְצוּיִין יֵשׁ לָהֶן שִׁכְחָה.

Rebbi Jeremiah asked: If it was marked in his mind, is it as if it were marked[4]? If it stood in the shadow[5] of a date palm, the date palm marks it. If two of them were dripping, each of them marks the other[6]. If the entire field was of dripping olive trees? Let us hear from the following: "Rebbi Yose says, there is no law of the forgotten sheaf for olives." Rebbi Simeon bar Yaqim[7] said, Rebbi Yose said this only in former times when olives were scarce because Hadrian, the evil one, had come and devastated the entire land[8]. But today when olive trees are everywhere, they are under the law of the forgotten sheaf.

4 If the olive grower gave the tree a private name in his mind, is that as good as a publicly known name (or, at least, a name known to his workers).

5 Maimonides (*Mattenot Aniïm* 5:24) reads בצד "next to", which probably is the correct reading.

6 These three cases are agreed on;

the question is about the next case.

7 An Amora of the third generation, student of R. Johanan and colleague of R. Eleazar, mentioned as R. Simeon bar Elyaqim in the Babli.

8 In the war of Bar Kokhba.

שְׁפְכָּנִי נוֹטֵף שֶׁמֶן. וְהָתַנִּינָן נְטִיפָה אֶלָּא שֶׁהִיא עוֹשָׂה שֶׁמֶן הַרְבֵּה. וְהָתְנָן בְּמַעֲשָׂיו שֶׁהוּא עוֹשֶׂה הַרְבֵּה. אֶלָּא שְׁפְכוֹנִי שֶׁהוּא עוֹשֶׂה שֶׁמֶן הַרְבֶּה. נְטוּפָה נוֹטֵף שֶׁמֶן. מַעֲשָׂיו שֶׁהוּא עוֹשֶׂה הַרְבֶּה. שֶׁהוּא עוֹשֶׂה זֵיתִים הַרְבֶּה. בֵּישָׁנִי אִית דִּבְעֵי מֵימַר בֵּישָׁנִי מַמָּשׁ. אִית דִּבְעֵי מֵימַר דְּהוּא מַבְעִית לְחַבְרֵיהּ עַד דְּיַעֲבִיד אַרְבָּעָה כִפְלֵיסִין כִּי הַהִיא דְּתַנֵּינָן תַּמָּן כָּל־עוֹמְרֵי הַשָּׂדֶה שֶׁל קַב קַב וְאֶחָד שֶׁל אַרְבַּעַת קַבִּין וּשְׁכָחוֹ. מִכֵּיוָן שֶׁהוּא עוֹשֶׂה יוֹתֵר מֵחֲבֵרוֹ כְּמִי שֶׁהוּא מְסוּיָּם. עַד דְּיַעֲבִיד כָּל־שָׁנָה וְשָׁנָה. וּמִכֵּיוָן שֶׁהוּא עוֹשֶׂה רוּבָּן שֶׁל שָׁנִים כְּמִי שֶׁהוּא מְסוּיָּם.

Šofkānī drips oil. But did we not state "dripping," so it must be that it yields much oil. But did we not state: "By its production, if it yields a lot." So, *Šofkānī*[9] yields much oil. *Nĕṭūfah*[10] drips oil. Its production, it yields a lot, *viz.*, it produces a lot of olives. *Bêšānī*, some say, really from Beth She'an[11]; some say, it puts the other trees to shame[12] by producing fourfold, similar to what we have stated: If all sheaves of the field are of one *qab*, except one which is of four *qab* and was forgotten. Since it produces more than others, it is considered marked. On condition that it produces every year? Since it produces most years it is considered marked.

9 Root שפך "to pour out."

10 Root נטף "to drip."

11 Biblical בית שאן, Talmudic בישן

12 Root בוש "ashamed," taken in causative sense, "to put to shame."

בִּמְקוֹמוֹ שֶׁהוּא עוֹמֵד בְּצַד הַגַּת אוֹ בְצַד הַפִּרְצָה. מַתְנִיתָא דְּבֵית שַׁמַּאי דְּבֵית שַׁמַּאי אוֹמְרִין הֶבְקֵר לָעֲנִיִּים הֶבְקֵר. אָמַר רִבִּי יוֹסֵי דִּבְרֵי הַכֹּל הִיא תַּמָּן דָּבָר תָּלוּשׁ בְּצַד דָּבָר מְחוּבָּר. בְּרַם הָכָא דָּבָר מְחוּבָּר בְּצַד דָּבָר מְחוּבָּר.

"By its place, if it stood next to the wine-press or near a hole in the wall." Is our Mishnah following the House of Shammai, since the House of Shammai say, property abandoned to the poor is abandoned[13]? Rebbi Yose[14] said, it is everybody's opinion; there it is movable near immovable, here it is immovable near immovable.

13 If the Mishnah did accept the ruling of the House of Shammai as generally accepted practice, it would be more than astonishing. However, the quote from the House of Shammai (Mishnah 6:1) seems to be wrong; it would have to be Mishnah 6:2: "The sheaf that was near a closure, a stack, cattle, or vessels; if it was forgotten, the House of Shammai say, it is not a forgotten sheaf, but the House of Hillel say, it is a forgotten sheaf." In contrast, everybody seems to agree that an olive tree standing near a closure is not forgotten.

14 The Amora.

רִבִּי יוֹסֵי אוֹמֵר אֵין שִׁכְחָה לְזֵיתִים. אָמַר רִבִּי שִׁמְעוֹן בֶּן יָקִים לֹא אָמַר רִבִּי יוֹסֵי אֶלָּא בָרִאשׁוֹנָה שֶׁלֹּא הָיוּ הַזֵּיתִים מְצוּיִין שֶׁבָּא אַדְרִייָנוּס הָרָשָׁע וְהֶחֱרִיב אֶת כָּל הָאָרֶץ. אֲבָל עַכְשָׁיו שֶׁהַזֵּיתִים מְצוּיִין יֵשׁ לָהֶן שִׁכְחָה.

"[15]Rebbi Yose says, there is no law of the forgotten sheaf for olives." Rebbi Simeon bar Yaqim said, Rebbi Yose said this only in former times when olives were scarce because Hadrian, the evil one, had come and devastated the entire land. But today when olive trees are everywhere, they are under the law of the forgotten sheaf.

15 Repeated from above.

אָמַר רִבִּי יוֹסֵי לֹא חִייֵב אָדָם שִׁכְחָה לְזֵיתִים אֶלָּא רִבִּי עֲקִיבָה דוּ דָרַשׁ אַחֲרֶיךָ אַחֲרֶיךָ. מֵעַתָּה אֵין שִׁכְחָה לְזֵיתִים כְּרִבִּי יוֹסֵי דְּלֹא דָרַשׁ אַחֲרֶיךָ. הָתִיבוּן הֲרֵי עוֹמֶר שִׁכְחָה הֲרֵי לֹא כְתִיב אַחֲרֶיךָ. מִכֵּיוָן שֶׁכְּתִיב לֹא תָשׁוּב לְקַחְתּוֹ כְּמִי שֶׁכְּתִיב אַחֲרֶיךָ.

Rebbi Yose[16] said, nobody applied the law of forgotten sheaves to olive trees except Rebbi Aqiba, for he drew inferences from "behind you, behind you." Then there should be no "forgotten sheaf" for olive trees following Rebbi Yose who does not draw inferences from "behind you.[17]" They objected, is not a sheaf subject to "forgotten sheaves", and there it is not written "behind you." Since it is written (*Deut.* 24:19): "Do not return to take it," it is as if "behind you" were written there.

16 The Amora. The reference here is to Halakhah 6:4 which specifically excludes single olives from the law of forgotten sheaves. The next reference to "Rebbi Yose" is to the Tanna.

17 It says in *Deut.* 24:20-21: "If you shake your olive tree, do not pick single olives *behind you*; they shall be for the stranger, the orphan, and the widow. If you harvest your vineyard, do not pick unripe berries *behind you*; they shall be for the stranger, the orphan, and the widow." *Behind you* must refer to things forgotten, since one harvests always in front of himself.

רִבִּי יוֹנָה בְּעֵי הָהֵן זַיִת נְטִיפָה הוֹאִיל וְהוּא מְסוּיָּים עַל דַּעְתֵּיהּ דְּרִבִּי יוֹסֵי אֲפִילוּ הִתְחִיל בּוֹ כְּמִי שֶׁלֹּא הִתְחִיל בּוֹ.

Rebbi Jonah had a problem[18]: That dripping olive tree, since it is marked, in the opinion of Rebbi Yose even if he started with it it, should it be as if he had not started with it?

18 The problem refers to the next Mishnah which states that once one started to harvest an olive tree, even if it was marked by some of the peculiarities enumerated, it becomes subject to the law of forgotten sheaves. Rebbi Yose denies any applicability of that law to olive trees. Since practice does not follow R. Yose, the question is not resolved.

(fol. 19d) **משנה ב:** זַיִת שֶׁנִּמְצָא עוֹמֵד בֵּין שָׁלֹשׁ שׁוּרוֹת שֶׁל שְׁנֵי מַלְבֵּנִים וּשְׁכָחוֹ אֵינוֹ שִׁכְחָה. זַיִת שֶׁיֵּשׁ בּוֹ סְאָתַיִם וּשְׁכָחוֹ אֵינוֹ שִׁכְחָה. בְּמַה דְּבָרִים אֲמוּרִים שֶׁלֹּא הִתְחִיל בּוֹ אֲבָל הִתְחִיל בּוֹ אֲפִילוּ כְּזַיִת הַנְּטוּפָה בְשַׁעְתּוֹ וּשְׁכָחוֹ יֵשׁ לוֹ שִׁכְחָה. כָּל־זְמָן שֶׁיֵּשׁ לוֹ תַחְתָּיו יֵשׁ לוֹ בְרֹאשׁוֹ. רִבִּי מֵאִיר אוֹמֵר מִשֶּׁתֵּלֵךְ הַמַּחְבָּא.

An olive tree standing between three rows of two rectangles, when forgotten, is not subject to the law of forgotten sheaves[19]. An olive tree which yields two *seah*[20], when forgotten, is not legally forgotten. When does this apply[21]? Only if he did not start with it, but if he started harvesting it, even a *dripping olive tree* in its time, when forgotten, is subject to the law of the forgotten sheaf. Whenever he[22] has under it, he has at its crown. Rebbi Meïr says, from the moment that the *mahba* is used[23].

19 Maimonides explains in his Mishnah commentary that the trees are planted in checkerboard fashion, that each "white" square has a tree while the "black" squares are planted with vegetables; we still say that the middle one is obscured by the surrounding trees, disregarding the vegetable beds. R. Isaac Simponti accepts this explanation but takes the rectangles to denote distance, not necessarily that they are planted. [However, in his Code (*Mattenot Aniïm* 3:25) Maimonides accepts the explanation, also given by R. Simson, that the olive tree is a single tree surrounded on three sides by three rows of trees, each row consisting of two trees, so that the surrounding trees hinder the access to the single tree. R. Simson rejects the idea that the tree should not be subject to the law because of difficulty of access.]

20 Olives, not oil.

21 This question does not refer to the tree yielding two *seah* but to the marked trees mentioned in Mishnah 1. After one started harvesting, these are not protected unless they yield two *seah*.

22 Maimonides, in his commentary and his Code (*Mattenot Aniïm* 1:12)

refers "him" to the poor. Once they have permission to search for olives under the tree, they may take the olives that are still on the tree, but not before (even though ususally olives are not harvested by climbing the tree but by shaking it.) R. Simson and R. Abraham ben David (*Mattenot Aniïm* 1:12) refer "him" to the owner; as long as anything under the tree (the main harvest) is not legally forgotten, everything on the tree is his, independent of his state of mind regarding the olives remaining on the tree.

23 According to Maimonides, the *maḥba* is an instrument with which the branches of the olive tree are shaken to remove the olives still clinging to the branches. In all manuscripts of his tradition, the spelling is מחבה as a feminine, in accord with the feminine form of the verb. R. Simson and R. Abraham ben David explain *maḥba* as the leaves which hide olives and must be removed. Since Maimonides lived in olive growing societies, his explanation should be accepted. The root underlying מחבא seems to be Arabic خبأ "to grow abundantly" (but cf. text at note 44).

(fol. 20a) **הלכה ב:** אָמַר רִבִּי לָעְזָר כֵּינִי מַתְנִיתָא שֶׁל שְׁנֵי מַלְבֵּנִים וּשְׁכָחוֹ. מַה נָן קַיָּמִין אִם מִשּׁוּם דָּבָר מְסוּיָּם אֵין כַּאן זֵתִים. אִם מִשּׁוּם שׁוּרָה הוּא עַצְמוֹ נִידּוֹן כְּשׁוּרָה. אֶלָּא עַל יְדֵי שׁוּרָה עַל יְדֵי שׁוּרוֹת.

Halakhah 2: Rebbi Eleazar said, so says the Mishnah: "of two rectangles" and he forgot it[24]. What are we dealing with? If it is because it is marked, are there not other olive trees[25]? If it is because it is in a row[26], it is considered a row in itself[27]. It must be because of row and of rows[28].

24 The last expression, "and he forgot it," is missing in the Rome manuscript. (However, "and he forgot it" is in the parallel Tosephta *Peah* 3:10). Rebbi Eleazar wants to emphasize that the correct reading is *two*, not *three* as in *Yalqut Shimoni* 937. Other explanations by J. N. Epstein in מבוא לנוסח המשנה pp. 92-93 are unconvincing.

25 They also should be exempt since they are adjacent to a marked tree. *Two* is also the reading in Tosephta *Peah* 3:10, *Sifri Deut.* 284.

26 If it is aligned in a long row of seven trees and therefore not privileged, which is impossible since it may be considered the head of a row of four.

27 Since it is not aligned with anything, it cannot be exempt from the law as a row.

28 It is in the middle of a row and its row is the middle row, following the explanation of Maimonides in the commentary to the Mishnah. The central position marks it.

אָמַר רִבִּי יוֹסֵי בְּזַיִת נוּדְייָן הִיא מַתְנִיתָא. אָמַר רִבִּי יוֹסֵי לֹא סוֹף דָּבָר נוּדְייָן אֶלָּא אֲפִילוּ שְׁאָר כָּל־הַזֵּיתִים מִכֵּיוָן שֶׁדַּרְכָּן לִיבָּחֵן כְּנוּדְייָן אֲפִילוּ שְׁאָר כָּל־הַזֵּיתִים אֵין לָהֶן שִׁכְחָה.

Rebbi Yose said[29], the Mishnah deals with an olive tree that can be shaken[30]. Rebbi Yose[31] said, not only one that can be shaken; since olive trees usually are first checked by shaking, none can be under the law of forgotten sheaves.

29 It is unlikely that "R. Yose" here is correct, since the next paragraphs refer to R. Joḥanan. R. S. Cirillo has אמר ר' יוסי אמר ר' יוחנן but this clearly is Babli style (in the Yerushalmi it could be either אמר ר' יוסי or אמר ר' יוסא ר' יוחנן (בשם ר' יוחנן) and, therefore, it is his interpolation.

30 I. e., the entire harvest can be done by shaking the tree; it is not necessary to climb up on a ladder to remove the olives still hanging.

31 This is either R. Yose the late Amora giving a ruling that in practice asserts the position of R. Yose the Tanna, or it is a justification of the position of the Tanna R. Yose from a practical, rather than a theoretical, point of view.

אִית תַּנָּאֵי תַּנֵּי שֶׁנִּמְצָא. אִית תַּנָּאֵי תַּנֵּי שֶׁנִּמְצָא עוֹמֵד. מָאן דְּאָמַר שֶׁנִּמְצָא מְסַייֵעַ לְרִבִּי יוֹחָנָן. מָאן דְּאָמַר שֶׁנִּמְצָא עוֹמֵד מְסַייֵעַ לְרִבִּי אֶלְעָזָר. מַתְנִיתָא

מְסַייְעָא לְרִבִּי יוֹחָנָן דְּתַנֵּי בְּמַה דְבָרִים אֲמוּרִים בִּזְמָן שֶׁאֵין מַכִּירוֹ. אֲבָל אִם הָיָה מַכִּירוֹ מְרַדֵּף אַחֲרָיו עַד מֵאָה.

Some Tannaïm[32] state: "it is found." Some Tannaïm state: "It is found standing." He who says "it is found" supports Rebbi Joḥanan[33]. He who says "it is found standing" supports Rebbi Eleazar[34]. A *baraita*[35] supports Rebbi Joḥanan: "When has this been said? If he does not recognize it. But if he recognizes it, he runs after it even 100 cubits[36]."

32 These Tannaïm are not the Sages of the period known as tannaïtic but are scholars who memorized tannaïtic statements (which at this time were not written down) to produce them when asked about them. The different versions are those of our Mishnah.

33 It turns out after the fact that the tree can be harvested simply by shaking.

34 It is known beforehand that the tree is standing at a certain privileged place.

35 Tosephta *Peah* 3:10. The text here follows the Rome manuscript which is identical with that of the Tosephta. The Venice print has the positions of "recognizes" and "does not recognize" switched.

36 If the tree has a distinguishing mark, as in the case described by R. Eleazar, the entire Mishnah does not apply. Hence, we must deal with a particular property discovered after the fact.

הָא אִם יֵשׁ בּוֹ סְאָתַיִם וּשְׁכָחוֹ אֵינוֹ שִׁכְחָה. לֹא עַל הָדָא אִיתְאֲמָרַת אֶלָּא עַל קַדְמִייָתָא כָּל־זַיִת שֶׁיֵּשׁ לוֹ שֵׁם בַּשָּׂדֶה כְּזַיִת נְטוּפָה בְּשַׁעְתּוֹ וּשְׁכָחוֹ אֵינוֹ שִׁכְחָה עָלֶיהָ. הָא אִם יֵשׁ בּוֹ סְאָתַיִם וּשְׁכָחוֹ.

Hence[37], if it yields two *seah*, if it was forgotten it is not legally forgotten. It does not refer to this but to the first Mishnah: "Every olive tree that has a special name on the field, for example 'a dripping olive tree' in its time, if it was forgotten, it is not legally forgotten. Hence, if it yields two *seah*, if it was forgotten . . ." [38]

37 Here starts the discussion of the second sentence of the Mishnah.

38 Maimonides in his Mishnah commentary construes as follows: "Every olive tree that has a special name on the field, for example 'a dripping olive tree' in its time, when forgotten is not legally forgotten. When has this been said? Only if he did not start with it; but if he started harvesting it, even a *dripping olive tree* in its time, when forgotten is legally forgotten. But if it yields two *seah*, when forgotten it is not legally forgotten."

כָּל־זְמָן שֶׁיֵּשׁ לוֹ תַחְתָּיו יֵשׁ לוֹ בְרֹאשׁוֹ. פָּתַר לָהּ תְּרֵין פִּיתְרִין. כָּל־זְמָן שֶׁיֵּשׁ לוֹ תַחְתָּיו יֵשׁ לוֹ בְרֹאשׁוֹ קוֹדֶם לָכֵן אַף עַל פִּי שֶׁאֵין לוֹ תַחְתָּיו יֵשׁ לוֹ בְרֹאשׁוֹ. פָּתַר חוֹרָן כָּל־זְמָן שֶׁיֵּשׁ לוֹ תַחְתָּיו אֵין לוֹ בְרֹאשׁוֹ הִילְכָא הַמַּחְבָּא אַף עַל פִּי שֶׁאֵין לוֹ בְרֹאשׁוֹ יֵשׁ לוֹ תַחְתָּיו.

"Whenever he has under it, he has at its crown." One may explain this in two ways. Whenever he has under it, he has at its crown; hence, before that even if there is nothing under it, he has at its crown[39]. Another explanation: Whenever he[40] has under it, he has nothing at its crown[41]; by the time the *mahba* was used, even though he has nothing at its crown he has under the tree[42].

39 The poor may take the olives remaining on the branches even though the owner is not finished with collecting all olives shaken from the tree (Maimonides *Mattenot Aniïm* 1:12).

40 The owner.

41 Since he will not start collecting the olives that fell off the tree until he has removed the remaining ones from the tree mechanically.

42 At that time, the poor may search the tree since the owner has completed his harvest.

תַּנֵּי מִשּׁוּם בֵּית שַׁמַּאי מְשֶׁיְּנַּיחַ אֶת הַבִּרְכַּר וּגְמָרוֹ הֲרֵי זֶה יֵשׁ לוֹ בְרֹאשׁוֹ. רִבִּי אַבָּהוּ בְשֵׁם רִבִּי שִׁמְעוֹן בֶּן לָקִישׁ בַּר כַּדָּה[43]. אָמַר רִבִּי אָבָּהוּ שֶׁהוּא מְשַׁיֵּיר אֶת הַמַּחְבוּיִין. וּדְעוּ וּרְאוּ מִכָּל־הַמַּחֲבוֹאִים אֲשֶׁר יִתְחַבֵּא שָׁם.

It was stated[44] in the name of the House of Shammai: When he puts away the knee cushion[45] and finishes, then he still has at the top. Rebbi Abbahu in the name of Rebbi Simeon ben Laqish: The remainder[46] of the harvest. Rebbi Abbahu said, [47]that which takes care of the hidden ones: (*1Sam.* 23:23) "Find out and see all the hiding places where he could hide."

43 Manuscript readings of R. Abraham ben David בְּדַבְרָה "on the grazing area," i. e., if the area is given over to animals to graze the harvest is finished.

44 Explaining the statement of R. Meïr and the word *maḥba*.

45 Used to collect all the olives shaken from the tree. (Second explanation of *Arukh*.)

46 Arabic כִּדַּה "poor soil", אַכִּדַּה "leftover pasture".

47 *Maḥba* is . . .

(fol. 19d) **משנה ג**: אֵי זֶהוּ פֶּרֶט הַנּוֹשֵׁר בִּשְׁעַת הַבְּצִירָה. הָיָה בוֹצֵר עָקַר אֶת הָאֶשְׁכּוֹל הִיסְבַּךְ בֶּעָלִים וְנָפַל בָּאָרֶץ וְנִפְרַט הֲרֵי זֶה שֶׁל בַּעַל הַבַּיִת. הַמֵּנִיחַ כַּלְכָּלָה תַּחַת הַגֶּפֶן בְּשָׁעָה שֶׁהוּא בוֹצֵר הֲרֵי זֶה גוֹזֵל אֶת הָעֲנִיִּים. עַל זֶה נֶאֱמַר אַל תַּסֵּג גְּבוּל עוֹלָם.

Mishnah 3: What are dropped berries[48]? Anything that drops during vintage. If he was gathering grapes, cut off the bunch, it got mixed up in the leaves, fell to the ground and scattered[49], that belongs to the proprietor. He who puts a basket under the vine while he is gathering grapes robs the poor, and about him it was said[50] (*Prov.* 22:28, 23:10): "Do not displace an eternal boundary."

48 Here starts the discussion of the duty to give single berries to the poor, *Lev.* 19:10.

49 By accident.

50 Cf. Mishnah 5:5.

(fol. 20a) **הלכה ג**: הָדָא אָמְרָה פֶּרֶט בְּנְשִׁירָתוֹ קָדֵשׁ. לֵית הָדָא פְּשִׁיטָא שְׁאִילְתֵּיהּ דְּחִילְפַי דְּחִילְפַי שְׁאַל לֶקֶט בִּנְשִׁירָתוֹ מַהוּ שֶׁיְּקַדֵּשׁ. אָמַר רִבִּי שְׁמוּאֵל בַּר אֶבוּדוּמָא שַׁנְיָא הִיא שֶׁהוּא גָּרַם לוֹ שֶׁלֹּא יֵרֵד לָאָרֶץ.

Halakhah 3: This means that dropped berries become sanctified[51] in the act of falling down. Does this not simply answer Hilfai[52]'s question, since Hilfai asked: Do gleanings become sanctified in the act of falling down? Rebbi Samuel ben Eudaimon said: There is a difference, because he prevented them from reaching the ground[53].

51 As food of the poor for which they do not have to give heave or tithes. If the berries were not the property of the poor while falling down, the vintner could not be accused of actively robbing the poor by putting a basket under the vine.

52 In the Babylonian Talmud, he is called Ilfa. He studied together with R. Johanan, was as great as R. Johanan in learning but preferred to earn a living in trade. He objected to the use of *baraitot* and *toseftot* and maintained that all necessary information could be obtained from the Mishnah.

53 Even if dropped berries become exempt from heave and tithes only when they touch the ground, still the vintner is guilty of robbery since without his intervention the berries would have touched the ground. However, it is reasonable to say that the berries do not become sanctified in falling and that the vintner, in addition to being a robber of the poor, is still under the obligation of giving heave and tithes from what he collected.

(fol. 19d) **משנה ד**: וְאֵי זוּ הִיא עוֹלֶלֶת כָּל־שֶׁאֵין לָהּ לֹא כָתֵף וְלֹא נָטֵף אִם יֵשׁ לָהּ כָּתֵף וְנָטֵף שֶׁל בַּעַל הַבַּיִת. אִם סָפֵק לָעֲנִיִּים. עוֹלֶלֶת שֶׁבְּאַרְכּוּבָה אִם נִקְרַעַת[54] עִם הָאֶשְׁכּוֹל שֶׁל בַּעַל הַבַּיִת וְאִם לָאו הֲרֵי הוּא שֶׁל עֲנִיִּים. גַּרְגַּר יְחִידִי רִבִּי יְהוּדָה אוֹמֵר אֶשְׁכּוֹל. וַחֲכָמִים אוֹמְרִים עוֹלֶלֶת.

Mishnah 4: What is a gleaning[55] of grapes? Anything that has no shoulder and no dropping[56]. If it has either shoulder or dropping it belongs to the proprietor, in case of doubt it belongs to the poor. A gleaning on a cut branch, if it can be cut off together with a bunch it belongs to the proprietor, otherwise to the poor. An isolated berry, Rebbi Jehudah says, it is considered a bunch[57], but the sages say, a gleaning.

54 All manuscript sources of the Mishnah except the Leyden manuscript have either נקרצת or נקצרת.

55 In the Torah, עלל is used exclusively for vines (*Lev*. 19:10, *Deut*. 24:21). In Arabic, the root means "going over the harvest a second time" in general.

56 The Halakhah explains these terms.

57 According to the Halakhah more than three isolated berries together form a bunch for R. Jehudah.

הלכה ד: אֵי זוּ הִיא עוֹלֵלוֹת כָּל־שֶׁאֵין לָהּ לֹא כָתֵף וְלֹא נָטֵף יֵשׁ לָהּ כָּתֵף אֲבָל לֹא נָטֵף נָטֵף אֲבָל לֹא כָתֵף לְבַעַל הַבַּיִת. וְאִם סָפֵק לָעֲנִיִּים. אֵי זוּ הִיא כָתֵף פְּסִיגִין זוּ עַל גַּבֵּי זוּ. אֵי זוּ הִיא נָטֵף תְּלוּיוֹת בְּשִׁיזְרָה וְיוֹרְדוֹת.

Halakhah 4: (Tosephta *Peah* 3:11): "What are gleanings? Anything that has no shoulder and no dropping. If it has shoulder but no dropping, dropping but no shoulder, it belongs to the proprietor, if it is doubtful it belongs to the poor. What is a shoulder? Spread out[58] one on top of the other. What is a dropping? They hang downward on the spine."

58 The etymology and meaning of פסיגין is not very clear. I am comparing it with Arabic פסג "to spread one's legs." The meaning of the sentence is that grapes must also grow upward from the spine.

רִבִּי בָּא בְשֵׁם רַב יְהוּדָה וְהֵן שֶׁיְּהוּ כוּלָּן נוֹגְעוֹת בְּפַס יָדוֹ. לֹא כֵן אָמַר רִבִּי חִייָא מַעֲשֶׂה שֶׁשָּׁקְלוּ עוֹלֵלוֹת שֶׁבַע לִיטְרִיּוֹת בְּצִיפּוֹרִי. אָמַר רִבִּי חִינְנָה שֶׁאִים נְתָנָהּ עַל גַּבֵּי טַבְלָה וְהֵן שֶׁיְּהוּ כוּלָּן נוֹגְעוֹת בְּטַבְלָה.

Rebbi Abba in the name of Rav Jehudah: Only if they all touch the palm of his hand[59]. But did not Rebbi Ḥiyya say, it happened that they weighed a gleaning in Sepphoris and it was seven pounds[60]? Rebbi Ḥinena said, if they put it on a board, every grape must touch the board[61].

59 A rudimentary bunch qualifies only as gleanings if it is so small that it fits into one hand.

60 Greek λίτρα, Latin *libra*, "a pound" of 12 oz.

61 Latin *tabula* "board, plank"; also "plot in a vineyard."

בֶּן לֵוִי שֶׁנִּתְמַנֶּה לוֹ מַעֲשֵׂר טֵבֶל וּמָצָא בְתוֹכוֹ עוֹלֵלוֹת הֲרֵי זֶה עוֹשֶׂה אוֹתָן תְּרוּמַת מַעֲשֵׂר בְּמָקוֹם אַחֵר. וְעוֹלֵלוֹת לָאו שֶׁל עָנִי הוּא. רִבִּי אָבִין בְּשֵׁם רַבָּנִין דְּתַמָּן אֲנִי אוֹמֵר עִם הַנִּקְרָצוֹת עִם הָאֶשְׁכּוֹלוֹת.

A Levite who received unprepared tithes[62] and found in them gleanings may use them for the heave of the tithes even on other places. But do not gleanings belong to the poor? Rebbi Avin in the name of the rabbis from there[63]: I say that they are gleanings cut with the bunches[64].

62 First Tithes of which the heave of the tithe was not given to the Cohen. Tithe may not be eaten before the heave of the tithe is separated (*Num.* 18:26). The heave of the farmer has no minimum spelled out from the Torah, but it must be given from the harvest itself. The heave of the tithe is fixed at 10% but it may be given from anywhere (*Terumot* 2:1); hence, the Levite may use any fruit he has for that tithe.

63 Babylonia.

64 As spelled out in the Mishnah. The Levite does not commit a sin since he is not using property acquired illegally to satisfy a religious duty. The Tosephta (*Peah* 3:14) simply states: "A Levite to whom grapes were given, among which he found gleanings, does not have to worry whether they might belong to the poor."

אָמַר רִבִּי סִימוֹן טַעֲמָא דְּרִבִּי יְהוּדָה וְנִשְׁאַר בּוֹ עוֹלֵלוֹת כְּנוֹקֶף זַיִת שְׁנַיִם שְׁלֹשָׁה גַּרְגְּרִים. יוֹתֵר מִכֵּן אֶשְׁכּוֹל.

Rebbi Simon said, the reason of Rebbi Jehudah (*Is.* 17:6): "There will remain in it gleanings as when one plucks olives, two or three kernels[65]." More than that is a grape.

65 Meaning that one, two, or three berries on one branch really belong to the poor even according to Rebbi Jehudah, but four or more, even though they grow out right from the stem and do not form bunches, are not called "berries" but "grape."

דֶּלְמָה רִבִּי אַבָּהוּ וְרִבִּי יוֹסֵי בֶּן חֲנִינָא וְרִבִּי שִׁמְעוֹן בֶּן לָקִישׁ עֲבְרוּ עַל כֶּרֶם דּוֹרוֹן אַפִּיק לוֹן אָרִיסָא חָדָא פֶּרְסִיקָא אֲכְלוֹן אִינּוּן וְחַמְרֵיהוֹן וְאַייַתְּרוֹן. וְשַׁעֲרוּנָהּ כְּהָדֵין לָפִיסָא דִכְפַר חֲנַנְיָה מַחֲזִיק סְאָה שֶׁל עֲדָשִׁים. בָּתַר יוֹמִין עֲבְרוּן תַּמָּן אַפִּיק לוֹן תְּרֵין תְּלָת לְגַוָא יָדֵיהּ. אָמְרוּ לֵיהּ מִן הַהוּא אִילָנָא אֲנָן בְּעַיי אֲמַר לוֹן מִינֵיהּ אִינּוּן. וְקָרוֹן עֲלוֹי אֶרֶץ פְּרִי לִמְלֵחָה מֵרָעַת יוֹשְׁבֵי בָהּ.

Clarification[66]. Rebbi Abbahu, Rebbi Yose ben Ḥanina, and Rebbi Simeon ben Laqish passed by the orchard of Doron[67]. The sharecropper brought them one peach[68]; they and their donkeys ate from it and left some over. They estimated it to be like a dish[69] from Kefar Ḥananiah[70] that contains a *seah* of lentils. After a time they passed by there, he brought them two or three peaches in one hand. They said to him, we would like some from that tree. He said to them, they are from it. On that, they quoted (*Ps.* 107:34): "A fruit-bearing land into salt flats, because of the evil of its inhabitants."

66 The following digressions are induced by the story told before of a few grapes in Sepphoris weighing together seven pounds. Most of these stories are also quoted, in changed form, in Babli *Ketubot* 111b-112a; the

first ones also, very much changed, in *Baba Batra* 91b.

כרם usually means "vineyard," but in *Jud.* 15:5 כרם זית is a plantation of olive trees.

67 It is not clear whether this is a personal or topographical name.

68 Greek περσικὸν μῆλον, τὸ, also περσικός, ὁ, "Persian apple."

69 Greek λοπάς, -άδος, ἡ, "plate."

70 A place in Galilee famous for its pottery, possibly Kafr Anan.

אָמַר רִבִּי חֲנִינָא כַּד סְלָקַת לְהָכָא נְסִיבִית אֵיזוֹרִי וְאֵיזוֹרֵיהּ דִּבְרִי וְאֵיזוֹרֵיהּ דְּחַמְרִי מִקְפָּא בִּירְתָא דְּחָרוּבְתֵּיהּ דְּאַרְעָא דְּיִשְׂרָאֵל וְלָא מָטוּן. קְצַת חַד חָרוּב וּנְגַד מְלֹא יָדוֹי דְּבַשׁ.

Rebbi Ḥanina said, when I immigrated here, I took my belt, my son's belt, and the belt of my donkey to measure around a young carob tree of the Land of Israel and it was not enough. I cut one carob pod and it filled my hand with honey[71].

71 Carob syrup. In general, "honey" may mean both bee's honey or syrup. In Arabic, דבש denotes only "sugary matter produced from a fruit, syrup, molasses".

אָמַר רִבִּי יוֹחָנָן יָפֶה סִיפְסוּף שֶׁאָכַלְנוּ בְיַלְדוּתֵינוּ מִפֶּרְסִיקִין שֶׁאָכַלְנוּ בְּזִקְנוּתֵינוּ דְּבְיוֹמוֹי אִישְׁתַּנֵּי עָלְמָא.

Rebbi Joḥanan said, the second quality fruit[72] we ate in our youth tasted better that the peaches we ate in our old age, because during his lifetime the world changed[73].

72 Cf. Arabic ספסאף "rejects, bad quality, junk."

73 He was born under the Principate, lived through the hyperinflation and the shrinking economy of the Military Anarchy, and died under Diocletian's military absolutism. (Cf. Babli *Baba batra* 91b.)

אָמַר רִבִּי חִייָא בַּר בָּא סְאָה אַרְבֵּלִית הָיְתָה מוֹצִיאָה סְאָה סוֹלֶת סְאָה קֶמַח סְאָה קֵיבָר סְאָה סוּבִּין סְאָה מוּרְסָן סְאָה גְנִינִין. וּכְדוֹן אֲפִילוּ חָדָא בְחָדָא לָא קַיְימָא.

Rebbi Ḥiyya bar Abba said, one *seah* of Arbel[74] grain did yield one *seah* of fine flour, one *seah* of white flour, one *seah* of dark flour, one *seah* of bran, one *seah* of coarse bran, and one *seah* of wheat germ. But today, we do not even get one for one[75].

74 On the high plain above Tiberias.

75 A *seah* of grain contains empty space between grains. In milling, by necessity something is lost. One *seah* of grain yields much less than a *seah* of flour. Cf. Babli *Ketubot* 112a, *Sotah* 17b.

רִבִּי חוּנָא בְשֵׁם רִבִּי אָבִין קִנָּמוֹן מַאֲכַל עִזִּים הָיָה הָיוּ יִשְׂרָאֵל מְגַדְּלִין אוֹתוֹ. רִבִּי חוּנָא בְשֵׁם רִבִּי אָבִין שְׁנֵי תְמִידִין שֶׁהָיוּ מַקְרִיבִין בְּכָל־יוֹם הָיוּ מַרְכִּיבִין אוֹתָן עַל (fol. 20b) גַּבֵּי גָמָל וְרַגְלֵיהֶן נוֹגְעוֹת בָּאָרֶץ. רִבִּי חוּנָא בְשֵׁם רִבִּי אִידִי מַעֲשֶׂה בְאֶחָד שֶׁקָּשַׁר עֵז לִתְאֵינָה וּבָא וּמָצָא דְבַשׁ וְחָלָב מְעוּרָבִין.

Rebbi Ḥuna in the name of Rebbi Avin: Cinnamon was goat feed when the Jews were growing it. Rebbi Ḥuna in the name of Rebbi Abin: The two daily offerings[76] which were sacrificed every day used to be carried by a camel and their legs touched the ground. Rebbi Ḥuna in the name of Rebbi Idi: It happened that someone tied his goat to a fig tree; when he returned, he found honey[71] and milk mixed[77].

76 Two yearling sheep.

77 Babli *Ketubot* 111b, in the name of Rami bar Ezechiel, brother of Rav Jehudah, a wanderer between Galilee and Babylonia.

רִבִּי אָמַר לְרַב פְּרִירִי לֵית אַתְּ חֲמֵי לִי הַהִיא סְגוּלָה דְגוֹ כַּרְמָךְ. אֲמַר לֵיהּ אִין נְפַק בְּעֵי מְחִימַיְיָא לֵיהּ עַד דְּהוּא רָחִיק צָפָה בֵיהּ כְּמִין תּוֹר אֲמַר לֵיהּ לֵית הָדֵין תּוֹרָא מְחַבֵּל כַּרְמָא אֲמַר לֵיהּ הָדֵין תּוֹרָא דְּאַתְּ סְבַר הוּא סְגוּלָה. וּקְרָא עֲלוֹי עַד שֶׁהַמֶּלֶךְ בִּמְסִיבּוֹ נִירְדִּי נָתַן רֵיחוֹ. בֵּית מוּקְדְּשָׁא חָרִיב וְאַתְּ קָאִית בְּקַשְׁיוּתָךְ. מִיַּד אִיתְבְּעוּן וְלָא אַשְׁכַּח.

Rebbi said to Rav Periri[78]: Would you show me the bunch of grapes in your vineyard? He said to him, if you come out, I will show it. When he was still far away, he spied something like an ox. He said to him, does not the ox destroy the vineyard? He said to him, what you take for an ox is the bunch of grapes. He quoted for it (*Cant.* 1:12): "As long as the King was at his round table, my nard gave its fragrance[79];" the Temple is destroyed and you persist in your obstinacy? Immediately, they looked for it and it was never found again.

78 He appears only here and the title "Rav" is impossible for anybody in the Yeshivah of Rebbi except Rav himself. R. S. Cirillo changes the name to Rebbi Pedat (who however lived long after Rebbi), R. Eliahu Fulda and R. Moses Margalit use "Rebbi Peridah," a mythical figure from the Babylonian Talmud who is reputed to have lived for over 400 years. He would fit into the story but one might doubt that Rebbi would hurt him. I wonder whether the person in question is not Rav himself and פרירי is an (Aramaic-Arabic فورار) address of endearment "my lamb". In that case, one has to translate: Rebbi said to Rav: My lamb, will you not show me. . . . Since Rav was a relative of the Heads of the Diaspora and rich, he could have owned real estate whose yield would sustain him during his years of study.

79 Meaning that the land will give its extraordinary yield only as long as the Shekhinah is in the Temple.

אַיְיתוּן קוֹמוֹי תְּרֵין פוּגְלִין מִבֵּין רֵישׁ שַׁתָּא לְצוֹמָא רַבָּא וַהֲוָה אֲפוּקֵי שְׁמִיטְתָא וַהֲוָה בְּהוֹן טְעוּנֵיהּ דְּגַמְלָא אֲמַר לוֹן וְלֵית אֲסִיר וְלָאו סְפִחִין אִינּוּן. אֲמַר לֵיהּ בְּפוּקֵי רֵישׁ שַׁתָּא אִיזְדַּרְעוּן. בְּאוֹתָהּ שָׁעָה הִתִּיר רִבִּי לִיקַּח יֶרֶק בְּמוֹצָאֵי שְׁבִיעִית מִיַּד.

They brought before him two radishes from between New Year's Day and the Great Fast[80]. It was the year after a Sabbatical, and they were a full camel's load. He said to them, are they not forbidden as aftergrowth[81]? He said to him, they were sown at the end of New Year's Day. At that moment did Rebbi permit to buy vegetables immediately after the end of the Sabbatical year.

80 Yom Kippur, the Tenth of Tishre. The radishes probably were offered for sale on Yom Kippur Eve.

81 One may not use any plant grown in the Sabbatical year for commercial purposes (and one may not use any produce if nothing of the same kind is left on the fields for wildlife.) Hence, the free growth of the Sabbatical is forbidden in commercial transactions even after the end of the Sabbatical year.

בְּעוֹן קוֹמוֹי מַהוּ הָדֵין דִּכְתִיב עָבְשׁוּ פְרוּדוֹת תַּחַת מֶגְרְפוֹתֵיהֶם. אָמַר לוֹן תַּחַת שֶׁהָיִינוּ גּוֹרְפִין דְּבַשׁ הֲרֵי אָנוּ גּוֹרְפִין רַקְבּוּבִית. מַעֲשֶׂה בְּאֶחָד שֶׁהָיָה לוֹ שׁוּרָה שֶׁל תְּאֵינִים וּבָא וּמָצָא גֶּדֶר שֶׁל דְּבַשׁ מַקִּיפָן.

They asked before him, what is that which is written (*Joel* 1:17): "Dried figs became mouldy under their shovels." He said to them, we were raking honey, now we are raking rotten things instead. It happened that somebody had a row of fig trees; when he came, he found them surrounded by a fence of honey.

חַד בַּר נַשׁ הֲוָה זְרַע חַקְלָא לֶפֶת וַהֲוָה מְקַטֵּעַ וּמַזְבִּין. מַעֲשֶׂה בְשׁוּעָל שֶׁבָּא וְקִינֵּן בְּרֹאשָׁהּ שֶׁל לֶפֶת. מַעֲשֶׂה בְשִׁיחִין בְּקֶלַח אֶחָד שֶׁל חַרְדָּל שֶׁהָיוּ בוֹ שְׁלֹשָׁה בַדִּין

וְנִפְשַׁח אֶחָד מֵהֶן וְסִיכְּכוּ סוּכַּת הַיּוֹצְרִין וּמָצְאוּ בּוֹ שְׁלֹשֶׁת קַבִּין שֶׁל חַרְדָּל. אָמַר רַבִּי שִׁמְעוֹן בֶּן חֲלַפְתָּא קֶלַח אֶחָד שֶׁל חַרְדָּל הָיָה לִי בְּתוֹךְ שֶׁלִּי וְהָיִיתִי עוֹלֶה בוֹ כְּעוֹלֶה בְרֹאשׁ הַתְּאֵינָה.

One person sowed turnips on his field; he used to cut them off and sell them[82]. It happened that a fox made his nest in a turnip's head. It happened in Shiḥin[83] that one stalk of mustard plant had three leaves; one leaf was split off to cover a potter's hut and they found on it three *qab*[84] of mustard seed. Rebbi Simeon ben Ḥalaphta said, I had a stem of mustard plant on my property and I climbed on it the way one climbs a fig tree.

82 It is still possible to replant the top of a large radish with a small part of the root and it will regrow a root, but not more than once.

83 A village near Sepphoris renowned for its pottery. This story also appears in *Ketubot*.

84 About 7 quarts.

מַעֲשֶׂה בְּאֶחָד שֶׁזָּרַע סְאָה שֶׁל אֲפוּנִין וְעָשָׂת שְׁלֹשׁ מְאוֹת סְאִין. אָמְרוּ לוֹ הִתְחִיל הַקָּדוֹשׁ בָּרוּךְ הוּא לְבָרֶכְךָ. אָמַר לוֹן אֲזָלוּן לְכוֹן דִּי יִנְחַת טַלָּא בִישָׁא עֲלֵיהּ דִּי לָא כֵן בְּכְפֵילָא הֲוָת מַעֲבִיד.

It happened that someone sowed a *seah* of peas and it produced 300 *seah*. They said to him, the Holy One, praise to Him, has started to bless you. He answered, get away from here, if bad dew had not descended on it, it would have produced twice as much.

אָמַר רַבִּי שִׁמְעוֹן בֶּן חֲלַפוּתָא הֲוָה מַעֲשֶׂה שֶׁאָמַר רַבִּי יְהוּדָה לִבְנוֹ בְּסִיכְנִין עֲלֵה וַהֲבֵא לָנוּ גְרוֹגְרוֹת מִן הֶחָבִית עָלָה וְהוֹשִׁיט יָדוֹ וּמְצָאָהּ שֶׁל דְּבַשׁ אָמַר לוֹ אַבָּא שֶׁל דְּבַשׁ הִיא. אָמַר לוֹ הַשְׁקַע יָדֶיךָ וְאַתְּ מַעֲלֶה גְרוֹגְרוֹת. מַעֲשֶׂה שֶׁאָמַר רַבִּי יוֹסֵי לִבְנוֹ בְּצִיפּוֹרִין עֲלֵה וַהֲבֵא לָנוּ גְרוֹגְרוֹת מִן הָעֲלִיָּה. עָלָה וּמָצָא אֶת הָעֲלִיָּה

צָף עֲלֶיהָ דְּבַשׁ. רִבִּי חֲנַנְיָה הֲוָה מַזְבֵּן דְּבַשׁ דִּדְבוֹרִיין וַהֲוָה לֵיהּ דְּבַשׁ דְּצַלְיין בָּתַר יוֹמִין עֲבְרוּן תַּמָּן אֲמַר לוֹן בְּגִין לָא מִטְעָיָא לְכוֹן הֲווֹן יָדְעִין הַהוּא דוּבְשָׁא דִיהָבִית לְכוֹן דְּצַלְיין יִינוּן. אָמְרוּ לֵיהּ מִינֵיהּ אֲנָן בְּעֵי דּוּ טָב לַעֲבִידְתִּין וְאַפְרֵישׁ טִימִיתֵיהּ וּבְנָא בֵיהּ בֵּי מִדְרְשָׁא דְּצִיפּוֹרִין.

Rebbi Simeon ben Ḥalaphta said, it happened that Rebbi Jehudah said to his son in Sikhnin[85]: Go and bring us dried figs from the barrel. He went and put his hand into the barrel, found it full of honey and said: Father, it is a barrel of honey. He said to him, put your hands deep into it and you will bring up the dried figs. It happened that Rebbi Yose said to his son in Sepphoris: Go and bring us dried figs from the upper floor. He went and found that honey was floating on the upper floor. Rebbi Ḥananiah was a dealer in bee's honey; he also had honey obtained by roasting[86]. After a time they passed by him. He said to them, in order not to trick you, you should know that the honey that I gave you was from roasting. They said, from that one we want more because it is good for our purposes. He set aside its value[87] and built with it the House of Study of Sepphoris.

85 A town in Galilee, birthplace of R. Joshua.

86 Following Levy, all the dictionaries identify *ẓeli* as a kind of dates, since vegetable honey is made from dates. However, the previous stories were all about the fact that earlier (before the war of Bar Kokhba but long after the destruction of the Temple) even figs produced sap so rich in sugar that it could be used as honey substitute. So one possible translation would be "of *ẓeli* figs"; it is unclear what kind they are. The translation assumes that it was bee's honey, which may be obtained from the honey combs by heating. Then the "roasted" honey was lower quality honey obtained by roasting honey combs from which the first quality had been extracted by moderate heat, and honesty required that the customer be informed that the

honey sold was of second quality only. "To roast" is Hebrew צלה, Arabic צלי. The word could also be derived from Arabic צויל "to clean out by washing", צולה "chaff", giving a similar meaning.

87 Greek τιμή, "value." He set aside the difference in value between premium bee's honey and *ẓeli* honey.

רִבִּי לֶעְזָר בֵּי רִבִּי שִׁמְעוֹן אֲזַל לְחַד אֲתַר. אַיְיתוּן קוֹמוֹי כְּרוּב מְצַמֵּק. אֲמַר לוֹן סַגִּין דְּבַשׁ יְהַבְתּוּן בֵּיהּ. אֲמְרִין לֵיהּ לָא יְהָבִינוּן בֵּיהּ מִינֵיהּ וּבֵיהּ הוּא.

Rebbi Eleazar ben Rebbi Simeon went to a place where they brought him shrunk cabbage[88]. He said to them, you put a lot of honey into it. They said to him, we did not put anything in, it is in its natural state.

88 Either dried in the air or roasted over a fire.

(fol. 19d) **משנה ה**: הַמֵּידַל בַּגְּפָנִים כְּשֵׁם שֶׁהוּא מֵידַל בְּתוֹךְ שֶׁלּוֹ כָּךְ הוּא מֵידַל בְּשֶׁל עֲנִיִּים דִּבְרֵי רִבִּי יְהוּדָה. רִבִּי מֵאִיר אוֹמֵר בְּשֶׁלּוֹ הוּא רְשַׁאי וְאֵינוֹ רְשַׁאי בְּשֶׁל עֲנִיִּים.

Mishnah 5: He who thins out vines[89], just as he thins out his own so he thins out those of the poor, the words of Rebbi Jehudah[90]. Rebbi Meïr says, he may do so for his own but he is not empowered for those of the poor.

89 So that the rest of them should grow more and larger grapes. The "vines of the poor" are those on which single berries are visible. One cannot say that it refers to the part of the vine that is designated as *peah* since thinning is done early in the growing season and *peah* is designated at the end of the harvest.

90 The Halakhah explains that R. Jehudah considers the poor as partners of the proprietor while R. Meïr considers them as buyers.

(fol. 20b) **הלכה ה**: הַכֹּל מוֹדִין בְּמוֹכֵר לַחֲבֵירוֹ עֲשָׂרָה אֶשְׁכּוֹלוֹת שֶׁיְּהֵא אָסוּר לִיגַּע בָּהֶן. הַכֹּל מוֹדִין בְּשׁוּתָּף כְּשֵׁם שֶׁהוּא מֵידַל בְּתוֹךְ שֶׁלּוֹ כָּךְ הוּא מֵידַל בְּתוֹךְ שֶׁל חֲבֵירוֹ. רִבִּי יְהוּדָה עֲבַד לֵיהּ כְּשׁוּתָּף וְרִבִּי מֵאִיר עֲבַד לֵיהּ כְּמוֹכֵר. אֲמַר לֵיהּ רִבִּי אִימִּי הַגַּע עַצְמָךְ שֶׁאֲכָלָתַן חַיָּה. אִין תְּעַבְדִּינֵיהּ כְּשׁוּתָּף יְהֵא חַיָּב לְשַׁלֵּם לוֹ.

Halakhah 5: Everybody agrees that he who sells ten bunches to somebody else may not touch them[91]. Everybody agrees in a partnership that just as he thins out his, so he thins out that of his partner[92]. Rebbi Jehudah considers him to be a partner, Rebbi Meïr considers him to be a seller[93]. Rebbi Immi said to him[94]: Think about it, if a wild animal ate it, if you consider him a partner he is required to pay him[95]!

91 To thin out after the sale.

92 Since it is a necessary part of tending the vineyard.

93 The last clause is missing in the Venice print and the Leyden manuscript; it is added from R. S. Cirillo and the Rome manuscript on the testimony of R. Simson of Sens that it was in his Yerushalmi text.

94 The person addressed is not indicated. The usual partner of Rebbi Immi was Rebbi Yasa (Assi).

95 If the wild animal ate all the gleanings of the poor person then, as in any partnership, the damage should be borne jointly by the two partners; hence, the farmer should pay to the poor person his part of the loss. (Since individual poor persons have no standing in court in this matter, probably he should give the equivalent to the local administrator of charity.)

אֲמַר רִבִּי יוֹחָנָן נִרְאֵית מוּחְלֶפֶת שִׁיטָּתוֹ שֶׁל רִבִּי יְהוּדָה. תַּמָּן הוּא אוֹמֵר בֵּין כָּךְ וּבֵין כָּךְ נוֹטְלָן וּמֵנִיחָן עַל הַגֶּדֶר וְהֶעָנִי בָּא וְנוֹטֵל אֶת שֶׁלּוֹ. וְכֹא הוּא אֲמַר הָכֵן. מִתּוֹךְ שֶׁהוּא מְעַכֵּן הֵן עוֹשׂוֹת יוֹתֵר לַשָּׁנָה הַבָּאָה. וְאָמַר אוּף הָכָא מִכֵּיוָן שֶׁהוּא מַרְבְּעָהּ הִיא עוֹשָׂה יוֹתֵר לַשָּׁנָה הַבָּאָה. אֲמַר לֵיהּ מָצוּי הוּא לְזוֹרְעָהּ יֶרֶק וּלְהַבְרִיחָהּ מִן הָעֲנִיִּים.

Rebbi Johanan said, it seems that Rebbi Jehudah changed his opinion. There[96] he says, in both cases he takes them, deposits them on the fence and the poor comes and takes what is his; but here he says so[97]! Because he squeezees them, they will produce more the next year. I should say also here, because he fertilizes it, it will produce more the next year. He said to him, it happens frequently[98] that he will sow vegetables and shelter them from the poor.

96 Halakhah 5:3, speaking of the farmer who wants to irrigate or fertilize his field immediately after harvest, before the poor had an opportunity to search for gleanings. There, the same question is asked in the other direction and answered differently.

97 That he can eliminate the part of the poor in the course of regular care of his vineyard.

98 A vine is a perennial and will always produce grapes, so the poor can wait for the next crop. But a field is subject to regular crop rotation and it is to be expected that every third year or so the field will be sown with vegetables not harvested at one time, exempt from *peah*. Hence, the interest of the poor in not in the next crop.

(fol. 19d) **משנה ו**: כֶּרֶם רְבָעִי בֵּית שַׁמַּאי אוֹמֵר אֵין לוֹ חוֹמֶשׁ וְאֵין לוֹ בֵּיעוּר. וּבֵית הִלֵּל אוֹמֵר יֵשׁ לוֹ. בֵּית שַׁמַּאי אוֹמֵר יֵשׁ לוֹ פֶּרֶט וְיֵשׁ לוֹ עוֹלֵלוֹת וַעֲנִיִּים פּוֹדִין לְעַצְמָן. וּבֵית הִלֵּל אוֹמֵר כּוּלּוֹ לְגַת.

Mishnah 6: A vineyard in its fourth year[99], the House of Shammai say, it is not subject to a fifth and is not subject to removal; but the House of Hillel say, it is. The House of Shammai say, it is subject to single berries and gleanings[100] and the poor redeem for themselves, but the House of Hillel say, all goes to the winepress[101].

99 It is forbidden to harvest a newly planted vineyard the first three years. In the fourth year, the grapes can be harvested but they (or the wine produced from them) must be brought to the Temple and be consumed in Jerusalem in a festive manner (*Lev.* 19:23-24). If there is too much to be taken on a journey, it may be redeemed and the money taken to Jerusalem. The House of Hillel compare the yield of the fourth year to the Second Tithe that also has to be eaten in Jerusalem, since produce of the Second Tithe that is redeemed is subject to a surcharge of one fifth (from above, 25% from below). There are two kinds of removal the vineyard of the fourth year may be subject to; if it is compared to the Second Tithe it must be removed from the house at the end of the third and sixth years of every Sabbatical period; if the produce was that of a Sabbatical year, one may take it but only as long as wild animals find similar food on the field (in this case, in other unharvested vineyards) and it must be removed by being consumed before that time. The House of Shammai consider the yield of the fourth year as profane food, subject only to what is expressly spelled out in the verse.

The argument of the House of Hillel, that the verse compares the vineyard in its fourth year to the Second Tithe, is given in Babli *Qiddušin* 54b, Sifra *Qedošim Parašah* 3 #8.

100 As any other profane food.

101 Since the second tithe is not subject to any gifts to the poor, neither is the yield of the fourth year.

(fol. 20b) **הלכה ו:** תַּנֵּי רִבִּי אוֹמֵר לֹא אָמְרוּ בֵּית שַׁמַּאי אֶלָּא בִשְׁבִיעִית אֲבָל בִּשְׁאָר שְׁנֵי שָׁבוּעַ [102]בֵּית שַׁמַּאי אוֹמְרִים יֵשׁ לוֹ חוֹמֶשׁ וְיֵשׁ לוֹ בִּיעוּר. עַל דַּעְתֵּיהּ דְּהָהֵן תַּנָּייָה לֹא לָמְדוּ נֶטַע רְבָעִי אֶלָּא מִמַּעֲשֵׂר שֵׁנִי כְּמַה דְתֵימַר אֵין מַעֲשֵׂר שֵׁנִי בִּשְׁבִיעִית. וְדִכְוָותָהּ אֵין נֶטַע רְבָעִי בִּשְׁבִיעִית. מֵעַתָּה אַל יְהִי לוֹ קְדוּשָּׁה וּקְדוּשָּׁתוֹ מֵאֵילָיו לָמְדוּ. קוֹדֶשׁ הִילּוּלִים. הֲרֵי הוּא כְקוֹדֶשׁ שֶׁקּוֹרִן עָלָיו. וִיהֵא מוּתָּר לְאוֹנֵן. תַּנֵּי מַגִּיד שֶׁהוּא אָסוּר לְאוֹנֵן. וִיהֵא חַייָב בְּבֵיעוּר. בְּגִין דְּרִבִּי שִׁמְעוֹן פּוֹטֵר מִן הַבֵּיעוּר. וְיִפָּדֶה בִמְחוּבָּר לְקַרְקַע.

Halakhah 6: It was stated[103]: Rebbi says, the House of Shammai said this only in the Sabbatical year, but in all other years of the sabbatical cycle, the House of Shammai say that it is subject to a fifth and subject to removal. According to that Tanna, they learned the rules of the vineyard of the fourth year only from the Second Tithe; since you say that there is no Second Tithe in the Sabbatical year[104], so there is no fourth year after planting[105] in the Sabbatical year. But then should there be no holiness in it? Its holiness comes from the verse (*Lev*. 19:24): "Holy for praises," it has the status of those holy fruits over which praises are said[106]. And should it be permitted to the fresh mourner[107]? It is stated: This[108] implies that it is forbidden to the fresh mourner. And should it be subject to removal? Since Rebbi Simeon frees it from removal[109]. And should it be redeemed while still connected to the ground[110]?

102 This text follows the parallel *Maäser Šeni* 5:3, the Venice text here has: שבית שמאי יש לו . . . .

103 In a different form, Tosephta *Maäser Šeni* 5:17. The entire discussion is found in Yerushalmi *Maäser Šeni* 5:3.

104 Since there is no private property of agricultural produce in the Sabbatical year, there may not be special uses for the farmer's family.

105 The Mishnah speaks of כרם רבעי, a vineyard in its fourth year. The *baraitot* all speak of נטע רבעי, a planting (a planted tree) in its fourth year. The extension of the Biblical commandment about the vineyard to all trees is discussed in *Maäser Šeni*, Chap. 5.

106 The First Fruits, for which the praises said in the Temple are spelled out in *Deut*. 26.

107 The mourner in the period between the death of a close relative and the burial, when he is forbidden any sanctified food even if he is not ritually defiled, *Deut*. 26:14.

108 The verse declaring the vineyard of the fourth year as "holy for praises." Cf. Sifra *Qedošim Parašah* 3 #9.

109 The House of Shammai will agree with Rebbi Simeon who states in

Mishnah *Bikkurim* 2:2 that First Fruits and the vineyard of the fourth year are not subject to either kind of removal.

110 This question is not answered. The Tosefta *Maäser Šeni* 5:19 states categorically that there can be no redemption while the grapes are still on the vine. However, see in *Tosefta Kifšutah Maäser Šeni* p. 786 the list of authorities who claim that this is only the required procedure, but that a redemption, if done on the vine, is valid after the fact.

תַּנֵּי רַבָּן שִׁמְעוֹן בֶּן גַּמְלִיאֵל אֶחָד שְׁבִיעִית וְאֶחָד שְׁאָר שְׁנֵי שָׁבוּעַ בֵּית שַׁמַּאי אוֹמְרִים אֵין לוֹ חוֹמֶשׁ וְאֵין לוֹ בֵּיעוּר. עַל דַּעְתֵּיהּ דְּהָדֵין תַּנָּייָה לֹא לָמְדוּ נֶטַע רְבָעִי מִמַּעֲשֵׂר שֵׁנִי כָּל־עִיקָּר. מֵעַתָּה אַל יְהִי לוֹ קְדוּשָּׁה וּקְדוּשָּׁתוֹ מֵאֵילָיו לָמְדוּ. קוֹדֶשׁ הִילּוּלִים. הֲרֵי הוּא כְקוֹדֶשׁ שֶׁקּוֹרִן עָלָיו אֶת הַהַלֵּל. וִיהֵא מוּתָּר לְאוֹנֵן. תַּנֵּי מַגִּיד שֶׁהוּא אָסוּר לְאוֹנֵן. וִיהֵא חַיָּיב בְּבֵיעוּר. בְּגִין דְּרִבִּי שִׁמְעוֹן פּוֹטֵר מִן הַבֵּיעוּר. וְיִפָּדֶה בִּמְחוּבָּר לְקַרְקַע.

Rabban Simeon ben Gamliel stated: Both in the Sabbatical year and in the rest of the years of the sabbatical cycle, the House of Shammai say, there is no fifth and no removal. According to that Tanna, they did not at all learn the rules of the fourth year after planting from the Second Tithe. But then[111] should there be no holiness in it? Its holiness comes from the verse (*Lev.* 19:24): "Holy for praises;" it has the status of those holy fruits over which praises are said. And should it be permitted to the fresh mourner? It is stated: This implies that it is forbidden to the fresh mourner. And should it be subject to removal? Since Rebbi Simeon frees it from removal. And should it be redeemed while still connected to the ground?

111 If it is profane food. The rest of the paragraph is identical with the previous one except for the insertion of את ההלל missing here in the first version (but found in *Maäser Šeni* 5:3).

רִבִּי זְעִירָה בְּעֵי קוֹמֵי רִבִּי אַבָּהוּ מְנַיִין שֶׁהוּא טָעוּן פִּדְיוֹן קוֹדֶשׁ הִילּוּלִים קוֹדֶשׁ חִילּוּלִים לָא מִתְמַנְעִין רַבָּנִין בֵּין הֵ״א לְחֵי״ת.

Rebbi Zeïra asked before Rebbi Abbahu: From where that it needs redemption[112]? (*Lev.* 19:24) "Holy for praises," holy for redemption. The rabbis never refrain from identifying ה and ח.[113]

112 If the produce cannot be bodily transported to the place of the Temple. The argument is quoted in Babli *Berakhot* 35a. The word פדיון "redemption" is missing in the Leyden manuscript and the Venice print; it has been added from the parallel text in *Maäser Šeni*.

113 In all Jewish dialects except Eastern European Ashkenazic, ח (*ḥ*) is very close to ה. In Medieval German Jewish, as well in Talmudic Babylonian Jewish, *h* and *ḥ* were identical and הַ, חַ were used as rhyming sounds. The current Ashkenazic identification of the sounds of ח,כ (*ḥ*, *k*) comes from the fact that Polish has only one *ch* sound; this was adopted by the Jews from their Gentile surroundings. While Biblical Hebrew probably had the two Semitic ח sounds, corresponding to Arabic ح ،خ , one *ḥ* as in יצחק Isaac (Septuagint Ισαακ), the other *k* as in רחל Rachel (Septuagint Ραχηλ), in Mishnaic times these distinctions had disappeared long ago.

תַּנֵּי רִבִּי אַיְיבוּ בַּר נַגָּרִי קוֹמֵי רִבִּי לָא דְּרִבִּי יִשְׁמָעֵאל אִם גָּאֹל יִגְאַל אִישׁ מִמַּעַשְׂרוֹ חֲמִשִׁיתוֹ יוֹסֵף עָלָיו. פְּרָט לְנֶטַע רְבָעִי שֶׁאֵין חַיָּבִין עָלָיו חוֹמֶשׁ. וְחָזַר וְתַנָּא קוֹמוֹי שְׁתֵּי גְאוּלּוֹת הֵן אַחַת לְמַעֲשֵׂר שֵׁנִי וְאַחַת לְנֶטַע רְבָעִי.

Rebbi Ayvu bar Naggari stated before Rebbi La following Rebbi Ismael (*Lev.* 27:31): "If a man redeems part of his tithes, he should add its fifth to it." That excludes the fourth year after planting; one is not obligated by it for a fifth. Then he turned around and stated: There are two terms of redemption[114], one for the Second Tithe and one for the fourth year after planting.

114 גְאֹל יְגָאֵל. One of these statements follows Rebbi, the other Rabban Simeon ben Gamliel.

תַּמָּן תַּנֵּינָן רִבִּי יוּדָה אוֹמֵר אֵין לְנָכְרִי כֶּרֶם רְבָעִי. וַחֲכָמִים אוֹמְרִים יֵשׁ לוֹ. אָמַר רִבִּי לָעְזָר כֵּינִי מַתְנִיתָא אֵין לְנָכְרִי כֶּרֶם רְבָעִי כָּל־עִיקָּר. רִבִּי בִּיבִי אָמַר [115] קוֹמֵי רִבִּי זְעִירָא בְּשֵׁם רִבִּי לָעְזָר אַתְיָא דְּרִבִּי יוּדָה כְּבֵית שַׁמַּאי עַל דַּעְתֵּיהּ דְּרִבִּי כְּמָה דְּבֵית שַׁמַּאי אָמַר לֹא לָמְדוּ נֶטַע רְבָעִי אֶלָּא מִמַּעֲשֵׂר שֵׁנִי כְּמָה דְּתֵימַר אֵין מַעֲשֵׂר שֵׁנִי בִּשְׁבִיעִית. וְדִכְוָתָהּ אֵין נֶטַע רְבָעִי בִּשְׁבִיעִית. כֵּן רִבִּי יְהוּדָה אוֹמֵר לֹא לָמְדוּ נֶטַע רְבָעִי אֶלָּא מִמַּעֲשֵׂר שֵׁנִי כְּמָה דְּתֵימַר אֵין מַעֲשֵׂר שֵׁנִי בְּסוּרְיָא וְדִכְוָתָהּ אֵין נֶטַע רְבָעִי בְּסוּרְיָא. אָמַר לֵיהּ חֲמִי מַה אָמַר לֹא אָמַר אֵין לוֹ חוֹמֶשׁ וְאֵין לוֹ בֵּיעוּר הָא שְׁאָר כָּל־הַדְּבָרִים יֵשׁ לוֹ. רִבִּי יְהוּדָה אוֹמֵר אֵין לְנָכְרִי כֶּרֶם רְבָעִי בְּסוּרְיָא.

There we have stated[116]: Rebbi Jehudah says, there is no vineyard in the fourth year for the Gentile, but the Sages say there is[117]. Rebbi Eleazar said, so says the Mishnah: There is never a vineyard in the fourth year for the Gentile[118]. Rebbi Bibi said before Rebbi Zeïra in the name of Rebbi Eleazar: According to the opinion of Rebbi, the statement of Rebbi Jehudah turns out to be like the statement of the House of Shammai. Since the House of Shammai said that they learned the rules of the vineyard of the fourth year only from the Second Tithe; since you say that there is no Second Tithe in the Sabbatical year, so there is no fourth year after planting in the Sabbatical year. Similarly, Rebbi Jehudah said that they learned the rules of the vineyard of the fourth year only from the Second Tithe; since you say that there is no Second Tithe in Syria[119], so there is no fourth year after planting in Syria. He said to him, look what he[120] said! He said only, it is not subject to a fifth and is not subject to removal[121], hence, it is subject to all other rules; Rebbi Jehudah[122] says, there is no vineyard in the fourth year for the Gentile in Syria.

115 Reading of the Rome ms. The Venice print has a superfluous בעי.

116 Mishnah *Terumot* 3:9: "The heave of Gentile and Samaritan is heave, their tithes are tithes, their dedication is dedication. Rebbi Jehudah says, there is no vineyard in the fourth year for the Gentile, but the Sages say, there is." Even though the Gentile is not required to give heave, tithes, or to dedicate anything to the Temple, if he does it voluntarily, it must be treated according to all rules applying to heave, tithes, and dedications from Jews.

117 This is connected with the disagreement between R. Meïr and R. Jehudah/R. Simeon whether the possession by a Gentile of arable land in the Land of Israel does free its produce from duties of heave and tithes or not, cf. Chapter 4, Notes 129-131. The Babli (*Menaḥot* 66b) declares R. Jehudah to agree with R. Meïr that the Gentile's arable land is subject to all duties, but this is not the opinion of the Yerushalmi.

118 It is difficult to understand what R. Eleazar adds. R. S. Cirillo has: "There is no 'vineyard of the fourth year' at all in Syria," interpreting the Mishnah in terms of Tosephta *Terumot* 2:13, where R. Jehudah is quoted that "a Gentile in Syria has no 'vineyard of the fourth year'." This follows the interpretation of R. Simson that R. Jehudah cannot speak of a Gentile in the Land of Israel, based on the Babli quoted in the preceding Note. However, R. Simson's argument does not apply to the Yerushalmi; the direct testimony of R. Salomon ben Adrat (*Responsa attributed to Nachmanides* 156) confirms the Yerushalmi text as it appears here, in *Maäser Šeni*, and in the Rome manuscript. It is true that in the end, one speaks only of Syria, but this cannot apply to R. Jehudah's statement in the Mishnah or to R. Eleazar's addition.

119 Syria has a special status as far as agricultural laws are concerned. The definition of "Syria" here means all territory that was not conquered by the 12 tribes under Joshua and the early Judges but was included in David's kingdom. Since it was never incorporated in the Kingdom of Israel, it is not subject to the agricultural laws from the Torah. But since it was part of King David's empire, these laws apply, either as Rabbinical ordinance or as popular usage. In any case, all rules must be interpreted leniently in Syria. (In consequence of the persecution of Jews in Palestine,

particularly under the Christian Roman empire, the center of Jewish population slowly moved from Galilee to Syria.)

120 The House of Shammai, taken as a collective singular.

121 They did not say simply: The rules of the vineyard do not apply at all.

122 Tosephta *Terumot* 2:13; this is R. Zeïra's proof against R. Bibi, that R. Jehudah does not negate the obligation of the fourth year for Jews in Syria. However, the paragraph after the next will show that the Yerushalmi follows R. Bibi, that there is no such obligation in Syria.

שְׁמוּאֵל בַּר אַבָּא בְּעֵי הָא בֵית שַׁמַּאי אָמַר לֹא לָמְדוּ נֶטַע רְבָעִי אֶלָּא מִמַּעֲשֵׂר שֵׁנִי כְּמָה דְתֵימַר אֵין מַעֲשֵׂר שֵׁנִי בִשְׁבִיעִית. וְדִכְוָתָהּ אֵין נֶטַע רְבָעִי בִשְׁבִיעִית. וְדִכְוָתָהּ שְׁלִישִׁית וְשִׁישִּׁית הוֹאִיל וְאֵין בָּהֶן מַעֲשֵׂר שֵׁנִי לֹא יְהֵא בָהֶן נֶטַע רְבָעִי. אָמַר רִבִּי יוֹסֵי שְׁלִישִׁית וְשִׁישִּׁית אַף עַל פִּי שֶׁאֵין בָּהֶן מַעֲשֵׂר שֵׁנִי (fol. 20c) יֵשׁ בָּהֶן מַעֲשֵׂר עָנִי. שְׁבִיעִית אֵין בָּהּ מַעֲשֵׂר כָּל־עִיקָּר.

Samuel bar Abba[123] asked: Since the House of Shammai said that they learned the rules of the vineyard of the fourth year only from the Second Tithe; since you say that there is no Second Tithe in the Sabbatical year, there is no fourth year after planting in the Sabbatical year. Similarly, in the third and sixth years of the sabbatical cycle, since there is no Second Tithe[124], there should not be any fourth year after planting. Rebbi Yose[125] said, even though there is no Second Tithe in the third and sixth years, there is the tithe for the poor. In the Sabbatical year, there are no tithes at all.

123 A Galilean Amora of the third generation, student of R. Joḥanan, Rebbi Assi, and Rebbi Zeïra. He is not identical with the Babylonian Samuel, whose full name also was Samuel bar Abba.

124 The second tithe is not called Second Tithe but Tithe of the Poor; cf. Chapter 1, Note 127.

125 The organizing principle for this and the following group of paragraphs is that Rebbi Yose solves the problems.

חֵיפָא שְׁאַל הָא[126] רִבִּי יוּדָה אָמַר לֹא לָֽמְדוּ נֶטַע רְבָעִי אֶלָּא מִמַּעֲשֵׂר שֵׁנִי כְּמַה דְתֵימַר אֵין מַעֲשֵׂר שֵׁנִי בְסוּרְיָא. וְדִכְוָתָהּ אֵין נֶטַע רְבָעִי בְסוּרְיָא. דִּכְוָתָהּ לֹא לָֽמְדוּ תְרוּמַת תּוֹדָה אֶלָּא מִתְּרוּמַת מַעֲשֵׂר כְּמַה דְתֵימַר אֵין תְּרוּמַת מַעֲשֵׂר בַּמִּדְבָּר וְדִכְוָתֵיהּ לֹא תְהֵא תְרוּמַת תּוֹדָה בַּמִּדְבָּר. אָמַר רִבִּי יוֹסֵי לֹא לָֽמְדוּ מִמֶּנָּה אֶלָּא לְשִׁיעוּרִין.

Ḥeipha[127] asked: Since Rebbi Jehudah said that they learned the rules of the vineyard of the fourth year only from the Second Tithe; since you say that there is no Second Tithe in Syria, there is no fourth year after planting in Syria[128]. Similarly, they learned the rules of the heave of the thanksgiving sacrifice[129] only from the heave of the tithe; since you say that there was no heave of the tithe[130] in the desert, will it follow that there was no heave of the thanksgiving sacrifice in the desert? Rebbi Yose said, they learned from it only in regard of quantities.

126 Text of *Maäser Šeni*. Venice print: את, which is chronologically impossible.

127 He seems to be identical with the Babylonian Fourth generation Amora 'Aipha ben Raḥaba from Pumbedita. He and his brother Abime were known as "the sharp-minded ones from Pumbedita."

128 Even for Jews, following R. Jehudah in the Mishnah and against R. Jehudah in the Tosephta. This is accepted as genuine interpretation of R. Jehudah's position.

129 The rules of the thanksgiving sacrifice (*Lev*. 7:11-15) note only that four kinds of bread have to be brought and that one loaf each has to be given as heave to the officiating priest. The number of required loaves is not specified. The first heave has no fixed amount from the Torah; in the words of Samuel, one grain is enough for an entire silo. But since the number 1 is spelled out here and it is called heave, the natural inference is that the heave is the heave of the tithe given to the Levite, of which the Levite has to give 10% to the priest (*Num*. 18:26). Hence, 1 is 10% of the required amount, and from each kind of bread 10 loaves have to be brought to the Temple

(*Sifra Ẓav* 7:1).

130 Since there were no tithes during the 40 years in the desert; tithes are only imposed in the Land of Israel.

תַּנֵּי רִבִּי יוֹסֵי בֵּי רִבִּי יוּדָה רִבִּי לָעְזָר בֵּי רִבִּי שִׁמְעוֹן אוֹמֵר לֹא נִתְחַייְבוּ יִשְׂרָאֵל בְּנֶטַע רְבָעִי אֶלָּא לְאַחַר אַרְבַּע עֶשְׂרֵה שָׁנָה שֶׁבַע שֶׁכִּיבְּשׁוּ וְשֶׁבַע שֶׁחִילְּקוּ. אָמַר רַב חִסְדָּא אַתְיָא דְּרִבִּי יוֹסֵי בֵּי רִבִּי יוּדָה כְּשִׁיטַּת דְּרִבִּי יוּדָה אָבוֹי. כְּמָה דְּרִבִּי יוּדָה אוֹמֵר לֹא לָמְדוּ נֶטַע רְבָעִי אֶלָּא מִמַּעֲשֵׂר שֵׁנִי כְּמָה דְּתֵימַר אֵין מַעֲשֵׂר שֵׁנִי אֶלָּא לְאַחַר אַרְבַּע עֶשְׂרֵה שָׁנָה. וְדִכְוָותָהּ אֵין נֶטַע רְבָעִי אֶלָּא לְאַחַר אַרְבַּע עֶשְׂרֵה שָׁנָה. אָמַר רִבִּי יוֹסֵי וְהוּא בְשִׁיטַּת בְּנוֹ סוּרְיָא לְמֵדָה מֵאַרְבַּע עֶשְׂרֵה שָׁנָה אֵין אַרְבַּע עֶשְׂרֵה שָׁנָה לְמֵדָה מִסּוּרְיָא.

Rebbi Yose ben Rebbi Jehudah[131] stated: Rebbi Eleazar ben Rebbi Simeon said, Israel did become obligated for the fourth year after planting only after 14 years, seven during which they conquered and seven during which they divided up the land[132]. Rav Ḥisda said, it turns out that the argument of Rebbi Yose ben Rebbi Jehudah is identical with that of his father Rebbi Jehudah. Just as Rebbi Jehudah said that they learned the rules of the vineyard of the fourth year only from the Second Tithe, since you say that the Second Tithe started only after 14 years, similarly there was no fourth year after planting until after 14 years. Rebbi Yose said, he follows his son's argument; Syria was inferred from "after 14 years[133];" "after 14 years" was not inferred from Syria.

131 A son of R. Jehudah (bar Illaï) and companion of Rebbi.

132 The computation which proves that the time from the death of Moses till the end of the land distribution under Joshua and the assembly at Shiloh was 14 years is given in *Seder Olam* (Chap. 11, in the author's edition pp. 116-118.)

133 If they were not obligated while they were in the Land before its distribution, then certainly they are not obligated in Syria which was conquered only by a king, not by the

community of tribes, held only temporarily, and never was distributed among the tribes.

כְּתִיב וּבַשָּׁנָה הַחֲמִישִׁית תֹּאכְלוּ אֶת פִּרְיוֹ. רִבִּי יוֹסֵי הַגָּלִילִי אוֹמֵר הֲרֵי אַתְּ כְּמוֹסִיף פֵּירוֹת חֲמִישִׁית עַל פֵּירוֹת רְבִיעִית מָה פֵּירוֹת חֲמִישִׁית לִבְעָלִים. אַף פֵּירוֹת רְבִיעִית לִבְעָלִים. רִבִּי זְעִירָא רִבִּי יָסָא בְשֵׁם רִבִּי יוֹחָנָן אַתְיָא דְּרִבִּי יוֹסֵי הַגָּלִילִי כְּרִבִּי יְהוּדָה. כְּמָא דְּרִבִּי יְהוּדָה עוֹשֶׂה אוֹתוֹ כִּנְכָסָיו כֵּן רִבִּי יוֹסֵי הַגָּלִילִי עוֹשֶׂה אוֹתוֹ כִּנְכָסָיו.

It is written (*Lev*. 19:25): "In the fifth year, you shall eat its yield[134]." Rebbi Yose the Galilean says, here one adds the fruits of the fifth to the fruits of the fourth year. Just as the fruits of the fifth year are for the proprietors, so the fruits of the fourth year are for the proprietors. Rebbi Zeïra, Rebbi Yasa, in the name of Rebbi Joḥanan: It turns out that Rebbi Yose the Galilean argues like Rebbi Jehudah. Just as Rebbi Jehudah makes it his property[135], so Rebbi Yose the Galilean makes it his property.

134 This verse following the one which declares the yield of the fourth year of a new vineyard "holy for praises" reads: "But in the fifth year, you shall eat its fruit, to increase its yield to you." Hence, the harvest is directly given to the owner of the vineyard. Also, "increase" presupposes prior yield for the owner.

135 This may refer to the earlier statement of R. Jehudah that the status of the yield of the fourth year is derived from the laws of Second Tithe and, as private property, is subject to the rules of single berries and gleanings. It also may refer to Mishnah *Qiddušin* 2:8 where R. Jehudah states that Second Tithe when wilfully and illegally diverted to profane use, such as bridal money to acquire a wife, becomes valid private property and the marriage is contracted, but if the same act was done in error, without intent to change the status of the Tithe, the Second Tithe remains holy, does not become profane, and the marriage is not contracted.

רִבִּי יִרְמְיָה בְּעֵי קוֹמֵי רִבִּי זְעִירָא כְּדִבְרֵי מִי שֶׁהוּא עוֹשֶׂה אוֹתוֹ כִּנְכָסָיו מַהוּ שֶׁיְּהֵא חַיָּיב בְּמַעְשְׂרוֹת. אָמַר לֵיהּ כַּיי דְּאָמַר רִבִּי יְהוֹשֻׁעַ בֶּן לֵוִי דְּאָמַר רִבִּי אָבִין בְּשֵׁם רִבִּי יְהוֹשֻׁעַ בֶּן לֵוִי לֹא סוֹף דָּבָר הֲלָכָה זוּ אֶלָּא כָּל־הֲלָכָה שֶׁהִיא רוֹפֶפֶת בְּבֵית דִּין וְאֵין אַתְּ יוֹדֵעַ מַה טִיבָהּ צֵא וּרְאֵה מַה הַצִּיבּוּר נוֹהֵג וּנְהוֹג. וַאֲנָן חָמֵיי צִיבּוּרָא דְּלָא מַפְרְשִׁין. אָמַר רִבִּי מָנָא אִילּוּ נֶאֱמַר כְּבֵית שַׁמַּאי וְיֵשׁ צִיבּוּר כְּבֵית שַׁמַּאי. אָמַר רִבִּי אָבִין כְּלוּם לָמְדוּ נֶטַע רְבָעִי אֶלָּא מִמַּעֲשֵׂר שֵׁנִי כְּמַה דְּתֵימַר אֵין מַעֲשֵׂר שֵׁנִי חַיָּיב בְּמַעְשְׂרוֹת. וְדִכְוָותָהּ אֵין נֶטַע רְבָעִי חַיָּיב בְּמַעְשְׂרוֹת.

Rebbi Jeremiah asked before Rebbi Zeïra: According to those who declare it his property, should it not be subject to tithes? He said to him, according to what Rebbi Joshua ben Levi said[136], as Rebbi Abin said in the name of Rebbi Joshua ben Levi, not only this practice, but in any practical question which is weak in court and you do not know how to decide, go out and see how the public acts, and act accordingly[137]. And we see that they do not give[138]. Rebbi Mana said, that is, if the practice would follow the House of Shammai. But is there any public that acts according to the House of Shammai? Rebbi Abin said, they learned the rules of the vineyard of the fourth year only from the Second Tithe; just as you say that the Second Tithe is not subject to tithes, so the yield of the fourth year is not subject to tithes[139].

136 *Yebamot* 7:2. This refers to the laws indicated in *Lev.* 22:10-14. A non-priestly woman married to a priest may eat *terumah*. If she is divorced, or she becomes a widow without issue, she returns to her former non-priestly status and may not eat *terumah*. The Mishnah states that the servants of a non-priestly woman who was married to a priest and became a widow while pregnant with her first child, should not eat *terumah*. The first Mishnah had explained that there are two kinds of property a bride brings to her husband. For "property of dowry" נכסי מלוג the ownership resides with the wife. "Iron

cattle" צאן ברזל becomes the husband's property completely in exchange for an obligation to return full value in case of dissolution of the marriage. In the Halakhah, the Mishnah is interpreted to mean that *her servants* are "property of dowry" servants, but "iron cattle" servants are *his* and entitled to eat *terumah* since only their value has to be returned. She herself may not eat *terumah* unless and until she gives birth to a male child. On this, R. Abin says in the name of R. Joshua ben Levi that one has to follow what people do, and they do not let *any* slaves brought by the wife eat in such a situation.

137 In Babli *Berakhot* 45a, this is ascribed to Abbaie, an acquaintance of R. Abin.

138 R. Zeïra seems to indicate that practice follows the House of Shammai in the interpretation of R. Jehudah. However, practice must follow the House of Hillel who consider the Second Tithe as Heaven's money.

139 According to the House of Hillel.

רִבִּי בָּא רִבִּי חִייָא בְּשֵׁם רִבִּי יוֹחָנָן עִיסַּת מַעֲשֵׂר שֵׁנִי בִּירוּשָׁלַ͏ִם כְּרִבִּי מֵאִיר פְּטוּרָה מִן הַחַלָּה כְּרִבִּי יְהוּדָה חַייֶבֶת בְּחַלָּה. אָמַר רִבִּי יוֹנָה לֹא אָמְרוּ אֶלָּא בִּירוּשָׁלַ͏ִם אֲבָל בִּגְבוּלִין לֹא.

Rebbi Abba, Rebbi Ḥiyya, in the name of Rebbi Joḥanan[140]: A dough of Second Tithe in Jerusalem, following Rebbi Meïr,[141] is free from *ḥallah*, following Rebbi Jehudah[142] it is subject to *ḥallah*. Rebbi Jonah said, they said this only for Jerusalem, but not for the countryside[143].

140 In Babli *Pesaḥim* 37b, this is stated by R. Assi, another student of R. Joḥanan.

141 Who in Mishnah *Qiddušin* 2:8 disagrees with R. Jehudah and states that one never may use the Second Tithe for bridal money since it belongs to Heaven rather than to the owner. The law of *ḥallah* (*Num*. 15:20) states that it must be given to the priest as heave from *your dough*, and for R. Meïr it is not *yours*.

142 In the Babli, R. Jehudah's opinion is classified as that of the Sages, i. e. the operative practice, in accordance with the opinion of the

Yerushalmi.

143 Outside of Jerusalem, produce from Second Tithe may be eaten only if redeemed. Then the produce becomes profane and the sanctity is transferred to the money. Hence, even R. Meir must agree that the dough must acquire profane status and, therefore, is subject to *ḥallah*.

רִבִּי בָּא בַּר כֹּהֶן בְּעָא קוֹמֵי רִבִּי יוֹסֵי כְּדִבְרֵי מִי שֶׁהוּא מְחַייֵב בְּפֶרֶט מַהוּ שֶׁתְּהֵא חַייֶבֶת בְּחַלָּה. אָמַר לֵיהּ וְלֹא רִבִּי יוּדָה הִיא וְסָבְרִינָן מֵימַר כָּל־הָדָא הִלְכְתָא רִבִּי יוּדָה כְּבֵית שַׁמַּאי.

Rebbi Abba bar Cohen asked before Rebbi Yose: He who declares it[144] obligated for single berries, does he also declare it obligated for *ḥallah*? He said to him, is that not Rebbi Jehudah? And it is our opinion that in all this practice, Rebbi Jehudah follows the House of Shammai[145].

144 This must refer to the Second Tithe, not the fruit of the fourth year of a tree, since *ḥallah* is only due from dough made from grain.

145 Who declare both the Second Tithe and the growth of the fourth year as private property, subject to all its laws.

(fol. 19d) **משנה ז**: כֶּרֶם שֶׁכּוּלּוֹ עוֹלֵלוֹת רִבִּי אֱלִעֶזֶר אוֹמֵר לְבַעַל הַבַּיִת וְרִבִּי עֲקִיבָא אוֹמֵר לָעֲנִיִּים. אָמַר רִבִּי אֱלִיעֶזֶר כִּי תִבְצוֹר לֹא תְעוֹלֵל אִם אֵין בָּצִיר מְנַיִין עוֹלֵלוֹת אָמַר לוֹ רִבִּי עֲקִיבָא וְכַרְמְךָ לֹא תְעוֹלֵל אֲפִילוּ כּוּלּוֹ עוֹלֵלוֹת אִם כֵּן לָמָּה נֶאֱמַר כִּי תִבְצוֹר לֹא תְעוֹלֵל אֵין לָעֲנִיִּים בְּעוֹלֵלוֹת קוֹדֶם לְבָצִיר.

Mishnah 7: A vineyard that produces only gleanings, Rebbi Eliezer says, they are for the proprietor, Rebbi Aqiba says, for the poor. Rebbi Eliezer said (*Deut*. 24:21): "When you gather your grapes . . . do not take the gleanings after it." If there is no vintage, where are the gleanings? Rebbi Aqiba told him (*Lev.* 19:10): "Do not take gleanings from your vineyard," even if it is all gleanings. If that is so, why does it say "when you gather your grapes . . . do not take the gleanings after it;" the poor have no right to the gleanings[146] before the vintage.

146 Nor to enter the vineyard before the time of the harvest. The grapes might still grow to sit one row on top of the other so that at harvest time they are no longer gleanings.

(fol. 20c) **הלכה ז**: וְדִכְוָותָהּ אִם אֵין בָּצִיר אֵין פֶּרֶט עַד שֶׁיְּהֵא בָּצִיר בְּצַד הַבָּצִיר. אֲכָלָתַן חַיָּה לֹא.

Halakhah 7: Similarly, if there is no harvest there are no single berries[147], until there should be vintage[148] along vintage, not if a wild animal ate it.

147 Following R. Eliezer. Since in *Lev.* 19:10, gleaning and single berries are mentioned in one verse, they must follow the same rules.

148 When the proprietor gathers, the poor can have their grape gathering from the gleanings. However, if animals ate all grape bunches before the harvest, R. Eliezer declares the gleanings to belong to the proprietor.

וְכַמָּה הוּא בָּצִיר דְּבֵית שִׁילָא אָמְרֵי שְׁלֹשָׁה אֶשְׁכּוֹלוֹת שֶׁהֵן עוֹשִׂין רְבִיעַ.

How much is a vintage? In the school of Shila[149] they said, three bunches that make a quarter[150] of wine.

149 An Amora of the first generation in Nahardea who already had his school when Rav returned from Galilee. In the Babli, he usually is given the title Rav, which however is an anachronistic usage by later

generations.

150 A quarter of a *log*, about 3.8 fl. oz. or 133 cm^3; cf. *Berakhot* p. 296.

וְהָא רִבִּי עֲקִיבָה מְקַיֵּים תְּרֵי קְרָאֵי. וּמָה דְרִבִּי לִיעֶזֶר וְכַרְמְךָ לֹא תְעוֹלֵל שֶׁלֹּא תֹאמַר הוֹאִיל וְאֵין לָעֲנִיִּים בְּעוֹלֵלוֹת קוֹדֶם לְבָצִיר זָכָה בָהֶן בַּעַל הַבַּיִת לְפוּם כָּךְ צָרִיךְ מֵימַר וְכַרְמְךָ לֹא תְעוֹלֵל.

Rebbi Aqiba certainly explains both verses. How does Rebbi Eliezer explain "do not take gleanings from your vineyard"? So you should not say that, since the poor have no rights before harvest time, the proprietor acquired rights to them[151], it is necessary to say "do not take gleanings from your vineyard[152]."

151 That the owner of the vineyard could come and take all the unripe gleanings for himself before harvest time.

152 Anytime before, during, and after the harvest.

(fol. 19d) **משנה ח**: הַמַּקְדִּישׁ אֶת כַּרְמוֹ עַד שֶׁלֹּא נוֹדְעוּ הָעוֹלֵלוֹת אֵין הָעוֹלֵלוֹת לָעֲנִיִּים. וּמִשְּׁנוֹדְעוּ הָעוֹלֵלוֹת הָעוֹלֵלוֹת לָעֲנִיִּים. רִבִּי יוֹסֵי אוֹמֵר יִתְּנוּ שְׂכַר גִּידּוּלִין לְהֶקְדֵּשׁ. וְאֵי זוּ הִיא שִׁכְחָה בְּעָרִיס כָּל־שֶׁאֵינוֹ יָכוֹל לִפְשׁוֹט אֶת יָדָיו לִיטְּלָהּ. וּבְרוֹגָלִיּוֹת מִשֶּׁיַּעֲבוֹר מִמֶּנָּה.

Mishnah 8: If someone dedicates[153] his vineyard before gleanings are recognizable, the gleanings do not belong to the poor[154]. But after the gleanings are recognizable, the gleanings belong to the poor. Rebbi Yose said, they should give the value of their growth to the Temple[155]. What are forgotten grapes? On a trellis, anything he cannot stretch out his hands and take[156]. On a single growing vine, once he is done with it.

153 Donates it to the Temple. Temple property is exempt from the laws of tithes and gifts to the poor and it is sinful to use any Temple property without first redeeming it by paying for it.

154 Since nobody can give away what he does not possess, the owner of the vineyard cannot give away the property of the poor. As long as the gleanings are not recognizable, the poor have no rights to them.

155 To avoid using Temple property unlawfully, the poor who harvest the grapes have to give to the Temple the difference in value of the grapes now and at the time of dedication. (One cannot explain the statement to mean that they should pay part of the cost of tending the vineyard since the vineyard in the Sabbatical year may not be worked on.)

156 Since on a trellis the branches are stretched out widely, once he has moved he may not return. But single vines standing separately are units by themselves and they become forgotten only if the vintner moves to the next vine.

(fol. 20c) **הלכה ח**: תַּמָּן תַּנֵּינָן מַתִּירִין בְּגֻמְזִיּוֹת שֶׁל הֶקְדֵּשׁ. אָמְרוּ לָהֶן חֲכָמִים אֵין אַתֶּם מוֹדִין לָנוּ בְּגִידּוּלֵי הֶקְדֵּשׁ שֶׁהֶן אֲסוּרִין. אָמְרוּ לָהֶן אֲבוֹתֵינוּ כְּשֶׁהִקְדִּישׁוּ לֹא הִקְדִּישׁוּ אֶלָּא קוֹרוֹת מִפְּנֵי בַּעֲלֵי אֶגְרוֹף שֶׁהָיוּ בָאִין וְנוֹטְלִין אוֹתָן בִּזְרוֹעַ. מַה רַבָּנִין סָבְרִין מֵימַר קוֹרוֹת וּפֵירוֹת הִקְדִּישׁוּ[157]. וַאֲפִילוּ תֵּימַר קוֹרוֹת וּפֵירוֹת קוֹרוֹת הִקְדִּישׁוּ וּפֵירוֹת לֹא הִקְדִּישׁוּ. צְרִיכָה לְרַבָּנִין הַמַּקְדִּישׁ שְׂדֵה אִילָן מַהוּ שֶׁיְּשַׁיֵּיר לוֹ בְּגִידּוּלֵיהֶן. נִישְׁמְעִינָהּ מִן הָדָא מִשְּׁנוֹדְעוּ הָעוֹלֵלוֹת הָעוֹלֵלוֹת לָעֲנִיִּים. שַׁנְיָיא הִיא שֶׁאֵין אָדָם מַקְדִּישׁ דָּבָר שֶׁאֵינוֹ שֶׁלּוֹ. מֵעַתָּה אֲפִילוּ לֹא נוֹדְעוּ הָעוֹלֵלוֹת יְהוּ הָעוֹלֵלוֹת שֶׁל עֲנִיִּים. שַׁנְיָיא הִיא שֶׁהִיא כֶּרֶם הֶקְדֵּשׁ כְּהָדָא דְתַנֵּי הַנּוֹטֵעַ כֶּרֶם לְהֶקְדֵּשׁ פָּטוּר מִן הָעָרְלָה וּמִן הָרְבָעִי וּמִן הָעוֹלֵלוֹת וְחַיָּיב בִּשְׁבִיעִית.

Halakhah 8: There[158] we have stated: "They permitted the use of sycamore figs[159] from Temple trees. The[160] Sages told them: Do you not agree with us that fruits from Temple property are forbidden? They said to them, when our forefathers dedicated them, they dedicated only the tree stems because of strong men who came and took them by force[161]." Do the rabbis mean to say that they dedicated tree stems and their fruits? Even if you say that they dedicated only the stems but not the fruits, the rabbis wonder whether if somebody dedicates an orchard, he may reserve the growth for himself[162]. Let us hear from the following: "After the gleanings are recognizable, they belong to the poor." That is different because nobody may dedicate anything that is not his own. Does that not mean that even if the gleanings were not yet recognizable, they should belong to the poor[163]? That is different, because it is a vineyard for the Temple, as it was stated[164]: "If somebody plants a vineyard for the Temple[165] it is exempt from *orlah*[166], from the fourth year, and from gleanings, but it is subject to the Sabbatical year[167]."

157 Text of the parallel in *Pesaḥim* 4:9; here the text reads לא הקדישו.

158 Mishnah *Pesaḥim* 4:8 (Yerushalmi 4:9), Tosephta *Pesaḥim* 3:19. Taking the fruits from dedicated sycamores is one of the three things the people of Jericho did and against which the Sages protested. In the Babli, the discussion is *Pesaḥim* 56 a/b. The entire Halakhah also appears in *Pesaḥim* 4:9.

159 גמזין in Arabic. The Gaonic interpretation is "growth that comes out of the tree trunk." (Pliny, *Naturalis Historia*, Book XIII, §56, already notes that the fruits of the "Egyptian fig" sit on the stem, not on branches.) The fruits are of such inferior quality that they do not qualify as objects of trade. (Cf. *Tosefta Kifšutah* I, p. 361.)

160 Tosephta *Pesaḥim* 3:22.

161 Sycamores produce inferior fruits but superior building material. The "strong men" are probably the Hasmonean rulers. The people protected their sycamore groves by putting them out of bounds of any human government.

162 In Mishnah *Meïlah* 3:6, the anonymous Tanna declares that taking the fruits of a Temple tree does not constitute the crime of *meïlah* (larceny

committed on Temple property.) In contrast, R. Yose declares the fruits to be covered by *meïlah*, therefore he requires in our Mishnah the poor to pay for the expenditures of tending the vines during the growing season. As the Babli (*Pesaḥim* 56b) points out, the Sages of the Tosephta, while agreeing that no felony is committed taking the sycamore figs, nevertheless must assume that taking them means overstepping a prohibition. However, this prohibition is not written in the Torah. While any condition that goes against a commandment of the Torah is invalid (Halakhah 6:9), a condition that goes against a rabbinic prohibition may be valid. It is unresolved whether the ancestors of the people of Jericho had the right to reserve for themselves the use of the sycamore figs.

163 If the people of Jericho could not reserve the fruits, then it is clear that future growth is implicit in today's tree, and the future gleanings should belong to the poor and not to the Temple.

164 Tosephta *Peah* 3:15.

165 I. e., if he dedicates a newly planted vineyard to the Temple.

166 The prohibition to use the fruit of a newly planted tree during the first three years refers to the individual Jewish owner; it does not apply to the Temple which is common property.

167 In which everybody is free to take its fruits.

רִבִּי זְעִירָא בְשֵׁם רִבִּי יוֹחָנָן וְשָׁבְתָה הָאָרֶץ שַׁבָּת לַיי. דָּבָר שֶׁהוּא לַיי קְדוּשַּׁת שְׁבִיעִית חָלָה עָלָיו. רִבִּי חִייָא בַּר אַבָּא בְּעָא קוֹמֵי רִבִּי מָנָא לְאוֹכְלוֹ בְּלִי פְּדִיוֹן אֵיפְשָׁר שֶׁאֵיפְשָׁר לְהֶקְדֵּשׁ לָצֵאת בְּלֹא פְדִיוֹן. לִפְדּוֹתוֹ וּלְאוֹכְלוֹ נִמְצָא כְּלוֹקֵחַ לוֹ קוֹרְדּוֹם מִדְּמֵי שְׁבִיעִית. אָמַר לֵיהּ הַגִּזְבָּר מַחֲלִיפוֹ בְּיַד אַחֵר. אָמַר רִבִּי מַתַּנְיָה וְלָמָּה לֵי נָן [פָּתְרִין לָהּ דִּבְרֵי הַכֹּל] כַּיי דָּמַר רִבִּי יוֹחָנָן דִּבְרֵי רִבִּי יוֹסֵי מִפְּנֵי שֶׁקָּדַם נִדְרוֹ לְהֶבְקֵירוֹ. וְכָא מִפְּנֵי שֶׁקָּדַם הֶבְקֵר נִדְרוֹ לְהֶקְדֵּשׁוֹ.

Rebbi Zeïra[168] in the name of Rebbi Joḥanan (*Lev.* 25:2): "The land shall observe a Sabbath for the Eternal." The sanctity of the Sabbatical year falls[169] on anything that is the Eternal's. Rebbi Ḥiyya bar Abba asked before Rebbi Mana: It is impossible[170] to eat it[171] without redemption since Temple property cannot exit[172] without redemption. If one redeems and eats it, it would be as if one bought an axe with money from the Sabbatical[173]! He said to him, the treasurer[174] exchanges it through a third person. Rebbi Mattaniah[175] said, why do we not explain it[176] according to everybody, as Rebbi Joḥanan said[177]: The words of Rebbi Yose: because his vow precedes his declaration of abandonment. And here[178], because his vow of abandonment precedes his dedication[179].

168 This paragraph explains the action of the Sabbatical year on Temple property. The text follows the parallel in *Pesaḥim* 4:9 (fol. 31b).

169 Hence, the status of ownership has no influence on the duties of the Sabbatical year.

170 In Mishnaic Hebrew, אפשר means "it is possible," but איפשר is a contraction of אֵי אפשר and means "it is impossible."

171 Any produce from Temple property collected in the Sabbatical year.

172 Its sacred status without the sanctity being transmitted to the money that goes into the Temple treasury.

173 Since it is written (*Lev*. 25:6): "The rest of the Land should be for you to eat," we infer that the spontaneous growth is there to be eaten, not to be traded. It is possible to trade produce of the Sabbatical year as long as the final use is for food. The Temple has no need for money for food since the public sacrifices must be paid from the Temple tax of half a *šeqel* and private sacrifices are paid by the donors. Valuables donated to the Temple are used for building upkeep, vessels, and implements. Any monetary gain from Sabbatical produce for these purposes is forbidden; how can the Temple accept illegal money?

174 The Temple treasurer. He has the right and the obligation to sell all Temple property which is not directly used for sacrifices in order to raise money for the upkeep of the Temple. The Sabbatical produce is not sold but directly exchanged for vessels or implements needed by the Temple. This exchange is permitted; it removes the holiness of Temple property but has no influence on the Sabbatical status of the produce. Then the third

party may sell the produce as Sabbatical food (Explanation by R. Z. Frankel.) The third party probably is chosen before any harvest of the Sabbatical year to avoid leading ignorant people into sin.

175 He belongs to the last generation of Galilean Amoraïm, later than R. Ḥiyya bar Abba.

176 That the laws of the Sabbatical year apply to Temple property.

177 This refers to Mishnah *Nedarim* 4:10: "If they were on the road (a person A and another B who had made a vow not to use anything belonging to A). If B has nothing to eat, A gives food to a third person as a gift and B may use it. If no third person is with them, A puts the food up on a fence or a rock and says: This is abandoned to anybody who wants it. B may take and eat it, but Rebbi Yose forbids it." On this, R. Johanan notes in Halakha 4:10 that R. Yose forbids only because the food was forbidden to B before it was declared abandoned; the abandonment is invalid relative to B. But if something was abandoned before any vow was made, R. Yose agrees that the vow cannot retroactively influence the status of abandoned property. Cf. Chapter 6, Note 17.

178 In the case of the vineyard, the abandonment of the gleanings is written in the Torah and certainly precedes any dedication.

179 The abandonment of the Sabbatical year is not invalidated by the dedication. Hence, the produce of the Sabbatical year should not need redemption.

אָמַר רִבִּי יוֹחָנָן מַעֲשֶׂה הָיָה וְהוֹרוּ כְּרִבִּי יוֹסֵי.

Rebbi Joḥanan said, it happened and they gave instructions following Rebbi Yose[180].

180 Who requires in the Mishnah that the Temple be reimbursed for the produce grown in its possession, deciding with R. Ḥiyya bar Abba and against R. Mattaniah.

לֵית הָדָא פְלִיגָא עַל רִבִּי יוֹחָנָן דְּרִבִּי יוֹחָנָן אָמַר מִכֵּיוָן שֶׁעָבַר עָלָיו וּשְׁכָחוֹ הֲרֵי הוּא שִׁכְחָה. שַׁנְיָיא הִיא בְּעָרִיס שֶׁדַּרְכּוֹ לִבָּחֵן. וַאֲפִילוּ עַל רִבִּי הוֹשַׁעְיָא לֵית

הִיא פְלִיגָא דְּרִבִּי הוֹשַׁעְיָא אָמַר רוֹמֵס הָיִיתִי זֵיתִים עִם רִבִּי חִייָא הַגָּדוֹל וְאָמַר לִי כָּל־זַיִת שֶׁאַתְּ יָכוֹל לִפְשׁוֹט יָדָךְ וְלִיטְּלוֹ אֵינוֹ שִׁכְחָה. שַׁנְיָיא הִיא שֶׁכָּל־רוֹגְלִיּוֹת וְרוֹגְלִיּוֹת אוּמָן בִּפְנֵי עַצְמוֹ.

Does this[180] not contradict Rebbi Joḥanan, since Rebbi Joḥanan said, if he passed it over and forgot it, it is forgotten[181]. There is a difference, for a trellis is usually checked. And it does not even contradict Rebbi Hoshaia, for Rebbi Hoshaia said, when I was mashing olives with the great Rebbi Ḥiyya, he told me that any olive you can reach when stretching out your hand is not forgotten[182]. There is a difference, since any single free-standing vine is a separate planting.

180 This refers to the last sentence in the Mishnah: What is forgotten on the vine?

181 And it is stated that for a trellis, one can go over the branches as many times as he wants as long as he does not move away.

182 But the Mishnah says that one may go around a free-standing vine as many times as he wants, as long as he does not move away.

מאימתי פרק שמיני

(fol. 20c) **משנה א**: מֵאֵימָתַי כָּל־אָדָם מוּתָּרִים בְּלֶקֶט מִשֶּׁיֵּלְכוּ הַנְּמוּשׁוֹת. בְּפֶרֶט וּבְעוֹלְלוֹת מִשֶּׁיֵּלְכוּ הָעֲנִיִּים בַּכֶּרֶם וְיָבוֹאוּ. וּבְזֵיתִים מִשֶּׁתֵּרֵד רְבִיעָה שְׁנִיָּה. אָמַר רִבִּי יְהוּדָה וַהֲלֹא יֵשׁ שֶׁאֵין מוֹסְקִין אֶת זֵיתֵיהֶן אֶלָּא לְאַחַר רְבִיעָה שְׁנִיָּה אֶלָּא כְּדֵי שֶׁיְּהֵא עָנִי יוֹצֵא וְלֹא יְהֵא מֵבִיא אֶלָּא בְּאַרְבָּעָה אִיסָּרוֹת.

Mishnah 1: When is everybody[1] permitted to take gleanings of grain? After the second wave of seekers[2] is gone. Single grapes and gleanings of grapes, after the poor have come to the vineyard and gone. Olives after the second wave of rainfall[3]. Rebbi Jehudah said, are there not people who do not harvest their olives until after the second wave of rainfall? Rather when a poor man goes out and does not collect more than the value of four *assarii*[4].

1 Even rich people and even the proprietor himself.

2 A *nif'al* participle from מוש "look up last." (In Arabic, מוש means "collecting gleanings from grapes.") If the word is derived from משש "to grope," it designates old people who walk around groping. Both etymologies are considered in the Halakhah.

3 In Israel, the first rainfall of the fall season is expected about the seventh of Marḥeshwan; the second rainfall is anytime between Markheshwan 17 and Kislew 1 (after that date, the year would be considered one of draught.)

4 An *assarius* or *as* is 1/24 of a silver denar. One silver denar was worth 1/25 of a gold denar whose gold content in good times was about 4.3 grams. It is stated that the minimum amount necessary for one meal of a poor person in Mishnaic was 1 *as*. If a poor man cannot collect the value of two meals for both himself and his wife, he will not waste his time collecting.

(fol. 20d) **הלכה א**: אָמַר רִבִּי יוֹחָנָן לָמָּה נִקְרְאוּ שְׁמָן נְמוּשׁוֹת שֶׁהֵן בָּאוֹת בְּסוֹף. אַבָּא שָׁאוּל הָיָה קוֹרֵא אוֹתָן מְשׁוּשׁוֹת. אִית תַּנָּיֵי תַּנֵּי נְמוּשׁוֹת. וְאִית תַּנָּיֵי תַּנֵּי מְשׁוּשׁוֹת. מָאן דְּאָמַר נְמוּשׁוֹת שֶׁהֵן בָּאִין בְּסוֹף. וּמָאן דְּאָמַר מְשׁוּשׁוֹת שֶׁהֵן מְמַשְׁמְשִׁין וּבָאִין. רִבִּי חוּנָא בְּשֵׁם מְנַחֵם רִבִּי יוֹחָנָן בֶּן נוּרִי הָיָה יוֹצֵא מִן הַנְּמוּשׁוֹת וּמֵבִיא פַּרְנָסָתוֹ שֶׁל כָּל־הַשָּׁנָה.

Halakhah 1: Rebbi Joḥanan said, why are they called *něműšōt*, because they come at the end[5]. Abba Shaul used to call them "gropers." Some formulate in the Mishnah *něműšōt*, some formulate *měšűšōt*. He who says *něműšōt*, because they come at the end. Those who say *měšűšōt*, because they grope to come. Rebbi Ḥuna in the name of Menaḥem[6]: Rebbi Joḥanan ben Nuri[7] used to go out with the second wave of seekers and returned with his needs for the entire year.

5 In the Babli (*Baba meẓi'a* 21b), this explanation is given in the name of R. Simeon ben Laqish. The feminine form both of the noun and the verb may indicate that the late collectors were mainly women. The use of the masculine later in the same context may be irrelevant since the Yerushalmi in general prefers the masculine singular for all genders and numbers.

6 Probably Rebbi Menaḥem, a student of R. Joḥanan and R. Simeon ben Laqish.

7 Tanna of the third generation, a student of R. Eliezer and colleague of R. Ḥalaphta, the father of R. Yose. On the recommendation of R. Joshua, Rabban Gamliel later appointed him overseer of the Academy of Jabneh. He is the paradigm of the God-fearing poor.

תַּנֵּי מַתְּנֹת עֲנִיִּים שֶׁבַּשָּׂדֶה שֶׁאֵין עֲנִיִּים מַקְפִּידִין עֲלֵיהֶן הֲרֵי הֵן שֶׁל בַּעַל הַבַּיִת. רִבִּי בּוּן בַּר חִייָא בְּעִי וְיֵשׁ אָדָם קוֹרֵא שֵׁם לְפֵאָה לְעַצְמָן. תַּנֵּי רִבִּי שִׁמְעוֹן בֶּן יוֹחַאי לֶעָנִי וְלַגֵּר תַּעֲזוֹב אוֹתָם וְלֹא לָעוֹרְבִין וְלָעֲטַלֵּפִים.

It was stated: The gifts to the poor standing on the field about which the poor do not care[8] belong to the proprietor. Rebbi Abun bar Ḥiyya asked, may a person give the name of *peah* to take for himself[9]? Rebbi Simeon bar Iohai stated: (*Lev.* 19:10,22) "Abandon them to the poor and the stranger," not ravens and bats[10].

8 They did not come to collect them at the appointed times, or they did not collect them when they did come.

9 Since it was stated in Halakhah 1:6 that even a farmer who qualifies as poor has to abandon his *peah* to the poor in general, how can he then be authorized to take it for himself?

10 It is better that food be used for humans who care about it. Since the obligation of these gifts to the poor is to "abandon" them, not to "give" them, the farmer is not required to give the value of *peah*, gleanings, etc., to the treasury of charities.

בְּפֶרֶט וּבְעוֹלֵלוֹת מִשֶּׁיֵּלְכוּ הָעֲנִיִּים בַּכֶּרֶם וְיָבוֹאוּ. וְלָא תַנֵּינָן נְמוּשׁוֹת עַל יְדֵי שֶׁהֵן חֲבִיבִין הֵן בָּאִין עַל עָתָר.

"Single grapes and gleanings of grapes, after the poor have come to the vineyard and gone." We did not state "the second wave of seekers;" since these are so desirable they all come immediately.

וּבְזֵיתִים מִשֶּׁתֵּרֵד רְבִיעָה שְׁנִיָּה. וְלָא תַנֵּינָן נְמוּשׁוֹת מִפְּנֵי שֶׁהֵן צִינָּה וְאֵינָן יוֹצְאִין אֶלָּא בַּחוּרִים.

"Olives after the second wave of rainfall." We did not state "the second wave of seekers;" since when it is cold, only young people will go out.

וְקוֹדֶם לָכֵן אֵינוֹ אָסוּר מִשּׁוּם גֶּזֶל. בְּשִׁיטָּתוֹ הֱשִׁיבוּהוּ לֹא אַתֶּם שֶׁאַתֶּם אוֹמְרִין מִפְּנֵי שֶׁהוּא צִינָּה אֵינָן יוֹצְאִין אֶלָּא בַּחוּרִין שֶׁמִּתּוֹךְ שֶׁהוּא יוֹדֵעַ שֶׁ[אֵין][11] מֵבִיא פַּרְנָסָתוֹ אַף הוּא אֵינוֹ יוֹצֵא.

And before that[12], is it not forbidden because of robbery? They received their answer according to their reasoning: You who say that because of the cold only young people will go out[13], for you, since he knows[14] that he will not bring home enough for his upkeep, he will not go out.

11 Reading of R. Simson of Sens, the Venice print has הוא.

12 The argument refers to the last part of the Mishnah, where R. Jehudah disputes the date of the second downpour and connects the date to the value of olives to be gleaned. If less than that amount is found, it is assumed that the poor abandoned the rest and it becomes abandoned to everybody (*Baba Meẓi'a* 2:1). But if there is more, is it not still the possession of the poor and forbidden to everybody else?

13 Since you require to wait until after the second downpour, you seem to think that the poor have given up on those few farmers who harvest their olives only after the second downpour.

14 The second gleaner.

(fol. 20c) **משנה ב**: נֶאֱמָנִים עַל הַלֶּקֶט וְעַל הַשִּׁכְחָה וְעַל הַפֵּיאָה בְּשַׁעְתָּן וְעַל מַעֲשַׂר עָנִי בְּכָל־שְׁנָתוֹ וּבֶן לֵוִי נֶאֱמָן לְעוֹלָם. וְאֵינָן נֶאֱמָנִין אֶלָּא עַל דָּבָר שֶׁכֵּן דֶּרֶךְ בְּנֵי אָדָם לִהְיוֹת נוֹהֲגִין כֵּן.

Mishnah 2: They[15] can be trusted about gleanings, forgotten sheaves, and *peah* at harvest time, and about the tithe of the poor its entire year[16]; the Levite can always be trusted[17]. But they can be trusted only about things that people are in the habit of doing[18].

15 The poor can be trusted that they received produce as one of the gifts to the poor and that everybody (including a rich person buying from a poor one) is able to eat them, without separating heave and heave of tithes, and not commit a sin.

16 The third and sixth years of a Sabbatical cycle.

17 Since he receives the First Tithe every year; even though he is required to separate from this 10% as heave of tithes, we do not suspect him of being derelict in his duty, even if he is unlearned in this matter.

18 This is explained in the following two Mishnaiot.

(fol. 20d) **הלכה ב:** עַד אֵיכָן. אָמַר רִבִּי חֲנִינָא עַד מָקוֹם שֶׁדַּרְכּוֹ לֵילֵךְ וְלָבִיא בוֹ בַיּוֹם. מַעֲשֶׂה וְהֶאֱמִין רִבִּי לַחֲמִשָּׁה אַחִין בַּחֲמִשָּׁה כּוֹרִין שֶׁל חִטִּים. וְאֵיפְשָׁר כֵּן אֶלָּא מִיכָּא צִיבְחָר וּמִיכָּא צִיבְחָר כּוֹרָא[19] סָלַק.

Halakhah 2: How far[20]? Rebbi Ḥanina said, to a place where he usually[21] goes and returns the same day. It happened that Rebbi trusted five brothers about five *kor*[22] of wheat. Is that not impossible? A little here and a little there adds up to a *kor*.

19 Reading of the Rome manuscript. The Venice print has unintelligible בו דא.

20 If the poor person testifies that he collected the grain at a certain place, how far away may that place be so that we still may trust him.

21 I. e., with his usual speed and endurance.

22 Each one of them returning with one *kor*, about 380 liter!

רִבִּי לָעְזָר דְּרוֹמַיָּה בְּעֵי קוֹמֵי רִבִּי יוֹסֵי. מַתְנִיתִין דְּרִבִּי אֱלִיעֶזֶר דְּרִבִּי אֱלִיעֶזֶר אוֹמֵר נֶאֱמָן עַל הַשֵּׁנִי נֶאֱמָן עַל הָרִאשׁוֹן. אָמַר רִבִּי יוֹסֵי דִּבְרֵי הַכֹּל הִיא שַׁנְיָיא הִיא שֶׁאֵין אָדָם עוֹשֶׂה בִּדְבַר עֶרְוָה. רִבִּי לָעְזָר בְּשֵׁם רִבִּי הוֹשַׁעְיָא כְּשֵׁם שֶׁלֹּא נֶחְשְׁדוּ יִשְׂרָאֵל עַל תְּרוּמָה גְדוֹלָה כָּךְ לֹא נֶחְשַׁד בֶּן לֵוִי עַל תְּרוּמַת מַעֲשֵׂר. אָמַר רִבִּי הוֹשַׁעְיָה מַתְנִיתִין אָמַר כֵּן וּבֶן לֵוִי נֶאֱמָן לְעוֹלָם.

Rebbi Eleazer from the South[23] asked before Rebbi Yose: Does our Mishnah follow Rebbi Eliezer, since Rebbi Eliezer said[24], if he can be trusted for the Second, he can be trusted for the First? Rebbi Yose said, it is everybody's opinion. Here it is different since nobody fools around with deadly sins[25]. Rebbi Eleazar in the name of Rebbi Hoshaia: Just as Jews are not suspected in matters of the great heave[26], so Levites are not suspected in matters of the heave of tithes. Rebbi Hoshaia said, our Mishnah says so: The Levite can always be trusted.

23 A fifth generation Amora from the South, the region around Lod, student of the Galilean R. Yose.

24 The statement is in Tosephtah *Maäser Šeni* 3:16; it belongs to the topic of tractate *Demai* and is discussed in *Demai* 4:5: "If one was seen separating the Second Tithe, he is trustworthy also for the First Tithe, the words of R. Eliezer. But the Sages say, if he can be trusted for the First, he can be trusted for the Second, but if he can be trusted for the Second, he cannot yet be trusted for the First." Eating First Tithe without separating its heave of the tithe is a deadly sin. Eating unredeemed Second Tithe is a transgression but no deadly sin. For the Sages, essentially everybody can be trusted in matters of the heave of the tithe but only people checked out for trustworthiness can give reliable information about the Second Tithe.

25 There is no question of minor transgression; eating food that is not a gift to the poor without separating out "great" heave and heave of the tithe is a deadly sin and people will not knowingly engage in it or lead others into a deadly sin.

26 The first heave given from the harvest before tithes.

רִבִּי מָנָא בְּעֵי וּבֶן לֵוִי נֶאֱמָן לְעוֹלָם אֲפִילוּ בִשְׁבִיעִית.

Rebbi Mana asked, can the Levite always be trusted, even in the Sabbatical year[27]?

27 In the six years in which he receives the First Tithe, we understand that he is trustworthy because he will not lightly commit a mortal sin. But in the Sabbatical year, in which no tithes are given, there seems to be no reason to give the Levite a privileged position. The question is not answered.

אָמַר רִבִּי בּוּן בַּר חִיָּיא נֶאֱמָן בֶּן לֵוִי לוֹמַר מַעֲשֵׂר בָּרוּר הוּא לְפוֹטְרוֹ מִן הַשֵּׁנִי. אֲבָל בְּאוֹמֵר נִיתָּן לִי אוֹ בְּאוֹמֵר מִשֶּׁלּוֹ הֵן אֵינָן נֶאֱמָנִין דּוּ מַתְנִיתָא אֵינָן נֶאֱמָנִין אֶלָּא עַל דָּבָר שֶׁכֵּן דֶּרֶךְ בְּנֵי אָדָם נוֹהֲגִין כֵּן. כֵּינִי מַתְנִיתָא אֵינָן נֶאֱמָנִין אֶלָּא עַל דָּבָר שֶׁכֵּן דֶּרֶךְ בְּנֵי אָדָם נוֹתְנִין[28] כֵּן.

Rebbi Abun bar Ḥiyya said, the Levite may be trusted if he says, this is certainly tithe, to free it from Second Tithe. But if he says: It was given to me[29], or if he says that it is from his own crop[30], they cannot be trusted. That is the Mishnah: But they can be trusted only about things that people are in the habit of doing. So is the Mishnah: But they can be trusted only about things that people are in the habit of giving[31].

28 Reading of the Rome manuscript and R. S. Cirillo. The Venice print and Leyden manuscript have בהגין, identical with the Mishnah text.

29 As a gift, not as obligatory tithe.

30 Of which he is not entitled to take the gifts to the poor. The Levite may take his own First Tithe.

31 That means "the habit" does not refer to the Levite or the poor but to the farmer.

(fol. 20c) **משנה ג**: נֶאֱמָנִין עַל הַחִטִּים וְאֵינָן נֶאֱמָנִין לֹא עַל הַקֶּמַח וְלֹא עַל הַפַּת. נֶאֱמָנִין עַל הַשְּׂעוֹרָה[32] שֶׁל אוֹרֶז וְאֵינָן[33] נֶאֱמָנִין עָלָיו בֵּין חַי בֵּין מְבוּשָּׁל. נֶאֱמָנִין עַל הַפּוֹל וְאֵינָן נֶאֱמָנִין עַל הַגְּרִיסִין בֵּין חַיִּין בֵּין מְבוּשָּׁלִין. נֶאֱמָנִין עַל הַשֶּׁמֶן לוֹמַר שֶׁל מַעֲשֵׂר עָנִי וְאֵינָן נֶאֱמָנִין עָלָיו לוֹמַר שֶׁל זֵיתֵי נִיקּוּף הוּא.

They are trustworthy about wheat but not flour or bread[34]. They are trustworthy about panicles of rice[35] but not if it is either raw or cooked. They are trustworthy about beans but not bean groats, either raw or cooked. They are trustworthy about oil[36] if they say it is from the tithe of the poor, but not if they say it is made from picked olives[37].

32 Reading of the Rome manuscript, the Mishnah manuscripts of the Yerushalmi tradition, and the first hand of the Leyden manuscript. The second hand and the print have: הסעודה.

33 Missing from the Venice print, the word is in all manuscripts.

34 Since gifts to the poor are only given in unhulled, without supporting evidence one can trust the poor only for the grain itself to exempt it from heave and tithes.

35 Only if the rice is on the panicles and not hulled. "Raw" in the

next clause refers to hulled rice.

36 Olive oil, which is given after pressing.

37 Since oil is made only from olives that are ripe enough to fall off when the tree is shaken.

(fol. 20d) **הלכה ג**: מַהוּ שֶׁיְּהֵא נֶאֱמָן לוֹמַר חִיטִּים נִיתַּן לִי וְעָשִׂיתִי אוֹתָן קֶמַח. חִטִּים נִיתַּן לִי וְעָשִׂיתִי אוֹתָן פַּת. פְּשִׁיטָא לֵיהּ שֶׁהוּא נֶאֱמָן. הָיוּ הַכֹּל יוֹדְעִין שֶׁרוֹב בְּנֵי אָדָם מַכְנִיסוֹ לֶקֶט אֲפִילוּ כֵן אֵינוֹ נֶאֱמָן. תַּנֵּי רִבִּי יוּדָן אוֹמֵר מָקוֹם שֶׁנָּהֲגוּ לִהְיוֹת דּוֹרְכִין אֶת הָעוֹלֵלוֹת יְהֵא עָנִי נֶאֱמָן לוֹמַר יַיִן זֶה שֶׁל עוֹלֵלוֹת הוּא. וְדִכְוָותֵיהּ מָקוֹם שֶׁנָּהֲגוּ לִהְיוֹת מוֹסְקִין זֵיתֵי נִיקוּף יְהֵא הֶעָנִי נֶאֱמָן לוֹמַר שֶׁמֶן זֶה שֶׁל זֵיתֵי נִיקוּף הוּא.

Halakhah 3: Should the poor be trustworthy if they say: It was given me as grain and I turned it into flour, it was given me as grain and I turned it into bread? It is clear to him[38] that he is trustworthy. Even if everybody knew that most people store gleanings, he is not trustworthy[39]. It was stated: "Rebbi Jehudah says[40], at a place where one presses gleanings of grapes, the poor shall be trusted when they say, this wine is from gleanings of grapes." Similarly, at a place where one presses picked olives, the poor should be trusted when they say, this oil is from picked olives.

38 The anonymous person who asked the question. Since the testimony is really on the grain, the poor must be trusted.

39 If most farmers collect gleanings and later distribute them, the poor cannot be trusted in their statements about grain they did not collect themselves.

40 Tosephta *Peah* 4:1. There the wording is: The poor person *is* trustworthy. The last sentence extends the argument of R. Jehudah to olive oil.

(fol. 20c) **משנה ד**: נֶאֱמָנִין עַל יָרָק חַי וְאֵינָן נֶאֱמָנִין עַל הַמְּבוּשָּׁל אֶלָּא אִם כֵּן הָיָה לוֹ דָבָר מְמוּעָט שֶׁכֵּן דֶּרֶךְ בַּעַל הַבַּיִת לִהְיוֹת מוֹצִיא מִלְּפָסוֹ.

Mishnah 4: They are trustworthy in regard to fresh vegetables[41] but not for cooked ones except if it was a small amount, since it is the way of householders to bring out from their pans.

41 That it is from the tithe of the poor since vegetables are not subject to *peah* and the other gifts connected with *peah*.

(fol. 20d) **הלכה ד**: אִילֵּין דְּבֵית אַסִּי בִּשְׁלוּן יָרָק אִנְשׁוּן מְתַקְנֵיהּ סְלַק גַּמְלִיאֵל זוּגָא וְתַקְנֵיהּ מִן גַּוָא לְפַסָּא.

Halakhah 4: In the house of Assi they cooked vegetables but had forgotten to put them in order[42]. Gamliel the twin came and fixed them in the pot[43].

42 To give at least the heave and the tithes so that the vegetables could be eaten by non-priests.

43 He removed the required amount from the cooked vegetables. This shows that it is possible for the poor to receive their tithe from the pot and one should not object to the formulation of the Mishnah that a testimony about cooked vegetables is irrelevant since tithes certainly were given before the cooking started. We also learn that separating heave and tithes after cooking legitimizes the small amounts absorbed by the walls of the (clay) pot.

(fol. 20c) **משנה ה**: אֵין פּוֹחְתִין לָעֲנִיִּים בְּגוֹרֶן מֵחֲצִי קַב חִטִּים (fol. 20d) וְקַב שְׂעוֹרִים. רִבִּי מֵאִיר אוֹמֵר חֲצִי קַב. קַב וָחֵצִי כּוּסְמִין וְקַב גְּרוֹגְרוֹת אוֹ מְנֶה דְבֵילָה. רִבִּי עֲקִיבָה אוֹמֵר פְּרָס. חֲצִי לוֹג יַיִן רִבִּי עֲקִיבָה אוֹמֵר רְבִיעִית. רְבִיעִית שֶׁמֶן רִבִּי עֲקִיבָה אוֹמֵר שְׁמִינִית. וּשְׁאָר כָּל־הַפֵּירוֹת אָמַר אַבָּא שָׁאוּל

Mishnah 5: One may not give to the poor from the threshing floor[44] less than half a *qab*[45] of wheat or a *qab* of barley; Rebbi Meïr says, half a *qab*. One and a half *qab* of spelt, a *qab* of dried figs or a mina[46] of fig cake; Rebbi Aqiba says, half. Half a *log* of wine; Rebbi Aqiba says, a quarter. A quarter of a *log* of olive oil; Rebbi Aqiba says, an eighth. About all other produce, Abba Shaul says enough so he may sell it and buy food for two meals from the proceeds.

44 The tithe of the poor, which is *given*, rather than *abandoned*, and for which it is in the hand of the farmer to whom to give and how much. A certain minimum has to be handed out each time. What to do if this reduces the number of poor who can receive something is treated in the next Mishnah.

45 One sixth of a *seah* and four *log*, 2.13 liter; cf. Chapter 3, Note 108.

46 The weight of 100 silver denar. According to Maimonides in his Commentary, a denar is 96 grains or 6.22 grams. This would make a mina equal to 622 g, about twice the weight of 100 Severan silver denars. R. Isaac Simponti in his commentary identifies the mina with the lb. of 16 oz. (following Rashi *Erubin* 29a), and the *log* as 12 fl. oz. (.426 liter). Cf. Note 75.

(fol. 20d) **הלכה ה**: תַּנֵּי רוֹבַע אוֹרֶז כּוּלָה תַּבְלִין לִיטְרָא יֶרֶק שְׁלֹשֶׁת קַבִּין חֲרוּבִין חֲצִי לוֹג יַיִן רְבִיעִית שֶׁמֶן. עֲשָׂרָה אֱגוֹזִין חֲמִשָּׁה אֲפַרְסְקִין שְׁנֵי רִימּוֹנִין וְאֶתְרוֹג אֶחָד. מַה טַעְמָא וְאָכְלוּ בִשְׁעָרֶיךָ וְשָׂבֵעוּ. תֵּן לוֹ כְדֵי שׂוֹבְעוֹ. חִזְקִיָּה שְׁאַל לְאָבוֹי מְנָא אִילֵּין שִׁיעוּרַיָּא אָמַר לָהֶן אֲהֶן צְרָרָא סָמַךְ הָדָא בְרַתָּא. רִבִּי חֲנַנְיָה הֲוָה יְתִיב קוֹמֵי רִבִּי אִלַּי וְהוּא אֲמַר טַעֲמִין וְהוּא סְתַר. אֲמַר טַעֲמִין וְהוּא סָתַר אֲמַר לֵיהּ לָא בְּלַן מִיסְתּוֹר אֶלָּא מִבְנֵי.

Halakhah 5: It was stated[47]: A quarter[48] of rice, an *ukla*[49] of spices, a pound[50] of vegetables, three *qab* carob, half a *log* of wine, a quarter of a *log* of olive oil, ten nuts, five peaches, two pomegranates, one *etrog*[51]. What is the reason? (*Deut*. 26:12) "They shall eat in your gates and be satiated," give him to satisfy him. Ḥizqiah asked his father: From where do we get all these amounts[52]? He said to them[53], a pebble supports a tower[54]. Rebbi Ḥananiah was sitting before Rebbi Ilaï, the latter was giving a reason and the former destroyed it, the latter was giving a reason and the former destroyed it, until he said to him, is it not depraved to destroy instead of building up?

47 A similar list appears in Babli *Erubin* 29a in the name of R. Simeon ben Eleazar.

48 A quarter *qab* equalling one *log* fluid.

49 1/8 of a *log*.

50 A Roman pound of 12 ounces, 345 g.

51 *Citrus medica*, also used on the feast of Tabernacles.

52 Some of them do not appear sufficient for a meal; the amounts seem to be inconsistent with their derivation from the verse.

53 R. Ḥiyya, the father, said to Jehudah and Ḥizqiah, his twin sons.

54 A slight allusion may be the justification for an elaborate set of rules.

אָמַר רִבִּי מָנָא תַּנְיָא אַרְבַּע לִיטְרִין.

Rebbi Mana said, one should state "four pounds.[55]"

55 As a minum gift of vegetables, not one pound as in the Baraitha.

אָמַר רִבִּי לָעְזָר וְכֵן לְעֵירוּב. אָמַר רִבִּי חִינְנָא הָדָא דְתֵימַר בְּיַיִן אֲבָל בְּשֶׁמֶן מְעָרְבִין בּוֹ מָזוֹן שְׁתֵּי סְעוּדוֹת. תַּנֵּי מְעָרְבִין בְּחוֹמֶץ מָזוֹן שְׁתֵּי סְעוּדוֹת. תַּנֵּי מְעָרְבִין בְּשֶׁמֶן מָזוֹן שְׁתֵּי סְעוּדוֹת. רִבִּי יִרְמְיָה בְּשֵׁם רִבִּי שְׁמוּאֵל בַּר רַב יִצְחָק כְּדֵי לִטְבּוֹל בְּיֶרֶק הַנֶּאֱגַד שְׁתֵּי סְעוּדוֹת. רִבִּי יִצְחָק עֲטוֹשָׁיָא אָמַר קוֹמֵי רִבִּי זְעִירָא בְּשֵׁם דְּבֵי רִבִּי יַנַּאי אֲפוּנִין חַיִין מְעָרְבִין בָּהֶן מָזוֹן שְׁתֵּי סְעוּדוֹת. לְמִי נִצְרְכָה לְרִבִּי מֵאִיר שֶׁלֹּא תֹאמַר הוֹאִיל וְהֵן מַסְרִיחִין (fol. 21a) אֶת הַפֶּה אֵין מְעָרְבִין בָּהֶן. דָּג מְלִיחַ מְעָרְבִין בּוֹ. בָּשָׂר מְלִיחַ מְעָרְבִין בּוֹ. בָּשָׂר חַי דְּתַנֵּינָן הַבַּבְלִיִּים אוֹכְלִים אוֹתוֹ כְּשֶׁהוּא חַי מִפְּנֵי שֶׁדַּעְתָּן מְקוּלְקֶלֶת. רִבִּי יוּדָן בְּעֵי הָדָא

כלקירא הוּא וְאִילֵּין כּוּתָאֵי אָכְלֵי מִינָּהּ חַיָּיה הִיא מְעָרְבִין בָּהּ. שְׁמוּאֵל בַּר שִׁילַת בְּשֵׁם רַב פְּעָפוּעִין וְגַדְגְּנִיּוֹת וַחֲלוּגְלוּגוֹת מְעָרְבִין בָּהֶן. בְּעוֹן קוֹמֵי הֵיידָן וִינּוּן אָמַר לוֹן קַקּוּלֵי וְהִנְדְּקִיקֵי וּפַרְפָּחִינֵי.

Rebbi Eleazar said, the same is valid for an *eruv*[56]. Rebbi Ḥinena said, this is for wine, but oil for an *eruv* must be enough for two meals. It was stated: One may use for *eruv* vinegar enough for two meals. It was stated: One may use for *eruv* oil enough for two meals. Rebbi Jeremiah in the name of Rebbi Samuel bar Rav Isaac: For dipping in it bundled vegetables for two meals. Rebbi Isaac Aṭoshaya[57] said before Rebbi Zeïra in the name of the House of Rebbi Yannai: One may use for *eruv* raw peas enough for two meals. For whom is this statement necessary? For Rebbi Meïr[58], that one should not say because they produce bad mouth odor one may not use them for *eruv*. One may use salted fish for *eruv*. One may use salted meat for *eruv*. Fresh meat, as we have stated[59]: The Babylonians eat it raw because their taste is strange. Rebbi Judan asked: May one use χαλκίς[60] for *eruv* since the Samaritans eat it raw? Samuel bar Shilat[61] in the name of Rav: One may use for *eruv pa'apu'in, gudganiot,* and *ḥaluglugot*. They asked him: what are these? He said to them, καυκαλίς[62], melilot[63], and purslain[64].

56 The entire paragraph is also in *Erubin* 3:1, the parallel in Babli *Erubin* 28a. On the Sabbath, one may not venture out from one's town more than 2000 cubits in each direction. [This is a commonly accepted practice; the Biblical commandment (*Ex.* 16:29): "Nobody shall leave his place on the Sabbath" is interpreted to mean a distance of 12 *mil*, 24000 cubits.] If somebody needs to go up to 4000 cubits in a certain direction, he may go on Friday afternoon to a distance of 2000 and deposit there food for two meals as *eruv* for himself. Then he "acquires Sabbath rest" at that spot and may go 2000 cubits from that place in any direction, even if he was not actually there at nightfall Friday evening. Every built-up area is counted as 4

cubits, but the person with an *eruv* may not go even one step in the opposite direction outside the built-up area. Since the Mishnah states that the poor should get food for two meals as a minumum, these minima also apply to *eruv*.

57 From a place 'Aṭoša, probably not far from Tiberias. He transmits traditions from R. Joḥanan and most of the latter's students.

58 Tosephta *Erubin* 6(9):4. Yerushalmi *Erubin* 3:11, Babli *Erubin* 29a. There R. Meïr decides that onions are not fit for *eruv* (the Babli applies this only to the leaves, not the bulbs.)

59 Mishnah *Menaḥot* 11:7, referring to the ram given as sin-offering on a Day of Atonement that falls on the Sabbath; it must be eaten by the priests before the next morning but cannot be cooked. The priests from Babylonia (in the opinion of the Babli, those from Alexandria) ate it raw after the fast. The text of our Mishnah has "because their taste is refined" as a euphemism.

60 This word and its meaning are difficult to determine. The Rome manuscript has בלבידה, the Venice text in *Erubin* בלבודה. These two readings constitute a majority and should be accepted. Levy, followed by all other modern dictionaries, assumes the ב to be an error for כ and reads χαλκίς, a kind of herring, also mentioned as כלכיד in Yerushalmi *Niddah* 6:1. However, in the Babli (*Avodah zarah* 39b, Tosephta *Avodah zarah* 4:11 printed edition, and elsewhere), this appears as בילבית, but in both manuscripts of the Tosephta, the Munich manuscript of the Babli, and the *editio princeps* of Alfassi, it is בילכית. Rabbenu Ḥananel explains: a small kosher fish.

61 In the Babli, he appears as Rav Samuel bar Shilat, a student of Rav, renowned as *the* devoted school teacher.

62 A plant, *melilotus officinalis*. In Arabic, קָקֻל is cardamom, קָקְלִי an alkaline plant; cf. I. Löw, *Die Flora der Juden*, Vol. 1, p. 490.

63 Arabic חנדקוקא, a kind of tall clover, only barely digestible. Rashi explains in *Berakhot* 57b *cierges*, "candles", a name used, as also its German equivalent *Kerze*, to designate tall annual plants.

64 Arabic פרפ̇ה. In both Talmudim, the last identification is ascribed to Rebbi's slave girl (about her see *Berakhot* Chap. 3, Note 175).

(fol. 20d) **משנה ו**: מִידָּה זוּ אֲמוּרָה בְּכֹהֲנִים וּבִלְוִיִּם וּבְיִשְׂרָאֵל הָיָה מַצִּיל נוֹתֵן מֶחֱצָה וְנוֹטֵל מֶחֱצָה. הָיָה מְמוּעָט נוֹתֵן לִפְנֵיהֶן וְהֵן מְחַלְּקִין בֵּינֵיהֶן.

Mishnah 6: These measures[65] apply to priests, Levites, and Israel. If he wanted to save[66], he gives half and takes half. If it was little[67], he puts it before them and they divide it up among themselves.

65 The amounts specified in the previous Mishnah apply to all poor persons equally, as well as the Levites and priests who come to get the First Tithe.

66 If he wanted to save from his tithe of the poor to give to his own poor relatives, he must publicly distribute half of it to the general poor who come to collect, in a nondiscriminatory manner; the other half he gives to his poor relatives in private.

67 If the tithe of the poor (or half of it) was not sufficient to give the minimal amount to every poor person who appeared, he does not distribute but lets the poor divide it among themselves.

(fol. 21a) **הלכה ו**: רִבִּי יוֹנָה פּוֹתֵר מַתְנִיתָא בְּיוֹתֵר מִכְּשִׁיעוּר הָיָה מַצִּיל נוֹטֵל מֶחֱצָה וְנוֹתֵן מֶחֱצָה אֲבָל בִּכְשִׁיעוּר הוּא נוֹתֵן לִפְנֵיהֶן וְהֵן מְחַלְּקִין בֵּינֵיהֶן. רִבִּי חִזְקִיָּה פּוֹתֵר מַתְנִיתָא בִּכְשִׁיעוּר בִּיקֵּשׁ לְהַצִּיל נוֹטֵל מֶחֱצָה וְנוֹתֵן מֶחֱצָה שֶׁמִּתּוֹךְ שֶׁנּוֹטֵל מֶחֱצָה וְנוֹתֵן מֶחֱצָה נַעֲשָׂה דָּבָר מוּעָט הוּא נוֹתֵן לִפְנֵיהֶן וְהֵן מְחַלְּקִין בֵּינֵיהֶן.

Halakhah 6: Rebbi Jonah refers the Mishnah to the case when he has more than the measure: If he wanted to save, he takes away half and gives half, but if he has only the measure[68], he puts it before them and they divide it up among themselves. Rebbi Ḥizqiah refers the Mishnah to the case when he has the exact measure: If he wants to save, he takes away one half and gives one half; since if he takes away one half and gives one half it becomes less, he puts it before them and they divide it up among themselves[69].

68 After taking off half for his own family, he can no longer give to every poor what is due to him by Mishnah 5. Maimonides (*Mattenot Aniïm* 6:11) accepts the position of R. Jonah.

69 R. Ḥizqiah permits the farmer to reduce by his own deliberate action the amount available for the general poor below the required minimum. [In the Tosephta (*Peah* 4:2) it is reported in the name of R. Eliezer that the farmer may reserve two thirds for his family.]

תַּנֵּי הַמְסַבְּבִים עַל הַפְּתָחִים אֵין נִזְקָקִין לָהֶן לְכָל־דָּבָר. אָמַר רִבִּי יוֹנָה וּבִלְבַד דְּלֹא יִפְחוֹת לֵיהּ מִן אגרון[70] דִּילֵיהּ.

It was stated[71]: "One does not bother at all[72] with those who beg at doors." Rebbi Jonah said, only if he would not get less than his collection[73].

70 Reading of the Rome manuscript. The Venice print has ארגדון, the Leyden ms. ארגרון. The word אגרון is not in the Talmudic dictionaries but was used by Rabbenu Saadiah Gaon as title of a book, "collection." D. Sperber (Roman Palestine 200 - 400, Ramat Gan 1974), devotes an entire chapter (XXII) to this passage. He prefers the reading ארגרון which he identifies with Greek ἀργύριον "small silver coin".

71 Tosephta *Peah* 4:8, formulated in singular as in Babli *Baba Batra* 9a, where the same conclusion is reached here that if he does not collect a minimum, one may give him from public money up to the minimum but not more than that.

72 This refers both to public assistance, detailed in the next Mishnah, and the public distribution of the tithe of the poor. The "doors" here are doors of residences, not of barns. Since a tax is collected (both in money and in foodstuffs) for public charity, private persons do not have an obligation over and above that which is stated in the Mishnah.

73 The poor should not have less than the minimum needed to keep him alive. [Explanation of R. Moses Margalit. Sperber (*loc. cit.*) gives economical reasons for the apparent relaxation of the Tannaitic rule in R. Jonah's time (ca. 350 C. E.)] The singular might be addressed to the householder who in R. Jonah's time was supposed not to let the beggar at his door go away totally emptyhanded.

הָכָא אַתְּ אֲמַר אֵין פּוֹחֲתִין לָעֲנִיִּים בְּגוֹרֶן. וְכָא אַתְּ אֲמַר אֵין פּוֹחֲתִין לְעָנִי הָעוֹבֵר מִמָּקוֹם לְמָקוֹם. רַב הוּנָא אָמַר צֵא מֵהֶן שְׁלִישׁ לִיצִיאָה. רִבִּי יוֹסֵי בֵּי רִבִּי בּוּן מַפִּיק לְאִילֵּין נַחְתּוֹמַיָּא כְּהָדָא דְּרַב הוּנָא וּבִלְחוּד כְּהָדֵין שִׁיעוּרָא.

Here[74] you say, one may not give to the poor less than this from the threshing floor. And there[75] you say, one may not give to the poor who is travelling from one place to another less than[76] that. Rav Huna said, deduct one third for expenses[77]. Rebbi Yose ben Rebbi Abun gave to the bakers according to the statement of Rav Huna, but only for these measures[78].

74 Mishnah 5; the minimum gift is one half *qab*, and the same Mishnah states later that the general principle is "food for two meals."

75 Mishnah 7; one may not give to the poor person who is travelling from one place to another less than a loaf of bread in the value of a *pondion*, i. e., a *dupondius* (half an obolus, one twelfth of a silver denar) if four *seah* cost a *sela'* (tetradrachma). 4 *seah* are 24 *qab* and a tetradrachma is 24 oboli.

76 The price of the loaf of bread is exactly the price of the grain that the poor gets at the barn. Some weight is lost in milling, and some expense is incurred in baking, and the baker has to make a living. So it seems that the stranger is treated better than the local poor, which is against all rules. [Not all the water used for the dough evaporates in baking, which increases the weight somewhat.]

77 The loaf which the stranger gets is not made from half a *qab* of wheat flour but only from a third of a *qab* so that miller and baker can make a living. In Babli *Erubin* 82a, it is Rav Ḥisda, a student of Rav Huna, who explains that processing costs 1/3 from above, or 1/2 from below.

78 For greater amounts, the price to be paid to miller and baker may be less and is negotiable without being unfair to the baker.

רִבִּי בָּא בַּר בָּא בַּר מָמָל בְּעָא קוֹמֵי רִבִּי לָא רָאוּ אוֹתוֹ יוֹצֵא מִן הָעִיר וְנִכְנַס לֵיהּ אָמַר לֵיהּ הַנּוֹתֵן נוֹתֵן וְהַלּוֹקֵחַ יָחוּשׁ לְעַצְמוֹ.

Rebbi Abba bar Abba bar Mamal[79] asked before Rebbi Ilaï: What if they saw him[80] leave the town and enter it again? He said to him, he who gives shall give and he who takes should be afraid for himself[81].

79 A son of the more renowned Rebbi Abba bar Mamal.

80 The travelling poor, who comes back to take twice at the same place.

81 For committing the sin of stealing from other needy people, as explained in Mishnah 9. In handing out charity, the giver should err on the side of generosity.

(fol. 20d) **משנה ז**: אֵין פּוֹחֲתִין לְעָנִי הָעוֹבֵר מִמָּקוֹם לְמָקוֹם מִכִּכָּר בְּפוֹנְדְּיוֹן מֵאַרְבַּע סְאִין בְּסֶלַע. לָן נוֹתְנִין לוֹ פַּרְנָסַת לִינָה. שָׁבַת נוֹתְנִין לוֹ מָזוֹן שָׁלֹשׁ סְעוּדוֹת. מִי שֶׁיֵּשׁ לוֹ מָזוֹן שְׁתֵּי סְעוּדוֹת לֹא יִטּוֹל מִן הַתַּמְחוּי. מָזוֹן אַרְבַּע עֶשְׂרֵה סְעוּדוֹת לֹא יִטּוֹל מִן הַקּוּפָּה. וְהַקּוּפָּה נִגְבֵּית בִּשְׁנַיִם וּמִתְחַלֶּקֶת בִּשְׁלֹשָׁה.

Mishnah 7: One does not give to the poor who is travelling from one place to another less than a loaf that costs a dupondius at a time when four *seah* cost a *sela'*[75]. If he stays overnight, one provides him with a bed for sleeping[82]. If he stays over the Sabbath, one gives him food for three meals. He who has food for two meals should not take from the *tamhui*[83], if for fourteen meals, he should not take from the charity chest. The chest is collected by two people[84] and distributed by three[86].

82 A mattress and cover.

83 A basket from which food is distributed to the poor; it was collected for this purpose by the overseers of charity from the households of the town. The word is derived from a Semitic root that in Arabic is ḥmḥ "to mix", since all food was put together in one big basket or plate (Accadic *tamahu* "to grasp, hold in one's hand".)

84 Since the contribution of money for welfare is a local tax and forcibly

collected as a tax, it can never be in the hands of only one person.

85 The overseers of charity must act as a court to judge eligibility; they must be three, the minimum number of judges in a Jewish court.

(fol. 21a) **הלכה ז:** תַּמְחוּי בְּכָל־יוֹם קוּפָּה מֵעֶרֶב שַׁבָּת לְעֶרֶב שַׁבָּת. תַּמְחוּי לְכָל־אָדָם. קוּפָּה אֵינָהּ אֶלָּא לְאַנְשֵׁי אוֹתָהּ הָעִיר בִּלְבָד.

Halakhah 7: *Tamḥui*[86] is collected every day, the chest every Friday. *Tamḥui* is for everybody[87], the chest is only for local people.

86 Tosephta *Peah* 4:9, Babli *Baba Batra* 8b.

87 Including the travellers.

רִבִּי חוּנָא אָמַר תַּמְחוּי בִּשְׁלֹשָׁה שֶׁהוּא עַל אָתָר. רִבִּי חֶלְבּוֹ בְּשֵׁם רִבִּי בָּא בַּר זַבְדָּא אֵין מַעֲמִידִין פַּרְנָסִין פָּחוּת מִשְּׁלֹשָׁה. אִיתָא[88] חָמֵי דִּינֵי מְמוֹנוֹת בִּשְׁלֹשָׁה דִּינֵי נְפָשׁוֹת לֹא כָּל־שֶׁכֵּן. וְיִהְיוּ עֶשְׂרִים וּשְׁלֹשָׁה. עַד דְּהוּא מַצְמִית לוֹן הוּא מִסְכֵּן.

Rebbi Ḥuna said, the *tamḥui* is collected by three people, because it it given out on the spot. Rebbi Ḥelbo in the name of Rebbi Abba bar Zavda, one does not appoint less than three providers[89]. Come and look, money matters are judged by three, matters of life and death not so much more? But then they should be 23[90]. Until one assembles them, he[91] is in danger.

88 Reading of the Rome manuscript, this is the standard language of the Yerushalmi. Venice print: אנא "please."

89 Who spend public money or distribute food to support the poor.

90 The number of judges of a criminal court (mainly acting as a jury.)

91 The hungry poor.

רִבִּי יוֹסֵי בְּשֵׁם רִבִּי יוֹחָנָן אֵין מַעֲמִידִין שְׁנֵי אַחִים פַּרְנָסִים. רִבִּי יוֹסֵי עֲבַר חַד מִן תְּרֵין אַחִין. עָאַל וְאָמַר קוֹמֵיהוֹן לֹא נִמְצָא לְאִישׁ פְּלוֹנִי דְּבַר עֲבֵירָה אֶלָּא שֶׁאֵין מַעֲמִידִין שְׁנֵי אַחִים פַּרְנָסִים.

Rebbi Yose in the name of Rebbi Johanan: One does not appoint two brothers as providers[92]. Rebbi Yose removed one of two brothers. He came and said before them[93]: There was not anything wrong with Mr. X, only one does not appoint two brothers as providers.

92 The Babli (*Baba Batra* 8b) quotes R. Ḥanina (a very early Galilean Amora) to the effect that Rebbi appointed two brothers as overseers of charity at the same time.

93 In public assembly before the entire town.

רִבִּי יוֹסֵי עֲאַל לְכֶפְרָא בְּעָא מוּקְמָא לוֹן פַּרְנָסִין וְלָא קַבְּלִין עֲלֵיהוֹן. עֲאַל וְאָמַר קוֹמֵיהוֹן בֶּן בָּבָי עַל הַפְּקִיעַ. וּמָה אִם זֶה שֶׁנִּתְמַנֶּה עַל הַפְּתִילָה זָכָה לְהִימָּנוֹת עִם גְּדוֹלֵי הַדּוֹר. אַתֶּם שֶׁאַתֶּם מִתְמַנִּין עַל חַיֵּי נְפָשׁוֹת לֹא כָּל־שֶׁכֵּן. רִבִּי חַגַּיי כַּד הֲוָה מֵקִים פַּרְנָסִין הֲוָה מַטְעִין לוֹן אוֹרֶיְתָא לוֹמַר שֶׁכָּל־שְׂרָרָה שֶׁנִּיתְּנָה מִתּוֹרָה נִיתְּנָה. בִּי מְלָכִים יִמְלוֹכוּ. בִּי שָׂרִים יָשׂוֹרוּ. רִבִּי חִיָּיא בַּר בָּא מֵקִים אַרְכוֹנִין.

Rebbi Yose went up to Kufra[94] and wanted to appoint providers there, but they did not accept. He came and said before them[95]: "Ben Bavai over the oakum." If this one had been appointed over the wicks and therefore merited to be counted with the leaders of his generation, you who are being appointed over the lives of people[96], so much more. Rebbi Ḥaggai, when he inducted providers, let them carry the Torah, to indicate that every public office is given by the Torah (*Prov*. 8:15-16): "Through me, kings rule, through me, princes become princes." Rebbi Ḥiyya bar Abba appointed magistrates[97].

94 Possibly Koufeir near Hasbeya in South Lebanon.

95 Mishnah *Šeqalim* 5:1 lists the small permanent staff of the Temple, probably in the last times of its existence. Ben Babai administered the oakum, bought with public money, from which the wicks for the

candelabra were made.

96 The poor who would starve without assistance.

97 Greek ἄρχων. He also inducted them to their offices by giving them the Torah scroll to carry.

רִבִּי לִיעֶזֶר הֲוָה פַּרְנָס. חַד זְמַן נְחִית לְבֵייתֵיהּ אֲמַר לוֹן מַאי עֲבִידְתּוּן אֲמַר לֵיהּ אֲתָא חַד סִיעָא וְאָכְלוּן וְשָׁתוּן וּצְלוֹן עֲלָךְ. אֲמַר לוֹן לֵיכָּא אֲגַר טָב. נְחַת זְמַן תִּנְיָין אֲמַר לוֹן מַאי עֲבִידְתּוּן אָמְרוּ לֵיהּ אֲתָא חַד סִיעָא חוֹרִי וְאָכְלוּן וְשָׁתוּן וְאַקְלוּנָךְ. אֲמַר לוֹן כְּדוֹן אִיכָּא אֲגַר טָב.

Rebbi Eliezer was provider. Once, he returned to his house and said to them: What happened? He said to him, there came a group, they ate and drank and prayed for you. He said to them, that does not give much reward. Another time, he came to his house and said to them: What happened? They said to him, there came another group, they ate and drank and cursed you. He said to them, that gives much reward.

רִבִּי עֲקִיבָה בְּעוֹן מְמַנִּיתֵיהּ פַּרְנָס. אֲמַר לוֹן נִמְלָךְ גּוֹ בֵּיתֵיהּ הָלְכוּן בַּתְרֵיהּ שָׁמְעוּן דְּיֵימַר עַל מְנָת מִתְקַל עַל מְנָת מִבְזָיָיא.

They wanted to appoint Rebbi Aqiba as provider. He said that he had to take counsel with his house[98]. They followed him and heard him say: In order to be cursed, in order to be insulted[99].

98 The house is his wife, who may be referred to only in indirect speech.

99 His wife warned him of what would happen to him and he agreed that these things must be expected when a provider takes office.

רִבִּי בָּא בַּר זַבְדָּא אָמַר אִיתְפַּלְגוּן רַב וְרִבִּי יוֹחָנָן חַד אָמַר מְדַקְדְּקִין בִּכְסוּת וְאֵין מְדַקְדְּקִין בְּחַיֵּי נְפָשׁוֹת. וְחָרָנָה אָמַר אַף בִּכְסוּת אֵין מְדַקְדְּקִין מִפְּנֵי בְרִיתוֹ שֶׁל אַבְרָהָם אָבִינוּ. מַתְנִיתָא פְלִיגָא עַל מָאן דְּאָמַר אַף בִּכְסוּת אֵין מְדַקְדְּקִין פָּתַר לֵיהּ לְפִי כְבוֹדוֹ. וְתַנֵּי כֵן בַּמֶּה דְבָרִים אֲמוּרִים בִּזְמַן שֶׁאֵין מַכִּירִין אוֹתוֹ. אֲבָל בִּזְמַן שֶׁמַּכִּירִין אוֹתוֹ אַף מְכַסִּין אוֹתוֹ וְהַכֹּל לְפִי כְבוֹדוֹ.

וְהָתַנֵּי לִמְזוֹנוֹת שְׁלֹשִׁים יוֹם. לִכְסוּת שִׁשָּׁה חֳדָשִׁים. פָּתַר לָהּ לִיתֵּן[100]. וְהָתַנֵּי לִמְזוֹנוֹת שְׁלֹשִׁים יוֹם לְפִיסִּין וְלִצְדָקוֹת שְׁנֵים עָשָׂר חוֹדֶשׁ הָא קַדְמִייָתָא לִיטּוֹל. עוֹד הִיא לִיתֵּן. מַהוּ לְפִיסִּין וְלִצְדָקוֹת שְׁנֵים עָשָׂר חוֹדֶשׁ בִּשְׂכַר סוֹפְרִים וּמַשְׁנִים.

Rebbi Abba bar Zavda said: Rav and Rebbi Johanan disagreed[101]. One said, one checks out before giving clothing but one does not check out for necessities of life[102]. The other said, even before giving clothing one does not check out, because of the covenant of the patriarch Abraham[103]. A *baraita* disagrees with him who says that even before giving clothing one does not check out. He explains it for giving him according to his status, as we have stated[104]: "When has this been said? If they do not know him. But if they know him, they also clothe him, everything befitting his status." But was it not stated[105]: "For food thirty days, for clothing six months." Explain it, to contribute. But was it not stated: "For food thirty days, for assessments[106] and charity twelve months?" This means to contribute, the earlier must mean to receive. It still means to contribute; what does it mean, for assessments and charity twelve months? For the salaries of scribes[107] and teachers[108].

100 Reading of the Rome manuscript. The Venice print has ליטול; this is contradicted by the following reference, עוֹד הִיא לִיתֵּן, which presupposes a ליתן earlier.

101 In the Babli, *Baba Batra* 9a, Rav Huna (the student of Rav) says that one checks for food but not for clothing and Rav Jehudah (student mainly of Samuel) says that one checks for clothing but not for food. Maimonides (*Mattenot Aniïm* 7:6) decides for Rav Jehudah. It seems that nobody in Babylonia accepted the theory that one does not check in either case.

102 I. e., food for the hungry.

103 That no Jew should have to go naked.

104 Tosephta *Peah* 4:8: "One does not give to the poor who is travelling from one place to another less than a loaf that costs a *dupondius* at a time when four *seah* cost a *sela'*. If he stays overnight, one provides for him

bedding, oil, and legumes. If he stays over the Sabbath, one gives him food for three meals, oil, legumes, fish, and vegetables. When has this been said? If they do not know him. But if they know him, they also clothe him, everything befitting his status (his prior status before he lost his money)."

105 A similar text is in Tosephta *Peah* 4:9: "*Tamḥui* is collected every day, the chest every Friday. *Tamḥui* is for everybody, the chest is only for local people. If he stayed there for thirty days, he is like the local residents for the charity chest, but for clothing six months. For the poor (Erfurt manuscript: the taxes) of the town twelve months." The last sentence certainly refers to an obligation to pay taxes; the sentence before the last is ambiguous as to whether it speaks of a duty to contribute or a right to take.

106 Meaning of the Syriac word **פסא**. Compare also Arabic **פסא** "to tear something up."

107 Scribes of the courts who also were notaries and teachers of advanced students.

108 Elementary school teachers, since the upkeep of elementary schools is a communal obligation from the times of the High Priest Joshua ben Gamla.

(fol. 20d) **משנה ח**: מִי שֶׁיֵּשׁ לוֹ מָאתַיִם זוּז לֹא יִטּוֹל לֶקֶט שִׁכְחָה וּפֵיאָה וּמַעְשַׂר עָנִי. הָיוּ לוֹ מָאתַיִם חָסֵר דֵּינָר אֲפִילוּ אֶלֶף נוֹתְנִים לוֹ כְּאַחַת הֲרֵי זֶה יִטּוֹל. הָיוּ מְמוּשְׁכָּנִין בִּכְתוּבַּת אִשְׁתּוֹ אוֹ לְבַעַל חוֹבוֹ הֲרֵי זֶה יִטּוֹל. אֵין מְחַייְבִין אוֹתוֹ לִמְכּוֹר אֶת בֵּיתוֹ וְאֶת כְּלֵי תַשְׁמִישָׁיו.

Mishnah 8: He who owns 200 *zuz*[109] should not take gleanings, forgotten sheaves, *peah*, and tithes of the poor. If he had 199, even if a thousand people gave him at the same time, he should take. If they were mortgaged for his wife's *ketubah*[110] or for a creditor, he may take. One does not require him to sell his house or the vessels of daily use[111].

109 This is the usual name for the silver denar. [According to the definition of *Shulḥan Arukh* that a *pĕruṭah*, 1/192 of a denar, is one-half grain of sterling silver, 200 *zuz* would be 80 oz. of sterling silver. Its buying power would be much more since in Antiquity the ratio of silver to gold was at most 1:12; it was an amount on which a person could live comfortably for one full year.]

110 Cf. Chapter 3, Note 151. The *ketubah* is a general lien on all his property. The Mishnah supposes that specific money is set aside for the satisfaction of the *ketubah*. This is permitted only in special cases such as an impending divorce or death. In the same way, the surety for a loan here is not a general mortgaging of property but a definite lien attached to cash.

111 The rules of this Mishnah apply only to one who takes gleanings, forgotten sheaves, *peah*, and tithes of the poor. The protection does not apply to people asking for public assistance.

(fol. 21a) **הלכה ח**: חַד תַּלְמִיד מִן דְּרִבִּי הָיוּ לוֹ מָאתַיִם חָסֵר דֵּינָר וַהֲוָה רִבִּי יְלִיף זְכִי עִימֵּיהּ חָדָא לִתְלַת שְׁנֵי מַעֲשֵׂר מִסְכֵּנִין. עַבְדּוּן בֵּיהּ תַּלְמִידוֹי עֵינָא בִּישָׁא וּמְלוֹן לֵיהּ. אֲתָא בְּעֵי מַזְכֵּי עִימֵּיהּ אֲמַר לֵיהּ רִבִּי אִית לִי שִׁיעוּרָא. אָמַר זֶה מַכַּת פְּרוּשִׁים נָגְעוּ בוֹ. רְמַז לְתַלְמִידוֹי וְאַעֲלוּנֵיהּ לְקַפֵּילִין וְחַסְרוּנֵיהּ חַד קְרַט וּזְכָה עִימֵּיהּ הֵיךְ מַה דַּהֲוָה יְלִיף.

Halakhah 8: A student of Rebbi had 199 denar; Rebbi used to let him receive the tithe of the poor once every three years. His students cast an evil eye on him and completed for him[112]. The next time, when he wanted to let him receive, he said: My teacher, I have the measure. He said, this one was hit by a beast of prey[113]. He gave a hint to his student who took him to a store[114], made him spend a carat[115], then he (Rebbi) let him receive as he was used to do.

112 That he had exactly 200 denar.

113 In Mishnah *Sotah* 3:4, a list is given of those who destroy the world, and beasts of prey (not "the pious") are part of the list. The story is repeated there. The main definition given for "hit by a beast of prey" are tricks by learned people who think that by

scrupulously observing all formal legal rules they can hurt other people with impunity, for example those who advise heirs how to manipulate their property legally so that nothing is left to sustain their father's widow (assuming she is not their mother.) The derivation here assumes that the Hebrew has the same root as Arabic פרשׁ "to devour, tear apart," said of a beast of prey.

114 Greek καπηλεῖον.

115 $^1/_{24}$ of a denar, in Mishnaic Hebrew called איסר. The student still had 199 $^{23}/_{24}$ denar left, so he could take the tithe and still keep most of the gift that was maliciously given to him. (Note that while the story is told in Aramaic, Rebbi is quoted speaking only pure Hebrew. This fits in with what we know about Rebbi's household from other sources.)

מִשְׁפַּחַת אנטבילא הָיְתָה בירושָׁלַ.ם וְהָיְתָה מִתְייַחֶסֶת שֶׁל אָרְנָן הַיְבוּסִי. פַּעַם אַחַת פָּסְקוּ לָהֶן חֲכָמִים שֵׁשׁ מֵאוֹת כִּכְּרֵי זָהָב שֶׁלֹּא לְהוֹצִיאָן חוּץ לִירוּשָׁלַ.ם דַּהֲווֹן דָּרְשִׁין בִּשְׁעָרֶיךָ בִּשְׁעָרֶיךָ לְרַבּוֹת יְרוּשָׁלַ.ם.

A[116] family from Nevallat[117] in Jerusalem traced its descent from Ornan the Yebusite[118]. Once the Sages alotted them six hundred talents of gold[119] to avoid causing them to leave Jerusalem, since they interpreted "in your gates, in your gates[120]," to include Jerusalem.

116 This and the following stories illustrate the principle that if one knows the recipient of charity one has to support him so that his prior dignity is not impaired.

117 In Tosephta *Peah* 4:11, the reading is בית נבלטה, in *Sifri Deut.* 110, 303 בית נבטלה. The best explanation is given by I. Löw; the reference is to a town in Benjamin, *Neh.* 11:34.

118 The last king of the Yebusites who sold the Temple site to David (*2Sam.* 24:20-24, *1Chr.* 21:15).

119 The enormous sum of 1'800'000 gold sheqel. In the Tosephta it is 300 gold sheqel (Erfurt manuscript: 600), in the Rome manuscript 600 talents silver gold, a confluence of two versions. The number given in the Yerushalmi also appears in *Sifri Deut.* 110, but in #303 it is 600 talents of silver. The amount given here probably is an adaptation of the original amount to the hyperinflation of the military anarchy; it would correspond approximately to 1'800 honest gold

sheqel.

120 The repetition of "in your gates" in *Deut.* 26:12, 16:11,14, 14:21,27,29 is taken to include Jerusalem. The verse *Deut.* 26:12, referring to tithes one has to give to the Levite, the stranger, the orphan, and the widow, so that "they should eat in your gates and be satisfied," is explained in *Sifri Deut.* 303: "'In your gates' teaches that one may not export tithes from the Land of Israel. They said that a family from Nevallat was in Jerusalem and the Sages alotted them six hundred talents of silver and did not want to permit them to leave Jerusalem." (Similar in *Sifri Deut.* 110). In *Sifri Deut.* 71, the repetition "in your gates, in your gates" is explained as reference to dedicated animals that may be slaughtered outside of Jerusalem; hence, a special inclusion of Jerusalem is needed.

וְהָתַנֵּי מַעֲשֶׂה בְּהִלֵּל שֶׁלָּקַח לְעָנִי בֶּן טוֹבִים סוּס אֶחָד לְהִתְעַמֵּל בּוֹ וְעֶבֶד לְשַׁמְּשׁוֹ. שׁוּב מַעֲשֶׂה בְּאַנְשֵׁי הַגָּלִיל שֶׁהָיוּ מַעֲלִין לְזָקֵן אֶחָד לִיטְרָא בָּשָׂר פִּי[121] צִפּוֹרִין בְּכָל יוֹם. וְאֵיפְשַׁר כֵּן אֶלָּא דְלֹא הֲוָה אֲכַל אִם חוֹרָנִין.

Also[122], we have stated: It happened that Hillel took for a poor son of a prominent family a horse for his exercise and a slave to serve him. Also, it happened that the people of Galilee brought a Sepphoris pound of meat[123] to an old man every day. Is this not impossible[124]? It was because he did not eat except in company.

121 Reading of the Rome manuscript. Venice print: בשר צפרים "bird meat".

122 Tosephta *Peah* 4:11, *Ketubot* 67b.

123 In Babli and Tosephta, the text reads: "Daily a pound of meat for a poor man from Sepphoris". We do not know how much a Sepphoris pound was; it is also mentioned in *Sifri Deut.* 317. Rashi in Babli *Ketubot* 67b reads: בליטרא בשר, "meat for a pound (of coins)." However, the pound as unit of currency is not found before Charlemagne.

124 That an old man would need so much meat.

תַּנֵּי מִשְׁתַּמֵּשׁ בִּכְלֵי זָהָב נוֹתְנִין לוֹ כְלֵי כֶסֶף. כְּלֵי כֶסֶף נוֹתְנִין לוֹ כְלֵי נְחוֹשֶׁת כְּלֵי נְחוֹשֶׁת נוֹתְנִין לוֹ כְלֵי זְכוּכִית. אָמַר רִבִּי מָנָא כְּלֵי כֶסֶף וּכְלֵי זְכוּכִית בְּגוּפֵיהֶן. וְהָתַנֵּי הָיָה מִשְׁתַּמֵּשׁ בִּכְלֵי מֵילַת נוֹתְנִין לוֹ כְלֵי מֵילַת. כָּאן בְּגוּפוֹ וְכָאן בְּשֶׁאֵינוֹ גוּפוֹ.

It was stated[125]: "If he was used to golden vessels, one gives him silver vessels, silver vessels one gives him brass vessels, brass vessels one gives him glass vessels." Rebbi Mana said, silver vessels and glass vessels of personal use[126]. But was it not stated: If he was used to silk clothes, one gives him silk clothes. Here it is on his body, there it is not on his body.

125 Tosephta *Peah* 4:11: "If he was used to golden vessels, he has to sell them and use silver vessels," in Babli *Ketubot* 68a: "If he was used to golden vessels, he should use silver vessels." Tosephta and Babli make a condition for public support that he first should sell his luxury items; the Yerushalmi speaks of what public charity has to provide for him.

126 If the Mishnah said, one does not require him to sell the vessels of daily use, that refers only to utensils used on his body, like combs etc. The Tosephta that requires him to sell his precious belongings refers to tableware and other vessels that are not used on his body.

Glass vessels were luxury items in ancient Rome. One has to assume that the cheap glass vessels referred to here are those products of Phoenician glass making that were not of export quality.

חַד מִן אִילֵּין דִּנְשִׂייוּתָא אִיתְנְחָת מִן נִכְסוֹי וַהֲווֹן זָכִין לֵיהּ בְּמָאן דְּחֶסֶף וְהוּא אָכַל וּמוֹתִיב. אָמַר לֵיהּ אַסְיָא עִיקָּר תַּבְשִׁילָא לָא מִן גַּוָּא לְפַסָּא הוּא אֲכִיל מִן לְפַצָּא.

One from the family of the Patriarch lost his possessions; they provided for him in pottery vessels, he ate and threw up[127]. The doctor told him, is not the main preparation of food in the cooking pan? Eat out of the pan[128]!

127 Since he was so disgusted by the ugly tableware.

128 Greek λοπάς, cf. Chapter 7, Note 69. There was no difference heard between ס = *s* and צ = *ss*.

עַד כְּדוֹן בְּבַעַל חוֹב שֶׁהוּא דוֹחֵק אֲפִילוּ בְּבַעַל חוֹב שֶׁאֵינוֹ דוֹחֵק. נִישְׁמְעִינָהּ מִן הָדָא הָיוּ מְמוּשְׁכָּנִין בִּכְתוּבַּת אִשְׁתּוֹ אוֹ לְבַעַל חוֹבוֹ. וְדָא אִשָּׁה לֹא כְּבַעַל חוֹב שֶׁאֵינוֹ דוֹחֵק הוּא אֵין מְחַייְבִין אוֹתוֹ (fol. 21b) לִמְכּוֹר.

So[129] far a creditor who pushes for payment. Also for a creditor who does not push for payment? Let us hear from the following: "If they were mortgaged for his wife's *ketubah* or for a creditor." Is the wife not like a creditor who does not push for payment[130]? "One does not require him to sell."

129 This refers to the part of the Mishnah which prescribes that mortgaged debts can be deducted from the net worth before the limit of 200 *zuz* is computed.

130 Since the *ketubah* is not due as long as she is married.

אָמַר רִבִּי חֲנִינָא צָרִיךְ אָדָם שֶׁיְּהוּ לוֹ שְׁנֵי עֲטִיפִין אֶחָד לְחוֹל וְאֶחָד לְשַׁבָּת. מַה טַעְמָא וְרָחַצְתְּ וָסַכְתְּ וְשַׂמְתְּ שִׂמְלוֹתַיִךְ וְכִי עֲרוּמָּה הָיְתָה אֶלָּא אֵילּוּ בִגְדֵי שַׁבָּתָהּ. כַּד דְּרָשָׁהּ רִבִּי שִׂמְלַאי בְּצִיבּוּרָא בָּכוּן חֲבֵרַייָא לְקוּבְלֵיהּ אָמְרוּ לֵיהּ רִבִּי כַּעֲטִיפוֹתֵינוּ בְּחוֹל כֵּן עֲטִיפוֹתֵינוּ בְּשַׁבָּת. אָמַר לוֹן אַף עַל פִּי כֵן צְרִיכִין אַתֶּם לְשַׁנּוֹת מִן הָדָא וְרָחַצְתְּ וְסַכְתְּ וְשַׂמְתְּ שִׂמְלוֹתַיִךְ עָלַיִךְ וְיוֹרַדְתְּ הַגּוֹרֶן. ויורדתי כְּתִיב אָמַר לָהּ זְכוּתִי תֵּרֵד עִמָּךְ. וְעַרְטִילָא הֲוָות אֶלָּא אָמְרָה לָהּ לְבוּשׁ מָאנַךְ דְּשׁוּבְתָּא.

Rebbi Ḥanina said: A person has to have two outer garments, one for weekdays and one for the Sabbath. What is the reason (*Ruth* 3:3): "Wash, rub yourself with oil, and put on your clothes[131]." Was she naked? But that refers to her Sabbath clothes. When Rebbi Simlai preached this in public, the companions[132] cried and said to him, our teacher, as our garments are on weekdays so our garments are on the Sabbath. He said to them, nevertheless, you have to change, from this: "Wash, rub yourself with oil, and put your clothes on yourself and descend to the threshing floor." (It is written "I will decend," she said to her, my merits will go down with you.[133] Was she naked? No, she said to her: put on your Sabbath garments.)

131 In Babli Sabbath 113b, this is a saying of R. Eleazar, a frequent tradent of sayings by R. Ḥanina. The explanation of Rashi is taken straight from this Yerushalmi or from the (Yerushalmi) parallel in Midrash *Ruth rabba* 5:12. The speaker is Naomi, the person addressed Ruth. It is spelled out in *Ruth* that they were poor enough to go and collect gleanings; hence, even if somebody is on welfare he needs separate outer garments for weekdays and Sabbath, and these must be provided by public assistance. Hence, this paragraph belongs to the current Halakhah.

132 The members of his *yeshivah*.

133 This aggadic insert is appropriate in Midrash *Ruth* but is intrusive here. However, R. Simlai, the famous preacher, will not let the occasion for a sermon pass by.

(fol. 20d) **משנה ט**: מִי שֶׁיֵּשׁ לוֹ חֲמִשִּׁים זוּז וְהוּא נוֹשֵׂא וְנוֹתֵן בָּהֶן הֲרֵי זֶה לֹא יִטּוֹל. וְכָל־מִי שֶׁאֵינוֹ צָרִיךְ לִיטּוֹל וְנוֹטֵל אֵינוֹ מֵת מִן הַזִּקְנָה עַד שֶׁיִּצְטָרֵךְ לַבְּרִיּוֹת. וְכָל־מִי שֶׁצָּרִיךְ לִיטּוֹל וְאֵינוֹ נוֹטֵל אֵינוֹ מֵת מִן הַזִּקְנָה עַד שֶׁיְּפַרְנֵס לַאֲחֵרִים מִשֶּׁלּוֹ. וְעַל זֶה נֶאֱמַר בָּרוּךְ הַגֶּבֶר אֲשֶׁר יִבְטַח בַּיי וְהָיָה יי מִבְטַחוֹ. וְכֵן דַּיָּיָן שֶׁדָּן דִּין אֱמֶת לַאֲמִיתּוֹ. וְכָל־מִי שֶׁאֵינוֹ לֹא חִיגֵּר וְלֹא סוּמָא וְלֹא פִּיסֵּחַ וְעוֹשֶׂה עַצְמוֹ כְּאֶחָד מֵהֶם אֵינוֹ מֵת מִן הַזִּקְנָה עַד שֶׁיִּהְיֶה כְּאֶחָד מֵהֶם שֶׁנֶּאֱמַר צֶדֶק צֶדֶק תִּרְדּוֹף וְכָל־דַּיָּין שֶׁלּוֹקֵחַ שׁוֹחַד וּמַטֶּה אֶת הַדִּין אֵינוֹ מֵת מִן הַזִּקְנָה עַד שֶׁיִּכְהוּ עֵינָיו כֵּהוֹת שֶׁנֶּאֱמַר וְשׁוֹחַד לֹא תִקָּח כִּי הַשּׁוֹחַד יְעַוֵּר עֵינֵי פִקְחִים[134] וגו'.

Mishnah 9: He who has 50 *zuz* and uses them for trade should not take[135]. One who has no need to take but takes will not die of old age until he needs the creatures[136]. One who has need to take but does not take will not die of old age until he can provide for others from what is his; for him is was said (*Jer*. 17:7): "Blessed be the man who will be confident in the Eternal, the Eternal will be his trust." The same applies to a judge who delivers strictly true judgment[137]. But one who is neither lame nor blind nor limping and presents himself as such will not die from old age until he will be one of them, as it is said (*Deut*. 16:20): "Justice, justice you shall pursue." But every judge who takes bribes and bends the law will not die from old age until his eyes are dimmed, as it is said (*Ex*. 23:8): "Do not take bribes, for bribes blind the eyes of the seeing."[138]

134 Reading of the Rome manuscript and the Mishnah manuscripts in the Maimonides tradition. The Leyden manuscript and Venice print have חכמים, a conflation of two verses: (*Ex*. 23:8) "Do not take bribes, for bribes blind the seeing and adulterate just sayings." (*Deut*. 16:19) "Do not take bribes, for bribes blind the wise and adulterate just sayings."

135 Neither the agricultural gifts to the poor nor public assistance.

136 I. e., people.

137 While compromise is usually preferred, he who negotiates a compromise does not have the same responsibility as one who has to deliver unassailable true judgment.

138 The blinding of the seeing can also be applied to welfare fraud, as it was stated in Halakhah 6 that certifying eligibility for welfare is a judicial task.

In the most trustworthy Mishnah manuscripts, the text after the quote from Jeremiah is missing. In others, only the reference to honest and dishonest judges is added. It is clear from the disconnected text that the insertion about simulants is the last. Since these additions are not discussed in the Halakhah, it seems that they are late additions to emphasize the end of the tractate (probably being added by the compilers of the Yerushalmi.)

(fol. 21b) **הלכה ט**: הָדָא אָמְרָה חַמְשִׁין עָבְדִין טָבִין מִן מָאתַיִם דְּלָא עָבְדִין.

Halakhah 9: This means that 50 at work are better than 200 not at work.

הַמְסַמֵּא אֶת עֵינוֹ וְהַמְנַפֵּחַ אֶת שׁוֹקָיו וְהַמְצַבֶּא אֶת כְּרֵיסוֹ אֵינוֹ נִפְטָר מִן הָעוֹלָם עַד שֶׁיְּהוּ לוֹ כֵן.

He who blinds his eye[139] or swells his legs or blows up his belly does not leave this world until it really happens to him[140].

139 He fakes blindness or swelling.

140 A slightly different version in Tosephta *Peah* 4:14 and Babli *Ketubot* 68a.

שְׁמוּאֵל עֲרַק מִן אָבוֹי אֲזַל וְקָם לֵיהּ בֵּין תְּרֵין צְרִיפִין דְּמִסְכֵּנִין שְׁמַע קָלְהוֹן אָמְרִין בְּהָדֵין אַרְגֶּנְטִין[141] אֲנָן אָכְלִין יוֹמָא דֵין בְּאַרְגֶּנְטוֹרִין דַּהֲבָא בְּאַרְגֶּנְטוֹרִין כַּסְפָּא. אֲעַל וַאֲמַר קוֹמֵי אָבוֹי. אֲמַר לֵיהּ צְרִיכִין אָנוּ לְהַחֲזִיק טוֹבָה לָרַמָּאִין שֶׁבָּהֶם.

Samuel ran away from his father and stayed between two huts of the poor. He heard their voices saying, on which silver[142] will we eat today, on golden silverplate[143] or silver silverplate? He returned and told his father about it. He said to him, we have to give thanks to the dishonest among them[144].

141 Reading of *Arukh* and R. S. Cirillo. Venice print: **אגנטין**

142 Latin *argentum*.

143 Latin *argentarius, -a, -um*, adj. "of silver".

144 Since we know that some who pose as poor are not poor, we can be discriminating and give only to those we judge worthy.

דִּלְמָא רִבִּי יוֹחָנָן וְרִבִּי שִׁמְעוֹן בֶּן לָקִישׁ עָלוֹן מִיסְחֵי בְּהָדֵין דֵּימוֹסִין דְּטִיבֵּרְיָא פְּגַע בּוֹן חַד מִסְכֵּן אֲמַר לוֹן זְכִין בִּי אָמְרוּ לֵיהּ מִי חָזְרוּן מִי חָזְרוּן. אַשְׁכְּחוּנֵיהּ

מית. אָמְרוּ הוֹאִיל וְלָא זְכִינָן בֵּיהּ בְּחַיָּיו נִיטְפַּל בֵּיהּ בְּמִיתוּתֵיהּ. כִּי מִיטְפְּלוּן בֵּיהּ אַשְׁכְּחוּן כִּיס דֵּינַרָיָא תְּלוּ בֵיהּ. אָמְרוּ הָדָא דְאָמַר רִבִּי אַבָּהוּ אָמַר רִבִּי לָעְזָר צְרִיכִין אָנוּ לְהַחֲזִיק טוֹבָה לָרַמָּאִין שֶׁבָּהֶן שֶׁאִילוּלֵי הָרַמָּאִין שֶׁבָּהֶן הָיָה אֶחָד תּוֹבֵעַ צְדָקָה מִן הָאָדָם וְלֹא נוֹתֵן לוֹ מִיַּד נֶאֱנָשׁ.

Clarification. Rebbi Johanan and Rebbi Simeon ben Laqish went to bathe in the public baths[145] of Tiberias. A poor man met them and said to them: acquire merit by me. They said to him, when we return, when we return. When they returned, they found him dead. They said, since we did not acquire merit during his lifetime, let us care for him in his death. While they were occupied with him, they found a pouch of denars hanging on him. They said, that is what Rebbi Abbahu said in the name of Rebbi Eleazar[146]: We have to give thanks to the dishonest among them, because if there were no dishonest persons among them, if one of them was requesting alms from a man and he would not give him, he would be punished immediately.

145 Greek, cf. *Berakhot* p. 299.

146 Parallels in Babli *Ketubot* 68a, *Lev. rabba* 34, *Ruth rabba* 5.

אַבָּא בַּר אַבָּא יְהַב לִשְׁמוּאֵל בְּרֵיהּ פְּרִיטִין דִּפְלַג לְמִיסְכֵּינַיָּא נְפַק וְאַשְׁכַּח חַד מִסְכֵּן אֲכַל קוּפָּד וּשְׁתֵי חֲמַר. אֲעַל וַאֲמַר קוֹמוֹי אָבוֹי. אֲמַר לֵיהּ הַב יְתִיר דְּנַפְשֵׁיהּ מְרָתֵיהּ.

Abba bar Abba[147] gave coins to his son Samuel to distribute to the poor. He found one poor who ate red meat and drank wine. He returned and told his father about it. The latter said to him, give him more since his soul is bitter[148].

147 The father of Samuel, rabbi of Nahardea and descendant of R. Joshua's nephew.

148 He has expensive tastes and lacks the money to indulge them.

רִבִּי יַעֲקֹב בַּר אִידִי וְרִבִּי יִצְחָק בַּר נַחְמָן הֲווֹן פַּרְנָסִין וַהֲווֹן יְהָבִין לְרִבִּי חָמָא אָבוֹי דְּרִבִּי אוֹשַׁעְיָא חַד דֵּינָר וְהוּא יְהַב לֵיהּ לְחוֹרָנִין. רִבִּי זְכַרְיָה חַתְנֵיהּ דְּרִבִּי לֵוִי הָיוּ הַכֹּל מְלִיזִין עָלָיו אָמְרוּ דְּלֹא צָרִיךְ וְהוּא נְסַב. כַּד דְּמַךְ בְּדְקוּן וְאַשְׁכְּחוּן דַּהֲוָה מְפְלִיג לֵיהּ לְחוֹרָנִין.

Rebbi Jacob bar Idi and Rebbi Isaac bar Naḥman were providers[149] and gave a denar to Rebbi Ḥama[150] the father of Rabbi Oshaia, but he gave it away to others. All were saying evil things about Rebbi Zachariah[151], the son-in-law of Rebbi Levi; they said that he was taking while he did not need it. When he died, they checked and found that he was splitting it up for others.

149 Administrators of public charity. From here to the penultimate paragraph, the text also appears in *Šeqalim* 5:6, in a text with fewer scribal errors. In doubtful cases, the spelling of *Šeqalim* is followed.

150 R. Ḥama bar Bissa, of the generation of transition from Tannaïm to Amoraïm, from the region of Lod. His son belongs to the first Amoraïm.

151 Amora of the third and fourth generations. His father-in-law was the preacher in Tiberias in R. Joḥanan's time.

רִבִּי חִינְנָא בַּר פַּפָּא הָיָה מַפְלִיג מִינֵיהּ בְּלֵילְיָא. חַד זְמַן פְּגַע בּוֹ רַבְּהוֹן דְּרוּחַיָּא. אָמַר לֵיהּ לָא כָּךְ אוּלְפָן רִבִּי לֹא תַשִּׂיג גְּבוּל רֵעֲךָ. אָמַר לֵיהּ וְלֹא כֵן כְּתִיב מַתָּן בַּסֵּתֶר יִכְפֶּה אָף וַהֲוָה מִסְתַּפֵּיהּ מִינֵיהּ וַעֲרַק מִן קוֹמוֹי.

Rebbi Ḥinena bar Pappai used to distribute his charity in the night. Once the prince of spirits encountered him. He said to him, did not our teacher[152] teach us (*Deut* 19:14): "Do not displace your neighbor's boundaries." He said to him, but is it not written (*Prov.* 21:14): "A gift in secret appeases anger." He was afraid of him and fled from him.

152 Moses. The implication is that humans should leave the night for spirits since it is dangerous to go out then (Mishnah *Avot* 3:8).

אָמַר רִבִּי יוֹנָה אַשְׁרֵי נוֹתֵן לְדָל אֵין כְּתִיב כָּאן אֶלָּא אַשְׁרֵי מַשְׂכִּיל אֶל דָּל. וְהוּא שֶׁמִּסְתַּכֵּל בַּמִּצְוָה הֵיאַךְ לַעֲשׂוֹתָהּ. כֵּיצַד הָיָה רִבִּי יוֹנָה עוֹשֶׂה כְּשֶׁהָיָה רוֹאֶה בֶּן טוֹבִים שֶׁיָּרַד מִנְּכָסָיו הָיָה אוֹמֵר לוֹ בְּנִי בִּשְׁבִיל שֶׁשָּׁמַעְתִּי שֶׁנָּפְלָה לָךְ יְרוּשָּׁה מִמָּקוֹם אַחֵר טוֹל וְאַתְּ פּוֹרֵעַ. מִן דְּהֲוָה נְסַב לֵיהּ אָמַר לֵיהּ מַתָּנָה.

Rebbi Jonah said, it is not written, "hail to him who gives to the needy," but (*Ps.* 41:2): "Hail to him who is considerate to the needy;" this refers to him who fulfills this commandment intelligently. How did Rebbi Jonah do it? When he saw a son of a prominent family who had lost his property, he used to say to him: My son, since I heard that an inheritance fell to you at another place, take and you will pay back. When he had taken it, he said to him, it is a gift.

אָמַר רִבִּי חִיָּיא בַּר אָדָא אִית הֲווֹ סַבִּין בְּיוֹמֵינוּ מָן דַּהֲוָה יְהָבִין לוֹן מִבֵּין רֵישׁ שַׁתָּא לְצוֹמָא רַבָּא הֲווֹן נָסְבִין. מִן בָּתַר כֵּן לָא הֲווֹן נָסְבִין אָמְרֵי רְשׁוּתָא גַּבָּן.

Rebbi Ḥiyya bar Ada said, in our days there were old people who used to take if somebody gave to them between New Year's Day and the Great Fastday. After that, they were not taking. They said, there[153] is permission for us.

153 During the days of repentance, between *Rosh Hashanah* and *Yom Kippur*, the givers need the merit that comes with giving gifts to the needy; hence, the gifts are given wholeheartedly.

נְחֶמְיָה אִישׁ שִׁיחִין פְּגַע בֵּיהּ יְרוּשַׁלְמִי אֶחָד אֲמַר לֵיהּ זְכִי עִימִּי הָדָא תַּרְנְגוֹלְתָא. אֲמַר לֵיהּ הֵי לָךְ טִימִיתֵיהּ וְזִיל זְבִין קוּפָּד וְאָכַל וָמֵת. וְאָמַר בּוֹאוּ וְסִפְדוּ לַהֲרוּגוֹ שֶׁל נְחֶמְיָה.

Neḥemiah from Shiḥin[153] met a Jerusalemite who said to him, acquire merit by giving me that chicken. He said to him, here is its value[154], go buy red meat; he ate and died[155]. He said, come and eulogize him whom Neḥemiah killed.

153 A Tanna of the third generation, sometimes mentioned with the School of Rebbi Aqiba. Kefar Shiḥin was South of Sepphoris in Lower Galilee.

154 Greek τιμή "value," cf. *Berakhot* p. 604.

155 Being unaccustomed to red meat.

נָחוּם אִישׁ גַּם זוֹ הָיָה מוֹלִיךְ דּוֹרוֹן לְבֵית חָמוֹי פָּגַע בֵּיהּ מוּכֵּה שְׁחִין אֶחָד אָמַר לוֹ זְכֵה עִמִּי מִמָּה דְּאִית גַּבָּךְ. אָמַר לֵיהּ מִיחְזַר חָזַר וְאַשְׁכְּחֵיהּ מֵית. וַהֲוָה אֲמַר לְקַבְלֵיהּ עֵינֵיהּ דְּחָמוּנָךְ וְלָא יְהָבוּן לָךְ יִסְתַּמְיָן. יָדֵיהּ דְּלָא פָּשְׁטָן מִיתֵּן לָךְ יִתְקַטְּעוּן. רַגְלָיָא דְּלָא רְהָטִין מִיתֵּן לָךְ יִתְבָּרָן. וּמָטָתֵיהּ כֵּן. סְלִיק לְגַבֵּיהּ רִבִּי עֲקִיבָה אָמַר לֵיהּ אִי לִי שֶׁאֲנִי רוֹאֶה אוֹתָךְ כֵּן. אָמַר לֵיהּ אוֹי לִי שֶׁאֵינִי רוֹאֶה אוֹתָךְ כֵּן. אָמַר לֵיהּ מַה אַתְּ מְקַלְלֵנִי. אָמַר לֵיהּ וּמַה אַתְּ מְבָעֵט בְּיִיסוּרִין.

Naḥum from Gimzo[156] was carrying a gift[157] to the house of his father-in-law when he met a person afflicted with boils[158] who asked him, acquire merit[159] from what you have on you. He said to him, when I shall return. He returned and found him dead. He said before him, his[160] eyes which saw you and did not give to you shall go blind, his hands which did not stretch out to give to you shall be cut off, his feet which did not run to give to you shall be broken. This happened to him. Rebbi Aqiba came to visit him and said, woe to me that I see you in this state. He answered, woe to me that I do not see you in this state. He asked, why do you curse me? He answered, why are you contemptuous of suffering[161]?

156 A Tanna of the third generation, teacher of R. Aqiba. Gimzo is a village near Lod. His surname was changed into גם זו "this also" since his motto was "this also will be for the best", גם זו לטובה.

157 Greek δῶρον, τό, "gift".

158 A dirt infection, sign of poverty.

159 Give me a charitable gift.

160 Meaning, "my". It is Talmudic usage that all bad things said about one's own person are formulated in the third person, cf. *Berakhot* Chapter 3, notes 195-196.

161 Since suffering for sins in this world leaves you innocent and with much merit in the World to Come.

רִבִּי הוֹשַׁעְיָא רַבָּה הֲוָה רַבֵּיהּ דִּבְרֵיהּ חַד דְּסַגְיָא נְהוֹרָא וַהֲוָה יְלִיף אֲכַל עִימֵּיהּ בְּכָל־יוֹם. חַד זְמַן הֲוָה אֳרְחִין וְלָא מְטָא מֵיכוֹל עִימֵּיהּ. בְּרוּמְשָׁא סְלִיק לְגַבֵּיהּ לֹא יִכְעוֹס מָרִי עָלַי בְּגִין דַּהֲוָה לִי אֳרְחִין וְלָא בְּעֵי מִיבְזְיָא אִיקָרֵיהּ דְּמָרִי. בְּגִין כֵּן לָא אֲכְלִית עִמָּךְ יוֹמָא דֵין. אֲמַר לֵיהּ אַתָּה פִּייַסְתָּ לְמָאן דְּמִיתְחָמִי וְלָא חָמִי דֵּין דְּחָמִי וְלָא מִיתְחָמִי יְקַבֵּל פִּייוּסָךְ. אֲמַר לֵיהּ הָדָא מְנָא לָךְ אֲמַר לֵיהּ מֵרִבִּי אֱלִיעֶזֶר בֶּן יַעֲקֹב. דְּרִבִּי אֱלִיעֶזֶר בֶּן יַעֲקֹב עַל חַד דְּסַגְיָא נְהוֹרָא לְקַרְתֵּיהּ יְתַב לֵיהּ רִבִּי אֱלִיעֶזֶר בֶּן יַעֲקֹב לְרַע מִינֵּיהּ דִּי אָמְרִין דְּאִילוּלֵי דְּהוּא בַּר נַשָׁה רַבָּא לָא יְתִיב לֵיהּ רִבִּי אֱלִיעֶזֶר בֶּן יַעֲקֹב לְרַע מִינֵּיהּ. עָבְדוּן לֵיהּ פַּרְנָסָה דְּאִיקָר. אֲמַר לָהוּ מַהוּ הָכֵין. אָמְרוּ לֵיהּ רִבִּי אֱלִיעֶזֶר בֶּן יַעֲקֹב יְתִיב לְרַע מִינָּךְ. וּצְלִי עֲלוֹי הָדָא צְלוֹתָא אַתָּה גָּמַלְתָּ חֶסֶד לְמָאן דְּמִיתְחָמִי וְלָא חָמִי. דֵּין דְּחָמִי וְלָא מִיתְחָמִי יְקַבֵּל פִּיוּסָךְ וְיִגְמוֹל יָתָךְ חֶסֶד.

The teacher of the great Rebbi Hoshaia's son was blind and he used to invite him to eat with him every day. One day there were guests and he[162] did not ask him to eat with him. In the evening, he went to him and said: Please, Sir, do not be angry with me. Since I had guests, I did not want risking injuring the Sir's honor[163], therefore I did not eat with you today. He said to him, you assuaged him who is seen but does not see; may He be appeased by you Who sees but is not seen[164]. He asked him, from where do you have this? He said, from Rebbi Eliezer ben Jacob[165]. For there came a blind man to Rebbi Eliezer ben Jacob's town; Rebbi Eliezer ben Jacob sat below him[166] so that they should say if he were not a great person, Rebbi Eliezer ben Jacob would not sit below him. They provided for him in honor. He asked them, what is this? They told him, because Rebbi Eliezer ben Jacob sat below you. He prayed for him the following prayer: You did a good deed for one who is seen but does not see; He Who sees but is not seen may be appeased by you and do good for you.

162 R. Hoshaia did not invite the blind man to table.

163 It seems that handicapped persons were treated as social outcasts.

164 God. The expression is the translation of *Targum Yerushalmi* for אל ראי, חי ראי (*Gen.* 16.13, 24:62).

165 He is R. Eliezer ben Jacob II, a contemporary of the last students of R. Aqiba, not to be confused with R. Eliezer ben Jacob I, a Tanna of the first generation whom practice always follows.

166 Indicating that the blind man was his superior in knowledge.

דֵּלְמָא רִבִּי חָמָא בַּר חֲנִינָא וְרִבִּי הוֹשַׁעְיָה הֲוֹון מְטַייְלִין בְּאִילֵּין כְּנִישְׁתָּא דְלוֹד. אָמַר רִבִּי חָמָא בַּר חֲנִינָא לְרִבִּי הוֹשַׁעְיָה כַּמָּה מָמוֹן שִׁיקְעוּ אֲבוֹתַי כָּאן. אָמַר לֵיהּ כַּמָּה נְפָשׁוֹת שִׁיקְעוּ אֲבוֹתֶיךָ כָּאן. לָא הֲוָא אִית בַּר נַשׁ דְּלָעְיִין בְּאוֹרָיְתָא.

Clarification. Rebbi Ḥama bar Ḥanina and Rebbi Hoshaiah were strolling through the synagogue of Lod. Rebbi Ḥama bar Ḥanina said to Rebbi Hoshaiah: How much money did my forefathers invest here! He answered him: How many souls did your forefathers invest here, there is no one in here who studies Torah[167]!

167 All the money spent on building the synagogue could have been spent either on saving the poor from starvation or to support students of Torah (probably, including building houses of study for these students.)

רִבִּי אָחָא בְשֵׁם רִבִּי חִנְּנָא כֵּינִי מַתְנִיתָא כָּל־מִי שֶׁצָּרִיךְ לִיטּוֹל וְאֵינוֹ נוֹטֵל הֲרֵי זֶה שׁוֹפֵךְ דָּמִים וְאָסוּר לְהִתְרַחֵם עָלָיו. עַל נַפְשֵׁיהּ לֹא חַיֵּיס עַל חוֹרָנִין לֹא כָּל־שֶׁכֵּן. כָּל־מִי שֶׁאֵינוֹ צָרִיךְ לִיטּוֹל וְנוֹטֵל אֵינוֹ מֵת מִן הַזִּקְנָה עַד שֶׁיִּצְטָרֵךְ לַבְּרִיּוֹת. וְכָל־מִי שֶׁצָּרִיךְ לִיטּוֹל וְאֵינוֹ נוֹטֵל אֵינוֹ מֵת מִן הַזִּקְנָה עַד שֶׁיְּפַרְנֵס לַאֲחֵרִים מִשֶּׁלּוֹ וְעַל זֶה נֶאֱמַר בָּרוּךְ הַגֶּבֶר אֲשֶׁר יִבְטַח בַּיי וְהָיָה יי מִבְטַחוֹ.

Rebbi Aḥa in the name of Rebbi Ḥinena, so is the Mishnah: Everybody who needs to take and does not take commits suicide[168] and one may not have mercy on him. If he does not care for himself, would he care for others? Everybody who has no need to take but takes will not die of old age until he needs the creatures. Everybody who needs to take but does not take will not die of old age until he can provide for others from what is his; on him is was said (*Jer.* 17:7): "Blessed be the man who will be confident in the Eternal; the Eternal will be his trust."

168 If he cannot survive without the help of others, one should not give private charity to one who refuses public charity. But one who can survive and does not take any charity is characterized in the last sentence of the rewritten Mishnah.

Introduction to Tractate Demay

Demay is the technical term for produce bought from a source that cannot be trusted to faithfully give tithes. It was determined during the Second Commonwealth that all farmers could be trusted to give the heave to the Cohen since it was generally known that eating produce from which the heave was not taken is a deadly sin. In addition, the heave has no fixed amount in Biblical law and, therefore, the farmer could fulfill his obligation at very little cost. The situation is different for tithes which are two times ten percent. It was found that a sizeable minority of farmers did not give tithes. The First Tithe is given to a Levite (or a Cohen); this is purely a monetary claim and, therefore, cannot be claimed from a buyer, since any Levite claiming the tithe would have to prove that actually the producer of that crop did not give tithes, which for produce bought on the market is impossible. Hence, the buyer does not have to give First Tithe from what he bought. However, the Levite would have been obliged to give 10% of the First Tithe as *heave of the tithe* to the Cohen (*Num.* 18), and this heave of the tithe follows the same rule as heave itself: Its consumption by a non-Cohen, or consumption in impurity, is a deadly sin. Hence, the buyer from a noncertified source must give 1% (one-tenth of one-tenth) as heave of the tithe in order to avoid committing a deadly sin.

The Second Tithe, due in years 1, 2, 4, 5 of the Sabbatical cycle, is for the farmer himself, to be eaten in purity in Jerusalem. However, it may be redeemed for money (*Deut.* 14:25), and in the absence of a Temple it may be redeemed for a token sum. Hence, there is no great hardship involved if the buyer has to separate the Second Tithe mentally and then redeem it for a penny. The Tithe of the Poor, taking the place of the Second Tithe in years 3 and 6 of the Sabbatical cycle, is again a monetary obligation for which a claimant would have no proof and, therefore, it does not have to be given.

Since all the obligations to give the heave of the tithe and to redeem the Second Tithe are imposed only to be sure that no sin is committed, there are several leniencies in the interpretation of the laws available to the buyer of *demay* not available for produce that certainly has not been tithed. The fine points of the law are discussed at length in the tractate. In the last chapter, some arithmetic niceties of the laws are explored for their intellectual value.

The etymology of the word דמאי is given by the Yerushalmi *Maäser Šeni* 5:13 as דמי - דמי "maybe yes, maybe no." Eliezer Ben Jehudah compares the semantic relation of the Hebrew root דמה "to compare" and the adjective דמי "uncertain" to that of Arabic شَبَه שבה "to compare" to شُبْهَة שבהה "doubt, incertitude; vague, equivocal." All derivations of the term from non-Semitic words have to be rejected.

An important topic also treated in *Demay* is that of applicability of the laws of tithes. The boundaries of the Holy Land given in *Num.* 34

extend far to the North of the territory actually occupied by Israel in the time of Joshua and Judges. The vestiges of the original distribution of land disappeared with the Babylonian exile. The returnees under Ezra and Neḥemiah accepted again the duties of tithes and Sabbaticals by a solemn covenant (*Neh.* 10). By its nature, this covenant was restricted to the territories settled by the returnees (Judea) and those never emptied of a Jewish population (Galilee, Western Bashan, and possibly Samaria.) The strict rules, therefore, apply only to those territories. In the remainder of the Holy Land and the territories within the pentateuchal boundaries incorporated into David's empire (Syria), the rules apply in relaxed form, as a remainder of the stringent rules or as a sign of hope that the full rules will be established again in the times of the Messiah. The boundaries of the different domains are discussed in Chapter Two. The readings in the text of localities in border territories have been checked against those in the synagogue mosaic in the Beth Shean valley; the interpretation follows *Caphtor Waperaḥ*, A. Neubauer, S. Klein, and M. Avi-Yona.

The circle of people observing all rules of tithing was always restricted. Since it was necessary to identify sellers of tithed produce, an official category of "trustworthy" sellers was established. A more restricted category still was that of people adhering to the rules of ritual purity even 200 years and more after the destruction of the Temple when many of these rules could no longer be observed to the letter. These people were given the title of חבר *ḥaver* "member of the fellowship" after they formally accepted the rules of fellowship before a court composed of fellows. Those who were neither *ḥaver* nor trustworthy, are called עם הארץ *am haärez̧* "vulgar person". The rules of trustworthiness and *ḥaverut*, and the rules of relations between *ḥaverim*, trustworthies, and *amē haärez̧*, are a major topic of tractate *Demay*. Many stringent rules spelled out in the Mishnah are greatly attenuated in the Halakhot, and the picture that emerges from the Yerushalmi is one of harmonious coexistence, quite in contrast to the picture of antagonism and strict separation given in the Babylonian Talmud on basis of Mishnaic rules. Since trustworthiness and fellowship in the Israeli sense were impossible in Babylonia, the picture given by the Yerushalmi has to be accepted as authentic and the status of the עם הארץ in rabbinic society has to be re-evaluated. In Babylonia, the meaning of עם הארץ is "uneducated", totally different from the meaning of the term in the Yerushalmi. While the Babli frowns upon marriages between the educated and the *am haärez̧*, the Yerushalmi insists that it is sinful for the observant Jew to separate himself from his "vulgar" brethren if this would lead the *am haärez̧* into sin (Halakhah 2:1).

The material dependence of the Babylonian Talmud on the Yerushalmi was demonstrated in the Introduction to the first volume in this series. In Note 89 of Chapter 1, a dependence of Babylonian Amoraic technical terminology on the Yerushalmi is uncovered.

The commentaries used are the same as for Tractate Peah.

הקלים פרק ראשון

(fol. 21c) **משנה א.** הַקַּלִּים שֶׁבִּדְמַאי הַשִּׁיתִין וְהָרִימִין וְהָעֻזְרְדִין וּבְנוֹת שׁוּחַ וּבְנוֹת שִׁקְמָה וְנוֹבְלוֹת הַתְּמָרָה וְהַגּוּפְנָן וְהַנִּצְפָּה. וּבִיהוּדָה הָעוֹג וְהַחוֹמֶץ וְהַכּוּסְבָּר. רִבִּי יְהוּדָה אוֹמֵר כָּל־הַשִּׁיתִים פְּטוּרוֹת חוּץ מִשֶּׁל דִּיפְרָא. וְכָל־הָרִימִין פְּטוּרִין חוּץ מֵרִימֵי שִׁיקְמָנָה[1]. וְכָל־בְּנוֹת שִׁקְמָה פְּטוּרוֹת חוּץ מִשֶּׁל הַמְּסוּטָּפוֹת.

Mishnah 1: The easy ones for *demay*[2] are *shitin*[3], lotus fruit[4], the fruit of the service tree, white figs[5], and sycamore figs, fallen dates[6], fennel[7], and capers[8]. Also in Judea sumac, vinegar, and coriander. Rebbi Jehudah says, all *shitin* are free except those from a tree bearing fruit twice a year, all lotus fruit are free except lotus fruit from Shiqmanah[9], and all sycamore fruits are free except those cracked open[10].

1 Reading of the Leyden manuscript. In the Venice print, as well as the Kaufmann manuscript of the Mishnah, שיקמה, perhaps by dittography from the next sentence. In the Rome manuscript, שיקמונה.

2 The definition of *demay* is given in the Introduction. The "easy ones" are those to which the laws of *demay* do not apply and which may be bought from any source without separating heave or tithe.

3 S. Lieberman has convincingly argued that שיתין is a contraction of שחיתין "garbage fruit" in the Galilean dialect which had no ח sound (compare *Peah* 2:5, Note 86.) It will be explained that these are figs growing under the leaves. Since figs need much sun to ripen, normally figs grow on top of the leaves, exposed to the sun. Those growing under the leaves remain hard and inedible at harvest time and are not usually harvested. Hence, these

figs are to be considered abandoned property after the harvest and are not subject to any laws of heave and tithes.

4 Definition of Maimonides, Arabic אַלְנַבְּק. In some Mishnah and Tosephta manuscripts the reading is דימין and *Caftor Waperach*, ed. Luncz, Jerusalem 1899, p. 526, notes that in Falastini Arabic the fruit is called אַלדום.

5 Identification of R. Joḥanan in the Babli (*Berakhot* 40b).

6 Either fallen because they are rotten or wormy inside or knocked down by a windstorm.

7 See later, Note 55; cf. I. Löw, *Flora der Juden* 3, p. 462. Maimonides declares it to be "a relative of dill." The Arukh declares it to be wild grapes, Italian *lambrusco*. This follows the Babli (*Berakhot* 40b) which defines it to be grapes that ripen only after the harvest.

8 Concurrent definition of Arukh (*cappero*) and Maimonides. This refers to the fruit only.

9 Identified as a village Sycaminon at the foot of Mt. Carmel, South of Haifa.

10 Cracked open while still on the tree, they will become sweet enough to qualify as human food. The others are only considered animal fodder. The sweetness of cracked sycamores was already noted by Pliny, *Naturalis Historia*, Book XIII, §56. In all these instances, R. Jehudah insists that the fruits do not grow wild and/or are not abandoned.

הלכה א: אָמַר רִבִּי יוֹחָנָן לְפִי שֶׁרוֹב הַמִּינִין הַלָּלוּ אֵין בָּאִין אֶלָּא מִן הַהֶבְקֵר לְפִיכָךְ מָנוּ אוֹתָן חֲכָמִים.

Halakhah 1: Rebbi Joḥanan said, the Sages enumerated them because the majority of these kinds are collected only from abandoned property[11].

11 Either they are leftovers after the harvest and actually abandoned, or they are from shrubs and trees that are never harvested and, therefore, the fruits can be treated as abandoned even though they grow on private property.

רִבִּי שִׁמְעוֹן בֶּן לָקִישׁ אָמַר לֹא שָׁנוּ אֶלָּא דְּמַאי אֲבָל וַדָּאִין חַייָבִין. רִבִּי יוֹחָנָן אָמַר לָא שַׁנְייָא בֵּין דְּמַאי וּבֵין וַדַּאי פְּטוּרִין. וְקַשְׁיָא עַל דְּרִבִּי יוֹחָנָן. לֹא שָׁנוּ אֶלָּא דְּמַאי אֲבָל וַדַּאי חַייָבִין .אָמַר רִבִּי לָא לְפִי שֶׁבְּכָל־מָקוֹם וּמָקוֹם לֹא חָשִׁיב אֶלָּא דְּמַאי וְהָכָא לֹא אֲתִינָן אֶלָּא וַדַּאי.

Rebbi Simeon ben Laqish said, only *demay* is mentioned, hence one is obligated[12] if they are certain. Rebbi Joḥanan said, they are free whether *demay* or certain[13]. It is difficult for Rebbi Joḥanan, didn't they mention only *demay?* Hence if it is certain, is it not obligated[14]? Rebbi La said, since at every place[15] he considers only *demay*, here he quotes only *demay*.

12 If it is certain that the tithes were not given, one is obligated to give them in full in any case, including the kinds mentioned in the Mishnah. Only if it is *demay* can one get away with giving only 1%. (This argument appears anonymously in Babli *Berakhot* 40b.)

13 The kinds enumerated in the Mishnah are not subject to any tithes.

14 R. Joḥanan's position would be acceptable if the Mishnah were in one of the tractates *Terumot* or *Ma'serot*, but here it refers explicitly to *demay*.

15 In this tractate. The mention of *demay* is a mnemotechnic device which starts tractate *Demay*. It has no intrinsic meaning.

מַתְנִיתָא מְסַייְעָא לְרִבִּי יוֹחָנָן מִגְּזִיב וּלְהַלָּן פָּטוּר מִן הַדְּמַאי. שַׁנְייָא הִיא מִגְּזִיב וּלְהַלָּן בֵּין דְּמַאי בֵּין וַדַּאי. אוּף הָכָא לָא שַׁנְייָא בֵּין דְּמַאי בֵּין וַדַּאי.

The Mishnah supports Rebbi Joḥanan: "From Akhzib[16] and further on[17] it is free from *demay*." Is not from Akhzib and further on no difference between *demay* and certainty? Here also there is no difference between *demay* and certainty[18].

16 A place whose ruins are on the seashore, just South of the Lebanese border, mentioned in *Jos.* 19:29, *Jud.* 1:31. Along the seashore, Kezib or Akhzib denotes the northernmost point of contiguous settlement by Jews during the Second Commenwealth. As explained in the Introduction, agricultural land outside this area is in principle free from all obligations imposed on the Land. (Exceptions are discussed in Chapter 2, Halakhah 1 and, for the Tithe of the Poor only, in Tractates *Ma'serot* and *Ševiït*.)

17 To the North, into Phoenician territory.

18 Certainty that no tithes were given.

מַתְנִיתָא פְלִיגָא עַל רִבִּי שִׁמְעוֹן בֶּן לָקִישׁ. אִם הָיוּ נִשְׁמָרִין חַיָּבִין עִיקָּרָן לֹא מִן הַהֶבְקֵר הֵן בָּאִין. פָּתַר לָהּ אַחַר רוֹב מְשַׁמְּרִין. אִתָא חֲמֵי אִם רוֹב מְשַׁמְּרִין דִּבְרֵי הַכֹּל חַיָּבִין בֵּין דְּמַאי בֵּין וַדַּאי. אִם אֵין רוֹב מְשַׁמְּרִין דִּבְרֵי הַכֹּל פְּטוּרִין בֵּין דְּמַאי בֵּין וַדַּאי. מֶחֱצָה עַל מֶחֱצָה לֵית יָכִיל דְּתַנֵּינָן מֶחֱצָה עַל מֶחֱצָה דְּמַאי. אָמַר רִבִּי זְעִירָא לֹא סוֹף דָּבָר הַקַּלִּים שֶׁבִּדְמַאי אֶלָּא אֲפִילוּ דְמַאי עַצְמוֹ.

A *baraita*[19] disagrees with Rebbi Simeon ben Laqish: "If they were kept in storage they are obligated." Did they not essentially come from abandoned property? He explains it, if most people keep them in storage[20]. Come and see, if most people keep them in storage, it is everybody's opinion[21] that they are obligated, be it *demay* or certain. If most people do not keep them in storage, it is everybody's opinion that they are free, be it *demay* or certain. Half and half you cannot consider[22] since we have stated[23]: "Half and half is *demay*." Rebbi Zeïra said, not only the easy ones for *demay* but even *demay* itself[24].

19 Tosephta *Demay* 1:1: "The easy ones for *demay*, *shitin*, lotus fruit, and the fruit of the service tree, may be trusted everywhere to be free (from obligation of tithes), but if they are kept in storage they are obligated."

20 At such a place, nobody abandons the fruits and they are not free from tithes.

21 Both R. Joḥanan and R. Simeon

ben Laqish.

22 This would be the only practical point of difference between R. Joḥanan, who frees the fruits from tithes, and R. Simeon ben Laqish, who submits them to tithes.

23 Mishnah *Makhshirin* 2:10: "If someone finds produce on the road, if most people store it in their houses, it is free" (since, then, everybody must give heave and tithes at his barn and the few things lost on the road are included,) "if most people transport it to sell on the market, it is obligated" (since the seller may nibble from it occasionally without tithes and the future buyer, who has no relationship to the harvester, is obligated for tithes,) "half and half is *demay*." Hence, there seems to be no way to relax the standard for a fifty-fifty doubt.

24 The Mishnah *Makhshirin* does not deal with our case, but with commercial produce; hence, it has no implications here and we may reduce the difference between R. Joḥanan and R. Simeon ben Laqish to this particular case.

תַּנֵּי נִכְנַס לְעִיר שֶׁרוּבָּהּ גּוֹיִם סָפֵק רוֹב מְשַׁמְּרִין סָפֵק אֵין רוֹב מְשַׁמְּרִין דִּבְרֵי הַכֹּל חַייָבִין בֵּין דְּמַאי בֵּין וַדַּאי. נִכְנַס לְעִיר שֶׁרוּבָּהּ יִשְׂרָאֵל סָפֵק רוֹב מְשַׁמְּרִין סָפֵק אֵין רוֹב מְשַׁמְּרִין דִּבְרֵי הַכֹּל פְּטוּרִין בֵּין דְּמַאי בֵּין וַדַּאי. סָפֵק רוֹב גּוֹיִם סָפֵק רוֹב יִשְׂרָאֵל סָפֵק רוֹב מְשַׁמְּרִין סָפֵק אֵין רוֹב מְשַׁמְּרִין מַחְלוֹקֶת רִבִּי יוֹחָנָן וְרִבִּי שִׁמְעוֹן בֶּן לָקִישׁ.

It was stated[25]: If one enters a town inhabited mostly by Gentiles, if there is a doubt whether the majority keep them in storage[26] or not, everybody agrees[27] that they are obligated, be it *demay* or certain[28]. If one enters a town inhabited mostly by Jews, if there is a doubt whether the majority keep them in storage or not, everybody agrees that they are free, be it *demay* or certain[29]. If there is any doubt whether there is a majority of Gentiles or a majority of Jews, that is the disagreement between Rebbi Joḥanan and Rebbi Simeon ben Laqish.

25 As R. M. Margalit points out, this passage seems to be Amoraic, not Tannaitic as usually associated with the expression "stated."

26 The kinds mentioned in the Mishnah.

27 In Halakhah 2:1, in reference to a list in the Mishnah about produce that must be treated as *demay* everywhere, even outside the Land of Israel, since usually these are produce of the Land. There R. Joḥanan asserts that the requirement to treat them as *demay* equally applies to fruits bought from Gentiles or from Jews, but R. Eleazar only treats produce bought from Jews as *demay* and insists that produce bought from Gentiles is certainly not in order and one also has to give the heave. Everybody agrees with R. Meïr that Gentile ownership of land in the domain settled by the returnees from Babylonia does not free the land from the obligation of heaves and tithes, against the ruling of the Babli (cf. *Peah*, Chapter 4, Notes 129-131). "Everybody" referred to here, however, are R. Joḥanan and R. Simeon ben Laqish, whose disagreement is explained in a second case.

28 *Demay* always for R. Joḥanan, certain for R. Eleazar if bought from a Gentile. Even these are "easy ones", since the Gentiles certainly did not give heave and tithes; the twofold doubt which is the basis of the leniencies of *demay*, as explained in the Introduction, does not apply. There is only a single doubt, viz., whether the produce is obligated for tithes or not, and this, being of Biblical origin, must in case of doubt be resolved in a restrictive way.

29 As explained in the preceding paragraph.

אֵילּוּ הֵן הַשִּׁיתִים רִבִּי שִׁמְעוֹן בְּרֵיהּ דְּרִבִּי אַבָּא אֵילּוּ שֶׁהֵן יוֹצְאוֹת מִתַּחַת הֶעָלִין.

These[30] are the *shitim*: Rebbi Simeon, the son of Rebbi Abba[31]: Those appearing under the leaves.

30 Here starts the detailed discussion of the Mishnah.

31 In the Rome manuscript: R. Ayvu. However, R. Ayvu was a later aggadic preacher and nothing is known of his family. R. Simeon bar Abba was a Galilean scholar of the second generation, a relative of Samuel of

Nahardea; he was a great scholar and always very poor. When Nahardea was destroyed by Odenatus, two of Samuel's daughters were taken captive and redeemed in Galilee. R. Simeon bar Abba married first one, then after the early death of his wife the other, who also died soon.

הַבְּכִירוֹת וְהַמְסוּייָפוֹת הֲרֵי אֵילוּ פְטוּרוֹת. וְאֵילוּ הֵן הַבְּכִירוֹת עַד שֶׁלֹּא הוֹשִׁיב שׁוֹמֵר. וּבְשׁוֹמֵר הַדָּבָר תָּלוּי. אָמַר רִבִּי יוֹסֵי בְּשֶׁאֵין בָּהּ כְּדֵי טַפֵּילַת שׁוֹמֵר. אֵילוּ הֵן הַמְסוּייָפוֹת מִשֶּׁיְּקַפְּלוּ הַמְקְצוֹעוֹת. רִבִּי לְעַיי אָמַר מִשּׁוּם רִבִּי לִיעֶזֶר הַבְּכִירוֹת הֲרֵי אֵילוּ חַייָבוֹת מִפְּנֵי שֶׁהֵן בְּחֶזְקַת מִשְׁתַּמְּרוֹת. רִבִּי יוֹסֵי בֵּין חַלְפוּתָא אָמַר הַשִּׁיתִין שֶׁבְּצִיפּוֹרִין הֲרֵי אֵילוּ חַייָבוֹת מִפְּנֵי שֶׁהֵן בְּחֶזְקַת מִשְׁתַּמְּרוֹת.

"[32]Early[33] and late fruits are exempt. These are the early fruits, before one appoints a watchman." But does this depend on the watchman[34]? Rebbi Yose said, if they are not worth the attention of a watchman. "These are the late fruits, after they folded up the mats[35]. Rebbi Illaï said in the name of Rebbi Eliezer, the early ones are obligated because of an assumption that they are being watched[36]." Rebbi Yose ben Ḥalaphta said, *shitin* in Sepphoris are obligated because of an assumption that they are watched[37].

32 Tosephta *Demay* 1:3: "Early and late fruits in a garden are obligated; on the field they are exempt. These are the early fruits, before one appoints a watchman, the late fruits, after they folded up the mats. Rebbi Illaï said in the name of Rebbi Eliezer, the early ones are obligated because of an assumption that they are being watched."

33 They are ripe before there is a market for them. The late ones are unripe at harvest time, so they are abandoned on the field. Here one speaks of valuable fruits, not those mentioned in the Mishnah.

34 Since it is an individual decision, it is not a legal standard.

35 To store the fruits on the field, to shield them from dirt and dust

before they are transported to the farmhouse.

36 Since there always is a market for *primeurs*.

37 Probably, to make vegetable rennet. This statement is also Tannaitic; it is not in our Tosephta but may come from a Yerushalmi version of the Tosephta.

נִסְתַּייְפוּ הַתְּאֵינִים וְהוּא מְשַׁמֵּר שָׂדֵהוּ מִפְּנֵי עֲנָבִים. עֲנָבִים וְהוּא מְשַׁמֵּר שָׂדֵהוּ מִפְּנֵי הַיֶּרֶק אִם נִכְנַס הוּא הַפּוֹעֵל וּבַעַל הַבַּיִת מַקְפִּיד עָלָיו אֲסוּרוֹת מִשּׁוּם גֶּזֶל.

If the fig harvest was finished and he watches his field because of grapes, grape harvest and he watches his field because of vegetables, if a worker enters there and the owner is offended, they are forbidden because of robbery[38].

38 (There is a similar text in Tosephta *Ma'serot* 3:12 and Babli *Pesaḥim* 6b, but it deals with the obligation to give tithes.) By Biblical ordinance (*Deut*. 23:25), a worker is entitled to eat from the produce he is harvesting. This implies that without the owner's consent he cannot eat from produce he is not harvesting. Hence, if the owner objects to his workers going through those parts of his property that are already harvested, the owner retains all property rights to the unripe produce still standing on the field and, *a fortiori*, the unripe produce is not abandoned, may not be taken by other people, and is not freed from the obligations of heave and tithes.

עוּלָּא בַּר יִשְׁמָעֵאל בְּשֵׁם רִבִּי יוֹחָנָן רִבִּי וְרִבִּי יוֹסֵי בֵּי רִבִּי יוּדָה נִכְנְסוּ לוֹכַל בִּמְסוּייָפוֹת וְצָוַוח בָּהֶן הַשּׁוֹמֵר וּמָשַׁךְ רִבִּי יוֹסֵי בֵּי רִבִּי יְהוּדָה אֶת יָדָיו. אָמַר לוֹ רִבִּי אֱכוֹל שֶׁכְּבָר נִתְייָאֲשׁוּ הַבְּעָלִים מֵהֶן. רִבִּי יוֹחָנָן בְּעֵי צָווַח וְאַתְּ אָמַר הָכֵן. אָמַר רִבִּי יוֹנָה יְאוּת הוּא מַקְשֵׁי. וְהָא מַתְנִיתָא פְלִיגָא הַסִּיאָה וְהָאֵזוֹב וְהַקּוּרְנִית שֶׁבְּחָצֵר אִם הָיוּ נִשְׁמָרִין חַייָבִין. הָא בְגִינָּה אֲפִילוּ נִישְׁמָרִין פְּטוּרִין. תַּמָּן יָכוֹל הוּא לוֹמַר לוֹ הֲרֵי כָל־הָעוֹלָם כּוּלּוֹ לְפָנֶיךָ בְּרַם הָכָא כַלְכָּלָה אַחַת הִיא וַאֲנִי מְשַׁמְּרָהּ לְבַעַל מְלַאכְתִּי.

Ulla bar Ismael[39] in the name of Rebbi Joḥanan: Rebbi and Rebbi Yose ben Rebbi Jehudah[40] entered to eat of late fruits; the watchman shouted at them, and Rebbi Yose ben Rebbi Jehudah stopped. Rebbi told him: eat, because the owners already gave up their expectations for them[41]! Rebbi Joḥanan asked: He shouted, and you say so[42]? Rebbi Jonah said, he objects rightfully. But does not a Mishnah disagree: "[43]Calamint, hyssop, and thyme in the courtyard are obligated if they are tended." Hence, in the garden they are free even if they are watched. There[44], he may say, the entire world is before you, but here, there is one basketful and I am watching it for my employer.

39 In the Babli, he is simply called Ulla. A student of R. Joḥanan, he was a frequent traveller to Babylonia and an important link between the Galilean and Babylonian sages. He died during one of his trips there.

40 A son of R. Jehudah bar Illaï, constant companion of Rebbi, and influential in the composition of the Mishnah.

41 **יאוש** is the technical term for giving up hope to regain a lost article. Rebbi seems to imply that the law made them give up hope. (Arabic **איאס** "giving up hope".)

42 The *baraita* of the previous paragraph bars people from taking late fruits if they are guarded. How could Rebbi permit taking these fruits?

43 *Ma'serot* 3:9. The plants mentioned are weeds used as spices. If they are close to the house and tended, they are kitchen herbs and as private property obligated for tithes. In all other circumstances, they are treated as weeds and free from heave and tithes.

44 Spice-weeds are everywhere but late fruits are watched; Rebbi was in error when he applied the ruling of the Mishnah in *Ma'serot* to his case.

תַּנֵּי רִבִּי יוֹסֵי בֵּי רִבִּי יוּדָה הַנּוֹבְלוֹת הַנִּמְכָּרוֹת עִם הַתְּמָרִים הֲרֵי אֵלּוּ פְּטוּרוֹת. מַה שְׁתֵּי קוּפּוֹת זוּ בְּצַד זוּ אוֹ זוּ עַל גַּבֵּי זוּ וְלָא שַׁנְייָא הִיא זוּ בְּצַד זוּ הִיא זוּ עַל גַּבֵּי זוּ. אֶלָּא כִּי נָן קַייָמִין בִּמְעוֹרָבוֹת כְּשֶׁהִטִּילוּ שְׂאוֹר אוֹ בְּשֶׁלֹּא הִטִּילוּ שְׂאוֹר.

רִבִּי מָנָא אָמַר בְּשֶׁהִטִּילוּ שְׂאוֹר אֲנָן קַייָמִין. אִם בְּשֶׁהִטִּילוּ שְׂאוֹר בִּפְנֵי עַצְמָן יְהוּ חַייָבוֹת. לֵית יָכִיל דְּאָמַר רִבִּי יוֹחָנָן מִפְּנֵי שֶׁרוֹב הַמִּינִין הָאֵילוּ אֵינָן בָּאִין אֶלָּא מִן הַהֶבְקֵר לְפִיכָךְ מָנוּ אוֹתָן חֲכָמִים. רִבִּי חֲנִינָא אָמַר בְּשֶׁלֹּא הִטִּילוּ שְׂאוֹר אֲנָן קַייָמִין. אִם בְּשֶׁלֹּא הִטִּילוּ שְׂאוֹר אֲנָן קַייָמִין אֲפִילוּ בִּמְעוֹרָבוֹת יְהוּ פְּטוּרוֹת. לֵית יָכִיל דְּתַנֵּי רִבִּי יִשְׁמָעֵאל בֵּי רִבִּי יוֹסֵי אָמַר מִשּׁוּם אָבִיו אֶשְׁכּוֹל שֶׁבִּיכֵּר בּוֹ גַּרְגִּיר יְחִידִי כּוּלּוֹ חִיבּוּר לְמַעְשְׂרוֹת. רִבִּי יוֹסֵי בֵּי רִבִּי בּוּן אָמַר רִבִּי זְעִירָא וְרִבִּי הִילָּא חַד אָמַר כְּהָדֵין וְחַד אָמַר כְּהָדֵין. וַחֲכָמִים (fol. 21d) אוֹמְרִים לֹא כְדִבְרֵי זֶה וְלֹא כְדִבְרֵי זֶה אֶלָּא אֶת שֶׁהִטִּילוּ שְׂאוֹר חַייָבוֹת וְאֶת שֶׁלֹּא הִטִּילוּ שְׂאוֹר פְּטוּרוֹת.

It was stated[45]: "Rebbi Yose ben Rebbi Jehudah says, fallen dates sold with regular dates are free[46]." Is it about two boxes, one beside the other or one on top of the other[47]? No, here we deal with a mixed bunch. Did they start to ferment[48] or did they not start to ferment? Rebbi Mana said, we deal with fermenting ones. If they started to ferment, they should be obligated for themselves[49]! You cannot say that, since Rebbi Johanan said, the Sages detailed them because the majority of these kinds are collected only from abandoned property[50]. Rebbi Ḥanina said, we deal with nonfermenting ones. If we deal with nonfermenting ones they should be free even when mixed[51]. You cannot say that, since it was stated[52]: "Rebbi Ismael ben Rebbi Yose said in his father's name that a bunch of grapes of which one berry ripened, is all connected for tithes[53]." Rebbi Yose ben Rebbi Abun said, Rebbi Zeïra and Rebbi Illaï, one adopted the first opinion, the other the second opinion. But the Sages say one does not follow either of them; those fermenting are obligated, those not fermenting are free[54].

45 Tosephta *Demay* 1:1. The next sentence there reads: "But the Sages say, they are free as long as they do not ferment; once they start to ferment they are obligated." Fermented dates are used for date wine.

46 "Free" means not under the laws of either heave and tithes or those of *demay*. "Obligated" means that they fall under both kinds of laws. The reading "free" is in all Yerushalmi manuscripts except that of R. S. Cirillo, but the latter most probably represents an emendation by its author. In all Tosephta texts, the reading is "obligated." Since the reading is "free" in both the Leyden and the Rome manuscripts, it must be very old. Nevertheless, it must represent a scribal error, and the reading must be "obligated;" otherwise the statement would be superfluous and contradicting the following discussion.

47 Is it restricted to a case where the buyer can directly check what he is getting (if good and fallen dates are in separate boxes)?

48 In that case, the fallen dates can be used to make date liquor and are commercially valuable. If they are fallen and did not start to ferment probably they are not sweet enough to qualify as human food and are valueless.

49 And subject to *demay* even if not mixed with good dates.

50 Abandoned property is exempt even if valuable.

51 Since they have no value.

52 This statement does not appear in any other collection.

53 One good grape makes the entire bunch subject to the laws of heave and tithes. Hence, one good fruit in a box makes the entire box subject to the laws of heave and tithes.

54 An adaptation of the Tosephta text quoted at the start of this paragraph, turned into a statement of Amoraic practice, adopted by Maimonides (*Maäser* 13:1). The statement of the Mishnah is qualified to apply only to dates that are so devoid of sugar that they do not ferment.

וְהַגּוּפְנָן שְׁמֵירָה. מַה בֵּין בִּיהוּדָה בֵּין בַּגָּלִיל. מִן מַה דְמַתְלִין לָהּ מְתַל בְּגָלִילָא. שׁוּמֵירָא שְׁמַר מָרָהּ מִן מְתַל לָךְ עִם תַּבְלָיָא. הָדָא אֲמְרָה בְּגָלִיל פָּטוּר וּבִיהוּדָה חַיָּיב.

Gufnān is *šāmērāh*[55]. What is the difference between Judea and Galilee? Since one has a popular saying in Galilee: *šāmērāh, šĕmar mārāh* (its owner should watch it), would anybody compare it to spices[56]? That means, in Galilee it is free but in Judea it is obligated.

55 Arabic שַׁמְרָה, fennel.

56 That a weed can be used in the kitchen does not make it a spice. Hence, in Galilee where fennel grows wild, it is not a cultivated plant, in contrast to arid Judea where it needs tending.

כּוּסְבְּרָא כּוּסְבָּרְתָא. מַה בֵּין בִּיהוּדָה בֵּין בַּגָּלִיל. מִן מַה דְּמַתְלִין לָהּ מְתַל דָּרוֹמָא. כּוּסְבְּרָא כּוּסְבָּרְתָא מִן מְתַלִיךְ עִם תַּבְלָיְיָא. הָדָא אָמְרָה בְּגָלִיל חַיֶּיבֶת וּבִיהוּדָה פְּטוּרָה.

Coriander is *kusbārātā*[57]. What is the difference between Judea and Galilee? Since one has a popular saying in the South: Coriander is *kusbārātā*[58], would anybody compare it to spices? That means, in Galilee it is obligated but in Judea it is free.

57 Formally, the feminine form of the word for coriander, but, as seen in the next Note, denoting a weed.

58 Taking the Arabic *kuzbara(t)* for a guide, this form means wild growing adiantum (or it may mean *kuzbarat altalab*, pimpernel, *kuzbarat kadra'*, chervil, *kuzbarat alṣakr*, haircap-moss, *kuzbarat alḥamām*, Fumaria officinalis). *Kusbārātā* is not considered cultivated.

תַּנֵּי אָמַר רִבִּי יוּדָה בָּרִאשׁוֹנָה הָיָה חוֹמֶץ שֶׁבִּיהוּדָה פָּטוּר מִן הַמַּעְשְׂרוֹת. שֶׁהָיוּ עוֹשִׂין יֵינָן בְּטָהֳרָה לִנְסָכִים וְלֹא הָיָה מַחְמִיץ וְהָיוּ מְבִיאִין מִן הַתֶּמֶד. וְעַכְשָׁיו שֶׁהַיַּיִן מַחְמִיץ חַיָּיב. מַחְלְפָה שִׁיטָּתֵיהּ דְּרִבִּי יוּדָה דְּתַנֵּינָן תַּמָּן הַמְתַמֵּד וְנָתַן מַיִם בְּמִידָּה וּמָצָא כְדֵי מִידָּתוֹ פָּטוּר. וְרִבִּי יְהוּדָה מְחַיֵּיב. וְכָא הוּא אָמַר הָכֵן. אָמַר רִבִּי לָא בָּרִאשׁוֹנָה הָיוּ עֲנָבִים מְרוּבּוֹת וְלֹא הָיוּ חַרְצָנִים חֲשׁוּבוֹת וְעַכְשָׁיו שֶׁאֵין עֲנָבִים מְרוּבּוֹת חַרְצָנִים חֲשׁוּבוֹת.

It was stated: "Rebbi Jehudah said, in earlier times, vinegar in Judea was exempt from tithes. Since they made all their wine in purity for Temple offerings[59], it never got sour; they made vinegar from the skins of grapes. But now, since wine turns sour[60], it is obligated." The argument of Rebbi Jehudah is inverted since we stated there[61]: "If one makes after-wine and puts in a given volume of water, if he finds exactly the same volume it is free, but Rebbi Jehudah obligates him[62]." And here he says so! Rebbi La said, in earlier times when grapes were plentiful, their skins were not counted as anything[63], but now that grapes are not plentiful, the skins are important.

59 In the time of the Second Temple, all wine and oil for the Temple had to come from Judea since the two blocks of Jewish settlement, Judea and Galilee, were not contiguous. Hence it was impossible to transport wine or oil from Galilee to Judea without passing over impure Gentile territory, since even Samaritan Samaria was separated from Galilee by a strip of land occupied by Gentiles.

60 Wine-vinegar is really wine turned sour; it is subject to all rules of wine. A similar anonymous statement appears in Tosephta *Demay* 1:2: "In earlier times, vinegar was exempt in Jehudah since it was presumed to be made from after-wine, but now it is presumed to be from wine and is obligated."

61 Mishnah *Ma'serot* 5:6.

62 According to the first Tanna, after-wine is water which absorbed some taste from the grape skins. According to Rebbi Jehudah, it is wine mixed with water. Since they always drank their wine mixed with water, this is regular wine and subject to its rules. This contradicts Rebbi Jehudah's statement in the earlier *baraita*.

63 Afterwine was worthless and thus not subject to tithes; now it is traded as merchandise.

רִבִּי הוּנָא אָמַר רִבִּי יִרְמְיָה בְּעֵי לֵית הָדָא פְלִיגָא עַל רִבִּי שִׁמְעוֹן בֶּן לָקִישׁ.
וְיִרְבּוּ כָּל־הָרִימִין עַל רִימֵי שִׁקְמָא וְיִהְיוּ פְטוּרִין. אָמַר רִבִּי יוֹסֵי תִּיפְתָּר בְּמָקוֹם

שֶׁרוֹב מְשַׁמְּרִין. רִבִּי יוֹסֵי בִּרְבִּי בְּעֵי וְאֵין כָּל־הָעוֹלָם כּוּלּוֹ לְפָנָיו וְיִרְבּוּ כָּל־הָרִימִין עַל רִימֵי אוֹתוֹ מָקוֹם וְיִהְיוּ פְּטוּרִין.

Rebbi Huna said: Rebbi Jeremiah asked, does this not contradict Rebbi Simeon ben Laqish[64]? Should not all lotus fruit be more than the lotus fruit of Shiqmana, should they not be free? Rebbi Yose said, explain it at a place where most people store it[65]. Rebbi Yose the Great[66] asked: Is not the entire world before him, should not all lotus fruit be more than the lotus fruit of this place and be free?

64 This question seems directed both to the problem of vinegar just discussed and the statement of R. Jehudah in the Mishnah, that all lotus fruit is exempt except that of Shiqmana, since R. Jehudah and the anonymous Tosephta exempt all vinegar, even when it is known not to have been tithed. Similarly, a doubt whether lotus fruit is valued at some place should not make them obligated since there still is a twofold doubt: perhaps these fruits come from another place, and if they do come from Shiqmana, perhaps they are not gathered to be stored. This is exactly the case in which R. Simeon ben Laqish declares them to be free. There is no problem for R. Johanan since he equates the rules for untithed and *demay* in all these cases.

65 Not only do they store it but, since it is an object of trade only at this place. There is no doubt that the fruits in question are local.

66 Not known otherwise. Possibly it should read: Rebbi Yose ben Rebbi X. But the second name is also missing in the Rome manuscript. The question is not answered.

(fol. 21c) **משנה ב**: הַדְּמַאי אֵין לוֹ חוֹמֶשׁ וְאֵין לוֹ בִּיעוּר וְנֶאֱכַל לְאוֹנֵן וְנִכְנַס לִירוּשָׁלַ͏ִם וְיוֹצֵא וּמְאַבְּדִין אֶת מִיעוּטוֹ בַּדְּרָכִים וְנוֹתְנוֹ לְעַם הָאָרֶץ וְאוֹכְלוֹ כְּנֶגְדּוֹ וּמְחַלֵּל אוֹתוֹ כֶּסֶף עַל כֶּסֶף וּנְחוֹשֶׁת עַל נְחוֹשֶׁת כֶּסֶף עַל נְחוֹשֶׁת וּנְחוֹשֶׁת

עַל הַפֵּירוֹת וּבִלְבַד שֶׁיַּחֲזוֹר וְיִפְדֶּה אֶת הַפֵּירוֹת דִּבְרֵי רִבִּי מֵאִיר. וַחֲכָמִים אוֹמְרִים יֵעָלוּ הַפֵּירוֹת וְיֵאָכְלוּ בִּירוּשָׁלַ͏ִם.

Mishnah 2: *Demay*[67] is not subject to a fifth[68] or to elimination[69], it may be eaten by a strict mourner[70], it may enter Jerusalem and leave it[71], and one may destroy a small part of it on the road[72]; he may give it to the *am haärez* if he eats correspondingly[73], he may redeem silver for silver, copper for copper, silver for copper[74], and copper for produce[75] if he again redeems the produce, the words of Rebbi Meïr. But the Sages say, produce should be brought up and eaten in Jerusalem.

67 The subject is the Second Tithe. How far the Mishnah might be applicable to the heave of the tithe will be discussed in the Halakhah.

68 If the Second Tithe is redeemed by money so that the produce itself becomes profane, one fifth (from above, a quarter from below) must be added (*Lev*. 27:31). This does not apply to the Second Tithe of *Demay*.

69 The Second Tithe must be consumed at the latest during the year when the Tithe of the Poor is due, i. e., the tithes of years 1, 2 of the Sabbatical cycle must be eaten before the end of year 3, those of years 4,5 by the end of year 6 (*Deut*. 26:13).

70 The אונן, the strict mourner, is a close relative of a deceased person from the time of death to the end of the day of burial when he must concentrate on the duties of burial and is excluded from all other religious rites (*Deut*. 26:14). Since the Second Tithe of *demay* does not have the sanctity of Second Tithe, it is not deemed subject to that prohibition.

71 Genuine Second Tithe may not leave Jerusalem after having entered but must be consumed there. This is the position of the anonymous Tanna in Mishnah *Maäser Šeni* 3:5. [According to Rabban Simeon ben Gamliel, all Second Tithe may leave Jerusalem. In the Babli (*Baba Mezia'* 54b) the prohibition is given rabbinic character only. Maimonides (*Maäser Šeni* 2:9) restricts this part of the Mishnah to *demay* itself, not the Second Tithe taken from *demay*, on the basis of a discussion in tractate *Maäser Šeni* 3:4, as explained by the commentators of

Maimonides.]

72 Genuine Second Tithe must be brought to Jerusalem intact. The Halakhah will define "small part".

73 The *am haärez̧* is a person who cannot be presumed to eat his food, other than sacrifices, in ritual purity; cf. the definition of *am haärez̧* in the Introduction. The Second Tithe is not a sacrifice but nevertheless must be eaten in ritual purity (*Deut.* 24:16); hence, genuine Second Tithe may not be shared with the *am haärez̧*. For the Second Tithe of *demay*, if it is too little for a meal, the owner may give that to the *am haärez̧* in preference to have it entirely wasted, but nevertheless the owner has to spend of his own money to buy pure food in the same amount to eat in purity (Maimonides *Maäser Šeni* 3:9).

74 Genuine Second Tithe must be redeemed with silver coins (*Deut.* 14:25); it may not be redeemed in copper, neither may the silver be exchanged for copper. [As a matter of practice, it is permitted to exchange silver coins for gold coins to reduce their weight (*Maäser Šeni* 2:7).]

75 Outside of Jerusalem; R. Meïr permits these vegetables to be redeemed again; the Sages require them to be eaten in Jerusalem. By contrast, everybody agrees that it is possible to exchange coins many times for other coins.

(fol. 21d) **הלכה ב**: לֹא כְּיוֹחָנָן כֹּהֵן גָּדוֹל הֶעֱבִיר[76] הוֹדָיַית הַמַּעֲשֵׂר. הֶעֱבִירָן שֶׁלֹּא יִתְוַדּוּ. הָא לְבָעֵר צָרִיךְ לְבָעֵר וּבְוַדַּאי. אֲבָל בִּדְמַאי אֵינוֹ צָרִיךְ לְבָעֵר.

Halakhah 2: Not following the High Priest Joḥanan who abolished the declaration of tithes[77]. He abolished the declaration but one still has to eliminate, i. e., eliminate the sure tithes. But *demay* one does not have to eliminate[78].

76 Reading of all manuscripts. The print has a typographical error הבעיר.

77 Mishnah *Maäser Šeni* 5:13: "The High Priest Joḥanan removed the declaration of tithes." Since at the return from Babylonia the priests returned *en masse* but almost no Levites came, the returnees decreed to give the First Tithe to the Cohen (who automatically also is a Levite.) The

declaration of tithes, to be recited when the Second Tithe was brought to Jerusalem, is *Deut.* 26:13-14: "You shall say before the Eternal, your God: I have eliminated the holy matter from my house, I gave it to the Levite (the First Tithe), the stranger, the orphan, and the widow (the Tithe of the Poor), following all Your ordinances that You commanded me, I did not transgress Your ordinances and I did not forget. I did not eat from it in my strict mourning, I did not eliminate it (by eating) in impurity, I did not give of it to the dead. I listened to the voice of the Eternal, my God, I did all that You commanded me." The High Priest found it inappropriate to declare that tithes were given to the Levite when in fact they went to the Cohen.

78 There is no contradiction to the Mishnah in *Maäser Šeni.*

תַּנֵּי נֶאֱכַל בָּאֲנִינָה וְאֵינוֹ נֶאֱכַל בְּטוּמְאָה. מַה בֵּין אֲנִינָה וּמַה בֵּין טוּמְאָה. אָמַר רַב נַחְמָן טוּמְאָה מְצוּיָה אֲנִינָה אֵינָהּ מְצוּיָה. גָּֽזְרוּ עַל דָּבָר שֶׁהוּא מָצוּי וְלֹא גָֽזְרוּ עַל דָּבָר שֶׁאֵינוֹ מָצוּי. אָמַר רִבִּי יוֹסֵי אֲפִילוּ כְּסָפֵק טֶבֶל לֹא עָשׂוּ אוֹתוֹ. אִילּוּ בְּסָפֵק טֶבֶל [79]נִיתְקַן מַחְמַת שֵׁנִי סָפֵק לֹא נִתְקַן שֶׁמָּא אֵינוֹ אָסוּר לְאוֹנֵן. בְּרַם הָכָא מוּתָּר לְאוֹנֵן.

It was stated: It may be eaten in strict mourning but not in impurity. What is the difference between strict mourning and impurity? Rav Naḥman said, impurity is frequent, strict mourning is infrequent. They made a decree for a frequent situation, they did not decree for an infrequent situation[80]. Rebbi Yose said, they did not even make it similar to a doubt of *ṭevel*[81]. Since for a doubt of *ṭevel*, whether Second Tithe was given in order, or maybe Second Tithe was not given in order, is that not forbidden for the strict mourner[82]? But here, it is permitted to the mourner.

79 It seems that here a second ספק has been omitted.

80 This principle is also invoked several times in the Babli, cf. *Ketubot* 56b, *Nazir* 55a.

81 *Ṭevel* is defined in *Peah,*

82 Since a doubt in matters of Biblical prohibitions always must be treated as prohibition.

Chapter 1, Note 303. Produce that may be Ṭevel must be treated as if the holy parts were still in it.

תַּמָּן תַּנֵּינָן הַתְּרוּמָה וּתְרוּמַת מַעֲשֵׂר וּתְרוּמַת מַעֲשֵׂר שֶׁל דְּמַאי. וְהָכָא אַתְּ אָמַר הָכֵן. אָמַר רִבִּי זְעִירָא תַּמָּן תַּנֵּינָן תְּרוּמַת מַעֲשֵׂר שֶׁל דְּמַאי. בְּרַם הָכָא מַעֲשֵׂר שֵׁנִי שֶׁל דְּמַאי. אָמַר רִבִּי אִימִּי אֵין הַמִּשְׁנָה הַזֶּה יוֹצֵא יְדֵי תְּרוּמַת מַעֲשֵׂר שֶׁל דְּמַאי. מַהוּ כְדוֹן תַּמָּן רִבִּי מֵאִיר בְּרַם הָכָא רַבָּנִין. רִבִּי זְעִירָא אָמַר בְּשֵׁם רַבָּנִין בְּדִין הָיָה תְּרוּמַת מַעֲשֵׂר שֶׁל דְּמַאי שֶׁלֹּא יַפְרִישׁ עָלֶיהָ חוֹמֶשׁ וְלָמָּה אָמְרוּ שֶׁיַּפְרִישׁ מִפְּנֵי גְדֵירָהּ שֶׁאִם אַתְּ אוֹמֵר לוֹ שֶׁלֹּא יַפְרִישׁ אַף הוּא אֵינוֹ נוֹהֵג בָּהּ בִּקְדוּשָּׁה. כְּדוֹן הָיָה מַעֲשֵׂר שֵׁנִי שֶׁל דְּמַאי שֶׁיַּפְרִישׁ עָלֶיהָ חוֹמֶשׁ וְלָמָּה אָמַר שֶׁלֹּא יַפְרִישׁ מִפְּנֵי גְדֵירוֹ שֶׁאִם אוֹמֵר אַתְּ לוֹ שֶׁיַּפְרִישׁ אַף הוּא אֵינוֹ מַפְרִישׁ כָּל־עִיקָּר.

There, we have stated[83]: "Heave, the heave of the tithe, and the heave of the tithe of *demay*." And here you say so[84]! Rebbi Zeïra said, there we have stated heave of the tithe of *demay* but here Second Tithe of *demay*[85]. Rebbi Immi said, the Mishnah does not stop to deal with the heave of the tithe of *demay*. What is that? There it is Rebbi Meïr, but here the rabbis[86]. Rebbi Zeïra said in the name of the rabbis[87]: It would have been logical that for the heave of the tithe of *demay* one would not have to add a fifth[88]; why did they say that one has to add a fifth? Because of a fence for it[89], for if you tell him that he does not have to add, he will not treat it as holy. It would have been logical that for the Second Tithe of *demay* one would have to add a fifth[90]; why did they say that one does not have to add a fifth? Because of a fence for it, for if you tell him that he has to add, he will not separate it at all[91].

83 Mishnah *Baba Meẓia'* 3:7. The Mishnah enumerates five cases in which one has to add a fifth to the redemption money.

84 If the Mishnah here also deals with the heave of the tithe of *demay*, it would be an obvious contradiction of one Mishnah against the other.

85 The Mishnah does not deal with heave at all.

86 Usually, an anonymous Mishnah gives the opinion of R. Meïr. R. Immi asserts that as an exception, this Mishnah does not.

87 He gives the argument to support his own position. Since it is undisputed, it represents practice.

88 Since one does not add a fifth for *demay* as stated in the Mishnah.

89 Rabbinic ordinances are always described as "a fence around the Law" (Mishnah *Abot* 1:1). Babylonian גזירה "rabbinic ordinance" is a derivative of Galilean גדירה "fence", *z* for ð.

90 If one adds one for the heave of the tithe, since the Second Tithe also has to be consumed in purity.

91 One requires the separation of Second Tithe of *demay*, in contrast to the First Tithe and the tithe of the poor, since the Second Tithe will not burden the buyer. Anything that makes it burdensome (and, in the absence of the Temple, when the coin used for redemption has to be destroyed, also costly) will cause people to ignore their duty.

רִבִּי בּוּן בַּר חִיָּיא בְּעָא קוֹמֵי רִבִּי לָא לָמָּה לִי דְמַאי אֲפִילוּ וַדַּאי. לָמָּה לִי מִיעוּט אֲפִילוּ רוֹב. וְלֹא כֵן תַּנֵּי אֵין מְבִיאִין תְּרוּמָה מִן הַגּוֹרֶן לָעִיר וְלֹא מִן הַמִּדְבָּר לְיִישׁוּב אֶלָּא אִם כֵּן הָיְתָה בְמָקוֹם שֶׁהָיְתָה גְרָרְתָהּ מְבִיאָהּ וְנוֹטֵל דָּמִים מִן הַשֵּׁבֶט. אָמַר לֵיהּ וְאֵינוֹ מִצְוָה לְהָשִׁיב אֲבֵידָה. אָמַר רִבִּי יוֹסֵי מִצְוָה הִיא לְהָשִׁיב אֲבֵידָה בְּדָבָר מוּעָט. וְאֵינוֹ מִצְוָה לְהָשִׁיב אֲבֵידָה בְּדָבָר מְרוּבָּה. וּבְוַדַּאי אֲבָל בִּדְמַאי אֵינוֹ מִצְוָה לְהָשִׁיב אֲבֵידָה. דְּתַנֵּינָן וּמְאַבְּדִין אֶת מִיעוּטוֹ בַּדְּרָכִים. עַד כְּדוֹן בְּשֶׁאֵין בְּיָדוֹ מָעוֹת. הָיוּ בְיָדוֹ מָעוֹת רִבִּי נְחוּמִי בְּרֵיהּ דְּרִבִּי חִיָּיא בַּר בָּא אָמַר (אַבָּא[92]) הָיוּ מָעוֹת בְּדִיסַקְיָא וְלֹא הָיָה מְחַלְּלוֹ. אַתְיָא דְּרִבִּי חִיָּיא בְּרִבִּי וָוא כְּרִבִּי זְעִירָא וּדְרִבִּי אָחָא כְּרִבִּי אִמִּי.

Rebbi Abun bar Ḥiyya asked before Rebbi La[93]: Why *demay* and not also what is certain[94], why a little bit, maybe the greater part? Did we not state: One does not bring the heave from the threshing floor to town, nor from the prairie to cultivated land[95], except in a place where [an animal[96]] would drag it away; in that case he brings it and takes money from the tribe[97]. He[98] said to him, is it not a commandment to return a find? Rebbi Yose said, it is a commandment to return a find in small matters[99]; it is not a commandment to return in large matters, except if it is certain; it is not a commandment to return *demay* since we have stated: "one may destroy a small part of it on the road". So far, if he had no money in hand[100]. If he had money in hand? Rebbi Neḥumai[101], the son of Rebbi Ḥiyya bar Abba, said, my father had money in a double sack[102] and he did not redeem. It turns out that Rebbi Ḥiyya bar Abba holds with Rebbi Zeïra[103] and Rebbi Aḥa[104] with Rebbi Immi.

92 Reading of R. Simson of Sens; the word fell out by haplography.

93 Here starts the discussion of the Mishnah: "one may destroy a small part of it on the road." The question is again whether this refers only to the Second Tithe or also to the heave of the tithe. It seems that the same interpretation given to the question of the fifth applies here also.

94 Heave or Second Tithe, which are unquestionably holy, being given straight from the harvest, or on information that the produce is still *ṭevel*.

95 The recipient of heave is required to collect it where it is due and remove it himself.

96 While there is no direct manuscript evidence, it seems that היתה גררתה is a misspelling for חיה גררתה. The reading היתה is an old one since R. Simson of Sens reads היתה גדודתה and explains "it was in danger of armies (or groups of robbers)." גררתה seems to be the better reading.

97 The Cohen who took the heave has to pay the cost of transportation. The question presupposes that the Mishnah also applies to the heave of the tithe from *demay*.

98 Rebbi La to Rebbi Abun. If the heave is abandoned until some Cohen will come to pick it up, it probably will be lost.

99 If presenting the heave to the

Cohen involves little effort and little expenditure, one is certainly obligated to hand over the heave to the Cohen to prevent it from being lost. However, if the effort or expenditure were large, one has no such obligation. (Explanation of R. Eliahu Wilna.)

100 If someone has difficulty handling the Second Tithe, rather than let some of it get lost as authorized in the Mishnah, would it not be better to have the owner redeem it for money which will not get spoiled or lost? Should we restrict the Mishnah to the most unlikely case where the owner has no money for redemption?

101 Nothing else is known about him. Neḥumai is a Babylonian name; the family of R. Ḥiyya bar Abba was Babylonian.

102 Byzantine Greek δισάκκιον "double sack", hanging down on both sides of a donkey; cf. *Berakhot* p. 319.

103 Since he permits the Second Tithe of *demay* to go to waste, he explains the Mishnah here to refer exclusively to Second Tithe. Since in the times of R. Ḥiyya bar Abba heave already had to be burned because all Cohanim were ritually impure in the absence of the ashes of the red heifer, the reference could not possibly be to heave.

104 Since Rebbi Aḥa is not mentioned in the entire Halakhah, this must be a scribal error for Rebbi La, who explains the Mishnah in *Baba Meẓia'* by the duty of conserving other people's property in the same way as something found. Hence, R. La accepts that the Mishnah here also speaks of the heave of the tithe of *demay*, as proposed by R. Immi.

דְּבֵי רִבִּי יַנַּאי אָמְרוּ פָּחוֹת מֵאֹכֶל מוּתָּר לְאַבֵּד בְּפָרוּס אֲבָל בְּשָׁלֵם עַד כִּגְרוֹגֶרֶת. רִבִּי יוֹחָנָן בְּשֵׁם רִבִּי שִׁמְעוֹן בֶּן יוֹצָדָק בְּשָׁלֵם עַד כִּגְרוֹגֶרֶת בְּפָרוּס אֲפִילוּ כַּמָּה מוּתָּר. מַה פְּלִיגִין. רִבִּי מָנָא אָמַר לֹא פְלִיגִין. דְּבֵי רִבִּי יַנַּאי אָמְרוּ פָּחוֹת מֵאוֹכֶל מוּתָּר לְאַבֵּד בְּפָרוּס אֲבָל בְּשָׁלֵם עַד כִּגְרוֹגֶרֶת. רִבִּי יוֹחָנָן אָמַר בְּשֵׁם רִבִּי שִׁמְעוֹן בֶּן יוֹצָדָק בֵּין בְּפָרוּס בֵּין בְּשָׁלֵם עַד כִּגְרוֹגֶרֶת.

In the house of Rebbi Yannai they said, if it is in crumbs one is permitted to waste in amounts less than a meal[105], but whole foods only up to the volume of a dried fig. Rebbi Joḥanan in the name of R. Simeon ben Yoẓadaq: If it is whole, up to the volume of a dried fig, in crumbs any amount[106]. Is that their difference? Rebbi Mana said, is not the following their difference: In the house of Rebbi Yannai they said, if it is in crumbs one is permitted to waste in amounts less than a meal, whole foods only up to the volume of a dried fig. Rebbi Joḥanan in the name of R. Simeon ben Yoẓadaq, whether it be whole or in crumbs, up to the volume of a dried fig.

105 Generally taken to be the volume of a chicken egg.

106 In this version, R. Joḥanan is more lenient than the House of R. Yannai; in the alternative version he is more restrictive. Maimonides interprets "up to" as "less than," R. Abraham ben David as "not more than."

רִבִּי הוֹשַׁעְיָא בְּעֵי מָהוּ לְאַבֵּד כָּל־שֶׁהוּא וּלְאַבֵּד. וְנוֹתְנוֹ לְעַם הָאָרֶץ לוֹכַל כְּנֶגְדּוֹ בִּדְמַאי. הָא בְּוַדַּאי לֹא שֶׁאֵין מוֹסְרִין וַדַּאי לְעַם הָאָרֶץ.

Rebbi Hoshaia asked: May one allow a small amount to go to waste[107]? One may give it to the *am haärez* and eat from *demay* accordingly. But not for certain food[108], since one does not hand over certain food to the *am haärez*.

107 If one has to give only a small amount, less than the volume of a dried fig, and he has no other use for it, may he give it to the *am haärez* or does he have the right to directly throw it away? (R. Eliahu Fulda and his followers change לאבד into להפריש, "to separate", but this emendation is unnecessary.) Since the question is not answered it should be answered in the negative (Maimonides *Maäser Šeni* 3:9, with concurrence of R. Abraham ben David.)

108 Food for which it is certain that it has to be consumed in ritual purity.

(fol. 21c) **משנה ג**: הַלּוֹקֵחַ לְזֶרַע וְלִבְהֵמָה קֶמַח לְעוֹרוֹת וְשֶׁמֶן לְנֵר שֶׁמֶן לָסוּךְ בּוֹ אֶת הַכֵּלִים פָּטוּר מִן הַדְּמַאי. מִן גְּזִיב וּלְהַלָּן פָּטוּר מִן הַדְּמַאי. חַלַּת עַם הָאָרֶץ וְהַמְּדוּמָע וְהַלָּקוּחַ בְּכֶסֶף מַעֲשֵׂר שְׁיָרֵי מְנָחוֹת פְּטוּרִין מִן הַדְּמַאי. וְשֶׁמֶן עָרֵב בֵּית שַׁמַּאי מְחַיְּיבִין וּבֵית הִלֵּל פּוֹטְרִין.

Mishnah 3: He who buys as seeds or animal fodder, flour for tanning, oil for lighting, or oil to rub on vessels[109], is free from *demay*[110]. From Akhzib and further he is free from *demay*[111]. *Ḥallah*[112] of the *am haärez*, food containing heave[113], food bought with money of the Second Tithe, and the remainders of flour sacrifices[114] are free from *demay*. Sweet oil[115], the House of Shammai declare it obligated but the House of Hillel declare it free.

109 However, oil used as lotion is subject to *demay*, since rubbing on is everywhere equated to drinking.

110 The obligation of heave and tithes falls only on foodstuffs, not on industrial materials.

111 Explained in Halakhah 1.

112 The heave of the dough made for bread, which is given to the Cohen.

113 Which either has to be consumed by the priest or heave has to be taken from it as certain heave. Heave is called דמע in *Ex*. 22:28.

114 The offering of a handful for the altar was taken and the rest eaten by male Cohanim in the Temple precinct under the strict rules of sacrifices. For all of these, *demay* was never intended as it would make no sense.

115 Perfumed oil for the House of Shammai is a lotion, for the House of Hillel it is a perfume. Cf. Note 155.

(fol. 21d) **הלכה ג**: מִכֵּיוָן שֶׁלְּקָחוֹ לְזֶרַע לֹא שַׁנְיָיא הִיא דָּבָר שֶׁזַּרְעוֹ כָּלֶה הִיא דָּבָר שֶׁאֵין זַרְעוֹ כָּלֶה. אָמַר רִבִּי יוֹחָנָן וְתַנֵּי כֵּן לְקָחָן לְזֶרַע וְחִישֵּׁב עֲלֵיהֶן לַאֲכִילָה בָּאִין מַחֲשָׁבָה. לְקָחָן לַאֲכִילָה וְחִישֵּׁב עֲלֵיהֶן לְזֶרַע לֹא הַכֹּל מִמֶּנּוּ.

Halakhah 3: Since he bought it as seeds there is no difference whether it is something of which the seed disappears or something of which the seed does not disappear[116]. Rebbi Johanan said, we have stated this[117]: "If he bought as seeds and then changed his mind to use them for consumption, they enter[118] by thought. If he bought for consumption and then changed his mind to use them as seeds, not all is from him[119]."

116 In contrast to certain heave, where seeds which do not disappear in the new growth never lose their status as heave (Mishnah *Terumot* 9:5).

117 Tosephta *Demay* 1:18, the first part of the statement discussed in the next paragraph.

118 They enter into the obligation of *demay* by his thought.

119 Meaning, nothing results from his thought; his intentions may introduce the obligation of *demay* but cannot remove it.

תַּנֵּי אֵין זוֹרְעִין טֶבֶל וְאֵין[120] מְחַפִּין טֶבֶל אֲבָל מְחַפִּין עִם הַגּוֹי טֶבֶל. הַשֹּׁכֵחַ וְזָרַע טֶבֶל פָּטוּר שֶׁכְּבָר אָבַד. בְּדָבָר שֶׁאֵין דַּרְכּוֹ לְהִתְלַקֵּט אֲבָל בְּדָבָר שֶׁדַּרְכּוֹ לְהִתְלַקֵּט קוֹנְסִין אוֹתוֹ שֶׁיְּלַקֵּט אוֹתוֹ בְּלֹא צֶמַח. אֲבָל אִם צוֹמֵחַ נַעֲשֶׂה כְּדָבָר שֶׁאֵין דַּרְכּוֹ לְהִתְלַקֵּט.

It was stated[121]: One does not sow *ṭevel*, one may not cover *ṭevel*[122], but one covers *ṭevel* with a Gentile[123]. If one forgot and sowed *ṭevel*, he is free[124], for it is already lost if it is something that usually is not collected;, but for something that usually is collected[125], he is fined to collect it before it sprouts. But if it sprouted, it turns into something that usually is not collected.

120 Reading of Rome manuscript. The Venice text and Leyden manuscript have אבל, which is contradicted by the next clause.

121 Tosephta *Demay* 1:18: "One does not sow *ṭevel*, nor does one cover

ṭevel; one does not work *ṭevel* with a Gentile. A Jew who forgot and sowed *ṭevel*, before it sprouted he is obligated, after it sprouted he is free because it already is lost." The language of the Yerushalmi (Rome ms.) is preferable; since if one does not work on *ṭevel* with a Gentile, it is obvious that one cannot do it alone. [Maimonides (*Maäser* 3:6) omits the mention of the Gentile, possibly because of the two contradictory sources.]

122 Produce lying on the ground (or in a ditch) may not be covered with earth before heaves have been given.

123 In joint ownership.

124 From giving heave and tithes from the seeds, since they no longer exist.

125 Which can be recovered from the soil in usable (edible) state. In that case, he must remove the produce from the soil, give heaves, and only then may he return the remainder to the ground.

אָמְרוּ רִבִּי יוֹחָנָן כַּד הֲוָה אֲכַל אֲפִילוּ קוֹפָּד אֲפִילוּ בֵּיעָה הֲוָה מְתַקֵּן. אָמְרוּ לֵיהּ תַּלְמִידוֹי לֹא כֵן אִילְפָן רִבִּי עַשֵּׂר תְּעַשֵּׂר אֶת כָּל־תְּבוּאַת זַרְעֶךָ. דּוּ חָשַׁשׁ לַמַּשְׁקִין שֶׁיֵּשׁ בָּהֶן.

They said that Rebbi Johanan was putting in order[126] everything he ate, even red meat, even an egg. His students said to him: Did our teacher not teach us (*Deut.* 14:22): "You shall certainly tithe all the yield of your field[127]." He was worried about the fluids[128] in it.

126 If anything of *demay* was used in cooking, he gave heave of the tithe and redeemed the Second Tithe for everything. "Putting in order" everywhere means giving heave and tithes to permit the food for consumption.

127 Excluding anything not vegetal.

128 Wine and oils used in cooking; because of the part absorbed in the meat, he gave heave from everything.

רִבִּי יִרְמְיָה שְׁלַח לְרִבִּי זְעִירָא חָדָא מְסָאנָא דִתְאֵנִים דְּלָא מְתַקְּנָא. וַהֲוָה רִבִּי יִרְמְיָה סְבַר מֵימַר מַה רִבִּי זְעִירָא מֵיכוּל דְּלָא מְתַקְּנָא. וַהֲוָה רִבִּי זְעִירָא סְבַר מֵימַר מַה אֵיפְשַׁר דְּרִבִּי יִרְמְיָה מְשַׁלְּחָה לִי מִילָּא דְּלָא מְתַקְּנָא. מַה בֵּין דֵּין

לְדֵין אִיתַּכְלַת טֵבֶל. לְמָחָר קָם עִימֵּיהּ אֲמַר לֵיהּ הַהִיא מְסָנְתָא דְּשָׁלַחְתְּ לִי אֶתְמֹל מְתַקְּנָא הֲוָת. אֲמַר לֵיהּ אֲמְרִית מַה רִבִּי זְעִירָא מֵיכוּל מִילָּא דְּלָא מְתַקְּנָה. אֲמַר לֵיהּ אוּף אֲנָא אֲמְרִית כֵּן הֲוָה רִבִּי יִרְמְיָה מְשַׁלְּחָה לִי מִילָּה דְּלָא מְתַקְּנֵיהּ. רִבִּי אַבָּא בַּר זְמִינָא[129] בְּשֵׁם רִבִּי זְעִירָא אָמַר אִין הֲווֹן קַדְמָאֵי בְּנֵי מַלְאָכִים אֲנָן בְּנֵי נַשׁ. וְאִין הֲווֹן בְּנֵי נַשׁ אֲנָן חֲמָרִין. אָמַר רִבִּי מָנָא בְּהַהִיא שַׁתָּא אָמְרִין אֲפִילוּ לַחֲמָרְתֵיהּ דְּרִבִּי פִּינְחָס בֶּן יָאִיר לָא אִידְמִינָן.

Rebbi Jeremiah sent Rebbi Zeïra a basket of figs that were not put in order. Rebbi Jeremiah said to himself, would Rebbi Zeïra eat anything that was not put in order? Rebbi Zeïra said to himself, it is impossible that Rebbi Jeremiah would send me anything that was not put in order. In the meantime, *ṭevel* was eaten. The next day, when he was with him, he asked him: Was that basket you sent me put in order? He answered him, I said, would Rebbi Zeïra eat anything that was not put in order? He answered, I also said, would Rebbi Jeremiah send me anything that was not put in order[130]? Rebbi Abba bar Zemina[131] said in the name of Rebbi Zeïra: If the earlier generations were angels, we are men; if they were men, we are donkeys[132]. Rebbi Mana said, at that moment[133] they said, we are not even comparable to the she-ass of Rebbi Phineas ben Yaïr[134].

129 Text of the Rome manuscript, this is also the name quoted in several other passages in the Yerushalmi. The Venice/Leyden text has זמינה.

130 The moral of the story is that among observant Jews it is necessary to spell out whether food is tithed or not. Food originating with the *am haärez* is automatically put in order by the rules of *demay*; this story extends the duty of *demay* to food from the observant unless there is a declaration.

131 An Amora of the Fourth Generation, student of R. Zeïra.

132 Quoted in Babli *Sabbat* 112b. The parallel is *Šeqalim* fol. 48c, Midrash *Gen. rabba* 60.

133 When *ṭevel* was eaten and nobody suspected that it was not in order.

134 A Tanna of the Fifth Generation, son-in-law of R. Simeon bar Ioḥai. No halakhic statements of his are known. He is the paradigm of a holy man.

חֲמָרְתֵיהּ דְּרִבִּי פִּינְחָס בֶּן יָאִיר גְּנָבוּנָהּ לִיסְטֵיֵי בְּלֵילְיָא עָבְדָת טְמוּרָה גַּבָּן תְּלָתָא יוֹמִין דְּלָא טַעֲמָא כְּלוּם. בָּתַר תְּלָתָא יוֹמִין אִיתְמַלְּכוּן מַחֲזָרְתָהּ לְמָרָהּ. אָמְרִין נִישַׁלְחִינָהּ לְמָרָהּ דְּלָא לִימוּת לְגַבָּן וְתִיסְרִי מְעָרְתָא. אַפְקוּנָהּ וְקָמַת עַל תּוּרְעַת דְּמָרָהּ שׁוּרִייַת מְנַהֲקָה אֲמַר לוֹן פּוּתְחוּן לַהֲדָא עֲלִיבְתָא דְּאִית לָהּ תְּלָתָה יוֹמִין דְּלָא טְעִימַת כְּלוּם. פְּתְחוּן לָהּ וַעֲלַת לָהּ. אֲמַר לוֹן יְהָבוּן[135] לָהּ כְּלוּם תֵּיכוּל. יְהָבוּן קוֹמָהּ שְׂעָרִין וְלָא בְעִית מֵיכוּל. אָמְרֵי לֵיהּ רִבִּי (fol. 22a) לָא בְעִית מֵיכוּל. אֲמַר לוֹן מְתַקְּנָן אִינּוּן. אָמְרוּ לֵיהּ אִין. אֲמַר לוֹן וַאֲרֵימִיתֵּן דְּמַיָּן. אָמְרוּ לֵיהּ וְלֹא כֵן אִילְפָן רִבִּי הַלּוֹקֵחַ לְזֶרַע וְלִבְהֵמָה קֶמַח לְעוֹרוֹת וְשֶׁמֶן לְנֵר שֶׁמֶן לָסוּךְ בּוֹ אֶת הַכֵּלִים פָּטוּר מִן הַדְּמַאי. אֲמַר לוֹן מַה נֵיעֲבִיד לְהָדָא עֲלִיבְתָא דְּהִיא מַחְמְרָה עַל גַּרְמָהּ סַגִּין. וַאֲרִימוּן דְּמַיָּן וְאָכְלַת.

Thieves stole the she-ass of Rebbi Phineas ben Yaïr at night. She was hidden with them for three days during which she did not eat anything. After three days, they took counsel to return her to her master. They said, let us send her to her master lest she die with us and foul up the cave. They let her out; she stood at her master's door and started braying. He said to them[136], open to that poor creature because for three days now she did not taste anything. They opened for her and she entered. He said to them, give her something to eat. They put oats before her but she did not eat. They said to him, rabbi, she does not want to eat. He asked them, did you put it in order? They said: Yes. He asked them, did you remove its *demay*? They said, did the rabbi not teach us: "He who buys for seeds or animals, flour for tanning, oil for lighting, or oil to rub vessels, is free from *demay*." He said to them, what can we do with this poor creature since she is very restrictive for herself[137]? They removed the *demay* and she ate.

135 Reading of Midrash and *Šeqalim*. The Venice print has יתבון "they sat".

136 "He" is always R. Phineas, "they" his family and servants.

137 The she-ass refused to eat anything she could not eat if she were a Jewish human. A Babylonian version of the second part of the story is in Babli *Ḥulin* 7a/b; the first part of the story is told of the she-ass of R. Ḥanina ben Dosa in *Aboth de Rabbi Nathan*, Version 1, end of Chapter 8. Both stories are referred to in Babli *Šabbat* 112b. The Yerushalmi version is also in *Gen. rabba* 60.

תְּרֵין מִסְכֵּינִין אַפְקְדוּן תְּרֵין סְאִין דִשְׂעָרִין גַּבֵּי רִבִּי פִּינְחָס בֶּן יָאִיר זְרָעוֹן וְחַצְדוֹן. וְאַעֲלוֹן בְּעֵיָין מֵיסַב שְׂעָרֵיהוֹן. אֲמַר לוֹן אַייתוּן גַּמְלַיָּא וְחֲמָרַיָּא וּסְבוּן שְׂעָרֵיהוֹן.

Two poor people entrusted two *se'ah* of barley to Rebbi Phineas ben Yaïr; he sowed them and harvested them. They came to him and wanted to take their barley. He said to them, bring camels and donkeys to carry their barley[138].

138 This story and the following one are told, in Hebrew, also in Midrash *Deut. rabba* 3(4). There, he replanted the crop for seven years.

רִבִּי פִּינְחָס בֶּן יָאִיר אֲזַל לְחַד אֲתַר אֲתוּן לְגַבֵּיהּ אָמְרוּן לֵיהּ עַכְבָּרַיָּא אָכַל עִיבּוּרָן. גְּזַר עֲלֵיהֹן וְצַמְתּוּן שָׁרוּן מְצַפְצְפִין אֲמַר לוֹן יָדְעִין אַתּוּן מַה אִינּוּן אָמְרִין אָמְרוּ לֵיהּ לָא. אֲמַר לוֹן אָמְרוּ דְלָא מְתַקְּנָא. אָמְרוּ לֵיהּ עוֹרְבָן וְעָרְבוֹן וְלָא אַנְכּוּן.

Rebbi Phineas ben Yaïr went to a place where they[139] came to him and said, the rats are eating our grain. He commanded them[140]; they assembled and started to whistle. He asked them, do you understand what they are saying? They said, no. He said to them, they say that it is not put in order. They said to him, be our guarantor. He promised[141] and they had no further losses.

139 The farmers of that place.

140 The rats.

141 That the rats would leave if all tithes were taken. It is implied that the townspeople complied and correctly gave all heave and tithes.

מַרְגְּלִי מִן דְּמַלְכָּא סַרְקִיָּא נָפְלַת וּבָלְעַת חַד עַכְבָּר. אֲתָא לְגַבֵּי רִבִּי פִּינְחָס בֶּן יָאִיר אֲמַר לֵיהּ מִן אֲנָא חֲבַר. אֲמַר לֵיהּ לִשְׁמָךְ טָבָא אָתִית. גָּזַר עֲלֵיהֹן וְצַמְתּוּן. חָמָא חַד מְגַבַּע וְאָתֵי אֲמַר גַּבֵּי הָהֵן נִיהוּ וּגְזַר עֲלוֹי וּפְלָטָהּ.

A pearl of the king of Saracens[142] fell and was swallowed by a rat. He came to Rebbi Phineas ben Yaïr, who said to him, am I a sorcerer? He answered, I came because of your good name. He commanded them[140]; they assembled. He saw one coming that was hunchbacked. He said, it is in this one; he gave the rat a command and it spat out the pearl.

142 It is not clear whether Arabs were already called Saracens at that time; related words are Arabic שרק "Eastern" and סראק "big robber."

רִבִּי פִּינְחָס בֶּן יָאִיר אֲזַל לְחַד אֲתַר אֲתוֹן לְגַבֵּיהּ אָמְרוֹן לֵיהּ לֵית מַבּוּעָן מְסַפֵּק לוֹן. אֲמַר לוֹן דִּילְמָא לָא אַתּוּן מְתַקְּנִין. אָמְרוּ לֵיהּ עוֹרְבָן וְעָרְבוֹן וְאַסְפֵּק לָהוּ.

Rebbi Phineas ben Yaïr went to a place where they[139] came to him and said, our water source is not sufficient for us. He said to them, perhaps you do not put in order? They said to him, be our guarantor. He promised them[141] and it became sufficient for them.

רִבִּי פִּינְחָס בֶּן יָאִיר הֲוָה אֲזִיל לְבֵית וַעַד וַהֲוָה גִּינַיי גְּבִיר. אֲמַר לֵיהּ גִּינַיי גִּינַיי מַה אַתְּ מְנַע לִי מִבֵּית וַעֲדָה וּפְלַג קוֹמוֹי וַעֲבַר. אֲמַר לֵיהּ תַּלְמִידָיו יָכְלִין אֲנָן עָבְרִין. אֲמַר לוֹן מַאן דְּיָדַע בְּנַפְשֵׁיהּ דְּלָא אֲקִיל לְבַר נַשׁ מִיִּשְׂרָאֵל מִן יוֹמוֹי יַעֲבוֹר וְלָא מִנְּכֶה.

Rebbi Phineas ben Yaïr went to the House of Assembly[143] when Ginai[144] overflowed. He said: Ginai, Ginai, why do you prevent me from going to the House of Assembly? It split before him and he crossed it. His students asked him, may we cross also? He said to them, he who knows of himself that he never slighted a Jew may cross and will not be harmed.

143 Probably the place at Ḥamat Gader at which the intercalation of months was decided.

144 A river, called "river Ginai" in the Babli, *Ḥulin* 7a, probably *Wadi Jenin.*

רִבִּי בְּעֵי מִישְׁרֵי שְׁמִיטְתָא סְלַק רִבִּי פִּינְחָס בֶּן יָאִיר לְגַבֵּיהּ. אֲמַר לֵיהּ מַה עִיבּוּרַיָּא עֲבִידִין. אֲמַר לֵיהּ עוּלְשִׁין יָפוֹת. מַה עִיבּוּרַיָּא עֲבִידִין. אֲמַר לֵיהּ עוּלְשִׁין יָפוֹת. וִידַע רִבִּי דְּלֵית הוּא מַסְכְּמָה עִימֵּיהּ. אֲמַר לֵיהּ מִישְׁגָּח רִבִּי מֵיכוֹל עִימִּין צִיבְחַר פְּטַל יוֹמָא דֵין. אֲמַר לֵיהּ אִין. מִי נְחֵית חֲמָא מוּלְוָתָא דְּרִבִּי קַיְימִין. אֲמַר כָּל־אִילֵּין יְהוּדָאֵי זְנִין אֵיפְשַׁר דְּלָא חֲמֵי סְבַר אַפּוֹי מִן כְּדוֹן. אָזְלִין וְאָמְרִין לְרִבִּי וּשְׁלַח רִבִּי בְּעֵי מְפַיְיסָתֵיהּ. מָטוֹן בֵּיהּ גַּבֵּי קַרְתֵּיהּ אֲמַר בְּנֵי קַרְתֵּיהּ קוֹרְבִין לִי וְנָחֲתוּ בְּנֵי קַרְתָּא וְאַקְפוּן עֲלוֹי. אֲמַר לוֹן רִבִּי בְּעֵי מְפַיְיסָתֵיהּ. שַׁבְקוּנֵיהּ וַאֲזוּל לוֹן. אֲמַר בְּנֵי דוֹדִי קוֹרְבָן לִי. נָחֲתַת אֵישְׁתָא מִן שְׁמַיָּא וְאַקְפַת עֲלוֹי. אָזְלוּן וְאָמְרִין לְרִבִּי אָמַר הוֹאִיל וְלֹא זְכִינָן נִישְׂבַּע מִינֵיהּ בְּעָלְמָא הָדֵין נִיזְכֵּי נִישְׂבַּע מִינֵיהּ בְּעָלְמָא דְּאָתֵי.

Rebbi wanted to permit the Sabbatical year[145]. Rebbi Phineas ben Yaïr went to him. He said to him: how is the grain doing? He[146] answered him: endives[147] are doing fine. He said to him: how is the grain doing?

He answered him: endives are doing fine. From this, Rebbi understood that he did not agree with him. He said to him: Would the rabbi care to eat a bite with me today? He said to him, yes. When he came, he saw the she-mules[148] of Rebbi standing. He said, are all these fed by Jews? He will not see me again! They went and told this to Rebbi. Rebbi sent and wanted to pacify him. They found him in his city. He said, the people of my city should come close to me. The people of his city came and surrounded him. They said to them, Rebbi wants to make peace with him. They left him and went away. He said, my cousins[149] should come close to me. Fire descended from Heaven and surrounded him. They returned and told Rebbi. He said, since we did not have merit to eat our fill from him in this world, may we be worthy to eat our fill from him in the World to Come.

145 Since in the absence of a Temple and the distribution of land as ordered in the Torah, the Sabbatical year is observed as a Rabbinic ordinance, Rebbi wanted to allow cultivation of the land to help pay real estate taxes that were imposed irrespective of the yield. A generation later, R. Yannai did permit the cultivation of land for the payment of taxes and delivery of requisitioned produce to the Roman army (Yerushalmi *Ševiït* 4:2, Babli *Sanhedrin* 26a, cf. Rashi there.) The parallel to the entire story is in *Taäniot* 3:1.

146 R. Phineas ben Yaïr.

147 They are irrelevant for taxes or the army.

148 Latin *mulus*. *Yoma* 8:5, it is stated that a white mule's kick is life-threatening. Hence, white mules should not be kept by Jews.

149 In *Taäniot*: "My sons."

רִבִּי חַגַּיי בְּשֵׁם רִבִּי שְׁמוּאֵל בַּר נַחְמָן מַעֲשֶׂה בְּחָסִיד אֶחָד שֶׁהָיָה חוֹפֵר בּוֹרוֹת שִׁיחִין וּמְעָרוֹת לָעוֹבְרִים וְשָׁבִים. פַּעַם אַחַת הָיְתָה בִתּוֹ עוֹבֶרֶת לִינָּשֵׂא וּשְׁטָפָהּ

נָהָר. וַהֲוֹון כָּל־עַמָּא עָלְלִין לְגַבֵּיהּ בְּעָיֵין מְנַחֲמָתֵיהּ וְלָא קְבֵיל עֲלוֹי מִתְנַחֲמָה. אֲעַל רִבִּי פִּינְחָס בֶּן יָאִיר לְגַבֵּיהּ בְּעֵי מְנַחֲמָתֵיהּ וְלָא קְבֵיל עֲלוֹי מִתְנַחֲמָה. אֲמַר לוֹן דֵּין הוּא חֲסִידְכוֹן. אֲמְרוּ לֵיהּ רִבִּי כָּךְ וְכָךְ הָיָה עוֹשֶׂה כָּךְ וְכָךְ אִירְעוֹן. אֲמַר אֵיפְשַׁר שֶׁהָיָה מְכַבֵּד אֶת בּוֹרְאוֹ בְּמַיִם וְהוּא מְקַפְּחוֹ בְּמַיִם. מִיַּד נֶפְלָה הֲבָרָה בְּעִיר בָּאַת בִּתּוֹ שֶׁל אוֹתוֹ הָאִישׁ. אִית דְּאָמְרֵי בְּסִיכְּתָא אִיתְעֲרִייַת. וְאִית דְּאָמְרֵי מַלְאַךְ יָרַד בִּדְמוּת רִבִּי פִּינְחָס בֶּן יָאִיר וְהִצִּילָהּ.

Rebbi Ḥaggai in the name of Rebbi Samuel bar Naḥman[150]: It happened that a pious person used to dig cisterns, ditches, and caves for travellers. Once, his daughter travelled to marry and she was swept away by a river. All people came to him and wanted to console him, but he refused to be consoled. Rebbi Phineas ben Yaïr came to him and wanted to console him, but he refused to be consoled. He told them, is that your pious man? They said to him: Rabbi, such and such he did, such and such happened to him. He replied: It is impossible that he would honor his Creator by water and He hurts him by water! Immediately, there started a rumor in the town that the pious man's daughter had returned. Some say, she got trapped in a hedge of thorns, others say that an angel came in the appearance of Rebbi Phineas ben Yaïr and saved her.

150 The text also appears in *Šeqalim* 5:2 and in slightly different form in Midrash *Deut. rabba* 3.

רִבִּי חֲנִינָא בֶּן דוֹסָא הֲוָה יְתִיב אֲכִיל בְּלֵילֵי שַׁבָּת פְּחַת פְּתוֹרָא קוֹמוֹי. אֲמְרוּ לֵיהּ מַהוּ כֵן. אֲמְרָה לֵיהּ תַּבְלִין שָׁאַלְתִּי מִשְּׁכֶנְתִּי וְלֹא עִישַּׂרְתִּיו. וְהִזְכִּיר תֵּינְיָין וְעָלָה הַשּׁוּלְחָן מֵאֵלָיו.

Rebbi Ḥanina ben Dosa was sitting down to eat on Friday night when the table sank before him. They said to him[151], what is that? She said to him, I borrowed spices from my neighbor and forgot to give tithes[152] from it. He mentioned a condition[153] and the table rose by itself.

151 Since the Yerushalmi is notoriously inexact with genders and numbers, it might mean: He asked her (his wife).

152 It follows that the Yerushalmi requires tithing of spices, whereas the Babli requires it only when the spice may serve as food in itself; cf. *Tosafot* and *Tosafot Yešenim* to *Yoma* 87b.

153 He mentioned the place from which he would give tithes after the Sabbath; this is an acceptable form of tithing of *demay* during the twilight hours of Friday night (Mishnah *Sabbath* 2:6). The story is inserted to show that a just person will not stumble unwittingly over a prohibition.

רִבִּי טַרְפוֹן הֲוָה יְתִיב אֲכִיל וּנְפַל פִּיתּוּתָא מִינֵיהּ. אָֽמְרוּ לֵיהּ מַהוּ כֵן. אָמַר לָהוּ קוֹרְדּוֹם שָׁאַלְתִּי וְעָשִׂיתִי עַל גַּבֵּי טְהוֹרוֹת.

Rebbi Tarphon sat down to eat when he dropped his bread. They asked him, what is this? He said to them, I borrowed an axe and I prepared food in purity with it[154].

154 Apparently the axe was not ritually pure and the bread that was made impure by this fell before he could eat it. As a Pharisee, R. Tarphon ate all his food in purity.

יַיִן לְמוּרִייֵס וְיַיִן לַאֲלוֹנְטִית קִטְנִיּוֹת לַעֲשׂוֹתוֹ טְחִינִין חַיָּבִין בִּדְמַאי וְאֵין צָרִיךְ לוֹמַר בְּוַדַּאי הֵן עַצְמָן פְּטוּרִין מִן הַדְּמַאי. מַה נָן קַיָּמִין אִין כְּרִבִּי אֲפִילוּ בִדְמַאי יְהוֹ חַיָּבִין אִין כְּרִבִּי אֶלְעָזָר בֵּי רִבִּי שִׁמְעוֹן אֲפִילוּ בְּוַדַּאי יְהוֹ פְּטוּרִין. אֶלָּא רִבִּי אֲנָן אָֽמְרִין בְּקַלִּין שֶׁהֵקִילוּ בִדְמַאי.

"[155]Wine for brine[156], wine for perfume[157], legumes to make into powder[158] are subject to *demay*, not to mention if they are certain. They themselves[159] are free from *demay*." Where are we standing? According to Rebbi, they should be subject to *demay*, according to Rebbi Eleazar ben Rebbi Simeon, even if certain they should be free[160]. But we follow Rebbi, we say we are dealing with the easy ones, for which they eased the rules of *demay*.

155 A similar text in Tosephta *Demay* 1:24. There, the text continues: "If one buys wine and oil to put on abscesses, black peas to make powder, they are subject to *demay* but R. Simeon ben Eleazar declares it free."

156 Latin *muries, muria*, shortened from Greek ἁλμυρίς, ίδος, ἡ, "salty thing; salt land; saltiness" (E. G.).

157 Latin *olentia*, cf. *Berakhot* pp. 87, 510. According to the Babli (*Šabbat* 140 a) a mixture of olive oil, wine, and balsamum.

158 Pea or bean meal to be used as powder.

159 If one buys them ready-made.

160 The disagreement between Rebbi and R. Eleazar ben R. Simeon is stated in *Terumot* 11:1 (fol. 47c) "Wine of *terumah* {heave} to use for brine, Rebbi permits it {since the wine remains wine}, R. Eleazar ben R. Simeon forbids it {since it is a use of the heave not for direct consumption.} Hence, Rebbi forbids such brine for non-Cohanim {since the sanctity of the heave permeates all}, R. Simeon ben Eleazar permits it to non-Cohanim {since the wine has disappeared.}" Here also, if the wine etc. has disappeared, and if brine bought on the market is not subject to *demay*, for R. Eleazar ben R. Simeon even wine bought expressly for the production of brine cannot be subject to *demay*.

יַיִן לְקִילוֹר קֶמַח לַעֲשׂוֹתוֹ מְלוּגְמָא חַיָּבִין בְּוַדַּאי וְאֵין צָרִיךְ לוֹמַר בִּדְמַאי הֵן עַצְמָן פְּטוּרִין מִן הַוַּדַּאי. הָכָא אַתְּ אֲמַר פְּטוּרִין מִן הַוַּדַּאי וְהָכָא אַתְּ אֲמַר פְּטוּרִין מִן הַדְּמַאי. כָּאן עַל גַּב גּוּפוֹ הוּא בָטֵל וְכָאן כֵּיוָן שֶׁהוּא נוֹתְנוֹ הוּא בָטֵל.

"Wine for eye medication[161], flour to make into wound dressing[162], are obligated if they are certain and one does not have to mention that they are under the rules of *demay*. They themselves are free if certain." Here you say, free if certain, and there[163] you say, free from *demay*. Here it disappears by itself, there it disappears when used.

161 Greek κολλύριον. The text in Tosephta *Demay* 1:25 reads: "He who buys wine to put into eye medication or flour to put into wound dressing, is free from *demay* and obligated if it is certain. They themselves are free from *demay*." It seems that this is a Babylonian text.

162 Greek μάλαγμα. If wine and flour are produced, they are subject to the duties of heave and tithes, no matter what the final use is. But if one buys medication which definitely is not food, no obligation exists even if heave was not given from grain or wine.

163 In the previous paragraph, where wine and flour are used for exempt foods, but foods nevertheless. In medication, wine and flour are denatured; in foods, only their status is changed.

וְהָתַנֵּי קִילוֹר שֶׁל עֲבוֹדָה זָרָה אָסוּר בַּהֲנָייָה. שַׁנְייָא הִיא דִּכְתִיב לֹא יִדְבַּק בְּיָדְךָ מְאוּמָה מִן הַחֵרֶם. מַה בֵּינָן לִשְׁמָרִים שֶׁל גּוֹי אִילּוּ שְׁמָרִים שֶׁל גּוֹי שֶׁמָּא אֵינָן אֲסוּרִין בַּהֲנָייָה. הָא שְׁמָרִים שֶׁיָּבְשׁוּ אֵין בָּהֶן מִשּׁוּם הֲנָיַית עֲבוֹדָה זָרָה.

Did we not state: "Eye medication from a pagan temple is forbidden to use?"[164] There is a difference, since it is written (*Deut*. 13:16): "Nothing banned should stick to your hands." What is the difference between this and grape skins from Gentiles? Are these not also forbidden to use[165]? But dried skins are not forbidden because of idolatrous use[166].

164 This implies that eye medication is valuable; why should it be free from heave and tithes?

165 Since the pagan Gentile is assumed to have offered a libation from his newly pressed wine to his gods, all pagan wine is forbidden for any use whatsoever. (This is different from the prohibition to drink any Gentile wine, even from non-pagans.)

166 As stated in Mishnah *Avodah zarah* 2:4, skins remaining after

pressing grapes for wine are forbidden to use if moist but not if completely dry. The question is not answered, probably because the answer is obvious: totally dry eye medication is unusable.

מִן גְּזִיב וּלְהַלָּן פָּטוּר מִן הַדְּמַאי. כְּזִיב עַצְמָהּ מַה הִיא. תַּנֵּי גְּזִיב עַצְמָהּ פְּטוּרִין מִן הַדְּמַאי.

"[167]From Akhzib and further on it is free from *demay*." What is the status of Akhzib itself? It was stated (Tosephta *Demay* 1:4): "Akhzib itself is free from *demay*."

167 Continuation of the discussion of the Mishnah.

הַלּוֹקֵחַ מִן הַחֲמֶרֶת בְּצוֹר וּמִן הַמְּגוֹרֶת בְּצִידָן חַיָּב הָא מִן הַמְּגוֹרֶת בְּצוֹר וּמִן הַחֲמֶרֶת בְּצִידָן פָּטוּר. מֵחֲמוֹר יְחִידִי בְצוֹר. חֲמֶרֶת שֶׁנִּכְנְסָה לְצוֹר דֶּרֶךְ כְּזִיב. אִתָא חֲמֵי אִילּוּ עָמְדָה לָהּ בִּכְזִיב פְּטוּרָה עַכְשָׁיו שֶׁנִּכְנְסָה לְצוֹר חַיֶּיבֶת.

"He who buys from a donkey caravan at Tyre and from the chest[168] at Sidon is obligated[169]." Hence, from the donkey caravan at Sidon and from the chest at Tyre it is free. From a single donkey at Tyre[170]. A donkey caravan that entered Tyre through Akhzib? Come and see, if it were standing at Akhziv it would be free, now that it entered Tyre would it be obligated?

168 The drawer of a trader, who sells staple goods which may come from any nearby region that is a major producer, including Galilee. It seems that in Tyre, which is much closer to Galilee, Galilean grain was usually sold directly by the transporter who brought the grain, not by the local merchant (Maimonides *Maäser* 13:6).

169 Quote from a Tosephta. In our Tosephta, *Demay* 1:10, the statement is inverted: "He who buys from a donkey caravan at Tyre and from the chest at Sidon is free, from the chest at Tyre and the donkey caravan at Sidon is obligated. R. Yose ben R. Jehudah says,

he who buys from the chest at Tyre is free, and certainly from the donkey caravan. From one donkey driver at Tyre he is obligated. R. Jehudah says, the donkey caravan that descends to Akhzib is obligated because it may be assumed that it comes from Galilee. {If it "descends", it comes either from Galilee or from Tyre.} But the Sages say, it is in its prior state, free until you have ascertained from where it comes."

170 The status is not indicated. Since the Yerushalmi contradicts the Tosephta the inference is that it is free (Maimonides *Maäser* 13:6).

אָמַר רִבִּי יוֹחָנָן בְּשָׁעָה שֶׁגָּזְרוּ עַל הַדְּמַאי לֹא גָזְרוּ עַל הַדְּבָרִים הַלָּלוּ. אָמַר רִבִּי הוֹשַׁעְיָא אֵימַת קֳדָשִׁים עָלָיו וְאֵינוֹ נוֹתֵן לַכֹּהֵן דָּבָר שֶׁאֵינוֹ מְתוּקָּן. וְחַלַּת עַם הָאָרֶץ עַל דַּעְתֵּיהּ דְּרִבִּי הוֹשַׁעְיָא בְּחַלַּת עַם הָאָרֶץ הִיא מַתְנִיתָא. אֲבָל חָבֵר שֶׁלָּקַח עִיסָּה מֵעַם הָאָרֶץ וְהִפְרִישׁ חַלָּתָהּ לֹא. עַל דַּעְתֵּיהּ דְּרִבִּי יוֹחָנָן הִיא הָדָא הִיא הָדָא. וְהַמְדוּמָּע עַל דַּעְתֵּיהּ דְּרִבִּי הוֹשַׁעְיָא בְּפֵירוֹת עַם הָאָרֶץ הִיא מַתְנִיתָא. אֲבָל חָבֵר שֶׁלָּקַח פֵּירוֹת מֵעַם הָאָרֶץ וְנִדְמְעוּ לֹא. עַל דַּעְתֵּיהּ דְּרִבִּי יוֹחָנָן הִיא הָדָא הִיא הָדָא. מַאן נְפַק מִבֵּינֵיהוֹן סְאָה עוֹלָה מִתּוֹךְ מֵאָה עַל דַּעְתֵּיהּ דְּרִבִּי יוֹחָנָן חַיֶּיבֶת עַל דַּעְתֵּיהּ דְּרִבִּי הוֹשַׁעְיָא פְטוּרָה.

Rebbi Joḥanan said: When they decreed *demay*, they did not decree about these matters[171]. Rebbi Hoshaia said, the fear of sacred things is on him and he will not give to the Cohen anything that is not in order[172]. "*Ḥallah* of the *am haärez*," according to R. Hoshaia, the Mishnah deals with the *ḥallah* of an *am haärez*. But a *ḥaver* who bought dough from an *am haärez* and gave *ḥallah* is not covered[173]. According to R. Joḥanan, the two cases are identical. "And food containing heave," according to R. Hoshaia, the Mishnah deals with produce of an *am haärez*. But if a *ḥaver* bought produce from an *am haärez* and it became mixed with heave, he is not covered. According to R. Joḥanan, the two cases are identical. What is the difference between them[174]? One *seah* that was lifted from among

100 *seah*[175], according to R. Joḥanan it is obligated, according to R. Hoshaia it is free.

171 The cases enumerated at the end of the Mishnah, "*Ḥallah* of the *am haäreẓ*, food containing heave, food bought with money of the Second Tithe, and the remainders of flour sacrifices are free from *demay*" were never included in a duty of *demay*; there is no need for an explanation why these are excluded.

172 Any one of these is connected with the Sanctuary and their consumption in violation of the rules is a deadly sin, the farmer's sin if he tricks the Cohen into thinking that the produce was brought in order. Hence, it is rational to exclude these items from *demay* even if the original decree did not mention this exclusion.

173 His heave of the tithes must include 10% of the amount given as *ḥallah*, since his case is not mentioned in the Mishnah.

174 Is there a case where the difference is in the opposite direction, that R. Joḥanan requires putting in order and R. Hoshaia does not?

175 If heave fell into profane food (of the same kind, so that the heave is no longer recognizable) the entire food becomes מדומע and is no longer usable by laymen. But if the volume of the profane food is at least 100 times that of the heave, one may lift food in the volume of the heave out of the mixture and declare this now to be the heave; the rest is profane and may be used by everybody. This is true only if the rest is truly profane food which may be used by everybody. Hence, before designating the lifted amount as heave, the owner has to be sure that the rest is profane, so he has to remove the heave of the tithe from it first. According to R. Hoshaia, the owner will do that, so that the remainder is in order even in the hands of the unobservant. R. Joḥanan does not accept the argument and any produce in the hands of the unobservant remains *demay*.

וְתַנֵּי וְכוּלָּן שֶׁקָּרָא שֵׁם לִתְרוּמַת מַעֲשֵׂר אוֹ לְמַעֲשֵׂר שֵׁנִי שֶׁלָּהֶן מַה שֶּׁעָשָׂה עָשׂוּי. עַל דַּעְתֵּיהּ דְּרִבִּי יוֹחָנָן נִיחָא. עַל דַּעְתֵּיהּ דְּרִבִּי הוֹשַׁעְיָא מְתוּקָּנִין וְאַתְּ אֲמַר הָכֵן. מִפְּנֵי אֶחָד שֶׁאֵינוֹ מְתוּקָּן שֶׁאֵין אֵימַת קֳדָשִׁים עָלָיו. תַּנֵּי וְכוּלָּן שֶׁקָּרָא שֵׁם

לִתְרוּמַת מַעֲשֵׂר אוֹ לְמַעֲשֵׂר שֵׁנִי שֶׁלָּהֶן מַה שֶּׁעָשָׂה עָשׂוּי מִפְּנֵי אֶחָד שֶׁאֵינוֹ מְתוּקָּן.

It was stated: "All of these[176], if he gave a name to their heave of the tithe or Second Tithe, what he did is done.[177]" According to R. Joḥanan, this is fine[178]. According to R. Hoshaia, they are in order, and you say so[179]? Because of one who is unscrupulous about sacred things[180]. It was stated[181]: "All of these, if he gave a name to their heave of the tithe or Second Tithe, what he did is done, because of one who does not put in order."

176 Mentioned in the Mishnah as not under the laws of *demay*.

177 A similar text is in Tosephta *Demay* 1:28 which, however, as noted by R. S. Lieberman, deals exclusively with matters of the Temple and, therefore, excludes the heave of the tithe.

178 He is not required to give, but if he gives there is no objection.

179 Since one cannot give heave from produce that was already tithed and if he is sure the produce was tithed, he should declare that calling anything from it heave of the tithe is invalid.

180 According to R. Hoshaia, his assertion is one of probability that the produce will be in order, so that one may base one's actions on it, not of total certainty.

181 A *baraita* was found expressing the last argument.

רִבִּי בּוּן בַּר חִייָא בְּעָא קוֹמֵי רִבִּי זְעִירָא עַד כְּדוֹן בְּכֶסֶף מַעֲשֵׂר שֶׁל דְּמַאי אֲפִילוּ בְוַדַּאי.

Rebbi Abun bar Ḥiyya asked[183] before Rebbi Zeïra: So far with money of tithes of *demay*? Even if it is certain!

182 He asked whether the exemption of food bought with money of the Second Tithe refers only to money from *demay* or also includes regular tithe. The answer is that all tithe money is exempt (R. Simson.)

תַּנֵּי כּוּלָּן שֶׁקָּרָא שֵׁם לִתְרוּמַת מַעֲשֵׂר (fol. 22b) אוֹ לְמַעֲשֵׂר שֵׁנִי שֶׁלָּהֶן מַה שֶּׁעָשָׂה עָשׂוּי. רִבִּי לָעְזָר אוֹמֵר חוּץ מִשְּׁיָרֵי מְנָחוֹת. רִבִּי יִרְמְיָה אָמַר הַשְּׁאָר בְּמַחְלוֹקֶת. רִבִּי יוֹסֵי בָּעֵי הַיידָא מַחְלוֹקֶת. מַה נָן קַייָמִין אִין כְּרִבִּי מֵאִיר הִיא מַעֲשֵׂר הִיא שְׁיָרֵי מְנָחוֹת לֹא עָשָׂה כְּלוּם. אִין כְּרִבִּי יְהוּדָה מַה שֶּׁעָשָׂה עָשׂוּי. אָמַר רִבִּי מָנָא אָזְלִית לְקֵיסָרִין וְשָׁמְעִית רִבִּי חִזְקִיָּה יָתִיב וּמַתְנֵי הַמְקַדֵּשׁ בְּחֶלְקוֹ בְּקָדְשֵׁי קָדָשִׁים אוֹ בְקָדָשִׁים קַלִּים אֵינָהּ מְקוּדֶּשֶׁת. רִבִּי לָעְזָר אוֹמֵר דִּבְרֵי הַכֹּל. רִבִּי יוֹחָנָן אָמַר בְּמַחְלוֹקֶת. וְאָמְרִית לֵיהּ מְנָן שָׁמַע רִבִּי הָדָא מִילְּתָא וְאָמַר לִי מִן רִבִּי יִרְמְיָה. וְאָמְרִית יְאוּת רִבִּי יִרְמְיָה דְּהוּא שְׁמִיעַ הָדָא דְּרִבִּי לָעְזָר דִּבְרֵי הַכֹּל הִיא דְּאָמַר בְּמַחְלוֹקֶת. רִבִּי יוֹסֵי דְּלָא שְׁמִיעַ לֵיהּ צְרִיכָא לֵיהּ דּוּ אָמַר הַיידָא מַחְלוֹקֶת. אִין כְּרִבִּי מֵאִיר הִיא מַעֲשֵׂר שֵׁנִי הִיא שְׁיָרֵי מְנָחוֹת הִיא לֹא עָשָׂה כְּלוּם. אִין כְּרִבִּי יְהוּדָה מַה שֶּׁעָשָׂה עָשׂוּי.

It[183] was stated: "All of these, if he gave a name to their heave of the tithe or Second Tithe, what he did is done." Rebbi Eleazar said, with the exception of the remainders of flour sacrifices[184]. Rebbi Jeremiah said, the rest is in dispute. Rebbi Yose asked, what dispute? Where are we standing, if according to Rebbi Meïr[185], both for tithes and for the remainders of flour sacrifices, he did not do anything. If according to Rebbi Jehudah[186], what he did is done. Rebbi Mana said, I went to Caesarea and heard Rebbi Ḥizqiah who was sitting there, stating: "If a priest marries by means of his share in the holiest sacrifices or simple holy sacrifices, the marriage is not valid." Rebbi Eleazar said, that is everybody's opinion. Rebbi Joḥanan said, it is in dispute[187]. I said to him, from whom did the rabbi hear this, and he said, from Rebbi Jeremiah. I said, this explains the matter! Rebbi Jeremiah, who heard that Rebbi Eleazar said, it is everybody's opinion, he says it is in dispute[188]. Rebbi Yose, who did not hear that, asked which dispute? If according to Rebbi

Meïr, both for Second Tithe and for the remainders of flour sacrifices, he did not do anything, if according to Rebbi Jehudah, what he did is done.

183 The entire paragraph is also in *Qiddušin* 2:8, fol. 63a, which is its main place.

184 Since the flour sacrifice must be eaten by male priests in the Temple precinct but heave of the tithe can be eaten by all members of the Cohen's family anywhere, it is clear that strict sanctity cannot be replaced by a less stringent one.

185 The dispute is in Mishnah *Qiddušin* 2:8: "If a priest marries by his share in the holiest sacrifices or simple holy sacrifices, the marriage is not valid. With Second Tithes, be it with or without knowledge, the marriage is not valid, the words of R. Meïr. Rebbi Jehudah said, if in error, the marriage is not valid, if with knowledge, the marriage is valid." In order to marry, the groom has to give the bride something valuable of his property while declaring before two witnesses that by accepting the gift she is married to him (cf. *Peah* Chapter 6, Note 46). Rebbi Meïr declares that holiest sacrifices, the Cohen's share of simple sacrifices, and the Second Tithe are all Heaven's property offered, as the case may be, to the Cohen, his family, or the layman and his family for consumption in Jerusalem. Hence, for R. Meïr, the basic conditions for a valid marriage are not satisfied.

186 R. Jehudah agrees that under normal circumstances, Second Tithe in Jerusalem cannot be redeemed. However, since it must be redeemed if it became ritually impure, it can also be redeemed unlawfully. His position is explained in *Peah*, Chapter 7, Note 135.

187 Rebbi Jehudah states that the Cohen's share of the sacrifices is his personal property. Hence, at least as far as simple sacrifices are concerned, the woman becomes his wife through the marriage and can legally consume the meat given to her. In that case, R. Jehudah also asserts that Second Tithe is always the owner's property, even before redemption. However, it cannot be used as a marriage gift as is since there is a lien on it that it should be used only for consumption, and that lien must first be removed by redemption.

188 Transferring R. Joḥanan's opinion from the Mishnah in *Qiddušin* to *Demay*.

תַּנֵּי אָמַר רִבִּי יוּדָה לֹא פָּטְרוּ בֵית הִלֵּל אֶלָּא שֶׁמֶן שֶׁל פִּילְיָיטוֹן בִּלְבַד. אֲחֵרִים אוֹמְרִים בְּשֵׁם רִבִּי נָתָן מְחַייְבִין הָיוּ בֵית הִלֵּל בְּשֶׁמֶן וֶורֶד וְיירִינוֹן.

It was stated[189]: Rebbi Jehudah said, the House of Hillel freed only spikenard oil[190]. Others say in the name of Rebbi Nathan, the House of Hillel obligated oil perfumed with rose or iris[191].

189 This is the discussion of the last statement in the Mishnah. A different text, in the name of R. Nathan and not mentioning iris, is Tosephta *Demay* 1:26-27. As R. S. Lieberman points out, it follows that putting some (not too much) natural perfume in oil does not make the oil unfit for human consumption even though it is destined for rubbing into the skin.

190 Latin *foliatum*, cf. Pliny, *Hist. Nat.* XIII, 2.

191 Greek ἴρινον "made from the iris".

(fol. 21c) **משנה ד**: הַדְּמַאי מְעָרְבִין בּוֹ וּמִשְׁתַּתְּפִין בּוֹ מְבָרְכִין עָלָיו וּמְזַמְּנִין עָלָיו וּמַפְרִישִׁין אוֹתוֹ עָרוֹם וּבֵין הַשְּׁמָשׁוֹת. וְאִם הִקְדִּים מַעֲשֵׂר שֵׁנִי לָרִאשׁוֹן אֵין בְּכָךְ כְּלוּם. שֶׁמֶן שֶׁהַגִּירְדִּי סָךְ בְּאֶצְבְּעוֹתָיו חַייָב בִּדְמַאי. וְשֶׁהַסּוֹרֵק נוֹתֵן בַּצֶּמֶר פָּטוּר מִן הַדְּמַאי.

Mishnah 4: With *demay*, one may make *eruv*[192], participate[193], recite grace[194], and recite grace in a group[195]. One may separate it while naked[196] or at twilight[197]. And if one lifted the Second Tithe before the First, it is also acceptable[198]. The oil the weaver puts on his hands[200] is obligated for *demay*, that which the carder puts on wool is free from *demay*.

192 There are two kinds of *eruv* ("mixing") on the Sabbath. If many houses open into a common courtyard, in order to carry from the houses to the

courtyard it is necessary to turn the courtyard into common property. This is done by putting into the courtyard some food to which all houses contributed. The second kind is "mixing of domains", explained in *Peah*, Chapter 8, Note 56.

193 In order to turn a dead-end street into a common domain in which one may carry on the Sabbath, the residents of the courtyards opening into the dead-end street have to *participate* in giving food for a common meal. Since the rules for the dead-end street are different from those for a courtyard, the word *eruv* is not used.

194 Even if *demay* wine has not been put in order and one wants to use it for the cup of blessing. If a transgression of a Biblical commandment were involved, using it for a benediction would constitute blasphemy.

195 The longer form of Grace with an additional invocation.

196 In contrast to separating heave and tithes from certain produce, *demay* does not require a benediction and no invocation of the Name, and, hence, may be separated while one is naked (Cf. *Berakhot* Halakhah 8:2).

197 Friday night after sundown when it is still light but possibly already Sabbath. Certain food cannot be put in order then because this would make it usable now when before it was not at the start of the Sabbath. But *demay* which in any case is food of the poor, may be put in order during twilight (Mishnah *Šabbat* 2:7).

198 For untithed food, lifting the Second Tithe before the First is forbidden; here it is permitted. Maimonides points out that in any case the heave of the tithe must be a full one percent of the original amount.

199 He rubs it in so that his hands should not be hurt by handling the thread; rubbing in everywhere is given the status of drinking.

(fol. 22b) **הלכה ד**: מַפְרִישִׁין אוֹתוֹ עָרוֹם שֶׁאֵין טָעוּן בְּרָכָה.

Halakhah 4: One may separate it while naked because it does not need a benediction.

מִבֵּין הַשְּׁמָשׁוֹת הָדָא דְתַנֵּינָן סָפֵק חֲשֵׁיכָה סָפֵק אֵינָהּ חֲשֵׁיכָה.

Around twilight, that is what we have stated[201]: "If it is doubtful whether it is night or not."

200 Mishnah *Šabbat* 2:7: "If it is doubtful whether it is night or not, one does not tithe the certain, one does not immerse vessels (to remove impurity), one does not kindle lights, but one may tithe the *demay*, make an *eruv*, and cover warm food (to keep it warm for the next morning.)"

תַּנֵּי רִבִּי חֲלַפְתָּא בֶּן שָׁאוּל מְחַלְּלִין דְּמַאי בְּמֶרְחַץ שֶׁאֵינוֹ טָעוּן בְּרָכָה. הָא וַדַּאי טָעוּן בְּרָכָה. רִבִּי מָנָא בְּעֵי קוֹמֵי רִבִּי יוּדָן כֵּיצַד הוּא מְבָרֵךְ אִם הָיוּ פֵּירוֹת עַל פִּדְיוֹן מַעֲשֵׂר שֵׁנִי אִם הָיוּ מָעוֹת עַל חִילּוּל מַעֲשֵׂר שֵׁנִי.

Rebbi Ḥalaphta ben Shaul stated: One may redeem *demay* in the bathhouse[201] since it does not need a benediction. Hence, if the produce is certain it needs a benediction. Rebbi Mana asked before Rebbi Judan, what does he recite? If it was produce, "on the redemption of Second Tithe[202]," if it was money[203], "on turning Second Tithe profane."

201 Where most people are naked, even if he himself is not.

202 Praised are You, Eternal, our God, King of the Universe, Who sanctified us by His commandments and commanded us on the redemption of Second Tithe.

203 Money from the redemption of Second tithe which is sacred and, therefore, cannot be exchanged for other coins, or for produce in Jerusalem to consume in purity, without a ceremony of profaning the first coins and substituting new ones as holy.

אִם הִקְדִּים מִשֵּׁנִי לָרִאשׁוֹן אֵין בְּכָךְ כְּלוּם הָא בַּתְּחִילָּה לֹא. רִבִּי בָּא בְּרֵיהּ דְּרִבִּי חִיָּא בַּר וָוא רִבִּי חִיָּא בְּשֵׁם רִבִּי יוֹחָנָן מוּתָּר לְהַקְדִּים שֵׁנִי לָרִאשׁוֹן בִּדְמַאי. רִבִּי יַעֲקֹב בַּר אָחָא בַּר אִידִי בְּשֵׁם רִבִּי יְהוֹשֻׁעַ בֶּן לֵוִי לֹא יַעֲשֶׂה וְאִם עָשָׂה מַה שֶּׁעָשָׂה עָשׂוּי.

"If one lifted the Second Tithe before the First, it is also acceptable." Hence, one should not do it on purpose[204]. Rebbi Abba, son of Rebbi Ḥiyya bar Abba, Rebbi Ḥiyya[205] in the name of Rebbi Joḥanan, one may make the Second precede the First in *demay*[206]. Rebbi Jacob bar Aḥa bar Idi[207] in the name of Rebbi Joshua ben Levi: One should not do it, but if he did, what he did is valid.

204 Since it is formulated as a conditional, if it happened, nothing bad has happened. It does not say that one is invited to do it.

205 R. Ḥiyya bar Abba.

206 This is accepted by Maimonides, *Maäser* 9:6, even though for practical decisions one prefers R. Joshua ben Levi over R. Joḥanan, probably because the practical rule which the Halakhah gives, in the paragraph following the next, works only according to R. Joḥanan.

207 He cannot be identical either with R. Jacob bar Aḥa of the fourth generation, or with R. Jacob bar Idi, companion of R. Joḥanan. He is quoted only here and nothing else is known about him.

מַהוּ לִיקְבֹּעַ שֵׁנִי בִּמְקוֹם רִאשׁוֹן. רִבִּי יוֹסֵי בֶּן שָׁאוּל אַיְיתֵי אָרִיסֵיהּ פֵּירֵי. אָמַר לֵיהּ צֵא וּקְבַע שֵׁנִי. חָזַר וְאָמַר לֵיהּ צֵא וּקְבַע רִאשׁוֹן וְחָשׁ לוֹמַר שֶׁמָּא קָבַע שֵׁנִי בִּמְקוֹם רִאשׁוֹן. הָדָא אָמְרָה שֶׁמּוּתָּר לִיקְבֹּעַ שֵׁנִי בִּמְקוֹם רִאשׁוֹן.

May one determine the Second in place of the First[208]? His sharecropper brought fruits to Rebbi Yose ben Shaul. He said to him, go and fix a place for the Second. He returned, and he told him, go and fix a place for the First. Should he not worry that maybe the Second was fixed at a place reserved for the First[209]? This means that it is permitted to determine the Second in place of[210] the First.

208 This is not a question about *demay* but about produce from which no tithes were taken. It is forbidden to change the order in which the tithes

are to be taken; if one takes the Second before the First, one may not recite in the Temple the declaration of tithes, containing the assertion (*Deut*. 26:13); "I did not overstep Your commandments." Here, the question is whether this also applies simply to the designation of the place from which the tithe will be taken in the future. This is important if somebody wants to consume fruits or wine for which he will give tithes in the future from some other batch, under circumstances that prevent the actual separation now, e. g., on the Sabbath. Then he must spell out the location from which tithes will be taken. Does this preliminary determination also have to follow the strict rules of precedence?

209 If the tithes had actually been taken, would some of the produce now designated as Second Tithe actually have become First and would then be forbidden to the owner? Note that the sharecropper understood Hebrew, not only Aramaic; he was educated and did not object to what he was told.

210 I. e., prior to.

עוּלָּא בַּר יִשְׁמָעֵאל בְּשֵׁם רִבִּי יוֹחָנָן פּוֹטֵר הוּא אָדָם אֶת טִבְלוֹ בִּסְאָה אַחַת שֶׁל טֶבֶל. כֵּיצַד הוּא עוֹשֶׂה מֵבִיא סְאָה אַחַת שֶׁל טֶבֶל וְעוֹשֶׂה אוֹתָהּ שֵׁנִי וּפוֹדֶה אוֹתָהּ וְחוֹזֵר וְעוֹשֶׂה אוֹתָהּ תְּרוּמַת מַעֲשֵׂר לְמָקוֹם אַחֵר. נְחַת עוּלָּא לְתַמָּן וְאָמְרָהּ בְּשֵׁם רִבִּי יוֹחָנָן וְחָבְרוּן עֲלוֹי. הֵתִיב רַב שֵׁשֶׁת וְהָא מַתְנִיתָא פְּלִיגָא הָיוּ לְפָנָיו שְׁתֵּי כַלְכָּלוֹת שֶׁל טֶבֶל. וְתַנֵּי עֲלָהּ נוֹטֵל מִן הַשְּׁנִייָה שְׁנֵי תְּאֵינִים וּשְׁנֵי עִישּׂוּרִין וְעִישּׂוּרִין שֶׁל עִישּׂוּר. וְיִטּוֹל שְׁתֵּי תְאֵינִים וְיַעֲשֶׂה אוֹתָן שֵׁנִי וְיִפְדֶּה וְיַחְזוֹר וְיַעֲשֶׂם תְּרוּמַת מַעֲשֵׂר לְמָקוֹם אַחֵר. אָמַר רִבִּי מָנָא וְאֵין שֵׁנִי שֶׁבָּרִאשׁוֹנָה טָבוּל לְרִאשׁוֹן שֶׁבִּשְׁנִייָה. אָמַר רִבִּי חֲנַנְיָה תַּמָּן כְּדֵי שֶׁהוּא טוֹבֵל לָרִאשׁוֹן וְלַשֵּׁנִי. בְּרַם הָכָא שֵׁנִי שֶׁנִּיתְקַן מֵחֲמַת רִאשׁוֹן אַתְּ חוֹזֵר וְעוֹשֶׂה אוֹתוֹ רִאשׁוֹן.

Ulla bar Ismael in the name of Rebbi Joḥanan: A person may free his *ṭevel*[211] with one *seah* of *ṭevel*. How does he do it? He brings one *seah* of *ṭevel* and declares it to be Second (Tithe), redeems it[212], and returns to make it heave of the tithe for any other place. Ulla descended there[213] and said this in the name of Rebbi Joḥanan, but they united against him.

Rav Sheshet objected, does not a Mishnah contradict: "If there were before him two baskets full of figs[214]." And we have stated about this[215]: "He takes from the second basket two figs and two tenths, and a tenth of a tenth." Why can he not take two figs, declare them to be Second (Tithe), redeem them, and return to make them heave of the tithe for any other place[216]? Rebbi Mana said, is not the Second Tithe in the first basket containing First Tithe of the second basket[217]? Rebbi Ḥananiah said, there[218] it is *ṭevel* for the First and Second. But here, Second Tithe that was put in order after First, can you return and make it First[219]?

211 Produce from which tithes were not yet given. In general, *ṭevel* denotes produce from which nothing yet was given but, as R. Abraham ben David points out in his notes to Maimonides, *Maäser* 7:3, one must assume that heave already was taken; otherwise, the entire operation would be impossible.

212 Since the heave of the tithe was not yet taken, the redeemed Second Tithe is now *ṭevel* for the First Tithe only and can be used as First Tithe or as heave of the tithe. Since this Second Tithe is different from the produce to be tithed, no transgression was committed in designating the Second Tithe first.

213 Babylonia.

214 *Demay* 7:6: "If he had before him two baskets of *ṭevel*; if he said, the tithes of one of them are in the other, the tithes of the first one are given. Of the first in the second and of the second in the first, the tithes of the first one are given. The tithes of each of the baskets are in the other one, he named them correctly." In the second case, the second basket is not in order since the first basket is in order and one may under no circumstances give tithes from produce from which tithes were already given. In the third case, however, the fixing of the places of tithes is simultaneous for both baskets and that is possible since it was permitted in the first case (and we have established that there is no sin in giving names or fixing places simultaneously as long as the actual lifting of the tithes is done in good order.)

215 Tosephta *Demay* 8:15: "If two baskets of *ṭevel* were before him, each containing 100 figs, if their heave was taken and the tithes of each, the first gives its tithes. If he takes the tithes of each from the other, the first does not give tithes (as explained in the previous note). He takes two figs, two tithes, and a tenth of a tenth." If he takes the tithes from each basket, he takes from each basket 19 figs (10 for First Tithe, 9 for Second Tithe, since heave was already taken.) If he takes all tithes from one basket, he takes 20 for First Tithe, 16 for Second Tithe. Hence, he has to add another 2 figs to get to the required 38 figs. Then from the First Tithe, he takes one tenth as heave of the tithe.

216 Following the recipe of R. Johanan.

217 Since everything comes from the second basket, the second basket would have to be fixed first but then it will be unusable to fix any other. Hence, the method of R. Johanan is not applicable here.

218 In the case of Ulla.

219 Since First was already taken, one cannot take something that is exempt from further obligations in order to make it heave of the tithe anywhere. (The explanations to this paragraph given in the commentaries, from R. Simson of Sens to R. S. Lieberman, are unintelligible.)

שֶׁמֶן שֶׁהַגִּירְדִּי סָךְ בְּאֶצְבְּעוֹתָיו חַיָּיב בִּדְמַאי. וְשֶׁהַסּוֹרֵק נוֹתֵן בַּצֶּמֶר פָּטוּר מִן הַדְּמַאי. מַה בֵּין זֶה לָזֶה. זֶה עַל גַּב גּוּפוֹ בָּטֵל. וְזֶה עַל גַּב צֶמֶר הוּא בָטֵל.

"The oil that the weaver puts on his hands is obligated for *demay*, that which the carder puts on wool is free from *demay*." What is the difference between one case and the other? The first disappears on his body[220], the latter disappears on the wool.

220 It supports the body and is titheable as food.

אלו דברים פרק שני

(fol. 22b) **משנה א.** אֵלּוּ דְּבָרִים מִתְעַשְּׂרִין דְּמַאי בְּכָל־מָקוֹם. הַדְּבֵילָה וְהַתְּמָרִים וְהֶחָרוּבִין הָאוֹרֶז וְהַכַּמּוֹן. הָאוֹרֶז שֶׁבְּחוּצָה לָאָרֶץ כָּל־הַמִּשְׁתַּמֵּשׁ מִמֶּנּוּ פָּטוּר.

Mishnah 1: The following must be tithed as *demay* everywhere[1]: Fig cakes, dates, carobs, rice, and cumin. Rice from outside the Land[2] is free for everybody who uses it.

1 Every place that ever belonged to the Biblical Land of the Twelve Tribes, but only if the produce is from a kind which grows in the Land of Israel. These kinds are export articles and one may expect to find them in all surrounding countries.

2 Rice from strains not grown in the Land are free from *demay* even if imported and used in the land occupied by the returnees from Babylonia.

הלכה א: תַּמָּן תַּנֵּינָן שׁוּם בַּעַל בֶּכִי וּבָצֵל שֶׁל רִכְפָּה וּגְרִיסִין הַקִּילְקִין וַעֲדָשִׁים הַמִּצְרִיּוֹת. הַמִּינִין הַלָּלוּ עַל יְדֵי שֶׁיֵּשׁ כְּיוֹצֵא בָהֶן בְּאֶרֶץ יִשְׂרָאֵל צָֽרְכוּ חֲכָמִים לִיתֵּן לָהֶן סִימָן. אֲבָל הָאֶלַּצְרִין וְהָאַפִּסְטֶקִּין וְהָאִצְטְרוֹבֶלִין עַל יְדֵי שֶׁאֵין כְּיוֹצֵא בָהֶן בְּאֶרֶץ יִשְׂרָאֵל לֹא צָֽרְכוּ חֲכָמִים לִיתֵּן לָהֶן סִימָן. אָמַר רִבִּי אָבִין הָדָא מַתְנִיתָא חִילּוּפָא חִיּוּב הַמִּינִן הָאֵלּוּ עַל יְדֵי שֶׁאֵין כְּיוֹצֵא בָהֶן בְּחוּצָה לָאָרֶץ צָֽרְכוּ חֲכָמִים לִמְנוֹתָן. וְהָא דְבֵילָה בְּבוּצְרָה. שְׁחוּקָה הִיא. וְהָא תְמָרִין בְּאַלֶכְסַנְדְּרִיָּא. דְּקִיקִין אִינּוּן. וְהָא חָרוּב בְּכִיאָרֵי גִּידוּד הוּא. וְהָא אוֹרֶז בְּחוּלְתָא אַכְּתַר הוּא סִימּוּק הוּא. וְהָא כָּמוּן בְּקִיפְּרוֹס. עָקוּם הוּא.

Halakhah 1: There, we have stated[3]: "Garlic from Baalbek, onions from Rikhpah[4], split beans from Cilicia, and Egyptian lentils." Because these kinds[5] also grow in the Land of Israel, the Sages had to attach marks to them[6]. "But filberts, pistachios, and pine nuts, since these kinds do not grow in the Land of Israel, the Sages did not have to attach marks to them.[7]" Rebbi Abun said, the Mishnah is the opposite regarding the obligation of these kinds; since these kinds do not grow outside of the Land, the Sages had to enumerate them[8]. But is there not fig cake from Bosra[9]? It is pounded. But dates from Alexandria? They are thin. But carob from Kiari[4]? It is cut. But rice from the Ḥolata[10]? It has more numerous kernels and is reddish. But cumin from Cyprus? It is curved.

3 Mishnah *Ma'serot* 4:8. All these kinds are not subject to tithes since they are not produced in the Land of Israel.

4 This place has not been identified.

5 Garlic, onions, beans, and lentils, but not these sorts.

6 Greek σημεῖον "mark, symbol."

7 Tosephta *Ma'serot* 4:10, from a statement of R. Yose. There (in all Tosephta manuscripts) it is implied that these nuts are also produced in the Land of Israel, but Baalbek onions etc. do not grow in the Land. R. Isaac ben Malchisedek Simponti notes that he has Yerushalmi manuscripts of both traditions.

8 That they are subject to *demay* even outside the Land, in contrast to the first Mishnah which enumerated the kinds exempt from *demay* even if grown in the Land.

8 This probably is Bosra or Bostra, on the main road that goes South from Damascus, just outside the boundaries of the domain settled by the returnees from Babylonia.

9 Rice from the dunes (חולה) of Antiochia is mentioned at the end of this Halakhah (fol. 22d), but there it is implied that it is undistinguishable from rice grown in the Land, in opposition to the text here. (אכחר is Arabic אכ̇תר "more numerous", there are more kernels to a stalk.) R. Simson of

Sens reads: Rice from Ḥolata Aktar? It is reddish. No locality Ḥolata Aktar is known. It is also impossible to identify חולתה with Ḥuleh, since according to all versions of the Tosephta detailing the borders of the land settled by the returnees from Babylonia, Lake Ḥuleh is inside the Land.

אָמַר רִבִּי לָעְזָר לֹא שָׁנוּ אֶלָּא הַלּוֹקֵחַ מִן הַגּוֹי אֲבָל הַלּוֹקֵחַ מִיִּשְׂרָאֵל דְּמַאי. רִבִּי יוֹחָנָן (fol. 22c) אָמַר לֹא שַׁנְיָיא הִיא הַלּוֹקֵחַ מִיִּשְׂרָאֵל הִיא הַלּוֹקֵחַ מִן הַגּוֹי דְּמַאי. רִבִּי לָעְזָר סָבַר מֵימַר רוֹב אֶרֶץ יִשְׂרָאֵל נְתוּנָה בְּיַד גּוֹיִם. רִבִּי יוֹחָנָן סָבַר מֵימַר רוֹב אֶרֶץ יִשְׂרָאֵל נְתוּנָה בְּיַד יִשְׂרָאֵל. וַאֲפִילוּ יִסְבּוֹר רִבִּי לָעְזָר כְּרִבִּי יוֹחָנָן רוֹב אֶרֶץ יִשְׂרָאֵל נְתוּנָה בְּיַד יִשְׂרָאֵל. רִבִּי לָעְזָר חָשׁ לְמִיעוּט. כְּהָדָא כּוֹרְכְיָא שֶׁהִיא מִסְתַּפֶּקֶת יוֹם אֶחָד מִן הָאָסוּר נַעֲשֶׂה אוֹתוֹ הַיּוֹם הוֹכִיחַ לְכָל־הַיָּמִים. רִבִּי יוֹסֵי בְּעֵי מֵעַתָּה גֵּר שֶׁבָּא לְהִתְגַּייֵר אֵין מְקַבְּלִין אוֹתוֹ אֲנִי אוֹמֵר מֵעַמּוֹן וּמוֹאָב הוּא. וְנַעֲשֶׂה אוֹתוֹ הַגֵּר הוֹכִיחַ לְכָל־הַגֵּרִים. אֶלָּא כֵּינִי הָא רִבִּי לָעְזָר סָבַר מֵימַר רוֹב אֶרֶץ יִשְׂרָאֵל נְתוּנָה בְּיַד גּוֹיִם. וְרִבִּי יוֹחָנָן סָבַר מֵימַר רוֹב אֶרֶץ יִשְׂרָאֵל נְתוּנָה בְּיַד יִשְׂרָאֵל.

Rebbi Lazar said, they stated the Mishnah only for him who buys from a Gentile, but for him who buys from a Jew it is *demay*[11]. Rebbi Joḥanan said, there is no difference, whether one buys from a Jew or from a Gentile it is *demay*. Rebbi Eleazar holds that most of the Land of Israel is in the hands of the Gentiles[12]. Rebbi Joḥanan holds that most of the Land of Israel is in the hands of Jews. But even if Rebbi Eleazar agrees with Rebbi Joḥanan that most of the Land of Israel is in the hands of Jews, Rebbi Eleazar is anxious about a minority. Like that fortification[13], if for one day it got supplies from a forbidden source, that day will become proof for all days. Rebbi Yose asked: If that is so, a prospective proselyte who comes to convert should not be accepted[14]; I say he is from Ammon and Moab, and one proselyte would become proof for all proselytes. Hence, Rebbi Eleazar must hold that most of the Land of Israel is in the hands of Gentiles and Rebbi Joḥanan must hold that most of the Land of Israel is in the hands of Jews.

11 This is the text in all Yerushalmi manuscripts but it cannot be correct. Since the Mishnah speaks of *demay*, if the text is allowed to stand there would be no difference between R. Eleazar and R. Joḥanan. So either R. Eleazar must say that produce of a Gentile is certain and only that of a Jew is *demay* (following R. Meïr who declares that a Gentile cannot acquire arable land in the Land of Israel to exempt it from heave and tithes) or that the produce of the Jew is certain and that of the Gentile is *demay*. The second version is impossible since only a Jew will be expected to give heave and tithes but not a Gentile. In light of the following it is also impossible to assume that the Gentile is only the seller, not the producer. So only the first possibility remains. (Since practice follows R. Joḥanan, as indicated in the next paragraph, the problem is not mentioned in Maimonides and we do not know his reading.)

11 Any produce is assumed to be untithed except if it is known to come from a Jewish producer.

12 Palisades, Greek χάραξ (cf. *Berakhot* p. 663). In the Babli it appears as ברך. The garrison in the palisades is Gentile and lives off the *annona*, a tax to be paid in agricultural products. They will sell their surplus; if all surroundings are Jewish, one buys their surplus as if it were Jewish produce, but not if some of the farmers sending their *annona* to the garrison are Gentiles. Then a testimony that one day the supply came from a Gentile source makes all their surplus subject to all tithes for him who holds that produce grown by a Gentile in the Land is subject to heave and tithes.

13 He can be accepted but would be prohibited from marrying a Jewish woman, *Deut*. 23:4. Since practice rules this out, according to Mishnah *Yadaim* 4:4, every male proselyte is permitted to marry a Jewish woman and the alternative reason given for R. Eleazar is unacceptable.

וְעוֹד מִן הָדָא רִבִּי זְעִירָא שְׁלַח שְׁאַל לְרִבִּי אֲלֶכְסַנְדְּרָא דִּצְדוֹקָא אִילֵּין נִיקְלֶווֹסִין דְּהָכָא מַה אַתּוּן מְשַׁעֲרִין בְּהוֹן רוֹב מִן הַגּוֹיִם אוֹ רוּבָּן מִיִּשְׂרָאֵל. אָמַר לֵיהּ לֵית אֲנָן יָכְלִין מְשַׁעֲרִין בְּהוֹן.

Moreover from the following: Rebbi Zeïra sent to ask Rebbi Alexander from Ẓedoqa[15], those Nicolaus dates from here, what do you estimate about them, mostly from Gentiles or mostly from Jews? He said to him, we are not able to estimate about them[16].

15 An unidentified place in Galilee. Nothing is known about this R. Alexander.

16 If there were a need, they certainly would have decided. Hence, practice follows R. Joḥanan.

מַתְנִיתָא מְסַייְעָה לְדֵין וּמַתְנִיתָא מְסַייְעָה לְרִבִּי לָעְזָר. הַתַּגָּר בְּכָל־מָקוֹם דְּמַאי. אֵימָתַי בִּזְמַן שֶׁרוֹב מִכְנָסוֹ מִיִּשְׂרָאֵל אֲבָל אִם הָיָה לוֹקֵחַ מִן הַגּוֹי וַדַּאי. מַתְנִיתָא מְסַייְעָה לְרִבִּי יוֹחָנָן. תַּנֵּי רִבִּי נְחֶמְיָה אָמַר אֶחָד גּוֹי וְאֶחָד יִשְׂרָאֵל כּוּתִי וְאֶחָד עַם הָאָרֶץ פְּעָמִים שֶׁהוּא לוֹקֵחַ פַּעַם אַחַת מִן הַגּוֹי פַּעַם אַחַת מִיִּשְׂרָאֵל דְּמַאי.

One statement supports this and a second statement supports Rebbi Eleazar. "The trader's produce everywhere is *demay*. When is that? If most of his supply is from Jews. But if he buys from Gentiles, it is certain[17]." A statement supports Rebbi Joḥanan: "Rebbi Neḥemiah stated: "Whether from a Gentile, a Jewish Samaritan[18], or an *am haareẓ* seller, if at times he buys from the Gentile, at times from the Jew, it is *demay*."

17 This supports our reconstruction of R. Eleazar's text above, Note 11.

18 All commentators change the text here, to treat ישראל either as a separate entry or to move it as qualifier to עם הארץ. However, there is no manuscript evidence for such a change. Rather Rebbi Neḥemiah seems to take sides in the quarrel on whether to consider Samaritans as Jews and

sides with Rabban Simeon ben Gamliel (*Ketubot* 3:1, fol. 27a) against Rebbi; cf. also Chapter 3, Note 98. A Samaritan observes all Biblical laws. However, since his brand of Judaism was adopted by the Sadducees, we know that he takes the verse (*Lev.* 19:14): "Do not put an obstacle before a blind man" literally, not as a general injunction not to trap the unwary; he will not take heave and tithes from his harvest for sale. His produce is certainly subject to all the laws if we accept Samaritans as Jews.

רִבִּי חִייָא בַּר אָדָא בְּעָא קוֹמֵי רִבִּי מָנָא מִמִּי לָקַח הָאִישׁ הַזֶּה נֹאמַר מִיִּשְׂרָאֵל דְּמַאי מִן הַגּוֹי וַדַּאי. תִּיפְתָּר שֶׁהָיָה הַתַּגָּר גּוֹי. וְיִשְׂרָאֵל וְגוֹי מַטִּילִין לְפָנָיו דְּמַי. הָתִיב רַב הוֹשַׁעְיָא וְהָא מַתְנִיתָא מְסַייְעָא לְרִבִּי יוֹחָנָן דְּתַנֵּי אָמַר רִבִּי יוּדָא לֹא הִזְכִּירוּ רִימּוֹנֵי בַּדָּן וַחֲצִיר גֶּבַע אֶלָּא שֶׁהֵן מִתְעַשְּׂרִין וַדַּאי בְּכָל־מָקוֹם. מַה נָּן קַייָמִין. אִם בְּלוֹקֵחַ מִיִּשְׂרָאֵל כְּהָדָא דְתַנֵּינָן וַדַּאי. אֶלָּא כִּי נָן קַייָמִין בְּלוֹקֵחַ מִן הַגּוֹי. הָא שְׁאָר כָּל־הַדְּבָרִים דְּמַאי. אָמַר רִבִּי שְׁמוּאֵל בַּר רַב יִצְחָק בְּוַדַּאי אֲנָן קַייָמִין וּבְלוֹקֵחַ מִיִּשְׂרָאֵל אֲנָן קַייָמִין. תִּיפְתָּר שֶׁהָיָה אֲגוֹרָנֵימוֹס גָּדוֹל וְדָחַק עָלָיו לִהְיוֹת מוֹכֵר בְּזוֹל. וְהִתִּירוּ לוֹ לִהְיוֹת מוֹכֵר טְבָלִים וְהַלּוֹקֵחַ יָחוּשׁ לְעַצְמוֹ.

Rebbi Ḥiyya bar Ada asked before Rebbi Mana: From whom did this man buy[19]? If from a Jew it is *demay*, from a Gentile certain. Explain that if the trader was a Gentile and both Jew and Gentile deliver to him[20], it is *demay*. Rav Hoshaia objected, does not the Mishnah support Rebbi Joḥanan? As it was stated[21]: "Rebbi Jehudah said, they only mentioned pomegranates from Badan and grain from Geba because they must be tithed as certain everywhere." What are we talking about? If he bought from a Jew, can it be pronounced certain? But we must deal with a Gentile. Hence, all other things are tithed as *demay*. Rebbi Samuel bar Rav Isaac said, we deal with certain produce from a Jew. Explain it that there was a powerful overseer of markets[22] who exerted pressure to sell at low prices, and they[23] permitted him to sell *ṭevel* and let the buyer beware for himself.

19 The trader who has no single source of supply.

20 The farmers bring him their produce and he does not care who it is.

21 *Kelim* 17:5. Badan (*Wadi Badyah*) and Geba were places in Samaria (Tosephta *Kelim Baba Meẓi'a* 6:10). While these varieties were mainly grown in Samaria, some were grown by Jews. But since the Jews were a minority among the Samaritans, the produce must be treated as Samaritan, subject to tithes but certainly not tithed.

22 Greek ἀγορανόμος, the market supervisor. Usually, his function was only to act as police for correct weights and measures and fair trading practices.

23 The local rabbis, to save the livelihoods of the Jewish merchants. If the buyer buys below regular cost, it is common prudence to assume that the produce is untithed.

אֵי זֶהוּ הַתַּגָּר. כָּל־שֶׁהֵבִיא וְשִׁנָּה וְשִׁלֵּשׁ. רִבִּי יוֹנָה בְּעֵי הֵבִיא שְׁלֹשָׁה מַשּׂוֹאִין כְּאַחַת אֵין זֶה תַּגָּר. זֶה אַחַר זֶה תַּגָּר. רִבִּי יוֹנָה בְּעֵי לְמַפְרֵיעוֹ הוּא נַעֲשֶׂה תַּגָּר אוֹ מִכָּן וּלְהַבָּא. מַה נַפְקָא מִבֵּינֵיהוֹן. בָּא וְהִתְקִין. אִין תֵּימַר מִכָּן וּלְהַבָּא מְעַשֵּׂר זֶה עַל זֶה. רִבִּי מָנָא בְּעֵי הוּא וּבְנוֹ וּפוֹעֲלוֹ מַהוּ שֶׁיִּצְטָרְפוּ לְג׳ מַשּׂוֹאִין כְּאַחַת. רִבִּי יוֹנָה בְּעֵי סְפִינָה הַבָּאָה מֵרוֹמֵי כַּמָּה מִינִין יֵשׁ בָּהּ אַתְּ רוֹאֶה אוֹתָהּ כְּאִילּוּ הִיא אֶחָד[24].

Who is a trader[25]? Everyone who brought, repeated, and came a third time. Rebbi Jonah asked, if he brought three loads together, is he not a trader[26]; one after the other, is he a trader? Rebbi Jonah asked, does he become a trader retroactively or only for the future? What is the difference? If someone came and brought his things in order, if you say only for the future, can he tithe from one on the other[27]! Rebbi Mana asked: Can he, his son, and his worker combine for three loads[28]? Rebbi Jonah asked, a ship that comes from Rome and carries many kinds, do you count this only as one[29]?

24 Reading of the Rome manuscript; Venice print: אחר.

25 Discussion of the *baraita* supporting R. Eleazar.

26 "Three loads" means that he either brings three carriers or three donkeys with him, each with a full load. A rhetorical question to show that this would be an unreasonable restriction.

27 If somebody bought before he became a professional trader, the produce is certain; after that, it is *demay*. Once he is a trader, one cannot tithe one *demay* for another since the one chosen may have been in order and the tithing is invalid. If the title of trader is not retroactive, he may give from the certain also for the *demay*. The question is not answered.

28 Since they are all extensions of the trader himself, would R. Jonah agree that these three do not count separately.

29 If the ship's owner is the seller, does he have professional status already the first time around or not?

הַפֵּירוֹת לֹא הִילְכוּ בָהֶן לֹא אַחַר הָרֵיחַ וְלֹא אַחַר הַמַּרְאֶה וְלֹא אַחַר הַטַּעַם וְלֹא אַחַר הַדָּמִים אֶלָּא אַחַר הָרוֹב. רִבִּי יַעֲקֹב בַּר אָחָא בְשֵׁם רִבִּי יוֹחָנָן אִם הָיָה יַיִן כְּגוֹן יַיִן חָדָשׁ וְיַיִן יָשָׁן הָלְכוּ בוֹ אַחַר הַטַּעַם.

"For fruits they did not consider either smell, or looks, or taste, or value, but only plurality[30]." Rebbi Jacob bar Aḥa in the name of Rebbi Joḥanan: If it was wine, for example new wine and old wine, they judged according to taste.

30 Tosephta *Demay* 4:11. If fruits are mixed the obligations of tithes follow the status of the group which forms a plurality.

אָמַר רִבִּי מָנָא אָזְלִית לְקֵיסָרִין וַחֲמִיתוֹן נְהִיגִין בְּהָדָא דְבֵילָתָא שׁוֹרַיי. שְׁאֵלִית לְרִבִּי יִצְחָק בַּר אֶלְעָזָר וְאָמַר לִי כָּךְ נָהַג זוּגָא שׁוֹרַיי. רִבִּי יִצְחָק בַּר אֶלְעָזָר בְּשֵׁם זוּגָא דְקֵיסָרִין כָּל־דַּחֲמֵי מַיָא שׁוֹרֵי. אִית דְּבָעֵי מֵימַר עַד מִגְדַּל מִלְחָא. וְאִית דְּבָעֵי מֵימַר עַד מְעָרַת טְלֵימוֹן. אָמַר רִבִּי אַבָּמָרִי מִילֵּיהוֹן דְּרַבָּנִין אָמְרֵי

כָּל־הַמִּינִין אֲסוּרִין בְּקֵיסָרִין. הַחִיטִּים וְהַפַּת וְהַיַּיִן וְהַשֶּׁמֶן וְהַתְּמָרִים הָאוֹרֶז וְהַכַּמּוֹן. וְלָא פְּרָשִׁינָן דְּבֵילָה. בְּגִין דְּתַנֵּיתָהּ. וְהָא תַנֵּינָן אוֹרֶז וְכַמּוֹן וּפְרַשְׁתְּנוּן. הֲנֵי שְׁיָרֵיהּ הִיא. הֲרֵי אֵלּוּ בִשְׁבִיעִית הֵיתֵר בִּשְׁאָר יְמֵי שָׁבוּעַ דְּמַאי. הֲרֵי אֵלּוּ בִשְׁבִיעִית הֵיתֵר וְיִהְיוּ בִּשְׁבִיעִית שְׁבִיעִית. יִשְׂרָאֵל מְשַׁמְּטִין וְגוֹי פָּטוּר יִשְׂרָאֵל וְגוֹיִם רָבִים עַל כּוּתִים. בִּשְׁאַר יְמֵי שָׁבוּעַ דְּמַאי דִיהוּדָאֵי יִשְׂרָאֵל מְתַקְּנָן וְגוֹיִם פְּטוּרִין יִשְׂרָאֵל וְגוֹיִם רָבִים[31] עַל כּוּתִים. עַד הֵיכָן. פּוּנְדְּקָא דַעֲמוּדָא פּוּנְדְּקָא דְטַיְבְּתָא[32] עַד כְּפַר סָבָא. וְצוּרָן וַדַּאי בְּקֵיסָרִין.

Rebbi Mana said, I went to Caesarea[33] and I saw them using fig cake as free. I asked Rebbi Isaac bar Eleazar; he said to me that Zeugos[34] used to permit it. Rebbi Isaac bar Eleazar in the name of Zeugos of Caesarea: All that sees the water[35] is free. Some want to say, up to the salt tower, some want to say, up to the Telamon cave[36]. Rebbi Abba Mari said, the words of the rabbis imply that all kinds are forbidden in Caesarea. "Wheat, bread, oil, dates, rice, and cumin[37]." Fig cakes are not included? It is in the Mishnah[38]. But we have also mentioned rice and cumin; these are in the Mishnah and we have spelled them out! Those are the ones which are left out. "These are permitted in the Sabbatical year, in all other years of the Sabbatical cycle they are *demay*." These are permitted in the Sabbatical year; why are they not Sabbatical fruits in the Sabbatical year? The Jews treat them as Sabbatical, the Gentiles are free, Jews and Gentiles outnumber Samaritans[39]. In all other years of the Sabbatical cycle they are *demay*, the Judean Jews put them in order, Gentiles are free, Jews and Gentiles outnumber Samaritans. How far? The inn of the pillars[40], the inn at Tayibeh[41], as far as Kefar Saba. Their juices are certain in Caesarea.

31 Reading of the Rome manuscript. The word is missing in the Venice print. For יהודאי, Rome reads יהו ודאי which is not impossible.

32 Reading of Rome manuscript. Leyden and Venice: רטיבתא "the moist one."

33 As shown in tractate *Berakhot*, Caesarea in the Yerushalmi is usually Caesarea Philippi near the source of the Jordan river. Caesarea here is Caesarea maritima, whose leading authority was R. Isaac ben Eleazar. The Land in which all duties on produce are due is the land occupied by the returnees from Babylonia, Judea and Galilee, and, if we accept Samaritans as Jews, their land, Samaria. In the plain East of Samaria, the region between the *via maris* connecting Damascus and Egypt and the sea was mostly malaria swamps, except for the healthy strip between the first dunes and the sea. Herod built an elevated highway from the *via maris* to the sea, where he built Caesarea maritima for a Gentile population, separate from the Jewish centers. Hence, the region of Caesarea and its sand marshes never fell under the laws attached to the Land.

34 An otherwise unknown sage. That the authority is such a minor figure again shows that we are not dealing with Caesarea Philippi. The fig cakes at Caesarea probably had a peculiar form so that they were immediately recognized.

35 In the Rome manuscript: ימה, "the sea." This might be the better reading.

36 Probably the salt pans at the Northern end of the sands. The place of the cave is unknown; the only caves in the neighborhood are (burial) caves in the petrified first row of dunes North of the aqueduct from the Carmel range. Τέλαμων is a Greek mythological figure; also "base of στήλη", Τελαμῶνες the name of colossal figures supporting pillars (E. G.).

37 First half of a *baraita* whose end is quoted later in the paragraph. The implication is that only these products are *demay* because they are imported; all others are free, since it does not simply say: everything in Caesarea is *demay*. In the synagogue mosaic from Reḥov, the text reads:

הפירות הללו מתעסרין דמיי בקסרין החטין והפת חלה לעולם והיין והשמן והתמרין והאורז והכמן הרי אלו מותרין בשביעית בקסרין ובישאר שני שבוע הן מתקנין דמיי ויש אוסרין בולבסין הלבנין מהר המלך.

"The following produce is tithed as *demay* in Cesarea: Wheat (bread always needs *ḥallah*), wine, oil, dates, rice, and cumin; these are permitted in the Sabbatical year, in the other years they must be fixed as *demay*. Some authorities forbid white bulbs (onions) from King's Mountain."

38 Which requires *demay* "everywhere." The sentence is the answer to the preceding question.

39 Since Samaritans will not hesitate to supply others for money with Sabbatical fruits that they themselves would not use; they are a minority and we may assume that all produce offered for sale at Cesarea is Gentile. Similarly, Jewish produce in the other years is *demay*; Gentile produce is *demay* because maybe it is locally grown and exempt; this outnumbers the produce that may be certain if produced by Samaritans.

40 Its position is unknown. In the mosaic of Reḥov, the text reads: ועד איכן סביב לקיסרין עד צוורנה ופנדקה דטיבתא ועמודה ודור וכפר סבה ואם יש מקום שקנו אותו ישראל חוששין לו רבותינו שלום. "What is the extent of the vicinity of Cesarea? As far as Ṣavranah, the inn at Ṭaybeta, the pillar, Dor, Kefar Sabah, and any land which a Jew ever bought, our teachers worry about it; Peace (upon you)." R. Saul Lieberman (*Tarbiẓ* 45, 54-63) concludes from the last sentence that the principle of applying the Laws of the Land to the territory held by the returnees from Babylonia meant that any real estate ever held by a Jew within the territory of Biblical Israel after the return is forever subject to the Laws of the Land.

41 On the *via maris* North of Kefar Saba (which probably was near modern Juljulia), which in its turn was North of Antipatris, the Northern border fortress of Judea.

רִבִּי אַבָּהוּ בְשֵׁם רִבִּי יוֹסֵי בַּר חֲנִינָא כּוּלְכָּסִין[42] הַנִּמְכָּרִין בְּקֵיסָרִין הֲרֵי אֵלּוּ אֲסוּרִין מִפְּנֵי שֶׁרוּבָּן בָּאִין מֵהַר הַמֶּלֶךְ. רִבִּי חִיָּיא בַּר אָדָא אָמַר בִּלְבָנִין. וְרַבָּנִין דְּקֵיסָרִין אָמְרִין בָּאֲדוּמִין.

Rebbi Abbahu in the name of Rebbi Yose bar Ḥanina: bulbs (onions) sold in Cesarea are forbidden because most of them come from King's Mountain[43]. Rebbi Ḥiyya bar Ada said, the white ones, but the rabbis of Cesarea say, the red ones.

42 Reading of Venice text. In the Leyden ms: בולכסין ; in the Reḥov mosaic correctly בולבסין, Greek βολβός, "root, bulb, onion"; Latin *bulbus* "bulb, onion" or other garden vegetable mentioned as *bulbus fabrilis* in *Ed. Diocl.*

43 Probably this is the hill region between Judea and Samaria proper.

רִבִּי זְעִירָא רִבִּי חִייָא בַּר אַבָּא[44] בְּשֵׁם רִבִּי יוֹחָנָן רִבִּי הִתִּיר בֵּית שְׁאַן מִפִּי יְהוֹשֻׁעַ בֶּן זֵירוּז בֶּן חָמִיו שֶׁל רִבִּי מֵאִיר שֶׁאָמַר אֲנִי רָאִיתִי אֶת רִבִּי מֵאִיר לוֹקֵחַ יֶרֶק מִן הַגִּינָּה בַּשְּׁבִיעִית וְהִתִּיר אֶת כּוּלָּהּ. אָמַר רִבִּי זְעִירָא הָדָא אָמְרָה אָסוּר לְבַר נַשׁ מֵיעֲבַד מִילָּה בְּצִיבּוּר אֲנִי אוֹמֵר אוֹתָהּ הַגִּינָּה הָיְתָה מְיוּחֶדֶת לוֹ דְּהִתִּיר אֶת כּוּלָּהּ. רִבִּי הִתִּיר בֵּית שְׁאַן רִבִּי הִתִּיר קֵיסָרִין רִבִּי הִתִּיר בֵּית גּוּבְרִין רִבִּי הִתִּיר כְּפַר צֶמַח. רִבִּי הִתִּיר לִיקַּח יֶרֶק בְּמוֹצָאֵי שְׁבִיעִית וְהָיוּ הַכֹּל מְלִיזִין עָלָיו. אָמַר לָהֶן בּוֹאוּ וּנְדַיֵּין כְּתִיב וְכִתַּת נְחַשׁ הַנְּחוֹשֶׁת. וְכִי לֹא עָמַד צַדִּיק מִמֹּשֶׁה וְעַד חִזְקִיָּהוּ לְהַעֲבִירוֹ. אֶלָּא אוֹתָהּ עֲטָרָה הִנִּיחַ לוֹ הַקָּדוֹשׁ בָּרוּךְ הוּא לְהִתְעַטֵּר בָּהּ. וַאֲנָן הָעֲטָרָה הַזֹּאת הִנִּיחַ הַקָּדוֹשׁ בָּרוּךְ הוּא לָנוּ לְהִתְעַטֵּר בָּהּ.

Rebbi Zeïra, Rebbi Ḥiyya bar Abba in the name of Rebbi Joḥanan: Rebbi permitted Beth Shean[45] on the testimony of Joshua ben Zeruz, the son of Rebbi Meïr's father-in-law, who said, I saw Rebbi Meïr buy vegetables from a garden in the Sabbatical year. He permitted all of it![46] Rebbi Zeïra said, this implies that nobody should act in public; I say that this garden was a particular case for him[47]; should he have permitted it completely[48]? Rebbi permitted Beth Shean[49], permitted Caesarea[50], permitted Bet Guvrin[51], permitted Kefar Ẓemaḥ[52]. Rebbi permitted to buy vegetables after the end of the Sabbatical year[53] and all were saying bad things about him[54]. He said to them, come and let us discuss the matter. It is written (*2Kings* 18:4): "He[55] smashed the brass snake." Was there no just person between Moses and Hezekiah to remove it? But the Holy One, praise to Him, reserved that crown to him so he could crown himself with it. We also had this crown reserved by the Holy One, praise to Him, to crown ourselves with it.

44 Reading of the Rome manuscript, the last two words missing in the Venice print. R. Ḥiyya the student of R. Joḥanan is always R. Ḥiyya bar Abba.

45 He permitted produce from the entire valley of Beth Shean in the Sabbatical year for commercial use because it seems not to have been settled by the returnees from Babylonia. In the Babli (*Ḥulin* 6b), the reading is that R. Meïr ate a leaf of vegetable without tithing for the same kind of argument.

46 Even though the testimony was only from one spot.

47 Maybe that particular plot of land never had a Jewish owner since Bet Shean was a Philistine city.

48 As the ruins of ancient synagogues with mosaic floors show, in the time of R. Zeïra the valley of Beth Shean was settled by Jews and should not have been permitted, but his authority was not sufficient to overturn Rebbi's ruling.

49 The Jews of Beth Shean (Scythopolis) were murdered in a progrom of 66 C. E. and we have no record of the re-establishment of a community in that city.

50 Caesarea maritima.

51 Near Lakhish, Northwest of Hebron.

52 Kafr Samekh just South of the Sea of Genezareth; it is counted in the neighborhood of Susita.

53 Mishnah *Ševiït* 6:4, Tosephta *Ševiït* 4:17. The reason is detailed in *Peah* 7:4, note 81.

54 In the Tosephta: His family united against him.

55 Hezekiah destroyed the brass snake Moses had made (*Num.* 21:9), because the people worshipped it as a divinity. The argument given here is also in Babli *Ḥulin* 6a.

רִבִּי יְהוֹשֻׁעַ בֶּן לֵוִי הֲוָה מְפַקֵּד לְטַלָּייָא לֹא תֵיזְבּוּן לִי יָרֶק אֶלָּא מִן גִּינְתָא דְּסִיסְרָא. קָם עִימֵּיהּ הַזָּכוּר לַטּוֹב אָמַר לֵיהּ זִיל אֱמַר לְרַבָּךְ לֵית הָדָא גִּינְתָא דְּסִיסְרָא דִיהוּדָיי הֲוָת וּקְטָלֵיהּ וּנְסָבָהּ מִינֵיהּ וְאִין בְּעִית מַחְמְרָא עַל נַפְשָׁךְ אִישְׁתְּרֵי לְחַבְרָךְ.

Rebbi Joshua ben Levi commanded his lads: Do not buy me vegetables except from Sisera's garden[56]. He, may he be remembered for the good[57] stood nearby and said to him: Go tell your teacher that this is not Sisera's garden; it did belong to a Jew but he killed him and took it away from him. If you want to be restrictive for yourself, permit it to your friend[58].

56 Sisera's headquarters were somewhere in the valley of Bet Shean. R. Joshua ben Levi wanted vegetables only from a place that was neither distributed by Joshua nor settled by the returnees from Babylonia; such a place certainly is free from all obligations on the Land.

57 A common appellation of Elijah. Since he did not die, one cannot mention for him the blessing of the dead, "may his remembrance be a blessing."

58 Elijah rebuked R. Joshua ben Levi on two points: The names attached to plots are no guarantee for their past, and restrictive action should be taken in private, not declared publicly. The story shows clearly that R. Joshua ben Levi was living in Bet Shean valley, South of Galilee.

רִבִּי יוֹסֵי דִכְפַר דָּן בְּשֵׁם רִבִּי בֶּן מְעָדְיָה הַמִּינִין הָאֲסוּרִין בְּבֵית שְׁאָן. הַקֶּצַח וְהַשּׁוּמְשׁוּם וְהַחַרְדָּל וְהַשּׁוּם וְהַבּוּלְבָּסִין הָאֲפוּנִין הַשְּׁחוֹרִין וּבְצָלִים הַנִּמְכָּרִים וּבְנֵי הַמְּדִינָה הַנִּמְכָּרִים בְּמִידָּה וּפוּל הַמִּצְרִי הַנֶּאֱגָד בְּשִׁיפָה מֵינְתָה הַנֶּאֱגָד בִּפְנֵי עַצְמָהּ וְהָאִיסְטְפֶּנִינֵי לְעוֹלָם וְקֶפַלּוֹטוֹת מִן הָעֲצֶרֶת וְעַד חֲנוּכָּה. אָמַר רִבִּי זְעִירָא מִן הָעֲצֶרֶת וְעַד חֲנוּכָּה אִיסּוּר רָבָה עַל הַהֵיתֵר. מִן הַחֲנוּכָּה וְעַד הָעֲצֶרֶת הֵיתֵר רָבָה עַל הָאִיסּוּר. וּלְעִנְיַן סְפִחִים מֵרֹאשׁ הַשָּׁנָה וְעַד חֲנוּכָּה אִסּוּר סְפִחִין. מִן הַחֲנוּכָּה וְעַד הָעֲצֶרֶת הֵיתֵר סְפִחִין. מִן הָעֲצֶרֶת וְעַד רֹאשׁ הַשָּׁנָה צְרִיכָה. הַקִּישּׁוּאִין וְהַדִּילּוּעִין וְהָאֲבַטִּיחִין וְהַמְּלַפְּפוֹנוֹת וְהַיַּיִן וְהַשֶּׁמֶן וּתְמָרִים אֶפְסִיּוֹת וְיֵשׁ אוֹמֵר אַף הַתּוּרְמוּסִין וּפַת חַלָּה לְעוֹלָם הֲרֵי אֵילוּ בַּשְּׁבִיעִית שְׁבִיעִית. בִּשְׁאָר יְמֵי שָׁבוּעַ מַה. רִבִּי יוֹנָה אָמַר דְּמַאי רִבִּי יוֹסֵי אוֹמֵר וַדַּאי. וְלֹא לַמַּעְשְׂרוֹת פְּלִיגִין. מָה דְרִבִּי יוֹנָה אוֹמֵר דְּמַאי בְּלוֹקֵחַ מִן הַבַּלּוֹנְקֵי[59]. וּמָה דְרִבִּי (fol. 22d) יוֹסֵי אוֹמֵר וַדַּאי בְּלוֹקֵחַ מִן הַגִּינָּה.

Rebbi Yose of Kefar Dan in the name of Rebbi from Meadiah[60], the kinds forbidden in Beth Shean[61]: Nigella, sesame, mustard, garlic, bulbs, black peas, commercial onions[62], local ones that are sold by weight, Egyptian beans bound with bast, mint bundled separately, carrot[63] always, leeks[64] from Pentecost to Ḥanukkah. Rebbi Zeïra said, from Pentecost to Ḥanukkah the forbidden ones outnumber the permitted ones, from Ḥanukkah to Pentecost the permitted ones outnumber the forbidden ones. In the matter of aftergrowth[65], from New Year's Day to Ḥanukkah prohibition of aftergrowth, from Ḥanukkah to Pentecost permission of aftergrowth, from Pentecost to New Year's Day questionable. Zucchini, squash, water melon, apple melon[66], wine, oil, Ephesian dates, somebody also says lupines. Bread always requires *hallah*[67]. These are Sabbatical in a Sabbatical year. In the other years of the cycle? Rebbi Jonah said, *demay*; Rebbi Yose said, certain. They have no disagreement over tithes; Rebbi Jonah said *demay* for him who buys from a person making house calls[68], Rebbi Yose said certain for him who bought from the garden[69].

59 Also cf. reading of the Rome ms: הכליניקי. R. S. Lieberman proposes to read לכניקי, explained as [πλατεῖα] λαχανική "[market of] vegetable kind." One might read כליניקי as κλινικοί "physicians" [making house calls to patients in bed (κλίνη)]. For food the physician may be feeding his patient, cf. Chapter 3, Notes 18-19.

60 Nothing is known about these two authorities nor about their localities. In the Rome manuscript, the last place name is spelled מעזיה, showing that the vowel under ע is long.

61 The kinds of vegetables forbidden as objects of trade in the Sabbatical year because they are imported from regions under the Sabbatical law. The text is now confirmed by the mosaic inscription from the synagogue of Reḥov in the Beth Shean valley: הפירות הללו אסורין בבית שאן ובשאר שני שבוע מתאסרין (!) דמי הקישואין והאבטיחין והממלפפונות והמינתה

הנאגדת בפני עצמה ופול המצרי הנאגד בשיפה והקפלוטות מן העצרת עד החנוכה והזירעונין והקצע והשמשמין והחרדל והאורז והכמון והתורמסין היבשין והאפונין הגמלונין הנמכרין במידה והשום ובצלין בני מדינה הנמכרין במידה והבולבסין והתמרין אפסיות והיין והשמן בשביעית שביעית שני שבוע דמי והפת חלה לעולם. "The following are forbidden in Bet Shean and in the other years of the Sabbatical cycle they are tithed as *demay*: Green melon, water melon and sweet melon, mint {Greek μίνθα, μίνθη, Latin *menta, mentha*} bundled separately, Egyptian beans bundled with bast, leeks from Shavuot to Hanukkah, seeds of nigella, sesame, mustard, rice, cumin, dry lupines, large peas sold by measure {cf. Mishnah *Kilaim* 3:2}, garlic, local onions, βολβός {perhaps truffles}, Ephesian dates; wine and oil are Sabbatical produce in the Sabbatical year, in the other years *demay*. Bread always needs *ḥallah*."

62 Probably imported from Galilee or Samaria. The "local ones" must mean the ones of the same type as the local produce but since they are sold wholesale they are not considered local.

63 In the Beth Shean inscription, אסטפליני, Greek σταφυλῖνος "carrot, *Daucus carota*".

64 *Allium porrum L.*, called *allium capitatum*, corresponding to Greek κεφαλωτός [Pliny XX. 6. 22]; cf. *Berakhot* p. 484.

65 Produce that started growing by itself in the Sabbatical year and which is to be treated as Sabbatical in the following year (*Lev.* 25:5,11).

66 Latin *melopepo*, Greek μηλοπέπων. The modern meaning of the word, "cucumber", is found in Maimonides and *Caftor waPeraḥ* (ed. Luncz, Jerusalem 1899, p. 485), see Mishnah *Kilaim* 1:2. The identification of all these fruits from the *cucurbitaceae* family is tentative; see the detailed discussion in the commentary to Mishnah *Kilaim* 1:2.

67 *Ḥallah* is an obligation of the Land (Mishnah *Ḥallah* 2:1), but by rabbinical ordinance it has to be taken everywhere (Mishnah *Ḥallah* 4:8). It seems from the repeated insistence on the obligation to give *ḥallah* in the Yerushalmi and the mosaic from Reḥov that this rabbinic ordinance was not generally observed by the population of districts outside the holdings of the returnees from Babylonia.

68 Explanation of A. Kohut in *Aruch Completum*, cf. Arabic בלנקע "paved road." The produce bought on the road is of uncertain origin.

69 Local produce is from a Gentile grower, certainly exempt.

עַד הֵיכָן. פרשתא ורציפתא ונפשא דפגוטיה עד כפר קרנים וכפר קרנים כבית שאן.

How far[70]? (The cross roads of *Rẓyfta*, the mausoleum of *Pgvṭiah* and Kefar Karnaim, Kefar Karnaim being like Beth Shean.)

70 How far does the exemption of the Beth Shean valley extend? The text is garbled, the places have not been identified. The list is better preserved in the mosaic from Reḥov: אילו המקומות המותרין סביבות בית שאן מן הדרום שהיא פילי דקמפון עד חלקה חיורתה מן המערב שהיא פילי דזיירא עד סוף הרצפה מן הצפון שהיא פילי דסכותא עד כפר קרנוס וכפר קרנוס כבית שאן ומן המזרח שהיא פילי דזבלייה עד נפשיה דפנוקטייה ופילי דכפר זימרין ופילי דאגמה לפנים מן השער מותר ולחוץ אסור. "These are the places permitted in the neighborhood of Beth Shean: In the South, from the Stadium (*campus*) gate (πύλη) to the white smooth place (the shale rocks at the foot of the Gilboa mountains). In the West, from the Ziara gate to the end of the paved road. In the North, from the Sakota gate to Kefar Qarnos (quoted in *Lev. rabba* 17 as grazing place of Job's cattle; ms. Rome also reads קרנוס); Kefar Qarnos has the status of Beth Shean. In the East, from the dung gate to the mausoleum of Panokatia (?), the gates of Kefar Zimrin and the pond gate; inside the gate it is permitted, outside it is forbidden."

רִבִּי יוֹנָה בְשֵׁם רִבִּי שִׁמְעוֹן בֶּן זְכַרְיָה הַמִּינִין הָאֲסוּרִין בִּפְּנַיַּיס הָאֱגוֹזִין וְהָאוֹרֶז וְהַשּׁוּמְשְׁמִין וּפוּל הַמִּצְרִי. גַּמְלִייֵל זוּגָא אָמַר אַחְיָנִיּוֹת הַבְּכוּרוֹת. אָמַר רִבִּי יוֹנָה הָדָא דְּתֵימַר מִתַּרְנְגוֹל קֵיסָרִיוֹן וּלְמַעְלָן. אֲבָל מִתַּרְנְגוֹל קֵיסָרִיוֹן וּלְמַטָּן כְּאֶרֶץ יִשְׂרָאֵל הִיא. רִבִּי יוֹנָה בְּעֵי הָיְתָה שָׂדֵהוּ זְרוּעָה יֶרֶק וּבָא וּמְצָאָהּ אוֹרֶז. יֶרֶק מוּתָּר וְהָאוֹרֶז אָסוּר. אוֹרֶז מִלְּמַעְלָן וְיֶרֶק מִלְּמַטָּן יֶרֶק מוּתָּר וְהָאוֹרֶז אָסוּר. אֲבָל רוֹב הַשָּׂדוֹת הַלָּלוּ עוֹשׂוֹת הַמִּינִין הַלָּלוּ. וַאֲפִילוּ תֵימַר רוֹב הַשָּׂדוֹת הַלָּלוּ עוֹשׂוֹת רוֹב[71] הַמִּינִין הַלָּלוּ רוֹב הַמִּינִין הַלָּלוּ אֵינָן בָּאִין אֶלָּא מִן הָאִיסּוּר.

Rebbi Jonah in the name of Rebbi Simeon ben Zachariah[72]: The kinds forbidden in Paneas[73]: Walnuts, rice, sesame, and Egyption beans.

Gamliel the twin says, early ripening *atriplex*[74]. Rebbi Jonah said, that means, higher than the Rooster of Caesarea[75]. But below the Rooster of Caesarea it has the status of the Land of Israel. Rebbi Jonah asked: If his field was sown with vegetables and he came and found it full of rice, is the vegetable permitted and the rice forbidden? If the rice is high and the vegetable low, is the vegetable permitted and the rice forbidden? In fact, most of these fields produce these species! Even if you say that most of these fields produce these species, most of these kinds only come from forbidden areas[76].

71 A superfluous word, probably scribal error.

72 An otherwise unknown author.

73 Banias, at the Jordan source, a Greek town just upstream from Caesarea Philippi. The text of Reḥov reads: הפירות הללו אסורין בפניס בשביעית ובישאר שני שבוע הן מתעסרין דמיי משלם האורז והאגוזין והשמשמין ופול המצרי יש אומרין אוף אחוניות הבכירות הרי אלו בשביעית שביעית ובשאר שני שבוע הן מתעסרין ודיי ואפילו מן תרנגולה עלייה ולחוץ. "The following produce is forbidden at Paneas in the Sabbatical year; in the other years their are tithed as complete *demay*: Rice, walnuts, sesame, Egyptian beans; some also say early ripening *atriplex*. These have sabbatical status in the Sabbatical year, in the remaining years they must be tithed as certain, even outside the Upper Rooster." The identity of "complete *demay*" and "certain" is discussed by R. S. Lieberman in *Tarbiẓ* 45 (5776), 54-63. He quotes several passages in which "certain" means "to be treated as certain because of doubt."

74 Cf. *Berakhot* 6:2, Note 125.

75 In the Tosephta on the borders of the Holy Land (*Ševiït* 6:1, fol. 36c), one of the border marks is "the Upper Rooster over Cesarea Philippi"; from there to the Northeast is the Trachonitis and Syria, to the Southwest is the Holy Land.

76 Since the imports outnumber local produce, we have to follow the majority in all cases, as established earlier.

תַּנֵּי הָאוֹרֶז שֶׁבְּחוֹלַת אַנְטוֹכְיָא מוּתָּר בִּמְקוֹמוֹ. רִבִּי לְעָזָר בֵּי רִבִּי יוֹסֵי הִתִּיר עַד כדון. רִבִּי יוֹנָה בְּעֵי וּכְמִידָּתָהּ לְכָל־רוּחַ.

It was stated: The rice in the sands of Antiochia[77] is permitted in its place. Rebbi Eleazar ben Rebbi Yose permitted it as far as *Kdvn*[78]. Rebbi Jonah asked: This distance[79] in every direction?

77 Antakia on the Orontes. It seems that the rice from there was the same kind as that from the Holy Land; since the local production was enough and nothing or very little was imported, the decree of the Mishnah does not apply to Antiochia.

78 R. Simson of Sens reads בורן. The place is unidentified.

79 Measured from the dunes.

אֵילּוּ עֲיָירוֹת אֲסוּרוֹת בִּתְחוּם צוֹר שצת ובצת ופי מצובת וחנותא עֶלְיָיתָא וחניתא תַּחְתִּיָּה בריא[80] וראש מיא ועמון ומזי.

"The following are the forbidden towns in the district of Tyre[81]: *ṡẓt*[82], Al-Baṣa[83], the source at Ma'aṣuba[84], upper and lower Ḥanuta[85], Bet Badia[86], the water spring, Hamun[87], and Mazy[88]."

80 The Rome ms. and the Vienna ms. of the Tosephta read: בית בדיא

81 Even though the Mishnah states that Akhzib is the Northern border of the Land, there are isolated villages that always had a Jewish population and, therefore, are obliged to follow the rules of the Sabbatical. The list is in Tosephta *Ševiït* 4:9. The text of the Reḥov mosaic reads: העיירות האסורות בתחום צור שצת ובצת ופי מצובה וחנותה עלייתה וחנותה ארעייתה וביברה וראש מייה ואמון ומזה היא קסטלה וכל מה שקנו ישראל נאסר. "The towns forbidden in the district of Tyre: *ṡẓt*, Al-Baṣa, the source at Ma'aṣuba, upper and lower Ḥanuta, the house of Bara (or Badia), the water spring, Hamun, and Mazy, that is the water tower [*castellum*, cf. Y. Sussman, *Tarbiẓ* 45 (5736), 213-257]; and all that was acquired by Jews becomes forbidden."

82 Unidentified; in the Rome ms. שיצת, in the Tosephta mss. אשנץ, שנץ.

83 Just South of Rosh Haniqra.

84 Khirbet Ma'aṣuba, SE of Al-Baṣa.

85 Khirbet Ḥanuta, NE from Khirbet Ma'aṣuba.

86 Unidentified; in the Erfurt ms. of the Tosephta: בית כריא.

87 Khirbet Mazy is near Rosh Haniqra; Ḥamun (*Jos.* 19:28) is North of it at the source Ḥamul, so maybe ראש מיא and עמון are one and the same. In Galilean speech, ח, ע, א were undifferentiated.

88 Khirbet Mazy near Rosh Haniqra.

אָמַר רִבִּי מָנָא הָדָא דְּאַתְּ אָמַר בָּרִאשׁוֹנָה. אֲבָל עַכְשָׁיו יֵשׁ [עֲיָירוֹת אֲחֵרוֹת שֶׁהֶחֱזִיקוּ בָּהֶם יִשְׂרָאֵל שֶׁהֶם אֲסוּרוֹת. אֵילּוּ עֲיָירוֹת אֲסוּרוֹת בִּתְחוּם][89] סוּסִיתָה. עיינוש ועין תרע ורם ברין ועיון ויעדוט וכפר וחרוב ונוב וחספיה וּכְפַר צֶמַח. רִבִּי הִתִּיר כְּפַר צֶמַח. רִבִּי אִימִּי בְּעֵי וְלֹא מִמַּעֲלֵי מִסִּין הֵן. סָבַר רִבִּי אִימִּי מַעֲלֵי מִסִּין כְּמִי שֶׁנִּתְכַּבְּשׁוּ.

Rebbi Mana said, what you enumerate was earlier. But now there [are other towns that were held by Israel and they are forbidden. "[90]These are the towns forbidden in district] Susita[91]: Al 'Awaniš[92], Eyn Tara'[93], the heights of Barin[94], the spring Ya'riṭ, Kefar Yaḥrib[95], Nab, Ḥasfin[96], and Kefar Ẓemaḥ. Rebbi permitted Kefar Ẓemaḥ." Rebbi Immi asked: Are these not of the taxpayers[97]? Rebbi Immi is of the opinion that taxpayers count as if they were conquered.

89 Text of the Rome ms. and R. S. Cirillo, missing from the Leyden ms. and Venice text.

90 The text in Tosephta *Ševiït* 4:10 is: "Towns obligated for tithes in the district of Susita." R. S. Lieberman points out that the obligation of tithes also extends to places freed from the obligation of the Sabbatical year. The text of the mosaic of Reḥov: העיירות אסורות בתחום סוסיתה. עיינוש ועין חרה ודמבר ועיון ויערוט וכפר יחריב ונוב וחספייה וכפר צמח. ורבי התיר כפר צמח. "These are the towns forbidden in district Susita: Al 'Awaniš, Eyn Ḥara' (probably a pejorative name for a spring holy to a pagan deity), Dambar, Iyun (not the one in Lebanon) and Ya'ruṭ, Kefar Yaḥrib, Nab, Ḥasfin, and Kefar Ẓemaḥ. Rebbi permitted Kefar

Ẓemaḥ."

91 The city of Hippos overlooking the Eastern shore of lake Genezareth. Even though the description of the boundaries of the Land includes all of the Golan heights, Hippos and its surroundings were formerly Greek and exempt.

92 North of Susita. In the Erfurt ms. עינישת, in *Caphtor Waperaḥ* עושית.

93 Unidentified, the name is misspelled as seen in the Reḥov mosaic. Missing in the list of *Caphtor Waperaḥ*.

94 In the Rome ms. בריך, in the Vienna ms. of the Tosephta: ורומברך. Identified by S. Klein as Barīqa S. of Susita; in view of the Reḥov mosaic, that identification cannot be sustained.

95 These two are unidentified. Rome ms.: ועיין ויעריט וכפר יחריב. In the Tosephta ms. עין יעריט וכפר יערים.

96 Nab is E. of 'Awaniš and Ḥasfin N. of Nab (S. Klein).

97 Taxpayers of the mainly Jewish district.

אֵילּוּ עֲיָירוֹת שֶׁהָיוּ[98] מוּתָּרוֹת בִּתְחוּם נַבִּי. צור וציר וגשמיו וזיויון ויגדי חטם ודבב חרבתיה וכרכה דבר הזרג.

"The following are the towns that were permitted in the district of Naveh[99]: Ṣaria[100], Ṭeriya, Jasim[101], Zizun, the stone heaps of *ḥṭm*[102], Aldanba the ruin[103], the palisades of *Bar hzrg*[104]."

98 Reading of Rome ms. Leyden and Venice: שהן which is redundant in the syntax of the Yerushalmi. The reference is to the statement of R. Mana above that there were towns on the Golan heights which were permitted but in his time, when the center of Jewish settlement was moving from Galilee to the Golan heights, they became Jewish and forbidden.

99 Appears in the Yerushalmi also as Nineveh (*Taäniot* 1:1), in the center of the Bašan plateau. The text is also in Tosephta *Ševiït* 4:8. In the Tosephta: "Towns that were permitted in the district of Nave and became forbidden." As Arab village, Nowa. The text from Reḥov reads: העיירות שהן ספק בתחום נווה ציר וצייר וגשמיי וזיזון ורנב וחרבתה ואיגרי חותם וכרכרה דבר הרג. "The towns that are questionable (whether Jewish or Gentile) in the district of Naveh: Ṣaria, Ṭeriya, Jasim, Zizun, Regeb (?), the ruin and wall of *ḥṭm*, the

palisades of *Bar hrg*."

100 Tosephta mss.: ציר וצייר, Rome ms. צורן צייר. The identifications here are S. Klein's. The place is E. of Nave, N. of Ṭeriya.

101 The reading of the Rome Yerushalmi and Vienna Tosephta mss. is גשמי וזיזון, the Erfurt ms. has גושמי וזיזין. Jasim is N. of Naveh, Zizun to the SE.

102 In the Tosephta: ויגרי טב. For יגר, cf. *Gen*. 31.47. Identified by S. Klein as 'Otman, E. of Zizun.

103 Rome ms. ונדב חרבותה, Tosephta mss. ודנב חורבתא. Aldanba is E. of Naveh (S. Klein).

104 Rome ms.: דבר הורג. Tosephta mss.: דבית הרב. The place of this fortification has not been identified. S. Klein identifies the name *ḥzrg* as Nabatean (maybe from زرج "shoot of vine").

חַד טְעִין דְּצִימּוּקִין אֲעַל לְטִיבֵּרְיָא שְׁאַל גַּמְלִיאֵל זוּגָא לְרִבִּי בָּא בַּר כַּהֲנָא. אָמַר לֵיהּ אֵין כָּל־אֶרֶץ יִשְׂרָאֵל עָשׂוּי מַשּׂוּי אֶחָד שֶׁל צִימּוּקִין. וְאֵין כָּל־אֶרֶץ יִשְׂרָאֵל עָשׂוּי מַשּׂוּי אֶחָד שֶׁל צִימּוּקִין אֶלָּא כֵן[105] אָמַר לֵיהּ אֵין מָקוֹם בְּאֶרֶץ יִשְׂרָאֵל עוֹשֶׂה מַסּוּי שֶׁל צִימּוּקִין.

A load of raisins[106] came up to Tiberias. Gamliel the twin asked Rebbi Abba bar Kahana[107]. He said to him: All of the Land of Israel does not produce a load of raisins. Does all of the Land of Israel not produce a load of raisins? But so he said to him: No single place in the land of Israel produces a load of raisins.

105 Reading of Rome ms. Venice: עשׂוי שׁל צימוקין אלא נן.

106 Either a full donkey load or a full camel load. Since it says "ascended," it must have come up the Jordan valley from the Beth Shean valley, or from Transjordan. It seems from the following that the question was whether in a Sabbatical year one was permitted to trade in these raisins.

107 Rome ms: Rebbi Abba bar Zavda. This reading is more likely since the latter was the Halakhic authority.

חַד בַּר נַשׁ אַיְיתֵי הָדָא אַפְשְׁלָא דְקֶפְלוֹטִין לְרִבִּי יִצְחָק בַּר טֶבְלַיי. שְׁאַל לְרִבִּי יוֹחָנָן. אָמַר לֵיהּ פּוּק שְׁאַל לַחֲנַנְיָה בֶּן שְׁמוּאֵל דְּתַנְּתָהּ. נְפַק וּשְׁאַל לֵיהּ. אָמַר מַתְנֵי לָא יַחְמֵי לִי שְׁמוּעָה אָמַר לִי. דְּאָמַר רִבִּי יָסָא בְּשֵׁם רִבִּי יוֹחָנָן אִיתְפַּלְגוּן רִבִּי וְרִבִּי אֶלְעָזָר בֵּי רִבִּי שִׁמְעוֹן חַד אָמַר אַחַר מְקוֹמוֹ וְחָרְנָא אָמַר אַחַר מַעֲמָדוֹ. רִבִּי אַבָּהוּ אָמַר רִבִּי אוֹמֵר אַחַר מְקוֹמוֹ וְהוֹרֵי לֵיהּ כְּהָדָא דְרִבִּי אֶלְעָזָר בֵּי רִבִּי שִׁמְעוֹן אַחַר מַעֲמָדוֹ. הָדָא דְתֵימַר בְּאִילֵּין אַפְשְׁלָתָא בְּרַם בְּאִילֵּין טוֹעֲנַיָּא כָּל־עַמָּא מוֹדֵיי אַחַר מְקוֹמוֹ. הָיָה מְקוֹמוֹ וּמַעֲמָדוֹ הֵיתֵר וְהוּא עָתִיד לְהַעֲבִירוֹ דֶּרֶךְ אִיסּוּר אוֹתוֹ הָאִיסּוּר כְּמִי שֶׁלֹּא הֶעֱבִירוֹ. רִבִּי בָּא בַּר כֹּהֵן בְּעָא קוֹמֵי רִבִּי יוֹסֵי לֹא כֵן אָמַר רִבִּי חִייָא בְּשֵׁם רִבִּי יוֹחָנָן רִבִּי וַחֲבֵירוֹ הֲלָכָה כְּרִבִּי. וְאָמַר רִבִּי יוֹנָה וַאֲפִילוּ רִבִּי אֵצֶל רִבִּי לָעְזָר בֵּי רִבִּי שִׁמְעוֹן. אָמַר לֵיהּ מַה אַתְּ בָּעֵי מֵרִבִּי יוֹחָנָן. רִבִּי יוֹחָנָן כְּדַעְתֵּיהּ. דְּרִבִּי יוֹחָנָן אָמַר קַל הֵקִילוּ בַּשְּׁבִיעִית שֶׁהִיא מִדִּבְרֵיהֶם. אִית דְּבָעֵי מֵימַר נִצְטָרְפָה דַעְתּוֹ שֶׁל רִבִּי יוֹחָנָן עִם רִבִּי אֶלְעָזָר בֵּי רִבִּי שִׁמְעוֹן וְרָבוּ עַל רִבִּי.

A person brought a back-pack[108] of leeks to Rebbi Isaac bar Tevele. He asked Rebbi Johanan. He said to him, go and ask Ḥananiah ben Samuel[109] who knows statements about this. He went and asked. He said, they did not show me a statement, but he told me an Amoraic tradition, since Rebbi Yasa said in the name of Rebbi Johanan: Rebbi and Rebbi Eleazar ben Rebbi Simeon disagree: one says after its place of production, the other says, after its current stand. Rebbi Abbahu said that Rebbi said, after its place of production, and they taught him following Rebbi Eleazar ben Rebbi Simeon, after its current stand[110]. This means for back packs, but for animal loads everybody agrees after its place of production. If its place of production and of current placement are free but he is going to transport it through forbidden territory, that forbidden territory is as if he did not traverse it. Rebbi Abba bar Cohen asked before Rebbi Yose: Did not Rebbi Ḥiyya say in the name of Rebbi Joḥanan, between Rebbi and his colleague, practice follows Rebbi. But Rebbi Jonah said, even Rebbi with Rebbi Eleazar ben Rebbi Simeon[111]? He said to him, what do you want from Rebbi Joḥanan! Rebbi Joḥanan follows his own opinion, for Rebbi Joḥanan said, they were very lenient regarding the Sabbatical, which is of their words[112]. Some want to say[113], the opinion of Rebbi Joḥanan is added to that of Rebbi and they form a majority against Rebbi Eleazar ben Rebbi Simeon.

108 Rome ms: מַפשלחה; the *hif'il* of פשל means: to let hang down (in Arabic: to fail, be unsuccessful.)

109 A Tanna in the academy of R. Joḥanan, whose task was to memorize all known tannaïtic statements. R. Isaac bar Tevele is otherwise unknown.

110 Produce that may be from the Land of Israel is under the laws of the Sabbatical everywhere in the Land if carried by a human.

111 Since R. Eleazar ben R. Simeon was Rebbi's teacher; he could not be counted as a "colleague." It is said that after the death of R. Eleazar, Rebbi, who at that time was a widower, asked his widow to marry him. She answered: "Should a vessel that was used in the Sanctuary ever be used for profane purposes?"

112 Even though the observation of the Sabbatical year is among the duties that the returnees from Babylonia took upon themselves voluntarily (*Neh.* 10:32), it cannot be considered a Biblical commandment since it is intrinsically connected with the Jubilee year which presupposes that every family hold the grounds alotted to it in Joshua's distribution. Since there can be no Jubilee, the Sabbatical stands only on popular acceptance.

113 These object to R. Joḥanan and say that even if the Sabbatical cannot be considered a part of the Jubilee institution, at least it is to be kept in fulfillment of the vow registered by Nehemiah and, as such, it is Biblical.

(fol. 22b) **משנה ב**: הַמְקַבֵּל עָלָיו לִהְיוֹת נֶאֱמָן מְעַשֵּׂר אֶת שֶׁהוּא אוֹכֵל וְאֶת שֶׁהוּא מוֹכֵר וְאֶת שֶׁהוּא לוֹקֵחַ וְאֵינוֹ מִתְאָרֵחַ אֶצֶל עַם הָאָרֶץ. רַבִּי יְהוּדָה אוֹמֵר הַמִּתְאָרֵחַ אֶצֶל עַם הָאָרֶץ נֶאֱמָן. אָמְרוּ לוֹ עַל עַצְמוֹ אֵינוֹ נֶאֱמָן כֵּיצַד יְהֵא נֶאֱמָן עַל שֶׁל אֲחֵרִים.

Mishnah 2: He who takes it upon himself to be trustworthy[114] gives tithes for what he eats, what he sells, and what he buys, and he is not a guest of an *am haärez*. Rebbi Jehudah said, he who is a guest of an *am haärez* may be trustworthy. They said to him, for himself he is not trustworthy[115], how can he be trusted for others?

114 To guarantee that all his produce is tithed and free from the rules of *demay*.

115 Since it is assumed that the *am haärez* will serve him *demay* from which the heave of tithes was not taken, and by eating it he potentially commits a deadly sin, how can he be trusted by his customers that tithes were taken according to all rules?

(fol. 22d) **הלכה ב**: מַה שֶׁהוּא לוֹקֵחַ עַל מְנָת לֶאֱכוֹל. וְהָא תַנֵּינָן אֶת שֶׁהוּא אוֹכֵל. אֶלָּא אֶת שֶׁהוּא לוֹקֵחַ עַל מְנָת לִמְכּוֹר. וְהָתַנֵּינָן אֶת שֶׁהוּא מוֹכֵר אֶלָּא אֶת שֶׁהוּא לוֹקֵחַ עַל מְנָת לִמְכּוֹר וְאֶת שֶׁהוּא מוֹכֵר מִפֵּירוֹת מִכְנָסוֹ.

Halakhah 2: "What he buys," to eat it. But did we not state: "What he eats?" Hence, "what he buys" in order to sell it. But did we not state: "What he sells?" Hence, "what he buys" in order to sell it and "what he sells" from his own gathering.

תַּנֵּי אָמַר רַבִּי יוּדָה מִימֵיהֶן שֶׁל בַּעֲלֵי בָּתִּים לֹא נִמְנְעוּ לִהְיוֹת מִתְאָרְחִין אֶצֶל בַּעֲלֵי בָּתִּים חֲבֵירֵיהֶם. אַף עַל פִּי כֵן נוֹהֲגִין הָיוּ בְּפֵירוֹתֵיהֶן מְתוּקָּנִין לְתוֹךְ בָּתֵּיהֶן.

It was stated[116]: Rebbi Jehudah said, private persons never refrained from being guests of private persons of their acquaintance. Nevertheless, they used to put in order all their produce in their own houses.

116 Tosephta *Demay* 2:1. As usual, the opinion of the anonymous author of the Mishnah is attributed to R. Meïr. The position taken in the Mishnah and here by R. Jehudah in the Tosephta is the collective opinion of the Sages. The sentence here is R. Jehudah's (or the Sages') reply that one never objected to any private person's being the guest of an *am haäreẓ*. (What the observant person has to do in this case is described at the end of this Halakhah. The Yerushalmi accepts this relaxed standard for private persons but not for traders.)

אָמַר רִבִּי יוֹנָה חֲבֵירִין אֵינָן חֲשׁוּדִין לֹא לֶאֱכוֹל וְלֹא לְהַאֲכִיל. רִבִּי יוֹסֵי אוֹמֵר חֲבֵירִין חֲשׁוּדִין לֶאֱכוֹל וְאֵינָן חֲשׁוּדִין לְהַאֲכִיל. מַתְנִיתָא פְלִיגָא עַל רִבִּי יוֹסֵי. אָמְרוּ לוֹ עַל עַצְמוֹ אֵינוֹ נֶאֱמָן כֵּיצַד יְהֵא נֶאֱמָן עַל שֶׁל אֲחֵרִים. מִילֵּיהוֹן דְּרַבָּנִין מְסַייְעִין עַל רִבִּי יוֹסֵי. דְּאָמַר רִבִּי חֲנִינָא רִבִּי יָסָא בְשֵׁם רִבִּי יוֹחָנָן לֹא אָמַר רִבִּי יוּדָה אֶלָּא בְסוֹף אֲבָל בִּתְחִילָּה אוּף רִבִּי יוּדָה מוֹדֵי. אִין תֵּימַר חֲבֵירִים אֵין חֲשׁוּדִין לֹא לוֹכַל וְלֹא לְהַאֲכִיל מַה בֵּין בִּתְחִילָּה מַה בֵּין בְּסוֹף. דְּתַנֵּי הַמְקַבֵּל עָלָיו לִהְיוֹת נֶאֱמָן חוּץ מִדָּבָר אֶחָד אֵין מְקַבְּלִין אוֹתוֹ הֶחָשׁוּד עַל דָּבָר אֶחָד חָשׁוּד הוּא עַל הַכֹּל. רִבִּי יוּדָה אוֹמֵר אֵינוֹ חָשׁוּד אֶלָּא עַל אוֹתוֹ דָבָר בִּלְבַד.

Rebbi Jonah said, *ḥaverim*[117] are not suspected either to eat or to serve to others[118]. Rebbi Yose said, *ḥaverim* are suspected to eat but not to serve to others[119]. The Mishnah disagrees with Rebbi Yose: "They said to him, for himself he is not trustworthy, how can he be trusted for others?" The words of the rabbis support Rebbi Yose, for Rebbi Ḥanina, Rebbi Yasa, said in the name of Rebbi Joḥanan: Rebbi Jehudah spoke only of the end, but at the start even Rebbi Jehudah will agree.[120] If you say that *ḥaverim* are not suspected either to eat or to serve to others, what is the difference between start and end? As we have stated[121]: "He who takes it on himself to be trustworthy except for one thing cannot be accepted; he who is suspect in one thing is suspect in everything. Rebbi Jehudah said, he is only suspect in that thing alone."

117 As explained in the next Mishnah, a *ḥaver* is a person who takes it upon himself to observe the rules of ritual purity in his private life, away from the Sanctuary, and to avoid becoming impure if at all possible. With the disappearance of the last ways to cleanse oneself from the impurity induced by the dead (see the Notes to Mishnah *Berakhot* 1:1), fellowship was slowly transformed into the fraternity of those who followed ritual law scrupulously. Since Rebbi Jonah and Rebbi Yose are late Amoraïm, we have to assume that for them, fellowship and trustworthiness are practically identical; see the story about R. Simeon ben Laqish in the next Halakhah, Note 154.

118 According to R. Jonah, a *ḥaver* who is seen eating at an *am haäreẓ*'s home or inviting an *am haäreẓ* to eat with him loses his standing. There is no imputation that the home of the *am haäreẓ* would not be kosher, but his food may be impure and eating it might break the vow of fellowship. That would not apply to fruits eaten dry, for example. But the food presented by the *am haäreẓ* is *demay* by definition and it will be made clear that the vow of fellowship is a step above that of being trustworthy for tithes; hence, eating *demay* breaks trustworthiness and, *a fortiori*, fellowship. If one gives of one's food to an *am haäreẓ*, it becomes impure by contact with the impure person which is a sure break of the vow of fellowship.

119 R. Yose holds that a *ḥaver* who is seen eating from a source considered as *demay* does not lose his standing since he might have put his food in order mentally as explained at the end of the Halakhah. In the next Halakhah, however, the statement of R. Yose is qualified to apply to trustworthy persons only, not to recognized *ḥaverim*.

120 If somebody takes the vow (publicly, as explained later) of

trustworthiness, he must accept the rules spelled out in the Mishnah as the majority opinion. If later he is seen eating from the *am haäreẓ*'s, there is disagreement between R. Jehudah and the Sages.

121 A similar statement is in Tosephta *Demay* 2:3, reproduced Babli *Bekhorot* 30b, but speaking of fellowship instead of trustworthiness. Again, the anonymous opinion here is R. Meïr's in the Tosephta, and R. Jehudah's here is that of the anonymous majority there. (Maimonides *Miškav Umošav* 10:9 follows the Babli and, hence, the opinion expressed here by R. Jehudah.)

תַּנֵּי הַנֶּאֱמָן עַל הַטָּהֳרוֹת נֶאֱמָן עַל הַמַּעְשְׂרוֹת. תַּנִּיתָהּ רִבִּי יַנַּאי בֵּי רִבִּי יִשְׁמָעֵאל וְאָמַר טַעְמָא. הָדָא דְתֵימַר בְּמִתְאָרֵחַ אֶצְלוֹ אֲבָל בְּרַבִּים אֵינוֹ נֶאֱמָן עַד שֶׁיְּקַבֵּל עָלָיו בְּרַבִּים. רִבִּי אַמִּי בְשֵׁם רִבִּי יַנַּאי אֲפִילוּ אֲנִי אֵינִי נֶאֱמָן עַד שֶׁנְּקַבֵּל עָלָיו בְּרַבִּים. רִבִּי זְעִירָא רִבִּי יָסָא בְשֵׁם רִבִּי יוֹחָנָן אֲפִילוּ חָבֵר שֶׁשָּׁלַח לְחָבֵר צָרִיךְ לְעַשֵּׂר. רִבִּי זְעִירָא בְּעָא קוֹמֵי רִבִּי יָסָא כְּגוֹן אֲנִי לְרִבִּי שְׁמוּאֵל בַּר רַב יִצְחָק וְרִבִּי שְׁמוּאֵל בַּר רַב יִצְחָק לִי. אָמַר לֵיהּ מַה אַתְּ בְּעֵי מֵרִבִּי שְׁמוּאֵל בַּר רַב יִצְחָק דְּכָל־מַה דְּהוּא אוֹכֵל מִן שׁוּקָא הוּא אוֹכֵל.

It was stated: "He who is trustworthy for purity is trustworthy for tithes.[122]" Rebbi Yannai ben Rebbi Ismaël stated it and explained his reason: That means, if one is a guest of his, but for the public he is not trustworthy until he accepts it publicly[123]. Rebbi Ammi in the name of Rebbi Yannai: Even I am not trustworthy until we accept it in public[124]. Rebbi Zeïra, Rebbi Yasa, in the name of Rebbi Joḥanan: Even a *ḥaver* who sent to another *ḥaver*, the recipient must tithe[125]. Rebbi Zeïra asked before Rebbi Yasa, for example, I to Rebbi Samuel ben Rav Isaac, and Rebbi Samuel ben Rav Isaac to me? He answered him, what do you want from Rebbi Samuel ben Rav Isaac, because all he eats, he eats from the market[126].

122 This implies that one is not accepted for fellowship until he be trustworthy for tithes; see the next Halakhah.

123 Usually, "publicly" means before at least ten adult males. Similarly, the Tosephta (*Demay* 2:14) speaks of "him who accepts before the fellowship." However, the Babli (*Bekhorot* 20b) requires "before three people" (who form a court of law.)

124 The Tosephta (*Demay* 2:13) and the Babli (*Bekhorot* 30b) exempt a member of a Rabbinic court since he would not have been accepted into the court had he not given a vow of fellowship.

125 In order to avoid situations as that described in Halakhah 1:3 between R. Zeïra and R. Jeremiah, where each trusted the other to put the food in order.

126 He was Babylonian in origin and, in contrast to R. Zeïra, never acquired land in Galilee. Hence, all he ate was bought from the market as *demay* and immediately put in order.

הוּא נֶאֱמָן וְאִשְׁתּוֹ אֵינָהּ נֶאֱמֶנֶת לוֹקְחִין מִמֶּנּוּ וְאֵין מִתְאָרְחִין אֶצְלוֹ. אֲבָל אָמְרוּ הֲרֵי כְדָר עִם נָחָשׁ בִּכְפִיפָה. אִשְׁתּוֹ נֶאֱמֶנֶת וְהוּא אֵינוֹ נֶאֱמָן מִתְאָרְחִין אֶצְלוֹ וְאֵין לוֹקְחִין מִמֶּנּוּ אֲבָל אָמְרוּ תָּבוֹא מְאֵירָה לְמִי שֶׁאִשְׁתּוֹ נֶאֱמֶנֶת וְהוּא אֵינוֹ נֶאֱמָן.

"If[127] he is trustworthy but his wife is not, one buys from him[128] but one cannot be his guest. But they said, he is like one who lives with a snake in the same basket[129]. If his wife is trustworthy but he is not, one can be his guest but not buy from him. But they said, a curse should fall on him whose wife is trustworthy while he is not."

127 Tosephta *Demay* 3:9, in slightly different language. The curse on the man whose wife is trustworthy while he is not is missing there.

128 On the market.

129 Since she will serve him *demay* that was not brought in order if he forgot to ask.

תַּנֵּי לֹא יְשַׁמֵּשׁ חָבֵר בְּמִשְׁתֶּה עַם הָאָרֶץ וְלֹא בִסְעוּדַת עַם הָאָרֶץ אֶלָּא אִם כֵּן הָיָה הַכֹּל מְתוּקָּן וּמְעוּשָּׂר מִתַּחַת יָדוֹ וַאֲפִילוּ מֵינֶקֶת שֶׁל יַיִן. וְאִם שִׁימֵּשׁ חָבֵר בְּמִשְׁתֶּה עַם הָאָרֶץ וּבִסְעוּדַת עַם הָאָרֶץ הֲרֵי זוּ חֲזָקָה לְמַעְשְׂרוֹת. רָאוּ אוֹתוֹ מֵיסֵב אֵינָהּ חֲזָקָה אֲנִי אוֹמֵר עַל הַתְּנָאִין שֶׁבְּלִבּוֹ הוּא מֵיסֵב. בְּנוֹ מֵיסֵב אֶצְלוֹ צָרִיךְ לְעַשֵּׂר עַל יָדָיו. חֲבֵירוֹ אֵין צָרִיךְ לְעַשֵּׂר עַל יָדָיו.

It was stated[130]: "A *ḥaver*[131] should not serve as waiter at the wedding feast of an *am haäreẓ* or the dinner of an *am haäreẓ* except when everything was in order and tithed under his control, even[132] the wine ladle. But if[133] a *ḥaver* acted as waiter at the wedding feast of an *am haäreẓ* or the dinner of an *am haäreẓ* this is *prima facie* evidence for tithes. If one saw him[134] lying on a couch it would not be *prima facie* evidence, since I say that he is lying on the couch after making the required mental stipulations. If his son is lying down next to him, he has to tithe for him; he does not have to tithe for another *ḥaver*."

130 Similar text is in Tosephta *Demay* 3:6-7.

131 According to R. S. Lieberman, the "*ḥaver*" here is the trustworthy person, not necessarily a full member of the fellowship, but the language both here and in the Tosephta does not support this explanation. Maimonides, in Chapter 10 of *Maäser*, identifies trustworthy person and *ḥaver*, but he writes for practical use and in his time the difference between the two had disappeared since nobody was able to eat in purity. However, as will be explained in the next Halakhah, one facet of fellowship, the washing of one's hands before a meal, is still valid and this has to be added to the conditions of trustworthiness in any case.

132 Including the wine that might be in the ladle separate from the amphora from which the heave of the tithe is taken.

133 Since a *ḥaver* may not serve at a dinner of untithed food, his presence is a guarantee of the kosher status of the entire meal.

134 The *ḥaver* was not a waiter but a guest; his participation is not proof of

anything since before the meal he could have made a mental stipulation to give the necessary tithes for what he ate from his own provisions at home when he returned; this is an acceptable way of tithing *demay* in emergencies (Mishnah 7:1). But he is not responsible for anybody else at the dinner, except for his dependents.

(fol. 22b) **משנה ג**: הַמְקַבֵּל עָלָיו לִיהְיוֹת חָבֵר אֵינוֹ מוֹכֵר לְעַם הָאָרֶץ לַח וְיָבֵשׁ וְאֵינוֹ לוֹקֵחַ מִמֶּנּוּ לַח וְאֵינוֹ מִתְאָרֵחַ אֶצֶל עַם הָאָרֶץ וְלֹא מְאָרְחוֹ אֶצְלוֹ בִכְסוּתוֹ. רִבִּי יְהוּדָה אוֹמֵר אַף לֹא יְגַדֵּל בְּהֵמָה דַקָּה וְלֹא יְהֵא פָרוּץ בִּנְדָרִים וּבִשְׂחוֹק וְלֹא יְהֵא מִיטַּמֵּא לְמֵתִים וּמְשַׁמֵּשׁ בְּבֵית הַמִּדְרָשׁ. אָמְרוּ לוֹ לֹא בָאוּ אֵלּוּ לִכְלָל.

Mishnah 3: He who accepts upon himself to be a *ḥaver* will not sell to the *am haärez̧* wet or dry[135] and will not buy wet from him[136], is not guest of an *am haärez̧* and does not have him as a guest in his clothing[137]. Rebbi Jehudah says, moreover he should not raise animals of the flock[138], should not overstep bounds by vows[139] and laughter, should not defile himself with the dead[140], and be a regular in the house of study. They said to him, these are not included.

135 The entire essence of fellowship is to preserve food grown or raised in the Land of Israel from ritual impurity. Since the *am haärez̧* is characterized by his disregard for ritual purity (except in Jerusalem during the three annual pilgrimages when the Temple was standing, when "all of Israel are *ḥaverim*"), food sold to the *am haärez̧* will certainly become defiled.

136 There is a rabbinic decree (explained in the next Note) that any fluid which becomes impure in any degree becomes impure in the first degree. In particular, unwashed hands are always impure in the second degree; the *am haärez̧* can be assumed not to wash his hands before handling

either drinks or wet food (such as olives); the food therefore is impure in the first degree and unfit for the *ḥaver*. (Fluids that cause impurity are water, human body fluids, grape juice or wine, olive oil, and date honey.)

137 The impurities caused by certain human discharges, such as gonorrhea and menstrual blood, impart original impurity not only to the human himself but also to his clothes. Hence, the clothes of an *am haäreẓ* have to be considered sources of original impurity and a *ḥaver* can have an *am haäreẓ* person as a guest only if he sends him first to the ritual bath to be purified and then clothes him in his own pure clothing. The stages of impurity are, in order, 1) "grandfather of impurity," a dead person and the house in which there is a corpse, 2) original impurity, anything in contact with a corpse or in a house in which there is a corpse (with a few exceptions), and any other impurity described in the Torah, 3) impurity in the first degree, imparted by contact with original impurity or any impure fluid (because fluids might be in contact with impure human discharges, as above), 3) impurity in the second degree, imparted by contact with impurity of the first degree, also the status of any unwashed hands unless the person was careful that his hands should not touch anything absentmindedly, 4) impurity in the third degree, imparted by contact with impurity of the second degree, applicable to sacrifices and heave only, not to profane food (including profane food eaten under the rules of the heave), and 5) impurity in the fourth degree, imparted by contact with impurity of the third degree, applicable to sacrifices only, but not to heave or to profane food.

138 Sheep or goats. The prohibition applies only to goats whose grazing is destructive to young trees and should be permitted in semi-desert conditions only, never near cultivated land.

139 The scrupulous should not make vows for fear of not fulfilling them to the letter. Laughter might be considered a sacrilege; since nobody would laugh in the presence of a king, how could one laugh in the always present fear of the Almighty King of Kings.

140 Since priests may not defile themselves unless it be for a close relative (*Lev.* 21:1). However, for the majority view, burying the dead is a most sacred duty because its reward is entirely in the hands of Heaven since the object of the duty can no longer give thanks.

(fol. 22d) **הלכה ג**: אֵינוֹ לוֹקֵחַ הֵימֶנּוּ לַח. הָא יָבֵשׁ מוּתָּר שֶׁעַמֵּי הָאָרֶץ נֶאֱמָנִין עַל הֶכְשֵׁירוּת. וְתַנֵּי כֵן נֶאֱמָן עַם הָאָרֶץ לוֹמַר הַפֵּירוֹת הַלָּלוּ לֹא הוּכְשְׁרוּ. אֲבָל אֵינוֹ נֶאֱמָן לוֹמַר הוּכְשְׁרוּ אֶלָּא שֶׁלֹּא קִיבְּלוּ אֶת הַטּוּמְאָה.

Halakhah 3: "He will not buy wet from him," hence dry is permitted since the *amē haärez̦* are trustworthy as to preparation[141]. And it was stated: "The *am haärez̦* is trustworthy to say, these fruits were never prepared. But he is not trustworthy to say that they were prepared but did not accept impurity[142]."

141 Fluids always become impure by contact. Produce in the ground cannot become impure. Produce harvested dry can become impure if first it was "prepared" by contact with water (or any of the fluids mentioned above), *Lev.* 11:38. Since the *pu'al* verb יתן is written defective, orthographically identical to the active *pi'el* form, it is concluded that even passive wetting must have an active ingredient, *viz.*, that the wetting should be agreeable to the owner. Since the status of the produce depends on the owner and the rules were known to the *am haärez̦*, his word in this matter can be trusted.

142 If the produce is prepared, the *am haärez̦* by his person will make it most likely that it is impure.

הָא מִכְּלָל דּוּ מוֹדֵי עַל הַקַּמָּייָתָא. לֵית הָדָא פְלִיגָא עַל דְּרִבִּי יוֹנָה דְּרִבִּי יוֹנָה אָמַר חֲבֵירִין אֵינָן חֲשׁוּדִין לֹא לֶאֱכוֹל וְלֹא לְהַאֲכִיל שֶׁלֹּא יֵלֵךְ וִיטַמֵּא גוּפוֹ וְיָבֹא וִיטַמֵּא טָהֳרוֹת. וַאֲפִילוּ עַל דְּרִבִּי יוֹסֵי לֵית הָדָא פְלִיגָא. דְּרִבִּי יוֹסֵי אָמַר חֲבֵירִין חֲשׁוּדִין לוֹכַל וְאֵינָן חֲשׁוּדִין לְהַאֲכִיל. תַּמָּן לְטָהֳרוֹת אֲבָל הָכָא לְמַעְשְׂרוֹת. הַנֶּאֱמָן עַל הַטָּהֳרוֹת נֶאֱמָן עַל הַמַּעְשְׂרוֹת.

By the first statement he invalidated the second[143]. Does this not disagree with Rebbi Jonah, since Rebbi Jonah said, *ḥaverim* are not suspect to eat or to serve to others? He should not go, defile his body and come to defile pure food[144]. It does not disagree even with Rebbi Yose, since Rebbi Yose said, *ḥaverim* are suspect to eat but not to serve to others. There one speaks about purity but here about tithes[145]. "He who is trustworthy for purities is trustworthy for tithes[146]."

143 Rebbi Jehudah, who in Mishnah 2 permitted to be a guest at the *am haärez*'s, accepts all restrictions given in Mishnah 3. Why can he not accept that the *ḥaver* will eat only dry produce not prepared for impurity?

144 If the problem were only food, R. Jehudah could disagree. But since the chairs and couches in the house of the *am haärez* must be presumed to be originally impure (*Lev.* 15:6, 20), the *ḥaver* will not be able to remain undefiled in that house; returning, he might defile all pure food in his own house.

145 It follows that the "*ḥaver*" of R. Yose is not really a *ḥaver* but a person trustworthy for tithes.

146 See the previous Halakhah.

(fol. 23a) תַּנֵּי כָּל־הַבָּא צָרִיךְ לְקַבֵּל עָלָיו אֲפִילוּ חָבֵר תַּלְמִיד חָכָם אֲבָל חָכָם שֶׁיָּשַׁב בִּישִׁיבָה אֵינוֹ צָרִיךְ לְקַבֵּל עָלָיו שֶׁכְּבָר קִיבֵּל עָלָיו מִשָּׁעָה שֶׁיָּשַׁב. אָמַר רִבִּי לָא וְהוּא שֶׁקִּיבֵּל עָלָיו מִשָּׁעָה רִאשׁוֹנָה. רִבִּי יוֹסֵי בְּעֵי אִי מִשָּׁעָה רִאשׁוֹנָה לָמָּה לִי חָבֵר אֲפִילוּ עַם הָאָרֶץ. אַתְיָא דְּרִבִּי לָא כְּרִבִּי שִׁמְעוֹן בֶּן לָקִישׁ. דְּרִבִּי שִׁמְעוֹן בֶּן לָקִישׁ הֲוָה סְלַק לְגַבֵּי אִילֵּין דְּבֵי רִבִּי יַנַּאי וַהֲווֹ נְשַׁיָּא חַזְיָין לֵיהּ וְעָרְקִין מְקוֹמוֹי. אֲמַר לוֹן אָבָא לְכוֹן בְּיִיתָא עַם הָאָרֶץ אֲנִי אֵצֶל הַטָּהֳרוֹת.

It was stated[147]: "Everybody who comes has to accept[148], even a learned *ḥaver*[149]; but a rabbi[150] who has been sitting in rabbinical court does not have to accept because he did it at the moment he joined the court." Rebbi La said, only if he really accepted it from the first hour on[151]. Rebbi Yose asked, if it was from the first hour, what is the difference between a *ḥaver* and an *am haärez*? The position of Rebbi La parallels that of Rebbi Simeon ben Laqish, for Rebbi Simeon ben Laqish came to those of the house of Rebbi Yannai[152]; the women saw him and removed themselves from before him[153]. He said to them, I shall come to your house; I am an *am haärez* with respect to purities[154].

147 Tosephta *Demay* 2:13, Babli *Bekhorot* 30b.

148 As explained in the Tosephta of the next paragraph, he has publicly to accept the restrictions imposed on a *ḥaver*.

149 One is forced to explain this "*ḥaver*" by "trustworthy person."

150 The חכם everywhere is the acting rabbi.

151 Rebbi La, student of R. Simeon ben Laqish, represents the later generations when abstinence from ritually unclean food was no longer a prerequisite for a rabbinical position.

152 The yeshivah of R. Yannai, after the latter's death.

153 So that he should not come in contact with any of their clothes and become impure.

154 He was not a *ḥaver* in the sense of the Mishnah even though he was number two in the rabbinical establishment of his time.

תַּנֵּי הוּא נֶעֱנֶה לַחֲבוּרָה וּבָנָיו וּבְנֵי בֵיתוֹ נֶעֱנִין לוֹ. אִית תַּנָּיֵי תַּנֵּי הוּא וּבָנָיו וּבְנֵי בֵיתוֹ נֶעֱנִין לַחֲבוּרָה. וְלֹא פְלִיג. כָּאן בְּטִפּוּלִין לַאֲבִיהֶן כָּאן כְּשֶׁאֵינָן טִפּוּלִין לַאֲבִיהֶן. תַּנֵּי רִבִּי חֲלַפְתָּא בֶּן שָׁאוּל גְּדוֹלִים נֶעֱנִין לַחֲבוּרָה קְטַנִּים נֶעֱנִין לוֹ.

It was stated[155]: "He answers[156] to the fellowship, his sons and household answer to him." Some Tannaïm state: "He, his sons, and his household answer to the fellowship." They do not disagree: the first, if they are dependent on their father[156], the second, if they do not depend on their father. Rebbi Ḥalaphta ben Saul stated, adults answer to the fellowship, minors answer to him[157].

155 A different text with the same meaning in Tosephta *Demay* 2:14, a substantially different text in Babli *Bekhorot* 30b.

156 The acceptance of the rules of fellowship has to be in public in front of the resident *ḥaverim*; his wife, servants, and minor children will accept before him.

156 These answer to their father.

157 R. Ḥalaphta ben Saul disagrees with the explanation just given; according to him, only minors do not have to appear personally before the fellowship. In the Babli, Rabban Simeon ben Gamliel is reported to require appearance of the (adult) sons before the fellowship because that is the more impressive ceremony.

תַּנֵּי מַקְרִיבִין לִכְנָפַיִם וְאַחַר כָּךְ מְלַמְּדִין לְטָהֳרוֹת. אָמַר רִבִּי יִצְחָק בְּרִבִּי לָעְזָר כְּנָפַיִים מַדָּפוֹת הַסָּתוֹת טָהֳרוֹת מַעְשְׂרוֹת.

It was stated[158]: "One brings close[159] for 'wings'[160] and after that one teaches about purity[161]." Rebbi Isaac ben Eleazar said, wings, smells[162], pushings[163], purity[164], tithes.

158 In Tosephta *Demay* 2:11 and Babli *Bekhorot* 30b: "One accepts for 'wings' and after that one accepts for purities."

159 People who are interested in following the strict rules are first trained to follow the strict discipline of washing their hands before they are taught the intricacies of the rules of pure food.

160 "Wings" are the hands the person who is a candidate for fellowship has to promise to wash before eating (Rashi in *Bekhorot* 30b). The institution of washing one's hands for profane food follows the discipline of the heave (*Bikkurim* 2:1, fol. 64d). The washing required here is for any food since even dry food may become wet by saliva. The Babylonian version of the same discipline is to wash only for meals taken with bread (*Ḥulin* 106a), but there fellowship was unknown.

161 Pure food. Taking טהרות as a plural of abstraction.

162 From נדף "to give smell" (Maimonides to *Zavim* 4:6). The Biblical original impurities produced by a person with gonorrhea refer not only to things he touches but also those on which he sits or which he carries or moves otherwise. A lesser impurity is imparted to things above him but which he does not move. These are called מדף, "a smell of impurity." The list given is a syllabus of the different kinds of impurity the novice has to learn about.

163 Vessels and foodstuffs that the

zav, the person with gonorrhea, pushes or moves. These become impure even if never touched by the *zav*.

164 All other impurities treated in Mishnah tractate *Ṭahorot*.

בָּרִאשׁוֹנָה הָיוּ אוֹמְרִים חָבֵר שֶׁנַּעֲשָׂה גַּבַּיי דּוֹחִין אוֹתוֹ מֵחֲבוּרָתוֹ. חָזְרוּ לוֹמַר כָּל־זְמָן שֶׁהוּא גַּבַּיי דּוֹחִין אוֹתוֹ מֵחֲבוּרָתוֹ. יָצָא מִגַּבַּיְיָתוֹ הֲרֵי הוּא כְחָבֵר.

"In earlier times, they said: One removes from fellowship a *ḥaver* who became tax collector. They changed to say, one removes him from fellowship for the entire time he acts as tax collector. Once he left his collectorship, he is again treated as a *ḥaver*.[165]"

165 Tosephta *Demay* 3:4, Babli *Bekhorot* 31a. Since taxes in antiquity were usually farmed out, the tax collector had to pay the anticipated taxes up front to the government and then try to recover them from the population. Since he incurred expenses for the collection, he was forced to collect more than what he had paid to the government. Any amount taken above his expenses is possibly theft, and certainly any amount taken above the official rate is robbery. The tax collector would not be in business if he did not make money. Hence, he probably is a thief and a robber and disqualified as member of a religious fellowship. However, in the absence of bidders the Roman government would force people to become tax collectors; the prior rule was therefore no longer enforceable or applicable.

חִייָא בְּרִבִּי בּוּן בְּשֵׁם רִבִּי יוֹחָנָן חָבֵר שֶׁיָּצָא לְחוּצָה לָאָרֶץ אֵין דּוֹחִין אוֹתוֹ מֵחֲבוּרָתוֹ. הָא קָטָן אֵין צָרִיךְ קֵירוּב.

Ḥiyya ben Rebbi Abun[166] in the name of Rebbi Joḥanan: One does not remove from fellowship a *ḥaver* who went outside the Land[167]. Hence[168], a minor does not need to be brought close.

166 He probably is R. Ḥiyya ben Abba.

167 The land outside the Land of Israel is impure (*Amos* 7:17); the person

who leaves the Land automatically becomes impure. But this impurity is not from the Torah and is easily removed upon return; hence, leaving the Land on trips was not frowned upon (except for priests who had no compelling reason to go abroad.) Because of this impurity, the Israeli fellowship was impossible in Babylonia at all times.

168 The place of this sentence is not here but three paragraphs earlier (but it possibly is a statement by R. Joḥanan.) Since the minor takes the obligation of fellowship through his father, his father, not the fellowship, is required to teach him.

(fol. 22b) **משנה ד**: הַנַּחְתּוֹמִין לֹא חִייְבוּ אוֹתָן חֲכָמִים לְהַפְרִישׁ אֶלָּא כְדֵי תְּרוּמַת מַעֲשֵׂר וְחַלָּה. הַחֶנְוָנִין אֵינָן רְשָׁאִין לִמְכּוֹר אֶת הַדְּמַאי. וְכָל־הַמַּשְׁפִּיעִין בְּמִידָּה גַסָּה רְשָׁאִין לִמְכּוֹר אֶת הַדְּמַאי. וְאֵלּוּ הֵן הַמַּשְׁפִּיעִין בְּמִידָּה גַסָּה כְּגוֹן הַסִּיטוֹנוֹת וּמוֹכְרֵי תְבוּאָה.

Mishnah 4: The sages did not obligate bakers to separate more than the heave of the tithe and *ḥallah*[169]. Grocers are not permitted to sell *demay*. All who sell wholesale in large quantities may sell *demay*[170]. The following sell wholesale in large quantities, for example grain buyers[171] and sellers.

169 They do not have to take the Second Tithe, not even in order to redeem it, in order to keep prices down. The Halakhah will address the questions raised by such a policy.

170 Since the buyer knows that he buys *demay*.

171 Latin *sitona, ae, m.*, "purchaser of grain, commissioner, purveyor", from Greek σιτώνης "public buyer of grain," wholesale grain merchant who worked with or for the government (E. G.).

(fol. 23a) **הלכה ד**: תַּמָּן תַּנִּינָן הַלּוֹקֵחַ מִן הַנַּחְתּוֹם כֵּיצַד הוּא מְעַשֵּׂר. הָכָא אַתְּ אָמַר הַלּוֹקֵחַ מַפְרִישׁ וְהָכָא אַתְּ אָמַר הַנַּחְתּוֹם מַפְרִישׁ. רִבִּי יוֹנָה אָמַר אִיתְפַּלְּגוּן רִבִּי לָעְזָר וְרִבִּי יוֹחָנָן. חַד אָמַר כָּאן בְּעוֹשֶׂה בְטָהֳרָה וְכָאן בְּעוֹשֶׂה בְטוּמְאָה. וְחָרָנָה אָמַר כָּאן בְּמִידָּה דַקָּה וְכָאן בְּמִידָּה גַסָּה. וְלָא יָדְעִין מָאן דְּאָמַר דָּא וּמָאן דְּאָמַר דָּא. מִן מַה[176] דְּאָמַר רִבִּי יוֹחָנָן מִפְּנֵי הַטָּהֳרוֹת. הֲוֵי רִבִּי לָעְזָר הוּא דָמַר כָּאן בְּמִידָּה דַקָּה וְכָאן בְּמִידָּה גַסָּה. וְקַשְׁיָא עַל דְּרִבִּי יוֹחָנָן אִם בְּעוֹשֶׂה בְטָהֳרָה יַפְרִישׁ עַל הַכֹּל. בְּדִין הָיָה שֶׁלֹּא יַפְרִישׁ כְּלוּם שֶׁאֵין מוֹסְרִין וַדַּאי לְעַם הָאָרֶץ. וְקַשְׁיָא עַל דְּרִבִּי לָעְזָר אִם בְּמִידָּה דַקָּה יַפְרִישׁ עַל הַכֹּל. הַחֶנְוָנִין אֵין רְשָׁאִין לִמְכּוֹר דְּמַאי.

Halakhah 4: There[172], we have stated: "If one buys from the baker[173], how does he tithe?" There you say, the buyer separates, and here you say, the baker separates. Rebbi Jonah said, Rebbi Eleazar and Rebbi Johanan disagree. One says, here if he works in purity[174], there if he works in impurity[175]. The other says, here in retail, there in wholesale. We did not know who said what. Since Rebbi Johanan said[176], because of purity, it follows that Rebbi Eleazar is the one who said, here in retail, there in wholesale. It is difficult for Rebbi Johanan, if he works in purity, let him separate everything[177]. It would be logical that he should not give anything because one does not deliver certain grain[178] to the *am haärez*. It is difficult for Rebbi Eleazar, if it is in retail, let him separate everything. Grocers are not permitted to sell *demay*[179]!

172 Mishnah 5:1 requires that he who buys from a baker has to give *hallah*, heave of the tithe, and redeem the Second Tithe. The Mishnah here demands that the baker himself give *hallah* and heave of the tithe.

173 The baker is the craftsman who does the actual baking in his *tannur*, a stove in the form of a truncated cone, the fire burning on the bottom. The bread dough is brought in from the top and slapped onto the walls to be baked

into pittah; this motion of "slapping down" is expressed by the root בחת. The seller of baked goods, either the baker in a separate store adjacent to his baking establishment, or an independent dealer, is the פַּלְטֵר, from Greek πρατήρ. The baker will also bake other people's dough for a fee; that case is not considered here.

174 The baker is not a *ḥaver*, but he has hired a *ḥaver* to knead the dough so that it should not become impure. If the baker handles dry flour or dry bread, nothing happens since profane dry food can be made impure only by original impurity. Therefore, the *ḥaver* may take the heave of the tithe and *ḥallah*.

175 One does not trust him to handle impure heave and *ḥallah* following the rules.

176 In a related discussion, Halakhah 5:1. (The reading מה is from the Rome ms., Venice print: מאן.)

177 Why should he be exempt from Second Tithe?

178 Grain from which it is known with certainty that the Heave of the Tithe was not taken. The baker here must be an *am haärez̧* since we already have stated that the *ḥaver* may not sell *demay* at all. Hence, in the majority of cases, the Second Tithe, together with the heave of the tithe, are already taken and there would remain only *ḥallah* which is a duty upon bread dough only.

179 There is no reason why the bread retailer should be treated in any way different from other retailers.

חֲבֵרַייָא בְּשֵׁם רִבִּי לָעְזָר דְּרִבִּי מֵאִיר הִיא דְּרִבִּי מֵאִיר אָמַר לֹא הִתִּירוּ לִמְכּוֹר דְּמַאי אֶלָּא לְסִיטוֹן בִּלְבַד. הָתִיב רִבִּי יוֹסֵי וְהָא מַתְנִיתָא פְּלִיגָא אֵילּוּ הֵן הַמְשׁוּפָּעִין בְּמִידָּה גַּסָּה כְּגוֹן הַסִּיטוֹנוֹת וּמוֹכְרֵי תְבוּאָה. הוֹי אִית חוֹרָנִין. אָמַר רִבִּי יוֹסֵי לֹא עַל הָדָא רִבִּי אֶלְעָזָר[180] אָמַר הָדָא מִילְתָא אֶלָּא עַל הָדָא. דְּתַנֵּי בַּמֶּה דְּבָרִים אֲמוּרִים בִּזְמַן שֶׁהָיָה מוֹכֵר בַּחֲנוּתוֹ אוֹ עַל פֶּתַח חֲנוּתוֹ. אֲבָל אִם הָיָה מוֹכֵר בְּפַלְטֵר אוֹ בַּחֲנוּתוֹ שֶׁהִיא סְמוּכָה לְפַלְטֵר מְעַשֵּׂר עַל הַכֹּל עָלֶיהָ. חֲבֵרַייָא בְּשֵׁם רִבִּי לָעְזָר דְּרִבִּי מֵאִיר הִיא דְּרִבִּי מֵאִיר אָמַר לֹא הִתִּירוּ לִמְכּוֹר דְּמַאי אֶלָּא לְסִיטוֹן בִּלְבַד. הֵיידָן רִבִּי מֵאִיר הָהִיא דְתַנֵּינָן לְבַתְרָהּ. רִבִּי מֵאִיר אוֹמֵר אֶת שֶׁדַּרְכּוֹ לִמְדּוֹד בְּגַסָּה וּמְדָדוֹ בְּדַקָּה טְפֵילָה דַקָּה לְגַסָּה. תַּנֵּי רִבִּי חִייָא

כֵּן אֶת שֶׁדַּרְכּוֹ לְהִימָּדֵד בְּגַסָּה וּמְדָדוֹ בְּדַקָּה טְפֵילָה דַקָּה לְגַסָּה. וְכֵן פַּלְטֵר מִידָּה דַקָּה וְחָנוּת מִידָּה גַסָּה טְפֵילָה הִיא הַגַּסָּה לַדַּקָּה.

The colleagues in the name of Rebbi Eleazar: It[181] is Rebbi Meïr's, since Rebbi Meïr said, they permitted to sell *demay* only to the commissioned grain merchant[182]. Rebbi Yose objected, does not the Mishnah disagree? "The following sell wholesale in large quantities, *for example* commissioners and grain merchants." Hence, there must be others! Rebbi Yose said, this is not what Rebbi Eleazar referred to, but the following, as we have stated[183]: "When is this statement operative, if he sells in his bakeshop or at the door of his bakeshop. But if he was selling in the bakery or in his bakeshop adjacent to the bakery, he must give all tithes on it." The colleagues in the name of Rebbi Eleazar: It is Rebbi Meïr's, since Rebbi Meïr said, they only permitted to the commissioned grain merchant to sell *demay*. Which (statement of) Rebbi Meïr? The one we have stated next[184]: "Rebbi Meïr says, something which usually he measured wholesale and he measured retail, the retail is adjunct to the wholesale." Rebbi Ḥiyya[185] stated: "Something which usually is measured wholesale and he measured it retail, the retail is adjunct to the wholesale[186]." And so the bakery is retail but the bakeshop is wholesale, there[187] the wholesale is adjunct to the retail.

180 Reading of the Rome ms. Venice and Leyden have ר' אילא who is mentioned in the paragraph in disagreement with the colleagues.

181 The statement of Mishnah 2:4.

182 But not any other wholesaler of foodstuffs. The full statement is quoted in Babli *Baba Meẓi'a* 56a.

183 Tosephta *Demay* 3:10, on the statement of the Mishnah, "The Sages did not obligate bakers to separate more than the heave of the tithe and *ḥallah*," in slightly different wording.

184 The next Mishnah, in

abbreviated form.

185 The Great Rebbi Ḥiyya, collector of Tosephtot. His formulation, which in contrast to the Mishnah refers not to the standing of the seller but to the goods sold, is in Tosephta *Demay* 3:10.

186 Somebody who buys a retail quantity from a wholesaler must expect to receive *demay*.

187 If the bakery, or the baker's workshop physically connected to the retail operation, would sell wholesale, it nevertheless would be a retail operation.

חֲבֵרַיָּא בְּשֵׁם רִבִּי יוֹחָנָן מִפְּנֵי הַתִּינוֹקוֹת דְּלָא יֵיכְלוּן טֶבֶל. רִבִּי לָא בְּשֵׁם רִבִּי יוֹחָנָן מִידָּה דַקָּה הוֹאִיל וְהַמּוֹכֵר מִשְׂתַּכֵּר הַמּוֹכֵר מַפְרִישׁ. מִידָּה גַסָּה הוֹאִיל וְהַלּוֹקֵחַ מִשְׂתַּכֵּר הַלּוֹקֵחַ מַפְרִישׁ. מַתְנִיתִין מְסַייֵעַ לְדֵין וּמַתְנִיתִין מְסַייֵעַ לְדֵין. מַתְנִיתִין מְסַייֵעַ לַחֲבֵרַיָּא רִבִּי נְחֶמְיָה אָמַר אֶת שֶׁהוּא טָפֵל לְדַקָּה כְדַקָּה וְאֶת שֶׁהוּא טָפֵל לְגַסָּה כְגַסָּה. מַתְנִיתִין מְסַייֵעַ לְרִבִּי לָא תַּנֵּי רִבִּי יִשְׁמָעֵאל בְּנוֹ שֶׁל רִבִּי יוֹחָנָן בֶּן בְּרוֹקָה אָמַר מָדַד לוֹ בְדַקָּה חַייָב אֲפִילוּ לֹא מָדַד לוֹ אֶלָּא סְאָה וְרוֹבַע צָרִיךְ לְעַשֵּׂר אֶת אוֹתוֹ הָרוֹבַע. אָמַר רִבִּי זְעִירָא חֶשְׁבּוֹן שָׂכָר בֵּינֵיהֶן. מָדַד לוֹ סְאָה לְעִנְיָן רְבָעִין הוֹאִיל וְהַמּוֹכֵר מִשְׂתַּכֵּר הַמּוֹכֵר מַפְרִישׁ. מָכַר לוֹ רְבָעִים לְעִנְיָין סְאָה הוֹאִיל וְהַלּוֹקֵחַ מִשְׂתַּכֵּר הַלּוֹקֵחַ מַפְרִישׁ.

The colleagues in the name of Rebbi Joḥanan[188]: Because of the children lest they should eat *ṭevel*. Rebbi La in the name of Rebbi Joḥanan, in retail, because the seller takes the large margin, the seller separates[189]. In wholesale, because the buyer will take the large margin, the buyer separates. One statement supports one and another statement supports the other. A statement supports the colleagues: "Rebbi Neḥemiah said, that which is connected to a retail outlet is like retail, connected to a wholesale outlet it is wholesale.[190]" A statement supports Rebbi La. It was stated: "Rebbi Ismael ben Rebbi Joḥanan ben Beroqa[191] said, if he measured with a retail measure, he is obligated. Even if he did measure only one seah and a quarter *qab*[192], he must tithe the quarter *qab*." Rebbi Zeïra said, computation of gain is between them[193]. If he measured for him the *seah* at the rate of quarter *qabs*, since the seller takes the large margin, the seller separates. If he measures the quarter *qab* at the rate of *seahs*, since the buyer will take the large margin, the buyer separates.

188 Here starts the discussion of the Mishnah's statement that the retailer but not the wholesaler must tithe *demay*. The colleagues say that it is a religious law to protect the innocent. Rebbi La says, it is a commercial law that the one who takes the larger margin is better able to absorb the costs.

189 He separates heave of tithes and Second Tithe and redeems the Second Tithe.

190 Anything which the retailer sells must be tithed because it is accessible to the general public, but anything the wholesaler sells, even an occasional retail quantity to the limited circle of his customers, may be *demay*. The opposite statement is ascribed to R. Neḥemiah in the Tosephta, *Demay* 3:11: "R. Neḥemiah says, anything sold in retail quantity is retail, in wholesale quantity it is wholesale," supporting R. La.

191 A Tanna of the fourth generation, associate of Rabban Simeon ben Gamliel.

192 $^1/_4$*qab* = $^1/_{24}$*seah*.

193 The argument between R. Neḥemiah here and R. Ismael ben R. Johanan ben Beroqa is whether price plays any role. R. Ismael negates the role of price; R. Neḥemiah's argument is detailed by R. Zeïra.

(fol. 22b) **משנה ה:** רִבִּי מֵאִיר אוֹמֵר אֶת שֶׁדַּרְכּוֹ לִמֻּדֵּד בְּדַקָּה וּמְדָדוֹ בְגַסָּה טְפֵילָה גַסָּה לְדַקָּה בְּגַסָּה וּמְדָדוֹ בְּדַקָּה טְפֵילָה דַקָּה לְגַסָּה[194]. אֵי זוֹ הִיא מִידָּה גַסָּה בְּיָבֵשׁ שְׁלוֹשָׁה קַבִּין וּבְלַח דֵּינָר. רִבִּי יוֹסֵי אוֹמֵר סַלֵּי תְאֵינִים וְסַלֵּי עֲנָבִים וְקוּפּוֹת שֶׁל יָרָק כָּל־שֶׁהוּא מוֹכְרָן אֲכַסָּרָא פָּטוּר.

Mishnah 5: Rebbi Meïr says, something which usually is sold retail and he sold wholesale, the wholesale is adjunct to the retail[195]; something which usually is sold wholesale and he sold retail, the retail is adjunct to the wholesale. What is wholesale? For dry produce, three *qab*[196], for liquids, the value of one *denar*[197]. Rebbi Yose says, baskets of figs, baskets of grapes, and boxes of vegetables, all these if sold *en bloc*[198] are free.

194 Reading of all Mishnah and Yerushalmi manuscripts. The Venice print is garbled at this point: את שדרכו למדוד בדקה ומדדו בגסה בגסה ומדדו בדקה בא טפילה דקה בגסה.

195 And must be tithed; in the following case, the retail quantity may be sold as *demay*.

196 About 6.4 liter or 1.7 US gals.

197 According to Maimonides, one gold denar which equals 24 or 25 silver denar.

198 *Arukh* gives two interpretations. 1) "Anything that is neither weighed nor measured is called אכסרה." 2) "'At a loss', for in Arabic loss (or damage) is called כ̇סארה خسارة". The first interpretation seems to be appropriate here; according to the second one, all produce should be exempted if sold at a loss. Since the Halakhah does not discuss R. Yose's statement, his opinion is not followed in practice.

(fol. 23a) **הלכה ה**: עַל דַּעְתֵּיהּ דְּהָדֵין תַּנָּייָא נָֽתְנוּ שֵׁיעוּר לְיָבֵשׁ לֹא נָֽתְנוּ שֵׁיעוּר לְלַח. נָֽתְנוּ דָמִים לְלַח וְלֹא נָֽתְנוּ דָמִים לְיָבֵשׁ. תַּנֵּי רִבִּי חִיָּיא הִין מִידָּה גַּסָּה מִן הַהִין וּלְמַטָּן מִידָּה דַּקָּה. נִימָן[199] מִידָּה דַקָּה מִנִּימָן לְמַעְלָן מִידָּה גַּסָּה. עַל דַּעְתֵּיהּ דְּהָדֵין תַּנָּייָא נָֽתְנוּ שֵׁיעוּר לְלַח לֹא נָֽתְנוּ שֵׁיעוּר לְיָבֵשׁ נָֽתְנוּ דָמִים לְיָבֵשׁ וְלֹא נָֽתְנוּ דָמִים לְלַח.

Halakhah 5: In the opinion of this Tanna, they gave a measure for dry produce but not for fluids, they gave a value for fluids but not for dry produce. Rebbi Ḥiyya stated[200]: "A *hin*[201] is wholesale, less than a *hin* is retail. A *nummus*[202] is retail, more than a *nummus* is wholesale." In the opinion of that Tanna, they gave a measure for fluids but not for dry produce, they gave a value for dry produce but not for fluids.

199 Reading of the Rome ms. Venice print and Leyden ms. have טמן, easily explained as reading error ני → ט.

200 Tosephta *Demay* 3:12.

201 A fluid measure, half a *seah*, equal to the three *qab* mentioned in the Mishnah as dry measure.

202 In R. Ḥiyya's time of honest coinage and stable prices. Latin *nummus*, also called *nummus sestertius*, "a small coin."

רִבִּי יוֹחָנָן בְּשֵׁם רִבִּי שִׁמְעוֹן בֶּן יְצָדָק תְּנַיי בֵית דִּין הוּא שֶׁתְּהֵא תְּרוּמַת מַעֲשֵׂר שֶׁל מוֹכֵר וּמַעֲשֵׂר שֵׁנִי מִשֶּׁל לוֹקֵחַ. מַה נָן קַייָמִין אִם בְּמִדָּה דַקָּה הוֹאִיל וְהַמּוֹכֵר מִשְׂתַּכֵּר הַמּוֹכֵר מַפְרִישׁ. אִם בְּמִדָּה גַסָּה הוֹאִיל וְהַלּוֹקֵחַ מִשְׂתַּכֵּר הַלּוֹקֵחַ מַפְרִישׁ. אָמַר רִבִּי בּוּן בַּר חִייָא תִּיפְתָּר בְּאוֹמֵר לוֹ מִכְּנִיסוֹ. אָמַר רִבִּי יוֹסֵי אֲפִילוּ תֵימַר שֶׁלֹּא מֵהַכְנִיסוֹ כְּאוֹמֵר בְּדַעְתּוֹ נִתְקוֹן אַף עַל פִּי כֵן אָמְרוּ לוֹ תְּנַיי בֵית דִּין הוּא שֶׁתְּהֵא תְּרוּמַת מַעֲשֵׂר מִשֶּׁל מוֹכֵר וּמַעֲשֵׂר שֵׁנִי מִשֶּׁל לוֹקֵחַ.

Rebbi Joḥanan in the name of Rebbi Simeon ben Yoẓadaq: It is a condition imposed by the Court that the heave of the tithe is on the seller and Second Tithe on the buyer. Where do we stand? If in retail, because the seller takes the large margin, the seller separates. If in wholesale, because the buyer will take the large margin, the buyer separates[203]. Rebbi Abun bar Ḥiyya said, explain it if he says it is of his own harvest[204]. Rebbi Yose said, even if you say it is not his own harvest, if he says in my opinion it was brought in order[205], even so they tell him that it is a condition imposed by the Court that the heave of the tithe be on the seller and Second Tithe on the buyer.

203 In both cases, one party pays for both heave and Second Tithe.

204 Not classifiable as either wholesale or retail.

206 If the seller says that the produce is in order it only means that the heave of the tithe was taken (reading and interpretation of R. Abraham ben David.) Maimonides does not read נתקון here but נְתַקֵּן, "let us put in order;" if both parties agree to put the produce in order at the point of sale, the heave is on the seller and the Second Tithe on the buyer, irrespective of a wholesale or retail transaction. (Maimonides *Maäser* 10:5).

רִבִּי לָעְזָר בְּשֵׁם רִבִּי הוֹשַׁעְיָה תְּנַיי בֵּית דִּין הוּא הַחֵלֶב מִשֶּׁל טַבָּח וְגִיד הַנָּשֶׁה מִשֶּׁל לוֹקֵחַ. הִנְהִיג רִבִּי אַבָּהוּ בְּקֵיסָרִין שֶׁיְּהוּ שְׁנֵיהֶן מִשֶּׁל לוֹקֵחַ. בְּגִין דִּיהֲווֹן מַרְבִּין טַבָּאוֹת.

Rebbi Eleazar in the name of Rebbi Hoshaiah: It is a condition imposed by the Court that the fat[206] be on the butcher and the sciatic tendon[207] on the buyer. Rebbi Abbahu made it common usage in Caesarea that both should be on the buyer, so that they would amply take out.

206 That fat of a four-legged animal, which in a sacrifice would go on the altar, is forbidden for profane use (*Lev.* 3:17). It has to be cut out before the piece of meat is sold.

207 It may not be eaten (*Gen.* 32:33). It must be cut out together with all the fat in which it is embedded. The butcher would naturally cut out only the minimum of fat in order to maximize his profit.

מאכילין פרק שלישי

(fol. 23a) **משנה א**: מַאֲכִילִין אֶת הָעֲנִיִּים דְּמַאי וְאֶת הָאַכְסַנְיָה דְּמַאי. רַבָּן גַּמְלִיאֵל הָיָה מַאֲכִיל אֶת פּוֹעֲלִין דְּמַאי. גַּבָּאֵי צְדָקָה בֵּית שַׁמַּאי אוֹמְרִין נוֹתְנִין אֶת הַמְעוּשָּׂר לְשֶׁאֵינוֹ מְעַשֵּׂר וְאֶת שֶׁאֵינוֹ מְעוּשָּׂר לִמְעַשֵּׂר נִמְצְאוּ כָּל־אָדָם אוֹכְלִין מְתוּקָּן. וַחֲכָמִים אוֹמְרִים גּוֹבִין סְתָם וּמְחַלְּקִין סְתָם וְהָרוֹצֶה לְתַקֵּן יְתַקֵּן.

Mishnah 1: One lets the poor and the stranger[1] eat *demay*. Rabban Gamliel let his laborers[2] eat *demay*. The House of Shammai say, the administrators of charity give the tithed food to those who do not tithe, and the untithed food to those who tithe, so that it turns out that everybody eats produce that is in order[3]. But the Sages say, one collects[4] without asking and one distributes without asking, and he who wants to put in order should put in order.

1 Greek ξένος, meaning either a non-resident or a passer-by (*Berakhot* p. 619).

2 If these were not poor, they would not be working as day laborers. However, since it was usual that the employer feed his journeymen, Rabban Gamliel saved by giving them *demay*, and this is not permitted.

3 It is stated explicitly in a *baraita*, quoted in Babli *Eruvin* 17b, that the House of Shammai disagree with the first sentence of the Mishnah and forbid to give *demay* to the poor.

4 *Tamḥui* and chest, as described in *Peah* 8:7, is collected and distributed without inquiring into the degree of religious observance of either donor or recipient.

(fol. 23b) **הלכה א**: אָמַר רִבִּי יוֹנָה מַתְנִיתִין בַּעֲנִיֵּי חֲבֵרִים וּבְאַכְסַנְיָה כְּרִבִּי יְהוֹשֻׁעַ. תַּנֵּי מַעֲשֶׂה בְּרִבִּי יְהוֹשֻׁעַ שֶׁהָלַךְ אַחַר רַבָּן יוֹחָנָן בֶּן זַכַּאי לִבְרוֹר[5] חַיִל וְהָיוּ אוֹתָן בְּנֵי הָעֲיָירוֹת מְבִיאִין לָהֶן פֵּירוֹת. אָמַר לָהֶן רִבִּי יְהוֹשֻׁעַ אִם לָנוּ כָּאן חַייָבִין אָנוּ לְעַשֵּׂר. וְאִם לָאו אֵין אָנוּ חַייָבִין לְעַשֵּׂר. רִבִּי יוֹסֵי אוֹמֵר בַּעֲנִיֵּי עַם הָאָרֶץ הִיא מַתְנִיתָא. אִם אָמַר אַתְּ בַּעֲנִיֵּי חֲבֵירִים נִמְצֵאת נוֹעֵל דֶּלֶת בִּפְנֵי עַם הָאָרֶץ. מַה מְקַיֵּים רִבִּי יוֹסֵי לְאַכְסַנְיָיה כְּהָדָא דְתַנֵּי הַגָּרִים עִמָּכֶם לְרַבּוֹת אֶת הָאַכְסַנְיָיה. רִבִּי אֱלִיעֶזֶר אוֹמֵר זוֹ אַכְסַנְיָה שֶׁל גּוֹי.

Halakhah 1: Rebbi Jonah said, our Mishnah speaks about poor *ḥaverim*, and about guests following Rebbi Joshua. It was stated[6]: "It happened that Rebbi Joshua went to Rabban Joḥanan ben Zakkai in Beror Ḥayil[7], and some local people brought them fruits. Rebbi Joshua said to them, if they[8] stay overnight, we are obliged to tithe; otherwise, we are not obliged to tithe." Rebbi Yose said, the Mishnah speaks about *am haärez̧* poor. If you restrict to poor *ḥaverim*, you lock the door before *am haärez̧* poor[9]. How does Rebbi Yose hold about "the stranger?[10]" Following what was stated: "(*Lev.* 25:45) 'Those who dwell among you,' to include the stranger; Rebbi Eliezer said, that means the Gentile stranger.[11]"

5 Reading of the Rome ms. and all Medieval sources. Venice has לכלי, in the parallel *Ma'serot* 2:3, fol. 49d, לבני.

6 Tosephta *Ma'serot* 2:1: "Donkey drivers and private persons on the road from place to place may eat and they are free (from the obligation to tithe) until they reach their destination. Therefore, if their host gave them a separate room and they stayed there overnight, they have to tithe, otherwise they are exempt. It happened that Rebbi Joshua went to Rabban Joḥanan ben Zakkai at Beror Ḥayil, and some inhabitants of these localities brought them figs. They asked him, do we have to tithe? He said to them, if we stay overnight, we are obligated to tithe; otherwise, we are not obligated to tithe." Because R. Joshua was such an important personality, he and his students certainly were placed in a

separate room; therefore, staying overnight alone creates the obligation of tithes. The obligation for heave and tithes only starts with the storage of the harvest. Since R. Joshua would not travel without a large group of students, keeping him overnight creates the duty to give heave and tithes. This is the explicit interpretation given in Yerushalmi *Ma'serot* 2:3.

7 Neither name nor location of this place are certain but it is known that it was the home town of Rabban Joḥanan ben Zakkai.

8 His students.

9 If it becomes expensive to give to the *am haärez̧* poor, nobody will give to them.

10 For R. Jonah, there is no problem; since the traveller is not really poor it is necessary to say that the Mishnah applies only to *ḥaverim* who will put their food in order. But why does R. Yose need to mention the traveller?

11 It is permitted to buy oneself goodwill with *demay* even though one may not satisfy a formal obligation with *demay*.

תַּנֵּי צָרִיךְ לְהוֹדִיעַ. עַל דַּעְתֵּיהּ דְּרִבִּי יוֹנָה דּוּ אָמַר בַּעֲנִיֵּי חֲבֵירִים הִיא מַתְנִיתָא נִיחָא. עַל דַּעְתֵּיהּ דְּרִבִּי יוֹסֵי דּוּ אָמַר בַּעֲנִיֵּי עַם הָאָרֶץ הִיא מַתְנִיתָא אֲפִילוּ מוֹדִיעוֹ מָהוּ מוֹעִיל. בִּפְנֵי אֶחָד שֶׁאֵינוֹ מְתַקֵּן.

It was stated: "One has to declare." In the opinion of Rebbi Jonah, it is understood[12] that the Mishnah speaks about poor *ḥaverim*. In the opinion of Rebbi Yose, the Mishnah speaks about *am haärez̧* poor; even if he informs him, what does he gain[13]? Because of one who does not put in order?

12 One has to inform him that he receives *demay* so that he may bring it in order.

13 Since the *am haärez̧* does not care, what has one gained by informing the recipient? The answer is that only a minority of the *amē haärez̧* do not care, so why should he hurt the decent majority because of the actions of a few nonobservant persons?

אָמַר רִבִּי מָנָא הָדָא אָמְרָה אִילֵּין דִּיהֲווֹן בְּבֵיתִין אָסוּר לִיתֵּן מִדְּמֵי שְׁבִיעִית שֶׁאֵינוֹ אֶלָּא פּוֹרֵעַ חוֹב מִדְּמֵי שְׁבִיעִית. כְּהָדָא דְתַנֵּי אֶחָד שְׁבִיעִית וְאֶחָד מַעֲשֵׂר שֵׁנִי אֵין נִפְרָעִין מֵהֶן מִלְוֶה וְחוֹב. וְאֵין עוֹשִׂין מֵהֶן שׁוֹשְׁבִינוּת. וְאֵין מְשַׁלְּמִין מֵהֶן תַּשְׁלוּמִין. וְאֵין פּוֹסְקִין מֵהֶן צְדָקָה לָעֲנִיִּים בְּבֵית הַכְּנֶסֶת. אֲבָל מְשַׁלְּמִין לָהֶן דָּבָר שֶׁל גְּמִילוּת חֶסֶד. וְצָרִיךְ לְהוֹדִיעַ.

Rebbi Mana said, this means that he who gives in his home[12] may not give from Sabbatical value because he would pay his debt with Sabbatical value. As it was stated[13]: "Neither Sabbatical produce nor Second Tithe may be used to satisfy a loan or a debt. One does not use them for best men's meals[14]. One does not pay with them obligatory payments. One does not use them to pledge for charity in the synagogue. But one may use them for goodwill; then one has to notify."

12 He does not give to the administrators of charity but invites the poor to his house. What he feeds them is still restricted only to *demay* if he informs the recipients. He may not use Sabbatical produce or its value for charity.

13 Tosephta *Ševiït* 7:9, with text very close to our text here.

14 Since these meals are due in reciprocity, they constitute a debt that can not be satisfied either with Sabbatical fruits, which are ownerless even if grown on the farmer's own field, or Second Tithe, which is Heaven's money.

תַּמָּן תַּנִּינָן פּוֹעֵל שֶׁאֵינוֹ מַאֲמִין לְבַעַל הַבַּיִת. תַּמָּן אַתְּ אָמַר הַפּוֹעֵל מַפְרִישׁ. וְכָה אַתְּ אָמַר בַּעַל הַבַּיִת מַפְרִישׁ. אָמַר רִבִּי יוֹנָה תַּמָּן בְּמַאֲכִילוֹ מִן הַמְּנוּיִין בְּרַם הָכָא בְּמַאֲכִילוֹ מִן הָאָבוּס.

There[15] we have stated: "The worker who does not trust the employer." There you say, the worker separates. But here you say that the employer separates[16]. Rebbi Jonah said, there if he serves him counted portions, here if he lets him eat from the bowl[17].

15 Mishnah *Demay* 7:3: "A worker who does not trust his employer should take one fig and say: This fig and the nine following shall be tithe on the 90 remaining that I will eat; this one will be heave of the tithe, the others will be redeemed by coins. (Mishnah 4) Then he saves one fig (assuming the employer gave him 100 for lunch.) Rabban Simeon ben Gamliel said, he should not save (but buy one with his own money and give it to the Cohen) because he reduces the work of the employer (by eating less than the allotted ration, he has less strength to work.) Rebbi Yose said, he should not save because this is a condition of the Court (that the employer must pay for the heave of the tithe.)"

The argument here refers to what Rabban Gamliel did. Since he is mentioned by name, what he did is not accepted. The Sages conclude that the employer must give his farmhands fully tithed food.

16 Since the action of Rabban Gamliel is not quoted as opinion of the Sages.

17 Cooked food, or figs and dates, in a big bowl from which each farmhand scoops up what he can. Then it is impossible for the worker to determine what the heave of tithe should be.

רִבִּי זְרִיקָן שִׁמְעוֹן בַּר וָוא בְּשֵׁם רִבִּי יוֹחָנָן רוֹפֵא חָבֵר שֶׁהָיָה מַאֲכִיל לְחוֹלֶה עַם הָאָרֶץ נוֹתֵן לְתוֹךְ יָדוֹ וְאֵינוֹ נוֹתֵן לְתוֹךְ פִּיו בִּדְמַאי. אֲבָל בְּוַדַּאי אֲפִילוּ לְתוֹךְ יָדוֹ אָסוּר. מִשֶּׁל חוֹלֶה אֲבָל מִשֶּׁל רוֹפֵא אָסוּר. בְּיִשְׂרָאֵל אֲבָל בִּבְנֵי נֹחַ אֲפִילוּ בְּוַדַּאי מוּתָּר. מִשֶּׁל חוֹלֶה אֲבָל מִשֶּׁל רוֹפֵא אָסוּר. אִם הָיָה אֵבֶר מִן הַחַי אֲפִילוּ מִשֶּׁל חוֹלֶה אָסוּר שֶׁלֹּא יָבוֹא לִידֵי תְקָלָה.

Rebbi Zeriqan, Simeon bar Abba, in the name of Rebbi Joḥanan: A medical doctor who is a *ḥaver*, if he feeds a sick person who is an *am haärez*, shall put the food into his patient's hand[18] but not into his mouth. That is, if it is *demay,* but if it is certain[19], it is forbidden even to put it in his hand. This means, if it is the patient's property, but the doctor's is forbidden[20] for a Jew; for a descendant of Noah[21] it is permitted even if it is certain and the patient's property, but the doctor's is forbidden. But if it was a limb taken from a living animal it is forbidden even if it is the patient's property, that he should not be caused to stumble[22].

18 The *am haärez̩* will eat *demay* but the *ḥaver* is forbidden to serve others anything not fully tithed.

19 That no heave of the tithe has been given. In that case, the doctor would commit a sin and lose his fellowship standing in handing such food to the *am haärez̩* since it would clearly be forbidden (assuming that the sickness is not life-threatening and some other remedy is available.)

20 Since the *ḥaver*, or even simply the person trustworthy for tithes, is not permitted to serve others anything that is not in order.

"Descendant of Noah" means a Gentile, since all mankind is descended from Noah. The expression is used here to indicate that all of mankind are obligated by the Seven Commandments given to Noah (prohibition of murder, idolatry, incest and adultery, eating limbs taken from a living animal, blasphemy, and anarchism.)

21 Since parts cut from live animals are forbidden not only to Jews but to all mankind (Babli *Sanhedrin* 57b, cf. Rashi on *Gen.* 9:4).

וְקַשְׁיָא עַל דְּבֵית שַׁמַּאי בְּגִין דּוּ כָּשֵׁר יַפְסִיד. נוֹתֵן לוֹ כְּדֵי תִּיקּוּנוֹ. מַה טַעַם דְּבֵית שַׁמַּאי אֲפִילוּ תִגְדְּרֶנּוּ עַכְשָׁיו יָכוֹל אַתְּ לְגוֹדְרוֹ לְאַחַר זְמַן אֵין אַתְּ יָכוֹל לְגָדְרוֹ. מַה טַעַם דְּרַבָּנִין אִם מְדַקְדֵּק אַתְּ אַחֲרָיו אַף הוּא מְמָעֵט בִּצְדָקָה.

It is difficult for the House of Shammai[22], should he lose because he is worthy[23]? He adds what he has to put in order. What is the reason of the House of Shammai? Even if you regulate him now, can you regulate him in the future[24]? You cannot regulate him. What is the reason of the rabbis? If you investigate him[25] he will reduce his charity giving.

22 Here starts the discussion of the rules for the administrators of charity.

23 Assuming that everybody gets the same, the observant end up with less to eat than the nonobservant. Hence, the observant should get slightly more than the nonobservant.

24 If he takes it home untithed, the

am haärez will eat it untithed, and it will turn out that the administrator has led a fellow Jew into sin by giving him untithed food.

25 If you ask people whether they follow the rules of fellowship or not, the nonobservant will not give and you have committed two evils: you have reduced the amount of food available for the poor and you have prevented fellow Jews from fulfilling the commandment of charitable giving.

גַּבָּאֵי צְדָקָה בְּיוֹם טוֹב לֹא יְהוּ מַכְרִיזִין כְּדֶרֶךְ שֶׁמַּכְרִיזִין בְּחוֹל. אֲבָל גּוֹבִין בְּצִינְעָה וְנוֹתְנִין לְתוֹךְ חֵיקוֹ וּמְחַלְּקִין לְכָל־שְׁכוּנָה וּשְׁכוּנָה בִּפְנֵי עַצְמָהּ. גַּבָּאֵי קוּפָּה בַּשְּׁבִיעִית לֹא יְהוּ מְדַקְדְּקִין בַּחֲצֵרוֹת שֶׁל אוֹכְלֵי שְׁבִיעִית. נָתְנוּ לָהֶן פַּת מוּתָּר שֶׁלֹּא נֶחְשְׁדוּ יִשְׂרָאֵל לִהְיוֹת נוֹתְנִין אֶלָּא מָעוֹת אוֹ בֵּצוֹת. רִבִּי חֲנַנְיָה בְּשֵׁם רִבִּי פִּינְחָס הָדָא דְתֵימַר בְּמָקוֹם שֶׁזּוֹרְעִים וְלֹא אוֹכְלִין. לֶאֱכוֹל אֵינָן חֲשׁוּדִין לֹא כָּל־שֶׁכֵּן לְהַאֲכִיל.

"[26]The administrators of charity should not publicly announce on a holiday[27] in the way they announce on weekdays, but they collect in private, carry it in their bosom, and distribute for each quarter separately. The administrators of the charity chest[28] should not be inquisitive in the courtyards of those who eat from the yield[29] of the Sabbatical year. If one gave them bread it is permitted, because Jews are not suspected of giving anything other than money or eggs[30]." Rebbi Ḥananiah in the name of Rebbi Phineas: That means, at a place where people sow[31] but do not eat. Since they are not suspected to eat, *a fortiori* not to feed.

26 Tosephta *Demay* 3:16,17.

27 On weekdays, they announce in the synagogue how many poor they have to feed and how much they need from every householder. On holidays, when money transactions are forbidden, even charity cannot be collected publicly.

28 See *Peah* 8:7. In the Tosephta, this is the majority opinion, against R. Meïr who holds that one does not take from questionable sources during the

Sabbatical year.

29 Everybody may eat from the yield of the Sabbatical year the spontaneous growth of fallow fields. Here, the reference is to produce grown for cash in the Sabbatical.

30 Money received for a crop in the Sabbatical year or eggs, not subject to Sabbatical rules, bought with such money. If somebody gives bread, one may assume that it was not from grain grown for cash in the Sabbatical year.

31 For cash, to be able to pay their taxes.

כֹּהֲנִים הַמְגַבְּלִין בְּטָהֳרָה לֹא יְהוּ מְדַקְדְּקִין בַּחֲצֵרוֹת שֶׁל אוֹכְלֵי שְׁבִיעִית. אִית תַּנָּיֵי תַּנֵּי מְדַקְדְּקִין. אָמַר רִבִּי פִינְחָס מָאן דְּאָמַר מְדַקְדְּקִין מִפְּנֵי חַלָּתָן מָאן דְּאָמַר אֵין מְדַקְדְּקִין מַבְרִיחוֹ מִן הַקַּלָּה וּמַכְנִיסוֹ לַחֲמוּרָה. טֶבֶל בְּעָוֹן מִיתָה שְׁבִיעִית בְּלֹא תַעֲשֶׂה.

"Cohanim who prepare dough in purity[32] should not be inquisitive in the courtyards of those who eat from the yield of the Sabbatical year." Some Tannaïm[33] stated: "They should be inquisitive." Rebbi Phineas said, he who says that they should be inquisitive, because of their *ḥallah*[34]; he who says that they should not be inquisitive, for he would save him from the simple sin and lead him to a deadly one. *Ṭevel* is a deadly sin, the Sabbatical year is a simple prohibition[35].

32 Since *ḥallah* has to be taken from bread dough under the rules of the heave and be eaten in purity, and the *am haärez̧* by his touch would give primary impurity to the wet dough, as explained in Halakhah 2:3, it was customary to hire a Cohen to knead the dough in purity, take *ḥallah* to eat it, and then hand the dough over to the *am haärez̧* to bake it.

33 Tosephta *Demay* 3:17.

34 Produce of the Sabbatical year, being legally abandoned property, is exempt from heave and tithes. But dough prepared from grain grown in the Sabbatical year, even if the grain was legally harvested, is always subject to *ḥallah*. So the Tosephta requires the Cohen not only to take *ḥallah*, but also to check whether the grain might be

demay.

35 If the Cohen would refuse to knead the dough of the nonobservant and to take *ḥallah*, the nonobservant would knead the dough himself and not give *ḥallah*. However, dough from which *ḥallah* was not taken is *ṭevel*, and its consumption is as bad a sin as consuming grain from which heave was not taken. Since the Cohen by his action leads the nonobservant into sin, the sin is the Cohen's.

כֵּיצַד הוּא עוֹשֶׂה אָמַר רִבִּי הוּנָא מֵבִיא כֹּהֵן חָשׁוּד וּמַטְבִּילָהּ וּמַאֲכִילָהּ לוֹ. וְלֹא נִמְצָא מוֹסֵר טָהֳרוֹת לְעַם הָאָרֶץ. אָמַר רִבִּי מָנָא מֵבִיא כֹּהֵן חָשׁוּד וּמַטְבִּילָהּ וּמְשַׁמְּרוֹ עַד הָעֶרֶב וּמַאֲכִילָהּ לוֹ. וְלֹא נִמְצָא מַחֲזִיק יְדֵי עוֹבְרֵי עֲבֵירָה. רִבִּי שִׁמְעוֹן בַּר כַּרְסָנִי[36] בְּשֵׁם רִבִּי אָחָא מְשַׁמְּרָהּ עַד עֶרֶב הַפֶּסַח וְשׂוֹרְפָהּ.

What does he do[37]? Rebbi Huna said, he brings a suspect Cohen[38], lets him immerse himself, and serves it to him. But then does he not deliver pure foods to an *am haäreẓ*[39]? Rebbi Mana said, he brings a suspect Cohen, lets him immerse himself, watches him until sundown and then serves it to him. But then does he not support the sinners? Rebbi Simeon from Carsan in the name of Rebbi Aḥa: He keeps it until the day before Passover and then burns it[40].

36 Reading of the Rome ms. Venice and Leyden: בר סני The Rome reading is supported by the few other places in which this author is quoted; cf. *Ḥallah* 4:3, *Šabbat* 1:8, *Eruvin* 1:7. The tradent was a student of R. Aḥa; nothing more is known about him.

37 The Cohen who has taken *ḥallah* from dough he suspects to be from grain raised during the Sabbatical year, from which one cannot partake.

38 He is suspected to eat from produce commercially grown in the Sabbatical year. Still, the observant Cohen must make sure that he eats *ḥallah* in purity; hence, he has to send him to the *miqweh* (and, as R. Mana points out, watch him in purity until sundown.) See Mishnah *Berakhot* 1:1.

39 Who can be assumed to make everything impure (except in Jerusalem, during the time of the

Temple, on holidays when "all of Israel are *ḥaverim*.") In this case, the observant Cohen would lead the nonobservant into sin.

40 Pure *terumah* and *ḥallah* must be eaten; they may be burned only if they are either impure or on Passover eve if they contain leavened material. Since it is forbidden to make holy things impure intentionally, the Cohen has to keep *ḥallah* in purity until he is forced to burn it on Passover eve.

(fol. 23a) **משנה ב:** הָרוֹצֶה לַחֲזוֹם עָלֵי יֶרֶק לְהָקֵל מִמַּשָּׂאוֹ לֹא יַשְׁלִיךְ עַד שֶׁיְּעַשֵּׂר. הַלּוֹקֵחַ יֶרֶק מִן הַשּׁוּק וְנִמְלַךְ לְהַחֲזִיר לֹא יַחֲזִיר עַד שֶׁיְּעַשֵּׂר. שֶׁאֵינוֹ מְעֻשָּׂר אֶלָּא מִנְיָין. הָיָה עוֹמֵד וְלוֹקֵחַ וְרָאָה טוֹעַן אֶחָד יָפֶה מִמֶּנּוּ מוּתָּר לְהַחֲזִיר מִפְּנֵי שֶׁלֹּא מָשַׁךְ.

Mishnah 2: He who wants to cut off greens of vegetables[41] in order to lighten his load should not throw them away before he tithed. He who buys vegetables on the market[42] and then decides to return them should not return them before he tithed, because nothing is missing[43] but counting[44]. If he stopped to buy but saw another, better, load, he may change his mind because[45] he did not take it up.

41 For example turnip greens which usually are not used but may be used as vegetables by the poor. Hence, since it is likely that the leaves will be collected as food, the preparation of the vegetables for transportation and sale signifies the end of the harvest and requires tithing from then on.

42 These vegetables have a fixed price per unit. The moment the buyer takes up a bunch, he is obliged to pay a fixed amount. Hence, the act of lifting up the bunch transfers property rights to the buyer in exchange for a debt incurred. Since now the bunch belongs to the buyer, he cannot return it untithed without losing his standing as being trustworthy for tithes.

43 The Mishnah manuscripts of the Yerushalmi tradition and the Munich

ms. of the Babli have מעושר. The manuscripts of the Babylonian tradition and the Rome ms. have מחוסר, which explains the word used here. In Galilee, ח was pronounced like ה and ע.

44 The number of bunches the buyer took up.

45 Or better: As long as he did not lift up any of the bunches. Then they never were his property and he is not responsible.

(fol. 23b) **הלכה ב**: אָמַר רִבִּי לָעְזָר דְּרִבִּי מֵאִיר הִיא. דְּרִבִּי מֵאִיר אָמַר לֹא הִתִּירוּ לִמְכּוֹר דְּמַאי אֶלָּא לְסִיטוֹן בִּלְבַד. אָמַר רִבִּי יוֹחָנָן דִּבְרֵי הַכֹּל הִיא שַׁנְיָיא הִיא שֶׁהַזּוֹכֶה זוֹכֶה בְדַקָּה וְאֵין הַמַּבְקִיר מַבְקִיר בְּגַסָּה. וְלֵית הָדָא פְלִיגָא עַל דְּרִבִּי מֵאִיר דְּרִבִּי מֵאִיר דוּ אָמַר כֵּיוָן שֶׁאָדָם מַבְקִיר דָּבָר וְיָצָא מֵרְשׁוּתוֹ הֶבְקֵרוֹ הֶבְקֵר. שַׁנְיָיא הִיא שֶׁהַזּוֹכֶה זוֹכֶה בְדַקָּה וְאֵין הַמַּבְקִיר מַבְקִיר בְּגַסָּה. וַאֲפִילוּ עַל רִבִּי יוֹסֵי לֵית הָדָא פְלִיגָא דְּרִבִּי יוֹסֵי אָמַר אֵין הֶבְקֵר יוֹצֵא מִתַּחַת יְדֵי הַבְּעָלִים אֶלָּא בִזְכִייָה אֵין הֶבְקֵרוֹ הֶבְקֵר. שַׁנְיָיא הִיא שֶׁהַמַּבְקִיר מַבְקִיר בְּגַסָּה וְאֵין הַזּוֹכֶה זוֹכֶה בְדַקָּה.

Halakhah 2: Rebbi Eleazar said[46], it is Rebbi Meïr's, since Rebbi Meïr said, they permitted to sell *demay* only to the commissioned grain wholesaler. Rebbi Johanan said, it is according to everybody; there is a difference because the one who takes it up takes it up in retail quantity and the one who abandons does not abandon wholesale[47]. But does this not disagree with Rebbi Meïr[48], since Rebbi Meïr is the one who says that as soon as a person abandons anything of his property, it is legally abandoned as soon as it leaves his power. There is a difference because the one who takes it up takes it up in retail quantity and the one who abandons does not abandon wholesale. It does not even disagree with Rebbi Yose, for Rebbi Yose says that nothing may leave the power of its owners except if it is taken up; otherwise it was not legally abandoned. There is a difference here, because the one who abandons abandons wholesale, and the one who takes it up, takes up only retail quantities[49].

46 The discussion refers to the first statement of the Mishnah that he who separates greens from bunches of vegetables must tithe first. Since the leaves are thrown away, they are legally abandoned, and anybody who collects abandoned property is free from all obligations of tithing. This being the case, how could the poor who collect the leaves possibly incur any guilt in not tithing and why should the transporter be liable for tithes?

Rebbi Meïr's statement was discussed in Halakhah 2:4.

47 Hence, while he might get away without tithing from the point of view of Biblical law, he cannot get away if he wants to retain his standing as being trustworthy for tithes.

48 This disagreement between R. Meïr and R. Yose is discussed in *Peah* 6:1 (Babli *Nedarim* 43a-44a).

49 According to R. Yose, if a large quantity was abandoned, it does not become abandoned property by being collected in small quantities by different persons.

חִזְקִיָּה אָמַר אֵינוֹ הֶבְקֵר[50] מְחוּסָּר לְבַעֲלִין אֶלָּא בִזְכִיָּה מִנְיָין.

Ḥizqiah said[51], nothing is missing for the owners but the credit by counting.

50 This word, while in the mss., must be considered an intrusion from the preceding sentences.

51 The reference is to the middle part of the Mishnah, that if somebody took from the farmer's stall (who is neither wholesaler nor retail grocer) a bunch with a clearly marked price, he cannot return it without tithing. Ḥizqiah notes that מעושר should be מחוסר as noted before. In normative Hebrew, זכייה מניין would be a construct state זכית מנין.

כֵּיצַד הוּא עוֹשֶׂה נוֹטֵל מִן הָעֶלְיוֹן וּמְתַקֵּן. וְאֵינוֹ אָסוּר מִשּׁוּם גָּזֵל. כְּהָדָא רִבִּי שִׁמְעוֹן בַּר כַּהֲנָא הֲוָה מַסְמִיךְ לְרִבִּי לְעָזָר עֲבָרוֹן עַל חַד כֶּרֶם. אָמַר לֵיהּ אַיְיתִי לִי חַד קִיסָּם מֵיחֲצַד שִׁינַּיי. חָזַר וְאָמַר לֵיהּ לֹא תֵּיתִי לִי כְלוּם אָמַר דְּאִין אַיְיתֵי כָּל־בַּר נַשׁ וּבַר נַשׁ מֵיעֲבַד כֵּן הָא אָזִיל סִייָגָא דְּגוּבְרָא. רִבִּי חַגַּיי הֲוָה מַסְמִיךְ

לְרִבִּי זְעִירָא עָבַר חַד טָעִין חַד מֵיבַל דְּקִיסִין. אָמַר לֵיהּ אַיְיתִי לִי חַד קִיסֵם מֵיחֲצַדָן שִׁינַּיי. חָזַר וְאָמַר לֵיהּ לֹא תֵּיתִי לִי כְּלוּם דְּאִין אָתֵי כָּל־בַּר נַשׁ וּבַר נַשׁ מֵיעֲבַד כֵּן הָא אָזֵילָא מִיבְלָא דְּגוּבְרָא. לָא רִבִּי זְעִירָא כָּשֵׁר כָּל־כֵּן. אֶלָּא מִילִּין דְּיוֹצְרָן שְׁמַע (fol. 23c) לָן נֵעַבְדִּינָן. רִבִּי אַבָּהוּ בְּשֵׁם רִבִּי יוֹחָנָן כֵּיוָן שֶׁמָּשַׁךְ קָנֶה לֹא הָיָה חָסֵר אֶלָּא מִמְנֵי לֵיהּ. כֵּיצַד הוּא עוֹשֶׂה נוֹתֵן דְּמֵי אַחַת מֵהֶן וּמְתַקֵּן.

How does he do it[52]? He takes from the uppermost layer and puts it in order. Is that not forbidden because of robbery[53]? Like that of Rebbi Simeon bar Cahana[54] who was supporting Rebbi Eliezer[55]. They passed by a vineyard. He said to him, bring me a sliver[56] as a toothpick. He changed his mind and told him, do not bring me anything; if everybody would do that, the fence of this man would be gone. Rebbi Ḥaggai was supporting Rebbi Zeïra. A person passed by who was carrying a load of chips. He said to him, bring me a chip as a toothpick. He changed his mind and told him, do not bring me anything; if everybody would do that, the load of this man would be gone. Is not Rebbi Zeïra particularly pious? No, he told us that we should observe the words of our Creator. Rebbi Abbahu in the name of Rebbi Joḥanan: When he took one stalk, nothing was missing but counting them[57]. How does he do it? He pays for one of them[58] and puts it in order.

52 How does one give tithes from the vegetables one returns to the market stall.

53 If he declares one of the vegetables as tithes, he takes away from the seller. Even if we say that the seller as retailer should be required to tithe himself, if enough customers act like this one, there will be only tithe and heave of the tithe left, and nothing to sell, without the seller having made a single sale. (There are other complications which will be discussed in the next paragraph.)

54 A Tanna of the third generation, student of R. Eliezer.

55 Rebbi Eliezer was leaning on his arm while walking.

56 Taking the sliver from the wooden fence, since taking property worth less than a *peruṭa* (one sixth or one eighth of a copper *as*) is not considered robbing.

57 Rebbi Joḥanan repeats the opinion of his teacher Ḥizqiah.

58 If the seller is paid, no robbery has occured. The one stalk now is taken as heave of the tithe. The rest of the bunch is permitted to a *ḥaver* without tithing and the seller can sell it as such.

וְלֹא נִמְצָא עוֹשֶׂה תְקָלָה לַבָּאִים אַחֲרָיו. עוֹשֶׂה אוֹתָן צִיבּוּר לְפָנָיו. וְיִקְבַּע אוֹתָן לְתוֹךְ פֵּירוֹתָיו. וְלֹא כֵן תַּנֵּי קוֹבֵעַ הוּא אָדָם מַעְשְׂרוֹתָיו שֶׁל חֲבֵירוֹ לְתוֹךְ פֵּירוֹתָיו וַאֲפִילוּ עוֹשֶׂה תְקָלָה לַבָּאִים אַחֲרָיו. אָמַר רִבִּי חִינְנָא תִּקְּנוּ בְלוֹקֵחַ וְלֹא תִקְּנוּ בְּמַחֲזִיר.

But does it not turn out that he creates an obstacle for those who come after him[59]? Let him make a separate heap. But why can he not fix them in his own produce[60]? Did we not state[61]: "A person may fix his tithes for someone else, even if he creates an obstacle for those who come after him." Rebbi Ḥinena said, they made that ordinance for the buyer[62] but not for him who returns [produce].

59 If the produce is *demay* or *ṭevel*. One may not give heave from produce already tithed and if the next buyer would use from the already tithed produce for heave of the tithe, that act would be void and he would in fact be eating *ṭevel*.

60 Why should the buyer give the seller money to be able to put that bunch in order; let him return it as is with a remark that the prospective buyer will give the heave of the tithe (and redemption of the Second Tithe) from his own produce at home.

61 There is a similar text in Tosephta *Maäser Šeni* 4:8: "One may give the heave of the tithe for produce of an *am haärez*, even if this creates an obstacle for those who will come later," meaning later buyers from the *am haärez* who is the seller; the buyers might treat the produce that was put in

order as *demay* and use it for illegitimate tithing of other produce.

62 This particular exception was meant only for the *ḥaver* who has no choice but to buy from an *am haärez̧* seller, in the absence of a *ḥaver* on the market. Since the *ḥaver* is prohibited from buying produce that is not in order, he is forced to stipulate that he will put the seller's produce in order before concluding the deal. He naturally will tell the seller that his produce will be put in order, but he has absolutely no guarantee that the seller will transmit this information to the other buyers. However, since everything will be fine if the seller really warns the next buyers not to use his produce for tithing, no blame can be attached to the *ḥaver* who uses his own to put the *am haärez̧*'s produce in order. But this is permitted only to a bona fide buyer, not to one who changes his mind after already acquiring the produce.

כֵּינִי מַתְנִיתָא הָיָה עוֹמֵד וּבוֹרֵר. עַד כְּדוֹן בְּאוֹתוֹ הַמִּין אֲפִילוּ מִין אַחֵר.

So says the Mishnah[63]: "If he stood selecting." So far, of the same kind. Also, from a different kind.

63 This refers to the last part of the Mishnah: "If he stopped *to buy* but saw another, better batch, he may change his mind because he did not take it up." Since "to buy" has a connotation of "taking it," the word is changed to "selecting."

(fol. 23a) **משנה ג**: הַמּוֹצִיא פֵּירוֹת בַּדֶּרֶךְ וּנְטָלָן לְאָכְלָן וְנִמְלַךְ לְהַצְנִיעַ לֹא (fol. 23b) יַצְנִיעַ עַד שֶׁיְּעַשֵּׂר. אִם מִתְּחִילָּה נְטָלָן בִּשְׁבִיל שֶׁלֹּא יֹאבְדוּ פָּטוּר. כָּל־דָּבָר שֶׁאֵין אָדָם רַשַּׁאי לְמוֹכְרוֹ דְּמַאי לֹא יִשְׁלַח לַחֲבֵירוֹ דְּמַאי. רִבִּי יוֹסֵי מַתִּיר בְּוַדַּאי וּבִלְבַד שֶׁיּוֹדִיעֶנּוּ.

Mishnah 3: He who finds produce on the road and takes it to eat it[64], but then changed his mind to store it, should not store it until he tithed it[65]. If from the start he took it up only so that it should not be spoiled[66], he is free. Anything a person is not permitted to sell as *demay*, he may not send to a friend as *demay*. Rebbi Yose permits certain produce[67] on condition that he inform him.

64 To eat it on the spot. One may assume that the produce was lost before it was brought to the farmer's house to be stored. Hence, no heave or tithes are due.

65 Since the first act of storing subjects the produce to heave and tithes.

66 One may not let food lie on the road to be spoiled by people trampling upon it. If he simply takes that produce and puts it near the road where it will not go to waste, he did not acquire anything and has no obligation for heave and tithes.

67 Produce from which at least the heave of tithe certainly was not taken, may be sent as is to another person on condition that the latter would be informed, since he will not have certain produce lying around his house without putting it in order immediately.

(fol. 23c) **הלכה ג**: תַּנֵּי אֵין מַעֲבִירִין עַל הָאוֹכְלִין. רִבִּי יַעֲקֹב בַּר זַבְדִי בְּשֵׁם רִבִּי אַבָּהוּ הָא דָמַר בָּרִאשׁוֹנָה. אֲבָל עַכְשָׁיו מוּתָּר מִפְּנֵי הַכְּשָׁפִים.

Halakhah 3: It was stated: "One does not pass by foodstuffs.[69]" Rebbi Jacob bar Zavdi in the name of Rebbi Abbahu: That means, in earlier times. But now it is permitted because of sorcery[70].

69 But one has to take them up from the road and put them in a safe place. The statement of R. Abbahu is credited in the Babli (*Erubin* 64b) to R. Joḥanan in the name of R. Simeon bar Iohai.

70 As one might come under a spell and get hurt by taking it up.

תַּמָּן תַּנִּינָן הַהוֹפֵךְ אֶת הַגָּלָל בִּרְשׁוּת הָרַבִּים וְהוּזַּק בָּהֶן אַחֵר חַייָב בְּנִזְקוֹ. תַּנֵּי וַאֲסוּרִין מִשּׁוּם גֶּזֶל. כַּהֲנָא אָמַר וְהוּא שֶׁהֲפָכָהּ עַל מְנָת לִזְכּוֹת בָּהּ. אֲבָל אִם הֲפָכָהּ עַל מְנָת שֶׁלֹּא לִזְכּוֹת בָּהּ לֹא בְדָא. וּלְעִנְייָן נְזִיקִין לֹא בְדָא שַׁנְייָה בֵּין הֲפָכָהּ עַל מְנָת לִזְכּוֹת בּוֹ בֵּין הֲפָכָהּ עַל מְנָת שֶׁלֹּא לִזְכּוֹת בּוֹ וְהוּזַּק בָּהֶן אַחֵר חַייָב בְּנִזְקוֹ. וְהָכָא אַתְּ אָמַר הָכֵן. אָמַר רִבִּי אָבִין תַּמָּן כְּתִיב בַּעַל הַבּוֹר יְשַׁלֵּם בַּעַל הַנֶּזֶק יְשַׁלֵּם. בְּרַם הָכָא עַשֵּׂר תְּעַשֵּׂר מִשֶּׁלָּךְ אַתְּ מְעַשֵּׂר וְאֵין אַתְּ מְעַשֵּׂר מִשֶּׁל אֲחֵרִים.

There[71], we have stated: "He who turns over cow dung in the public domain and a third party was hurt, is liable for damages." It was also stated[72]: "It is forbidden because of robbery." Cahana[73] said, only if he turned it over in order to acquire it. But if he did not turn it over in order to acquire it, about that one does not speak. But as regards damages, there is no difference whether he turned it over in order to acquire it or he did not turn it over in order to acquire it; if a third party was hurt, he is liable for damages[74]. And here, you say so? Rebbi Abun said, there it is written (*Ex.* 21:34): "The one responsible for the pit[75] shall pay," the one responsible for the damage shall pay. But here (*Deut.* 14:22): "You shall give tithes," you give tithes from your property but not from other people's property.

71 Mishnah *Baba Qama* 3:3.

72 Tosephta *Baba Qama* 2:8: "He who turns over cow dung in the public domain in order to acquire it, and another person was hurt by it, he is liable, and it is forbidden because of robbery. Rabban Simeon ben Gamliel says, it is not robbery to impair the public domain." The person who acquired the dung is liable but, since he acquired it, one is forbidden to take it from him, but he may take it from the owner of the cattle since it was in the public domain and an obstacle to travelers.

73 It is impossible to decide whether Cahana here is Rav Cahana I, a companion of Rav in Babylonia, or

Rav Cahana II; see note in *Berakhot* p. 247.

74 This contradicts statements of Ḥizqiah in Yerushalmi *Baba Qama* 3:3, fol. 3c, and of R. Eleazar in Babli *Baba Qama* 29b.

75 An unauthorized open pit in the public domain.

כָּל־דָּבָר שֶׁאֵין אָדָם רַשַּׁאי לְמוֹכְרוֹ דְמַאי לֹא יִשְׁלַח לַחֲבֵירוֹ דְמַאי. מִידָּה דַקָּה שֶׁאֵין אָדָם רַשַּׁאי לְמוֹכְרוֹ דְמַאי לֹא יִשְׁלַח לַחֲבֵירוֹ דְמַאי. מִידָּה גַסָּה שֶׁאָדָם רַשַּׁאי לְמוֹכְרוֹ דְמַאי יִשְׁלַח לַחֲבֵירוֹ דְמַאי. רִבִּי יוֹסֵי מַתִּיר בְּוַדַּאי בֵּין דַּקָּה בֵּין גַּסָּה וְאוֹסֵר בִּדְמַאי בְדַקָּה.

"Anything a person is not permitted to sell as *demay*, he may not send to a friend as *demay*." Retail quantities which one is not permitted to sell as *demay*, one may not send to a friend as *demay*. Wholesale quantities which one is permitted to sell as *demay*, one may send to a friend as *demay*. "Rebbi Yose permits certain produce," be it retail or wholesale quantities, but he forbids retail quantities that are *demay*[76].

76 Even if the recipient is informed, since it falls under the blanket prohibition of the Mishnah. The exception he makes is for certain produce only.

רִבִּי אַבָּהוּ בְשֵׁם רִבִּי יוֹחָנָן מִפְּנֵי גִידּוּרוֹ הִתִּירוּ דְמַאי בְגַסָּה.

Rebbi Abbahu in the name of Rebbi Joḥanan: They permitted *demay* in wholesale quantity because of its being fenced in[77].

77 Because everybody knows that wholesale quantities are *demay*, no *ḥaver* will refrain from giving the appropriate tithes.

דו מַתְנִיתָא רִבִּי יוֹסֵי אוֹמֵר סַלֵּי תְאֵינִים וְסַלֵּי עֲנָבִים וְקוּפוֹת שֶׁל יֶרֶק כָּל־זְמַן שֶׁהוּא מוֹכְרָן אֲכָסְרָא פָּטוּר. אָמַר רַבָּן שִׁמְעוֹן בֶּן גַּמְלִיאֵל שָׁלַח לִי רִבִּי יוֹסֵי

בִּירְבִּי אֶתְרוֹג וְאָמַר לִי זֶה בָּא בְיָדִי מִקֵּיסָרִין. וְלָמַדְתִּי בוֹ שְׁלֹשָׁה דְּבָרִים. שֶׁהוּא וַדַּאי. שֶׁהוּא טָמֵא. שֶׁלֹּא בָּא בְּיַד אַחֵר. שֶׁהוּא וַדַּאי. שֶׁפֵּירוֹת קֵיסָרִין וַדַּאי. שֶׁהוּא טָמֵא מַרְבִּיצִין עָלָיו מַיִם. שֶׁלֹּא בָּא בְּיַד אַחֵר שֶׁאִילּוּ בָא בְּיַד אַחֵר הָיִיתִי מְעַשֵּׂר מִזֶּה עַל זֶה. וִיעַשֵּׂר מִמֶּנּוּ עָלָיו. דּוּ חָשַׁשׁ לְהָדָא דְּבַר קַפָּרָא. דְּבַר קַפָּרָא אָמַר אֵין דֶּרֶךְ בְּנֵי אָדָם לִהְיוֹת מְשַׁלְּחִין לַחֲבֵירֵיהֶן דְּבָרִים חֲסֵרִין. וְלֹא מַתְנִיתִין הִיא רִבִּי יוֹסֵי מַתִּיר בְּוַדַּאי בִּלְבַד שֶׁיּוֹדִיעֶן. אָתָא מֵימַר לָךְ אַף עַל גַּב דּוּ פְּלֵיג עַל רַבָּנִין לָא עֲבַד עוּבְדָא דְכְוָותֵיהּ.

This is a *baraita*[78]: "Rebbi Yose says, baskets of figs, baskets of grapes, and boxes of vegetables, as long as they are sold *en bloc*, are free. [79]Rabban Simeon ben Gamliel said, the great Rebbi Yose sent me an *etrog* and said to me: this came into my hand from Caesarea[80]. I understood from this three things: That it was certain, could become impure, and he did not have another one. That it was certain, because the fruits of Caesarea are certain. That it could become impure, because they sprinkle water on it[81]. That he did not have another one, because if he had, he would have tithed from one on the other." Why could he not have tithed from itself on itself[82]? Because he was mindful of the saying of Bar Kappara, for Bar Kappara said that people do not send things that are defective to their friends. But is that not our Mishnah? "Rebbi Yose permits certain produce on condition that he inform him." This tells you that, even though he disagreed with the rabbis, he did not act according to his own opinion.

78 While the first sentence is Mishnah 2:5, Maimonides (*Maäser* 11:4) takes everything together as one statement. Rabban Simeon ben Gamliel in Tosephta *Demay* 2:12 quotes Rebbi Yose that the kinds mentioned in the Mishnah fall under the monetary limitations spelled out in Halakhah 2:5. Maimonides seems to think that the final statement in this paragraph (that

R. Yose himself did not act according to his own opinion but deferred to that of his colleagues), applies to the entire Tannaitic statement here. In the opinion of R. Abraham ben David, the first sentence is a quote from the Mishnah, but the following text is from some Tosephta collection. Hence, he thinks that practice should follow R. Yose in 2:5, but not in 3:3.

79 A similar text in Tosephta *Demay* 2:14: "Rabban Simeon ben Gamliel said, it happened that the great Rebbi Yose sent me an *etrog* (*citrus medica*) from Sepphoris and said to me: this came into my hand from Caesarea. And I understood from this three things: That it was certain, could become impure, and he did not have another one, because if he had, he would have tithed from one on the other." A discussion of this text appears in Tosaphot *'Avodah zarah* 58b-59a.

80 Since this was sent from Sepphoris in Galilee, it is likely to come from Caesarea Philippi on the slopes of the Golan heights; cf. Halakhah 2:1. However, the next paragraph might mean that the *etrog* came from Caesarea maritima.

81 Cf. commentary to Halakhah 2:3, Note 137.

82 Taken out a small piece as heave of the tithe.

רִבִּי זְעִירָא בְּעָא קוֹמֵי רִבִּי יָסָא וְלֹא מִפֵּירוֹת שֶׁהֵן מוּתָּרִין בְּקֵיסָרִין הוּא. אָמַר לֵיהּ וְלֹא רִבִּי הִתִּיר קֵיסָרִין. וְרַבָּן שִׁמְעוֹן בֶּן גַּמְלִיאֵל קוֹדֶם לְרִבִּי הָיָה.

Rebbi Zeïra asked before Rebbi Yasa: It this not from the fruits that are exempt at Caesarea[83]? He said to him, did not Rebbi permit fruits at Caesarea? But Rabban Simeon ben Gamliel preceded Rebbi[84]!

83 *Etrog* is not on the list given in Halakhah 2:1 of *demay* fruits at Caesarea. Hence, it is not excluded that the *etrog* came from the Land of Israel near Caesarea Philippi (Banias),

84 Since he was Rebbi's father.

(fol. 23b) **משנה ד**: הַמּוֹלִיךְ חִיטָּיו לִטְחוֹן עִם הַכּוּתִי אוֹ לִטְחוֹן עִם[85] עַם הָאָרֶץ בְּחֶזְקָתָן לְמַעְשְׂרוֹת וְלִשְׁבִיעִית. לִטְחוֹן הַנָּכְרִי דְּמַאי. הַמַּפְקִיד פֵּירוֹתָיו אֶצֶל הַכּוּתִי וְאֶצֶל עַם הָאָרֶץ בְּחֶזְקָתָן לְמַעְשְׂרוֹת וּלִשְׁבִיעִית וְאֶצֶל הַנָּכְרִי כְּפֵירוֹתָיו. רִבִּי שִׁמְעוֹן אוֹמֵר דְּמַאי.

Mishnah 4: Wheat brought to be milled[86] by a Samaritan or by an *am haärez* remains in its prior state for tithes[87] and Sabbatical year[88]. By a Gentile, it is *demay*[89]. Produce deposited with a Samaritan or with an *am haärez* remains in its prior state for tithes and Sabbatical year; with a Gentile, it is like his produce[90]. Rebbi Simeon says, it is *demay*[91].

85 Text of the Leyden manuscript, missing from the Venice print.

86 Reading of the Venice print and the Leyden manuscript. Most Mishnah manuscripts have הַמּוֹלִיךְ חִיטָּיו לְטָחוֹן כּוּתִי "he who brings his wheat to a Samaritan miller." This text is also confirmed by Rashi, *Gittin* 61b.

87 This must refer to the Second Tithe, since grain from which tithe was not taken is referred to as *tevel* or *demay*.

88 They are not suspected of switching grain they know belongs to a *haver*.

89 Since he does not care about these things, he will just deliver the correct quantity, irrespective of its source; it may be from the grain delivered by a nonobservant Jew.

90 Produce harvested by a Gentile is not subject to tithes and Sabbatical restrictions. However, produce bought by a Jew before it was warehoused is considered to come under the obligation of tithes when it is stored by the Jew. Hence, it depends on when the Jew acquires the Gentile's produce and one cannot simply say "obligated" or "not obligated."

91 If the Gentile accepts produce for storage, he also accepts from non-observant Jews and may store everything together. R. Simeon holds that the produce of the Gentile is exempt from tithes and heave; hence, his problem is only with Jewish produce in storage. [This is the interpretation of the Yerushalmi; according to the Babli (*Menahot* 67b) R. Simeon holds that the rabbis decreed *demay* for Gentile produce so that Jewish landowners

should not have an incentive to hand their land over to Gentile sharecroppers.]

(fol. 23c) **הלכה ד**: רִבִּי חִייָא בְשֵׁם רִבִּי יוֹחָנָן נִתְחַלְּפָה קוּפָּתוֹ אֶצֶל הַטָּחוֹן אִם הוּחְזַק עַם הָאָרֶץ לִהְיוֹת טוֹחֵן שָׁם בְּאוֹתוֹ הַיּוֹם חוֹשֵׁשׁ וְאִם לָאו אֵינוֹ חוֹשֵׁשׁ. וְיָחוּשׁ מַה בֵּינָהּ וּלְסֵירָקִי. לֹא כֵן תַּנֵּי סֵירָקִי שֶׁהָיְתָה מִסְתַּפֶּקֶת יוֹם אֶחָד מִן הָאָסוּר נַעֲשֶׂה אוֹתוֹ הַיּוֹם הוֹכִיחַ לְכָל־הַיָּמִים. סֵירָקִי אֵיפְשַׁר לָהּ שֶׁלֹּא לְהִסְתַּפֵּק. בְּרַם הָכָא לֹא הוּחְזַק עַם הָאָרֶץ לִהְיוֹת טוֹחֵן שָׁם בְּאוֹתוֹ הַיּוֹם.

Halakhah 4: Rebbi Ḥiyya in the name of Rebbi Joḥanan[92]: If his box was exchanged at the miller's, if it was established that an *am haärez̧* gave to be milled there that day, he has to worry[93]; otherwise, he does not have to worry. Should he not worry? What is the difference between this and the Saracens? Was it not stated: "If a group of Saracens one day provisioned themselves from forbidden supplies[94], then that day becomes a proof for all days[95]." It is impossible for Saracens not to supply themselves. But here it was not established that the *am haärez̧* was milling there that day[96].

92 The text is also in *Ketubot* 1:10, fol. 25d.

93 He has to worry that the grain is the *am haärez̧*'s and therefore *demay*; then he has to tithe a second time.

94 From Jewish suppliers who do not tithe.

95 All the produce they sell is *demay* even though the greater part of it may be Gentile and exempt. Hence, if we see that an *am haärez̧* uses that mill one day, why should we not assume that an *am haärez̧* uses it every day?

96 The Saracens showed that their persons are not to be trusted. In our case, we know that the *am haärez̧* cannot be trusted, which is nothing new and does not need proof. But the mill does not become an *amē haärez̧*' mill by that.

רִבִּי טַייְפָא סָמוּקָא בְּשֵׁם רִבִּי אַבָּהוּ כּוּתִין נֶאֱמָנִין עַל הַפִּיקָּדוֹן. וְלָא מַתְנִיתָא הִיא אֶצֶל הַכּוּתִי. מַתְנִיתִין עַד שֶׁלֹּא נֶחְשְׁדוּ אָתָא מֵימַר אֲפִילוּ מִשֶּׁנֶּחְשְׁדוּ. מַהוּ שֶׁיְּהֵא נֶאֱמָן לוֹמַר נְטַלְתִּיו וְהִנַּחְתִּי אֲחֵרִים מְתוּקָּנִין תַּחְתֵּיהֶן. אִם אַתְּ מַאֲמִינוֹ שֶׁנָּטַל הֶאֱמִינוֹ שֶׁנָּתַן. אִם אֵין אַתְּ מַאֲמִינוֹ שֶׁנָּטַל אַל תַּאֲמִינֵהוּ שֶׁנָּתַן. כּוּתִי אַתְּ מַאֲמִינוֹ שֶׁנָּתַן וְאֵין אַתְּ מַאֲמִינוֹ שֶׁנָּטַל. רִבִּי יוֹנָה בְּעֵי מַה נָן קַיָּמִין אִם בְּאוֹמֵר מִשֶּׁלִּי הֵן. אֲפִילוּ עַם הָאָרֶץ לֹא יְהֵא נֶאֱמָן. אִם בְּאוֹמֵר פְּלוֹנִי עִישֵּׂר לִי אֲפִילוּ כּוּתִי יְהֵא נֶאֱמָן. אָמַר רִבִּי בָּא תִּיפְתָּר כְּמָאן דְּאָמַר כּוּתִי כְּגוֹי. דְּאִיתְפַּלְּגוֹן כּוּתִי כְּגוֹי דִּבְרֵי רִבִּי רַבָּן שִׁמְעוֹן בֶּן גַּמְלִיאֵל אוֹמֵר כּוּתִי כְּיִשְׂרָאֵל לְכָל דָּבָר.

Rebbi Taypha the Red[97] in the name of Rebbi Abbahu: Samaritans can be trusted with deposits. Is that not the Mishnah: "With a Samaritan"? Our Mishnah before they became suspect, he comes to tell us even after they became suspect[98]. How is it, should he be trusted to say, I took it and replaced it by other deposits that were put in order? If you believe him in that he took it, you should believe him in what he gave. If you do not believe that he took, do not believe that he gave[99]. You believe a Samaritan that he gave[100] and you do not believe that he took. Rebbi Jonah asked: What are we talking about? If he says, they are my own, even an *am haärez* should not be trusted. If he says, X[101] took tithes for me, even the Samaritan should be believed. Rebbi Abba said, explain it according to him who says that a Samaritan is like a Gentile. As they disagreed: A Samaritan is like a Gentile, the words of Rebbi. Rabban Simeon ben Gamliel said, a Samaritan is like a Jew in every respect.

97 An Amora of the fourth generation, student of R. Abbahu and sometimes mentioned in connection with the Amora R. Yose.

98 The Yerushalmi always refers the question whether Samaritans are counted as Jews or as Gentiles to the disagreement between Rabban Simeon ben Gamliel and his son Rebbi, as reported below. However, it is stated

in *'Avodah zarah* 5:3, fol. 44d (quoted in Babli *Ḥulin* 6a) that in the times of Rebbis Ammi, Assi, and Abbahu, Samaritans were found to use Gentile wine (or to adopt Gentile behavior), and from that moment on Samaritans were considered as Gentiles. However it seems from the Yerushalmi that up to the end of the Talmudic period in Galilee, the separation of Jews and Samaritans was not universally accepted. (One also may assume that parts of Jewish Sadducee communities changed to a Samaritan affiliation after the destruction of the Temple.)

99 In the Tosephta (*Demay* 4:22), this argument is given in reference to deposits with an *am haärez*.

100 Grain from another source, but you do not believe him that he exchanged. In the Tosephta (*Demay* 4:24) one reads: "If he says, I took it and replaced it with some that was put in order, one does not worry either about tithes or about the Sabbatical."

101 A person recognized as a *ḥaver*.

הָכָא אַתְּ אָמַר לְטָחָן הַנָּכְרִי דְּמַיי. וְהָכָא אַתְּ אָמַר אֶצֶל הַנָּכְרִי כְּפֵירוֹתָיו. כָּאן קוּפָּה בְקוּפּוֹת וְכָאן פֵּירוֹת בְּפֵירוֹת.

Here you say, "by a Gentile miller, they are *demay*," there you say, "with a Gentile, they are like his produce." In the first case, a box among boxes[102], there, produce among his produce.

102 The miller may mistakenly have given his customers a wrong box. In the second sentence of the Mishnah, the produce is stored not in separate boxes but with the Gentile's produce.

רִבִּי יִרְמְיָה בְּעָא קוֹמֵי רִבִּי זְעִירָא[103] מַה כְּפֵירוֹתָיו מַמָּשׁ פְּטוֹר טֶבֶל בָּרוּר בְּמָקוֹם אַחֵר. אָמַר לֵיהּ וּלְכָל־דְּבָהּ. וְלֹא עַאל יְאוּת הֲוָה רִבִּי חֲנִינָא מַתְּרִיס לְקֳבֵיל רִבִּי אָחָא.

Rebbi Jeremiah asked before Rebbi Zeïra[104]: Does it mean, really like his produce? Freeing what would be *ṭevel* at another place[105]? He said to him, for all that is in it[106]. Rebbi Ḥanina was uselessly opposing Rebbi Aḥa[107].

103 Parallel in ʻ*Abodah zarah* 2:3, fol. 41b, where the reading is: רִבִּי חֲנִינָא בְּעָא קוֹמֵי רִבִּי מָנָא Since R. Ḥanina is mentioned in the conclusion, he should be mentioned here also. At the end, instead of מַתְּרִים לְקֳבֵל רִבִּי אָחָא it reads מַתְּרִים לְקִבְלֵיה, referring to Rebbi Mana. The Amora in that case must be R. Ḥanania, not R. Ḥanina. The last reading, "R. Aḥa," is not too likely either but not impossible.

104 The better reading is: R. Ḥanania before R. Mana; see the preceding note.

105 It would be a cheap way of tithing to deposit one's produce with a Gentile and then reclaiming it without taking heave and tithes!

106 It is only equal to the Gentile's produce if it is *in it*, i. e., if the produce was in order it does not become even *demay* at the Gentile's, but it cannot lose its status of either *demay* or *ṭevel*.

107 As explained above, this might be "R. Mana."

רִבִּי אָחָא רִבִּי חִייָא בַּר אָבוּן בְּשֵׁם רִבִּי יוֹסֵי בֶּן חֲנִינָא לֹא אָמַר רִבִּי שִׁמְעוֹן אֶלָּא כְדֵי קוּפָּתוֹ. הִפְקִיד אֶצְלוֹ שְׁתַּיִם אַחַת דְּמַאי וְאַחַת וַדַּאי. בְּקַייָמוֹת אֲבָל אִם נֶאֶכְלָה הָרִאשׁוֹנָה הַשְּׁנִיָּה דְּמַאי. נָטְלוּ מִמֶּנּוּ מֵאָה בְנֵי אָדָם מֵאָה סְאִין בַּת אַחַת כָּל־אֶחָד וְאֶחָד מְתַקֵּן דְּמַאי. נְתָנוּם לְאָדָם אַחֵר כְּבָר נִרְאוּ לִהְיוֹת וַדַּאי. נָטַל מִמֶּנּוּ אָדָם אֶחָד כַּמָּה סְאִין בַּת אַחַת הָרִאשׁוֹנָה דְּמַאי וְהַשְּׁאָר וַדַּאי. נְתָנָם לְמֵאָה בְנֵי אָדָם כְּבָר נִרְאוּ לִהְיוֹת וַדַּאי. וְהָתַנֵּי בְשֵׁם רִבִּי שִׁמְעוֹן בְּשֵׁם רִבִּי טַרְפוֹן עָשׂוּ פֵּירוֹת יִשְׂרָאֵל זֶה כְפֵירוֹת כּוּתִי זֶה דְּמַאי. עוֹד הִיא לֹא אָמַר רִבִּי שִׁמְעוֹן אֶלָּא עַד כְּדֵי קוּפָּתוֹ.

Rebbi Aḥa, Rebbi Ḥiyya bar Abin in the name of Rebbi Yose ben Ḥanina: Rebbi Simeon said, only for one box. If he handed over two boxes, one of them is *demay* and one is certain[108] if they are still in existence[109]; but if the first one was consumed, the second one is *demay*[110]. If a hundred people took from him 100 *seah* at one time, each one puts his produce in order as *demay*. If they gave it all to one person, it should be considered as certain[111]. If one person took many *seot* together, the first one is *demay*, the rest certain. If he then gave the rest to a hundred people, it should be considered as certain. Did we not state in the name of Rebbi Simeon in the name of Rebbi Ṭarphon: "They made the produce of this Jew like the produce of that Samaritan[112], *demay*." That again is the same; Rebbi Simeon said, only for one box.

108 We have to assume that here, "certain" does not mean that certainly the heave of the tithe was not taken, but to the contrary, that all heave and tithes were taken and the produce is ready to eat.

109 Then one remains *demay* and one is certain.

110 We do not say that this may be the one which was put in order.

111 Since R. Simeon suspects the Gentile only to substitute at most one box; if there are 100, of which 99 are in order, there is no reason to treat this as *demay*.

112 In the Tosephta (*Demay* 4:25): "Rabban Simeon ben Gamliel and Rebbi Simeon: The Jew's produce made this Gentile's produce *demay*." The word "Samaritan" in the Yerushalmi seems to be a scribal error. The question is about the interpretation of the Tosephta (or an equivalent *baraita*), and the answer is that the Tosephta is exactly parallel to the Mishnah and gives the reason for the Mishnah, but it does not extend R. Simeon's disagreement with the Tanna of the Mishnah.

אָמַר רִבִּי יְהוֹשֻׁעַ בֶּן קָבְסַיי כָּל־יָמַי הָיִיתִי קוֹרֵא הַפָּסוּק הַזֶּה וְהִזָּה הַטָּהוֹר עַל הַטָּמֵא טָהוֹר אֶחָד מַזֶּה עַל טָמֵא אֶחָד. עַד שֶׁלָּמַדְתִּיהָ מֵאוֹצָרָהּ שֶׁל יַבְנֶה וַחֲכָמִים אוֹמְרִים אֲפִילוּ כּוּלּוֹ גּוֹי וְיִשְׂרָאֵל אֶחָד מַטִּיל לְתוֹכוֹ דְּמַאי. הָדָא אָמְרָה שֶׁטָּהוֹר אֶחָד מַזֶּה עַל כַּמָּה טְמֵאִין דְּתַנֵּינָן אֶצֶל הַנָּכְרִי כְּפֵירוֹתָיו. אָמַר רִבִּי לָעְזָר חֲכָמִים שֶׁהֵן בְּשִׁיטַּת רִבִּי מֵאִיר. רִבִּי יוֹחָנָן אָמַר חֲכָמִים מַמָּשׁ. בְּעוֹן קָמֵי מַה טַעַם. אָמַר לוֹן כַּד תִּסָּאבוּן אֲנָא אֲמַר לְכוֹן. מַה הֲוָה מֵימַר לְכוֹן כְּמַה דְאָמַר מֵאֵילֵיהֶן קִבְּלוּ עֲלֵיהֶן אֶת הַמַּעְשְׂרוֹת. שְׁמוּאֵל בַּר בָּא בְּעֵי נִיחָא לְטָהֳרוֹת לֹא אָמַר לוֹן מִפְּנֵי גֶּדֶר טָהֳרוֹת. לְמַעְשְׂרוֹת לֹא אָמַר לוֹן מִפְּנֵי גֶּדֶר

מַעְשְׂרוֹת. לְקֳדָשִׁים לֹא אָמַר לוֹן וְאִילּוּ אָמַר לוֹן מַה הֲוָה מֵימַר לוֹן. גַּבֵּי מַעְשְׂרוֹת כְּמָאן דְּאָמַר מֵאֵילֵיהֶן קִבְּלוּ עֲלֵיהֶן אֶת הַמַּעְשְׂרוֹת.[113]

"[114]Rebbi Joshua ben Qabusai[115] said, all my life I read this verse (*Num.* 19:19): '*The* pure shall sprinkle on *the* impure,' that one pure person sprinkles on one impure person, until I learned it from the storage facility at Jabneh. This means that one pure person sprinkles on many impure persons.[116]"

"But the Sages say, it is *demay* even if all the contributors are Gentile except one Jew[117]." But we have stated: "With a Gentile, they are like his produce[118]." Rebbi Eleazar said, the Sages who follow the line of Rebbi Meïr. Rebbi Johanan said, these are really the Sages[119]. They asked him, what is the reason? He told them, if you get whitehaired, I might tell you[120]. What would he have told them? That they accepted tithes voluntarily[121]. Samuel bar Abba[122] asked: It is understandable that he did not tell them about pure food, because of a fence for pure food[123]. He did not tell them about tithes, as a fence for tithes. He did not tell them about sacrifices; if he had told them, what would he have told them[124]? For tithes, following him[126] who says that they accepted tithes voluntarily.

113 It seems that there is some confusion of two Tosephtot in the order of sentences here. The translation follows a reordered text:
אָמַר רִבִּי יְהוֹשֻׁעַ בֶּן קָבֵּסַיי כָּל־יָמַי הָיִיתִי קוֹרֵא הַפָּסוּק הַזֶּה וְהִזָּה הַטָּהוֹר עַל הַטָּמֵא טָהוֹר אֶחָד מַזֶּה עַל טָמֵא אֶחָד. עַד שֶׁלָּמַדְתִּיהָ מֵאוֹצָרָהּ שֶׁל יַבְנֶה. הָדָא אָמְרָה שֶׁטָּהוֹר אֶחָד מַזֶּה עַל כַּמָּה טְמֵאִין. וַחֲכָמִים אוֹמְרִים אֲפִילוּ כּוּלּוֹ גוֹי וְיִשְׂרָאֵל אֶחָד מַשִּׁיל לְתוֹכוֹ דְּמַאי. דְּתַנֵּינָן אֶצֶל הַנָּכְרִי כְּפֵירוֹתָיו. אָמַר רִבִּי לָעְזָר חֲכָמִים שֶׁהֵן בְּשִׁיטַּת רִבִּי מֵאִיר. רִבִּי יוֹחָנָן אָמַר חֲכָמִים מַמָּשׁ. בְּעוּן קָמֵי מַה טַעַם. אָמַר כַּד תְּסָאבוּן אֲנָא אֲמַר לְכוֹן. מַה הֲוָה מֵימַר לְכוֹן כְּמַה דְּאָמַר מֵאֵילֵיהֶן קִבְּלוּ עֲלֵיהֶן אֶת הַמַּעְשְׂרוֹת. שְׁמוּאֵל בַּר בָּא בְּעֵי נִיחָא לְטָהֳרוֹת לֹא אָמַר לוֹן מִפְּנֵי גֶּדֶר טָהֳרוֹת. לְמַעְשְׂרוֹת לֹא אָמַר לוֹן מִפְּנֵי גֶּדֶר מַעְשְׂרוֹת. לְקֳדָשִׁים לֹא אָמַר לוֹן וְאִילּוּ אָמַר לוֹן מַה הֲוָה מֵימַר לוֹן. גַּבֵּי מַעְשְׂרוֹת כְּמָאן דְּאָמַר מֵאֵילֵיהֶן קִבְּלוּ עֲלֵיהֶן אֶת הַמַּעְשְׂרוֹת.

114 Tosephta *Demay* 1:12-14

{commentary in braces}: "12. A storage facility into which Jews and Gentiles contribute; if the majority are Gentile it is certain, if the majority are Jewish, it is *demay*; these are the words of R. Meïr {who holds that produce of the Holy Land is subject to heave and tithes even if grown by a Gentile.} But the Sages say, it is *demay* even if all the contributors are Gentile except one Jew {since produce of the Holy Land is not subject to heave and tithes if grown by a Gentile.} 13. Rebbi Yose said, when are these words said, for a private storage facility, but at a government storage facility {for storing taxes paid in kind} one follows the majority. They said to him, you taught us about the storage facility of Jabneh, which is inside the walls, that it is *demay*, and most of the contributors are Samaritans {who are subject to tithes but certainly will not tithe what they personally do not use}; but a storage facility outside the Land, e. g., that of Ragab {a place in Jordan} is obligated only according to percentages {of the supply coming from the Land.} 13. Rebbi Joshua ben Qabusai said, all my life I read this verse (*Num.* 19:19): '*The* pure shall sprinkle on *the* impure,' and I did not understand it until the storage at Jabneh; I learned from the storage facility at Jabneh that one pure person sprinkles on many impure persons."

115 A Tanna of the Fourth generation, son-in-law of R. Aqiba. His father-in-law considers Samaritans as true converts (Babli *Qiddušin* 75b) but thinks one cannot intermarry with them because of their deviating interpretation of some incest prohibitions.

116 Since one rabbinic Jew makes *demay* in the presence of many Samaritans.

{In the Babli, *Nazir* 61b, the verse is taken to mean that only a person who may become impure by Biblical standards, i. e., a Jew, can sprinkle the water with the ashes of the red heifer to cleanse another Jew from the impurity of the dead. In *Sifry, Num.* 129, R. Aqiba infers that the water was purifying only if a pure person sprinkles on an impure one but sprinkling on a pure person makes him impure. This is accepted by the Yerushalmi, *Yoma* 1:2 (fol. 38d); a Babli source (*Yoma* 14a) quotes and follows a dissenting opinion of the Sages. *Sifry zuta, Ḥuqqat* 19, notes that only a pure person becomes impure; a person impure but not through a corpse is not influenced by being sprinkled. Since

Sifry zuta in general follows R. Ismael, this supports the position of the Yerushalmi that R. Aqiba's statement is accepted by everybody.}

117 Tosephta 1:12, given above.

118 Why is it not *demay* as in a storage facility?

119 They disagree with R. Meïr on the status of Gentile-grown produce and hold that it is exempt from all tithes.

120 But by that time, R. Johanan would have died long ago.

121 The returnees from Babylonia accepted the obligation of tithes voluntarily, since these obligations were originally bound to the land distributed by Joshua, and that distribution was obliterated by the exile. See the author's *The Scholar's Haggadah*, Northvale NJ 1995, p. 280-281. Since the obligation is similar in nature to a rabbinic ordinance, it follows the rules of leniency valid for such ordinances.

122 The Babylonian Sage Samuel.

123 He did not want to imply that heave does not have to be watched according to the standards of Biblical purity because of its rabbinic status, because then they would have disregarded the rules of purity altogether. The same applies to the tithes.

124 They seemed to have asked about some leniencies in the treatment of Gentiles' sacrifices; the question is not preserved. Samuel asked, why did he not answer that question since the answer could not have any practical consequence.

125 Rebbi Eleazar, *Sheviït* 6:1, fol. 36b.

רִבִּי יִרְמְיָה רִבִּי חִייָא בְּשֵׁם רִבִּי יוֹחָנָן מוֹדֶה רִבִּי שִׁמְעוֹן שֶׁהוּא מַפְרִישׁ מַעְשְׂרוֹתָיו מֵהֲלָכָה. הָא רִבִּי שִׁמְעוֹן אָמַר מַפְרִישׁ וְרַבָּנִין אָמְרֵי מַפְרִישׁ. (fol. 23d) מַה בֵּינֵיהוֹן. רִבִּי שִׁמְעוֹן אוֹמֵר מַפְרִישׁ וְנוֹטֵל דָּמִים מִן הַשֵּׁבֶט. רַבָּנִין אָמְרִין מַפְרִישׁ וְאֵינוֹ נוֹטֵל דָּמִים מִן הַשֵּׁבֶט. אֲפִילוּ כִּתְרוּמַת חוּצָה לָאָרֶץ אֵינָהּ אִילּוּ תְרוּמַת חוּצָה לָאָרֶץ שֶׁמָּא אֵינוֹ נוֹטֵל דָּמִים מִן הַשֵּׁבֶט. דִּילְמָא עַל עִיקָּר טִיבְלוֹ שֶׁל גּוֹי אִיתְאַמָּרַת. אֶלָּא בְגִין דְּתַנֵּי רִבִּי יְהוּדָה וְרִבִּי שִׁמְעוֹן אוֹמֵר יֵשׁ קִנְיָין לְגוֹי בְּאֶרֶץ יִשְׂרָאֵל לְפוֹטְרוֹ מִן הַמַּעְשְׂרוֹת עָלֶיהָ. רִבִּי יִרְמְיָה רִבִּי חִייָא בְּשֵׁם רִבִּי יוֹחָנָן מוֹדֶה רִבִּי שִׁמְעוֹן שֶׁהוּא מַפְרִישׁ מַעְשְׂרוֹתָיו מֵהֲלָכָה.

Rebbi Jeremiah, Rebbi Ḥiyya in the name of Rebbi Joḥanan: Rebbi Simeon agrees that one must separate tithes as a matter of practice[126]. Hence, Rebbi Simeon says that one separates, and the rabbis say that one separates[127]. What is the difference between them? Rebbi Simeon says, he separates and takes money from the tribe[128]. The rabbis say that he separates and does not take money from the tribe. But is it not even like heave from outside the Land, does he not take money from the tribe[129]? Maybe it was said on the principle of *ṭevel* for produce of the Gentile[130]? Since we have stated: Rebbi Jehudah and Rebbi Simeon say, a Gentile may acquire real estate in the Land of Israel to free it from the tithes imposed on it[131]. Rebbi Jeremiah, Rebbi Ḥiyya. in the name of Rebbi Joḥanan: Rebbi Simeon agrees that nevertheless he[132] must separate tithes as a matter of practice.

126 "Practice" in the language of the Yerushalmi is similar to the notion of "practice going back to Moses on Mount Sinai" in the Babli; it means a rule established by the returnees from Babylonia, the "Men of the Great Assembly," as part of the establishment of rabbinic Judaism. It is part of the original decree of *demay*.

127 Assuming that the statement of R. Joḥanan refers to the Mishnah, viz., that the Sages say produce deposited with a Gentile is like his own produce, the assertion that R. Simeon requires tithing is trivial since *demay* certainly must be tithed. The only inference to be drawn is from "agrees", which would imply that the Sages also require tithing and that the declaration of "his own produce" can only be used in a negative, not in a positive sense. Hence, the Sages also require tithing.

128 He separates heave of the tithe and sells it (cheaply, because there are few qualified buyers) to the Cohen. The Sages would require the heave to be given as a gift.

129 In those parts of the Land conquered and sanctified by Moses and Joshua but not settled by the returnees from Babylonia, heave and tithes were taken as a remembrance and sold to the

Cohanim. Outside the Biblical boundaries, no heave was ever taken (and could not be taken because that land is impure.)

130 The statement of R. Joḥanan never was meant as commentary on our Mishnah but as a remark on the status of produce grown by a Gentile in the Land of Israel. Hence, the inference about the stand taken by the Sages in our Mishnah is invalid.

131 They disagree with R. Meïr who holds that all land in the Land of Israel is subject to heave and tithes, irrespective of the owner; cf. *Peah* Chapter 4, Notes 129-131.

132 The Jew who buys produce grown in the Land by a Gentile. This obligation is one of tradition.

(fol. 23b) **משנה ה**: הַנּוֹתֵן לְפוּנְדְּקִית מְעַשֵּׂר אֶת שֶׁהוּא נוֹתֵן לָהּ וְאֶת שֶׁהוּא נוֹטֵל מִמֶּנָּה מִפְּנֵי שֶׁהִיא חֲשׁוּדָה לְחַלֵּף. אָמַר רִבִּי יוֹסֵי אֵין אָנוּ אַחֲרָאִין לְרַמָּאִין אֵינוֹ מְעַשֵּׂר אֶלָּא מַה שֶׁהוּא נוֹטֵל מִמֶּנָּה בִּלְבָד.

Mishnah 5: He who gives to the innkeeper's wife, tithes what he gives her and what he takes from her because she is suspected to switch[133]. Rebbi Yose said, we are not responsible for the dishonest[134]; he tithes only what he receives from her.

133 The motives imputed to the innkeeper's wife (or the female innkeeper) are not clear. She is supposed to cook for her guests the food they provide. The anonymous Tanna holds that a *ḥaver* never hands anything *demay* over to a fellow Jew. This Mishnah (and the next) are quoted in Babli *Ḥulin* 6a-b; there, the interpretation is that the innkeeper will try to please her guests and maybe substitute fresher produce or spices for him, whereas R. Yose takes a dim view of innkeepers and thinks that if she takes anything it is in order to steal.

134 If she steals and eats *ṭevel*, it is her own fault if she commits a deadly sin.

(fol. 23d) **הלכה ה**: רִבִּי יוֹסֵי וְרַבָּן שִׁמְעוֹן בֶּן גַּמְלִיאֵל שְׁנֵיהֶן אָמְרוּ דָּבָר אֶחָד. כְּמָה דְּרִבִּי יוֹסֵי אָמַר אֵין אָנוּ אַחֲרָאִין לְרַמָּאִין כֵּן רַבָּן שִׁמְעוֹן בֶּן גַּמְלִיאֵל אָמַר אֵין אָנוּ אַחֲרָאִין לְרַמָּאִין. מִסְתַּבְּרָה רִבִּי יוֹסֵי יוֹדֵי לְרַבָּן שִׁמְעוֹן בֶּן גַּמְלִיאֵל וְרַבָּן שִׁמְעוֹן בֶּן גַּמְלִיאֵל לֹא יוֹדֵי לְרִבִּי יוֹסֵי. רִבִּי יוֹסֵי יוֹדֵי לְרַבָּן שִׁמְעוֹן בֶּן גַּמְלִיאֵל שֶׁאֵין אָנוּ אַחֲרָאִין לְרַמָּאִין. וְרַבָּן שִׁמְעוֹן בֶּן גַּמְלִיאֵל לֹא יוֹדֵי לְרִבִּי יוֹסֵי. שֶׁאֵין דֶּרֶךְ חָבֵר לִהְיוֹת מוֹצִיא מִבֵּיתוֹ דָּבָר שֶׁאֵינוֹ מְתוּקָּן.

Halakhah 5: Both Rebbi Yose and Rabban Simeon ben Gamliel[135] said the same thing. Just as Rebbi Yose said, we are not responsible for the dishonest, so Rabban Simeon ben Gamliel said, we are not responsible for the dishonest. It is reasonable that Rebbi Yose will agree with Rabban Simeon ben Gamliel, but Rabban Simeon ben Gamliel will not agree with Rebbi Yose. Rebbi Yose will agree with Rabban Simeon ben Gamliel that we are not responsible for the dishonest. But Rabban Simeon ben Gamliel will not agree with Rebbi Yose, because it is not fitting for a *ḥaver* that anything not in order should leave his house[136].

135 Mishnah *Maäser Šeni* 5:1 states that a vineyard in the fourth year (whose fruits may not be eaten without redemption) is signalized by lumps of earth placed around it, and any orchard in the first three years after planting (whose fruits are forbidden for any use) by lumps of clay. Rabban Simeon ben Gamliel notes that this has to be done only in the Sabbatical year, when all growth is ownerless, but that in all other years, when taking from enclosed orchards and vineyards is theft, no signalizing is required since we are not responsible for the salvation of thieves.

136 This is quoted in the Babli (*Erubin* 32a, *Pesaḥim* 9a) in the name of R. Ḥanina (there called R. Ḥanina from Khusistan.)

(fol. 23b) **משנה ו**: הַנּוֹתֵן לַחֲמוֹתוֹ מְעַשֵּׂר אֶת שֶׁהוּא נוֹתֵן לָהּ וְאֶת שֶׁהוּא נוֹטֵל מִמֶּנָּה מִפְּנֵי שֶׁהִיא חֲשׁוּדָה לְחַלֵּף אֶת הַמִּתְקַלְקֵל. אָמַר רִבִּי יוּדָה רוֹצָה הִיא בְּתַקָּנַת בִּתָּהּ וּבוֹשָׁה מֵחֲתָנָהּ. וּמוֹדֶה רִבִּי יוּדָה בְנוֹתֵן לַחֲמוֹתוֹ שְׁבִיעִית שֶׁאֵינָהּ חֲשׁוּדָה לְהַחֲלִיף לְהַאֲכִיל אֶת בִּתָּהּ שְׁבִיעִית.

Mishnah 6: He[137] who gives to his mother-in-law tithes what he gives to her and what he receives from her because she is suspect to switch spoiled food[138]. Rebbi Jehudah says, she wants to put her daughter in a good light and is ashamed before her son-in-law. Rebbi Jehudah agrees that if he gives to his mother-in-law in the Sabbatical year she is not suspect of switching to feed her daughter from Sabbatical produce.

137 The *ḥaver* who married the daughter of an *am haärez*.

138 If something that the daughter cooks in her mother's kitchen is spoiled, the mother will take from her own stores to produce a perfect meal for her son-in-law. R. Jehudah does not disagree with the first sentence; he just gives the reasoning behind the rule.

(fol. 23d) **הלכה ו**: אָמַר רִבִּי יוֹחָנָן אַף קַדְמִיתָא עַל דַּעְתֵּיהּ דְּרִבִּי יְהוּדָה הִיא דְּרִבִּי יוּדָה אָמַר הַנּוֹתֵן לַחֲמוֹתוֹ כְּנוֹתֵן לְפוּנְדָּקִית. וְרַבָּנָן אָמְרִין הַנּוֹתֵן לַחֲמוֹתוֹ כְּנוֹתֵן לִשְׁכֶנְתּוֹ. כְּהָדָא דְתַנֵּי הַנּוֹתֵן לִשְׁכֶנְתּוֹ פַּת לֶאֱפוֹת בּוֹ תַּבְשִׁיל לַעֲשׂוֹת לוֹ אֵינוֹ חוֹשֵׁשׁ לֹא מִשּׁוּם שְׁבִיעִית וְלֹא מִשּׁוּם מַעְשְׂרוֹת. אֵימָתַי בִּזְמַן שֶׁנָּתַן לָהּ שְׂאוֹר וְתַבְלִין. אֲבָל אִם לֹא נָתַן לָהּ שְׂאוֹר וְתַבְלִין חוֹשֵׁשׁ מִשּׁוּם שְׁבִיעִית וּמִשּׁוּם מַעְשְׂרוֹת.

Halakhah 6: Rebbi Joḥanan said, the first sentence also gives the opinion of Rebbi Jehudah. But the rabbis say, one who gives to his mother-in-law is like one who gives to his neighbor. As we have stated[139]: "He who gives bread to his neighbor to bake for him, or a dish to cook for him, has to worry neither about the Sabbatical year nor about tithes.

That is, if he also gave her sour dough or spices. But if he did not give sour dough and spices, he worries about the Sabbatical year and about tithes."

139 Tosephta *Demay* 4:31, speaking of a *ḥaver* who gives something to bake or cook to his *am haärez̧* neighbor. The Tosephta is a little more explicit, reading in the last sentence: "he worries about the sour dough and spices for the Sabbatical year and tithes," not the foods he gave her.

מַה חֲמוֹתוֹ מִן הָאֵירוּסִין אוֹ מִן הַנִּישּׂוּאִין. נִשְׁמְעִינָהּ מִן הָדָא מוֹדֶה רִבִּי יוּדָה בְּנוֹתֵן לַחֲמוֹתוֹ שְׁבִיעִית שֶׁאֵינָהּ חֲשׁוּדָה לְהַחֲלִיף לְהַאֲכִיל אֶת בִּתָּהּ שְׁבִיעִית. שַׁנְיָיא הִיא תַּמָּן בֵּין מִן הָאֵירוּסִין בֵּין מִן הַנִּשּׂוּאִין. אוֹף הָכָא לָא שַׁנְיָיא בֵּין מִן הָאֵירוּסִין בֵּין מִן הַנִּשּׂוּאִין.

Does it mean his mother-in-law after the first[140] or the second marriage ceremony? Let us hear from the following: "Rebbi Jehudah agrees that if he gives to his mother-in-law in the Sabbatical year she is not suspect of switching to feed her daughter from Sabbatical produce[141]." Is there a difference between first and second marriage ceremony? Here also, there is no difference between first and second marriage ceremony.

140 Cf. *Peah* Chapter 6, Note 46.

141 In case the mother herself will not eat from Sabbatical produce used as merchandise.

הלקח פירות פרק רביעי

(fol. 23d) **משנה א**: הַלּוֹקֵחַ פֵּירוֹת מִמִּי שֶׁאֵינוֹ נֶאֱמָן עַל הַמַּעְשְׂרוֹת וְשָׁכַח לְעַשְּׂרָן שׁוֹאֲלוֹ בְשַׁבָּת וְאוֹכֵל עַל פִּיו. חֲשֵׁיכָה מוֹצָאֵי שַׁבָּת לֹא יֹאכַל עַד שֶׁיְּעַשֵּׂר.

Mishnah 1: He who buys produce from a person who is not trustworthy for tithes and forgot to tithe them[1] may ask the seller on the Sabbath and eats on the seller's information[2]. At nightfall, when Sabbath ends, he may not eat until he tithed.

1 Friday afternoon, and now, on the Sabbath, he has no other produce to eat.

2 Even though on weekdays, when tithing is possible, the seller's information would not be trusted.

הלכה א: חֲבֵרַיָּא בְשֵׁם רִבִּי יוֹחָנָן מִפְּנֵי כְבוֹד שַׁבָּת הִתִּירוּ. אִם מִפְּנֵי כְבוֹד שַׁבָּת לָמָּה לִי שׁוֹאֲלוֹ. עַל יְדֵי עִילֵּי עִילָּה[3]. רִבִּי בִּיבִי בְּשֵׁם רִבִּי חֲנִינָא אֵימַת שַׁבָּת עָלָיו וְהוּא אוֹמֵר אֱמֶת. וְאִם אֵימַת שַׁבָּת עָלָיו בְּדָה תַנֵּינָן חֲשֵׁיכָה מוֹצָאֵי שַׁבָּת לֹא יֹאכַל עַד שֶׁיְּעַשֵּׂר. מִפְּנֵי אֶחָד שֶׁאֵין אֵימַת שַׁבָּת עָלָיו. תַּנֵּי שׁוֹאֲלוֹ בְחוֹל לֹא יֹאכַל בְּשַׁבָּת. מָאן דְּאָמַר אֵימַת שַׁבָּת עָלָיו נִיחָא. מָאן דְּאָמַר מִפְּנֵי כְבוֹד שַׁבָּת אֲפִילוּ שׁוֹאֲלוֹ בְחוֹל יֹאכַל בְּשַׁבָּת.

Halakhah 1: The colleagues in the name of Rebbi Joḥanan: They permitted it because of the glory of the Sabbath. If it is because of the glory of the Sabbath, why does he have to ask him[4]? By way of finding a cause. Rebbi Bibi in the name of Rebbi Ḥanina: The fear of the Sabbath is on him[5] and he will speak the truth. If the fear of the Sabbath is on him, why did we state that at nightfall, when the Sabbath ends, he may not eat until he tithed? Because of one who does not fear the Sabbath. It was stated[6]: "If he asks him on weekdays, he may not eat on the Sabbath." According to him who says that the fear of the Sabbath is on him, this is fine. According to him who says that it is because of the glory of the Sabbath; when he asks him on weekdays, should he not eat on the Sabbath[7]?

3 Reading of Rome ms. and R. Simson. Venice: עולי עולה.

4 Since the seller is not trustworthy, his testimony is irrelevant. The answer is that some reason must be given to lift the strict rules of *demay* if those rules should be followed at all.

5 On the *am haärez*, who will not desecrate the Sabbath.

6 Tosephta *Demay* 5:1.

7 R. Johanan's argument seems weak. But in the next Halakhah, the tables are turned.

לֹא אָמַר אֶלָּא שׁוֹגֵג. הָא מֵזִיד אָסוּר דְּתַנֵּינָן שָׁכַח לְעַשְּׂרָן כְּשֶׁאֵין עִמּוֹ תְּנַאי אֲבָל אִם יֵשׁ עִמּוֹ תְּנַאי אוֹכֵל עַל תְּנָאוֹ שֶׁל חֲבֵירוֹ.

It was stated only for someone acting in error, not intentionally, as we have stated: If he forgot to tithe[8], if he had made no previous stipulation[9]. But with a stipulation, one eats even on the stipulation by a friend.

8 The leniencies are only admitted if somebody actually forgot to prepare, not if it was an intentional effort to seek leniencies.

9 This is explained in Mishnah 7:1: If somebody is invited to eat at another person's house and he does not trust his host with tithes, he can stipulate that after he returns home he will give tithes on what he ate there. While such a condition is forbidden for *tevel*, where heave can be given only from what clearly is in the tither's possession, this kind of stipulation is permitted for *demay*. It is even permitted for one person to make the stipulation for a whole group of people eating together.

משנה ב: לֹא מְצָאוֹ אָמַר לוֹ אֶחָד שֶׁאֵינוֹ נֶאֱמָן עַל הַמַּעְשְׂרוֹת מְעוּשָּׂרִין הֵן אוֹכֵל עַל פִּיו. חֲשֵׁיכָה מוֹצָאֵי שַׁבָּת לֹא יֹאכַל עַד שֶׁיְּעַשֵּׂר.

Mishnah 2: If he did not find the seller, but another person who is not trustworthy for tithes told him that it is tithed, he may eat on that information[10]. At nightfall when Sabbath ends, he may not eat until he tithed.

10 On the Sabbath only.

הלכה ב: מַהוּ שֶׁיֹּאכַל עַל שְׁאֵילַת חֲבֵירוֹ. הֵיךְ עֲבִידָא לָקְחוּ מִמֶּנּוּ שְׁנֵי בְנֵי אָדָם כְּאֶחָד שְׁאָלוֹ עַל אַחַת מֵהֶן הַשֵּׁנִי לֹא יֹאכַל עַד שֶׁיְּעַשֵּׂר אוֹ עַד שֶׁיִּשְׁאָלֶנּוּ. אֲנִי אוֹמֵר שֶׁל זֶה עִישֵּׂר וְשֶׁל זֶה לֹא עִישֵּׂר. לָקַח מִמֶּנּוּ אָדָם אֶחָד שְׁתֵּי כַלְכָּלוֹת כְּאַחַת שְׁאָלוֹ עַל אַחַת מֵהֶן הַשְּׁנִיָּה לֹא יֹאכַל עַד שֶׁיְּעַשֵּׂר אוֹ עַד שֶׁיִּשְׁאָלֶנּוּ אֲנִי אוֹמֵר זֶה עִישֵּׂר וְזֶה אֵינוֹ עִישֵּׂר. חֲשֵׁיכָה מוֹצָאֵי שַׁבָּת מְעַשֵּׂר מִזֶּה עַל זֶה. מָאן דְּאָמַר מִפְּנֵי כְבוֹד שַׁבָּת נִיחָא. מָאן דְּאָמַר אֵימַת שַׁבָּת עָלָיו לָמָּה לִי מְעַשֵּׂר מִזֶּה עַל זֶה.

Halakhah 2: May one eat on the question of another person? How is that understood? If two persons bought at the same time from him[11], if one of them asked him, the other may not eat until he tithed or also asked; I say he tithed one batch, but not the other. If one person bought from him two fig cakes and asked him about one of them, he may not eat from the second cake until he tithed or asked him; I say that he tithed one but not the other. At nightfall when Sabbath ends, he tithes from one on the other. According to him who says that it is because of the glory of the Sabbath, this is fine[13]. According to him who says that the fear of the Sabbath is on him, why should he be able to tithe from one on the other?

11 In the first two sentences, "he" and "him" always refer to the seller; in the last three to the buyer.

12 Both cakes remain *demay*, even though on the Sabbath a way was found to let the *ḥaver* buyer eat. But if we say that because of the fear of the Sabbath the *am haärez̧* will not lie if asked on the Sabbath proper, the cake on which the *am haärez̧* seller testified should be considered to be in order, not *demay*.

עַד כְּדוֹן בְּשֶׁאֵין לוֹ מֵאוֹתוֹ הַמִּין. וַאֲפִילוּ יֵשׁ לוֹ מֵאוֹתוֹ הַמִּין. הֵי צַד תֵּאוּב.

So far, if he has nothing of the same kind[13]. Even if he has of the same kind, that is a matter of preference.

13 We might assume that the leniencies expressed in the first two Mishnaiot apply only where the Sabbath enjoyment would be severely curtailed because nothing of the same kind is available in the buyer's house. However, even if other produce of the same kind is available the taste of that particular bunch might be preferred.

יוֹם טוֹב שֶׁהוּא סָמוּךְ לַשַּׁבָּת בֵּין מִלְּפָנֶיהָ בֵּין מֵאַחֲרֶיהָ וְכֵן שְׁנֵי יָמִים טוֹבִים שֶׁל גָּלִיּוֹת. מָאן דְּאָמַר קְדוּשָּׁה אַחַת הִיא אוֹכֵל. מָאן דְּאָמַר שְׁתֵּי קְדוּשּׁוֹת הֵן אֵינוֹ אוֹכֵל. אֲפִילוּ לְמָאן דְּאָמַר שְׁתֵּי קְדוּשּׁוֹת הֵן אוֹכֵל עַד שֶׁלֹּא נִרְאָה (fol. 24a) לְעַשֵּׂר בֵּינְתַיִם. וְתַנֵּי כֵן שׁוֹאֲלוֹ בְּיוֹם טוֹב אוֹכֵל בַּשַּׁבָּת. בַּשַּׁבָּת אוֹכֵל בְּיוֹם טוֹב. רִבִּי יוֹנָה בְשֵׁם רִבִּי זְעִירָא תִּיפְתָּר בְּפֵירוֹת שֶׁנִּסְמְכָה דַעְתּוֹ עֲלֵיהֶן מֵעֶרֶב שַׁבָּת. אֲבָל בְּפֵירוֹת שֶׁלֹּא נִסְמְכָה דַעְתּוֹ עֲלֵיהֶן מֵעֶרֶב שַׁבָּת לֹא בְדָא. אָמַר רִבִּי מָנָא מִילֵּיהוֹן דְּרַבָּנִין מְסַייְעִין לְרִבִּי יוֹנָה אַבָּא. דְּתַנֵּינָן תַּמָּן הַמַּדִּיר אֶת חֲבֵירוֹ שֶׁיֹּאכַל אֶצְלוֹ וְהוּא אֵינוֹ מַאֲמִינוֹ עַל הַמַּעְשְׂרוֹת. רִבִּי יַנַּאי בֵּי רִבִּי יִשְׁמָעֵאל בְּשֵׁם רִבִּי יוֹחָנָן בְּשַׁבָּת שֶׁל פְּרוֹטְגַּמִּייָא הִתִּירוּ מִפְּנֵי אֵיבָה. בְּשַׁבָּת שֶׁל פְּרוֹטְגַּמִּייָא לֹא כְפֵירוֹת שֶׁנִּסְמְכָה דַעְתּוֹ עֲלֵיהֶן מֵעֶרֶב שַׁבָּת. הוּא לֹא אָמַר אֶלָּא מִפְּנֵי אֵיבָה.

A holiday next to the Sabbath, be it before the Sabbath or after the Sabbath, and likewise the two holidays of the diaspora, according to him who says they are one sanctity, he may eat; according to him who says that they are two sanctities, he may not eat[14]. Even according to him who says that they are two sanctities, he may eat as long as there was no possibility to tithe between them[15]. It was stated[16]: "If he asks him on the holiday, he eats on the Sabbath; if he asks him on the Sabbath, he eats on the holiday." Rebbi Jonah in the name of Rebbi Zeïra, explain it regarding produce he had intended to use on Sabbath eve. But produce he had not intended on Sabbath eve (to use during the Sabbath) is not included[17]. Rebbi Mana said, the words of the rabbis support Rebbi Jonah, my father, since we have stated there[18]: "He who takes a vow regarding his friend that he will eat at his place but he does not trust him with the tithes." Rebbi Yannai ben Rebbi Ismaël in the name of Rebbi Joḥanan: On the Sabbath of the preliminary marriage[19] they permitted because of hatred. Is the Sabbath of the preliminary marriage not comparable to produce that on Sabbath eve he intended to use (later on the Sabbath)[20]? Nevertheless, he[21] only said "because of hatred."

14 Everybody agrees that the sanctity of Sabbath is greater than the sanctity of holidays and that the sanctity of the Biblical first day of holidays is greater than that of the rabbinic second day of the diaspora. Here the question is whether these different degrees of sanctity fit together smoothly or whether there is a clean break between them even if that break has no temporal extension. The problem is discussed in *Erubin* 3, fol. 21b, and *Yom Tov* 1:1, fol. 60a, Babli *Erubin* 38a-39a, in connection with *eruv teḥumin* as explained in *Peah*, Chapter Eight, Note 56. The question is now whether one may make one *eruv* for the Sabbath and another one for another direction for the Sunday following which is a holiday. If the

sanctities fit together smoothly, this is not possible. If there is a clean break, it is possible.

15 Even if it is possible to have two *eruvin*, it certainly is not possible to tithe. Hence, there is no legal "nightfall after the Sabbath" as envisaged by the Mishnah.

16 Tosephta *Demay* 5:1.

17 One cannot extend the validity of the query of an untrustworthy person beyond the original intent.

18 Mishnah 4:4: If an *am haäreẓ* declares that under the penalties of breaking a vow he will have no relations with the other person, a *ḥaver*, unless that other person comes to his house to eat with him on the Sabbath but the *ḥaver* does not trust the *am haäreẓ* with the tithes, the *ḥaver* may eat at *am haäreẓ*'s the place the first Sabbath even though he is not trustworthy for tithes, on condition that he tell him that all is tithed. On the second Sabbath, even though he makes a vow to abstain from all benefit from him, he shall not eat until he tithed. {Since tithing must be done before the Sabbath, it seems that the question also must be asked before the Sabbath.} This somewhat contrasts with Mishnah 7:1: "One who is invited by a person whom he does not trust with tithes says on Friday afternoon: Anything that I shall in the future separate for what I am going to eat shall be First and Second Tithes. The First Tithe shall become the heave of the tithe and the Second Tithe shall be redeemed with coins." Hence, it is possible to tithe mentally under the right circumstances. In the case of a holiday following a Sabbath, if one is mentally prepared, one may transfer the permission of Sabbath to the holiday.

19 πρωτογαμία, ἡ, Greek word in a Latin inscription from Carthage, "the Jewish celebration of the preliminary marriage" (cf. *Peah*, Chapter 6, Note 46). A big meal was given for the community on the Sabbath preceding קידושין and not to appear would have been an insult to the families of the young couple. The invited guest could retroactively tithe what he ate, according to Mishnah 7:1. If he forgot, he could rely on the assertion of the untrustworthy.

In medieval Germany, the festivity was called *spinholz* (from Italian *sposalizio*).

20 Since he already knew on Friday that he had to attend.

21 R. Joḥanan said, if it were not necessary for peace in the community, the rabbis would not have permitted to

accept the word of an untrustworthy person. Similarly, the permission to use on holidays the assertion of tithes by an untrustworthy person given on the Sabbath must be restricted to food also intended for the Sabbath.

שְׁאֲלוֹ שַׁבָּת רִאשׁוֹנָה וְלֹא בָא הַשְּׁנִייָה לֹא יֹאכַל עַד שֶׁיְּעַשֵּׂר אוֹ עַד שֶׁיִּשְׁאָלֶנּוּ. וְלֹא כְבָר שְׁאֲלוֹ. אָמַר רִבִּי יוֹנָה תַּמָּן בְּהַהוּא דִּשְׁאַל עַל נַפְשֵׁיהּ. בְּרַם הָכָא בְּהַהוּא דִשְׁאַל חוֹרָן עָלוֹי.

If he invited him the first Sabbath but he did not come, the second time he should not eat unless he tithes or asks him[22]. Did he not already ask him? Rebbi Jonah said, there he asked for himself. But here a third party asked about it.

22 Mishnah 4:4 states that on the first Sabbath he actually eats there he may rely on his host's word. But the second time around, the untrustworthy person's word is not good enough. Why is it accepted here since actually it is now the second time that the guest asks about tithing? The answer is that the first question did not concern him personally since he was somehow prevented from attending the meal.

וְרִבִּי יוֹנָה בְּעֵי מַהוּ שֶׁיִּשְׁאָלֶנּוּ דֶּרֶךְ עֲקַלָּתוֹן. רִבִּי יוֹנָה כְּדַעְתֵּיהּ. רִבִּי יוֹנָה זְבַן חִיטֵּי מִן דְּבַר חֲקוּלָה נְפַק לְגַבֵּיהּ אֲמַר לֵיהּ לָא דַאֲנָא חֲשֵׁיד לָךְ. אֶלָּא בְגִין דִּזְבַנִית מִינָּךְ חִטִּין וַחֲמִית אוֹכְלוֹסָא עֲלָךְ וְאָמְרִית דִּילְמָא דְאַנְשִׁיתֵיהּ מְתַקְּנָה מְתַקְּנָן הֲוַיְיָן. טְעַן מְחַזְּקָה עָלוֹי אֲמַר לֵיהּ מַה אַתְּ[23] חֲשַׁד לִי.

Rebbi Jonah asked: May he ask him in a roundabout way? Rebbi Jonah asks in this way. Rebbi Jonah bought wheat from Bar Ḥaqulah. He went to him and said, not that I suspect you, but since I bought wheat from you and I saw a multitude[24] with you, I said maybe you forgot to put them in order. Were they put in order? He complained strongly about him and said: Why do you suspect me?

23 Reading of Rome ms. Venice: אנא.

24 Greek ὄχλος "multitude, troups" (*Berakhot*, p. 612).

(fol. 23d) **משנה ג**: תְּרוּמַת מַעֲשֵׂר שֶׁל דְּמַאי שֶׁחָזְרָה לִמְקוֹמָהּ רִבִּי שִׁמְעוֹן הַשְּׁזוּרִי אוֹמֵר אַף בְּחוֹל שׁוֹאֲלוֹ וְאוֹכֵל עַל פִּיו.

Mishnah 3: Heave of the tithe that returned to its origin[25]. Rebbi Simeon from Shezur[26] said, even on weekdays he asks the seller and eats on his information.

25 If heave falls into profane food of the same kind, the entire lot cannot be eaten except by Cohanim. If heave falls into *ṭevel*, in general the produce cannot be fixed since heave cannot be used to take heave for other produce. (If the heave which falls into profane food is less than .99%, something can be done.) All rules are given in *Terumot* 5. If heave of the tithe falls into the produce from which it was taken, there results a major complication and a potential great monetary loss since Cohanim will pay little for produce containing heave. If the heave should be impure, the entire batch would be a total loss since, in the case which is described in the Mishnah, the heave (1%) falls into the remainder (99%) and, therefore, is turning everything into *dema'*. In that case, and since most *amē haärez̧* are supposed to tithe, if the untrustworthy seller asserts that heave was taken, no heave fell into the produce and all is permitted for profane use.

26 A Tanna, student of Rebbis Joshua, Eliezer, and Tarphon from lower Galilee, today's village of Sejur.

(fol. 24a) **הלכה ג**: תַּנֵּי תְּרוּמַת מַעֲשֵׂר שֶׁל דְּמַאי שֶׁחָזְרָה לִמְקוֹמָהּ מְדַמַּעַת שֶׁלֹּא לִמְקוֹמָהּ אֵינָהּ מְדַמַּעַת. רִבִּי שִׁמְעוֹן אוֹמֵר בֵּין לִמְקוֹמָהּ בֵּין שֶׁלֹּא לִמְקוֹמָהּ אֵינָהּ מְדַמַּעַת. רִבִּי בוּן בַּר חִיָּא בְּעָא קוֹמֵי רִבִּי זְעִירָא מָאן דְּאָמַר מְדַמַּעַת

מְדַמַּעַת. וּשְׁאֵינָהּ מְדַמַּעַת אֵינָהּ מְדַמַּעַת נִיחָא. מַאן דְּאָמַר לִמְקוֹמָהּ מְדַמַּעַת שֶׁלֹּא לִמְקוֹמָהּ אֵינָהּ מְדַמַּעַת. מַה בֵּין לִמְקוֹמָהּ מַה בֵּין שֶׁלֹּא לִמְקוֹמָהּ. עָל רִבִּי חַגַּיי. אָמְרִין בְּדֵין הוּא מֵימַר מֹשֶׁה דַּאֲנָא אֲמַר טַעֲמָא אֲמַר מֹשֶׁה דַּאֲנָא אֲמַר טַעֲמָא מַאן דְּאָמַר מְדַמַּעַת שֶׁהִיא מַתֶּרֶת אֶת הַשְּׁיָרַיִים לַאֲכִילָה. מָאן דְּאָמַר אֵינָהּ מְדַמַּעַת שֶׁאֵינָהּ מַתֶּרֶת אֶת הַשְּׁיָרַיִים לַאֲכִילָה. הוֹרֵי רִבִּי לָא כְּהָדָא דְּרִבִּי חַגַּיי. אָמַר רִבִּי זְעִירָא אֲתָא עוּבְדָא קוֹמֵי דְּרִבִּי חֲנִינָא וְהוֹרֵי כְּרִבִּי שִׁמְעוֹן שְׁזוּרִי. רִבִּי אָחָא בְּשֵׁם רִבִּי יוֹנָתָן אֵין הֲלָכָה כְּרִבִּי שִׁמְעוֹן שְׁזוּרִי.

Halakhah 3: It was stated: "Heave of the tithe from *demay* that returned to its origin makes *dema'*[27], not to its origin does not make *dema'*. Rebbi Simeon from Shezur said, both at its origin and not at its origin it does not make *dema'*." Rebbi Abun bar Ḥiyya asked before Rebbi Zeïra: For one who says, it makes *dema'*, it makes *dema'*; for one who says, it does not make *dema'*, it does not make *dema'*; this is reasonable[28]. But if one says, in its origin it makes *dema'*, not in its origin it does not make *dema'*; what is the difference between in its origin and not in its origin? Rebbi Ḥaggai came up. They said, this one will say, "by Moses, I shall explain the reason[29]." He said, by Moses, I shall explain the reason: He who says, it makes *dema'*, because it permits the rest to be eaten[30]. He who says, it does not make *dema'*, because it does not permit the rest to be eaten[31]. Rebbi La taught according to that of Rebbi Ḥaggai[32]. Rebbi Zeïra said: A case came before Rebbi Ḥanina and he taught according to Rebbi Simeon from Shezur. Rebbi Aḥa in the name of Rebbi Jonathan: Practice does not follow Rebbi Simeon from Shezur[33].

27 *Dema'* (a word of unclear etymology, *Ex. 22:28*) describes profane produce mixed with heave, which is unfit for human consumption if heave and food are impure, and is food only for Cohanim and their

families if both the heave and the food are pure. It can be put in order only if the amount of heave in the total is less than 1 in 101. Since heave from *demay* is genuinely holy only in a minority of cases, that heave does not necessarily create *dema'*. (Maimonides *Maäser* 12:4 and R. Abraham ben David *ad loc.*)

28 That means, I can understand R. Simeon from Shezur, that we always follow the majority of cases and, therefore, heave from *demay* cannot create *dema'*. I also could understand the position that, once the name of heave was attached to any produce, it must be treated like heave in all respects.

29 R. Ḥaggai's standard answer to questions of this type.

30 Since without tithing, *demay* may not be eaten by rabbinic ordinance, it should in this respect be treated like heave taken according to Biblical precept.

31 For other produce, it simply is food of questionable status.

32 He declares practice to follow the anonymous Tanna in the *baraita.*

33 In Babli *Ḥulin* 75b, both R. Ḥanina and R. Jonathan endorse the ruling of R. Simeon from Shezur as valid practice.

יוֹתֵר מִיכֵּן רִבִּי שִׁמְעוֹן הַשְּׁזוּרִי אוֹמֵר הִפְרִישׁ תְּרוּמַת מַעֲשֵׂר וְנִשְׂרְפָה הֲרֵי זֶה שׁוֹאֲלוֹ וְאוֹכֵל עַל פִּיו. לֹא בְדָא אָמַר רִבִּי זְעִירָא אֲתָא עוּבְדָא קוֹמֵי דְּרִבִּי חֲנִינָא וְהוֹרֵי כְּרִבִּי שִׁמְעוֹן שְׁזוּרִי. אָמַר רִבִּי אָבִין לֹא דָמְיָא הַהִיא שְׁאִילְתָּא לְהַהִיא קַדְמִיתָא. תַּמָּן לָא בְּגִין חֲשֵׁיד לָךְ. אֶלָּא בְגִין דְּזְבַנִית מִינָּךְ אֵיתְמוֹל חִטִּין וַחֲמִית אוֹכְלוֹסִין עָלָךְ וְאָמְרִית דִּילְמָא דְּאַנְשִׁיתָהּ מְתַקְּנָה מְתַקְּנָן הֲוִייָן. בְּרַם הָכָא בְּגִין דְּחֲשַׁדְתָּךְ וְתִיקַּנְתִּין וְאִיתּוֹקְדִין[34] מְתַקְּנָן הֲוִייָן. רִבִּי שְׁמוּאֵל בְּרֵיהּ דְּרִבִּי יוֹסֵי בֵּי רִבִּי בּוּן אָמַר תַּנֵּי בַּר קַפָּרָא כֵּן אֵימַת הַדִּימּוּעַ עָלָיו וְהוּא אָמַר אֱמֶת.

"In addition, Rebbi Simeon from Shezur said: If he separated the heave of the tithe and it was burned, he asks the seller and eats on his information[35]." Did Rebbi Zeïra not say that a similar case came before Rebbi Ḥanina and he taught according to Rebbi Simeon from Shezur? Rebbi Avin said, this question does not compare to the first question.

There it was, not that I suspect you, but since I bought wheat from you yesterday and I saw a multitude with you, I said maybe you forgot to put them in order. Were they put in order? But here, because I suspected you, I put them in order but they went up in fire. Were they put in order[36]? Rebbi Samuel, the son of Rebbi Yose ben Rebbi Abun[37] said that Bar Kappara stated: The fear of *dema'* is on him and he will tell the truth[38].

34 Reading of Rome ms. Venice: ואיתקרין ; see ספר ניר p. 32a, תוספתא כפשוטה p0. 246.

35 Tosephta *Demay* 5:2: "Heave of the tithe which returned to its origin. Rebbi Simeon from Shezur said, even on weekdays he asks the seller and eats on his information. In addition, Rebbi Simeon from Shezur said: If he separated heave and tithes and the produce was stolen, he asks the seller and eats what he separated on his information, because just as the fear of the Sabbath is on the *am haärez*, so the fear of *dema'* is on him." The different *baraita* here has to be interpreted in the same way, viz., that the main body of produce was burnt and he was left only with heave and tithes. Because of the monetary loss, he was permitted to treat heave and tithes as profane food on the untrustworthy seller's word.

36 How can he expect to get an honest answer if the question is an insult to the seller?

37 An Amora of the fifth generation, student of his father and of R. Nasa, also mentioned together with Rebbi Mattaniah.

38 Since everybody knows how bad the consequences of *dema'* are, even if he himself is only aware that he must separate the first heave, he will not be a party to such a grave sin. It follows that the Tosephta before us is in the tradition of Bar Kappara, and that it is part of the original statement of R. Simeon from Shezur.

(fol. 23d) **משנה ד**: הַמַּדִּיר אֶת חֲבֵירוֹ שֶׁיֹּאכַל אֶצְלוֹ וְהוּא אֵינוֹ מַאֲמִינוֹ עַל מַעְשְׂרוֹת אוֹכֵל עִמּוֹ בַּשַּׁבָּת הָרִאשׁוֹנָה אַף עַל פִּי שֶׁאֵינוֹ נֶאֱמָן עַל הַמַּעְשְׂרוֹת בִּלְבַד שֶׁיֹּאמַר לוֹ מְעוּשָּׂרִין הֵן. וּבְשַׁבָּת שְׁנִיָּה אַף עַל פִּי שֶׁהוּא נוֹדֵר הֵימֶנּוּ הֲנָיָה לֹא יֹאכַל עַד שֶׁיְּעַשֵּׂר.

Mishnah 4: He[39] who takes a vow concerning his friend that he should eat at his place but he does not trust him with the tithes, he may eat at his place the first Sabbath even though he is not trustworthy for tithes, on condition that he tell him that all is tithed. On the second Sabbath, even though he makes a vow to refuse any benefit from him, he shall not eat until he tithed."

39 See Note 18. Even though Mishnah 2:2 stated that the trustworthy person may not eat at an *am haäreẓ*'s place, in our case when the human relationship is endangered, when the *am haäreẓ* vowed to cease all relations with the trustworthy person unless he accepts his invitation, and it is on a Sabbath, when the fear of the Sabbath is on the *am haäreẓ*, an exception was made. But the following Sabbaths, he may eat only if either the *am haäreẓ* tithes before him or he tithes the *am haäreẓ*'s produce.

(fol. 24a) **הלכה ד**: רִבִּי יַנַּאי בֵּי רִבִּי יִשְׁמָעֵאל בְּשֵׁם רִבִּי יוֹחָנָן בְּשַׁבָּת שֶׁל פְּרוֹטֻגַּמִּיָא הִתִּירוּ מִפְּנֵי אֵיבָה. אָמַר רִבִּי אָבִין כָּאן הִתִּירוּ טְבָלִים מִשּׁוּם דַּרְכֵי שָׁלוֹם. רִבִּי חֲנִינָא אָמַר רִבִּי יִרְמְיָה בְּעֵי אִם מִפְּנֵי דַּרְכֵי שָׁלוֹם לָמָּה לִי בִּלְבַד שֶׁיֹּאמַר לוֹ מְעוּשָּׂרִין הֵן. שֶׁאֵלוּ בַּשַּׁבָּת הָרִאשׁוֹנָה וְלֹא בָא הַשְּׁנִיָּה מַהוּ שֶׁתֵּעָשֶׂה רִאשׁוֹנָה. אָמַר רַב חִסְדָּא כָּאן שָׁנִינוּ שֶׁאָסוּר לְחָבֵר שֶׁיֹּאכַל בִּסְעוּדָה שֶׁאֵין לָהּ שֵׁם.

Halakhah 4: Rebbi Yannai ben Rebbi Ismaël in the name of Rebbi Joḥanan: On the Sabbath of a *protogamia*[40] they permitted because of hatred. Rebbi Avin said, here they permitted *ṭevel* because of human relations. Rebbi Ḥanina said, Rebbi Jeremiah asked: If it is because of human relations, why is it only on condition that the host tell him that it was tithed[41]? If he invited him on the first Sabbath but he did not come, can the second Sabbath become the first[42]? Rav Ḥisda said, here we have learned that a *ḥaver* may not eat at a meal that has no name[43].

40 See Note 19.

41 Since probably the question about tithes will offend the host. No answer is given.

42 This refers back to the Mishnah, not to the *protogamia*. The question was answered in Halakhah 2.

43 A *ḥaver* may not eat at a meal offered by an *am haärez̧* except at a particular religious festivity, such as the *protogamia*. The statement refers to the pronouncement of R. Yannai, not the Mishnah. A similar statement, in the name of the Tanna R. Simeon, is in the Babli *Pesaḥim* 49a, with a different thrust since the Babli, in contrast to Mishnah and Yerushalmi, frowns upon marriages between *ḥaverim* and *amē haärez̧*. The restrictive statement here also is from a Babylonian author.

(fol. 23d) **משנה ה:** רִבִּי אֱלִיעֶזֶר[44] אוֹמֵר אֵין אָדָם צָרִיךְ לִקְרוֹת שֵׁם עַל מַעֲשֵׂר עָנִי שֶׁל דְּמַאי. וַחֲכָמִים אוֹמְרִים קוֹרֵא שֵׁם וְאֵינוֹ צָרִיךְ לְהַפְרִישׁ.

Mishnah 5: Rebbi Eliezer says, nobody has to give a name to the tithe of the poor from *demay*[45]. But the Sages say, he has to give a name but does not have to separate.

44 Reading of all manuscripts, Mishnah and Yerushalmi. In the Venice print by mistake: Eleazar.

45 The tithe of the poor is due in years 3 and 6 of the Sabbatical cycle. Since *demay* is only *ṭevel* by doubt, no poor man can go to court and sue to collect the tithe. The tithe of the poor is only a civil obligation and no sanctity is attached to it. R. Eliezer

says that in years 3 and 6 the tithe is nonexistent for *demay* but the Sages, according to Maimonides in his Mishnah Commentary, hold that in order to protect the separation and redemption of Second Tithe in other years, one has at least to indicate that the tithe of the poor, if given, would have to be at a fixed part of the stored produce (e. g., at the Northern or Southern end.)

(fol. 24a) **הלכה ה**: רִבִּי בָּא בַּר הוּנָא בְּשֵׁם רַב הָאוֹכֵל פֵּירוֹתָיו טְבוּלִין לְמַעֲשֵׂר עָנִי[46] חַיָּב מִיתָה. מַה טַעַם דְּרִבִּי לִיעֶזֶר מִכֵּיוָן שֶׁהוּא יוֹדֵעַ שֶׁהוּא בְּעָוֹון מִיתָה מַפְרִישׁ. מַה טַעַם דְּרַבָּנָן בְּלֹא כָךְ קוֹרֵא שֵׁם וְאֵינָן צְרִיךְ לְהַפְרִישׁ.

Halakhah 5: Rebbi Abba bar Huna[47] in the name of Rav: He who eats his produce without having separated the tithe of the poor commits a deadly sin[48]. What is the reason of Rebbi Eliezer? Because he[49] knows that it would be a deadly sin, he will separate it. What is the reason of the rabbis? He only has to give a name but does not have to separate it[47].

46 Reading of Midrash *Threni Rabbati* on *Thr*. 1:3, R. Simson of Sens and, it seems, that of Maimonides in *Maäkhalot Asurot* 10:20. The manuscripts and the Venice prints have מעשר שני, and this must have been Maimonides's reading in his youth when he wrote his Commentary to the Mishnah, since there he gives a totally different explanation for the Mishnah than that given by the Halakhah.

47 In the Babli, he is called Rabba bar Rav Huna, son of the Amora Rav Huna, and fourth head of the Yeshivah at Sura founded by Rav. In the Midrash (*Ekhah rabbati* on *Thr*. 1:3), this tradition is ascribed to Rav Bibi and Rav Huna. The title is incorrect; it should be רב but because of the elided א in the name Abba the text cannot be emended.

48 In the Babli, *Makkot* 16b, Rav is quoted as saying that such a person is whipped, implying that it is not a deadly sin.

49 The farmer knows that not separating the tithe of the poor makes his food a deadly affair; he will separate it. (Since most farmers consider themselves poor, he probably

will eat the tithe himself. If he is not actually poor he has overstepped a positive commandment, not a prohibition.) As a consequence, *demay* in the years of the tithe of the poor will not contain that tithe. Such an argument were impossible if we would read "Second Tithe" in the statement attributed to Rav.

49 It seems likely that the rabbis hold with Rav in the Babli, that eating *ṭevel* of which all heaves have been taken is never a deadly sin.

תַּנֵּי הַנֶּאֱמָן רָאוּ אוֹתוֹ מַפְרִישׁ שֵׁנִי. תַּנֵּי לַשֵּׁנִי נֶאֱמָן לָרִאשׁוֹן דִּבְרֵי רִבִּי אֱלִיעֶזֶר. וַחֲכָמִים אוֹמְרִים הַנֶּאֱמָן לָרִאשׁוֹן נֶאֱמָן לַשֵּׁנִי. הַנֶּאֱמָן לַשֵּׁנִי אֵינוֹ נֶאֱמָן לָרִאשׁוֹן. מַה טַעַם דְּרִבִּי אֱלִיעֶזֶר מִשּׁוּם שֶׁאֵינוֹ חָשׁוּד לְהַקְדִּים אוֹ מִשּׁוּם שֶׁהִפְרִישׁ שֵׁנִי חֲזָקָה שֶׁהִפְרִישׁ רִאשׁוֹן. וְהָתַנֵּינָן רִבִּי לִיעֶזֶר אוֹמֵר אֵין אָדָם צָרִיךְ לִקְרוֹת שֵׁם לְמַעְשַׂר עָנִי[50] שֶׁל דְּמַאי. הָא שֵׁנִי צָרִיךְ מַה אִם שֵׁנִי שֶׁאֵין לְרַבּוֹ טוֹבַת הֲנָיָה צָרִיךְ לְהַפְרִישׁ. רִאשׁוֹן שֶׁיֵּשׁ לְרַבּוֹ טוֹבַת הֲנָיָה לֹא כָל־שֶׁכֵּן.

It was stated[51]: He is trustworthy if they saw him separate the Second Tithe. It was stated: For the Second, he is trustworthy for the First, the words of Rebbi Eliezer. But the Sages say, if he trustworthy for the First, he is trustworthy for the Second. He who is trustworthy for the Second is not trustworthy for the First. What is the reason of Rebbi Eliezer?[52] Is it because he is not suspected of advancing the tithe[53], or because if he separated the Second it is a standing presumption that he separated the First[54]? But did we not state: "Rebbi Eliezer says, nobody has to give a name to the tithe of the poor from *demay*." Hence, for the Second it is needed[55]. Since he has to separate the Second, on which the owner earns no goodwill[56]; he certainly will separate the First, on which he earns goodwill[57]!

50 Reading of the Rome ms., missing in the Venice print, but clearly implied by the next sentence.

51 Tosephta *Maäser Šeni* 3:6: "If

somebody was seen separating the Second Tithe, he is trustworthy for the First Tithe, the words of R. Eliezer. But the Sages say, if he is trustworthy for the First, he is trustworthy for the Second; he who is trustworthy for the Second is not trustworthy for the First. If he separated heave, First and Second Tithes, and ate from it, he is trustworthy for that kind of food but not for any other kind, the words of Rebbi Eliezer. But the Sages say, even for that kind he is not trustworthy {unless he passes the formal tests of trustworthiness}; you cannot trust him for he might put in order for himself but leads others astray {by eating kosher produce but selling *ṭevel*.}"

The text here makes little sense. It seems that the first two words of the next clause are dittography. The implication is that the formal induction into *ḥaverut*, described in Chapter 2, does solve all problems in theory but not in practice since many people will be reluctant to wear a badge that proclaims their superiority over fellow Jews. Hence, we need some guidelines to recognize people who follow the rules without ostentation.

52 Since the Yerushalmi discusses R. Eliezer but not the Sages, it endorses R. Eliezer's stand in principle.

53 Cf. Chapter 1, Note 208.

54 Since not separating the heave of the tithe is much more severe a transgression than not separating the Second Tithe.

55 R. Eliezer certainly agrees that separating the Second Tithe is part of the procedure needed to fix *demay*.

56 Each time he redeems Second Tithe, he loses a *peruṭa*'s worth of value in the coin set aside for these redemptions. If all *peruṭot* in the coin are used up, he has to destroy it.

57 While he has to give the First Tithe to a Levite or a Cohen (at least as long as they had documentary proof that their male ancesters were admitted to service in the Temple), the choice of the person who receives his tithes is his and it is perfectly legitimate to use the First Tithe and the {pure} heave of the tithe to cement friendships and commercial ties.

הוֹצִיא לָהֶן מַעֲשֵׂר שֵׁנִי מִתּוֹךְ בֵּיתוֹ אָמַר לָהֶן פָּדוּי הוּא נֶאֱמָן. פְּדוּ לוֹ וּפְדוּ לָכֶם אֵינוֹ נֶאֱמָן. מַתְנִיתָא דְּרִבִּי לִיעֶזֶר דְּרִבִּי לִיעֶזֶר אוֹמֵר הַנֶּאֱמָן עַל הַשֵּׁנִי נֶאֱמָן עַל הָרִאשׁוֹן. אָמַר רִבִּי יוֹסֵי דִּבְרֵי הַכֹּל הִיא עָשׂוּ אוֹתוֹ כְתוֹסֶפֶת הַבִּיכּוּרִים מַה

תּוֹסֶפֶת הַבִּיכּוּרִים נֶאֱכֶלֶת בְּטָהֳרָה וּפְטוּרָה מִן הַדְּמַאי אַף זֶה נֶאֱכֶלֶת מִשּׁוּם שֵׁנִי וּפָטוּר מִשּׁוּם רִאשׁוֹן. אָתָא רִבִּי חֲנַנְיָה בְּשֵׁם רִבִּי אִיסִּי דְּרִבִּי לִיעֶזֶר הִיא.

"If somebody brought out Second Tithe from his house to somebody and said: 'It is redeemed,' he is trustworthy; 'redeem for me and yourself,'[58] he is not trustworthy[59]." The *baraita* is Rebbi Eliezer's, since Rebbi Eliezer said, he who is trustworthy for the Second is trustworthy for the First. Rebbi Yose said, everybody agrees, they made it like additions to First Fruits[60]. Just as additions to First Fruits are eaten in purity and are free from *demay*, so this is eaten as Second Tithe and is free from the First. Rebbi Ḥananiah confirmed in the name of Rebbi Issi[61]: it is Rebbi Eliezer's[62].

58 R. Abraham ben David (Maimonides, *Maäser* 12:5) reads פדוי לי ופדוי לכם "it is redeemed for me and is redeemed for you," interpreted to mean "it is redeemed following my standards and I hope that is good enough for you." He declares himself not to follow generally accepted standards and makes himself untrustworthy. The classical commentators follow this reading.

59 In the second case, when he says, redeem it for me, it is clear that Second Tithe was not given. Hence, if it is spelled out that he is not trustworthy, it implies that he is not trustworthy for First Tithe and the heave of the tithe. It follows that the first "trustworthy" has exactly the same meaning and in the first case he is declared to be trustworthy for First because he is believed to be trustworthy for Second.

60 First Fruits are presented to the Temple and eaten there by the Cohen under the laws of purity of sacrifices. First Fruits are chosen when the farmer sees a first fruit forming in his orchard; then he binds a string of bast around that twig to recognize the fruit later. If he thinks that it is shabby to bring just one fruit to the Temple, he will add other fruits of the same kind to his basket. The First Fruit itself, as a sacrifice, is exempt from all heaves and tithes; the additions are not. But if the

Cohen in the Temple asks the *am haärez* farmer whether the additional fruits are tithed, he is by law required to believe what the farmer tells him (Maimonides *Maäser* 13:14).

61 R. Assi.

62 There is no support in any Tannaitic material for R. Yose's creation of a new category of fruits exempt from *demay*. Hence, the *baraita* is R. Eliezer's and the Sages make trustworthiness dependent exclusively on the rules given in Chapter 2.

(fol. 23d) **משנה ו**: מִי שֶׁקָּרָא שֵׁם לִתְרוּמַת מַעֲשֵׂר שֶׁל דְּמַאי וּלְמַעֲשַׂר עָנִי שֶׁל וַדַּאי לֹא יִטְּלֵם בַּשַּׁבָּת וְאִם הָיָה כֹהֵן אוֹ עָנִי לְמוּדִים לוֹכַל מִמֶּנּוּ[63] אֶצְלוֹ יָבוֹאוּ וְיֹאכְלוּ וּבִלְבַד שֶׁיּוֹדִיעֵם.

Mishnah 6: He who gave a name[64] to his heave of the tithe of *demay*[65], or to the certain tithe of the poor, should not separate them[66] on the Sabbath. But if a Cohen or a poor person were used to eat from his food at his table, they may come and eat it[67] on condition that he inform them.

63 This word only appears in the Leyden ms and universally is declared a scribal error. However, the argument given at the end of the first paragraph of the Halakhah shows that it is genuinely part of the Yerushalmi Mishnah.

64 If he said, for example, that the heave of the tithe should be the Northernmost 1% of the produce, or the heave of the poor the 10% next to a given corner. If this is not done, nothing at all from that produce can be eaten on the Sabbath.

65 The heave of the tithe for certain *tevel* must be given by the Levite receiving the First Tithe, not the farmer. In contrast, the heave of the poor is given only from produce that is certain.

66 R. Simson of Sens proves from Mishnah 7:1, and it is also clear from

the next paragraph, that once a name is given to heave and tithes, the actual handling of it on the Sabbath is permitted. What is questionable is taking it and handing it over to the recipients since transfer of property on the Sabbath is not permitted.

67 He and they sit at the same table and eat from the same produce on condition that Cohen or poor eat from the corner that was declared to be their part. In that way, the produce is no longer *demay* or *ṭevel* and the owner may eat simultaneously with his guests as long as the guests know that they are eating heave or tithe.

(fol. 24a) **הלכה ו**: כֵּנִי מַתְנִיתָא לֹא יִתְּנֵם בְּשַׁבָּת דְּתַנֵּינָן תַּמָּן בֵּית שַׁמַּאי אוֹמְרִים אֵין מוֹלִיכִין חַלָּה וּמַתָּנוֹת לַכֹּהֵן בְּיוֹם טוֹב בֵּין שֶׁהוּרְמוּ מֵאֶמֶשׁ בֵּין שֶׁהוּרְמוּ מֵהַיּוֹם וּבֵית הִלֵּל מַתִּירִין. הָדָא יַלְפָא מִן הַהִיא וְהַהִיא יַלְפָא מִן הָדָא. הָדָא יַלְפָא מִן הַהִיא הִיא יוֹם טוֹב הִיא שַׁבָּת. וְהַהִיא יַלְפָא מִן הָדָא בְּלִימוּדִין אֲבָל בְּשֶׁאֵין לִימוּדִין לָא סְלַק עַל בַּר נַשׁ מֵיכוֹל פִּיסְתֵיהּ בְּבֵיתֵיהּ דְּחַבְרֵיהּ.

Halakhah 6: This is the Mishnah[68]: He should not hand them over on the Sabbath, since we have stated there: "The House of Shammai say that one does not bring *ḥallah* and *gifts*[69] to the Cohen on a holiday, whether they were separated the day before or on the day itself, but the House of Hillel do permit this." The first statement implies the second, the second implies the first. The first statement implies the second; there is no difference between holiday and Sabbath[70]. The second implies the first; that is, if they[71] are used to. But if they are not used to, no person comes[72] to eat his piece of bread at another's house.

68 A clarification of what the Mishnah means; cf. J. N. Epstein, מבוא לנוסח המשנה, 2nd ed., p. 445.

69 The parts of a profane, slaughtered animal that should be given to the Cohen (*Deut.* 18:3).

70 There is an obvious difference between holiday and Sabbath in that on holidays one is permitted to bake, hence to create *ḥallah*, and to slaughter, hence to create new gifts for the Cohen. But property may not be

transferred at all according to the House of Shammai, and according to the House of Hillel only in a roundabout way, when the Cohen eats his part at the table of the giver.

71 Cohen and poor person eating at the householder's Sabbath table. They may eat unseparated tithe or heave only if they are regular guests and the householder knows that they will come.

72 The text has two synonyms, סלק "comes up," על "ascends."

תַּנֵּי לֹא יְסָרֵב אָדָם בַּחֲבֵירוֹ לְאָרְחוֹ בְּשָׁעָה שֶׁהוּא יוֹדֵעַ שֶׁאֵינוֹ רוֹצֶה. וְלֹא יַרְבֶּה לוֹ בְּתַקְרוֹבֶת בְּשָׁעָה שֶׁהוּא יוֹדֵעַ שֶׁאֵינוֹ מְקַבֵּל. מַהוּ בְּתַקְרוֹבֶת יְדַע דְּהַהוּא רָחֵיץ וְהָא מַטְרַח עֲלוֹי. וּבִירוּשָׁלַם הֲוָה מַפִּיךְ פִּילְכֵּיהּ דִשְׂמָלָא לִימִינָא.

It was stated[73]: "One should not importune anybody to be his guest if he knows that the other person will not accept. He should not offer many gifts of closeness if he knows that the other person will not accept." What are gifts of closeness? He knows that the other person expects that he would exert himself for him. In Jerusalem one turned his clasp[74] from left to right.

73 Tosephta *Bava Qama* 7:8: "There are seven kinds of thieves and the worst of them is the thief of opinons: He who importunes another person to be his guest while he knows that the other will not accept, he who offers many gifts while he knows that the other will not accept, he who opens a new barrel for a guest when from its contents he will sell to a grocer, etc." In these cases, the person invited, offered gifts, or wine from a brand new barrel, thinks that the other party is ready to go to real expense on his behalf when in reality the pretending giver knows that it will cost him nothing. This paragraph is added because in the Mishnah, Cohen and poor have to be informed that they are eating heave and tithe which is forbidden to their host.

74 In the parallel text, *Avodah zarah* 1:3, fol. 39a, an unexplained word עיכלה is used, in *Ekhah rabbati* 4(2) יד אונקלי שלו . The commentary מתנות כהונה to *Ekhah rabbati* indicates that in his Yerushalmi manuscript the word is פיבליה, identified by A. Kohut

as Latin *fibula*, "clasp" to hold the toga together. The Yerushalmi spelling corresponds to the late Greek form φίβλα. Kohut conjectures that on the way to a dinner one wore the clasp inverted as a sign that no other invitation could be accepted. [Babylonian sources (Tosephta *Berakhot* 4:9, *Baba batra* 93b) deal with preparations of the host, not the guest, for the dinner. The word appearing here, פילכיה "his distaff, spindle" does not fit.]

תַּנֵּי אֵין מוֹלִיכִין לְבֵית הָאֵבֶל בִּכְלֵי זְכוּכִית צְבוּעָה מִפְּנֵי שֶׁהוּא טוֹעֲנוֹ טַעֲנַת חִנָּם.

It was stated: "One does not carry to the mourner's house in colored glass containers because he carries a false load[75]."

75 After a burial, the mourners may not prepare a meal for themselves but must receive their first meal from the neighbors. The Babli (*Moëd qaṭan* 27a) prescribes that all food be brought in simple baskets woven from leaves of the date palm (so that the poor also could take part in this good deed); the *baraita* there must be of Babylonian origin. Colored glass is frowned upon because is looks expensive but may contain very little food since it is opaque.

תַּנֵּי עִר שֶׁיֵּשׁ בָּהּ גּוֹיִם וְיִשְׂרָאֵל הַגַּבָּאִים גּוֹבִין מִשֶּׁל יִשְׂרָאֵל וּמִשֶּׁל גּוֹיִים וּמְפַרְנְסִין עֲנִיֵּי יִשְׂרָאֵל וַעֲנִיֵּי גוֹיִם וּמְבַקְּרִין חוֹלֵי יִשְׂרָאֵל וְחוֹלֵי גוֹיִם וְקוֹבְרִין מֵתֵי יִשְׂרָאֵל וּמֵתֵי גוֹיִם. וּמְנַחֲמִין אֲבֵילֵי יִשְׂרָאֵל וַאֲבֵילֵי גוֹיִם. וּמַכְנִיסִין כְּלֵי גוֹיִם וּכְלֵי יִשְׂרָאֵל מִפְּנֵי דַרְכֵי שָׁלוֹם.

It was stated[76]: "In a town where Gentiles and Jews live together, the overseers of charity collect from Jews and Gentiles and provide for Jewish and Gentile poor, visit Jewish and Gentile sick, bury Jewish and Gentile dead, and console Gentile and Jewish mourners. Also, one takes in vessels[77] from Gentiles and from Jews for the sake of peaceful coexistence."

76 Tosephta *Giṭṭin* 4:13-14, partially quoted in Babli *Giṭṭin* 61a. Since a Jewish community is required to have organized charity, if the Gentiles do not have similar services, the Jewish social services must be offered also to the Gentiles to advance intercommunal relations. The paragraph is inserted here probably from the parallel text in *Avodah zarah* 1:3, since the next paragraph is dependent on this one and belongs to *Avodah zarah*.

77 If one finds a usable vessel that has some distinguishing mark, if it was lost by a Jew it is the duty of a fellow Jew who finds it to take it with him, advertise for the loser, and return it (*Deut.* 22:1-3). This is extended to vessels lost by Gentiles for the sake of intercommunal peace.

גִּירְדָּאֵי שָׁאֲלוּן לְרִבִּי אִימִּי יוֹם מִשְׁתֶּה שֶׁל גּוֹיִם מַהוּ. סְבַר מִשְׁרֵי לוֹן מִן הָכָא מִפְּנֵי דַּרְכֵי שָׁלוֹם. אָמַר לוֹן רִבִּי בָּא וְהָתַנֵּי רִבִּי חִייָא יוֹם מִשְׁתֶּה שֶׁל גּוֹיִם אָסוּר. אָמַר רִבִּי אִימִּי אִילוּלֵי רִבִּי בָּא הָיָה לָנוּ לְהַתִּיר עֲבוֹדָה זָרָה שֶׁלָּהֶן וּבָרוּךְ שֶׁרִיחֲקָנוּ מֵיהֶם.

The weavers asked Rebbi Ammi, what about a Gentile wedding feast[78]? He wanted to permit it to them from this: "Because of peaceful coexistence." Rebbi Abba told them, did not Rebbi Ḥiyya state[79] that the holiday of a Gentile wedding feast is forbidden. Rebbi Ammi said, if it had not been for Rebbi Ba, we would have come to permit their strange worship[80]; praised be He Who distanced us from them.

78 Whether one may be a guest at such a celebration.

79 In Tosephta *Avodah zarah* 1:4 it is noted that one may not trade with a Gentile on the day of his wedding or the day he was appointed to a post in local government (since on these occasions religious ceremonies are unavoidable.)

80 I. e., idolatry.

(fol. 23d) **משנה ז**: הָאוֹמֵר לְמִי שֶׁאֵינוֹ נֶאֱמָן עַל הַמַּעְשְׂרוֹת קַח לִי מִמִּי שֶׁהוּא נֶאֱמָן וּמִי שֶׁהוּא מְעַשֵּׂר אֵינוֹ נֶאֱמָן. מֵאִישׁ פְּלוֹנִי הֲרֵי זֶה נֶאֱמָן. הָלַךְ לִיקַּח מִמֶּנּוּ אָמַר לוֹ לֹא מְצָאתִיו וְלָקַחְתִּי לָךְ מֵאֶחָד שֶׁהוּא נֶאֱמָן אֵינוֹ נֶאֱמָן.

Mishnah 7: He who tells somebody who is not trustworthy, buy for me from somebody who is trustworthy, or from somebody who tithes, is[81] not trustworthy; from X, he is trustworthy. If he went to buy from him and said, I did not find him, but I bought for you from somebody who is trustworthy, he is not trustworthy.

81 The untrustworthy person who was sent to buy produce. In such a case, the store from which he has to buy must be specified, otherwise all he bought is *demay*. If the untrustworthy emissary did not execute his job to the letter, the produce he bought is still *demay*.

(fol. 24a) **הלכה ז**: תַּנֵּי אָמַר רִבִּי יוֹסֵי אֲפִילוּ אָמַר לוֹ מִפְּלוֹנִי אֵינוֹ נֶאֱמָן עַד שֶׁיֹּאמַר קַח וַאֲנִי נוֹתֵן מָעוֹת. מַה טַעֲמָא דְּרִבִּי יוֹסֵי אֲנִי אוֹמֵר (fol. 24b) אֶחָד קָרוֹב מָצָא וְלָקַח מִמֶּנּוּ דְּתַנִּינָן תַּמָּן הִתְקַבֵּל לִי גִיטִּי בְּמָקוֹם פְּלוֹנִי אוֹכֶלֶת בִּתְרוּמָה עַד שֶׁיַּגִּיעַ גֵּט לְאוֹתוֹ מָקוֹם רִבִּי לָעְזָר אוֹסֵר מִיַּד. מַה טַעֲמָא דְּרִבִּי לָעְזָר אֲנִי אוֹמֵר אַחַר הַדֶּלֶת מְצָאוֹ. אָתָא דְּרִבִּי לָעְזָר כְּרִבִּי יוֹסֵי וּדְרִבִּי יוֹסֵי כְּרִבִּי לָעְזָר. דְּרִבִּי יוֹסֵי רִיבָּה מִן דְּרִבִּי לָעְזָר וְלֹא מוֹדֶה רִבִּי לָעְזָר שָׁם אָמַר לוֹ אַל תְּקַבְּלֵהוּ לִי אֶלָּא בְּמָקוֹם פְּלוֹנִי שֶׁהִיא אוֹכֶלֶת בִּתְרוּמָה עַד שֶׁיַּגִּיעַ גֵּט לְאוֹתוֹ מָקוֹם. וְהָכָא אֲפִילוּ אָמַר לוֹ מִפְּלוֹנִי אֵינוֹ נֶאֱמָן עַד שֶׁיֹּאמַר קַח וַאֲנִי נוֹתֵן מָעוֹת. מַה טַעֲמָא דְּרִבִּי יוֹסֵי אֲנִי אוֹמֵר אֶחָד קָרוֹב מָצָא וְלָקַח מִמֶּנּוּ.

Halakhah 7: It was stated[82]: "Rebbi Yose said, even if he specified, from X, he is not trustworthy, unless he said, you buy and I will pay." What is the reason of Rebbi Yose? I say that he found someone close by and bought from him, as we have stated there[83]: "Receive my bill of divorce at such and such a place; she may eat heave until the bill of divorce reaches that place. Rebbi Eleazar[84] prohibits her immediately." What is the reason of Rebbi Eleazar? I say that he found it behind the door. It turns out that Rebbi Eleazar is like Rebbi Yose and Rebbi Yose is like Rebbi Eleazar. Rebbi Yose says more than Rebbi Eleazar; does not Rebbi Eleazar agree that if she says to him, do not accept it except at such and such a place[85], that she continues eating until the bill of divorce reaches that place? But here, even if he says, only from X, he is not trustworthy, except if he said, you buy and I will pay.

82 In Tosephta *Demay* 5:3; the discussion here in the Halakhah is part of the statement: "He who says to somebody who is not trustworthy, buy for me from somebody who is trustworthy, or from somebody who tithes, is not trustworthy; from X, he is trustworthy. Rebbi Yose (the Tanna, ben Ḥalaphta) says, he is not trustworthy; maybe he found a source that is closer. Rebbi Yose agrees that if he said, go, eat the loaf, and I shall pay for it, go, drink a glass, and I shall pay for it, he is trustworthy."

83 Mishnah *Giṭṭin* 6:6. A bill of divorce is not valid until it is delivered into the hand of the wife (*Deut.* 24:1,3). However, the wife can appoint an agent and the hand of a duly appointed agent is like the hand of the principal. If she is the wife of a Cohen, she may eat heave as long as she is his wife but not when she is a divorcee. Hence, the exact moment when she is divorced is identical with the exact moment in which the wife of a Cohen may no longer eat heave.

84 R. Eleazar ben Shamua', one of the last students of R. Aqiba, discussed in the introduction to *Berakhot*. He is the authority for bills of divorce.

85 If the authorization contains such a restriction, the commission of the agent is not valid outside that place, and if the agent receives the bill of divorce at any other place she is not divorced.

(fol. 23d) **משנה ח**: הַנִּכְנָס לְעִיר וְאֵינוֹ מַכִּיר אָדָם שָׁם וְאוֹמֵר מִי כַּאן נֶאֱמָן מִי כַּאן מְעַשֵּׂר. אָמַר לוֹ אֶחָד אֲנִי אֵינִי נֶאֱמָן אִישׁ פְּלוֹנִי נֶאֱמָן הֲרֵי זֶה נֶאֱמָן. הָלַךְ וְלָקַח הֵימֶנּוּ. אָמַר לָהֶן מִי כַּאן מוֹכֵר יָשָׁן אָמַר לוֹ מִי שֶׁשְּׁלָחֲךָ אֶצְלִי אַף עַל פִּי שֶׁהֵן כְּגוֹמְלִין זֶה אֶת זֶה הֲרֵי אֵילוּ נֶאֱמָנִין.

Mishnah 8: If someone enters a town, does not know anybody there, and asks: Who is trustworthy here, who tithes? If somebody told him, I am not trustworthy, but Mr. X is trustworthy, he may be believed[86]. If he went and bought there and asked, who is selling old produce here[87]? If the seller said, the one who sent you to me, they may be believed even though they act as if they would do reciprocal favors to each other.

86 Even though the speaker himself is not trustworthy, in this case he may be believed, as explained in the Halakhah.

87 The meaning of "old produce" is difficult to establish. The traditional explanation, represented by Maimonides (*Maäser* 12:7). R. Abraham ben David, and Rashi (*Ketubot* 56b) is that the buyer is looking for old (better quality) wine and is ready to buy *demay* and tithe it if only he gets the quality desired. The interpretation of the Mishnah would be that the first informant, who directed the buyer to the second one's store, was not an uninterested bystander, but in effect was indirectly paid for steering the stranger to the second one's store. The plural "they may be believed" in the last sentence then would include the seller who asserted to the stranger that he was trustworthy by the rules. His trustworthiness is not invalidated by the kickback.

R. Simson of Sens refers "old produce" to that grown before the Sabbatical year if the question was asked in the Sabbatical. But the question here is about tithes, not the Sabbatical. Usually, "old" refers to grain that started to grow before the last Passover, since "new" grain, summer wheat planted after Passover, may not be eaten until after the next Passover (*Lev*. 23:14). But Rashi (*loc. cit.*) shows that this notion cannot apply here and summer wheat cannot be grown in the Land of Israel.

(fol. 24b) **הלכה ח**: וְעֵד אֶחָד נֶאֱמָן. אָמַר רִבִּי יוֹחָנָן קַל הֵקִילוּ בְּאַכְסַנְיָא מִפְּנֵי חַיֵּי נֶפֶשׁ.

Halakhah 8: But is a single witness trustworthy[88]? Rebbi Joḥanan said, they were very lenient for a guest because of the necessities of life.

88 Since the informant himself is not trustworthy, should not his information be treated as testimony which is invalid unless corroborated by two witnesses. The explanation of R. Joḥanan is ascribed to Rava (Rav Abba bar Rav Joseph bar Ḥama of the fourth generation) in the Babli (*Ketubot* 56b).

תַּנֵּי נִכְנַס לְעִיר וְאֵינוֹ מַכִּיר אָדָם אוֹ שֶׁהָיָה עוֹמֵד בְּגוֹרֶן וְאֵינוֹ מַכִּיר אָדָם שָׁם. הֲרֵי זֶה נִשְׁאַל בֵּין לְחָבֵר בֵּין לְעַם הָאָרֶץ דִּבְרֵי רַבָּן שִׁמְעוֹן בֶּן גַּמְלִיאֵל. רִבִּי אוֹמֵר אֵין נִשְׁאָלִין עַל הַתְּרוּמָה אֶלָּא לְחָבֵר בִּלְבַד. אַתְיָא דְּרִבִּי כְּרִבִּי מֵאִיר וּדְרַבָּן שִׁמְעוֹן בֶּן גַּמְלִיאֵל כְּשִׁיטָּתֵיהּ. דְּתַנֵּינָן תַּמָּן כָּל־הַמּוּמִין הָרְאוּיִן לָבוֹא בִידֵי אָדָם רוֹעִין יִשְׂרָאֵל נֶאֱמָנִין רוֹעִין כֹּהֲנִים אֵינָן נֶאֱמָנִין. רַבָּן שִׁמְעוֹן בֶּן גַּמְלִיאֵל אוֹמֵר נֶאֱמָן הוּא עַל שֶׁל חֲבֵירוֹ וְאֵינוֹ נֶאֱמָן עַל שֶׁל עַצְמוֹ. רִבִּי מֵאִיר אוֹמֵר הֶחָשׁוּד עַל הַדָּבָר לֹא דָנוֹ וְלֹא מְעִידוֹ. אָמַר רִבִּי יוֹנָה מַה פְלִיגוֹן לִיקַּח אֲבָל לְחַלֵּק אַף רַבָּן שִׁמְעוֹן בֶּן גַּמְלִיאֵל מוֹדֶה. מַה בֵּין לְחַלֵּק מַה בֵּין לִיקַּח. קוֹל יוֹצֵא לְחִילּוּק.

It was stated[89]: "He who enters a town and does not know anybody there, or stands by a threshing floor and does not know anybody there, may ask either a *ḥaver* or an *am haärez*, the words of Rabban Simeon ben Gamliel. Rebbi says, about heave one only may ask a *ḥaver*." It turns out that Rebbi follows Rebbi Meïr and Rabban Simeon ben Gamliel follows his own reasoning. As we have stated there[90]: "About any bodily defects that may be caused by humans, laymen shepherds are trustworthy, Cohen shepherds are not. Rabban Simeon ben Gamliel said, he is trustworthy about another's flock but not his own. Rebbi Meïr said, whoever is suspect[91] in a matter may neither judge nor testify about it." Rebbi Jonah said, they disagree only if it is a matter of taking, but in distributing even Rabban Simeon ben Gamliel agrees. What is the difference between taking and distributing? A distribution is public knowledge[92].

89 Tosephta *Demay* 5:4: "He who enters a town with heave in his hand, does not know anybody there, [or stands by a threshing floor with heave in his hand] {and wants to give the heave to a trustworthy Cohen,} and does not know anybody there, may ask either *ḥaverim* or *amē haäreẓ*, the words of Rabban Simeon ben Gamliel. Rebbi says, about heave one may only ask a *ḥaver*." One has to interpret the *baraita* in the Yerushalmi similarly, that the question is about heave. But the interpretation of the Yerushalmi, given by R. Jonah, is the opposite, that the stranger wants to know whether he may take without worry, not to whom to give.

The phrase in brackets is not in the Vienna ms. of the Tosephta and R. S. Liebermann explains this as scribal omission. However, while the thrust of the Tosephta is not that of the Yerushalmi, a Yerushalmi version would not have the phrase, or does not have the phrase, as asserted by R. Jonah at the end of this paragraph. The Vienna scribe probably did not make an error here.

90 Mishnah *Bekhorot* 5:4. The firstborn of a cow, sheep, or goat must be given to a Cohen. If it is without blemish, it is dedicated as sacrifice from birth. If it develops a defect, the Cohen may slaughter and eat it at home (*Deut.* 15:19-23). Hence, the Cohen has a monetary interest in finding a defect in such a firstborn.

91 And this includes absolutely all Cohanim in matters regarding firstborn animals.

92 Since a distribution of tithes is publicly announced, even the stranger would find enough information about the person who is making the distribution.

(fol. 23d) **משנה ט**: הַחַמָּרִים שֶׁנִּכְנְסוּ לָעִיר אָמַר אֶחָד מֵהֶן שֶׁלִּי חָדָשׁ וְשֶׁל חֲבֵירַי יָשָׁן. שֶׁלִּי אֵינוֹ מְתוּקָּן וְשֶׁל חֲבֵירַי מְתוּקָּן אֵינָן נֶאֱמָנִין. רִבִּי יְהוּדָה אוֹמֵר נֶאֱמָנִין.

Mishnah 9: Donkey drivers who entered a town and one of them said, my produce is new, my colleague's is old[93], mine is not in order, my colleague's is in order, are not to be believed[94]. Rebbi Jehudah says, they are to be believed.

93 All commentators agree that the meaning of "old" and "new" here is identical with the meaning in Mishnah 7.

94 Since they come in a group, they had ample time to devise a strategy by which each one of them gets the business of a specified place.

(fol. 24b) **הלכה ט**: תַּנֵּי הַנִּכְנַס לְעִיר וּמָצָא סִיעוֹת שֶׁל בְּנֵי אָדָם אָמַר מִי כָּאן נֶאֱמָן מִי כָּאן מְעַשֵּׂר. אָמַר לוֹ אֶחָד אֲנִי נֶאֱמָן. אִם אָמְרוּ לוֹ שֶׁהוּא נֶאֱמָן הֲרֵי זֶה נֶאֱמָן. אָמְרוּ לוֹ שֶׁאֵינוֹ נֶאֱמָן בְּפָנָיו אֵינוֹ נֶאֱמָן. שֶׁלֹּא בְּפָנָיו נֶאֱמָן. אָמַר רִבִּי יוֹנָה בְּבֶן עִיר בְּסִיעוֹת חֲבֵירִים וּבְאַכְסְנַאי בְּסִיעוֹת עַם הָאָרֶץ. וְקַשְׁיָא עַל דְּרִבִּי יוֹנָה חֲבֵירִין וְאַתְּ אָמַר אֵינוֹ נֶאֱמָן בְּפָנָיו.

Halakhah 9: It was stated[95]: "If somebody entered a town, found there groups of people, and asked, who is trustworthy here, who tithes here? If one person told him that he himself was trustworthy, and the others told him that he was trustworthy, that one is trustworthy. If they told him in the person's presence that he was not trustworthy, he is not trustworthy; but in his absence, he is trustworthy." Rebbi Jonah said, if that somebody was from that town, the group must be of *ḥaverim*, if he is a stranger, the group may be composed of *amē haärez̧*. It is difficult for Rebbi Yose, you say that *ḥaverim* are not trustworthy in his presence[96]?

95 Tosephta *Demay* 5:5 again has a thrust opposed to the *baraita* of the Yerushalmi: "If he was standing in a group of people and asked, who here is trustworthy, who here tithes? If one person told him that he himself was trustworthy, he is not trustworthy, about another one that he tithes, he is trustworthy. If they told him that this one tithes, in his presence he is not trustworthy; but in his absence, he is trustworthy; in a court of law, he is trustworthy." The question asked against the thesis of R. Jonah clearly refers to the last clause of the Tosephta, not the *baraita* quoted in the text.

96 As noted above, this refers to the Tosephta or a similar text, when somebody is declared trustworthy only if others declare him so in his absence. Does one suspect *ḥaverim* to lie in this matter to please somebody? The question is not answered.

מַה טַעַם דְּרִבִּי יְהוּדָה מִפְּנֵי חַיֵּיהֶן שֶׁל בְּנֵי הָעִיר. מַה טַעֲמֵיהוֹן דְּרַבָּנִין מְצוּיִים הֵן לְהִתְפַּרְנֵס מֵעִיר אַחֶרֶת.

What is the reason of Rebbi Jehudah? Because of the lives of the townspeople[97]. What is the reason of the rabbis? They can provision themselves in another town.

97 Donkey drivers should be encouraged to visit the place to increase the supply of foodstuffs. While we have translated עיר as "town," it is often used in the sense of "hamlet."

הלוקח מן הנחתום פרק חמישי

(fol. 24b) **משנה א**: הַלּוֹקֵחַ מִן הַנַּחְתּוֹם כֵּיצַד מְעַשֵּׂר. נוֹטֵל תְּרוּמַת מַעֲשֵׂר וְחַלָּה וְאוֹמֵר אֶחָד מִמֵּאָה שֶׁיֵּשׁ כָּאן הֲרֵי זֶה בְּצַד זֶה מַעֲשֵׂר וּשְׁאָר מַעֲשֵׂר סָמוּךְ לוֹ. זֶה שֶׁעָשִׂיתִי מַעֲשֵׂר עָשׂוּי תְּרוּמַת מַעֲשֵׂר עָלָיו וְהַשְּׁאָר חַלָּה וּמַעֲשֵׂר שֵׁנִי בִּצְפוֹנוֹ אוֹ בִּדְרוֹמוֹ וּמְחוּלָּל עַל הַמָּעוֹת.

He who buys from the baker[1], how does he tithe? He takes the heave of the tithe and *ḥallah*[2] and says: One percent here on that side is tithe, the rest of the tithe is adjacent to it. That which I turned into tithe is made heave of the tithe for it and the rest is *ḥallah*[3]. The Second Tithe is North (or South) of it and is redeemed by coins[4].

1 Who is not trusted for tithes and whose bread is *demay*. The seeming contradiction of this Mishnah and Mishnah 2:4 is discussed in Halakhah 2:4 and referred to again in the Halakhah here.

2 Heave of the tithe is 1%; *ḥallah*, if it can be eaten in ritual purity, has a rabbinic ratio of 2.0833% = 1/48. Today *ḥallah* is a symbolic little piece. All must be designated (but should not actually be separated) before the declaration.

3 The rest of first tithe does not have to be given or separated.

4 See Chapter 4, Note 56.

הלכה א: אַף עַל הַחַלָּה. וְחַלָּה חַייֶבֶת בִּדְמַאי. וְלֹא כֵן תַּנֵּינָן חַלַּת עַם הָאָרֶץ וְהַמְּדוּמָע פְּטוּרִין מִן הַדְּמַאי. רִבִּי אָחָא רִבִּי בּוּן בַּר חִייָא בְּשֵׁם רִבִּי יוֹסֵי בֶּן חֲנִינָא דְּבֵית שַׁמַּאי הִיא. וְתַנֵּי כֵן רִבִּי שִׁמְעוֹן בֶּן יְהוּדָה אוֹמֵר מִשּׁוּם רִבִּי שִׁמְעוֹן חַלָּה בֵּית שַׁמַּאי מְחַייְבִין וּבֵית הִלֵּל פּוֹטְרִין. כְּלוּם אָמְרוּ בֵית שַׁמַּאי אֶלָּא דָּבָר

שֶׁהוּא לִזְרִיעָה אִילּוּ הַלּוֹקֵחַ (fol. 24c) לְזֶרַע וְלִבְהֵמָה קֶמַח לְעוֹרוֹת שֶׁמֶן לְנֵר שֶׁמָּא אֵינוֹ פָטוּר מִדְּמַאי. אֶלָּא בִּמְגַבֵּל עִיסָּתוֹ בְּמֵי פֵירוֹת. לֹא כֵן אָמַר רִבִּי יוֹסֵי בֵּי רִבִּי חֲנִינָא דְּרִבִּי אֶלְעָזָר בֶּן יְהוּדָה אִישׁ בֵּירְתּוֹתָא הִיא הָא כְּרַבָּנִין לֹא. אֶלָּא כְּרִבִּי יוֹחָנָן דְּרִבִּי יוֹחָנָן אָמַר כָּאן בְּעוֹשֶׂה בְטָהֳרָה וְכָאן בְּעוֹשֶׂה בְטוּמְאָה. אֶלָּא כְּרִבִּי אֶלְעָזָר דְּרִבִּי אֶלְעָזָר אָמַר כָּאן וְכָאן בְּעוֹשֶׂה בְטָהֳרָה. אֶלָּא בְּמִתְאָרֵחַ אֶצְלוֹ. לֹא כֵן תַּנֵּי הַנֶּאֱמָן עַל הַטָּהֳרוֹת נֶאֱמָן עַל הַמַּעְשְׂרוֹת. וְתַנֵּיתָהּ רִבִּי יַנַּאי בֵּי רִבִּי יִשְׁמָעֵאל וְאָמַר הָדָא דְּתֵימַר בְּמִתְאָרֵחַ אֶצְלוֹ אֲבָל בְּרַבִּים אֵינוֹ נֶאֱמָן עַד שֶׁיְּקַבֵּל עָלָיו בְּרַבִּים. וְכֹא בְּרַבִּים אֲנָן קַייָמִין.

Halakhah 1: Also *ḥallah*? Is *ḥallah* due for *demay*? Did we not state[5]: "*Ḥallah* of the unobservant and food containing heave are free from *demay*." Rebbi Aḥa, Rebbi Abun bar Ḥiyya, in the name of Rebbi Yose ben Ḥanina: This is from the House of Shammai. We have stated accordingly[6]: "Rebbi Simeon ben Jehudah says in the name of Rebbi Simeon that the House of Shammai obligate for *ḥallah* and the House of Hillel exempt it." Did the House of Shammai include seed goods? But he who buys for sowing or animal feed, flour for tanning or oil for lighting, is he not free from *demay*[7]? But it must be for somebody who kneads his dough with fruit juice[8]. Did not Rebbi Yose ben Rebbi Ḥanina say that this follows Rebbi Eleazar ben Jehudah from Bartota[9], hence it does not follow the rabbis[10]. But it agrees with Rebbi Joḥanan, since Rebbi Joḥanan said[11], one case for him who works in purity and one case for him who works in impurity. But what following Rebbi Eleazar, since Rebbi Eleazar said, in both cases if he works in purity? It must be that he is a guest. Was it not stated[12]: "He who is trustworthy for purities is trustworthy for tithes?" Rebbi Yannai ben Rebbi Ismaël stated and said: That is, if one is his guest, but for the public he is not trustworthy unless he accepts it publicly. And here we deal with the public[13].

5 Mishnah 1:3. The opinions of Rebbis Joḥanan and Eleazar are detailed in Halakhah 1:3.

6 Not in other Tannaitic sources. But in Tosephta *Demay* 1:28 we read: "Replacements for heave and its fifth {from a layman who ate heave in error, who has to replace it together with a 25% fine, measured from below, *Lev.* 5:16}, the fifths of the fifth {if the layman then took the fifth by error, he has to restitute it with an additional fifth, *Lev.* 5:26}, the leftover of the *'omer* sacrifice, the two breads {leavened breads for the priests, offered on Pentecost}, the show breads, the leftovers of flour sacrifices, and additions to First Fruits; Rebbi Simeon ben Jehudah says in the name of Rebbi Simeon that the House of Shammai obligate but the House of Hillel exempt." It is difficult to make coherent sense of this Tosephta (cf. תוספתא כפשוטה p. 206-207), but the general tenor is that the House of Shammai treat as *demay* anything that may be food for human consumption.

7 Mishnah 1:3, accepted also by the House of Shammai.

8 Pure fruit juice, other than grape juice and olive oil, without a drop of water added, is not one of the fluids that make food ready to become ritually impure. Also, dough made with fruit juice is really cake dough, not bread dough, and therefore should not be subject to *ḥallah*. However, the Mishnah, *Ḥallah* 2:4, declares that dough made with fruit juice is subject to *ḥallah* even though it cannot become impure. [Maimonides, in his Code (*Bikkurim* 6:12), not in his Commentary to the Mishnah, restricts the obligation of *ḥallah* to dough made with grape juice and olive oil; he follows the Yerushalmi *Ḥallah* 2:2 which seems to indicate that practice does not follow the Mishnah.] If we follow the Mishnah in *Ḥallah*, we should require the person who buys such bread from the baker to separate *ḥallah* in order to make public the obligation to give *ḥallah* from such "bread."

9 Mishnah *Ṭebul Yom* 3:4: "Dough prepared with some fluid {i. e., that came into contact with some of the fluids that prepare food to become impure, cf. Chapter 2, Notes 136-137} and was kneaded with fruit juice {other than grape juice or olive oil} and was touched by a person who went to the ritual bath that day {but will be pure for heave and sacrifices only at sundown (*Lev.* 22:7)}, R. Eleazar ben Jehudah from Bartota said in the name of R. Joshua that he made all of it

unfit; R. Aqiba said in his {R. Joshua's} name that he made {heave} unfit {for consumption} only at the place he touched." Since practice follows R. Aqiba in his dispute with a single opponent, practice must be that fruit juice does not transmit impurity and, hence, does not impart impurity to *ḥallah*.

R. Eleazar ben Jehudah from Bartota, Tanna of the third generation, was a student of R. Joshua and teacher of Rabban Simeon ben Gamliel. The name Bartota has been tentatively identified in Upper Galilee.. R. Eleazar was known to give to charity more than he could afford, so that the administrators of charity tried to avoid being seen by him.

10 Since our Mishnah is anonymous, it is difficult to accept that it represents an opinion that clearly is not the practice.

11 In Halakhah 1:3, R. Joḥanan says that, if the baker hires a *ḥaver* to knead his dough in purity, he will also be careful with heave and tithes, and the baker should tithe. If he prepares his dough in impurity, the buyer should tithe, and this is the case here. R. Eleazar holds that the Mishnah means a wholesaler, who does not have to tithe, but Mishnah 1:3 deals either with a retail baker or a private person baking for his family and guests.

12 Quoted in Halakhah 2:2 together with the following sentences, *qq. v.*

13 Since the Mishnah states explicitly that one buys from the baker who offers baked goods to the public.

רִבִּי אָבִין רִבִּי שַׁמַּאי בְּשֵׁם רִבִּי אָחָא שְׁמַע לָהּ מִן דְּבַתְרָהּ. הָרוֹצֶא לְהַפְרִישׁ תְּרוּמָה וּתְרוּמַת מַעֲשֵׂר כְּאַחַת. כְּמַה דְּתֵימַר תַּמָּן חוּץ מִן הָרָאוּי לִיקָּדֵשׁ לְשֵׁם תְּרוּמָה וְהָכָא חוּץ מִן הָרָאוּי לִיקָּדֵשׁ לְשֵׁם חַלָּה.

Rebbi Abin, Rebbi Shammai, in the name of Rebbi Aḥa, understood this from the following[14]. "He who wants to separate heave and the heave of the tithe together." As you will say there, except for that which may become sanctified as heave, here also except for that which may become sanctified as *ḥallah*.

14 Mishnah 5:2 states that a person who wants to separate heave and heave of the tithe together must separate 1% for heave of the tithe. Heave of the tithe has to be given as 10% of the tithe which in itself is 10% of the produce left after heave was taken. Hence, the 1% mentioned in the next Mishnah is 1% of what is left after heave was taken. Similarly, the Mishnah does not imply that *ḥallah* is subject to the laws of *demay* but that the 1% for heave of the tithe is to be measured only after regular *ḥallah* was taken.

תַּנֵּינָן חַלָּה בֵּין רִאשׁוֹן לַשֵּׁנִי. רִבִּי יוֹנָה בְשֵׁם רִבִּי זְעִירָא זֹאת אָמַר חַלָּה אֵין בָּהּ מִשּׁוּם בַּל תְּאַחֵר. רִבִּי יוֹסֵי בְשֵׁם רִבִּי זְעִירָא אֵין מִשְׁנָה אֲמוּרָה עַל סֵדֶר וְלֹא בִדְמַאי אֲנָן קַיָּמִין. לֹא כֵן אָמַר רִבִּי בָּא בְּרֵיהּ דְּרִבִּי חִייָא בְּשֵׁם רִבִּי יוֹחָנָן מַתְנִיתִין בִדְמַאי הָא בְוַדַּאי לֹא. וְהָכָא בִדְמַאי אֲנָן קַיָּמִין. תַּנֵּי רִבִּי חִייָא אַף בְּוַדַּאי עָלֶיהָ רִבִּי יוֹנָה בְשֵׁם רִבִּי זְעִירָא זֹאת אוֹמֶרֶת חַלָּה אֵין בָּהּ מִשּׁוּם בַּל תְּאַחֵר. רִבִּי יוֹסֵי בְשֵׁם רִבִּי זְעִירָא אָמַר אֵין מִשְׁנָה אֲמוּרָה עַל סֵדֶר אֶלָּא תַקְדִּים חַלָּה לָרִאשׁוֹן. מֵעַתָּה תְהֵא חַלָּה חַייֶבֶת בְּמַעְשְׂרוֹת. וּמַעְשְׂרוֹת לֹא יְהוּ חַייָבִין בְּחַלָּה שֶׁכָּל־הַקּוֹדֵם אֶת חֲבֵירוֹ חֲבֵירוֹ מִתְחַייֵב בּוֹ. וְתַנֵּי כֵן הָעוֹשֶׂה עִיסָּה מִן הַטֶּבֶל בֵּין שֶׁהִקְדִּים חַלָּה לַתְּרוּמָה בֵּין שֶׁהִקְדִּים תְּרוּמָה לַחַלָּה מַה שֶּׁעָשָׂה עָשׂוּי. חַלָּה לֹא תֵאָכֵל עַד שֶׁיּוֹצִיא עָלֶיהָ תְרוּמָה. תְּרוּמָה לֹא תֵאָכֵל עַד שֶׁיַּפְרִישׁ עָלֶיהָ חַלָּה. וְלָמָּה קָדְמָה רִאשׁוֹן מִפְּנֵי שֶׁקָּדְמָה לַגּוֹרֶן. וַהֲרֵי שֵׁנִי קָדְמוֹ לַגּוֹרֶן. אָמַר רִבִּי מַתַּנְיָה בְּדִין הָיָה שֶׁתַּקְדִּים חַלָּה לַכֹּל. וְלָמָּה קָדְמָה רִאשׁוֹן מִפְּנֵי שֶׁקָּדְמָה לַגּוֹרֶן וְכָתוּב בּוֹ רֵאשִׁית. שֵׁנִי אַף עַל פִּי קָדְמוֹ לַגּוֹרֶן אֵין כְּתִיב בּוֹ רֵאשִׁית.

We have stated *ḥallah* between First and Second Tithes[15]. Rebbi Jonah in the name of Rebbi Zeïra: This means that *ḥallah* is not subject to "do not give too late[16]." Rebbi Yose in the name of Rebbi Zeïra: The Mishnah is not formulated in sequence, do we not deal with *demay*[17]? Did not Rebbi Abba, son of Rebbi Ḥiyya, say in the name of Rebbi

Joḥanan that the Mishnah deals with *demay*; hence, not with certain produce[18]? And here[19] we deal with *demay*. Rebbi Ḥiyya stated[20]: Also for certain. On that, Rebbi Jonah in the name of Rebbi Zeïra said, this means that *ḥallah* is not subject to "do not give too late." Rebbi Yose in the name of Rebbi Zeïra: The Mishnah is not formulated in sequence, should not *ḥallah* precede the First Tithe[21]? Then *ḥallah* should be subject to tithes but not tithes to *ḥallah*, because everything that precedes another, the other is obligated for it[22]. And we have stated in this respect[23]: "He who makes dough from *ṭevel*, whether he takes *ḥallah* before heave or heave before *ḥallah*, what he did is done. *Ḥallah* should not be eaten until he take heave for it, heave should not be eaten until he separate *ḥallah* for it." But why does First Tithe[24] have precedence? Because it started at the threshing floor. But does the Second Tithe not start at the threshing floor? Rebbi Mattaniah said, it would have been logical that *ḥallah* should precede everything else[25]. Why does First Heave have precedence? Because it started at the threshing floor and it is called "beginning[26]." Second Tithe, even though it started at the threshing floor, is not called "beginning."

15 The Mishnah prescribes taking heave of the tithe and *ḥallah* together, and only then to give a name to Second Tithe and to redeem it. Both tithes should have been given when the grain was first stored at the farm barn. The obligation of *ḥallah* comes much later, when grain is first made into flour and then the flour into bread dough.

16 "From your storage and your *dema'* you should not give too late," *Ex.* 22:28. From this one concludes that a person who gave heave of the tithe before the first heave cannot declare that he followed all the rules of tithing. No similar rule seems to exist for *ḥallah*.

17 Since heave and tithes should have been given at the threshing floor, any fixing of *demay* is in itself in the

wrong order.

18 This refers to Mishnah 1:4 which states that the order of separation for *demay* is irrelevant, that one may separate the heave of the tithe (which is part of the First Tithe) after the Second Tithe. R. Johanan notes that this is one of the special leniencies for *demay*.

19 In Mishnah 5:1.

20 Tosephta *Demay* 5:6: "He who wants to separate heave, heave of the tithe, and *ḥallah* together . . ." There the order of the declaration is heave, heave of the tithe, *ḥallah*, Second Tithe. Since the first heave is mentioned, one speaks about produce from which nothing at all was yet taken. Nevertheless, *ḥallah* appears between First and Second tithes.

21 Since *ḥallah* has the status of heave, once the obligation has started it should take the place of heave that *must* be given before any tithe.

22 Just as if one would transgress giving First Tithe before the heave, the heave given later must be not only from the remaining produce but also from the tithe, since anything that comes later needs to be put in order by fulfillment of the prior obligation. Then the requirement that *ḥallah* should be taken from dough made from grain from which heave and tithes were taken would be put on its head.

23 Tosephta *Terumot* 4:10. It follows that heave and *ḥallah* are coordinate, not subordinate one to the other. Hence, each of them needs to be put in order with respect to the other. But definitely this should give *ḥallah* a status prior to tithes.

24 I. e., the heave of the tithe that must be given from the First Tithe.

25 Not quite everything else, but everything else which has to be given for *demay*, i. e., comes after heave.

26 *Num*. 18:12. *Ḥallah* also is called "beginning" (*Num*. 15:20,21) but its obligation does not start at the threshing floor.

(fol. 24b) **משנה ב:** הָרוֹצֶה לְהַפְרִישׁ תְּרוּמָה וּתְרוּמַת מַעֲשֵׂר כְּאֶחָד נוֹטֵל אֶחָד
מִשְּׁלֹשִׁים וְשָׁלוֹשָׁה וּשְׁלִישׁ וְאוֹמֵר אֶחָד מִמֵּאָה מִמַּה שֶׁיֵּשׁ כָּאן הֲרֵי זֶה בְּצַד זֶה

חוּלִין וּשְׁאָר תְּרוּמָה עַל הַכֹּל. וּמֵהַחוּלִין[27] שֶׁיֵּשׁ כָּאן הֲרֵי זֶה בְּצַד זֶה מַעֲשֵׂר וּשְׁאָר מַעֲשֵׂר סָמוּךְ לוֹ. זֶה שֶׁעָשִׂיתִי מַעֲשֵׂר עָשׂוּי תְּרוּמַת מַעֲשֵׂר עָלָיו (וּשְׁאָר חַלָּה)[28] וּמַעֲשֵׂר שֵׁנִי בִּצְפוֹנוֹ אוֹ בִדְרוֹמוֹ וּמְחוּלָּל עַל הַמָּעוֹת.

Mishnah 2: He who wants to separate heave and heave of the tithe together takes one in thirty-three and one third[29] and says: One percent of what is here on this side is profane[30] and the remainder is heave for everything. The profane here on that side is tithe; the rest of the tithe is adjacent to it. That which I have declared as tithe is made heave of the tithe for it, (the rest is *ḥallah*,) the Second Tithe is either North or South of it and is redeemed by coins.

27 Text of the first hand in the Leyden ms. The Munich ms. of the Babli has מהחולין. The prints have מאה חולין which makes no sense.

28 In the best manuscripts of the Mishnah, and the Munich ms. of the Babli, this is missing. It came into the Mishnah from the Tosephta quoted at the start of the Halakhah. The only ms. of the Yerushalmi which does not have this addition is that of R. S. Cirillo; there the omission is probably the author's and not from a ms. before him.

29 Heave is 2% given by estimate, heave of the tithe is 1% exactly of the remainder, or .98% of the original amount. So together they would be 2.98% or 1 in 33.557, not 1 in 33.3333. This Mishnah follows the ruling of Abba Eleazar ben Gimel (*Terumot* 1:7, fol. 40d) that all heave may be given by estimate and that heave of the tithe may also be given by the owner himself, not only by the Levite who is the recipient of the First Tithe. Since the heaves are given by estimate, one has to increase the amount somewhat, to 3% or 1 in $33^1/_3$.

30 Since the first heave must be given before the heave of the tithe, the amount designated for heave of the tithe must be declared to be profane until after heave has been designated.

(fol. 24c) **הלכה ב**: תַּנֵּי הָרוֹצֶה לְהַפְרִישׁ תְּרוּמָה וּתְרוּמַת מַעֲשֵׂר וְחַלָּה כְּאַחַת נוֹטֵל כְּדֵי תְּרוּמָה וּתְרוּמַת מַעֲשֵׂר וְחַלָּה כְּאַחַת וְכַמָּה הֵן אֶחָד מֵעֶשְׂרִים. וְאוֹמֵר אֶחָד מִמֵּאָה מִמַּה שֶׁיֵּשׁ כָּאן הֲרֵי הֵן בְּצַד זֶה חוּלִין טֶבֶל וְעוֹד אֶחָד מֵאַרְבָּעִים וּשְׁמוֹנֶה סָמוּךְ לוֹ וְהַשְּׁאָר תְּרוּמָה עַל הַכֹּל. וּמֵהַחוּלִין שֶׁיֵּשׁ בּוֹ וְזֶה שֶׁעָשִׂיתִי חוּלִין טֶבֶל עָשׂוּי מַעֲשֵׂר וּשְׁאָר מַעֲשֵׂר סָמוּךְ לוֹ. זֶה שֶׁעָשִׂיתִי מַעֲשֵׂר עָשׂוּי תְּרוּמַת מַעֲשֵׂר עָלָיו. וּמַעֲשֵׂר שֵׁנִי בִּצְפוֹנוֹ אוֹ בִדְרוֹמוֹ מְחוּלָּל עַל הַמָּעוֹת.

Halakhah 2: "[31]He who wants to separate heave, heave of the tithe, and *ḥallah* together takes for heave, heave of the tithe, and *ḥallah*, that is one in 20[32], and says: One percent of what is here on this side[33] is profane *ṭevel* and another one in 48 next to it; the remainder is heave for everything. The profane which is in it and that which I made profane *ṭevel* is made tithe; the rest of the tithe is adjacent to it. That which I have declared as tithe is made heave of the tithe for it[34], the Second Tithe is North or South of it and is redeemed by coins."

31 Tosephta *Demay* 5:6.

32 The computation is not quite exact. If full amounts are taken, i. e., if it is possible to eat heave in ritual purity, heave is supposed to be 2%. Then heave of the tithe is 1% of the remaining 98%. The grain put in order therefore is 97.02% of the original amount. *Ḥallah* is $^1/_{48}$ of the dough (in our case, of the grain), or 2.0833% of the remainder, 2.02125% of the original amount. Hence, the total taken should be 5.00125% of the original amount, not 5% as stated in the Tosephta. However, $^1/_{800}$ of one percent is not a quantity that is verifiable by eyesight; as the Halakhah will state later, it is disregarded. Also, it is required that both heave and *ḥallah* be given by estimate, *not* by measurement; hence, the natural error in such an estimate is much larger than the small overshoot we should require for the heave of the tithe, as indicated in the Mishnah.

Today, when no heave can be eaten in the absence of the ashes of the red heifer, both heave and *ḥallah* are given in minute amounts to avoid destroying food. The modified declaration for putting in order *demay*, produce bought on a market in Israel, can be found in most of current prayer books printed in Israel. Produce sold by the farmers' cooperative *Tenuvah* in Israel (but not produce for export) is all tithed.

33 Of the 5% set aside, 1% is for heave of the tithe (to be generous, since it should be only .98%); 1 in 48 is *ḥallah* which also is a heave.

34 Both here and in the Tosephta, the declaration that the rest is *ḥallah* is missing. It should be deleted from the Mishnah and inserted here.

רִבִּי שְׁמוּאֵל בַּר נַחְמָן בְּשֵׁם רִבִּי יוֹנָתָן צָרִיךְ לְבָרֵךְ חָמֵשׁ בְּרָכוֹת. תַּנֵּי רִבִּי חִייָא כּוּלְּלָן בְּרָכָה אַחַת.

Rebbi Samuel bar Naḥman in the name of Rebbi Jonathan: He has to recite five benedictions[35]. Rebbi Ḥiyya stated: He subsumes them all in one benediction.

35 One for heave, one for the First Tithe, one for the heave of the tithe, one for Second Tithe, and one for *ḥallah*. Rebbi Ḥiyya prescribes a collective benediction: Praised are You, Eternal, our God, King of the Universe, Who sanctified us by His commandments and commanded us to separate heaves and tithes. (Maimonides *Maäser* 1:17).

עַד כְּדוֹן כֹּהֵן לֵוִי וְיִשְׂרָאֵל אֵין יֹאמַר תְּרוּמַת מַעֲשֵׂר נִמְצָא מַפְרִישׁ עַל דָּבָר שֶׁאֵינוֹ שֶׁלּוֹ.

So far for a Cohen or a Levi[36], but an Israel? If he will declare heave of the tithe, does he not separate for something that is not his[37]?

36 Normally the Israel farmer gives heave to the Cohen and tithe to the Levite (or Cohen, who also is a Levite) and then the Levite gives heave of the tithe to the Cohen. The Cohen himself, if he is a farmer, has to separate heave, tithe, and heave of the tithe, even though he keeps everything for himself, as is written (*Num.* 18:26): "You also shall separate the heave of the Eternal," and explained in *Sifry Num.* #120. He and the Levite are

owners both of the grain and the tithe, and can separate both heave and heave of the tithe. However, an Israel should not be owner of the tithe; how can he ever give heave of the tithe?

37 The question is not answered. If one follows Abba Eleazar ben Gimel, quoted in the Note to the Mishnah, there is no question. If one does not follow him, in fact an Israel cannot separate heave and heave of the tithe together.

מַעֲשֵׂר וְאַחַר כַּךְ תְּרוּמָה נִמְצָא מַקְדִּים. תְּרוּמָה וְאַחַר כַּךְ מַעֲשֵׂר נִמְצָא אוֹ פוֹחֵת מִמַּעְשְׂרוֹתָיו אוֹ מוֹסִיף עַל מַעְשְׂרוֹתָיו כְּהָדָא דְתַנֵּי הַפּוֹחֵת מִמַּעְשְׂרוֹתָיו מַעְשְׂרוֹתָיו מְתוּקָּנִין וּפֵירוֹתָיו מְקוּלְקָלִין. הַמַּעֲדִיף עַל מַעְשְׂרוֹתָיו מַעְשְׂרוֹתָיו מְקוּלְקָלִין וּפֵירוֹתָיו מְתוּקָּנִין. אָמַר רִבִּי יוֹסֵי בְּסָמוּךְ עַל תְּנַיי בֵּית דִּין הוּא. מַהוּ תְּנַיי בֵּית דִּין. עַד מָקוֹם שֶׁהַדַּעַת טוֹעָה.

If one gives tithe and after that heave, one has preceded[38]. First heave and after that tithe, might he not give too little tithe or add to his tithe[39]? As we have stated[40], he who gives too little tithe, his tithes are in order but his produce is damaged[41], if he gives too much tithe, his tithes are damaged[42] but his produce is in order. Rebbi Yose said, he relies on a stipulation by the Court. What is the stipulation by the Court? As far as one's mind might err[43].

38 It is forbidden to tithe before giving heave; this explains the language of the Mishnah.

39 Since tithe is supposed to be exactly 10%, and the heave of the tithe exactly 10% of the tithe, do Mishnah and Tosephta, which permit heave and heave of the tithe to be separated together by estimate, not lead into sin since it is almost impossible to guarantee that the heave of the tithe should be exactly 1% and, hence, the implied tithe should be exactly 10%?

40 Tosephta *Demay* 8:13; there the text is similar but the statements are switched in error.

41 Since the produce still contains some unseparated tithe and with it tithe of the heave; its consumption by a non-Cohen would be a deadly sin.

42 Since the superfluous part in it contains 10% Second Tithe or tithe of the poor.

43 Even in measurements, a perfect result is not possible. Hence, any estimate that is not clearly in error is accepted as exact and the pedantic argument from before is not accepted. This argument is not directly applicable to heave of the tithe; since the Torah prescribes exactly 1%, it is not clear from where the Court should have the authority to stipulate that we accept deviations from the Biblical norm. Hence, the stipulation must refer to tithe. While tithe has to be 10% by Biblical decree, and using the food before tithe was given is a deadly sin, tithe in the hand of the Levite or Cohen is profane food after heave of the tithe was given; in contrast to Second Tithe, which retains its status of holiness until consumed in Jerusalem or redeemed, First Tithe is the absolute possession of Cohen or Levite. Hence, the amount transferred to the Levite is a transfer of profane goods and subject to the eminent power of the Court which may declare property forfeit. Since the Court has the power to set the standards for tithe, the amount of heave of the tithe is a derivative of the amount set aside for tithe.

מַהוּ תְּנַיי בֵּית דִּין. אָמַר רִבִּי יוֹחָנָן כְּדֵי שֶׁיְּהֵא קוֹבֵעַ מַעֲשֵׂר רִאשׁוֹן בִּצְפוֹנוֹ וּמַעֲשֵׂר שֵׁנִי לִדְרוֹמוֹ וּתְרוּמַת מַעֲשֵׂר בִּצְפוֹן צְפוֹנוֹת. מַהוּ תְּנַיי בֵּית דִּין. הוּא לִכְשֶׁיִּפָּדֶה מַעֲשֵׂר שֵׁנִי שֶׁבְּעוֹדֶף פָּדוּי. עַד כְּדוֹן בְּיָבֵשׁ בְּלַח.

What is a stipulation by the Court? That one should fix the First Tithe to the North, Second Tithe to the South, and the heave of the tithe at the extreme North[44]. What is a stipulation by the Court? It is that if the Second Tithe is redeemed, that which is in excess is also redeemed[45]. All this refers to dry produce; for fluids[46]?

44 That one always should proceed in the same way any time one has produce to put in order as a matter of discipline lest one forget a step. For anybody following these rules, the first stipulation applies and good faith estimates are as valid as exact measurements. Consequently, if one

does not follow this particular way of doing things, even the first stipulation is not valid.

45 The possibility of estimating is given not only for First, but also for Second Tithe.

46 The method of Mishnah and Tosephta is not applicable to those fluids, wine and olive oil, which have to be tithed as Biblical commandment since these fluids will not remain static. The question is not answered; it seems that wine and olive oil must be tithed separately, the slow way.

הֲוָה לֵיהּ מֵאָה תְאֵינִין חַמְשִׁין רַבְרְבִין וְחַמְשִׁין דְּקִיקִין. אִין נְסַב מִן רַבְרְבָיָא צָרִיךְ מֵיסַב תְּשַׁע. מִן דְּקִיקָתָא צָרִיךְ מֵיסַב אַחַד עֶשְׂרֵה. נְסַב עֲשָׂרָה רַבְרְבָיָא אִית תַּמָּן חָדָא חוּלִין וְחָשׁ לוֹמַר שֶׁמָּא אוֹתָהּ חוּלִין עוֹשֶׂה אוֹתָהּ תְּרוּמַת מַעֲשֵׂר לְמָקוֹם אַחֵר. וּכְתִיב תְּרוּמַת יי מַעֲשֵׂר מִן הַמַּעֲשֵׂר. וְלֹא חוּלִין מִן הַמַּעֲשֵׂר. אָמַר רִבִּי בּוּן בַּר כַּהֲנָא מַתְנֶה וְאוֹמֵר מַעֲשֵׂר הַזֶּה שֶׁהַפֵּירוֹת הַלָּלוּ חַיָּיבוֹת הֲרֵי הוּא קָבוּעַ בִּתְחִילַּת כָּל־עוּקָץ וְעוּקָץ וּמְהַלֵּךְ עַד שֶׁהוּא מַגִּיעַ בְּכָל־עֶשֶׂר מֵסַב אִית בְּהוֹן חָדָא תְּרוּמַת מַעֲשֵׂר וְכָל־שֶׁהוּא חוּלִין.

If somebody had 100 figs, 50 large ones and 50 small ones. If he takes from the large ones, should he take nine? If he takes from the small ones, should he take eleven? If he takes ten large ones, there might be one profane among them and we would worry lest perhaps he use that one to make it heave of the tithe for another place, but it is written (*Num.* 18:26): "The heave of the Eternal, tithe from tithe," not profane from tithe[47]. Rebbi Abun bar Cahana[48] said, he stipulates and says, the tithe due from this produce should be fixed from the tip of each stem und continue until it reaches[49]; in each of the ten there is heave of the tithe and a tiny bit of profane.

47 Probably a scribal error; it would be more reasonable to say "not tithe from profane," since once produce is put in order, nothing of it can ever become heave or tithe again. But there is no manuscript evidence for this and

the problem is not taken up in *Sifry*.

48 Galilean Amora of the third generation, a student of R. Joḥanan who lived until the time of R. Mana.

49 If the total volume of all figs is V and that of the ten equal selected large figs is $\varepsilon + V/10$, then in each fig there is a volume of $\varepsilon/10$ profane and the rest is tithe. Hence, there is no fig selected that cannot be used for heave of the tithe.

עַד כְּדוֹן דָּבָר מְרוּבֶּה הָיָה דָּבָר מְמוּעָט הֲוָה לֵיהּ עֶשֶׂר תְּאֵינִין חָמֵשׁ רַבְרְבִין וְחָמֵשׁ דְּקִיקִין. אִין יְסַב מִן רַבְרְבָתָא צָרִיךְ מֵיסַב חָדָא פָּרָא צִיבְחַר. מִן דְּקִיקָתָא צָרִיךְ מֵיסַב חָדָא וְעוֹד צִיבְחַר. נְסַב חַד מִן רַבְרְבָתָא אִית תַּמָּן כָּל־שֶׁהוּא חוּלִין וְחָשׁ לוֹמַר שֶׁמָּא אוֹתָהּ הַחוּלִין עוֹשֶׂה תְּרוּמַת מַעֲשֵׂר לְמָקוֹם אַחֵר. וּכְתִיב תְּרוּמַת יי מַעֲשֵׂר מִן הַמַּעֲשֵׂר וְלֹא חוּלִין מִן הַמַּעֲשֵׂר. אָמַר רִבִּי אַבָּא קַרְתִּיגְנָייָא מַתְנֶה וְאוֹמֵר הַמַּעֲשֵׂר הַזֶּה שֶׁהַפֵּירוֹת הַלָּלוּ חַיָּיבוֹת הֲרֵי הוּא קָבוּעַ בִּתְחִילַּת הָעוּקֶץ וּמְסַיֵּים וְאוֹמֵר לַכֹּהֵן עַד כָּאן סִייַּמְתִּי.

That takes care of large quantities. If there was little, if he had ten figs, five large ones and five small ones? If he takes from the large ones, he has to take one minus[50] a little. From the little ones, he has to take one plus a little. If he took one of the large ones, it contains a little bit of profane and one has to worry that maybe he turns that profane part into heave of the tithe for another place, and it is written (*Num.* 18:26): "The heave of the Eternal, tithe from tithe," not profane from tithe. Rebbi Abba from Carthage said, he stipulates and says, the tithe due from this produce should be fixed from the tip of each stem and he marks it and says to the Cohen, as far as where I marked it[51].

50 Cf. Latin *parum*, adv., "too little, not enough."

51 The heave extends only from the stem to the mark on the fig.

הֲרֵי הוּא בְּצַד זֶה חוּלִין טֶבֶל. וְיֹאמַר הֲרֵי הוּא בְּצַד זֶה מַעֲשֵׂר. נִמְצָא מַקְדִּים. וְיֹאמַר הֲרֵי הוּא בְּצַד זֶה תְרוּמָה. נִמְצָא אוֹ פוֹחֵת עַל הַתְּרוּמָה אוֹ מוֹסִיף עַל הַתְּרוּמָה. מִתּוֹךְ שֶׁהוּא אוֹמֵר הֲרֵי הוּא בְּצַד זֶה חוּלִין טֶבֶל אוֹ פוֹחֵת עַל הַתְּרוּמָה אוֹ מוֹסִיף עַל הַתְּרוּמָה אֵין בְּכָךְ כְּלוּם.

"What is here on this side is profane *ṭevel*[52]." Why does he not say, what is here on this side is tithe? He would precede[53]. Why does he not say, that on this side is heave[54]? It would turn out that either he diminishes or increases the heave[55]. Since he says, what is here on this side is profane *ṭevel*, whether he diminishes or increases the heave does not matter.

52 Quote from the Tosephta at the start of the Halakhah; it is possible that it also refers to the Mishnah, where the word *ṭevel* is understood to qualify "profane." The question is, why is the language of the declaration so involved, and could it not be simplified by omitting this step?

53 He would give a name to the tithe before the heave, which is forbidden.

54 Not on the 1% mentioned in Mishnah and Tosephta, but the 2% left out of the designation.

55 This "heave" cannot refer to the first heave which has no measure from the Torah and must be given by an estimate; the 2% are only a guideline for the average person. It must refer to the heave of the tithe which should be exactly 1%. If everything is declared *ṭevel*, 10% can be declared to be tithe following the stipulation of the Court mentioned earlier and the stipulation will cover any deviation from the exact 1% for the grain actually separated from the harvest.

(fol. 24b) **משנה ג**: הַלּוֹקֵחַ מִן הַנַּחְתּוֹם מְעַשֵּׂר מִן הַחַמָּה עַל הַצּוֹנֶנֶת וּמִן הַצּוֹנֶנֶת עַל הַחַמָּה אֲפִילוּ מִטְּפוּסִים הַרְבֵּה דִּבְרֵי רִבִּי מֵאִיר. רִבִּי יְהוּדָה אוֹסֵר שֶׁאֲנִי אוֹמֵר חִטִּים שֶׁל אֶמֶשׁ הָיוּ מִשֶּׁל אֶחָד וְשֶׁל הַיּוֹם הָיוּ מִשֶּׁל אַחֵר. רִבִּי שִׁמְעוֹן אוֹסֵר בִּתְרוּמַת מַעֲשֵׂר וּמַתִּיר בְּחַלָּה.

Mishnah 3: He who buys from the baker may tithe from the warm on the cold and from the cold on the warm[56], even from many types[57], the words of Rebbi Meïr. Rebbi Jehudah forbids it; I say that the wheat of yesterday was from one source and today's is from another[58]. Rebbi Simeon forbids for heave of the tithe and permits for *ḥallah*[59].

56 That means, from old bread for fresh, even though it may be not only from two different batches but also from the lesser quality on the better, which is a questionable but legal practice, as will be explained in tractate *Terumot*.

57 Greek τύπος. It is not clear whether "type" or "shape" is the form of a baking pan or the form of bread baked on sheets. The commentators take "shape" to be the baking mould even though it forces Maimonides to note that the technique of baking bread had changed from Mishnaic times to his time. It seems more likely that "type" refers to the kind of the bread since different kinds of bread require different kinds of flour. This is the position of R. Jehudah.

58 One could be from a source that was tithed and another from a source that was not, since all the tithing here is for *demay*.

59 *Ḥallah* becomes obligated at the baker's; hence, everybody will agree that all bread from one baker can be fixed with one *ḥallah*. It follows that R. Jehudah, who does not mention *ḥallah*, will agree, and if R. Jehudah and R. Simeon disagree, R. Simeon must be the more restrictive since he forbids all tithing from one batch to another, even of the same day.

(fol. 24c) **הלכה ג**: עַד הֵיכָן תַּלְמִידוֹי שֶׁל רִבִּי חִייָא בְשֵׁם רִבִּי יְהוֹשֻׁעַ בֶּן לֵוִי עַד שְׁלֹשִׁים יוֹם. הֵיךְ עֲבִידָא לָקַח מִמֶּנּוּ בִּתְחִילַּת שְׁלֹשִׁים וּבְאֶמְצַע שְׁלֹשִׁים וּבְסוֹף

שְׁלֹשִׁים. רִאשׁוֹן עַל גַּבֵּי שֵׁנִי[60] מִין אֶחָד הוּא רִאשׁוֹן עַל גַּבֵּי שְׁלִישִׁי שְׁנֵי מִינִין הֵן.

Halakhah 3: How long? A student of Rebbi Ḥiyya in the name of Rebbi Joshua ben Levi, up to 30 days[61]. How is that? If he bought from him at the beginning of 30 days, in the middle, and at the end. The first and the second are one kind, the first and the third are two kinds.

60 Reading of R. Simson of Sens. Manuscripts and Venice print: שלישי. The question is how much difference can there be between two batches of bread so that they may be tithed together according to the anonymous Tanna. Probably one speaks here about flatbread with a long shelf life.

61 Not including the thirtieth day.

רִבִּי שִׁמְעוֹן אוֹסֵר בִּתְרוּמַת מַעֲשֵׂר וּמַתִּיר בְּחַלָּה. וְרִבִּי יְהוּדָה אוֹסֵר בְּחַלָּה. וְלֹא אֶצְלוֹ הִיא נִטְבֶּלֶת אֶלָּא בְּשׁוֹאֵל שְׂאוֹר טָמֵא לַעֲשׂוֹת עִסָּתוֹ. אֲפִילוּ כֵן לֹא אֶצְלוֹ הִיא נִטְבֶּלֶת. אֶלָּא בְשׁוֹאֵל כִּכָּר טָמֵא לְמַלְאוֹת תַּנּוּר. וְאִם בְּשׁוֹאֵל כִּכָּר טָמֵא לְמַלְאוֹת תַּנּוּרוֹ .מְעַשֵּׂר מִכָּל־כִּכָּר וְכִכָּר. אֶלָּא כְּרִבִּי יוֹחָנָן דְּרִבִּי יוֹחָנָן אָמַר כַּאן בְּעוֹשֶׂה בְטָהֳרָה כַּאן בְּעוֹשֶׂה בְטוּמְאָה. אֶלָּא כְרִבִּי אֶלְעָזָר דְּרִבִּי אֶלְעָזָר אָמַר כַּאן וְכַאן בְּעוֹשֶׂה בְטָהֳרָה. אָמַר רִבִּי יוּדָן אָבוֹי דְּרִבִּי מַתַּנְיָה בְּעוֹשֶׂה בְטוּמְאָה קַיְימִינָן וְאֶצְלוֹ הִיא נִטְבֶּלֶת. אַף רִבִּי יוּדָה מוֹדֶה בָהּ. וְתַנֵּי כֵן רִבִּי יוּדָה וְרִבִּי שִׁמְעוֹן אוֹסְרִין (fol. 24d) בִּתְרוּמַת מַעֲשֵׂר וּמַתִּירִין בְּחַלָּה. הָא רִבִּי יוּדָה אוֹסֵר בִּתְרוּמַת מַעְשְׂרָן וּמַתִּיר בְּחַלָּה. רִבִּי שִׁמְעוֹן אוֹסֵר בִּתְרוּמַת מַעֲשֵׂר וּמַתִּיר בְּחַלָּה. מַה בֵּינֵיהוֹ. עַל דַּעְתֵּיהּ דְּרִבִּי יוּדָה אֵינוֹ מַפְרִישׁ לֹא מִשֶּׁל הַיּוֹם עַל שֶׁל אֶמֶשׁ וְלֹא מִשֶּׁל אֶמֶשׁ עַל שֶׁל יוֹם מַפְרִישׁ מִן הַתַּנּוּר עַל הַתַּנּוּר. עַל דַּעְתֵּיהּ דְּרִבִּי שִׁמְעוֹן אֲפִילוּ מִן הַתַּנּוּר עַל הַתַּנּוּר אֵינוֹ מַפְרִישׁ.

"Rebbi Simeon forbids for heave of the tithe and permits for *ḥallah*[62]." Then Rebbi Jehudah forbids for *ḥallah*[63]. Does it not become *ṭevel* at his place[64]? But perhaps he borrows impure sour dough to make his bread-dough[65]. Even so, does it not become *ṭevel* at his place[66]? But perhaps he borrows an impure loaf[67] to fill up his oven. If he borrows an impure loaf to fill up his oven, must he then not tithe every single loaf[68]? That is for Rebbi Joḥanan, since Rebbi Joḥanan said, there[69] if he works in purity, here if he works in impurity. But for Rebbi Eleazar, who says that in both cases if he works in purity[70]? Rebbi Yudan, the father of Rebbi Mattaniah[71] said, we refer to one who works in impurity[72] and it becomes *ṭevel* at his place, and Rebbi Jehudah also agrees. We have stated accordingly: "Rebbi Jehudah and Rebbi Simeon forbid for heave of the tithe and permit for *ḥallah*." Hence, Rebbi Jehudah forbids for heave of the tithe and permits for *ḥallah*; Rebbi Simeon forbids for heave of the tithe and permits for *ḥallah*[73]. What is the difference between them? In the opinion of Rebbi Jehudah, one may not separate from today's for yesterday's or from yesterday's for today's, but one may separate from one oven batch on another oven batch[74]. In the opinion of Rebbi Simeon, even from one oven batch on another one may not separate.

62 Quote from the Mishnah.

63 Since R. Simeon is quoted as disagreeing with R. Jehudah (otherwise the Mishnah would say, R. Jehudah and R. Simeon say . . .); it seems that R. Jehudah forbids to give one *ḥallah* for different batches from the same bakery.

64 It is irrelevant from where the baker bought his flour; the obligation of *ḥallah* starts when he makes his dough and only depends on the baker's actions.

65 "Impure" does not mean literally impure, but that he bought from an *am haäreẓ* who does not care whether his food is ritually pure or not as long as it is not dedicated to the Temple. But the *am haäreẓ* does not take the heave of the tithe seriously, so we are back to the situation described by R. Jehudah that one batch of flour is from a source which was tithed, the other from a source not tithed.

66 The distinction made in the preceding sentence is relevant for heave of the tithe, irrelevant for *ḥallah*.

67 A loaf from another *am haärez̧* baker.

68 The other source could have given *ḥallah* on its dough and after baking the loaves are indistinguishable; one may not separate heave (*ḥallah*) from a loaf already put in order, and there would be no way out but to take *demay ḥallah* from every single loaf and not from one for all.

69 Mishnah 2:4, see Halakhah 2:4, 3:1.

70 How could R. Jehudah forbid taking one *ḥallah* for all?

71 A Galilean Amora of the third generation, father of the better known R. Mattaniah of the fourth generation. His teachers are unknown.

72 We also refer to one who works in impurity; he who cares for purity also cares for tithes.

73 What is the difference between them?

74 He states clearly that one may not tithe from one day to another; batches of the same day may be taken together.

(fol. 24b) **משנה ד**: הַלּוֹקֵחַ מִן הַפְּלָטֵר מְעַשֵּׂר מִכָּל־טִיפּוּס וְטִיפּוּס דִּבְרֵי רַבִּי מֵאִיר. רַבִּי יְהוּדָה אוֹמֵר מֵאֶחָד עַל הַכֹּל. וּמוֹדֶה רַבִּי יְהוּדָה בְּלוֹקֵחַ מִן הַמָּנְפּוֹל שֶׁהוּא מְעַשֵּׂר מִכָּל־אֶחָד וְאֶחָד.

Mishnah 4: He who buys from a merchant[75] tithes from each type[57] separately, the words of Rebbi Meïr. Rebbi Jehudah says, from one for everything. Rebbi Jehudah agrees about him who buys from a store with a monopoly[76] that he tithes from each single loaf.

75 Greek πρατήρ "seller"; he might buy from different bakeries, and everybody agrees that bread from different sources incurs different obligations of *ḥallah* and requires separate tithing.

76 Greek μονοπώλιον "right of monopoly," certain to have more than one source, as explained in the Halakhah.

(fol. 24d) **הלכה ד**: רִבִּי מֵאִיר אוֹמֵר נַחְתּוֹם עוֹשֶׂה טֶפּוֹס אֶחָד וּפְלָטֵר מִשְׁתַּמֵּשׁ בְּכַמָּה נַחְתּוֹמִים. רִבִּי יְהוּדָה אוֹמֵר נַחְתּוֹם עוֹשֶׂה כַמָּה טְפּוֹסִים וּפְלָטֵר מִשְׁתַּמֵּשׁ בְּנַחְתּוֹם אֶחָד.

Halakhah 4: Rebbi Meïr says, a baker makes one type and a merchant uses several bakers[77]. Rebbi Jehudah says, a baker makes several types and a merchant uses only one baker.

77 Quoted in Babli *Baba Meẓia'* 56a.

אֵי זֶהוּ מָנְפּוֹל. דְּבֵי רִבִּי מָנָא אָמְרֵי תִּשְׁעָה פְּלָטֵרִין וַעֲשָׂרָה נַחְתּוֹמִים תּוֹמָנְיָא מִן דְּתוֹמָנְיָא וְחַד מִן דִּתְרֵי.

What is a monopoly? At the House of Rebbi Yannai they say, nine sellers and ten bakers. Eight buy from eight and one from two[78].

78 A store has monopoly character if it outsells its closest rival by a ratio of two to one, or if it sells products from twice as many manufacturers.

רִבִּי יוֹנָה בְּעֵי הָיוּ לְפָנָיו שְׁנֵי טְפּסִים הוֹכִיחַ עַל עַצְמוֹ שֶׁהֵן שְׁנַיִים הוּשְׁווּ כוּלָּן לַעֲשׂוֹת טוּפּוֹס אֶחָד מְעַשֵּׂר מִכָּל־כִּכָּר וְכִכָּר. רִבִּי יוֹנָה בְּעֵי כְּמַה דְתֵימָא תִּשְׁעָה פְּלָטֵרִין וַעֲשָׂרָה נַחְתּוֹמִים תּוֹמָנְיָא מִן דְּתוֹמָנְיָא וְחַד מִן דִּתְרֵיי. וְדִכְווָתָהּ תִּשְׁעָה נַחְתּוֹמִים וַעֲשָׂרָה פְּלָטֵרִין תּוֹמָנְיָא מִן דְּתוֹמָנְיָא וְחַד מִן דִּתְרֵיי אוֹ תִשְׁעָה מִן דְּתִשְׁעָה וְחַד מִן כּוּלְּהוֹן מְעַשֵּׂר מִכָּל־כִּכָּר וְכִכָּר.

Rebbi Jonah asked: If he had before him two types, it would be evident that they are two. If all bakers agreed to make one and the same type, does he have to tithe each loaf separately[79]? Rebbi Jonah asked: As you said, nine stores and ten bakers, eight buy from eight and one from two. Similarly, nine bakers and ten stores; eight buy from eight and one from two, or nine from the nine and one buys from all of them? He must tithe each loaf separately.[80]

79 In that case, are all stores together one monopolist chain?

80 The definition of the monopoly is only a paradigm; the rule is applicable to every similar case.

(fol. 24b) **משנה ה**: הַלּוֹקֵחַ מִן הֶעָנִי וְכֵן הֶעָנִי שֶׁנִּיתְּנוּ לוֹ פְרוּסוֹת אוֹ פִילְחֵי דְבֵילָה מְעַשֵּׂר מִכָּל־אֶחָד וְאֶחָד. בִּתְמָרִים וּבִגְרוֹגְרוֹת בּוֹלֵל וְנוֹטֵל. אָמַר רִבִּי יְהוּדָה אֵימָתַי בִּזְמַן שֶׁמַּתָּנָה מְרוּבָּה. אֲבָל בִּזְמַן שֶׁמַּתָּנָה מְמוּעֶטֶת מְעַשֵּׂר מִכָּל־אֶחָד וְאֶחָד.

Mishnah 5: He who buys from a poor person, and similarly, the poor to whom bread slices or pieces of fig cake were given, tithe from each piece separately. But he mixes together dates and dried figs and then gives. Rebbi Jehudah said, when is that[81]? If the gift is large. But if the gift is small, he tithes from each single one.

81 Usually, statements of R. Jehudah introduced by "when is that?" give the reason for the preceding statement and do not express disagreement.

(fol. 24d) **הלכה ה**: רִבִּי יוֹסֵי בְּשֵׁם רִבִּי פְּדָיָה רִבִּי יוֹנָה בְּשֵׁם חִזְקִיָּה[82] אֵין בְּלִילָה אֶלָּא לְיַיִן וְשֶׁמֶן בִּלְבַד. רִבִּי יוֹחָנָן אָמַר עַד כְּזֵיתִין הַנִּבְלָלִין. מַתְנִיתִין פְּלִיגָא עַל רִבִּי יוֹחָנָן בִּתְמָרִים וּבִגְרוֹגְרוֹת בּוֹלֵל וְנוֹטֵל. פָּתַר לָהּ עַד כְּזֵתִין.

Halakhah 5: Rebbi Yose in the name of Rebbi Pedaiah, Rebbi Jonah in the name of Ḥizqiah, there is no mixing except for wine and oil[83]. Rebbi Joḥanan says, they can be mixed up to the size of olives. Our Mishnah disagrees with Rebbi Joḥanan: "But he mixes together dates and dried figs and then gives[84]." He explains it up to olive-sized bits.

82 Text of Rome ms. and R. Simson. Venice text: רִבִּי יוֹסֵי בְשֵׁם רִבִּי יוֹנָה בְשֵׁם חִזְקִיָּה which clearly is missing a name since Rebbis Yose and Jonah were colleagues.

83 Statement of Samuel in Babli *Roš Hašanah* 13b. It probably means that only fluids can be tithed when mixed because fluids from different sources quickly diffuse and material from each source is contained in every volume element in the fluid.

84 R. Johanan notes that dry matter may also be mixed if the parts are small enough. Dates and figs, fresh and dried, are much larger than olives. The answer is that figs and dates, in order to be tithed together, must be in pieces, each of them smaller than the volume of an olive. Then these pieces must be mixed. (Maimonides does not mention any cutting into pieces either in his Commentary to the Mishnah or in his Code (*Maäser'*4:8). R. Simson in his commentary requires that figs and dates be mashed together into cakes. This contradicts both the Yerushalmi and the Mishnah, because mashed figs are not גרוגרת but דבילה.)

רִבִּי יוֹסֵי בְשֵׁם רִבִּי זְעִירָא בִּדְמַאי הִתִּירוּ כְרִבִּי יְהוּדָה דְּתַנֵּינָן רִבִּי יְהוּדָה אוֹמֵר אֵימָתַי בִּזְמַן שֶׁמַּתָּנָה מְרוּבָּה. אֲבָל בִּזְמַן שֶׁמַּתָּנָה מְמוּעֶטֶת מְעַשֵּׂר מִכָּל־אֶחָד וְאֶחָד.

Rebbi Yose[85] in the name of Rebbi Zeïra: They permitted for *demay* following Rebbi Jehudah, since "Rebbi Jehudah says, when is that? If the gift is large[86]. But if the gift is small, he tithes from each single one."

85 He restricts his statement in the first paragraph, that fluids only may be tithed mixed, to cases where a Biblical commandment is involved. In his opinion, rabbinic *demay* was never under this rule.

86 The meaning of this condition is explained in the next paragraph.

דְּבֵי רִבִּי יַנַּאי אָמְרֵי בִשְׁעַת הַגּוֹרֶן שָׁנוּ שֶׁהַכֹּל הָיוּ נוֹתְנִין מִמֵּאָה סְאָה. הָיוּ הַכֹּל נוֹתְנִין מִמֵּאָה וְאֶחָד מֵחֲמִשִּׁים מְעַשֵּׂר מֵחֲמִשִּׁים. הָיוּ הַכֹּל נוֹתְנִין מֵחֲמִשִּׁים וְאֶחָד מֵאַרְבָּעִים מְעַשֵּׂר מֵאַרְבָּעִים. הָיוּ הַכֹּל נוֹתְנִין מֵאַרְבָּעִים וְאֶחָד מִשְּׁלֹשִׁים

מְעַשֵּׂר מִשְּׁלֹשִׁים. הָיוּ הַכֹּל נוֹתְנִין מֵעֶשְׂרִים וְאֶחָד מֵעֲשָׂרָה מְעַשֵּׂר מֵעֲשָׂרָה. הָיוּ הַכֹּל נוֹתְנִין מֵעֲשָׂרָה וְאֶחָד מֵאֶחָד מְעַשֵּׂר מִכָּל־אֶחָד וְאֶחָד.

In the House of Rebbi Yannai they said: The Mishnah speaks of threshing time[87], when everybody was giving from a hundred *seah*. If all were giving from a hundred *seah* but one only from fifty, he must tithe from fifty. If all were giving from fifty but one only from forty, he must tithe from forty. If all were giving from forty but one only from thirty, he must tithe from thirty. If all were giving from twenty but one only from ten, he must tithe from ten. If all were giving from ten but one only from one, he must tithe every single one.

87 When R. Jehudah makes a difference between large and small gifts, he refers only to times when the harvest is brought to the threshing floor or the barn and all farmers give equally. In that case, we say that probably they also gave tithes and the rules of *demay* allow for special leniencies. But if not all farmers at the place give in equal amounts, the poor recipient must split his gifts into packets corresponding in size to the smallest packet he received, and if this consists of a single fruit he must tithe all his gifts singly (or, giver by giver.) [The Tosephta (*Demay* 5:9) has another explanation, that "big gifts" are given only in years of a bumper crop; in that case, everybody may be assumed to tithe.]

(fol. 24b) **משנה ו:** הַלּוֹקֵחַ מִן הַסִּיטוֹן וְחָזַר וְלָקַח מִמֶּנּוּ שְׁנִיָּיה לֹא יְעַשֵּׂר מִזֶּה עַל זֶה אֲפִילוּ מֵאוֹתוֹ הַסּוּג אֲפִילוּ מֵאוֹתוֹ הַמִּין. נֶאֱמָן הַסִּיטוֹן לוֹמַר מִשֶּׁל אֶחָד הֵן.

Mishnah 6: He who buys from the grain wholesaler and later buys from him a second time should not tithe from one batch for any other, not even if they are from the same crate, not even if they are the same kind[88]. But the grain wholesaler is trustworthy to say that they are from the same source.

88 Since the wholesale commissioner surely buys from several farmers, two batches of the same kind of grain will probably come from two different sources and maybe one of them was already tithed but the other was not; then it is impossible to tithe from one for the other. Since the wholesaler has no monetary interest in telling whether the two batches of grain came from the same source or not, and as a wholesaler he sells *demay* with rabbinic permission, his statement may be believed.

(fol. 24d) **הלכה ו**: רִבִּי יִרְמְיָה בְּעֵי אֲפִילוּ הִשְׁבִּיחַ לוֹ מִקְחוֹ. אִינּוּן חִיטַּיָא דִּזְבַנִית מִינָּךְ אֶתְמוֹל טָבִין הֲוִין מֵאִינּוּן אִינּוּן.

Halakhah 6: Rebbi Jeremiah asked[89]: Even if he declares the buy to be good? "That wheat I bought from you yesterday was good!" "These are the same!"

89 Is the grain wholesaler also to be believed if the client expresses satisfaction with the earlier buy? In that case, the wholesaler has a monetary interest in the answer and should not be believed.

תַּנֵּי הַלּוֹקֵחַ מִן הַחֶנְוָנִי וְחָזַר וְלָקַח מִמֶּנּוּ שְׁנִיָּיה. אִם מַכִּיר הוּא אֶת הֶחָבִית שֶׁהִיא מְעַשֵּׂר מִמֶּנּוּ עָלָיו. הָא אִם אֵינוֹ מַכִּיר אֶת הֶחָבִית לֹא בְדָא. הָדָא דְתֵימַר בְּאִילֵּין אידתיקרימא בְּרַם בְּאִילֵּין שְׁפִיָּא אוּרְחָא מְפַנֵּיהוֹן אִילֵּין לְגַוְא אִילֵּין.

It was stated: "He who buys from the retail merchant and returns to buy a second time. If he recognizes that the amphora is the same, he tithes from one on the other[90]." But if he does not recognize it, he does not. That means, in the case of *'ydtyqrym'*[91], but not in the case of vessels (used to draw wine) which usually are refilled one from the other.

90 The Tosephta, *Demay* 5:11, has an opposite statement: "He who buys from the retail merchant and went back and bought a second time, even if he recognizes the amphora that it is the same, he may not tithe from one on the other."

91 This word has not been identified. The Rome ms. has אורתי קדמיתא, [Cirillo (ed. Luncz) has אולותוקרימא.] Lieberman (תוספתא כפשוטה p. 254-255) is correct in insisting that the word designates a kind of barrel; his emendation οἴνου κεράμια is unsupported by the evidence. D. Sperber (Sinai 78, 40-41) reads *ὀρθοκεράμια, "upright standing jar." But he takes שְׁפָיָיא to mean "flat lying vessels," not parallel to the usual שפיתא "vessel used to draw wine." It is difficult to imagine a clay vessel lying with its opening horizontal, even if closed by a clay stopper, without losing all its contents. Liebermann quotes a Syriac source showing that the שפיתא used to draw wine from the storage tank was also used to transport the wine from the producer to retail stores.

Perhaps the word is a combination of ὑδρία, ἡ "water pot", but also used for a vessel or urn of any kind, including "wine pot", and κέραμος, ὁ "clay", but also anything made of clay, including "wine jar" (E. G.).

(fol. 24b) **משנה ז:** הַלּוֹקֵחַ מִבַּעַל הַבַּיִת וְחָזַר וְלָקַח מִמֶּנּוּ שְׁנִייָה מְעַשֵּׂר מִזֶּה עַל זֶה אֲפִילוּ מִשְּׁתֵּי קוּפּוֹת אֲפִילוּ מִשְּׁתֵּי עֲיָירוֹת. בַּעַל הַבַּיִת שֶׁהָיָה מוֹכֵר יָרָק בַּשּׁוּק בִּזְמַן שֶׁהֵן מְבִיאִין לוֹ מִגַּנּוֹתָיו מְעַשֵּׂר מֵאַחַת עַל הַכֹּל וּמִגַּנּוֹת אֲחֵרוֹת מְעַשֵּׂר מִכָּל־אַחַת וְאַחַת.

Mishnah 7: He who buys from a farmer and then buys from him a second time tithes from one batch for the other, even if they are from two crates, even if the are from two different hamlets[92]. If the farmer sells vegetables on the market, in case that his supply comes from his own vegetable gardens, one tithes from one for all others, from other vegetable gardens, one has to tithe each bunch separately.

92 If the farmer tithes, *demay* is a formality for all his produce. If he does not tithe, all his produce needs tithing and it is possible to tithe from one for the other.

(fol. 24d) **הלכה ז**: רִבִּי יוֹנָה בְּעֵי וּכְרִבִּי מֵאִיר מְעַשֵּׂר מִכָּל־קֶלַח וְקֶלַח. דְּתַנֵּינָן תַּמָּן אָמַר רִבִּי מֵאִיר וְכִי מִפְּנֵי מַה טִימּוֹ אֶלָּא מִפְּנֵי מַשְׁקֶה הַפֶּה. כְּמָה דְּתֵימַר תַּמָּן דֶּרֶךְ אֲגוּדָה לִיתּוּר וְהוּא קְשׁוֹרָהּ בְּפִיו בְּרַם הָכָא דֶּרֶךְ אֲגוּדָה לִיתּוּר וְהוּא נוֹתֵן מַה שֶׁבִּפְנִים בַּחוּץ וּמַה שֶּׁבַּחוּץ בִּפְנִים.

Halakhah 7: Rebbi Jonah asked[93]: According to Rebbi Meïr, should he not tithe each stem separately? As we have stated there[94]: "Rebbi Meïr said, why did it become impure[95]? Only because of spittle!" As you will say, there it is usual to open bundles and he[96] binds using his mouth, but here, is it usual to open bundles to risk[97] having the outer ones inside and the inner ones outside?

93 The entire discussion is about the farmer who sells not only his own produce on the market.

94 Mishnah *Makhširin* 6:2: "All bundled vegetables on the market are impure. R. Jehudah declares the fresh ones pure. R. Meïr said, why did they declare them impure? Only because of spittle!" The first Tanna holds that on the market one sprinkles water on the vegetables to keep them fresh. Hence, they are subject to impurity and, since everybody touches them, we must assume that an unclean person may

have touched them and treat the vegetables as impure. R. Jehudah disagrees for those fresh vegetables which do not need refreshing; hence, they are not subject to impurity and it does not matter who touched them. R. Meïr restricts the impurity to bundles; since in binding them the farmer will have taken the string into his mouth the bundle was wetted intentionally, and, unless the farmer is a *ḥaver*, the bundle will certainly be impure. If the farmer is a *ḥaver*, the bundle still will probably become impure on the market.

95 Elided א, for טמאו.

96 The producer of the bundles.

97 Does the seller risk to open bundles? Is it not usual to have the good-looking vegetables outside and the lesser quality inside? Who would risk losing his sales by having less fresh vegetables visible from the outside?

אָמַר רִבִּי יוֹנָה לֹא סוֹף דָּבָר מִגִּנּוֹתָיו אֶלָּא אֲפִילוּ מִגִּנּוֹת אֲחֵרוֹת עִם מְעַשְּׂרִין הֵן לְדַעְתּוֹ מְעַשֵּׂר מִזֶּה עַל זֶה. וְאִם לָאו אֵינוֹ מְעַשֵּׂר מִזֶּה עַל זֶה.

Rebbi Jonah said, not only from his own vegetable gardens, but even from vegetable gardens of others, if they tithe under his instruction[98], he tithes from one for the other, but if they do not, he has to tithe each bunch separately.

98 Then all vegetables are either tithed or not tithed; in both cases, one can tithe *demay* without worry.

(fol. 24b) **משנה ח**: הַלּוֹקֵחַ טֶבֶל מִשְּׁנֵי מְקוֹמוֹת מְעַשֵּׂר מִזֶּה עַל זֶה אַף עַל פִּי שֶׁאָמְרוּ אֵין אָדָם רַשַּׁאי לִמְכּוֹר טֶבֶל אֶלָּא לְצוֹרֶךְ.

Mishnah 8: He who buys *ṭevel* from two sources may tithe from one for the other even though they said that nobody is permitted to sell *ṭevel* except in case of need[99].

99 If the first heave was not taken, it is clearly possible to take heave from one batch for the other, as long as they are of the same kind. The need to sell *ṭevel* arises if some grain that was tithed fell into a heap of *ṭevel*. In that case, heave can no longer be taken from that heap, because what one takes out may be from the profane grain and cannot become heave. Then it is necessary to take the heave for this heap from some other heap. But nobody can take heave for another person's property. Hence, a transfer of property may be necessary.

(fol. 24d) **הלכה ח**: אָמַר רִבִּי יוֹנָה כֵּינִי מַתְנִיתָא אֵין אָדָם רַשַּׁאי לִמְכּוֹר טֶבֶל אֶלָּא לְצוֹרֶךְ וּבִלְבַד לְחָבֵר. מֵעַתָּה עַם הָאָרֶץ שֶׁנִּתְעָרֵב טִבְלוֹ בְּחוּלִין אֵין לוֹ תַקָּנָה. כֵּיצַד הוּא עוֹשֶׂה הוֹלֵךְ אֵצֶל חָבֵר וְהוּא לוֹקֵחַ לוֹ טֶבֶל וּמְעַשְּׂרוֹ לוֹ.

Halakhah 8: Rebbi Jonah said, this is the Mishnah: Nobody is permitted to sell *ṭevel* except in case of need, and only to a *ḥaver*[100]. In that case, if *ṭevel* of an *am haärez̧* was mixed with profane, can that never be fixed? What shall he do? He goes to a *ḥaver* who buys *ṭevel* for him[101] and tithes for him.

100 Since the *ḥaver* not only must be observant but also knowlegeable in all the rules concerning *ṭevel*. [This **כיני מתניתא** is not discussed in the systematic study of the term in R. J. N. Epstein's מבוא לנוסח המשנה.]

101 R. Jonah implies that *ṭevel* can be sold to a *ḥaver* acting not only for himself but also as trustee for others.

(fol. 24b) **משנה ט**: מְעַשְּׂרִים מִשֶּׁל יִשְׂרָאֵל עַל שֶׁל גּוֹיִם וּמִשֶּׁל גּוֹיִם עַל שֶׁל יִשְׂרָאֵל. וּמִשֶּׁל יִשְׂרָאֵל עַל שֶׁל כּוּתִים. וּמִשֶּׁל כּוּתִים עַל שֶׁל כּוּתִים. רִבִּי לָֽעְזָר אוֹסֵר מִשֶּׁל כּוּתִים עַל שֶׁל כּוּתִים.

Mishnah 9: One tithes from a Jew's produce for that of a Gentile[102] and from a Gentile's for that of a Jew; from that of a Jew for that of a Samaritan, and from that of a Samaritan for that of a Samaritan. Rebbi Eleazar[103] prohibits from that of a Samaritan for that of a Samaritan.

102 This Mishnah represents only the opinion of R. Meïr, as stated in the Halakhah.

103 R. Eleazar bar Shamua, cf. מבוא לנוסח המשנה ע' תתשעז. The attribution is reasonable here since the first Tanna is identified as R. Meïr, contemporary of R. Eleazar. The reason of R. Eleazar is that Samaritans always tithe what they eat but not what they sell, but it could happen that a Samaritan farmer tithes for his own use and then for some reason sells that produce which is already in order and cannot be used to tithe any other. In the Tosephta (*Demay* 5:22), the statement and the reasoning behind it are attributed to R. Eliezer (ben Hyrkanos); this is reasonable there since his opponent is his contemporary, R. Ṭarphon.

(fol. 24d) **הלכה ט**: מַתְנִיתִין דְּרִבִּי מֵאִיר דְּרִבִּי מֵאִיר אָמַר אֵין קִנְיָין לְגוֹי בְּאֶרֶץ יִשְׂרָאֵל לְהַפְקִיעוֹ מִיַּד מַעֲשֵׂר. רִבִּי יוּדָה וְרִבִּי שִׁמְעוֹן אוֹמֵר יֵשׁ קִנְיָין לְגוֹי בְּאֶרֶץ יִשְׂרָאֵל לְפוֹטְרוֹ מִן הַמַּעֲשֵׂר. רִבִּי אִימִּי בְּשֵׁם רִבִּי שִׁמְעוֹן בֶּן לָקִישׁ טַעֲמָא דְּרִבִּי מֵאִיר וְהִתְנַחַלְתֶּם אוֹתָם לִבְנֵיכֶם אַחֲרֵיכֶם לָרֶשֶׁת אֲחוּזָּה. הֵקִישׁ אֲחוּזָּה לַעֲבָדִים. מַה עֲבָדִים אַתֶּם קוֹנִין מֵהֶן וְהֵן אֵינָן קוֹנִין מִכֶּם אַף אֲחוּזָּה אַתֶּם קוֹנִין מֵהֶן וְהֵן אֵינָן קוֹנִין מִכֶּם. אָמַר רִבִּי לָעְזָר בֵּי רִבִּי יוֹסֵי קוֹמֵי רִבִּי יָסָא וְדָא מְסַייְעָא לְרִבִּי מֵאִיר וְהָאָרֶץ לֹא תִמָּכֵר לִצְמִיתוּת כִּי לִי הָאָרֶץ. לְחוּלְטָנִית. אָמַר לֵיהּ כָּל־גַּרְמָהּ אָמְרָה דְּהִיא מְסַייְעָה לְרִבִּי שִׁמְעוֹן. לֹא תִמָּכֵר הָא אִם נִמְכְּרָה חֲלוּטָה הִיא.

Halakhah 9: The Mishnah[104] is Rebbi Meïr's, since Rebbi Meïr says that a Gentile may not acquire real estate in the Land of Israel to remove it from tithe; Rebbi Jehudah and Rebbi Simeon say, a Gentile may acquire real estate in the Land of Israel to free it from tithe. Rebbi Immi in the name of Rebbi Simeon ben Laqish: The reason of Rebbi Meïr (*Lev.* 25:46): "You shall transmit them[105] by inheritance to your sons after you, to inherit by the rules of real estate." This brackets real estate with slaves. Just as you may buy slaves from them but they cannot buy from you[106], so real estate you may buy from them but they cannot buy from you. Rebbi Eleazar ben Rebbi Yose said before Rebbi Yasa, the following supports Rebbi Meïr (*Lev.* 25:23): "The land shall not be sold permanently, because the land belongs to Me," absolutely[107]. He said to him, that in itself supports Rebbi Simeon. "It shall not be sold"[108], because if it was sold, it would be sold absolutely.

104 Parallels *Giṭṭin* 4:12, Babli *Giṭṭin* 47a; there the dispute is between two Amoraim, Rabba (in Babylonia, holding that Gentile land is subject to tithes) and R. Eleazar (in Galilee, holding that the Gentile's land is free from tithes.) The verses quoted also are totally different. Tosaphot (*Giṭṭin* 47a, s. v. אמר רבה) prove that in the opinion of the Babli, R. Meïr frees Gentile land from heave and tithes except if it is leased to a Jewish sharecropper. In Tosephta *Demay* 5:21, the position of R. Meïr is the same as here, the opposition consists of R. Jehudah, R. Simeon, R. Yose. The Tosephta is quoted in Babli *Menaḥot* 66b; there, R. Meïr and R. Jehudah agree with R. Meïr here; R. Simeon and R. Yose oppose. In the interpretation of the Babli *Menaḥot*, the disagreement is not about the status of the Land; it is universally held that ownership of real estate by a Gentile does not free the Land from its obligations. Rather, it is the ownership of the grain at the moment the obligation of heave and tithes starts, i. e., when the grain is stored. Since a Gentile is not subject to the laws of the Torah, R. Simeon and R. Jehudah hold that his grain cannot be subject to those laws. Cf. also *Peah*, Chapter 4, Notes 129-131.

105 Non-Jewish slaves.

106 In Babli *Yebamot* 46a, this is derived from the verse *Lev.* 25:45: "'Also from the children of the inhabitants that live among you, from them you may buy;' you, but not they." As a matter of practical law, since the

Jewish buyer of a non-Jewish slave is required to convert him, and the slave then is subject to the commandments of the Torah; if his owner would sell him to a Gentile, the slave automatically would go free.

107 This cryptic note refers to *Sifra Behar, Parashah* 4(8): לצמיתות לחולטנית, "permanently means absolutely." See R. Shaul Israeli, ספר ארץ חמדה[4], Jerusalem 1999, p. 195 ff.

108 If it could not be sold, there would be no sin in selling it, since the transaction would be void. But since selling agricultural real estate in the Land of Israel to a Gentile is a sin, by necessity the sale would be valid and would imply unrestricted transfer of title.

רִבִּי חוּנָא רוּבָּא דְצִיפּוֹרִין אָמַר הִנְהִיג רִבִּי חֲנִינָא בְצִיפּוֹרִין כְּהָדָא דְרִבִּי שִׁמְעוֹן. רִבִּי זְעִירָא אָמַר הִנְהִיג רִבִּי חֲנִינָא בְצִיפּוֹרִין כְּהָדָא דְרִבִּי שִׁמְעוֹן.

The Great Rebbi Ḥuna from Sepphoris said, Rebbi Ḥanina instituted in Sepphoris following Rebbi Simeon[109]. Rebbi Zeïra said, Rebbi Ḥanina instituted in Sepphoris following Rebbi Simeon.

109 That produce grown by a Gentile on his own land, or the land of another Gentile, is free from any duty of heave and tithes and cannot be used for any tithing. Since two authorities testify to it, this is the received practice. See in Note 104 that the names of R. Simeon's partners vary with the sources; this might be the reason that he alone is quoted.

רִבִּי זְעִירָא אָמַר קוֹמֵי רִבִּי אַבָּהוּ בְּשֵׁם רִבִּי לָעְזָר אַף עַל גַּב דְּרִבִּי מֵאִיר אָמַר אֵין קִנְיָין לְגוֹי בְּאֶרֶץ יִשְׂרָאֵל לְפוֹטְרוֹ מִן הַמַּעְשְׂרוֹת מוֹדֶה הוּא הָכָא דְּיֵשׁ לוֹ קִנְיַין נְכָסִים. אָמַר רִבִּי בָּא אוֹכֶלֶת פֵּירוֹת. וְהָתַנֵּינָן הַלּוֹקֵחַ מֵבִיא בִּיכּוּרִין מִפְּנֵי תִקּוּן הָעוֹלָם. וְיָבִיא בִיכּוּרִים דְּבַר תּוֹרָה.

Rebbi Zeïra said before Rebbi Abbahu in the name of Rebbi Eleazar: Even though Rebbi Meïr says that a Gentile may not acquire real estate in the Land of Israel to free it from tithes, he agrees here that he may acquire property rights. Rebbi Abba said, in order to eat its fruits. Did we not state: "The buyer[110] brings First Fruits for the good of the world." Why does he not bring it as a Biblical obligation?

110 Mishnah *Giṭṭin* 4:9. The Jew who bought agricultural land in Israel from a Gentile can bring its First Fruits to the Temple even though this is not his inheritance from the land distribution by Joshua. For Rebbi Meïr, who holds that possession by a Gentile cannot change the status of the Land relative to the duties imposed on it by the Torah, it should be clear that just as heave and tithe were not lifted from the Land, so the duty of First Fruits was not lifted. Why then is the bringing of First Fruits classified as a rabbinical ordinance, "for the good of the world," in order to encourage people to buy land in Israel, and not as original Biblical obligation?

רִבִּי יוֹנָה רִבִּי סִימוֹן בְּשֵׁם רִבִּי יְהוֹשֻׁעַ בֶּן לֵוִי הַלּוֹקֵחַ פֵּירוֹת תְּלוּשִׁין מִן הַגּוֹי מַפְרִישׁ תְּרוּמָה וּתְרוּמַת מַעֲשֵׂר מֵהֲלָכָה וְנוֹתֵן לַשֵּׁבֶט וְנוֹתֵן דָּמִים מִן הַשֵּׁבֶט. וְהַלּוֹקֵחַ פֵּירוֹת מְחוּבָּרִין מִן הַגּוֹי מַפְרִישׁ תְּרוּמָה וּתְרוּמַת מַעֲשֵׂר מֵהֲלָכָה וְנוֹתְנָן לַשֵּׁבֶט וְאֵינוֹ נוֹטֵל דָּמִים מִן הַשֵּׁבֶט. מַה טַעַם כִּי תִקְחוּ מֵאֵת בְּנֵי יִשְׂרָאֵל. מֵאֵת בְּנֵי יִשְׂרָאֵל אַתְּ מוֹצִיא וְאֵין אַתְּ מוֹצִיא מִיַּד מַכָּרֵי כְהוּנָּה וּלְוִייָה. וַאֲתְיָא כַּיי דָּמַר רִבִּי לָעְזָר כִּי תִקְחוּ מֵאֵת בְּנֵי יִשְׂרָאֵל. מֵאֵת בְּנֵי יִשְׂרָאֵל אַתְּ מוֹצִיא וְאֵין אַתְּ מוֹצִיא מִיַּד הַגּוֹי.

Rebbi Jonah, Rebbi Simon in the name of Rebbi Joshua ben Levi: He who buys loose produce from a Gentile separates heave and heave of the tithe as a matter of practice, gives it to the tribe, and receives money from the tribe[111]. But he who buys produce still in the ground from a Gentile separates heave and heave of the tithe as a matter of practice, gives it to the tribe, and does not take money from the tribe[112]. What is the reason? (*Num.* 18:26) "If you remove the tithe from the Children of Israel." From the Children of Israel you remove the tithe, but not from the acquaintances of Cohanim or Levites[113]. From the Children of Israel you remove the tithe, but not from the hand of a Gentile[114].

111 See Chapter 3, Notes 131-132. Since heave is taken as a matter of common practice, heave and heave of the tithe remain the property of the owner (Babli *Bekhorot* 11b). Since heave and heave of the tithe may be eaten only by Cohanim, presumably they will make a very low offer for the food, but they must pay.

112 Since the obligation of heave and tithes comes only when the harvest is stored, the obligation devolves on the Jew and the tithes are the immediate property of the Cohanim; the owner only has the choice of whom to give.

113 This refers to the second case, when the owner can decide to whom to give. However, it is possible that the sentence should read (*Sifry Zuṭa Qoraḥ* #26): "From the Children of Israel you remove the tithe, but not from Cohanim or Levites." In that case, the quote has no direct connection with the discussion here.

114 This refers to the first case, when the harvest was the Gentile's and no Biblical obligation of heave and tithes was incurred. The Babli (*Bekhorot* 11b) reports in the name of R. Joshua ben Levi that only heave, not heave of the tithe, must be given as a matter of practice. This is a serious disagreement between the two Talmudim.

אָמַר רִבִּי אָחָא בִּימֵי רִבִּי הוֹשַׁעְיָה בִּקְשׁוּ לְהִימָּנוֹת עַל הַר הַמֶּלֶךְ לְפוֹטְרוֹ מִן הַמַּעְשְׂרוֹת. אָמְרוּ יָבוֹא רִבִּי הוֹשַׁעְיָה. לֹא הִסְפִּיק לָבוֹא עַד שֶׁנִּטְרְפָה הַשָּׁעָה.

Rebbi Aḥa said, in the days of Rebbi Hoshaiah they wanted to vote on King's Mountain[115], to free it from tithes. They said, let Rebbi Hoshaiah come. Before he could come, the opportunity was lost[116].

115 A conquest of king Alexander Yannai, not part of the settlement of Judea and Galilee by the returnees from Babylonia, but part of the Jewish state in the later Hasmonean times. It seems that in early Amoraic times King's Mountain was entirely in Gentile hands.

116 A war was going on and the assembly was dispersed.

רִבִּי יוּדָה בַּר פָּזִי בְשֵׁם רִבִּי הוֹשַׁעְיָה הֲלָכָה כְּרִבִּי שִׁמְעוֹן דִּלֹא כֵן מַה נָן אָמְרֵי רִבִּי מֵאִיר וְרִבִּי שִׁמְעוֹן אֵין הֲלָכָה כְּרִבִּי שִׁמְעוֹן. אֶלָּא בְגִין דְּתַנֵּי אָמַר רִבִּי שִׁמְעוֹן שְׁזוּרִי מַעֲשֶׂה שֶׁנִּתְעָרְבוּ פֵּירוֹת טְבוּלִין בְּפֵירוֹתַי וְשָׁאַלְתִּי אֶת רִבִּי טַרְפוֹן. וְאָמַר לִי צֵא וְלוֹקְחֵם מִן הַגּוֹי וְעַשֵּׂר עֲלֵיהֶ. וְתַנֵּי עֲלֵיהּ רִבִּי יוּדָה וְרִבִּי שִׁמְעוֹן אוֹמֵר יֵשׁ קִנְיָין לְגוֹי בְּאֶרֶץ יִשְׂרָאֵל לְפוֹטְרוֹ מִן הַמַּעֲשֵׂר. דְּלָא תִיסְבּוֹר מֵימַר תְּרֵיי כָּל־קֳבֵל תְּרֵיי אִינּוּן. לְפוּם כָּךְ צָרַךְ לוֹמַר הֲלָכָה כְּרִבִּי שִׁמְעוֹן.

Rebbi Judah ben Pazi in the name of Rebbi Hoshaiah: Practice follows Rebbi Simeon. Otherwise, we would say, between Rebbi Meïr and Rebbi Simeon, practice does not follow Rebbi Simeon[117]. But because it was stated: "Rebbi Simeon from Shezur said, once some produce that was *ṭevel* was mixed up with my produce. I asked Rebbi Ṭarphon, and he told me: Go and buy from a Gentile[118] and tithe for it." On that we have stated: "Rebbi Jehudah and Rebbi Simeon say, a Gentile may acquire real estate in the Land of Israel to free it from tithe." Lest you think that this case has two[119] opposed by two[120]. Therefore, he had to say that practice follows Rebbi Simeon.

117 In the Babli, *Eruvin* 46b, the question about whose opinion prevails remains unanswered. In rabbinic tradition (*Maḥzor Vitry* p. 490, see the sources quoted there, note ט), between R. Meïr and R. Simeon practice follows the one who is more restrictive. However, R. Asher ben Yeḥiel (*Roš*, *Abodah Zarah* 2, #34) holds that between R. Meïr and R. Simeon practice follows R. Simeon.

118 R. Ṭarphon also holds that any produce grown in the Holy Land is subject to heave and tithes. The Gentile cannot separate heave and tithes; even if he wants to follow the Jewish rules and donate his tithes to Jewish priests, his heave is no heave. Hence, produce grown by a Gentile is certainly untithed and can be used to tithe other produce.

119 R. Ṭarphon and R. Meïr, belonging to two separate generations.

120 R. Simeon and R. Jehudah in our

text, R. Simeon and R. Yose in the Babli. All three belong to the same generation. [One has to wonder why one tries to insist here on the status of R. Simeon since it is agreed that both R. Jehudah and R. Yose have precedence over R. Meïr (Babli *Erubin* 46b, Yerushalmi *Terumot* 3:1, fol. 42a, *Pesaḥim* 4:1, fol. 30b), and even if one agrees to count R. Jehudah with R. Meïr as in the Babli text, R. Yose has precedence over R. Jehudah (Babli *Erubin* 46b, Yerushalmi *Yebamot* 4:11, fol. 6a).]

וְעוֹד מִן הָדָא דְּאָמַר רִבִּי זְעִירָא אַבָּא אֲנַטוֹלִי זְבִין פֵּירֵי מִן דַּאֲרַמָּאי אֲתָא לְגַבֵּי דְּרִבִּי יוּדָה בֶּן לֵוִי שְׁלַח לִמְנַחֵם בְּרֵיהּ דִּיתַקֵּן לֵיהּ וִיהַב לֵיהּ מַעְשְׂרֵיהּ. מִי אֲתִי קָם עִימֵּיהּ רִבִּי יְהוֹשֻׁעַ בֶּן לֵוִי אֲמַר לֵיהּ מָאן יַעֲבִיד דָּא אֶלָּא (fol. 25a) אָבוּךְ. מְחַלְּפָה שִׁיטָּתֵיהּ דְּרִבִּי יְהוֹשֻׁעַ בֶּן לֵוִי. תַּמָּן הוּא אוֹמֵר הַלּוֹקֵחַ פֵּירוֹת תְּלוּשִׁין מִן הַגּוֹי מַפְרִישׁ תְּרוּמָה וּתְרוּמַת מַעֲשֵׂר מֵהֲלָכָה וְנוֹתְנָן לַשֵּׁבֶט וְנוֹטֵל דָּמִין מִן הַשֵּׁבֶט. וְהָכָא הוּא אָמַר הָכֵין. אָמַר רִבִּי אַבָּא בַּר זְמִינָא קוֹמֵי רִבִּי זְעִירָא רִבִּי סִימוֹן לֹא אָמַר כֵן אֶלָּא מִי אֲתִי קָם עִימֵּיהּ רִבִּי יְהוֹשֻׁעַ בֶּן לֵוִי אֲמַר לֵיהּ לֵית אִילֵּין דְּאָבוּךְ. וְאִיקְפִּיד רִבִּי זְעִירָא.

In addition, from the following: Rebbi Zeïra said, Abba the Anatolian bought produce from an Aramean[121]; he came before Rebbi Judah ben Levi[122] who sent his son Menaḥem to put it in order; he[123] gave him his tithes. When he returned, Rebbi Joshua ben Levi met him and said, who else but your father would do such a thing[124]? The arguments of Rebbi Joshua ben Levi are inverted. There, he says that he who buys loose produce from a Gentile, separates heave and heave of the tithe as a matter of practice, gives them to the tribe, and receives money from the tribe; and here he says so! Rebbi Abba bar Zamina said before Rebbi Zeïra, Rebbi Simon does not say so, but when he returned, Rebbi Joshua ben Levi met him and said, this does not belong to your father[125]. Rebbi Zeïra was offended.

121 In both Talmudim, "Aramean" means Gentile.

122 A contemporary of R. Joshua ben Levi. Since the story implies that he was a Levite who could receive tithes, "ben Levi" simply means "Levite." The same probably applies to R. Joshua ben Levi, and no relationship between R. Jehudah and R. Joshua is implied except for the fact that both were Levites.

123 Abba gave to Menahem.

124 To tithe produce grown and harvested by a Gentile. Hence, R. Joshua ben Levi must agree with R. Simeon, and the former is the great authority.

125 The tithes were given by a misunderstanding that they were regular tithes. Since R. Joshua ben Levi requires that the Levite pay for these tithes, they cannot become the property of R. Judah ben Levi unless Menaḥem paid for them. In this version, R. Joshua ben Levi is consistent.

רִבִּי אָחָא רִבִּי תַנְחוּם בַּר חִייָא בְּשֵׁם רִבִּי יְהוֹשֻׁעַ בֶּן לֵוִי שְׁלֹשָׁה הֵן שֶׁהֵן מְעַשְּׂרִין שֶׁלֹּא בִרְשׁוּת. זֶה שֶׁנִּתְעָרֵב טִבְלוֹ בְחוּלִין. וְזֶה שֶׁהוּא לוֹקֵחַ מִפְּסִיקִיָּה שֶׁל כּוּתִין. אָמַר רִבִּי זְעִירָא זֹאת אוֹמֶרֶת שֶׁאֵינוֹ נוֹטֵל דָּמִין מִן הַשֵּׁבֶט. אִם אָמַר אַתְּ שֶׁהוּא נוֹטֵל דָּמִין מִן הַשֵּׁבֶט הֲרֵי בִרְשׁוּת תָּרַם.

Rebbi Aḥa, Rebbi Tanḥum bar Ḥiyya in the name of Rebbi Joshua ben Levi, three[126] may tithe without permission: He whose *ṭevel* was mixed with profane produce[127]. And he who buys from the division of the Samaritans[128]. Rebbi Zeïra said, this implies that he does not take money from the tribe. If you say that he takes money from the tribe, he tithed with permission[129]!

126 The list contains only two entries. But since the application here is to show that R. Zeïra was rightly offended, the case of produce bought from Gentiles has to be added.

127 As noted before, since every Jewish farmer did give the first heave which may be given in a minimal amount, it is impossible to buy on the market Jewish produce that can be used to fix a mixture of profane and *ṭevel* produce. Hence, any farmer who

uses his own *ṭevel* produce to take care of his neighbor's problem, does his neighbor a great favor and we are justified in decreeing that the neighbor's consent is implied and he does not have to be asked beforehand. "Permission" in the text means consent by the owner of the produce.

128 Mishnah *Taäniot* 3:4 explains that in Temple times, in Judea everybody has to be believed in matters of ritual purity of wine and olive oil used in the Temple. This implies that in Galilee only *ḥaverim* are trustworthy. The reason is explained in Halakhah *Taäniot* 3:4 (fol. 79c), because "the division of Samaritans" separates Judea from Galilee and it is impossible to bring wine and olive oil in purity from Galilee to Judea (since Samaritans, like Gentiles, do not bury still-births in cemeteries but anywhere at roadsides, and one cannot exclude the possibility that one might step over such a grave which imparts the impurity of the dead to wine and oil.) [In the Babli (*Taänit* 25a), it is asserted that a strip of Gentile land separates Galilee from Judea.] The division of the Samaritans therefore is the region of Samaria inhabited exclusively by Samaritans and produce from there is certainly *ṭevel* in all respects. Anybody who removes heave from this produce and turns it into regular *demay* removes a hidden stumbling block from the unwary buyer.

129 If money was to be given to the owner of the produce for heave and the heave of the tithe, he would be happy if somebody else did the work for him practically without cost to him. Hence, this would have the status of tithing with the knowledge of the owner; R. Simon cannot be correct in his transmission of the tradition of R. Joshua ben Levi and the latter must hold that practice follows R. Simeon.

אָמַר רִבִּי יוֹחָנָן טַעְמָא דְּרִבִּי לְעָזָר כְּשֵׁם שֶׁעָשׂוּ פֵּירוֹת אֶרֶץ יִשְׂרָאֵל דְּמַאי אַחַר רוּבָּן אֵין תּוֹרְמִין וּמְעַשְּׂרִין מִזֶּה עַל זֶה. כָּךְ עָשָׂה פֵּירוֹת כּוּתִי וַדַּאי אַחַר רוּבָּן אֵין תּוֹרְמִין וְלֹא מְעַשְּׂרִין מִזֶּה עַל זֶה.

Rebbi Joḥanan said, the reason of Rebbi Eleazar[130]: Just as they declared the produce of the Land of Israel *demay* notwithstanding the majority[131] and one may not give heave or tithe from one for the other, so they declared the produce of Samaritans certain[132], notwithstanding the majority one may not give heave or tithe from one for the other.

130 Discussion of the statement of R. Eleazar in the Mishnah.

131 Since most of the *amē haärez̧* farmers did tithe, there would have been no need for *demay*. Now that there is *demay*, we have to worry that the bunch before us is not in order but all others, the greater part, are in order. Therefore, *demay* may not be tithed from one batch on the other.

132 Since Samaritans are not obligated by their rules to give heave and tithe from produce they sell, we declare all their produce to be certain that no heave or tithes were given, even though there might be a sizeable minority, in particular in regions where Jews and Samaritans farm together, who tithe. Because of that minority, we may not permit tithing from one farmer's produce for that of another.

(fol. 24b) **משנה י:** עָצִיץ נָקוּב הֲרֵי הוּא כְּאֶרֶץ. תָּרַם מִן הָאָרֶץ עַל עָצִיץ נָקוּב וּמֵעָצִיץ נָקוּב עַל הָאָרֶץ תְּרוּמָתוֹ תְרוּמָה. וּמִשֶּׁאֵינוֹ נָקוּב עַל הַנָּקוּב תְּרוּמָה וְיַחְזוֹר וְיִתְרוֹם. מִן הַנָּקוּב עַל שֶׁאֵינוֹ נָקוּב תְּרוּמָה וְלֹא תֵאָכֵל עַד שֶׁיּוֹצִיא עָלֶיהָ תְרוּמָה וּמַעְשְׂרוֹת. תָּרַם מִן הַדְּמַאי עַל הַדְּמַאי וּמִדְּמַאי עַל הַוַּדַּאי תְּרוּמָה וְיַחְזוֹר וְיִתְרוֹם. מִן הַוַּדַּאי עַל הַדְּמַאי תְּרוּמָה וְלֹא תֵאָכֵל עַד שֶׁיּוֹצִיא עָלֶיהָ תְרוּמָה וּמַעְשְׂרוֹת.

A flower pot with a hole is like earth[133]. If he gave heave from the earth for a pot with a hole, or from a flower pot with a hole for produce of the earth, his heave is heave. From a pot without a hole[134] for one with a hole it is heave[135], but he must take heave a second time. From a pot with a hole for one without a hole[136], it is heave that should not be eaten unless heave and tithes were taken for it[137]. If he took heave from one *demay* for other *demay*, or from *demay* for certain produce, it is heave, but he must take heave a second time[138]. From certain produce for *demay*[139], it is heave that should not be eaten unless heave and tithes were taken for it.

133 If a root can grow out through the hole, the soil in the pot is considered part of the earth and in all respects the produce grown in such a pot is produce grown on a field.

134 The produce of a pot without hole is not "produce of the field;" there is no Biblical commandment to give heave and tithes from such produce. The amount separated for heave, therefore, is not heave in Biblical law; only the rabbis ordered that heave and tithes should be given also from produce not grown on the earth (*Kilaim* 7:6, fol. 31a.) But since it is not heave from the Biblical point of view, heave must be taken a second time from the produce subject to heave.

135 However, it does not create *dema'* (Tosephta *Demay* 5:25, Yerushalmi *Kilaim* 7:6).

136 Since the pot without a hole cannot cause heave to be given by Biblical law, the "heave" still is *ṭevel* and heave and tithes must be removed. The rest should be treated as heave by rabbinical decree, as in the previous case.

137 In Babli *Yebamot* 89b, it says "heave and tithes from another place," considering it similar to *dema'*. This definitely is not the position of the Yerushalmi.

138 Since we do not know whether the produce from which heave was taken was already tithed or not.

139 Since in the majority of cases *demay* was tithed, the heave taken would remain *ṭevel*. Hence, it must be treated as if it were certain *ṭevel*.

(fol. 25a) **הלכה י:** רִבִּי בּוּן בַּר חִייָא בְשֵׁם רִבִּי זְעִירָא עָצִיץ עָשׂוּ אוֹתוֹ סָפֵק. וְהָתַנֵּינָן עָצִיץ נָקוּב מְקַדֵּשׁ בְּכֶרֶם וְשֶׁאֵינוֹ נָקוּב אֵינוֹ מְקַדֵּשׁ בְּכֶרֶם מִסָּפֵק.

Halakhah 10: Rebbi Abun bar Ḥiyya in the name of Rebbi Zeïra: They declared a pot[140] to be of doubtful status. But did we not state: "A pot with a hole sanctifies in the vineyard[141], a pot without a hole does not sanctify in the vineyard[142]." Because of doubt[143].

140 A pot without a hole, since a pot with a hole is not doubtful at all.

141 Mishnah *Kilaim* 7:8. The language is from *Deut.* 22:9: "Do not sow two kinds in your vineyard, lest the fullness of the seeds that you are sowing together with the yield of the vineyard be sanctified." Sanctified here means that it becomes like dedicated sacrifice, forbidden for all use; קרבן "sacrifice" has the same meaning in non-sacrificial context (Mishnah *Nedarim 1:2, Matthew* 15:5).

142 The Mishnah implies that a pot without hole, put in the earth in a vineyard, certainly is not considered growing in the vineyard.

143 The Mishnah expresses the Biblical law, but because of doubt there is still a rabbinic prohibition to grow grain in a pot without holes in a vineyard (Maimonides *Kilaim* 5:16).

כְּמָה דְתֵימַר מִן הַוַּדַּאי עַל הַדְּמַאי תְּרוּמָה וְלֹא תֵיאָכֵל עַד שֶׁיּוֹצִיא עָלֶיהָ תְרוּמָה וּמַעְשְׂרוֹת. וְאָמַר מִן הַדְּמַאי עַל הַדְּמַאי כֵן. רִבִּי בּוּן בַּר חִיָּיא בְּשֵׁם רִבִּי שְׁמוּאֵל בַּר רַב יִצְחָק זֹאת אוֹמֶרֶת סְפֵק דִּימּוּעַ כִּסְפֵק תְּרוּמַת מַעֲשֵׂר שֶׁל דְּמַאי פָּטוּר מִן הַוַּדַּאי.

Just as you say, "from certain produce for *demay*, it is heave that should not be eaten unless heave and tithes were taken for it," should one say so also for "from one *demay* for other *demay*?[144]" Rebbi Abun bar Ḥiyya in the name of Rebbi Samuel bar Rav Isaac, this means that a case of doubtful *dema'* is like a case of doubt about heave of the tithe from *demay*; it is free from the rules of certain produce[145].

144 Since *demay* probably is in order, why should the two cases have different rules?

145 We do not know whether the produce is *dema'*, containing the forbidden heave of the tithe. Here all the leniencies of *demay* given in the first two chapters do apply.

המקבל פרק ששי

(fol. 25a) **משנה א**: הַמְקַבֵּל שָׂדֶה מִיִּשְׂרָאֵל מִן הַנָּכְרִי מִן הַכּוּתִי חוֹלֵק בִּפְנֵיהֶן. הַחוֹכֵר שָׂדֶה מִיִּשְׂרָאֵל תּוֹרֵם וְנוֹתֵן לוֹ. רִבִּי יְהוּדָה אוֹמֵר אֵימָתַי בִּזְמַן שֶׁנָּתַן לוֹ מֵאוֹתָהּ הַשָּׂדֶה וּמֵאוֹתוֹ הַמִּין. אֲבָל אִם נָתַן לוֹ מִשָּׂדֶה אַחֶרֶת אוֹ מִמִּין אַחֵר מְעַשֵּׂר וְנוֹתֵן לוֹ.

Mishnah 1: He who receives a field as sharecropper from a Jew, a Gentile, or a Samaritan, distributes in their presence[1]. He who leases[2] a field from a Jew separates heave and delivers to him. Rebbi Jehudah says, when is that? When he gives from that field and from that kind. But if he gives from another field or from another kind[3], he must tithe and give him.

1 The sharecropper does not have to give heave before taking his own share.

2 The contract calls for a fixed payment in kind independent of the actual yield. In that case, we do not allow anybody to liquidate his debts from his harvest without separating heave. But in a bid of the rabbis to attract Jewish farmers, the lessee is not required to tithe before he pays his rent. The lessor knows that he has to tithe.

3 In that case, the payment is simply a financial transaction and does not enjoy special status.

הלכה א: אָמַר רִבִּי יוֹחָנָן זוּ דִבְרֵי רַבָּן שִׁמְעוֹן בֶּן גַּמְלִיאֵל. אֲבָל דִּבְרֵי חֲכָמִים מִיִּשְׂרָאֵל חוֹלֵק מִן הַגּוֹי תּוֹרֵם. וְתַנֵּי כֵן הַחוֹכֵר שָׂדֶה מִן הַגּוֹי תּוֹרֵם וְנוֹתֵן לוֹ. אָמַר רַבָּן שִׁמְעוֹן בֶּן גַּמְלִיאֵל מַה אִם יִרְצֶה הַגּוֹי הַזֶּה שֶׁלֹּא לִתְרוֹם פֵּירוֹתָיו אֵינִי רַשַּׁאי אֶלָּא חוֹלֵק וּמֵנִיחַ לְפָנָיו.

Halakhah 1: Rebbi Johanan said, these are the words of Rabban Simeon ben Gamliel. But the words of the Sages are: From a Jew, he splits; from a Gentile, he gives heave. We have stated[4]: "He who leases a field from a Gentile separates heave and then gives to him. Rabban Simeon ben Gamliel said: If the Gentile does not wish to give heave, I have no right to it[5], but he[6] distributes and puts it before him."

4 Tosephta *Demay* 6:1: "He who receives a field as sharecropper from a Gentile tithes and gives to him. Rabban Simeon ben Gamliel said, what if the Gentile does not want to tithe his produce? But he distributes and gives before him." It is clear that the Yerushalmi does not speak about a lease for a fixed amount, because then the Gentile would not be interested in what the Jewish tenant does, but about a sharecropper who will diminish the landlord's part if he gives heave or tithes prior to distribution.

5 Since the Gentile is the owner and one may not give heave without authorization by the owner, it is impossible in Jewish law to give heave for the unwilling Gentile. Hence, the sharecropper may not give heave before he divides up the harvest.

6 The farmer distributes the harvest untithed in the presence of the landlord.

רִבִּי זְעִירָא רִבִּי יוֹחָנָן בְּשֵׁם רִבִּי יַנַּאי אַתֶּם גַּם אַתֶּם לְרַבּוֹת שְׁלוּחֲכֶם. מַה אַתֶּם בְּנֵי בְרִית אַף שְׁלוּחֲכֶם בְּנֵי בְרִית. אַתֶּם עוֹשִׂין שָׁלִיחַ וְאֵין הַגּוֹי עוֹשֶׂה שָׁלִיחַ. רִבִּי יָסָא סָבַר מֵימַר אֵין הַגּוֹי עוֹשֶׂה שָׁלִיחַ בְּיַד אַחֵר חֲבֵירוֹ הָא בְיִשְׂרָאֵל עוֹשֶׂה. אָמַר רִבִּי זְעִירָא וּמִינָהּ אַתֶּם[7] עוֹשִׂין שָׁלִיחַ וְלֹא בְיִשְׂרָאֵל. וְדִכְווָתָהּ אֵין הַגּוֹי עוֹשֶׂה שָׁלִיחַ אֲפִילוּ בְיִשְׂרָאֵל. הָתִיב רַב הוֹשַׁעְיָא וְהָא מַתְנִיתָא מְסַיְּיעָא לְרִבִּי יוֹחָנָן. אָמַר רַבָּן שִׁמְעוֹן בֶּן גַּמְלִיאֵל מַה אִם יִרְצֶה הַגּוֹי הַזֶּה שֶׁלֹּא לִתְרוֹם פֵּירוֹתָיו אֵינוֹ תוֹרֵם. אָמַר רִבִּי אַבָּא בְּמַאֲמִין עַל יָדָיו.

Rebbi Zeïra, Rebbi Johanan in the name of Rebbi Yannai (*Num*. 18:28): "You, also you," to include your plenipotentiary[8]. Just as you are in the covenant, so your plenipotentiary must be in the covenant. You appoint a plenipotentiary, the Gentile may not. Rebbi Yasa wanted to say that the Gentile cannot appoint as plenipotentiary another Gentile, but he can appoint a Jew. Rebbi Zeïra said, from the *baraita* itself: You appoint a plenipotentiary, does that not mean Jews? Similarly, the Gentile cannot appoint a plenipotentiary, not even a Jew. Rav Hoshaia objects: Does the *baraita* support Rebbi Joḥanan? "Rabban Simeon ben Gamliel said: If the Gentile does not wish to give heave from his produce, he cannot give heave[9]." Rebbi Abba said, if he confirms it after him[10].

7 Reading of the text in *Terumot* 1:1, fol. 40c. The reading here is אותן "they".

8 "So *you* shall lift, *also you*, the heave of the Eternal." The expression *also you* is superfluous; since "also" always means an addition, "also you" means a stand-in. Since he is titled "also you", it follows that he takes the place of the person authorizing him. The same explanation is given in *Terumot* 1:1 (fol. 40b/c), Babli *Qiddušin* 41b, *Baba Meẓia'* 22a.

9 In the opinion of Rabban Simeon ben Gamliel the Gentile cannot appoint a Jew as plenipotentiary for Jewish ritual.

10 This parallels the position of R. Isaac in Tosephta *Terumot* 1:15: "If a Gentile separated heave for a Jew, even with his permission, it is not heave. . . . Rebbi Isaac says, if a Gentile separated heave for a Jew and the owner confirms his action, it is heave." For a Jew, once permission is given, it does not require an additional action on the part of the owner. But the Gentile's action is not valid unless it is explicitly confirmed by the Jewish owner afterwards; the Gentile does the mechanical work and the Jew gives the separated amount the status of heave.

הַחוֹכֵר בְּפֵירוֹת הַשּׂוֹכֵר בְּמָעוֹת הַמְקַבֵּל לְמֶחֱצָה לִשְׁלִישׁ וְלִרְבִיעַ.

"'He who leases,' means he pays in produce, 'he who rents,' means he pays money, 'he who receives,' as sharecropper for a half, a third, or a quarter[11]."

11 The first two definitions are also found in Tosephta *Demay* 6:2.

עַד כְּדוֹן נָכְרִי כּוּתִי. נִישְׁמְעִינָהּ מִן הָדָא הַנּוֹתֵן שָׂדֵהוּ בְקַבָּלָה לְגוֹי וּלְכוּתִי וּלְמִי שֶׁאֵינוֹ נֶאֱמָן עַל הַמַּעְשְׂרוֹת עַד שֶׁלֹּא בָאוּ לְעוֹנַת הַמַּעְשְׂרוֹת אֵינוֹ צָרִיךְ לְעַשֵּׂר עַל יָדָיו מִשֶּׁבָּאוּ לְעוֹנַת הַמַּעְשְׂרוֹת צָרִיךְ לְעַשֵּׂר עַל יָדָיו. עַד כְּדוֹן בְּמָקוֹם שֶׁיִּשְׂרָאֵל מְצוּיִין. בְּמָקוֹם שֶׁאֵין יִשְׂרָאֵל מְצוּיִין. נִישְׁמְעִינָהּ מִן הָדָא רִבִּי סִימוֹן הָיוּ לוֹ שָׂדוֹת בְּהַר הַמֶּלֶךְ. שָׁאַל לְרִבִּי יוֹחָנָן אָמַר לֵיהּ (fol. 25b) יוֹבִירוּ וְאַל תַּשְׂכְּרֵם לְגוֹי. שָׁאַל לְרִבִּי יְהוֹשֻׁעַ בֶּן לֵוִי וְשָׁרָא לֵיהּ. סָבַר רִבִּי יְהוֹשֻׁעַ בֶּן לֵוִי מָקוֹם שֶׁאֵין יִשְׂרָאֵל מְצוּיִין כְּהָדָא סוּרְיָא. דְּהָדָא סוּרְיָא נִישְׁמְעִינָהּ מִן הָדָא רִבִּי חַגַּיי נְחַת לְחָמֶץ אֲתוֹן שָׁאֲלוֹן לֵיהּ אִילֵּין דְּבֵי עַשְׁתּוֹר בְּגִין דְּלֵית יִשְׂרָאֵל שְׁכִיחֵי וַאֲנָן מוֹגְרִין לְעַמִּים צְרִיכִין לְעַשֵּׂר אֲנָן עַל יְדֵיהוֹן. שְׁלַח שָׁאַל לְרִבִּי זְעִירָא. שָׁאַל רִבִּי זְעִירָא לְרִבִּי אִימִּי. אָמַר לֵיהּ אֵינוֹ צָרִיךְ לְעַשֵּׂר עַל יְדֵיהֶן. מִינָהּ אַתְּ שְׁמַע לְהַשְׂכִּיר כְּרִבִּי יוֹסֵי. וְעוֹד מִן הָדָא דְּאָמַר רִבִּי חֲנִינָא בְּרֵיהּ דְּרִבִּי אַבָּהוּ. אַבָּא הֲוָה לֵיהּ עוּבְדָּא שְׁלַח שָׁאַל לְרִבִּי חִיָּא וּלְרִבִּי יָסָא וּלְרִבִּי אִימִּי וְהוֹרוּן לֵיהּ לְהַשְׂכִּיר כְּרִבִּי יוֹסֵי הָא לְעַשֵּׂר עַל יְדֵיהֶן אֵינָן מְעַשְּׂרִין עַל יְדֵיהֶן.

So far a Gentile; a Samaritan? Let us hear from the following[12]: "He who gives a field to a Gentile sharecropper, a Samaritan, or somebody who is not trusted with tithes, before they come to the time of tithes[13] he does not have to tithe for him; after they come to the time of tithes he has to tithe for him." That is, at a place where Jews are present. At a place where no Jews are available[14]? Let us hear from the following: Rebbi Simon had fields at King's Mountain[15]. He asked Rebbi Joḥanan, who told him: Let them lie fallow, but do not lease them to a Gentile. He asked Rebbi Joshua ben Levi who permitted it to him. Rebbi Joshua ben Levi is of the opinion that a place where no Jews are available has the status of Syria[16]. For Syria, we hear from the following: Rebbi Ḥaggai descended into Homs. The family Astor asked him: Since no Jews are available here, we lease to Gentiles; do we have to tithe for them? He sent and asked Rebbi Zeïra. Rebbi Zeïra asked Rebbi Immi, who told him that they did not have to tithe. From this you hear that the rules of leasing follow Rebbi Yose[17]. Also from the following: Rebbi Ḥanina, the son of Rebbi Abbahu, said my father had a case; he sent and asked Rebbi Ḥiyya, Rebbi Yasa, and Rebbi Immi, and they taught him that the rules of leasing follow Rebbi Yose; hence, as far as tithing for them is concerned, they[18] do not tithe for them.

12 Tosephta *Demay* 7:25: "He who gives a field to a Gentile sharecropper, a Samaritan, or to somebody who is not trusted with tithes, even though one is not permitted to do so, he has to tithe for him." Here the obligation to tithe seems to be a kind of fine imposed upon someone who does not let his field to a trusted Jew. If it is imposed on someone who gives his field to a sharecropper, *a fortiori* on him who leases his field to a Gentile.

13 When the produce is prepared to be stored, the obligation of tithes begins.

14 There is no reason to impose a fine if no qualified Jewish farmers are available.

15 As noted earlier, in Amoraic times no Jews were left on King's Mountain. This entire piece also appears in *Avodah Zarah* 1:9, fol. 40b.

16 Cf. *Peah* Chapter 7, Note 119. The argument implies that Neḥemiah's covenant applies only to those regions of the Holy Land outside the immediate neighborhood of Jerusalem actually settled by Jews. The territory subject to tithes and Sabbatical therefore is variable over time [S. Klein, HUCA 5(1928) 197-260.]

17 Mishnah *Avodah Zarah* 1:9: "One does not lease houses in Israel to Gentiles, not to mention fields. In Syria one leases to them houses but not fields, and outside the Land one sells them houses and leases fields to them. These are the words of Rebbi Meïr. Rebbi Yose says, even in the Land of Israel one does lease houses to them and in Syria one sells to them houses and leases fields to them. Outside the Land one sells both to them." Since one may lease fields to Gentiles, the act of leasing does not remove a field from the duty of tithes. Hence, there is no such duty on the field itself and the Gentile's part does not have to be tithed by the Jewish landlord. The Yerushalmi's decision is repeated in Babli *Avodah Zarah* 21a.

18 The landlords do not have to tithe for their exempt tenants. (R. Ḥiyya here is R. Ḥiyya bar Abba.)

קִיבֵּל מִמֶּנּוּ שָׂדֶה לִקְצוֹר בְּחִיטִּים עֲנָבִים לִבְצוֹר בְּיַיִן זֵיתִם לִמְסוֹק בְּשֶׁמֶן מְעַשֵּׂר וְנוֹתֵן לוֹ. אִיתָא חֲמִי עַד שֶׁלֹּא זָרַע תּוֹרֵם מִשֶּׁזָּרַע מְעַשֵּׂר. אָמַר רִבִּי חִינְנָא תִּיקְּנוּ בִמְקַבֵּל שֶׁלֹּא תָבוּר אֶרֶץ יִשְׂרָאֵל. בְּרַם הָכָא זְרוּעָה הִיא.

"If[19] he received a field to harvest for wheat[20], grapes to harvest for wine, olives to harvest for oil, he tithes before he delivers." Come and see: Before he sows, he separates heave[21]; after it was sown, he tithes? Rebbi Ḥinena said, they made a special decree for the sharecropper, so that the Land of Israel should not lie fallow. But here it is already sown.

19 Tosephta *Demay* 1:6. The rule applies both to the sharecropper and to the lessee. Since the preceding Tosephta states the rules for sharecropper and lessee of a Jewish landlord, it follows that this Tosephta (and the one discussed in the following paragraph) deal with a Gentile landlord, which fits in the context of the present Halakhah.

20 That the agricultural worker takes his wages in the form of the finished product: threshed wheat grain, wine, or oil. This is after the obligation of tithes started.

21 At most, the lessee separates heave; the sharecropper does not give anything before splitting with the owner. This shows that the Tosephta speaks both of sharecropper and lessee.

קִיבֵּל מִמֶּנּוּ שָׂדֶה לִקְצוֹר בְּשַׁחֲרֵי שִׁבּוֹלִים[22] עֲנָבִים לִבְצוֹר בְּסַלֵּי עֲנָבִים זֵיתִם לִמְסוֹק בְּסַלֵּי זֵיתִים מֵנִיחַ כְּמוֹת שֶׁהֵן. הָא מֵאוֹתָהּ הַמִּין שֶׁלֹּא מֵאוֹתָהּ הַשָּׂדֶה מֵאוֹתָהּ הַשָּׂדֶה שֶׁלֹּא מֵאוֹתוֹ הַמִּין מְעַשֵּׂר וְנוֹתֵן לוֹ. תַּנֵּי רִבִּי חִייָא מֵאוֹתָהּ הַשָּׂדֶה בֵּין מֵאוֹתוֹ הַמִּין בֵּין מִמִּין אַחֵר תּוֹרֵם וְנוֹתֵן לוֹ. שָׂדֶה אַחֶרֶת בֵּין מֵאוֹתוֹ הַמִּין בֵּין מִמִּין אַחֵר מְעַשֵּׂר וְנוֹתֵן לוֹ. מַתְנִיתָא כְּרַבָּן שִׁמְעוֹן בֶּן גַּמְלִיאֵל. מַה דְתַנֵּי רִבִּי חִייָא כַּחֲכָמִים וּפְלִיגָא. אֲתִינָן מַתְנֵי מַתְנִיתִין בְּמָקוֹם פְּלוֹנִי שֶׁלֹּא[23] נָהֲגוּ שֶׁעוֹרִין כִּפְלַיִם כְּחִיטִּים. מַה דְתַנֵּי רִבִּי חִייָה בְּמָקוֹם שֶׁנָּהֲגוּ שֶׁעוֹרִין כִּפְלַיִם כְּחִיטִּים.

"If[24] he received a field to harvest for early ears, grapes to harvest for baskets of grapes, olives to harvest for baskets of olives, he delivers as is."

That means, if (he is paid) in the same kind; but from another field, or from that field but not from the same kind, he must tithe before he delivers. Rebbi Ḥiyya stated[25]: "From the same field, whether it be the same kind or another kind, he separates heave and delivers. From another field, whether it be the same kind or another kind, he tithes and delivers." The Mishnah follows Rabban Simeon ben Gamliel; what Rebbi Ḥiyya stated follows the Sages, and they disagree. We also may come and state that the Mishnah deals with some place where barley usually does not yield twice as much as wheat[26]; what Rebbi Ḥiyya stated refers to a place where barley usually yields twice as much as wheat.

22 Reading of the Rome ms. Text of Venice print: קבל ממנו שדה לקצור בשחרי

23 Reading of the Rome ms. In *Baba Meẓia'* 9:8, R. La's readings is: אין

24 Tosephta *Demay* 1:6. In this case, the payment is given before any obligation of heave and tithes was incurred.

25 This is the opinion of the Sages in Tosephta *Demay* 1:5.

26 This refers to another disagreement between the Sages and Rabban Simeon ben Gamliel (*Baba Meẓia'* 9:8): "He who receives a field to sow it with barley should not sow it with wheat; wheat, he may sow it with barley. Rabban Simeon ben Gamliel forbids it." In the opinion of the Yerushalmi, this depends on the relative cash value of the crops raised; if barley yields enough to offset its cheaper price relative to wheat, the lessee is permitted to change the crop. "The Mishnah" in our text means the opinion of Rabban Simeon ben Gamliel, representing actual practice. [In the opinion of the Babli (*Baba Meẓia'* 106b), wheat needs a more frequent crop rotation and lying fallow than barley and the landlord can always object.] Tosephta *Baba Meẓia'* 9:32, dealing with the subject matter of Mishnah 9:8, does not mention the point of view of Rabban Simeon ben Gamliel.

(fol. 25a) **משנה ב**: הַחוֹכֵר שָׂדֶה מִן הַנָּכְרִי מְעַשֵּׂר וְנוֹתֵן לוֹ. רִבִּי יְהוּדָה אוֹמֵר אַף הַמְקַבֵּל שְׂדֵי אֲבוֹתָיו מִן הַגּוֹי מְעַשֵּׂר וְנוֹתֵן לוֹ.

Mishnah 2: He who leases a field from a Gentile tithes and delivers to him. Rebbi Jehudah says, also he who is a sharecropper for a Gentile on a field that used to belong to his family tithes and delivers to him[27].

27 As an incentive to make it worthwhile for him to buy back the property from the Gentile.

(fol. 25b) **הלכה ב**: הָכָא אַתְּ אָמַר תּוֹרֵם וְנוֹתֵן לוֹ. וְכָא אַתְּ אָמַר מְעַשֵּׂר וְנוֹתֵן לוֹ. חֲבֵרַייָא בְשֵׁם רִבִּי יוֹחָנָן קָנְסוּ חֲכָמִים בְּחוֹכֵר מִן הַגּוֹיִם וְלֹא קָנְסוּ בְּחוֹכֵר מִיִּשְׂרָאֵל. רִבִּי לָא בְשֵׁם רִבִּי יוֹחָנָן תָּפְשָׂה מִידַּת הַדִּין בְּחוֹכֵר מִן הַגּוֹי וְלֹא תָפְשָׂה בְּחוֹכֵר מִיִּשְׂרָאֵל.

Halakhah 2: There[28] you say, he separates heave and delivers to him. Here you say, he tithes and delivers to him. The colleagues in the name of Rebbi Joḥanan: The Sages fined the one who leases from a Gentile[29] but they did not fine the one who leases from a Jew. Rebbi La in the name of Rebbi Joḥanan: The strict law[30] applies to him who leases from a Gentile but not to him who leases from a Jew.

28 In Mishnah 1, dealing with leases of agricultural land from a Jewish landlord.

29 To increase the cost of farming the Gentile's land, so that people would refrain from leasing and, if all landless farmers are Jews, to force the Gentile to sell out to a Jew.

30 That a *ḥaver*, or any observant Jew, should not deliver any produce not completely tithed to a third person.

מַתְנִיתָא מְסַייְעָא לְדֵין וּמַתְנִיתָא מְסַייְעָא לְדֵין. מַתְנִיתָא מְסַייְעָא לַחֲבֵרַייָא הַחוֹכֵר שָׂדֶה מִן הַגּוֹי תּוֹרֵם וְנוֹתֵן לוֹ. רִבִּי מֵאִיר אוֹמֵר מְעַשֵּׂר וְנוֹתֵן לוֹ הָא רַבָּנִין אָמְרִין קָנְסוּ חֲכָמִים בְּחוֹכֵר מִן הַגּוֹי. וְלֹא קָנְסוּ חֲכָמִים בְּחוֹכֵר מִיִּשְׂרָאֵל. וְיֵשׁ קְנָס בְּיִשְׂרָאֵל. אֶלָּא הָא הָכֵנִי רַבָּנִין אָמְרֵי תָּפְשָׂה מִידַּת הַדִּין בְּחוֹכֵר

מִיִּשְׂרָאֵל. וְרִבִּי מֵאִיר אוֹמֵר אֵין תֶּפְשָׂה מִידַּת הַדִּין בְּחוֹכֵר מִיִּשְׂרָאֵל. מַתְנִיתָא מְסַייְעָא לְרִבִּי לָא הַחוֹכֵר שָׂדֶה מִן הַגּוֹי מְעַשֵּׂר וְנוֹתֵן לוֹ. רִבִּי שִׁמְעוֹן אוֹמֵר תּוֹרֵם וְנוֹתֵן לוֹ. הָא רַבָּנִין אָמְרִין תֶּפְשָׂה מִידַּת הַדִּין בְּחוֹכֵר מִן הַגּוֹי וְלֹא תֶּפְשָׂה מִידַּת הַדִּין בְּחוֹכֵר מִיִּשְׂרָאֵל. רִבִּי שִׁמְעוֹן אוֹמֵר לֹא תֶּפְשָׂה מִידַּת הַדִּין בְּחוֹכֵר מִן הַגּוֹי. אִית בַּר נַשׁ דְּיֵימַר הָדָא מִילְתָא. אֶלָּא הָכֵינִי קָנְסוּ חֲכָמִים בְּחוֹכֵר מִן הַגּוֹי וְלֹא קָנְסוּ חֲכָמִים בְּחוֹכֵר מִיִּשְׂרָאֵל. רִבִּי שִׁמְעוֹן אוֹמֵר לֹא קָנְסוּ חֲכָמִים בְּחוֹכֵר מִן הַגּוֹי לְפִיכָךְ אִם חָזַר הַגּוֹי וְנִתְגַּייֵר אוֹ שֶׁמְּכָרָן לְיִשְׂרָאֵל אַחֵר מוּתָּר.

One *baraita* supports one and one *baraita* supports the other. One *baraita*[31] supports the colleagues. "He who leases a field from a Gentile separates heave and delivers to him. Rebbi Meïr says, he tithes and delivers to him." Could the rabbis say, the Sages fined him who leases from a Gentile but they did not fine him who leases from a Jew? How can a fine apply to leasing from a Jew? But so it is: The rabbis say, the strict law[32] applies to him who leases from a Jew, but Rebbi Meïr said, the strict law[33] does not apply to him who leases from a Jew. One *baraita* supports Rebbi La: "He[34] who leases a field from a Gentile tithes and delivers to him. Rebbi Simeon says, he separates heave and delivers to him." Could the rabbis say, the strict law applies to him who leases from a Gentile, but the strict law does not apply to him who leases from a Jew; Rebbi Simeon said, the strict law does not apply to him who leases from a Gentile? Can anybody make such a statement[35]? But so it is, the Sages fined him who leases from a Gentile but they did not fine him who leases from a Jew. Rebbi Simeon said, the Sages did not fine him who leases from a Gentile; hence, if the Gentile converted or sold to another Jew, it is permitted[36].

31 Tosephta *Demay* 5:2: "He who leases a field from a Gentile must tithe before delivering to him. Hence, if the lessee bought from a Gentile, or the Gentile sold his crop to another Jew, it is *demay*." The anonymous author of the Tosephta is R. Meïr in our *baraita*.

32 It is the law that only heave but no tithe has to be given as a precaution since the grain delivered by the lessee never was stored by him and, therefore, never was subject to tithes.

33 His strict law is that nobody may deliver produce into another's hand if that produce is not fully put in order.

34 Tosephta *Demay* 5:2: "He who splits the yield of a field with a Gentile tithes before delivering the Gentile's part. Rebbi Simeon says, he separates heave and delivers the Gentile's part. Hence, if the Gentile converted or sold to another Jew, he has to tithe before delivering." (R. S. Liebermann explains that Tosephta as dealing with the problem of retroactive clarification, ברירה, but that explanation is impossible since heave and tithes are due only at storage time, see מנחת ביכורים *ad loc.* In general, the commentaries on the entire paragraph rely too much on unsupported emendations to be taken seriously.)

35 A law is a law and cannot be abrogated for a special class of people.

36 It is retroactively permitted to the Jew to have leased the land from a Gentile when the Gentile sold his property to another Jew, since finally it again became Jewish land. Rebbi Simeon prefers to have the Gentiles convert with their land instead of driving them off by artificial obstacles.

מָאן דְּאָמַר תַּקָּנָה נִיחָא. מָאן דְּאָמַר קָנְסוּ בְיָדוֹ אָמַר רִבִּי יוֹחָנָן מִן הַמַּסִּיקִין שָׁנוּ מִתּוֹךְ שֶׁאַתְּ אָמַר לוֹ כֵן אַף הוּא דוֹחֵק עַצְמוֹ וּפוֹדֶה אוֹתָהּ.

Him[37] who says that the law applies, one can understand. He who says, they fined[38]? Rebbi Joḥanan said, one has stated this only in the case of oppressors. Since you say so to him, he exerts himself and buys the land back.

37 Here starts the discussion of the rule of R. Jehudah, who makes the situation of the sharecropper on his ancestral land worse than that of any other sharecropper.

38 Why should he be fined? R.

Joḥanan explains that the Gentile got the land not by paying for it but by expropriation of the Jew. In that case, the Jew should be pushed to ask for help from his fellow Jews to buy back his land. The statement of R. Joḥanan is quoted as a *baraita* in the Babli (*Baba Meẓia* 101a), with מציק instead of מסיק (identical sounds in Galilean dialect; Babylonian spelling as a rule is more historically correct.)

(fol. 25a) **משנה ג**: כֹּהֵן וְלֵוִי שֶׁקִּיבְּלוּ שָׂדֶה מִיִּשְׂרָאֵל כְּשֵׁם שֶׁחוֹלְקִין בְּחוּלִין כֵּן חוֹלְקִין בִּתְרוּמָה. רַבִּי אֱלִיעֶזֶר אוֹמֵר הַמַּעֲשֵׂר שֶׁלָּהֶן שֶׁעַל מְנָת כֵּן בָּאוּ.

Mishnah 3: A Cohen or a Levite who received a field (as sharecroppers) share in the tithe[39] in the same proportion as they share in a profane yield. Rebbi Eliezer says, the tithe[40] is theirs because they came because of it.

39 Cohen and Levite who are farmers are required to separate heave and tithe like everybody else. If they are the owners they may donate the sanctified parts to themselves.

40 The Cohen gets all the heave from this field and the Levite all the tithe since they expect it for their work.

(fol. 25b) **הלכה ג**: מְתִיבִין רַבָּנִין לְרַבִּי אֱלִיעֶזֶר בְּמָה קָנוּ. אָמַר לָהֶן אֵין אַתֶּם מוֹדִין לִי שֶׁאִם הִתְנוּ בֵּינֵיהֶן שֶׁהֵן חוֹלְקִין בְּמַעְשְׂרוֹת[41]. אֲפִילוּ הִתְנוּ בְּמָה קָנוּ. סְתָמוֹ נַעֲשֶׂה כְּאוֹמֵר תְּלוֹשׁ מִן הַקַּרְקַע הַזֶּה שֶׁתִּיקְנוּ לָךְ מַעְשְׂרוֹתָיו. אָמַר לֵיהּ אוֹפְנָא לֵית לוֹן אוֹפְנָא לֵית לִסְתָמָא נַעֲשֶׂה כְּאוֹמֵר תְּלוֹשׁ מִן הַקַּרְקַע הַזֶּה שֶׁיִּקַּח לָךְ אֶחָד מֵעֲשָׂרָה שֶׁבּוֹ.

Halakhah 3: The rabbis object to Rebbi Eliezer: How did they acquire[42]? He said to them, do you not agree with me that if they agreed[43] among themselves, tithes go to the workers? Even if they made a condition, how did they acquire? If there is nothing said, it is as if somebody said: Harvest from this land so that its tithes should be yours[44]. They said to him, there is no stipulation here; if nothing is said there is no stipulation. It is[45] as if he said, harvest this land on condition that you take one tenth for yourselves.

41 Reading of R. Simson: שהמעשרות שלהן.

42 If the landlord must give his heave to the tenant, there must be a legal reason why he has lost his right to give it to any Cohen he prefers (the usual example being that of a landlord whose daughter married a Cohen and who wants to give all his heave to his grandson the Cohen.)

43 In the sharecropping contract. In that case, the act which validates the contract also validates the stipulation. A Tosephta (*Demay* 7:1) authorizes that kind of stipulation.

44 This is the end of R. Eliezer's argument.

45 If there is a stipulation, it is a simple contract of payment for work done but not one for heave since the Cohen is not permitted to work for heave. Hence, there must be a contract for this to work.

תַּנֵּי כֹּהֵן מִכֹּהֵן לֵוִי מִלֵּוִי יִשְׂרָאֵל מִיִּשְׂרָאֵל חוֹלְקִין לְמַעְשְׂרוֹת. לְמִי נִצְרְכָה לְרִבִּי אֱלִיעֶזֶר אַף אַל גַּו דְּרִבִּי לִיעֶזֶר אוֹמֵר מַעֲשֵׂר[46] שֶׁלָּהֶן עַל מְנַת כֵּן בָּאוּ. מוֹדֵי הוּא הָכָא שֶׁהֵן חוֹלְקִין בְּמַעְשְׂרוֹת.

It was stated[47]: "A Cohen from a Cohen, a Levite from a Levite, an Israel[47] from an Israel, split the tithes." Who needs this statement? Rebbi Eliezer; even though Rebbi Eliezer says that the tithe is theirs because they came because of it, here he agrees that they divide up the tithes.

46 Reading of Rome ms. Venice: מחעשר.

47 Tosephta *Demay* 7:1: "An Israel (a Jew who is neither Cohen nor Levite) who received (as sharecropper) a field from an Israel, a Cohen from a Cohen, a Levite from a Levite, divide among themselves."

יִשְׂרָאֵל שֶׁקִּיבֵּל שָׂדֶה מִכֹּהֵן אָמַר לוֹ עַל מְנָת שֶׁיְּהוּ הַמַּעְשְׂרוֹת שֶׁלִּי אוֹ שֶׁלָּךְ אוֹ שֶׁלִּי וְשֶׁלָּךְ מוּתָּר. כֹּהֵן שֶׁקִּיבֵּל שָׂדֶה מִיִּשְׂרָאֵל אָמַר לוֹ עַל מְנָת שֶׁיְּהוּ הַמַּעְשְׂרוֹת שֶׁלִּי מוּתָּר. שֶׁלָּךְ אָסוּר. שֶׁלִּי וְשֶׁלָּךְ אָסוּר. קִיבְּלָהּ מִמֶּנּוּ כְּדֶרֶךְ הַמְקַבְּלִין מוּתָּר וְאִם לָאו אָסוּר. בְּלֹא כַךְ אֵין הַמַּעְשְׂרוֹת שֶׁלָּהֶן. אֶלָּא הָכֵנִי שֶׁלִּי שֶׁלִּי שֶׁלָּךְ שֶׁלִּי וְשֶׁלָּךְ אִם קִיבְּלָהּ מִמֶּנּוּ כְּדֶרֶךְ הַמְקַבְּלִין מוּתָּר וְאִם לָאו אָסוּר.

"An[48] Israel who received a field (as sharecropper) from a Cohen, if he[49] said to him, on condition that the tithes be mine, or yours, or mine and yours; this is permitted[50]. A Cohen who received a field (as sharecropper) from a Cohen, if he said to him, on condition that the tithes be mine, that is permitted. That they be yours, that is forbidden[51]. That they be mine and yours, that is forbidden. If he received it under the standard sharecropping contract[52], it is permitted, otherwise it is forbidden." Even without that, do not the tithes belong to them[53]? But so it must read: "My part is mine, your part is mine and yours, if he received it under the standard sharecropping contract, it is permitted, otherwise it is forbidden[54]."

48 In Tosephta *Demay* 7:3-4, one reads: "An Israel who received a field (as sharecropper) from a Cohen, if he said to him, on condition that the tithes be mine, or yours, or mine and yours; this is forbidden. A Cohen who received a field (as sharecropper) from an Israel, if he said to him, on condition that the tithes be mine, that is permitted. That they be yours, or that they be mine and yours, if he received it under the standard sharecropping contract, it is permitted, otherwise it is forbidden."

49 The landlord who is the active party in all these cases.

50 Since the tithes belong to the landlord, he can give them to whom he wants.

51 "Tithes" here naturally must include heave and heave of the tithe. What is forbidden is that the Cohen landlord gives the heaves to the Cohen sharecropper as part of the latter's wages for his services, since heave may never be used to liquidate an obligation.

52 Any distribution of heaves that

follows the local standard and is not different for a Cohen than for an Israel cannot be considered a special payment made with heave and is permitted.

53 To the landlord and the sharecropper, as explained in Mishnah 1. What does the *baraita* tell us as new information?

54 The Cohen landlord may reserve the heaves of his own field for himself only if this is common practice; otherwise, it is exploitation of the defenseless status of the sharecropper.

יִשְׂרָאֵל שֶׁקִּיבֵּל שָׂדֶה מִיִּשְׂרָאֵל עַל מְנַת שֶׁיְּהוּ הַמַּעְשְׂרוֹת שֶׁל זֶה אָסוּר. שֶׁאֶטְּלֵם אֲנִי וְאֶתְּנֵם לְזֶה מוּתָּר. וְלֹא דָא הִיא קַדְמִייָתָא. אָמַר רִבִּי אָחָא אִם תִּירְצֶה בֵּינֵיהֶן. אָמַר רִבִּי יוֹסֵי הָא דְתֵימַר מוּתָּר בְּשֶׁקִּיבְּלָהּ כְּדֶרֶךְ הַמְקַבְּלִין. וְהֵן דְּאַתְּ אָמַר אָסוּר בְּשֶׁלֹּא קִיבְּלָהּ מִמֶּנּוּ כְּדֶרֶךְ הַמְקַבְּלִין. אֲתִיָא דְּרִבִּי יוֹסֵי כְּרִבִּי יוֹחָנָן. וּדְרִבִּי אָחָא כְּרִבִּי יוֹסֵי בֵּי רִבִּי חֲנִינָא. דְּרִבִּי יוֹסֵי בֵּי רִבִּי חֲנִינָא אָמַר אָדָם נוֹתֵן מַעְשְׂרוֹת בְּטוֹבַת הֲנָייָה. רִבִּי יוֹחָנָן אָמַר אֵין אָדָם מֵבִיא מַעְשְׂרוֹתָיו בְּטוֹבַת הֲנָאָה. מַאי טַעְמָא דְּרִבִּי יוֹסֵי בֶּן חֲנִינָא וְאִישׁ אֶת קֳדָשָׁיו לוֹ יִהְיוּ. מַה עֲבַד לֵיהּ רִבִּי יוֹחָנָן יִתְּנֵם לְכָל־מִי שֶׁיִּרְצֶה.

"If an Israel received (as sharecropper) a field from another Israel on condition that the tithes go to a certain person, that clause is forbidden[55]; on condition that I shall take them and deliver them to a certain person, that clause is permitted.[56]" Is the second version not identical with the first? Rebbi Aḥa said, "if you agree" makes the difference[57]. Rebbi Yose[58] said, you say it is permitted if it follows the standard sharecropper's contract. You say it is forbidden if it does not follow the standard sharecropper's contract. It turns out that Rebbi Yose holds with Rebbi Joḥanan and Rebbi Aḥa with Rebbi Yose ben Rebbi Ḥanina. As Rebbi Yose ben Rebbi Ḥanina said, a person gives his tithes for the benefit of goodwill[59]. Rebbi Joḥanan said, a person may not give his tithes for the benefit of goodwill[60]. What is the reason of Rebbi Yose ben Rebbi Ḥanina? (*Num.* 5:10) "Everybody shall be the owner of his holy things."

What does Rebbi Joḥanan with this? He may give them to whomever he likes[61].

55 Distribution of tithes cannot become part of a financial package.

56 In the Tosephta (*Demay* 7:1) there is a positive prescription that between sharecropper and landlord of similar status, tithes must be evenly split. There is no prescription on how the tithes should be given to Levite or Cohen.

57 For R. Aḥa, the landlord may not prescribe the distribution of the sharecropper's tithes but he can ask the latter's consent to distribute them in a certain manner.

58 R. Yose agrees with the objection that the two clauses are indistinguishable; he must find another reason why one is permitted and the other forbidden.

59 While a person cannot trade his heaves or tithes, he can use them to create goodwill and so reap an indirect monetary benefit, or even a direct benefit if the party involved is not a Cohen. While an Israel may not take money from a Cohen for his heaves, he may take from an Israel for the promise to give all future heaves to the latter's grandson who is a Cohen. But since it is not possible to trade this kind of goodwill, it is not considered to be money in the Babli (*Nedarim* 64b-65a); hence, if the Cohen takes heave without consent of the owner, he cannot be sued for monetary damages (Maimonides *Terumot* 12:15). This is the only opinion mentioned in the Babli and the only one in *Sifry Naśo* (6). (Starting here, the next four paragraphs are also found in *Qiddušin* 2:10.)

60 Rebbi Joḥanan does not allow any monetary advantage from giving heaves and tithes.

61 No Cohen or Levy may take heave or tithe by force; only the owner can decide to whom to give [*Sifry Naśo* (6)].

מַתְנִיתָא פְלִיגָא עַל רִבִּי יוֹסֵי בֵּי רִבִּי חֲנִינָא קוֹנָם כֹּהֲנִים וּלְוִיִּם נֶהֱנִין לִי יִטְּלוּ בְּעַל כָּרְחוֹ. פָּתַר לָהּ בְּאוֹמֵר אֵי אֶיפְשִׁי לִיתֵּן מַתָּנוֹת כָּל־עִיקָּר. תֵּדַע לָךְ שֶׁהוּא כֵן דְּתַנֵּינָן כֹּהֲנִים אֵלּוּ לְוִיִּם אֵלּוּ נֶהֱנִין לִי יִטְּלוּ אֲחֵרִים. מַתְנִיתָא פְלִיגָא עַל רִבִּי יוֹחָנָן אֹמֵר הוּא יִשְׂרָאֵל לְיִשְׂרָאֵל הֵילָךְ סֶלַע זֶה וְתֵן בְּכוֹר זֶה לְבֶן בִּתִּי כֹהֵן. פָּתַר לָהּ בְּרוֹצֶה לִיתְּנוֹ לִשְׁנַיִם כֹּהֲנִים • בֶּן בִּתּוֹ אֶחָד מֵהֶן וְהוּא אָמַר הֵילָךְ סֶלַע זֶה וְתֵן כּוּלָּן לְבֶן בִּתִּי כֹהֵן.

A Mishnah disagrees with Rebbi Yose ben Rebbi Ḥaninah: "A vow that no Cohanim or Levites should have any advantage from me, they should take against his will[62]." He explains it about a person who says, I cannot possibly give them *any* gifts. You should know that this is so, since we have stated: "*These* Cohanim and Levites, let others take[63]." A *baraita* disagrees with Rebbi Joḥanan: "An Israel can say to another Israel, here you have a tetradrachma and give this first born to my daughter's son, a Cohen[64]." He explains, if he already wanted to give it to two Cohanim and that daughter's son was one of them; then one said, here you have a tetradrachma and give all of it to my daughter's son, a Cohen[65].

62 Mishnah *Nedarim* 3:11. This is one of the vows the husband cannot dissolve if made by his wife since dissolution is unnecessary; any recipient of the obligatory gifts to Cohen and Levite may take them by force in this case, and the owner has no monetary gain. It seems to disagree with R. Joḥanan who says that the owner has the choice of recipient. But since the owner does not want to give what he is obligated to, he transgresses commandments of the Torah and the situation can be saved only by others disregarding his rights.

63 Same Mishnah; if the vow excludes a certain group of people, he always can give to others.

64 Speaking of the firstborn of a cow or ewe. In the Babli (*Bekhorot* 27a) a similar statement is made for future heave. Both statements are taken together in Tosephta *Demay* 5:18: "An Israel may say to a Cohen {it seems that it should read: another Israel, but there is absolutely no manuscript evidence for that} here you have a tetradrachma and give heave to my daughter's son, the Cohen, or give a firstborn to my daughter's son, the Cohen." The Babli does not want to accept the statement about the firstborn since the Cohen might think the tetradrachma is redemption money and the firstborn does not have to be treated as a sacrifice.

65 Indirect usufruct is permitted by R. Joḥanan.

בָּעוּן קוֹמֵי רִבִּי זְעִירָא כְּהָדָא כֹּהֵן לְיִשְׂרָאֵל מַה. דְּרִבִּי יוֹסֵי אָמַר לֹא אֲגִיבוּן. רִבִּי חִזְקִיָּה בְּשֵׁם רִבִּי אָחָא אָמַר הָכֵין אֲמַר לוֹן עַל דַּעְתֵּיהּ דְּרִבִּי יוֹסֵי בֶּן חֲנִינָא כֹּהֵן לְיִשְׂרָאֵל לָמָּה הוּא אָסוּר לֹא מִפְּנֵי מַרְאִית הָעַיִן אַף רִבִּי יוֹחָנָן אִית לֵיהּ יִשְׂרָאֵל לְיִשְׂרָאֵל אָסוּר מִפְּנֵי מַרְאִית הָעַיִן. אָמַר רִבִּי יוֹסֵי בֵּי רִבִּי בּוּן חִילּוּל קֳדָשִׁים יֵשׁ כַּאן וְתֵימַר מִפְּנֵי מַרְאִית הָעַיִן. וְעוֹד מִן הָדָא דְתַנֵּי הַכֹּהֲנִים וְהַלְּוִיִּם הַמְסַייְעִין בְּבֵית הַגְּרָנוֹת אֵין לָהֶן לֹא תְרוּמָה וְלֹא מַעֲשֵׂר וְאִם נָתַן הֲרֵי זֶה (fol. 25c) חָלוּל שֶׁנֶּאֱמַר וְלֹא יְחַלְּלוּ אֶת קָדְשֵׁי בְּנֵי יִשְׂרָאֵל וְהֵן מְחַלְּלִין אוֹתָן יוֹתֵר מִכֵּן אָמְרוּ תְּרוּמָתָן אֵינוֹ תְרוּמָה וּמַעְשְׂרוֹתָן אֵינָן מַעְשְׂרוֹת וְהֶקְדֵּישָׁן אֵינָן הֶקְדֵּשׁ וַעֲלֵיהֶן הַכָּתוּב אוֹמֵר רָאשֶׁיהָ בְּשׁוֹחַד יִשְׁפּוֹטוּ וְכֹהֲנֶיהָ בִּמְחִיר יָבוֹאוּ. הַמָּקוֹם מֵבִיא עֲלֵיהֶן שָׁלֹשׁ פּוּרְעָנִיּוֹת. הַהוּא דִכְתִיב לָכֵן בִּגְלַלְכֶם צִיּוֹן שָׂדֶה תֵחָרֵשׁ וגו׳.

They asked before Rebbi Zeïra, in that situation[66], a Cohen to an Israel, what is the rule? At Rebbi Yose's they said that he did not answer. Rebbi Ḥizqiah in the name of Rebbi Aḥa said, so he said to them: In the opinion of Rebbi Yose ben Rebbi Ḥanina, why is a Cohen to an Israel forbidden, not because it looks badly[67]? Also Rebbi Joḥanan holds that from an Israel to an Israel it is forbidden because it looks badly[68]. Rebbi Yose ben Rebbi Abun said, there is desecration of sacrifices and you said because it looks badly? Because of the following, as it was stated[69]: "Cohanim and Levites who help at the threshing floor have no right either to heave or to tithe, and if the farmer gave, it is desecrated, as it is said (*Lev.* 22:15): 'They should not desecrate the sanctified things of the Children of Israel,' but they desecrate them! In addition, they said[70] that their heave is no heave, their tithes are no tithes, their dedications are no dedications, and about them the verse says (*Micha* 3:11): 'Their heads judge for bribes and their priests come for a price[71].' The Omnipresent brings over them three catastrophies; that is what is written (*Micha* 3:12): 'Therefore, because of you Zion will be ploughed over as a field, etc.'"

66 To give money to an Israel so that he should give his heave or the firstborn of his flock to a designated Cohen.

67 That people could think that he buys the gifts for himself; this would be forbidden. He should not do it lest he get a reputation as a sinner.

68 In the opinion of R. Yose ben R. Ḥanina the rabbis, not the Bible, prohibited the farmer from having any material gain from his heave and tithes.

69 Tosephta *Demay* 5:20, a slightly longer version.

70 By a decree of the Court, which has the power of removing property rights, anything that the Cohen receives is *ṭevel* and he has to give its heave and tithes to another Cohen. This is made explicit in the Tosephta.

71 And their prophets perform witchcraft for money. The three punishments for the three sins are: Zion will be ploughed as a field, Jerusalem will be desolate, and the Temple Mount a wooded hill.

מַתְנִיתָא פְלִיגָא עַל רִבִּי יוֹחָנָן הַמְקַדֵּשׁ בִּתְרוּמוֹת וּבְמַעְשְׂרוֹת וּבְמַתָּנוֹת וּבְמֵי חַטָּאת וּבְאֵפֶר חַטָּאת הֲרֵי זוֹ מְקוּדֶּשֶׁת אַף עַל פִּי יִשְׂרָאֵל. פָּתַר לָהּ בִּתְרוּמָה שֶׁנָּפְלָה לוֹ מִשֶּׁל אֲבִי אִמּוֹ כֹּהֵן.

A Mishnah disagrees with Rebbi Joḥanan[72]: "If somebody marries[73] giving heave, tithes, 'gifts'[74], water for sprinkling, or ashes of the red heifer[75], she is married, even if the groom is Israel." He explains it with heave he inherited from his maternal grandfather, a Cohen[76].

72 *Qiddušin* 2:10.

73 The first of the marriage ceremonies, קידושין, requires that the groom give the bride something of value and declare that with this gift she becomes his bride. Hence, the materials enumerated must have monetary value. If the groom is an Israel, how can heave have a monetary value if he does not even have the right to goodwill?

74 These "gifts" are parts of an animal slaughtered for profane food that are given to a Cohen (*Deut*. 18:3). They are profane food and may be sold by the Cohen to anybody.

75 The water and the ashes are used to cleanse people from the impurity imparted by a corpse. Water and ashes have no monetary value and it is a desecration to take money for sprinkling water with the ashes on

impure persons. However, it is permitted to take money for the time spent in transporting both (and keeping all the rules for this transport.) So the groom does not transfer ownership of the ashes since there is no ownership, but he transfers his claim to be paid for his exertions which is a lien on water and ashes (Babli *Qiddušin* 58b).

76 If the grandfather died before he had time to consume the heave, the grandson may sell the heave to another Cohen; in that case, everybody agrees that the heave has monetary value.

כֹּהֵן שֶׁמָּכַר שָׂדֶה לְיִשְׂרָאֵל וְאָמַר עַל מְנָת שֶׁיְּהוּ הַמַּעְשְׂרוֹת שֶׁלִּי הַמַּעְשְׂרוֹת שֶׁלּוֹ. מַהוּ שֶׁיִּמְכְּרֵם לְכֹהֵן. נִישְׁמְעִינָהּ מִן הָדָא. דְּאָמַר רִבִּי אַבָּהוּ בְּשֵׁם רִבִּי שִׁמְעוֹן בֶּן לָקִישׁ הַמּוֹכֵר מַעְשְׂרוֹת שָׂדֵהוּ לַחֲבֵירוֹ לֹא עָשָׂה כְלוּם. וּוְלָדֵי שִׁפְחָתוֹ לַחֲבֵירוֹ לֹא עָשָׂה כְלוּם. עוּבְּרֵי בְהֶמְתּוֹ לַחֲבֵירוֹ לֹא עָשָׂה כְלוּם. אֲוֵיר חוֹרֵבָתוֹ לַחֲבֵירוֹ לֹא עָשָׂה כְלוּם. אֶלָּא מוֹכֵר לוֹ שָׂדֶה וּמְשַׁיֵּיר לוֹ מַעְשְׂרוֹתֶיהָ. מוֹכֵר לוֹ שִׁפְחָה וּמְשַׁיֵּיר לוֹ וְולָדָהּ. מוֹכֵר לוֹ בְהֵמָה וּמְשַׁיֵּיר לוֹ עוּבְרָהּ. מוֹכֵר לוֹ חוֹרֵבָה וּמְשַׁיֵּיר לוֹ אֲוֵירָהּ. וְהֵיאַךְ אֵיפְשַׁר לָאָדָם לִמְכּוֹר אֲוֵיר חוֹרֵבָתוֹ לַחֲבֵירוֹ. תִּיפְתָּר בְּאוֹמֵר לוֹ תְּלוֹשׁ מִן הַחוֹרֵבָה הַזּוּ שֶׁהִקְנָה לָךְ אֲוֵירָהּ. וְכָא קַרְקַע לְפָנָיו שֶׁהוּא אוֹמֵר לוֹ תְּלוֹשׁ מִן הַקַּרְקַע הַזֶּה שֶׁתִּקְנֶה אֶחָד מֵעֲשָׂרָה שֶׁבּוֹ.

"[77]If a Cohen sold a field to an Israel and made the condition that the tithes should be his, the tithes are his." May he sell them to a Cohen[78]? Let us hear from the following. Rebbi Abbahu said in the name of Rebbi Simeon ben Laqish: He who sells the tithes of his field to another person did not do anything[79], the future children of his slave girl to another person, he did not do anything[80], the fetus of his animal to another person, he did not do anything, the airspace of his dry land to another person, he did not do anything[81]. But he may sell him a field and reserve the tithes for himself, a slave girl and reserve her children for himself, an animal and reserve her fetus for himself. Is it not impossible for a person to sell the airspace of his dry land to another person[82]? Explain it if he tells him, tear out some grasses in that dry land[83] to acquire its airspace. And here there is real estate before him and he says, pluck something from the ground so that you acquire one tenth of it.

77 Tosephta *Demay* 7:14; there the condition is that the buyer be trustworthy for tithes. A similar *baraita*, dealing with a Levite selling to an Israel, is in Babli *Baba Batra* 63a. Since a Cohen is required to separate heave and tithes but is permitted to take them for himself in order to eat the heaves in purity, his heaves are a kind of lien on the field and he may sell the field without selling the lien.

78 May the owner of these heaves sell them to another Cohen?

79 Since the tithes are not his; the goodwill represented by them is not money.

80 This and the following case are based on the principle that nobody can sell anything that does not yet exist.

81 Since the airspace is not material, it cannot be bodily acquired. However, if the seller grants the buyer the right to build in the airspace, he sells the right to set the building on walls or pillars and that is a valid transaction (Babli *Baba Batra* 64b, *Šulḥan Arukh Ḥošen Mišpaṭ* 212.)

82 Why does R. Abbahu include in the list something that seems to be obvious?

83 This is a positive action which everywhere confirms acquisition of real estate and liens on real estate. R. Abbahu has to inform us that here it does not work because the land is not an object of the sale. Similarly, in the case of the Cohen selling his right, the tithe is not fixed at 10% of the field but is only a lien that cannot thereby be acquired.

כֹּהֵן שֶׁמָּכַר שָׂדֶה לְיִשְׂרָאֵל וְאָמַר עַל מְנָת שֶׁיְּהוּ הַמַּעְשְׂרוֹת שֶׁלִּי הַמַּעְשְׂרוֹת שֶׁלּוֹ. מֵת אֵין לְבָנָיו בְּמַעְשְׂרוֹת. לִי וּלְבָנַי לִי וּלְיוֹרְשַׁי יֵשׁ לוֹ בְמַעְשְׂרוֹת וּלְבָנָיו בְּמַעְשְׂרוֹת וּלְיוֹרְשָׁיו בְּמַעְשְׂרוֹת. רִבִּי יוּדָן בַּר שָׁלוֹם בְּעָא קוֹמֵי דְּרִבִּי יוֹסֵי עַד כְּדוֹן בְּיוֹרְשִׁין שֶׁהֵן מִדְּבַר תּוֹרָה אֲפִילוּ בְיוֹרְשִׁין שֶׁאֵינָן מִדְּבַר תּוֹרָה.

"[84]If a Cohen sold a field to an Israel on condition that the tithes should be his, the tithes are his. If he dies, his sons have no right to the tithes. 'For me and my sons, for me and my heirs,' his sons have the tithes, his heirs have the tithes." Rebbi Yudan bar Shalom asked before Rebbi Yose:

So far only for heirs whose claim is from the Torah? Even for heirs whose claim is not from the Torah[85]!

84 Cf. Tosephta *Demay* 7:14; there the condition is that the buyer be trustworthy for tithes. There is no mention of heirs other than sons. A similar *baraita*, dealing with a Levite selling to an Israel, appears in Babli *Baba Batra* 63a. Since the Cohen may stipulate before the sale, he may stipulate anything he wishes.

85 For example, the husband inheriting from his wife whose marriage is only rabbinical, e. g. a man marrying an underage girl after her father's death.

שֶׁיְּהוּ כָּל־הַמַּעְשְׂרוֹת שֶׁלִּי כָּל־זְמַן שֶׁהוּא לְפָנָיו יְהוּ הַמַּעְשְׂרוֹת שֶׁלּוֹ כָּל־זְמַן שֶׁהוּא לְפָנָיו. מְכָרָהּ לְאַחֵר אֵין בְּמַעְשְׂרוֹת. חָזַר וּלְקָחָהּ מִמֶּנּוּ. תַּנֵּי רִבִּי חִיָּיא אֵין לוֹ בְּמַעְשְׂרוֹת. תַּנֵּי רִבִּי הוֹשַׁעְיָא יֵשׁ לוֹ בְּמַעְשְׂרוֹת. אַתְיָין אִילֵּין פְּלוּגְוָותָא כְּאִילֵּין פְּלוּגְוָותָא. דְּתַנֵּינָן תַּמָּן שֶׁהַמְגָרֵשׁ אֶת הָאִשָּׁה וְהֶחֱזִירָהּ עַל שֵׁם כְּתוּבָּתָהּ הָרִאשׁוֹנָה הֶחֱזִירָהּ. תַּנָּא רִבִּי חָנִין קוֹמֵי רִבִּי לָא תְּרֵין אֲמוֹרָאִין חַד אָמַר לִכְתוּבָּה אֲבָל לֹא לִתְנָאִין וְחָרָנָא אָמַר בֵּין לִכְתוּבָּה בֵּין לִתְנָאִין. מָאן דְּאָמַר לִכְתוּבָּה אֲבָל לֹא לִתְנָאִין יֵשׁ לוֹ בְּמַעְשְׂרוֹת. מָאן דְּאָמַר בֵּין לִכְתוּבָּה בֵּין לִתְנָאִין אֵין לוֹ בְּמַעְשְׂרוֹת. וְהָתַנֵּי קִיבֵּל שָׂדֶה מִכּוֹהֶנֶת הַמַּעְשְׂרוֹת שֶׁלָּהּ. נִישֵּׂאת לְיִשְׂרָאֵל חוֹלְקִין בְּמַעְשְׂרוֹת. נִתְאַרְמְלָה אוֹ נִתְגָּרְשָׁה חָזְרָה לִתְחִילָּתָהּ. כָּאן שֶׁמָּכַר כָּאן שֶׁקִּיבֵּל. וְהָתַנֵּי רִבִּי חִיָּיא מְכָרָהּ. אָמַר רִבִּי שְׁמוּאֵל בַּר אֶבְדּוּמָא תַּמָּן יָצָאת מֵרְשׁוּת שְׁנֵיהֶן. בְּרַם הָכָא יָצָאת מֵרְשׁוּת מוֹכֵר וְלֹא יָצָאת מֵרְשׁוּת לוֹקֵחַ.

"[86]That all tithes should be mine as long as you own it, he gets its tithes as long as the buyer owns it." When he sold it to a third party, he has no tithes. If the buyer then bought it back from the third party, Rebbi Ḥiyya states that he has no tithes, Rebbi Hoshaia states that the tithes are his. This disagreement turns out like the other disagreement, as we have stated there[87] "that he who divorces his wife and then remarries her, remarries her on the basis of the first *ketubah*." Rebbi Ḥanin[88] stated before Rebbi

La: Two Amoraïm, one says for *ketubah* but not for individual stipulations, and the other says, both for *ketubah* and individual stipulations. For him who says, for *ketubah* but not for individual stipulations, he has the tithes[89]. For him who says, both for *ketubah* and for individual stipulations, he has no tithes[90]. But did we not state[91]: "If somebody received (as sharecropper) from the daughter of a Cohen, she has the tithes[92]. If she married an Israel[93], they split the tithes. If she was widowed or divorced[94], she returns to her prior status." There when he sold, here when he received[95]. But did not Rebbi Ḥiyya state: "When she sold?[96]" Rebbi Samuel bar Eudaimon said, there it left the power of both parties; here, it left the power of the seller but not that of the buyer.

86 Tosephta *Demay* 7:14, the text is R. Ḥiyya's. A similar *baraita*, dealing with a Levite selling to an Israel, appears in Babli *Baba Batra* 63a, also following R. Ḥiyya only.

87 Mishnah *Ketubot* 9:13: "A woman who presents two letters of divorce and two *ketubot* collects two *ketubot*. Two *ketubot* and one letter of divorce, or one *ketubah* and two letters of divorce, or one *ketubah*, one letter of divorce, and a death, she collects only one *ketubah* since 'he who divorces his wife and then remarries her, remarries her on the basis of the first *ketubah*.'" The *ketubah* is explained in *Peah*, Chapter 3, Note 151. The individual stipulations are obligations the groom takes upon himself in addition to the obligatory *ketubah*.

88 An Amora of the third Galilean generation, student of R. Samuel bar Isaac; a frequent author of aggadic statements. The statement here, which appears in identical form in *Ketubot* 9:13 (fol. 33c), is his only known halakhic statement.

89 This refers to the Mishnah and the case that the husband dies and the widow presents two *ketubot* and one bill of divorce. If one assumes that the argument of the Mishnah applies only to the obligatory *ketubah*, she collects the amount of one obligatory *ketubah* but both individual stipulations; hence, the remarrying does not eliminate the validity of the first *ketubah*. In our case, the repurchasing of the field does not eliminate the first contract and the Cohen re-enters into his rights to tithes.

(The Babli, *Ketubot* 90a, which does not consider the case of *demay* presented by R. Hoshaia, holds that if the date of the letter of divorce is between the dates of the two *ketubot*, she collects both *ketubot* in full.)

90 In that case, the first *ketubah* is invalidated completely, as is the Cohen's contract of sale. (This is the only case considered by the Babli, *Baba Batra* 63a.)

91 Tosephta *Demay* 7:9; there it is spelled out: בת כהן .

92 Since heave is eaten not only by a Cohen but also by his entire family, her claim is as good as her father's.

93 She becomes a member of her husband's family and loses her priestly status. Hence, all rules for the Israel apply to her.

94 It is implied that she has no surviving descendants from her Israel husband. Otherwise, her status remains that of an Israel (*Lev.* 22:13).

95 Since the sharecropper never had title to the land, it is only her status that decides in matters of tithes.

96 This *baraita* is not in the Tosephta. R. Ḥiyya, who holds that the Cohen loses all his rights when the Israel sells the field to a third party, states that the daughter of a Cohen who sells her field to an Israel while retaining her rights to tithes, and who loses half of the tithes on her marriage to an Israel, can reclaim all her rights as a childless divorcee or widow. The problem is to reconcile the two statements of R. Ḥiyya; the answer is that in the second case the rights of the seller are only suspended, not eliminated.

כֹּהֵן שֶׁמָּכַר שָׂדֶה לְיִשְׂרָאֵל וְאָמַר עַל מְנָת שֶׁיְּהוּ הַמַּעְשְׂרוֹת שֶׁלּוֹ אַרְבַּע אוֹ חָמֵשׁ שָׁנִים יָכוֹל הוּא לְמְחוֹת בְּיָדוֹ שֶׁלֹּא לִיטְעָהּ כֶּרֶם שֶׁלֹּא לְזוֹרְעָהּ אִיסָּטִיס שֶׁלֹּא לַעֲשׂוֹתָהּ שְׂדֵה קָנִים. שֶׁלִּי לְעוֹלָם אֵינוֹ יָכוֹל לְמְחוֹת בְּיָדוֹ שֶׁלֹּא לִיטְעָהּ כֶּרֶם שֶׁלֹּא לְזוֹרְעָהּ אִיסָּטִיס שֶׁלֹּא לַעֲשׂוֹתָהּ שְׂדֵה קָנִים. אֲתָא עוּבְדָא קוֹמֵי רִבִּי אָחָא בַּר עוּלָּא וְחִייְבָהּ מִיתַּן לֵיהּ חַד מִן עֲשַׂרְתֵּי דְקָנְיָא.

"A[97] Cohen who sold a field to an Israel on condition that the tithes be his for four or five years can oppose the buyer's planting it as a vineyard[98], sowing woad[99], or turning it into a field of reeds[100]. Mine forever, he cannot oppose the buyer's planting it as a vineyard, sowing woad, or turning it into a field of reeds." There came a case before Rebbi

Aḥa bar Ulla[101] and he obligated him to turn over to him one tenth of the reeds.

97 Tosephta *Demay* 7:15.

98 Since the vineyard is *orlah* for the first three years and its fruits forbidden for all use, the Cohen would lose most of the tithes he had contracted for.

99 Greek ἰσάτις, Latin *isatis tinctoria*, a plant used to make dark blue dye. Since woad is not food, it is exempt from tithes and the Cohen would lose all income from the field.

100 Reeds were used to make pens and mats and were a commercial crop, exempt from tithes. As was established in the preceding paragraphs the Cohen, while forbidden to pay for tithes, may reserve some income from the field as a lien on the field; R. Aḥa bar Ulla interpreted the contract to mean that the Cohen reserved for himself one tenth of the yield, whether sacred or profane.

101 An Amora of the third and fourth generations. He was a Babylonian, student of Rav Ḥisda, who immigrated to Galilee and was still alive in the days of R. Jonah.

יִשְׂרָאֵל שֶׁמָּכַר שָׂדֶה לְכֹהֵן וְאָמַר לוֹ עַל מְנָת שֶׁיְּהוּ הַמַּעְשְׂרוֹת שֶׁלּוֹ אַרְבַּע וְחָמֵשׁ שָׁנִים מוּתָּר. לְעוֹלָם אָסוּר שֶׁאֵין כֹּהֵן עוֹשֶׂה כֹהֵן. כֹּהֵן שֶׁמָּכַר שָׂדֶה לְיִשְׂרָאֵל וְאָמַר לוֹ עַל מְנָת שֶׁיְּהוּ הַמַּעְשְׂרוֹת שֶׁלָּךְ אַרְבַּע אוֹ חָמֵשׁ שָׁנִים אָסוּר. הָכָא אַתְּ אָמַר מוּתָּר. וְהָכָא אַתְּ אָמַר אָסוּר. כָּאן זִיכֵּהוּ בְדָבָר שֶׁהוּא בִרְשׁוּתוֹ. וְכָאן זִיכֵּהוּ בְדָבָר שֶׁאֵינוֹ בִרְשׁוּתוֹ.

"If an[102] Israel sold a field to a Cohen on condition that the tithes be his[103] for four or five years, it is permitted. Forever, it is forbidden, since no Cohen can make a Cohen[104]. If a Cohen sold a field to an Israel on condition that the tithes be the Israel's for four or five years, it is forbidden[105]." There you say it is permitted, here you say it is forbidden! There, he gave him rights to something he had the right to dispose of, here, he gave him rights to something he had no right to dispose of.

102 Tosephta *Demay* 7:15, the first two sentences only.

103 That the Israel has the right to the tithes and may give them to any Cohen or Levite he pleases.

104 No Non-Cohen can have a permanent right to tithes. While the Israel obviously has the right to demand such a clause, since the Cohen as seller has the right to reserve the tithes for himself forever, here it is the buyer who is told that he may not agree to such a contract.

105 Since the Cohen is automatically the owner of his heave and tithes the moment he separates them from his harvest, but since the ownership is a gift from God and not the result of his farming, he may not desecrate heave and tithes by turning them over to an Israel.

(fol. 25a) **משנה ד**: יִשְׂרָאֵל שֶׁקִּיבֵּל מִכֹּהֵן וּמִלֵּוִי הַמַּעְשְׂרוֹת לִבְעָלִים. רִבִּי יִשְׁמָעֵאל אוֹמֵר הַקַּרְתָּנִי שֶׁקִּיבֵּל שָׂדֶה מִירוּשַׁלְמִי מַעֲשֵׂר שֵׁנִי שֶׁל יְרוּשַׁלְמִי. וַחֲכָמִים אוֹמְרִים יָכוֹל הוּא הַקַּרְתָּנִי לַעֲלוֹת וּלְאוֹכְלוֹ בִּירוּשָׁלַ͏ִם.

Mishnah 4: If an Israel received (as sharecropper) from a Cohen or a Levite, the tithes are for the owners[106]. Rebbi Ismael says, if a villager received a field from a Jerusalemite, the Second Tithe is the Jerusalemite's. But the Sages say, the villager can make pilgrimage[107] and eat his part in Jerusalem.

106 Everybody, including the Sages who oppose R. Eliezer in the previous Mishnah, agree that this is the standard stipulation and is valid.

107 He is encouraged to make the pilgrimage if there is a Temple. If there is no Temple, the entire rule is void since the Second Tithe *must* be redeemed.

(fol. 25d) **הלכה ד**: עַל דַּעְתֵּיהּ דְּרִבִּי יִשְׁמָעֵאל אִילּוּ כֹּהֵן טָמֵא שֶׁהָיָה שׁוּתָּף עִם כֹּהֵן טָהוֹר שֶׁמָּא אֵין חוֹלְקִין בְּמַעְשְׂרוֹת. תַּמָּן יָכוֹל הוּא לְמוֹכְרָן לְכֹהֵן טָהוֹר אַחֵר. בְּרַם הָכָא יָכוֹל הַקַּרְתָּנִי לַעֲלוֹת וּלְאוֹכְלוֹ בִּירוּשָׁלַ͏ִם.

Halakhah 4: According to the opinion of Rebbi Ismael, if an impure Cohen[108] and a pure Cohen were partners, would they not split the tithes? There he may sell the tithes to another pure Cohen[109], here can the villager make pilgrimage and eat his part in Jerusalem[110]?

108 A Cohen who does not follow the rules of ritual purity and, therefore, cannot ever eat heave. Nobody disputes the fact that he will receive his part of the tithes by Biblical decree.

109 Tithes and heave are private property but cannot be given over to a Non-Cohen.

110 Second Tithe cannot be sold; it must be eaten in Jerusalem. R. Ismael thinks that this is a burden on the farmer.

(fol. 25a) **משנה ה**: הַמְקַבֵּל זֵיתִים לַשֶּׁמֶן כְּשֵׁם שֶׁחוֹלְקִין בַּחוּלִּין כַּךְ חוֹלְקִין בִּתְרוּמָה. רִבִּי יְהוּדָה אוֹמֵר יִשְׂרָאֵל שֶׁקִּיבֵּל מִכֹּהֵן וּמִלֵּוִי זֵיתִים לַשֶּׁמֶן אוֹ לְמַחֲצִית שָׂכָר הַמַּעְשְׂרוֹת לַבְּעָלִים.

Mishnah 5: If somebody[111] receives olives to make oil, they split heave just as they split the profane. Rebbi Jehudah says, if an Israel received olives from a Cohen or a Levite for oil or for half the yield as his wages, the tithes are for the landlords.

111 Even an Israel who receives the field as sharecropper from a Cohen or a Levite.

(fol. 25c) **הלכה ה**: רִבִּי יוּדָה עֲבַד זֵתִים כְּקַרְקַע וְרַבָּנִין לָא עָבְדִין זֵתִים כְּקַרְקַע. מֵעַתָּה אִין יִסְבּוֹר רִבִּי יוּדָה[112] כְּרִבִּי לִיעֶזֶר. דְּרִבִּי לִיעֶזֶר אָמַר הַמַּעְשְׂרוֹת שֶׁלָּהֶן שֶׁעַל מְנָת כֵּן בָּאוּ. וְהָכָא כֹּהֵן וְלֵוִי שֶׁקִּיבְּלוּ שָׂדֶה מִיִּשְׂרָאֵל הַמַּעְשְׂרוֹת שֶׁלָּהֶן שֶׁעַל מְנָת כֵּן בָּאוּ.

Halakhah 5: Rebbi Jehudah treats olives like fields but the rabbis do not treat olives like fields[113]. Now it seems that Rebbi Judah is thinking like Rebbi Eliezer, as Rebbi Eliezer says[114], "the tithe is theirs because they came because of it." So here, if a Cohen or a Levite received a field (as sharecroppers), the tithes are theirs because they came because of them.

112 Reading of Rome ms. The word is missing in the Venice print but is required by the context.

113 It is not clear whether the rabbis exclude only olive groves from the rules of fields or any orchard. From the language of the Mishnah it seems that olives grown for pickling will come under the general rules of Mishnah 3.

114 In Mishnah 3.

פָּרָתוֹ שֶׁל כֹּהֵן שֶׁהָיְתָה שׁוּמָה אֵצֶל יִשְׂרָאֵל וְיָֽלְדָה בְּכוֹר הַבְּכוֹר לַכֹּהֵן דִּבְרֵי רִבִּי יְהוּדָה. וַחֲכָמִים אוֹמְרִים אֵין הַבְּכוֹר אֶלָּא לִשְׁנֵיהֶן. אָמַר לָהֶן רִבִּי יְהוּדָה אֵי אַתֶּם מוֹדִין לִי בְּמַעְשְׂרוֹת שָׂדֵהוּ שֶׁהוּא שֶׁלּוֹ. אָמַר לוֹ מִפְּנֵי שֶׁהַשָּׂדֶה גּוּפָהּ לַכֹּהֵן וְהַפָּרָה גוּפָהּ לִשְׁנֵיהֶן. אַף הַפָּרָה אִם הָיְתָה גוּפָהּ לַכֹּהֵן הַבְּכוֹר לַכֹּהֵן. וְתַנֵּי כֵן הַשָּׂם בְּאַחֲרָיוּת שְׁנֵיהֶן וְהַמּוֹכֵר בְּאַחֲרָיוּת הַנּוֹתֵן.

"[115]A cow of a Cohen that was put in an Israel's care and gave birth to a firstborn calf, the firstborn calf is the Cohen's, the words of Rebbi Jehudah. But the Sages say, the firstborn is their common property[116]. Rebbi Jehudah said to them, do you not agree with me that the tithes of his field are his? They said to him, because the body of the field is his property, but the body of the cow is joint property. If the body of the cow were sole property of the Cohen, the firstborn would be the Cohen's." We have stated accordingly, "*put in care* means joint responsibility, *selling* is the sole responsibility of him who gives."

115 Tosephta *Demay* 7:10. As explained later in this paragraph, the technical term "to put in care" is applied only to an animal that is the

joint property of the rancher and an investor.

117 The Israel who is the rancher may give his part of the firstborn calf to another Cohen.

כֹּהֵן שֶׁנָּתַן מָעוֹת לְיִשְׂרָאֵל לִיקַּח לוֹ בָהֶן פֵּירוֹת לְמַחֲצִית שָׂכָר אָמַר לוֹ הוֹתִירוּ אוֹ פָּחְתוּ שֶׁלִּי וְהַמַּעְשְׂרוֹת שֶׁלָּךְ מוּתָּר. יִשְׂרָאֵל שֶׁנָּתַן מָעוֹת לְכֹהֵן לִיקַּח לוֹ בָהֶן פֵּירוֹת לְמַחֲצִית שָׂכָר אָמַר לוֹ הוֹתִירוּ אוֹ פָּחְתוּ שֶׁלִּי וְהַמַּעְשְׂרוֹת שֶׁלָּךְ אִם נָתַן לוֹ שְׂכָרוֹ מוּתָּר וְאִם לָאו אָסוּר. יִשְׂרָאֵל שֶׁהָיָה מוֹכֵר זֵתִים בְּשִׁשִּׁים לוֹג טְבוּלִים. אָמַר לוֹ תְּנֵם לִי וַאֲנִי נוֹתֵן לָךְ שִׁשִּׁים לוֹג מְתוּקָּנִים מוּתָּר. שִׁשִּׁים לוֹג טְבוּלִין וַאֲנִי וְאַתְּ חוֹלְקִים אֶת הַמַּעְשְׂרוֹת אָסוּר. כְּדִי יְהַב לֵיהּ כּוּלֵּיהּ מוּתָּר. כְּדִי יְהַב לֵיהּ פַּלְגָּא אָסוּר. אָמַר רִבִּי יוֹסֵי כָּאן בְּמַרְוִיחַ לוֹ. וְתַנֵּי כָּאן אִם הָיָה מַרְוִיחַ לוֹ אָסוּר מִשּׁוּם רִבִּית וּמִשּׁוּם בִּזְיוֹן קֳדָשִׁים.

"If a[118] Cohen gave money to an Israel to buy produce for half the profit[119] and he (the Cohen) said to him: If they go up or down in price, it is on my account, and the tithes are yours, this is permitted. If an[120] Israel gave money to a Cohen to buy produce for half the profit and he (the Israel) said to him: If they go up or down in price, it is on my account, and the tithes are yours, if he had paid the wages, it is permitted, otherwise it is forbidden. An[121] Israel who sold olives against 60 *log* of *ṭevel*. If one[122] said to him, sell them to me and I shall give you 60 *log* that are in order, that is permitted. 60 *log ṭevel*, and both of us will share in the tithes, that is forbiden[123]." If he gives him everything, it is permitted, if he gives him half, it is forbidden? Rebbi Yose said, if he extends credit to him[124]. We also have stated in this respect: If he extends credit to him it is forbidden because of interest and because of degradation of holy things.

118 Tosephta *Demay* 7:7. In this case, the Cohen is the owner and heave and tithe are his. The tithe, after heave of the tithe is removed, is

profane in the hand of the Cohen and he may give them to anybody he wishes, even an Israel.

119 Not necessarily exactly half the profit, but, like a sharecropper, the Israel will be paid in kind rather than in money.

120 Tosephta *Demay* 7: 8. The Israel is the owner of everything, the Cohen is only his agent. Heave and tithes may not be part of the payment, otherwise the Cohen's standing would be that of a Cohen helping with the harvest; see Halakhah 3 above. Hence, the Cohen has to be paid in full before heave and tithe are given to him.

121 Tosephta *Demay* 5:18. R. Saul Lieberman conjectures that "sold" really means "leased his olive trees for one year," to be paid a fixed amount of olive oil as rent. One may assume that olives growing on trees are meant, to be harvested and pressed by the contractor. In that sense, "sold" is applicable.

122 A Cohen, who can take heave and tithes for himself. He may bid for the contract and offer better terms than a competing Israel.

123 This last sentence is not in the Tosephta. Again, the contractor is a Cohen willing to let the Israel have part of heave and tithe.

124 If the contractor is a Cohen and does not have to deliver the 60 *log* of oil immediately after they are pressed but only later, while another bidder would have to deliver promptly, not only does he give to the Israel landlord part of his tithes as hidden interest for the extension of credit but he uses tithes (of which heave of the tithe has not been removed and which still retains its holy status) to pay a debt and this is contempt of holy gifts. [In the Tosephta dealing with the first case, the Cohen who delivers 60 *log* of tithed oil, it is stated explicitly that there is no transgression either of the laws of interest or of those of honoring holy things.]

(fol. 25a) **משנה ו**: בֵּית שַׁמַּאי אוֹמְרִים לֹא יִמְכּוֹר אָדָם אֶת זֵיתָיו אֶלָּא לְחָבֵר. בֵּית הִלֵּל אוֹמְרִים אַף לִמְעַשֵּׂר[125]. וּצְנוּעֵי בֵּית הִלֵּל הָיוּ נוֹהֲגִין כְּדִבְרֵי בֵית שַׁמַּאי.

Mishnah 6: The House of Shammai say, one should sell one's olives only to a *ḥaver*[126]. The House of Hillel say, also to one who tithes. But the modest[127] ones of the House of Hillel used to follow the words of the House of Shammai.

125 Reading of the Rome ms. and all Mishnah manuscripts. The Leyden ms. and Venice print have למעשרות, almost certainly a scribal error.

126 The *ḥaver* will prepare his olive oil in ritual purity. The House of Shammai forbid causing impurity to food grown in the Land of Israel, but the House of Hillel permit this after the destruction of the Temple.

127 See end of Halakhah.

(fol. 25c) **הלכה ו**: אָמַר רִבִּי יוֹחָנָן טַעְמָא דְבֵית הִלֵּל דֶּרֶךְ בְּנֵי אָדָם לוֹכַל זֵיתֵיהֶן עֲטוּנִין אֶלָּא עַל יְדֵי עִילָּה. בֵּית הִלֵּל כְּדַעְתֵּיהּ דְּתַנֵּינָן לֹא יִמְכּוֹר לוֹ פָּרָה חוֹרֶשֶׁת בַּשְּׁבִיעִית. וּבֵית הִלֵּל מַתִּירִין מִפְּנֵי שֶׁיָּכוֹלָן לְשׁוֹחֲטָהּ. וְאוֹרְחֵי דְּבַר נַשׁ מֵיכוֹס תּוֹרָא דִידֵיהּ עַל יְדֵי עִילָּה. שָׁוִין שֶׁהוּא מוֹכֵר לוֹ שִׁיבֳּלִין לְעִיסָּתוֹ אַף עַל פִּי שֶׁיּוֹדֵעַ שֶׁאֵינוֹ עוֹשֶׂה אוֹתָן בְּטָהֳרָה.

Halakhah 6: Rebbi Joḥanan said, the reason of the House of Hillel is that people eat from their olives while they are being loaded into the oil vat[128], as a subterfuge. The House of Hillel follow their own opinion, as we have stated[129]: "One should not sell him a ploughing cow in the Sabbatical year, but the House of Hillel permit this because he may slaughter it." Do people really slaughter their cattle[130]? As a subterfuge. They agree that one may sell ears of grain[131] for dough even though one knows that the buyer will not prepare the dough in purity.

128 Olives when harvested are put into large vats called מעטן, to be transported to the oil press. Dry food cannot become impure. The olives can become impure only if their oil starts to flow; the lowest olives in the vat will start to exude fluid even before being emptied into the oil press. Then they and all olives wetted by them may become impure. But the top olives may

be eaten dry; it is possible that the buyer will eat some of them while in a state of purity even if the buyer is impure. Hence, there is no logical necessity that the sale will result in the olives made impure.

129 Mishnah *Ševiït* 5:8. The first sentence is labelled as opinion of the House of Shammai in the Mishnah. The House of Shammai argue that nobody would buy cattle trained for ploughing in a Sabbatical year unless he intends to use it then.

130 Cattle trained for ploughing and still vigorous are much too valuable to be slaughtered as food.

131 In the Rome ms. (and R. S. Cirillo), the reason is given: בדי חייו, necessities of life may be sold to everybody. The problems start only with large quantities, as indicated in the next paragraph.

תַּנֵּי שָׁוִין שֶׁאֵין מוֹכְרִין גָּדִישׁ שֶׁל חִטִּין וְעָבִט שֶׁל עֲנָבִים וּמַעֲטָן שֶׁל זֵיתִים אֶלָּא לְחָבֵר וּלְמִי שֶׁהוּא יוֹדֵעַ שֶׁהוּא עוֹשֶׂה אוֹתָן בְּטָהֳרָה. וְעָבִט שֶׁל עֲנָבִים לֹא תוֹרָה הִיא. לֵית הָדָא פְלִיגָא עַל רִבִּי יוֹחָנָן דְּרִבִּי יוֹחָנָן אָמַר כְּשֵׁם שֶׁאָמַר קָטָן חוּמְרִין כָּךְ אָמַר מַעֲטָן שֶׁל זֵיתִים חוּמְרִין. רִבִּי חִזְקִיָּה אָמַר רִבִּי יוֹנָה בְשֵׁם רִבִּי יִרְמְיָה מַה פְלִיגִין בְּחִיבּוּרִין. לְפִי שֶׁבְּכָל־מָקוֹם נָשׁוּךְ חִיבּוּר מָעוּךְ אֵינוֹ (fol. 25d) חִיבּוּר וְכָא אֲפִילוּ מָעוּךְ חִיבּוּר הָא הֶכְשֵׁירָן תּוֹרָה. קָם רִבִּי יוֹנָה עִם רִבִּי יִרְמְיָה אָמַר לוֹ אַתְּ אָמְרַתְּ הָדָא מִילְתָא אָמַר לֵיהּ אֵין מִנִּי אֲפִילוּ הֶכְשֵׁירָן וְהֵן חוּמְרִין. וְהָתַנֵּי שָׁוִין שֶׁאֵין מוֹכְרִין גָּדִישׁ שֶׁל חִטִּים וְעָבִט שֶׁל עֲנָבִים וּמַעֲטָן שֶׁל זֵיתִים אֶלָּא לְחָבֵר וּלְמִי שֶׁהוּא יוֹדֵעַ שֶׁהוּא עוֹשֶׂה אוֹתָן בְּטָהֳרָה. וְעָבִט שֶׁל עֲנָבִים לֹא תוֹרָה הִיא. וְדִכְוָותָהּ מַעֲטָן שֶׁל זֵתִים תּוֹרָה הִיא. מַיי כְדוֹן. תִּיפְתָּר כְּרִבִּי מֵאִיר דְּאָמַר רִבִּי מֵאִיר הַמּוֹהֵל כְּמַשְׁקֶה.

[132] It was stated[133]: "They agree that one does not sell a wheat stack, a grape vat[134], or an olive vat[135] to anybody but a *ḥaver* or to somebody who is known to process in purity." Is the grape vat not from the Torah[136]? This does not disagree with Rebbi Joḥanan[137]; just as Rebbi Joḥanan said, the little one is a restriction[138], so "vat of olives" is a restriction[139]. Rebbi Ḥizqiah said to Rebbi Jonah in the name of Rebbi Jeremiah: They disagree about connections. Because everywhere

"biting"[140] is a connection, squeezing is not a connection. But here even squeezing is a connection[141]; hence from the Torah they are enabled. Rebbi Jonah met Rebbi Jeremiah and asked him, did you say that? He said, that is not from me, even their enablings are restrictions. Did we not state[142]: "They agree that one does not sell a wheat stack, a grape vat, or an olive vat to anybody but a *ḥaver* or to somebody who is known to process in purity?" Is the grape vat not from the Torah? Then the olive vat should be from the Torah! What about this? Explain it following Rebbi Meïr, since Rebbi Meïr said, sap is counted as a fluid[143].

132 In the Venice text, Halakhah 7 starts here. It is clear that this discussion is the continuation of the previous paragraph and has no connection with Mishnah 7. The note in Leyden ms. and Venice print giving a new Halakhah here is clearly in error. For the rest of this chapter, numbers of Halakhot and Mishnaiot in these sources do not agree; the numbering here follows that of the relevant Mishnah.

133 Tosephta *Ma'serot* 3:13.

134 Grapes usually are harvested into baskets made from palm leaves. For transportation to the wine press, the baskets are then emptied into a vat, usually made of clay (or any other material that is impermeable.) If some grape berries are injured in harvesting and start oozing grape juice in the basket, that fluid will not make the grapes subject to ritual impurity since the oozing juice is lost and unwelcome to the vintner. However, in the vat the lowest grapes will be compressed by the weight of the upper layers of grapes and will start losing juice. Since that juice is poured into the winepress, it is welcome because it reduces the workload on the press. Hence, the juice will make all grapes in the vat subject to ritual impurity and selling the vat to a person unwilling to follow the rules of purity would help to make the vat impure.

135 The argument given for grapes essentially is valid also for olives harvested into boxes which then are emptied into a vat. The difference is that olives are not easily injured when poured into the vat, and when warmed by the weight of the olives on top will start oozing sap that contains little or

no oil. Hence, the olives become susceptible to impurity only if we consider the sap to be oil, since only seven kinds of fluid enable foods to be impure (cf. Chapter 2, Notes 136-137). The operative statement is Mishnah *Ṭahorot* 9:1: "When do olives become susceptible to impurity? When they start oozing sap in the vat but not in boxes, following the House of Shammai. Rebbi Simeon says, the term for oozing is three days. The House of Hillel say, if three olives cling together. Rabban Gamliel says, when the work is complete {i. e., if no more olives are added to the vat}, and the sages accept his position."

136 Since grape juice is one of the Seven Fluids, the impurity of grapes in the vat must be considered Biblical.

137 R. Joḥanan had explained in the previous paragraph that even the nonobservant may eat olives in purity from the vat!

138 "Restriction" means a restriction imposed by the rabbis, or the Men of the Great Assembly, not a direct Biblical ordinance. It is difficult to know what the reference means. In the opinion of R. Eliahu Fulda, one refers to a statement of R. Joḥanan reported in Babli *Qiddušin* 80a on Mishnah *Ṭahorot* 3:8: "If a toddler was found with a piece of dough near a dough made in purity, that dough is pure in the opinion of R. Meïr, impure in the opinion of the Sages, since toddlers will grab everything they see." On this R. Joḥanan notes that the impurity is rabbinic and one may not burn heave if it was made impure in this way. "Little one" then would refer to a toddler. According to R. Moses Margalit, the statement refers to Mishnah *Ṭevul Yom* 3:1: "All handles of food which would transmit impurity from its original source transmit impurity for *Ṭevul Yom.* Food that is almost separated, R. Meïr says, if he takes a large piece and a small one is lifted with it, the small piece goes with the large one. R. Jehudah says, if he takes a small piece and a large one is lifted with it, the large goes with the small one. R. Neḥemiah says, that refers to purity, the Sages say, to impurity." In this case, "small one" refers to a piece of food and R. Joḥanan notes that the restrictive attitude of the Sages represents a rabbinic decree, not an interpretation of Biblical law.

{A "handle" of a fruit is an inedible part by which the fruit may be moved, such as the stalk of a pear or an apple. The stalk is wood and not subject to impurity, but as handle it transmits impurity both from an impure person to the fruit and from an impure fruit to any person handling it. The detailed rules are spelled out in Tractate *Uqeẓin*.

Ṭevul Yom means a person who had been impure, had immersed himself in water for cleansing, and now is in an intermediate state until sundown when he will be pure (*Lev*. 22:7). In the state of *Ṭevul Yom*, any heave or sacrifices he touches become unusable; the Mishnah discusses transmission of that disability.}

139 Since olives and grapes cannot be compared for the fluids extracted from them.

140 "Biting" means that after touching, two different things cannot be cleanly separated. The standard example are two pieces of dough which after close contact cannot be cleanly separated again. Such a connection changes the two separate pieces into one for all considerations of impurity.

141 According to the House of Hillel in Mishnah *Ṭahorot* 9:1, if the olives are squeezed so that three cling together as one clump, their sap prepares for impurity and the olives are enabled to receive impurity in the Biblical sense.

142 R. Jonah asked from R. Jeremiah, how does he square his stand with that Tosephta?

143 R. Meïr holds with the House of Shammai that the sap, as a necessary precursor of the oil, has the Biblical status of olive oil. In that case, the mention of the vat of olives in the Tosephta would not be practice to be followed (neither would the prohibition of selling a wholesale quantity of wheat grain, where impurity can be imparted only if water is used in milling or if the flour later comes into contact with water.)

אָמַר רִבִּי זְעִירָא טַעְמָא דְבֵית שַׁמַּאי אֵין דֶּרֶךְ חָבֵר לִהְיוֹת מוֹכֵר זֵיתִים אֶלָּא לִמְעַשֵּׂר.

Rebbi Zeïra said, the reason of the House of Shammai is that a *ḥaver* should never sell olives to anybody but one who tithes[144].

144 The House of Shammai does not state like the House of Hillel that one may also sell to one who is certain to tithe but who is not formally a trustworthy person and therefore not obliged to tithe *demay* before selling, since a *ḥaver* is always bound by the rules of the trustworthy person.

מַהוּ צְנוּעֵי כְּשֵׁירֵי. אָמַר רַב חִסְדָּא כָּאן שָׁנִינוּ שֶׁהַכָּשֵׁר נִקְרָא צָנוּעַ.

Who are the modest ones[145]? Those of noble conduct. Rav Ḥisda said, here we have taught that those of noble conduct are called modest.

145 Mentioned in the Mishnah. This sentence appears as Halakhah 8 in the Venice print.

(fol. 25a) **משנה ז**: שְׁנַיִם שֶׁבָּצְרוּ כַּרְמֵיהֶן לְתוֹךְ גַּת אַחַת אֶחָד מְעַשֵּׂר וְאֶחָד שֶׁאֵינוֹ מְעַשֵּׂר הַמְּעַשֵּׂר מְעַשֵּׂר אֶת שֶׁלּוֹ וְחֶלְקוֹ בְּכָל־מָקוֹם שֶׁהוּא.

Mishnah 7: If two people put the yield of their vineyards into one wine press and one tithes but the other does not, then he who tithes must tithe his own and what could be his at any place[146].

146 The meaning is explained in the Halakhah.

(fol. 25d) **הלכה ז**: אָמַר רִבִּי לְעָזָר דְּרִבִּי מֵאִיר הִיא דְּרִבִּי מֵאִיר אָמַר לֹא הִתִּירוּ לִמְכּוֹר דְּמַאי אֶלָּא לְסִיטוֹן בִּלְבַד. הוּא פָּתַר לָהּ הַמְּעַשֵּׂר מְעַשֵּׂר אֶת שֶׁלּוֹ וַדַּאי וְחוּלְקוֹ בְּכָל־מָקוֹם שֶׁהוּא דְּמַאי. רִבִּי יוֹנָה בְּעֵי מוֹכֵר וַדַּאי וּמְתַקֵּן דְּמַאי. אֵין לָךְ אֶלָּא כְּהַהִיא דְּאָמַר רִבִּי יוֹחָנָן דִּבְרֵי הַכֹּל הִיא הַמְּעַשֵּׂר מְעַשֵּׂר אֶת שֶׁלּוֹ וַדַּאי וְחֵילְקוֹ בְּכָל־מָקוֹם שֶׁהוּא דְּמַאי וַחֲצִי חֶלְקוֹ שֶׁבְּיַד חֲבֵירוֹ מִשֶּׁלּוֹ דְּמַאי.

Halakhah 7[147]: Rebbi Eleazar said, this follows Rebbi Meïr, since Rebbi Meïr said, they permitted to sell *demay* only to the grain wholesaler[148]. He explains the Mishnah: The one who tithes must tithe his own part as certain[149], and that part of his which could be spread anywhere as *demay*[150]. Rebbi Jonah objected: He sells it as certain and tithes only *demay*[151]? It is only possible in the way Rebbi Joḥanan said, the Mishnah is the word of everybody: The one who tithes must tithe his own part as certain, and his part anywhere as *demay*; that means one half of his part in his partner's hand as *demay*[152].

147 In the Venice print Halakhah 9.

148 Cf. Halakhah 3:2. R. Eleazar considers the distribution of the finished wine to the two partners as a commercial transaction; hence, the one who tithes may not give to his partner anything that is not tithed.

149 That means, he must give heave and tithes from his own grapes before they are pressed. Otherwise, he would not know what is his.

150 The part of the grape juice he gets after pressing certainly contains juice from his partner's grapes of which it must be assumed that heave but not tithes were removed. Hence, he must tithe his grape juice as *demay*.

151 If this is considered a mutual sale, R. Meïr cannot be satisfied with treatment as *demay*, since it is required that everything be completely in order.

152 Since we assume that everybody gives heave and we may assume that not more than 50% of his grape juice comes from his partner's grapes, half of what he gets must be tithed as *demay* (assuming that both of them put exactly the same amount of grapes into the press; otherwise, he tithes an amount proportional to his partner's share in the whole.)

(fol. 25a) **משנה ח-ט**: שְׁנַיִם שֶׁקִּבְּלוּ אֶת הַשָּׂדֶה בַּאֲרִיסוּת אוֹ שֶׁיָּרְשׁוּ אוֹ שֶׁנִּשְׁתַּתְּפוּ יָכוֹל הוּא לוֹמַר לוֹ טוֹל אַתָּה חִטִּים שֶׁבְּמָקוֹם פְּלוֹנִי וַאֲנִי חִטִּים שֶׁבְּמָקוֹם פְּלוֹנִי אַתָּה יַיִן שֶׁבְּמָקוֹם פְּלוֹנִי וַאֲנִי יַיִן שֶׁבְּמָקוֹם פְּלוֹנִי. אֲבָל לֹא יֹאמַר לוֹ טוֹל אַתָּה חִטִּים וַאֲנִי שְׂעוֹרִים טוֹל אַתָּה יַיִן וַאֲנִי אֶטוֹל אֶת הַשֶּׁמֶן. חָבֵר וְעַם הָאָרֶץ שֶׁיָּרְשׁוּ אֲבִיהֶן עַם הָאָרֶץ יָכוֹל הוּא לוֹמַר לוֹ טוֹל אַתָּה חִטִּים שֶׁבְּמָקוֹם פְּלוֹנִי וַאֲנִי חִטִּים שֶׁבְּמָקוֹם פְּלוֹנִי. אַתָּה יַיִן שֶׁבְּמָקוֹם פְּלוֹנִי וַאֲנִי יַיִן שֶׁבְּמָקוֹם פְּלוֹנִי. אֲבָל לֹא יֹאמַר לוֹ טוֹל אַתָּה חִטִּים וַאֲנִי אֶטוֹל שְׂעוֹרִים טוֹל אַתָּה הַלַּח וַאֲנִי אֶת הַיָּבֵשׁ.

Mishnah 8-9: If two people received a field as sharecroppers or inherited it or bought it as partners, one can say to his partner, take your wheat on this side and I shall take on that side, take your wine from this side and I shall take from the other side. But he should not say to him, take the wheat and I shall take the barley, take the wine and I shall take the oil[153]. If a *ḥaver* and an *am haäreẓ* inherited from their *am haäreẓ* father, the *ḥaver* may say, take your wheat on this side and I shall take on that side, take wine from this side and I shall take from the other side. But he should not say to him, take wheat and I shall take barley, take the moist produce and I shall take the dry[154].

153 According to Maimonides in his Commentary, the first part does not refer to the laws of *demay* but to money matters. In his opinion, a splitting of the first kind, designating parts of the same crop for the benefit of either party, can be enforced in court on condition that it not hurt the other party, but a proposal of the second kind, exchanging rights to different kinds of crops, will not be supported by a court. To oppose a settlement that benefits one party without being in any way detrimental to the other is called "sin of Sodom."

According to R. Simson of Sens, all this deals with the laws of *demay;* in a division of the first kind, this is simply a necessary splitting of produce. The agreement must have been reached before the harvest, when no heaves and tithes were yet due. Hence, "wine" and "oil" must mean "grapes" and "olives;" nevertheless the unequal splitting is forbidden because it too closely resembles a sale that is questionable if one of the partners is a *ḥaver* and the other an *am haäreẓ*. The position of Maimonides seems to be more acceptable since the inheritance of *ḥaver* and *am haäreẓ* is treated in the following.

154 According to Maimonides, this concerns the *demay* aspects of the situation discussed above. The splitting is permitted since each partner is taking his own. This ruling follows the position taken in the Babli (*Baba Batra* 107a) as practice that brothers who split an inheritance cannot be considered as buying from one another. It is as if each of the brothers received

what was bequeathed to them even before their father's death. However, if they switch barley for wheat or oil for wine, they certainly have to be considered as buyers from one another and a *ḥaver* is not permitted to sell anything not fully tithed to an *am haärez̧*. The *ḥaver* would have a natural inclination to take dry produce not subject to ritual impurity. [In Tosephta *Demay* (6:8) even the splitting according to different places is forbidden if one side is pure and the other impure, since for the *ḥaver* these are two different kinds.]

(fol. 25d) **הלכה ט**: תַּנֵּי יִשְׂרָאֵל וְגוֹי שֶׁקָּנוּ שָׂדֶה בְסוּרְיָא הֲרֵי הוּא כְטֶבֶל וְכִמְעֻשָּׂר מְעוּרָבִין זֶה בְזֶה דִּבְרֵי רִבִּי. רַבָּן שִׁמְעוֹן בֶּן גַּמְלִיאֵל אוֹמֵר חֶלְקוֹ שֶׁל יִשְׂרָאֵל חַיָּב. חֶלְקוֹ שֶׁל גּוֹי פָּטוּר. רִבִּי יָסָא בְשֵׁם רִבִּי חֲנִינָא מַה פְלִיגִין בְּשֶׁחִלְּקוּ שָׂדֶה בְקָמָתָהּ. אֲבָל אִם חִלְּקוּ גָּדִישׁ אַף רַבָּן שִׁמְעוֹן בֶּן גַּמְלִיאֵל מוֹדֶה לְרִבִּי שֶׁכָּל־קֶלַח וְקֶלַח שֶׁל שׁוּתָּפוּת הוּא. אָמַר רִבִּי יוֹנָה רִבִּי יוֹסֵי בְשֵׁם רִבִּי יוֹחָנָן מַה פְלִיגִין בְּשֶׁחִלְּקוּ שָׂדֶה בְקָמָתָהּ. אֲבָל אִם חִלְּקוּ עֳמָרִים אַף רַבָּן שִׁמְעוֹן בֶּן גַּמְלִיאֵל מוֹדֶה לְרִבִּי שֶׁכָּל־קֶלַח וְקֶלַח שֶׁל שׁוּתָּפוּת הוּא. עַל דַּעְתֵּיהּ דְּרִבִּי יוֹנָה מַה בֵין גָּדִישׁ וּמַה בֵּין עֳמָרִים. בְּקוֹצֵר כָּל־שֶׁהוּא וּמֵנִיחַ לְפָנָיו. אָמַר רִבִּי הוֹשַׁעְיָא הָדָא דְתֵימָא שֶׁקָּנוּ עַל מְנָת שֶׁלֹּא לַחֲלוֹק. אֲבָל אִם קָנוּ עַל מְנָת לַחֲלוֹק אוּף רִבִּי מוֹדֶה לְרַבָּן שִׁמְעוֹן בֶּן גַּמְלִיאֵל שֶׁזֶּה חֵלֶק מַגִּיעַ לוֹ מִשָּׁעָה רִאשׁוֹנָה. אָמַר רִבִּי יוֹסֵי מִילֵּיהוֹן דְּרַבָּנִין פְלִיגִין דְּאָמַר רִבִּי אַבָּהוּ בְשֵׁם רִבִּי יוֹחָנָן הַשּׁוּתָּפִין מַחְלוֹקֶת רִבִּי וְרַבָּן שִׁמְעוֹן בֶּן גַּמְלִיאֵל. הָאַחִין הַשּׁוּתָּפִין לֹא לַחֲלוֹק הֵן.

Halakhah 9: It was stated[155]: "If a Jew and a Gentile bought a field in Syria, it is as if *ṭevel* and tithed produce were mixed together, the words of Rebbi[156]. Rebbi Simeon ben Gamliel says, the Jew's part is obligated, the Gentile's part is free." Rebbi Yasa in the name of Rebbi Ḥanina: When do they disagree? If they split the field while the grain was standing[157]. But if they split grain stacks, even Rabban Simeon ben Gamliel will agree with Rebbi that every single stalk belongs to the partnership[158]. Rebbi Jonah said, Rebbi Yose in the name of Rebbi Joḥanan: When do they disagree? If they split the field while the grain was standing. But if they split sheaves, even Rabban Simeon ben Gamliel will agree with Rebbi that every single stalk belongs to the partnership. According to Rebbi Jonah, what is the difference between stacks and sheaves[159]? If he harvests a small amount and shares with his partner. Rebbi Hoshaia said, that is, if they bought with the idea that they would not split. But if they bought with the idea that they always would split, Rebbi will agree with Rabban Simeon ben Gamliel that his part already belonged to him from the first moment[160]. Rebbi Yose said, the words of the rabbis disagree[161] since Rebbi Abbahu in the name of Rebbi Joḥanan said that partners are the subject of the disagreement between Rebbi and Rabban Simeon ben Gamliel[162]. Are brothers who split not like these partners[163]?

155 (Halakhah 10 in the Venice print.) Tosephta *Terumot* 2:10. The status of Syria is explained in *Peah*, Chapter 7, Note 119.

156 Since the Gentile is under no obligation for heave, the harvest itself is untitheable; heave and tithes must be given from obligated produce. The Jew's part of the crop must be tithed from a third, purely Jewish, source.

157 Standing grain is not subject to heave and tithes. Hence, if they split when the grain was standing, the partnership was dissolved before the obligation of heave started.

158 Since it was cut in common, they hold that there is no retroactive determination which part of the harvest really belonged to whom.

159 Grain is transported to the threshing floor in sheaves. Making sheaves therefore is the start of turning wheat into grain. Grain being subject to heave and tithes, at that time splitting can no longer determine the status of the harvest. For Rebbi, the start of the harvest determines, for Rabban Simeon only the binding of sheaves.

160 Retroactively the part of each partner was determined even though it is not determined by any place on the

common field. (Such retroactivity, in the Babli called ברירה, usually is admitted only for rabbinic obligations. The obligation of a field in Syria is rabbinic.)

161 They disprove the statement of R. Hoshaia.

162 This refers to Mishnah *Šeqalim* 1:7, *Bekhorot* 9:3, about the tithes on newborn calves and lambs and the *agio* to be paid the agents of the Temple when the yearly Temple tax of one-half *sheqel* was due (fee for the banker, amounting to $^1/_{24}$th of the coins exchanged, to exchange half-sheqels into full sheqels.) Partnerships are not subject to tithes on animals or to the *agio*; partners contribute full sheqels that need no exchanging. The Mishnah states at both places that the rules for *agio* and tithes are opposite. If heirs never divided up the inheritance, they are subject to tithes because the flock is still their father's, but are free from *agio* because they pay as one entity. If they divide the inheritance and afterwards form a new partnership they are free from tithes as partners but subject to *agio* because each one pays for himself. Rebbi Johanan points out that the rule on the undivided inheritance is not accepted by everybody.

163 If they split the inheritance, they inherited with the intent of splitting. If Rebbi would accept the argument of R. Hoshaia, he could not write in the Mishnah that the undivided inheritance is subject to tithe on animals.

(fol. 25a) **משנה י:** גֵּר וְגוֹי שֶׁיָּרְשׁוּ אֶת אֲבִיהֶם גּוֹי יָכוֹל הוּא לוֹמַר טוֹל אַתָּה עֲבוֹדָה זָרָה וַאֲנִי אֶטּוֹל אֶת הַמָּעוֹת אַתָּה יַיִן נֶסֶךְ וַאֲנִי פֵּירוֹת. אִם מִשֶּׁבָּאוּ לִרְשׁוּת הַגֵּר אָסוּר.

Mishnah 10: If a proselyte and a Gentile inherited from their Gentile father, the proselyte may say, take the idols and I shall take money, take the wine for libations and I shall take produce[164]. After they came into the proselyte's possession, this is forbidden.

164 Idols and wine that might be used for libations to the gods are forbidden for any and all usufruct; if they come into the hands of a Jew they must be destroyed. In Jewish view, the proselyte becomes a new person by converting; he has no legal family relationship with his prior kin. The part he inherits under Gentile law is not his until it is delivered into his hands. Therefore, he is permitted to try to get things that are useful to him. But the moment anything idolatrous came into his legal possession, he is bound to destroy it. The Yerushalmi treats this as reasonable legal construction. The Babli (*Avodah zarah* 64a) treats it as a special leniency, rather than a general law.

(fol. 25d) **הלכה י:** יִשְׂרָאֵל וְגוֹי שֶׁקָּנוּ בֵּיתוֹ שֶׁל גּוֹי וְהָיָה שָׁם יֵין נֶסֶךְ וַעֲבוֹדָה זָרָה וּמָעוֹת לֹא יֹאמַר לוֹ טוֹל אַתְּ יֵין נֶסֶךְ וַעֲבוֹדָה זָרָה וַאֲנִי מָעוֹת. אָמַר רִבִּי יוֹחָנָן לֹא סוֹף דָּבָר יֵין נֶסֶךְ וַעֲבוֹדָה זָרָה וּמָעוֹת אֶלָּא אֲפִילוּ הָיוּ שָׁם שְׁנֵי צְלָמִין אֶחָד עָשׂוּי כְּמִין דֶּלְפוֹקֵי וְאֶחָד שֶׁאֵינוֹ עָשׂוּי כְּמִין דֶּלְפוֹקֵי לֹא יֹאמַר לוֹ טוֹל אַתָּה אֶת שֶׁאֵינוֹ עָשׂוּי כְּמִין דֶּלְפוֹקֵי וַאֲנִי נוֹטֵל הֶעָשׂוּי כְּמִין דֶּלְפוֹקֵי. אָמַר רִבִּי זְעִירָא וְיָאוּת אִילּוּ חָבֵר וְעַם הָאָרֶץ שֶׁיָּרְשׁוּ אֶת אֲבִיהֶן עַם הָאָרֶץ וְהָיוּ שָׁם פֵּירוֹת מוּכְשָׁרִין וּפֵירוֹת שֶׁאֵינָן מוּכְשָׁרִין שֶׁמָּא אוֹמֵר לוֹ טוֹל אַתָּה אֶת הַמּוּכְשָׁרִין וַאֲנִי נוֹטֵל אֶת שֶׁאֵינָן מוּכְשָׁרִין. וְהָא מַתְנִיתִין פְּלִיגָא טוֹל אַתָּה עֲבוֹדָה זָרָה וַאֲנִי מָעוֹת אַתָּה יֵין נֶסֶךְ וַאֲנִי פֵּירוֹת. אָמַר סוֹפָא וְלֵית הִיא פְּלִיגָא אִם מִשֶּׁבָּאוּ לִרְשׁוּת הַגֵּר אָסוּר וְהָכָא מִכֵּיוָן שֶׁקָּנָה כְּמִי שֶׁנִּכְנַס לִרְשׁוּתוֹ.

Halakhah 10[164]: "If[165] a Jew and a Gentile bought a Gentile's house and found there idols, libation wine, and coins, he should not tell him, take the idols and libation wine, and I shall take the coins." Rebbi Joḥanan said, not only idols, libation wine, and coins, but even if there were two idols, one shaped as a tripod[166] and one not shaped as a tripod, he should not tell him, take the one that is not shaped as a tripod and I shall take the one shaped like a tripod[167]. Rebbi Zeïra said, that is correct, since even in the case of a *ḥaver* and an *am haärez* who inherited from their *am haärez* father and found there produce which might become impure and produce which might not, may he say to him, you take the produce which might become impure and I shall take that which might not[168]? But our Mishnah disagrees: "Take the idols and I shall take money, take the wine for libations and I shall take produce." But the end shows that there is no disagreement: "After they came into the possession of the proselyte, this is forbidden;" here, from the moment he acquired it it is as if it entered into his possession[169].

164 In the Venice print, Halakhah 11.

165 Tosephta *Demay* 6:13. The reason is explained at the end of the paragraph.

166 Greek δέλφιξ "tripod" [e. g. "three-legged pot", which might be dedicated to a temple.]

167 Both in the Tosephta and the statement of R. Johanan, the exchange would bring an illicit monetary gain through articles from which any usufruct is forbidden.

168 The produce that might become impure since it was in the hands of an *am haärez*, must be assumed to be impure and unfit for consumption by a *ḥaver*. According to Rashi (Babli *Ḥagigah* 25b), the *ḥaver* would be guilty of transgressing the prohibition to put an obstacle before a blind person if he steered his brother the *am haärez* to produce which, by the *ḥaver*'s rules, should not be eaten by a Jew.

169 In practical Jewish law, paying for real estate does not convey the title but only permits acquisition of the title. For actual possession, entering the property or some substitute symbolic action is required. However, since this real estate is acquired under Gentile law, concluding the contract has the force of conveying the title; hence, from the moment the title is transferred in Gentile law, the Jew can no longer try to give the unwanted articles to his Gentile partner. The implication is that a stipulation, contained in a transaction giving the idols to the Gentile and executed before the contract for sale of the real estate was drawn up, would be valid by the Yerushalmi's standards. This inference seems to be denied in the Babli, *Avodah zarah* 64a.

עֲקִילַס הַגֵּר חִילֵּק עִם אֶחָיו וְהֶחֱמִיר עַל עַצְמוֹ וְהוֹלִיךְ הֲנָייָה לְיַם הַמֶּלַח. תְּלָתָא אֲמוֹרִין חַד אָמַר דְּמֵי עֲבוֹדָה זָרָה הוֹלִיךְ לְיַם הַמֶּלַח. וְחָרָנָא אָמַר דְּמֵי חֶלְקוֹ שֶׁל עֲבוֹדָה זָרָה הוֹלִיךְ לְיַם הַמֶּלַח. וְחָרָנָא אָמַר עֲבוֹדָה זָרָה עַצְמָהּ הוֹלִיךְ לְיַם הַמֶּלַח. אֶלָּא בִּשְׁבִיל לַעֲקוֹר עֲבוֹדָה זָרָה מִבֵּית אַבָּא.

"Aquila the Proselyte[170] split with his brothers; he restricted himself and brought his gain to the Dead Sea." Three Amoraïm; one said that he brought the price of the idols to the Dead Sea, another said that he brought the price of his part in the idols to the Dead Sea, and another said that he brought the idols themselves to the Dead Sea, in order to remove them from his father's house.

170 Tosephta *Demay* 6:13. Aquila was a student of Rebbis Eliezer and Joshua and the author of a very literal translation of the Bible. He did not avail himself of the permission given in the Mishnah but took his share of the idols (or their price) and threw them into the Dead Sea, which was the ultimate way of making sure that nobody would derive any benefit from them.

(fol. 25a) **משנה יא**: הַמּוֹכֵר פֵּירוֹת בְּסוּרְיָא וְאָמַר מִשֶּׁל אֶרֶץ יִשְׂרָאֵל הֵן חַייָב לְעַשֵּׂר. מְעוּשָּׂרִין הֵן נֶאֱמָן שֶׁהַפֶּה שֶׁאָסַר הוּא הַפֶּה שֶׁהִתִּיר. מִשֶּׁלִּי הֵן חַייָב לְעַשֵּׂר. מְעוּשָּׂרִין הֵן נֶאֱמָן שֶׁהַפֶּה שֶׁאָסַר הוּא הַפֶּה שֶׁהִתִּיר. אִם יָדוּעַ הוּא שֶׁיֵּשׁ לוֹ שָׂדֶה בְּסוּרְיָא חַייָב לְעַשֵּׂר.

Mishnah 11: He who sells produce in Syria and says: 'They are from the Land of Israel,' must tithe them. 'They are tithed,' one believes him because the mouth that forbade is the mouth that permits[171]. 'They are from my field[172],' he must tithe them. 'They are tithed,' one believes him because the mouth that forbade is the mouth that permits. If it is known that he has a field in Syria, he must tithe[173].

171 A a general principle, a person who gives detrimental information about which no other source of information is available has the right to testify to circumstances that would remove the detrimental interpretation.

172 A field in Syria is subject to tithes only if it is the property of a Jew.

173 In that case, it is not his mouth which tells that he must tithe.

(fol. 25d) **הלכה יא**: תַּמָּן תַּנֵּינָן נֶאֱמָנִין עַל הַלֶּקֶט וְעַל הַשִּׁכְחָה וְעַל הַפֵּיאָה בְּשַׁעְתָּן. וְהָכָא אַתְּ אָמַר הָכֵן. תַּמָּן שֶׁתִּיקְנוֹ פָּטוּר בְּרַם הָכָא שֶׁתִּיקּוּנוֹ חַיָּיב. וְתַנֵּי כֵן אֶת שֶׁתִּיקְנוֹ פָּטוּר נֶאֱמָן לְהַחֲמִיר בְּרַם הָכָא פֵּירוּשׁוֹ לְהָקֵל נֶאֱמָן.

Halakhah 11[174]: There[175], we have stated: "They can be trusted about gleanings, forgotten sheaves, and *peah* at harvest time." And here you say so[176]? There, his assertion is for exemption, but here his assertion is for obligation. And we have stated so[177]: "If his assertion is for exemption, he may be trusted in restrictions." But here, he can be trusted even if his explanation is to make it easier[178].

174 Halakhah 12 in Venice print.

175 Mishnah *Peah* 8:2. There, everybody knows that the person is poor; hence, it is not the mouth which forbade the produce, asserting that it was not tithed, that could permit it without tithing as gifts to the poor. Nevertheless, the Mishnah asserts that the poor can be trusted.

176 In Syria, nobody is trusted if his negative information can be verified by other sources. [All commentators here follow the different interpretation of R. Eliahu Fulda which, however, is based on a forced emendation of the text.]

177 This *baraita* is not found in parallel sources, but a similar statement appears in the quote from the Tosephta in the next paragraph.

178 Hence, he can only be trusted if his initial information is not available from other sources.

תַּנֵּי גּוֹי שֶׁהָיָה צוֹוֵחַ וְאוֹמֵר בּוֹאוּ וּטְלוּ לָכֶם מִמֶּנִּי פֵּירוֹת הֵן פֵּירוֹת עָרְלָה הֵן פֵּירוֹת נֶטַע רְבָעִי אֵינוֹ נֶאֱמָן. אִם אָמַר מִגּוֹי פְּלוֹנִי הֵבֵאתִים נֶאֱמָן לְהַחֲמִיר

דִּבְרֵי רִבִּי. וַחֲכָמִים אוֹמְרִים דִּבְרֵי הַגּוֹי לֹא מַעֲלִין וְלֹא מוֹרִידִין. רִבִּי יוּדָן בְּעֵי הָיָה צוֹוֵחַ לְפִי תוּמּוֹ. רִבִּי יוּדָן בְּעֵי מִמָּה דְתֵימָה כּוּתִי כְגוֹי. דְּאִיתְפַּלְגוּן כּוּתִי כְגוֹי דִּבְרֵי רִבִּי. רַבָּן שִׁמְעוֹן בֶּן גַּמְלִיאֵל אוֹמֵר כּוּתִי כְיִשְׂרָאֵל לְכָל דָּבָר.

It was stated[179]: "A Gentile who was calling out, 'come and buy fruits from me, they are from an *orlah* tree[180], they are from a vineyard in its fourth year[181],' cannot be believed. If he says, 'I brought them from a certain Gentile,' he may be trusted for restrictions[182], the words of Rebbi. The Sages say, the words of a Gentile are irrelevant[183]." Rebbi Judan asked, what if he calls out when he is uninformed[184]? Rebbi Judan asked, what if one holds that a Samaritan is like a Gentile, since they disagreed: "A Samaritan is like a Gentile, the words of Rebbi. Rabban Simeon ben Gamliel says, a Samaritan is like a Jew in all respects[185]"?

179 Tosephta *Demai* 5:2: "A Gentile who was calling out, 'come and buy fruits, they are from Azeqa, from an *orlah* tree, from a vineyard in its fourth year,' cannot be believed because he intends to advertise. But if he says, 'I bought them from a certain Gentile,' he is to be trusted for restrictions, the words of Rebbi. Rabban Simeon ben Gamliel says, he cannot be trusted since the words of a Gentile are irrelevant."

180 A tree in the first three years after planting, when its fruits are forbidden for all use (*Lev.* 19:23).

181 See *Peah* 7:6.

182 He can be believed in that the produce is untithed; he cannot be believed that the produce is not subject to heave and tithes.

183 As far as Jewish religious obligations are concerned.

184 If he never heard of Jewish restrictions, or calls out in a place without any Jewish inhabitants. The questions are not answered, so they must be answered in a restrictive sense.

185 Cf. *Demay* 3:4, *Berakhot* 7:1.

אָמַר רִבִּי בּוּן בַּר חִיָּיא וְהוּא שֶׁיְּהֵא רוֹב מִכְנָסוֹ מִשֶּׁלּוֹ.

Rebbi Abun bar Ḥiyya said, that is only if most of what he takes in comes from his own[186].

186 This refers to the last statement in the Mishnah, that he will not be trusted for tithes if it is known that he has a field in Syria. If most of his fields are outside both Syria and the Holy Land, he still will be believed.

יִשְׂרָאֵל שֶׁהָיָה לוֹ אָרִיס בְּסוּרְיָא וְשִׁילַּח לוֹ פֵּירוֹת וְאָמַר הֲרֵי אֵילוּ מְעוּשָּׂרִין. אֲנִי אוֹמֵר מִן הַשּׁוּק לָקַח וְהוּא שֶׁיְּהֵא אוֹתוֹ הַמִּין מָצוּי בַשּׁוּק. לֹא סוֹף דָּבָר בְּשֶׁאֵין לוֹ מֵאוֹתוֹ הַמִּין תּוֹךְ שָׂדֵהוּ אֶלָּא אֲפִילוּ יֵשׁ לוֹ מֵאוֹתוֹ הַמִּין לְתוֹךְ שָׂדֵהוּ מִכֵּיוָן שֶׁאוֹתוֹ הַמִּין מָצוּי בַשּׁוּק מוּתָּר.

If a Jew had a sharecropper[187] in Syria who sent him fruits and said that they were tithed; I say that he bought them on the market, if that kind is found on the market. Not only if he does not grow that kind on his field, but even if he does grow that kind on his field; since that kind is found on the market it is permitted.

187 An *am haärez* who, in general, cannot be trusted in matters of tithes. But since in Syria most produce on the market comes from Gentile farmers who are exempt from tithes, it is to be assumed that the fruits come from a Gentile source and are permitted without tithing.

(fol. 25a) **משנה יב:** עַם הָאָרֶץ שֶׁאָמַר לְחָבֵר קַח לִי אֲגוּדַּת יֶרֶק קַח לִי קְלוֹסְקִין לוֹקֵחַ סְתָם פָּטוּר. אִם אָמַר זוֹ שֶׁלִּי וְזוֹ שֶׁל חֲבֵירִי וְנִתְעָרְבוּ חַייָב לְעַשֵּׂר אֲפִילוּ הֵן מֵאָה.

Mishnah 12: An *am haärez* who said to a *ḥaver*, buy for me a bunch of vegetables, buy for me a loaf[188], if he buys anonymously, he is free[189]. If he says, this one is for me[190] and that one is for my friend, if they became mixed up he has to tithe, even if there are a hundred.

188 Greek κόλλιξ, "roll, loaf of coarse bread."

189 Since the produce or the roll never was the property of the *haver*, he is not under the obligation to tithe before he delivers the goods. (Explanation of R. S. Lieberman.)

190 Therefore, if they became mixed up they become the *haver*'s property before delivery and must be tithed.

(fol. 25d) **הלכה יב**: מַתְנִיתִין דְּרַבִּי יוֹסֵי דְּתַנֵּי הַלּוֹקֵחַ סְתָם צָרִיךְ לְעַשֵּׂר. מַה נָן קַיָּמִין. אִם בְּשֶׁאָמַר לוֹ צֵא וּלְקַח לִי שְׁלוּחוֹ הוּא. צֵא וּלְקַח לָךְ שֶׁלּוֹ הֵן. אֶלָּא כִּי נָן קַיָּמִין בִּסְתָם רִבִּי יוּדָא אוֹמֵר לֹא נִתְכַּוֵּן הַמּוֹכֵר לְזַכּוֹת אֶלָּא לַלּוֹקֵחַ. רִבִּי יוֹסֵי אוֹמֵר לֹא נִתְכַּוֵּן הַמּוֹכֵר לְזַכּוֹת אֶלָּא לְבַעַל הַמָּעוֹת. לְפִיכָךְ אִם נָתַן אַחַת יְתֵירָה רִבִּי יוּדָה אוֹמֵר שֶׁל לוֹקֵחַ. רִבִּי יוֹסֵי אוֹמֵר שֶׁל שְׁנֵיהֶן. מְחִלְפָה שִׁיטָּתֵיהּ דְּרִבִּי יוֹסֵי. תַּמָּן הוּא אוֹמֵר לֹא נִתְכַּוֵּן הַמּוֹכֵר לְזַכּוֹת אֶלָּא לְבַעַל הַמָּעוֹת וְכָא אַתְּ אָמַר הָכֵין. כַּאן עַל יְדֵי מָעוֹתָיו שֶׁל זֶה וְעַל יְדֵי רַגְלָיו שֶׁל זֶה שְׁנֵיהֶן חוֹלְקִין.

Halakhah 12: Our Mishnah follows Rebbi Yose, as we have stated: "He who buys anonymously has to tithe[191]." What are we talking about? If he said to him, go and buy for me, he is his agent[192]; go and buy for yourself, they are his property[193]. But in our case nothing was spelled out. Rebbi Jehudah says that the seller wants the person who buys to get the property rights[194], Rebbi Yose says that the seller wants the owner of the money to get the property rights. Therefore, if he added a piece[195], Rebbi Jehudah says, it belongs to the buyer, Rebbi Yose says, it belongs to both of them. The argument of Rebbi Yose seems to be inverted. There he says that the seller wants the owner of the money to get the property rights, and here you say so[196]? Here the transaction is through the money of one and the feet of the other, therefore they split.

191 This statement itself is not found in other sources, but there are two versions of the underlying *baraita* that explain the situation. Tosephta

Demay 8:1: "If an *am haärez̧* said to a *ḥaver*, buy for me a bunch of vegetables, buy for me a loaf, Rebbi Yose says the *ḥaver* does not have to tithe, Rebbi Jehudah says he does." Babli *Erubin* 37b: " If an *am haärez̧* said to a *ḥaver*, buy for me a bunch of vegetables, buy for me a loaf, Rebbi Yose says the *ḥaver* does not have to tithe, but the Sages say he does."

192 According to all opinions, he should not have to tithe since in all respects he represents the *am haärez̧* who had commissioned him.

193 According to all opinions he has to tithe before he delivers to the *am haärez̧*. There seems to be no place for the disagreement between R. Yose and R. Jehudah.

194 Since in handing over the merchandise, the seller also agrees to transmit the rights to the merchandise, it matters to whom the seller wants to transmit those rights.

195 If the seller delivered a little more than was ordered for the price of the goods ordered, it depends on who is considered the recipient of the seller's gift. This depends on our interpretation of the disagreement between Rebbis Jehudah and Yose. A slightly different version is quoted in Babli *Ketubot* 98b. There, Rashi refers to Tosephta *Demay*; it should read: Yerushalmi *Demay*.

196 Why should the agent get anything if the property is given to the owner of the money? The Babli, *Ketubot* 98b, gives a different answer: If the unit price of the merchandise is fixed, then any addition is a gift and is jointly owned. If the unit price is not fixed, then the additional amount is part of the sale and totally belongs to the owner of the money.

תַּנֵּי רַבָּן שִׁמְעוֹן בֶּן גַּמְלִיאֵל אוֹמֵר אִם הֶחֱלִיף אֶת הַמָּעָה צָרִיךְ לְעַשֵּׂר. אָמַר רִבִּי יוֹסֵי הָדָא אָמַר הַנּוֹתֵן מָעוֹת לַחֲבֵירוֹ לְהַחֲלִיפָן וְאָבְדוּ חַיָּיב בְּאַחֲרָיוּתָן.

It was stated[197]: "Rabban Simeon ben Gamliel says, if he exchanged the coin he has to tithe." Rebbi Yose[198] said, this means that if somebody gives coins to another person to exchange them, when they are lost the recipient is answerable for their alienation.

197 Tosephta *Demay* 8:1. If the buyer took the coin for himself, it becomes his property and he owes the original owner money. Hence, if he

buys, he acquires the merchandise and as a *ḥaver*, he has to tithe.

198 The Amora. The alienation means that the coins fall in unauthorized hands (that they are lost or stolen.)

שְׁמוּאֵל אָמַר בְּמַחֲלִיק בְּיָדָיו. אָמַר רִבִּי לָעְזָר הוּא שֶׁנָּטַל חֶלְקוֹ בְסוֹף. אָמַר רִבִּי יוֹנָה צוּרְכָה לְדֵן וְצוּרְכָה לְדֵן. חִילֵּק בְּיָדוֹ וְנָטַל חֶלְקוֹ בַתְּחִילָּה אֵינוֹ צָרִיךְ לְעַשֵּׂר אֶלָּא עַל שֶׁלּוֹ. לֹא חִילֵּק בְּיָדוֹ וְנָטַל חֶלְקוֹ בַסּוֹף אֵינוֹ מְעַשֵּׂר אֶלָּא עַל שֶׁלּוֹ.

Samuel[199] says, if he distributes it himself[200]. Rebbi Eleazar said, only if he took his share last[201]. Rebbi Jonah said, both statements are necessary[202]. If he[203] distributes it himself and took his share first he only has to tithe his share. If he[204] did not distribute it but took his share last, he only has to tithe his share.

199 This refers to the last case in the Mishnah: he bought explicitly for himself and his partner but then the produce was mixed up.

200 If the seller gave the two lots separately the *ḥaver* did not acquire the *am haäreẓ*'s part and might not have to tithe.

201 In some situations, the *ḥaver* might have to tithe only his own share if he took it last.

202 Samuel and R. Eleazar do not disagree but speak about different scenarios.

203 The seller; the next "he" is the *ḥaver* buyer who never acquired the produce destined for the *am haäreẓ* and is not responsible for it.

204 The seller did not divide but the *ḥaver* who bought resolved in his mind that all produce would be the *am haäreẓ*'s except the last bunch that would be for himself.

תַּנֵּי אוֹמֵר הוּא אָדָם לְפוֹעֵל הֵילָךְ דֵּינַר זֶה אֱכוֹל בּוֹ. הֵילָךְ דֵּינַר זֶה שְׁתֵה בּוֹ וְאֵינוֹ חוֹשֵׁשׁ עַל שְׂכָרוֹ לֹא מִשּׁוּם שְׁבִיעִית וְלֹא מִשּׁוּם מַעְשְׂרוֹת וְלֹא מִשּׁוּם יֵיַן נֶסֶךְ. אֲבָל אִם אָמַר לוֹ צֵא וּלְקַח לָךְ כִּכָּר וַאֲנִי נוֹתֵן לָךְ דָּמִים. צֵא וּלְקַח לָךְ רְבִיעִית שֶׁל יַיִן וַאֲנִי נוֹתֵן לָךְ דָּמִים חוֹשְׁשִׁין עַל שְׂכָרוֹ מִשּׁוּם שְׁבִיעִית וּמִשּׁוּם

מַעְשְׂרוֹת וּמִשּׁוּם יַיִן נֶסֶךְ. אָמַר רִבִּי זְעִירָא נַעֲשֶׂה הַחֶנְווָנִי שְׁלוּחוֹ שֶׁל בַּעַל הַבַּיִת לִזְכּוֹת לַפּוֹעֵל. (fol. 26a) אָמַר רִבִּי הִילָא פּוֹעֵל זָכָה לְבַעַל הַבַּיִת מִשֶּׁל חֶנְווָנִי וְחוֹזֵר וְזוֹכֶה לְעַצְמוֹ. מַה נְפַק מִבֵּינֵיהוֹן. הָיָה הַחֶנְווָנִי חֵרֵשׁ עַל דַּעְתֵּיהּ דְּרִבִּי זְעִירָא לֹא חָשַׁשׁ שֶׁאֵין שְׁלִיחוּת לְחֵרֵשׁ. עַל דַּעְתֵּיהּ דְּרִבִּי הִילָא חוֹשֵׁשׁ.

It was stated[205]: "One may say to his worker[207]: Here you have a denar, use it for food, here you have a denar, use it for drink, and not be worried about either the Sabbatical year[208], tithes, or wine for libations[209]. But if he told him, go and buy yourself a loaf and I shall give you the money, go and buy yourself a *reviït* of wine and I shall give you the money, he has to worry[209] because of the Sabbatical year, tithes, and wine used for libations." Rebbi Zeïra said[210], the grocer becomes the plenipotentiary of the employer to let the worker acquire[211]. Rebbi Hila said, the worker acquired for the employer from the grocer[212] and then acquires it himself. What is the difference between them? If the grocer was deaf-mute. According to Rebbi Zeïra, he[213] does not have to worry because a deaf-mute cannot become a plenipotentiary[214]; according to Rebbi Hila, he has to worry.

205 Tosephta *Demay* 5:14, *Avodah zarah* 8:10, quoted in Babli *Avodah zarah* 63a, where, however, the second case is formulated so that the employer offers to pay the store for the purchases of the employee. The version discussed here, that the employer guarantees the employee's expenses, is also in Yerushalmi *Qiddušin* 2:1 (fol. 62c), together with the interpretations of Rebbis Zeïra and Hila (Illa, La).

206 In case the worker is either an *am haärez* or a Gentile.

207 That the *am haärez* worker would buy produce grown in the Sabbatical year which is forbidden for commercial transactions, or *demay* food and not tithe it. Since the money was given beforehand, it is spent on the responsibility of the worker alone.

208 If the worker is a Gentile, one assumes that he pours out a small libation before he drinks and the wine

is forbidden for usufruct since it was used for a pagan rite.

209 Since food and drink were bought on the employer's credit, it is sinful for the employer to let the employee transgress religious laws on his behalf, or to have the Gentile worker use on his behalf wine of which all usufruct is forbidden to a Jew.

210 Why does the employer sin when the employee buys forbidden foods with his money?

211 Hence, it is as if the employer himself gave the forbidden food to his employee and the employer is guilty of transgressing the prohibition to put a stone into the path of a blind man.

212 In most cases, the opinion of R. Hila is not materially different from that of R. Zeïra, but in his opinion the grocer does not have any responsibility. (In the Babli version, the role of the grocer is the only question and it leads to rather forced solutions. The position of R. Hila is explicitly rejected in the Babli, *Qiddušin* 8b, as explained in חידושי הרשב"א *ad loc.*)

213 The employer.

214 The deaf-mute cannot act without a guardian.

תַּנֵּי לֹא יֹאמַר אָדָם לַחֲבֵירוֹ הֵילָךְ מָאתַיִם דֵּינַר וּשְׁקוֹל עַל יָדַי לָאוֹצָר אֶלָּא אוֹמֵר הוּא לוֹ פֶּרְשֵׁנִי מִן הָאוֹצָר. וְכֵן לֹא יֹאמַר אָדָם לַחֲבֵירוֹ הֵילָךְ מָאתַיִם דֵּינַר וּשְׁקוֹל עַל יָדַי לָאוּמָנוּת אֶלָּא אוֹמֵר הוּא לוֹ פֶּרְשֵׁנִי מִן הָאוּמָנוּת.

It was stated[215]: "A person should not say to his friend, here you have 200 *zuz* and pay for me to the treasury, but he says to him, free me from the treasury[216]. Similarly, a person should not say to his friend, here you have 200 *zuz* and pay the *leiturgia*[217], but he says to him, free me from the *leiturgia*."

215 Tosephta *Demay* 6:4: "A Jew should not say to a Gentile, a Samaritan, or to one who cannot be trusted with tithes, here you have 200 *zuz* and pay for me to the treasury, but he says to him, free me from the treasury. Similarly, a person should not say to his friend, here you have 200 *zuz* and pay the *leiturgia*, but he says to him, separate me from the *leiturgia*." The parallel is in Babli *Avodah zarah* 71a.

216 The government requires taxes not in money but food and wine, where

the Jew cannot appoint a plenipotentiary who for him buys untithed produce or, if he is a Gentile, wine for libations. He has to formulate it so that the other party (those described in the Tosephta) will not be appointed plenipotentiary. In the interpretation of R. Solomon ben Adrat (תשובות הרשב״א חלק א, תרפו), the king has wine which he forces the citizens to buy at fixed prices. Since this is all wine for libations, the Jew is unable to buy the wine for himself, so he gives money to his Gentile friend and tells him, not to buy for him, but to free him from his obligation. It is possible that the treasury will be satisfied with money and will not insist on delivery of the wine, but if it delivers, the wine will be the Gentile's.

217 Greek λειτουργία, ἡ. "public service", offices and obligations forced upon private citizens by the government. Obligations included providing food and wine to officials or troups. The Jew himself could not satisfy his obligations with cheaper untithed produce and Gentile wine. (Cf. R. Solomon ben Adrat *loc. cit.*; בעל התרומות שער מו ח״ד יח in the name of Nachmanides.)

המזמין פרק שביעי

(fol. 26a) **משנה א**: הַמַּזְמִין אֶת חֲבֵירוֹ שֶׁיֹּאכַל אֶצְלוֹ וְהוּא אֵינוֹ מַאֲמִינוֹ עַל הַמַּעְשְׂרוֹת. אוֹמֵר מֵעֶרֶב שַׁבָּת מַה שֶּׁאֲנִי עָתִיד לְהַפְרִישׁ לְמָחָר הֲרֵי הוּא מַעֲשֵׂר וּשְׁאָר מַעֲשֵׂר סָמוּךְ לוֹ. זֶה שֶׁעָשִׂיתִי מַעֲשֵׂר עָשׂוּי תְּרוּמַת מַעֲשֵׂר עָלָיו וּמַעֲשֵׂר שֵׁנִי בִּצְפוֹנוֹ וּבִדְרוֹמוֹ וּמְחוּלָּל עַל הַמָּעוֹת.

Mishnah 1: If somebody invites his friend for a meal[1] but the latter does not trust him with tithes, the friend should say on Friday eve: That which I will separate in the future shall be tithe, the rest of tithe near to it[2]. That which I made tithe shall be the heave of the tithe for everything, and the Second Tithe shall be to the North (or South) and be redeemed by coins[3].

1   On the Sabbath, when tithing is forbidden.

2   The nine tenths of the tithe that one is not required to give.

3   It is understood that the prospective guest must have some coins at home, reserved for redemptions. Each time some Second Tithe is redeemed, a *peruṭah*, one-eighth of an obolus, must be deducted from the value of the coin. If all value has been used, the coin should be destroyed.

הלכה א: אָמַר רִבִּי יוֹחָנָן מַתְנִיתָא בִּדְמַאי הָא בְּוַדַּאי לֹא. מַתְנִיתָא אָמַר אֲפִילוּ בְּוַדַּאי זוֹ תַגִּינָן תַּמָּן הָיוּ לוֹ תְאֵנִים שֶׁל טֶבֶל בְּתוֹךְ בֵּיתוֹ וְהוּא בְּבֵית הַמִּדְרָשׁ אוֹ בַשָּׂדֶה. אִין תֵּימַר בִּדְמַאי אֲנַן קַייָמִין לֵית יָכִיל דְּתַגִּינָן הָיוּ דְמַאי מַה אָמַר רִבִּי יוֹחָנָן בִּדְמַאי לֹא בְּוַדַּאי לֹא אָמַר אֶלָּא מַתְנִיתָא בִּדְמַאי. מַה בֵּין דְּמַאי וּמַה בֵּין וַדַּאי. דְּמַאי אָדָם מַתְנֶה עַל דָּבָר שֶׁאֵינוֹ בִרְשׁוּתוֹ וַדַּאי אֵין אָדָם מַתְנֶה אֶלָּא עַל דָּבָר שֶׁהוּא בִרְשׁוּתוֹ.

Halakhah 1: Rebbi Joḥanan said: The Mishnah deals with *demay*. Hence, not with certain produce[4]? A Mishnah[5] says, even for certain produce, as we have stated there: "If he had *ṭevel* figs in his house and he was in the House of Study or on the field." If you want to say that we deal with *demay*, you cannot do so, since it is stated[6]: "If it was *demay*." What Rebbi Joḥanan said was that it deals with *demay*. He did not say, not with certain produce, but that this Mishnah deals with *demay*[7]. What is the difference between *demay* and certain produce? For *demay*, a person may make a proviso for something that is not in his possession; for certain produce, he may only make a proviso for something that is in his possession.

4 Either *ṭevel* or produce from which heave was taken but one is certain that no tithe was taken.

5 Mishnah 7:6. Since the possibility of tithing while he is out in his fields is discussed, that Mishnah must deal with weekdays. One discusses here only the possibility of tithing at a distance, which may apply also to produce which is certain. Tithing on the Sabbath is explicitly forbidden by Mishnah *Sabbath* 2:7, but the discussion here shows that the execution of a tithing plan already spelled out on Friday may be permitted.

6 Mishnah 7, a direct continuation of Mishnah 6.

7 R. Joḥanan asserted that this Mishnah deals with *demay*; he did not state that provisos can only be made for *demay*. Hence, the problem lies not in the possibility of a proviso but in its nature.

רִבִּי יַנַּאי הֲוָה לֵיהּ תְּנַאי וַדַּאי שְׁאַל לְרִבִּי חִייָא רוּבָּה מַהוּ מְתַקְּנָהּ בְּשׁוּבְתָא. אֲמַר לֵיהּ לְמַעַן תִּלְמַד לְיִרְאָה אֶת יי אֱלֹהֶיךָ כָּל־הַיָּמִים וַאֲפִילוּ בְּשַׁבָּת. מַהוּ דְחָמַת מֵיקַל בַּקָּשִׁי תָלוּי בִּי. אֲמַר לֵיהּ עָתִיד אַתְּ לְהַנְהִיג שְׂרָרָה עַל יִשְׂרָאֵל.

Rebbi Yannai had made a proviso for certain produce[8]. He asked the Great Rebbi Ḥiyya, may one fix this on the Sabbath? He said to him

(*Deut*. 14:23): "That you should learn to fear the Eternal, your God, all the days," including the Sabbath[9]. How did you see a way to be so lenient, my initiative[10] depends on me! He said to him, in the future you will carry leadership in Israel.

8 He had no time to tithe before the start of the Sabbath. (The Babli, *Yebamot* 93a, reports that his sharecropper used to bring him fruits every Friday afternoon, and that time he was so late that R. Yannai got nervous and made a proviso since the fruits would spoil if not eaten on the Sabbath.) Since provisos for certain produce were mentioned last, they are discussed first.

9 "You shall eat before the Eternal, your God, at the place that He shall choose to let His Name dwell there, the tithe of your grain, your wine, and your oil, the first-borns of your cattle and sheep, so that you should learn to fear the Eternal, your God, all the days." Since the verse speaks of tithes, one may tithe on the Sabbath. {In the parallel version in Babli *Yebamot* 93a/b, the verse is taken to prove that one should make provisos so that certain produce on the Sabbath does not diminish one's enjoyment of the Sabbath (interpretation of Rashi).}

10 The reading בלשי is attested to by all manuscript sources. The consensus of the commentators is that one should read בשלי, "it (a possible sin) hangs on me." But then the final בי would be unnecessary. I am taking the word parallel to Arabic בלש, "to initate, show initiative." R. Yannai is reluctant to follow the lenient ruling of R. Ḥiyya, who praises him for his independent and careful position. [J. Levy reads מַקִּיל בַּלָּשֵׁי "the stick of the investigators", the instrument of customs officials (Mishnah *Kelim* 15:4) used to check whether a load of grain does not hide taxable goods.]

רִבִּי הוֹשַׁעְיָא הֲוָה לֵיהּ תְּנַאי וַדַּאי. חָדָא אִיתָא בִשְׁלָא יֶרֶק אַנְשִׁייָת מְתַקְּנָה. אֲתַת לְגַבֵּי רִבִּי הוֹשַׁעְיָא וְשָׁלַח לְזַבְדִּי בֶּן לֵוִי דִּיתַקֵּן לֵילָא. רִבִּי אַבָּא בַּר מָמָל בְּעֵי וְלָא הֲוָה זַבְדִּי בֶּן לֵוִי צְרִיךְ מְזַכֵּיא לְרִבִּי הוֹשַׁעְיָא בְּיַרְקָא. רִבִּי זְעִירָא בְּעֵי מַה נָן קַיָּמִין. אִי בְּשֶׁיֵּשׁ לוֹ תְּנַאי עָלָיו וְעַל אֲחֵרִים אֵינוֹ צָרִיךְ לְזַכּוֹתוֹ בְּיֶרֶק. וְאִם בְּשֶׁאֵין לוֹ תְּנַאי לֹא עָלָיו וְלֹא עַל אֲחֵרִים צָרִיךְ לְזַכּוֹתוֹ בְּיֶרֶק. רִבִּי יַעֲקֹב בַּר זַבְדִּי בְשֵׁם רִבִּי אַבָּהוּ אִיתְתָּבַת וְלֹא זְכִי זַבְדִּי בֶּן לֵוִי לְרִבִּי הוֹשַׁעְיָא בְּיַרְקָא.

Rebbi Hoshaia had made a proviso for certain produce. One woman cooked vegetables she had forgotten to put in order. She came to Rebbi Hoshaia who sent Zavdi ben Levi[11] to put it in order for him and for her. Rebbi Abba bar Mamal asked, would Zavdi ben Levi not have to give Rebbi Hoshaia property rights on these vegetables[12]? Rebbi Zeïra asked, where do we hold? If his proviso was meant for him and for others, he does not have to give him property rights on the vegetable[13]. If his proviso was not meant for him and for others, he has to give him property rights on the vegetable. Rebbi Jacob bar Zavdi in the name of Rebbi Abbahu: It was answered, Zavdi ben Levi did not give Rebbi Hoshaia property rights on the vegetable[14].

11 An Amora of the first generation, possibly a son of Levi ben Sissi; most of his original statements are in Aggadah.

12 Since this is forbidden on the Sabbath, how could Zavdi ben Levi possibly tithe on R. Hoshaia's proviso, considering that for certain produce one may not make a proviso for produce not in one's possession.

13 What had been excluded was a proviso valid solely for another's produce, as described in the Mishnah. It is a general principle accepted in all of Talmudic legislation that anything one can do for himself he can do for himself and others. Hence, a proviso valid for him and for all Jews of his locality will be perfectly legal even under the restriction outlined at the start.

14 Hence, if one makes such a proviso (or, if the rabbi does,) it is advisable to make it for oneself and for all inhabitants of one's town, as in the formula for an *eruv*.

אָמַר רִבִּי יַנַּאי צָרִיךְ שֶׁיְּהֵא זָכוּר תְּנַייוֹ. שִׁמְעוֹן בַּר וָוא בְּשֵׁם רִבִּי יוֹחָנָן וְצָרִיךְ לְהַלְחִישׁ[15] בִּשְׂפָתָיו.

Rebbi Yannai said, he must remember his proviso. Simeon bar Abba in the name of Rebbi Joḥanan, he must whisper with his lips[16].

15 Reading of the Rome ms.; Venice and Leyden: להחליט "make it absolute."

16 Return to the discussion of the Mishnah. At the meal, the guest must remember that he tithes according to his prior proviso or whisper that he acts on that premise.

רִבִּי יִרְמְיָה בְּעָא קוֹמֵי רִבִּי זְעִירָא וְלֹא נִמְצָא כִּמְתַקֵּן בְּשַׁבָּת. אָמַר לֵיהּ אַדְהִיתְנֵיהּ[17]. רִבִּי יִרְמְיָה בְּעָא קוֹמֵי רִבִּי זְעִירָא וְאֵינוֹ אָסוּר מִפְּנֵי אוֹבְדָן אוֹכְלִים. אָמַר לֵיהּ מְפָרֵרִי כָּל־שֶׁהוּא וְאוֹכֵל. רִבִּי יִרְמְיָה בְּעָא קוֹמֵי רִבִּי זְעִירָא וְאֵינוֹ אָסוּר מִשּׁוּם גֶּזֶל. אָמַר לֵיהּ רוֹצֶה הוּא שֶׁיְּהֵא לוֹ נַחַת רוּחַ.

Rebbi Jeremiah[18] asked before Rebbi Zeïra: Is he not like somebody who makes repairs on the Sabbath[19]? He said to him, because of his proviso[20]. Rebbi Jeremiah asked before Rebbi Zeïra: Is it not forbidden because of destruction of edibles[20]? He said to him, he crumbles a small amount and eats[21]. Rebbi Jeremiah asked before Rebbi Zeïra: Is it not forbidden because of robbery[23]? He said to him, the host desires the satisfaction of his guest[24].

17 Reading of the Rome ms. Venice: אדהי תנא that may be read as one word "because he made a proviso."

18 All his questions deal with the problem that the rabbis cannot institute rules which contradict Biblical prohibitions; they can only abrogate rabbinical rules under certain circumstances.

19 To repair something otherwise unusable on the Sabbath is a capital crime under the heading of מכה בפטיש.

20 The essence of giving heave is to give it the name of heave, not the actual separation. Since the name was given on Friday, the actual separation is not the act that makes the food edible and is not Biblically forbidden.

21 It is a general prohibition, בל תשחית, to wantonly destroy usable things. In particular, foodstuffs may not be destroyed. The tiny amount the guest set aside for heave of the tithe must somehow be destroyed since under the circumstances it cannot be given to a Cohen.

22 These few crumbs even an *am haarez̩* guest might leave on his plate.

23 To take some of the host's property without the latter's knowledge

is a violation of the host's property rights and therefore should be forbidden (even if its value is less than a *peruṭa* and, hence, is not claimable in court).

24 Since without it, the guest would not eat at his place, the invitation implies the host's acquiescence to the guest's actions. Hence, it is not against the will of the host.

מִילֵּיהוֹן דְּרַבָּנִין פְּלִיגִין דְּאָמַר רִבִּי שְׁמוּאֵל בַּר רִבִּי יִצְחָק רִבִּי וְרִבִּי יוֹסֵי בֵּי רִבִּי יְהוּדָה נִתְאָרְחוּ אֵצֶל בַּעַל הַבַּיִת אֶחָד. אֲזַל לִישְׁנָא בִישָׁא אֲמַר לֵיהּ הַב דַּעְתָּךְ דְּאִינּוּן מְחַשְׁדוּנָךְ יְתִיב לֵיהּ מְעַיְינֵי לוֹן וַהֲווֹן עָבְדִין נַפְשִׁין מְזָרְקִין אִילֵּין לְאִילֵּין וּמְתַקְּנִין. וְאֵינוֹ רוֹצֶה הֲנָחַת רוּחַ. רוֹצֶה הוּא אֶלָּא דְלָא בְעֵי דְחַשְׁדוּנֵיהּ.

The words of the rabbis disagree since Rebbi Samuel bar Rebbi Isaac said: Rebbi and Rebbi Yose ben Rebbi Jehudah were guests of a private person. Evil rumors told the latter, watch out, they are suspecting you[25]! He sat near them and was watching them[26]. They pretended to throw food against each other and in that way were putting the food in order[27]. Does he not desire their satisfaction? He does, but he does not want to be suspected[28].

25 They do not trust you with tithes. It seems that they could not have refused the invitation, in particular as R. Yose ben R. Jehudah follows the teachings of his father, cf. Halakhah 2:2, second paragraph, even though he does not follow him in his opposition to anybody fixing the food which is another's property, as in the next paragraph.

26 The guests noticed that they were watched whether they would behave as if the host was an *am haärez*.

27 They threw little pieces of food against each other. These little pieces were not eaten but served as heave of the tithe without the host's knowledge.

28 The produce probably was tithed but since the host was not publicly part of the circle of the trustworthy persons, his food must be considered *demay*.

תַּנֵּי רִבִּי (fol. 26b) יוּדָה אוֹסֵר. מַה טַעְמָא דְּרִבִּי יְהוּדָה וְיֵשׁ אָדָם מַתְנֶה עַל דָּבָר שֶׁאֵינוֹ בִרְשׁוּתוֹ. מוֹדֶה רִבִּי יוּדָה שֶׁהוּא הוֹלֵךְ וְלוֹקֵחַ מִמָּקוֹם שֶׁלָּקַח זֶה וּמְעַשְּׂרָן. וְיֵשׁ אָדָם מַפְרִישׁ עַל דָּבָר שֶׁאֵינוֹ שֶׁלּוֹ. רִבִּי אַבָּהוּ בְּשֵׁם רִבִּי יוֹחָנָן עָשׂוּ אוֹתוֹ כְּמוֹכֵר פֵּירוֹת טְבוּלִין לַחֲבֵירוֹ. כְּהָדָא דְתַנֵּי הַמּוֹכֵר פֵּירוֹת טְבוּלִין לַחֲבֵירוֹ הֲרֵי זֶה רָץ אַחֲרָיו וּמְתַקְּנוֹ. לֹא מְצָאוֹ אִם יָדוּעַ שֶׁהַפֵּירוֹת קַיָּמִין מְעַשֵּׂר עֲלֵיהֶן וְאִם לָאו אֵינוֹ צָרִיךְ לְעַשֵּׂר עֲלֵיהֶן. סָפֵק קַיָּמִין סָפֵק אֵין קַיָּמִין מְעַשֵּׂר עֲלֵיהֶן וְקוֹרֵא שֵׁם לְמַעְשְׂרוֹתֵיהֶם.

It was stated[29]: "Rebbi Jehudah forbids[30]." What is the reason of Rebbi Jehudah? Can a person make a proviso about something not in his possession? "But Rebbi Jehudah agrees that he may go, buy from the place from which his host bought, and tithe." Can a person give for something that is not his? Rebbi Abbahu in the name of Rebbi Joḥanan: they considered him as one who sold *ṭevel* produce to another person, as was stated[31]: "He who sells *ṭevel* produce to another person has to run after him and put the produce in order. If he does not find him, if it is known that the produce still exists, he has to tithe for him[32]; if not, he does not have to tithe for him. If it is doubtful whether the produce exists or not, he tithes for it and gives a name to the tithes[33]."

29 Tosephta *Demay* 8:5: "R. Jehudah said, can a person make a proviso about something not in his possession? But Rebbi Jehudah agrees that he may go and buy from the place from which his host bought." Since the argument is Amoraic in our text, the Tosephta must represent a Babylonian edition.

30 He forbids these provisos even on weekdays and requires tithing by the guest before going to the party.

31 Tosephta *Maäser Šeni* 3:7, in slightly different language but identical meaning. R. Jehudah's restriction that the tithing must be from the same source as the *ṭevel* is not mentioned.

32 Also for something that is not in the tither's possession. The case discussed by R. Jehudah is parallel to the doubtful case here.

33 Since all tithes have to be named even if only the heave of the tithes actually has to be separated and given.

(fol. 26a) **משנה ב**: מָזְגוּ לוֹ אֶת הַכּוֹס אוֹמֵר מַה שֶׁאֲנִי עָתִיד לְשַׁיֵּיר בְּשׁוּלֵי הַכּוֹס הֲרֵי הוּא מַעֲשֵׂר וּשְׁאָר מַעֲשֵׂר סָמוּךְ לוֹ. זֶה שֶׁעָשִׂיתִי מַעֲשֵׂר עָשׂוּי תְּרוּמַת מַעֲשֵׂר עָלָיו וּמַעֲשֵׂר שֵׁנִי בְּפִיו וּמְחוּלָּל עַל הַמָּעוֹת.

Mishnah 2: When[34] they mixed him a cup, he says: What I shall leave at the rim of the cup shall be tithe, the rest of tithe near to it. What I made tithe shall be the heave of the tithe for everything, and the Second Tithe shall be on its top and be redeemed by coins.

34 This Mishnah is a continuation of the first and refers to the proviso he makes both on Friday and at the meal.

(fol. 26b) **הלכה ב**: כֵּינִי מַתְנִתָא לְעִנְייָן מְזִיגַת הַכּוֹס.

Halakhah 2: So is the Mishnah: Concerning the mixing of the cup[35].

35 Not that the proviso would be spelled out when they mix the cup, which would be on the Sabbath and forbidden; it is the proviso which has to be spelled out on Friday and then repeated, in a whisper, on the Sabbath.

מַה נָן קַייָמִין. אִם בְּאוֹמֵר מִכְּבָר מַשְׁקֶה מְעוּרָב הוּא. אִם בְּאוֹמֵר לִכְשֶׁיִּשְׁתֶּה לְמַפְרְעוֹ טֶבֶל שָׁתָה. אֶלָּא כִּי נָן קַייָמִין בְּאוֹמֵר מִכְּבָר לִכְשֶׁאֶשְׁתֶּה. וְלֹא נִמְצָא מְטַלְטֵל תְּרוּמָה טְמֵאָה בְּשַׁבָּת. אָמַר רִבִּי לְעָזָר מְשַׁיֵּיר כָּל־שֶׁהוּא חוּלִין כְּהַהִיא דְתַנֵּינָן תַּמָּן מְטַלְטְלִין תְּרוּמָה טְהוֹרָה [אִם הַטְּמֵאָה] אִם הַחוּלִין וְלֹא דָמְייָן. תַּמָּן טְמֵאָה לְצוֹרֶךְ טְהוֹרָה. בְּרַם הָכָא חוּלִין לְצוֹרֶךְ טְמֵאָה. אָמַר רִבִּי יוֹסֵי בֵּי רִבִּי בּוּן אִם יְצִיאָתוֹ מִן הַכּוֹס קָדִישׁ.

Where are we at? If he says it beforehand, the drink is mixed[36]. If he says, when I shall have drunk, before that he drank *ṭevel*[37]. What we are dealing with is that he says beforehand: When I shall have drunk[38]. But does he then not move impure heave on the Sabbath[39]? Rebbi Eleazar said, he leaves some profane[40], as what we have stated there[41]: "One moves pure heave with impure one and with profane food." But that does not compare. There, the impure is for the needs of the pure[42], but here the profane is for the needs of the impure[43]. Rebbi Yose ben Rebbi Abun said, when he sets down the cup it will be holy[44].

36 Since fluids move, if he declares the place of the heave at one moment, its molecules will have wandered away by the time he drinks, and he also drank of the heave, a deadly sin.

37 If he declares after he drank, he drank only *ṭevel*.

38 He must make the declaration beforehand in order to avoid drinking *ṭevel*. On the other hand, he cannot designate heave before he finished, in order to avoid drinking heave. Hence, he has to designate heave on Friday to be separated after he finished drinking.

39 Since he is eating at an *am haärez*'s, all the food is considered impure. Hence, the heave also is impure and must be destroyed. But this cannot be done on the Sabbath; the impure heave is therefore of no use on the Sabbath and under the rules of *muqẓeh* cannot be moved.

40 When he declares that the wine near the designated tithe should be tithe, he really does not want it to be all tithe but some drops of profane non-tithe must also remain. Since the profane wine may be moved, and since we have a principle that anything usable may be moved, the impure heave also can be moved.

41 Mishnah *Šabbat* 21:1: "One moves impure heave with pure and with profane food." It seems that the switch impure/pure in our text is a scribal error since the following argument requires the order of subjects in the Mishnah. In the parallel *Pesaḥim* 3:3 (fol. 30a), the quote of the Mishnah is correct. {Because of that switch, successive editors have mutilated the text in newer editions.}

42 There is no Yerushalmi on the Mishnah, and a parallel quote in

Pesaḥim 3:3 (fol. 30a) has exactly the same text. The explanation of the Yerushalmi seems to be the same as that of the Babli (*Šabbat* 142a), that impure heave can be moved on the Sabbath only if it is necessary to remove it in order to get at usable food, be it pure heave or profane.

43 Hence, there is no need to move the impure heave and it should not be permitted.

44 Since we have to stipulate from the start that wine should become heave only when the guest has finished drinking, one may also stipulate that this should happen only when the guest has put down the cup and does not move it again. Then the question does not arise.

תַּמָּן תַּנִּינָן הַלּוֹקֵחַ יַיִן מִבֵּין הַכּוּתִים. תַּנֵּי רִבִּי יוֹסֵי וְרִבִּי שִׁמְעוֹן אוֹסְרִין שֶׁמָּא תִיבָּקַע הַנּוֹד וְנִמְצָא זֶה שׁוֹתֶה טְבָלִים לְמַפְרֵעַ. וְהָדָא מַתְנִיתָא לֹא כְּרִבִּי יוֹסֵי וְרִבִּי שִׁמְעוֹן הִיא. אָמַר רִבִּי יַעֲקֹב בַּר אִידִי הַכֹּל מוֹדִין עַל הַכּוֹס שֶׁהוּא עַל אֲתַר.

There, we have stated[45]: "Is somebody buys wine from the Samaritans." It was stated[46]: "Rebbi Yose and Rebbi Simeon forbid it, for the wine bag may spring a leak and it will turn out retroactively that he drank *ṭevel*." Is our Mishnah not following Rebbi Yose and Rebbi Simeon[47]? Rebbi Jacob bar Idi said, all agree that the cup is at its place.

45 Mishnah 7:5. "He who buys wine from the Samaritans, since he buys wine which certainly is not tithed, he may declare that he will give designated amounts in the future and drink immediately." In the Tosephta, *Demay* 8:7, this is R. Meïr's opinion, restricted to somebody who bought on Friday and had no time to tithe it before sundown.

46 Tosephta *Demay* 8:7. R. Meïr's position is he never had a case of a broken wine bag; he would worry if a bag broke and was emptied without some drops remaining that could be designated as heave of the tithe.

47 The guest may drink before the heave was declared. Since the cup is filled at the place where one drinks, nothing bad can happen since even if something is spilled, the heave is in the drops clinging to the wall.

(fol. 26a) **משנה ג**: פּוֹעֵל שֶׁאֵינוֹ מַאֲמִין לְבַעַל הַבַּיִת נוֹטֵל גְּרוֹגֶרֶת אַחַת וְאוֹמֵר זוֹ וְתֵשַׁע הַבָּאוֹת אַחֲרֶיהָ עֲשׂוּיוֹת מַעֲשֵׂר עַל תִּשְׁעִים שֶׁאֲנִי אוֹכֵל וְזוֹ עֲשׂוּיָה תְרוּמַת מַעֲשֵׂר עֲלֵיהֶן. מַעֲשֵׂר שֵׁנִי בָּאַחֲרוֹנָה וּמְחוּלָּל עַל הַמָּעוֹת.

Mishnah 3: A worker[48] who does not believe his employer takes one dried fig[49] and says: This one and the next nine shall be tithe for ninety that I shall eat. This one is made heave of the tithe for them. The Second Tithe is at the end and it is redeemed by a coin[50].

48 An agricultural worker who is a *ḥaver* and has to be fed by his employer during the day.

49 Of those supplied by his untrustworthy employer. Again, the tithes have to be named but only the heave of the tithe has actually to be taken out and separated for *demay*.

50 One *peruṭah* in a coin.

(fol. 26b) **הלכה ג**: רִבִּי לָעְזָר בְּשֵׁם רִבִּי הוֹשַׁעְיָה עָשׂוּ אוֹתוֹ שֶׁאֵינוֹ מַעֲמִין לְבַעַל הַבַּיִת. פְּשִׁיטָא הָדָא מִילְּתָא נִשְׂרְפוּ הַפֵּירוֹת הַתְּרוּמָה בְטִיבּוּלָהּ. נִישְׂרְפָה הַתְּרוּמָה לִכְשֶׁיֵּאָכְלוּ הַפֵּירוֹת קָדְשָׁה הַתְּרוּמָה לְמַפְרֵעַ.

Halakhah 3: Rebbi Eleazar[51] in the name of Rebbi Hoshaiah: They considered him a worker who does not trust his employer. The following is obvious: If the produce was burned, the heave is *ṭevel*[52]. If the heave is burned, when the produce is eaten the heave will have been sanctified retroactively.

51 The paragraph does not belong here but in *Terumot* 2:4, where the text is identical except for בטילה instead of בטיבולה. The Mishnah in *Terumot* assumes that somebody gives a *seah* to a Levite and a *seah* to the poor; according to R. Meïr then he, or his worker, can eat eight *seah* based on the tithes he gave. The Sages permit only to eat according to the percentage of the tithe that still exists. Maimonides and R. Simson give two possible interpretations, one that the Mishnah there is a corollary to the Mishnah here and deals with a worker who receives food from his employer and

sees the employer give to the Levite and the poor but does not know whether he gave as tithes or as gifts. R. Hoshaiah declares that the position of the Sages in that Mishnah is identical with the position of the Tanna in our Mishnah.

52 Since heave is taken to permit the rest to be eaten, if nothing can be eaten there is no heave, and heave and tithes have to be separated anew from the remainder. This refers to the case where the produce burned before the heave was delivered to the Cohen. If the heave burned after he declared it, the farmer did his duty.

(fol. 26a) **משנה ד**: וְחוֹסֵךְ גְּרוֹגֶרֶת אַחַת. רַבָּן שִׁמְעוֹן בֶּן גַּמְלִיאֵל אוֹמֵר לֹא יַחְסוֹךְ מִפְּנֵי שֶׁהוּא מְמַעֵט אֶת מְלַאכְתּוֹ שֶׁל בַּעַל הַבַּיִת. וְרַבִּי יוֹסֵי אוֹמֵר לֹא יַחְסוֹךְ מִפְּנֵי שֶׁהוּא תְּנַאי בֵּית דִּין.

Mishnah 4: He saves one fig[53]. Rabban Simeon ben Gamliel says, he should not save because he reduces the work he will be able to do for his employer. But Rebbi Yose said, he should not save because that is a stipulation of the Court.

53 The worker of Mishnah 3. Since he has declared one fig to be heave of the tithe, that fig must be given to the Cohen. The anonymous Tanna requires the worker to give the fig from his allotment. Rabban Simeon ben Gamliel requires the worker to give a fig, but one he buys, not one given to him by his employer since he is required to eat all the food he receives from his employer in order to be strong. Rebbi Yose requires the employer to give a fig to the Cohen if the worker so requires since that is a stipulation of the Court and automatically incorporated in all work contracts.

(fol. 26b) **הלכה ד**: מָהוּ חָשַׂךְ מִן מֵיכְלֵיהּ הוּא מַפִּיק תְּרוּמַת מַעֲשֵׂר.

Halakhah 4: What did he save? From his food he separates the heave of the tithe.

תַּנֵּי לֹא יַחֲרוֹשׁ אָדָם בְּפָרָתוֹ בַלַּיְלָה וְיַשְׂכִּירֶנָּה בַיּוֹם וְלֹא יַעֲשֶׂה בְתוֹךְ שֶׁלּוֹ בַלַּיְלָה וְיַשְׂכִּיר עַצְמוֹ בַיּוֹם. לֹא יִרְעַב עַצְמוֹ וְלֹא יְסַגֵּף עַצְמוֹ מִפְּנֵי שֶׁהוּא מְמַעֵט בִּמְלַאכְתּוֹ שֶׁל בַּעַל הַבַּיִת.

It was stated[54]: "A man should not plough with his cow at night and rent her out during the day, he should not work for himself at night and rent himself out during the day, he should not starve himself and not torment himself because he reduces the work he will be able to do for his employer."

54 A similar text appears in Tosephta *Baba Meẓia'* 8:2: "A worker is not permitted to work for himself at night and rent himself out during the day, or plough with his cow in the evening and rent her out in the morning; he should not starve himself, torment himself, or give his food to his children, because he robs his employer of the work he will be able to do."

רִבִּי יוֹחָנָן אֲזַל לְחַד אֲתַר אַשְׁכַּח סַפְרָא אַיינֵיס אֲמַר לָהוּ מַהוּ כֵן. אָמְרוּ לֵיהּ צָיִים. אֲמַר לֵיהּ אָסוּר לָךְ. וּמַה אִם מְלַאכְתּוֹ שֶׁל בָּשָׂר וָדָם אַתְּ אָמַר אָסוּר מְלַאכְתּוֹ שֶׁל הַקָּדוֹשׁ בָּרוּךְ הוּא לֹא כָל־שֶׁכֵּן.

Rebbi Joḥanan went to some place where he found the schoolteacher weak[55]. He asked them, what has happened[56]? They said to him, he is fasting. He said to him, that is forbidden to you. If one says that it is forbidden for the work one does for flesh and blood, so much more for the work of the Holy One[57], praise to Him!

55 R. Simson reads אטימויים, *Hagahot Maimuniot* on Maimonides *Śekhirut* 13:6 reads אטימוס, ἄθυμος "feeble" (M. Sachs), in *Caftor Waperaḥ* Chap. 39, אטמיאס. The translation follows *Hagahot Maimuniot*.

56 It seems that he suspected the school board of not paying a living wage.

57 The elementary school teacher, who turns illiterates into literates and uncivilized into civilized, finishes the work of creation and therefore does God's work.

רַב חִייָא בַּר אַשִׁי בְּשֵׁם רַב תְּנַיי בֵּית דִּין שֶׁתְּהֵא תְרוּמַת מַעֲשֵׂר מִשֶּׁל פּוֹעֵל וּמַעֲשֵׂר שֵׁנִי שֶׁל בַּעַל הַבַּיִת.

Rav Ḥiyya bar Ashi in the name of Rav[58]: It is a stipulation of the Court that the heave of the tithe should be from the worker and the Second Tithe[59] from the employer.

58 Tosephta *Demay* 8:6: "R. Yose says that it is a stipulation of the Court that the heave of the tithe should be from the employer and the Second Tithe from the worker." R. Simson reads the text of the Tosephta in the Yerushalmi. *Caftor Waperaḥ* Chap. 39 quotes the Tosephta, not the Yerushalmi. Maimonides *Maäser* 9:11 follows the Tosephta as current practice. It seems that the Yerushalmi gives the position of the anonymous Tanna, in contrast to the Tosephta which explicitly refers to R. Yose; the reading in the Yerushalmi should not be changed for the (probably Babylonian) Tosephta. Rav explains the position of the anonymous Tanna as practice; he must assume that Rabban Simeon ben Gamliel and R. Yose disagree, so both are single opinions that are disregarded in face of a majority.

59 The *peruṭah* needed to redeem the second tithe.

(fol. 26a) **משנה ה**: הַלּוֹקֵחַ יַיִן מִבֵּין הַכּוּתִים אוֹמֵר שְׁנֵי לוֹגִין שֶׁאֲנִי עָתִיד לְהַפְרִישׁ הֲרֵי הֵן תְּרוּמָה. וַעֲשָׂרָה מַעֲשֵׂר וְתִשְׁעָה מַעֲשֵׂר שֵׁנִי וּמֵיחֵל וְשׁוֹתֶה.

Mishnah 5: If someone buys wine from Samaritans[60] he may say: Two *log* that I shall separate in the future are heave, ten tithe[61], and nine Second Tithe; then he redeems[62] and drinks.

60 If one accepts the Samaritans as Jews, the wine is kosher but it certainly is not tithed.

61 It really should be only 9.8 *log* per one hundred, but one does not require him to go into details.

Similarly, Second Tithe should be 10% of the remaining 89.2 *log*.

62 He redeems the Second Tithe with a *perutah* from a designated coin; the redemption is effected by his declaration.

(fol. 26b) **הלכה ה**: תַּנֵּי רִבִּי יוֹסֵי וְרִבִּי שִׁמְעוֹן אוֹסְרִין שֶׁמָּא תִיבָּקַע הַנּוֹד וְנִמְצָא שׁוֹתֶה טְבָלִים לְמַפְרֵעוֹ. לֹא כְטַעֲמֵיהּ דְּהָדֵין טַעֲמֵיהּ דְּהָדֵין. טַעֲמָא דְּרִבִּי יוֹסֵי שֶׁמָּא יַסִּייעַ. טַעֲמָא דְּרִבִּי שִׁמְעוֹן שֶׁמָּא יִשְׁכַּח וְיִשְׁתֶּה אֶת הַשְּׁאָר. כְּהָדָה דְתַנֵּי מַעֲשֵׂר שֵׁנִי שֶׁבְּחֵפֶץ זֶה מְחוּלָּל עַל סֶלַע שֶׁבְּכִיס זֶה חִילֵּל. רִבִּי יוֹסֵי אוֹמֵר לֹא חִילֵּל. מַאי טַעֲמָא דְּרִבִּי יוֹסֵי שֶׁאִם אָמַר עַל הַסֶּלַע הַיְּשָׁנָה וְעַל הַדֵּינָר הַיָּשָׁן שֶׁחִילֵּל. מוֹדִים חֲכָמִים לְרִבִּי יוֹסֵי שֶׁאִם אָמַר עַל הַסֶּלַע שֶׁאֶטּוֹל מִיַּד בְּנִי וְעַל הַדֵּינָר שֶׁאֶטּוֹל מִיַּד בְּנִי שֶׁלֹּא חִילֵּל. שֶׁלֹּא הָיוּ בְיָדוֹ בְּאוֹתָהּ שָׁעָה.

Halakhah 5: It was stated[63]: "Rebbi Yose and Rebbi Simeon prohibit to do so, maybe the wine bag will spring a leak and it turns out retroactively that he drank *tevel*." But the reason of one is not the reason of the other. The reason of Rebbi Yose is that maybe he will pour[64]. The reason of Rebbi Simeon is that maybe he will forget and drink the remainder[65]. As it was stated[66]: "The Second Tithe in this container should be redeemed by the tetradrachma in that wallet, it is redeemed. Rebbi Yose says, it is not redeemed." What is the reason of Rebbi Yose? "[67]If he said, the old tetradrachma or the old denar, he did redeem. The Sages admit to Rebbi Yose that if he said, the tetradrachma I shall take from my son's hand, or the denar I shall take from my son's hand, it is not redeemed since it was not in his hand at that time."

63 Tosephta *Demay* 8:7: "If someone buys wine from Samaritans on Fridays and he forgot to tithe, he may say: Two *log* that I shall separate in the future are heave, the next ten tithe, and the next nine Second Tithe; then he redeems and drinks immediately; the words of R. Meïr. R. Jehudah, R. Yose, and R. Simeon forbid it. They said to R. Meïr, do you not agree that if his wine bag would spring a leak he would drink *tevel*? He said to them, if it would spring a leak." R. Jehudah is not mentioned in the Halakhah; since he is

the senior among those who disagree, the argument with R. Meïr is his and does not obligate the other two authorities who agree with R. Jehudah on the practical rule but not on the theoretical reason. Note that in the version of the Tosephta, the wine bag is already transported to the buyer's house and, therefore, the risk of the bag springing a leak is minimized.

64 At home, he will pour out the contents of the leather wine bag into a clay amphora for storage. Then the text of his declaration is no longer applicable and the buyer drank *ṭevel.*

65 Then he actually drank heave and heave of the tithe!

66 A similar statement is in Tosephta *Maäser Šeni* 3:17: "If somebody said, the Second Tithe in this container should be redeemed by that *as,* and he did not define its place, R. Simeon says, he gave it its rightful name {and it is redeemed.} The Sages say, {it is not redeemed} until he says, at the North or South end." The next Tosephta shows that the "Sages" here follow the opinion of R. Yose. The problem is that without a clear definition, the owner may spend the redemption coin on other things. Therefore, one requires him to spell out where the coin will be taken and, since coins move around in a wallet, it is clear that he has to remove the coin from the wallet immediately and separate it.

67 Tosephta *Maäser Šeni* 4:12: "If somebody says, the Second Tithe shall be redeemed by a tetradrachma that will come out of this wallet, or the denar that will come out of that wallet, R. Yose says, he did not redeem, but the Sages say, he did redeem. R. Yose agrees with the Sages that if he says that the Second Tithe shall be redeemed by the new tetradrachma which will come out of this wallet, or the new denar that will come out of that wallet, he did redeem. The Sages admit to Rebbi Yose that if he said [it shall be redeemed] by the tetradrachma that was in my son's hand, the denar that was in my son's hand, it is not redeemed since perhaps it was not in his hand at that time." We have to assume that R. Yose agrees only in case the owner had only one new coin of that type at the moment of the declaration.

תַּמָּן תַּנֵּינָן הַמֵּנִיחַ פֵּירוֹת לִהְיוֹת מַפְרִישׁ עֲלֵיהֶן מַעֲשֵׂר שֵׁנִי. וְהָדָא מַתְנִיתָא דְּלֹא כְּרִבִּי יוֹסֵי וּכְרִבִּי שִׁמְעוֹן. אָמַר רִבִּי זְעִירָא תַּמָּן לְמַפְרֵעוֹ נִתְקַלְקְלוּ. בְּרַם הָכָא מֵאוֹבְדָן וְהֵילַךְ נִתְקַלְקְלוּ.

There, we have stated[68]: "If somebody puts aside produce . . . to serve for Second Tithe." Does[69] that Mishnah disagree with Rebbi Yose and Rebbi Simeon? Rebbi Zeïra said, there they become spoiled retroactively, but here they become spoiled only starting from the moment of loss[70].

68 Mishnah *Giṭṭin* 3:8: "If somebody puts aside produce to serve for heave or tithes, or coins to serve for Second Tithe, he refers to them {to redeem produce or to put produce in order with the intention that all sanctity should devolve on produce and coins set aside} based on the prior knowledge that they still exist. If they are lost, he worries for 24 hours, the words of R. Eleazar (ben Shamua'.)" In both the Babli (*Giṭṭin* 31a/b} and the Yerushalmi (*Giṭṭin* 3:8), there is a discussion whether the tithing is questionable for the 24 hours preceding the discovery of the loss or whether the tithing is not questionable only for the first 24 hours after produce or coins were set aside. In any case, there is no opposition noted by either R. Yose or R. Simeon. Since transporting wine from Samaria presumably takes less than 24 hours, such opposition would have been expected.

69 This and the next sentence are copied from *Giṭṭin*. Therefore, our *baraita* is referred to as "there", and the Mishnah as "here."

70 Even if the heave was lost, since it was legal heave at the time it saves the produce from ever being *ṭevel* again.

תַּמָּן תַּנֵּינָן פְּרוּטָה שֶׁל הֶקְדֵּשׁ שֶׁנָּפְלָה לְתוֹךְ הַכִּיס אוֹ שֶׁאָמַר פְּרוּטָה בְּכִיס זֶה הֶקְדֵּשׁ תַּנָּה עַל הָרִאשׁוֹנָה מָעַל בְּסָפֵק וְעַל הַשְּׁנִייָה מָעַל בְּוַדַּאי דִּבְרֵי רִבִּי עֲקִיבָא. וַחֲכָמִים אוֹמְרִים עַל כּוּלָּן מָעַל בְּסָפֵק וְעַל הָאַחֲרוֹנָה מָעַל בְּוַדַּאי. אָמַר רִבִּי יוּדָן אָבוֹי דְּרִבִּי מַתַּנְיָא הָדָא דְּתֵימַר כְּשֶׁהָיוּ עֶשֶׂר. אֲבָל הָיוּ שְׁתַּיִם עַל הָרִאשׁוֹנָה מָעַל בְּסָפֵק וְעַל הַשְּׁנִייָה מָעַל בְּוַדַּאי. רִבִּי שִׁמְעוֹן בֶּן לָקִישׁ בְּעָא קוֹמֵי רִבִּי יוֹחָנָן מַה בֵּין הָאוֹמֵר בַּכִּיס מַה בֵּין הָאוֹמֵר מִן הַכִּיס. רִבִּי שִׁמְעוֹן בֶּן לָקִישׁ אָמַר אֲפִילוּ הוֹצִיא אֶת כָּל־הַכִּיס לֹא יִמְעוֹל כְּמָה דְתֵימַר לְמַפְרֵעוֹ טֶבֶל שָׁתָה אוּף הָכָא לְמַפְרֵעוֹ חוּלִין הוֹצִיא אֶלָּא כָּאן תָּלוּי בְּהַפְרָשָׁה. אָמַר רִבִּי יוֹנָה

כָּאן וְכָאן תָּלוּי בְּהַפְרָשָׁה נַעֲשָׂה כְאוֹמֵר אַל יֵצֵא הַכִּיס הַזֶּה יְדֵי פְרוּטָה הֶקְדֵּשׁ. מֵחֲלְפָה שִׁיטָתֵיהּ דְּרִבִּי שִׁמְעוֹן בֶּן לָקִישׁ תַּמָּן הוּא אוֹמֵר מוֹעֲלִין בִּפְרוּטָה לְפִי חֶשְׁבּוֹן שְׁלֹשָׁה לוֹגִין. וְהָכָא הוּא אָמַר הָכֵין. מִן דְּאַצְרְכַתּ לֵיהּ חָזַר וּפַשְׁטָהּ.

There, we have stated[71]: "If a *peruṭah* of Temple property fell into somebody's wallet, or if somebody said, a *peruṭah* in this wallet shall be Temple property," it was stated that "with the first coin he committed probable larceny, with the second one certain larceny[72], the words of Rebbi Aqiba. But the Sages say, with any of them he committed probable larceny, except that with the last one he committed certain larceny." Rebbi Yudan, the father of Rebbi Mattania said, that is, if there were ten coins. But if there were only two, with the first coin he committed probable larceny, with the second one certain larceny. Rebbi Simeon ben Laqish asked before Rebbi Joḥanan: What is the difference between him who says "in the wallet" and him who says "from the wallet?[73]" Rebbi Simeon ben Laqish said, even if he spent the entire wallet he would not have committed larceny; just as you say 'that he drank *ṭevel* retroactively,' here also 'retroactively he spent profane money.[74]' But here it depends on the act of separation[75]. Rebbi Jonah said, in both cases it depends on the act of separation; it is as if he said, this wallet should not be freed from a *peruṭah* of Temple property[76]. Rebbi Simeon ben Laqish's argument is inverted. There[77], he says that one commits larceny with a *peruṭah* corresponding to the computation of three *log*. And here, he says so? After he asked, he returned and gave the simple answer[78].

71 Mishnah *Meïlah* 6:6: "If a *peruṭah* of Temple property fell into somebody's wallet, or if somebody said, a *peruṭah* in this wallet shall be Temple property, then the moment he spent the first coin he committed larceny, the words of Rebbi Aqiba. But the Sages say, not until he spent the entire wallet. Rebbi Aqiba agrees that if he said, 'a *peruṭah* from this wallet

shall be Temple property,' he may go and spend the entire contents of the wallet." מעל refers to the particular case of larceny involving Temple property, whose private use is forbidden even if it does not impair its value (*Lev.* 5:15). Our text is a *baraita* that combines the Mishnah with Tosephta *Meïlah* 3:1: "If a *peruṭah* of Temple property fell into somebody's wallet, or if somebody said, a *peruṭah* in this wallet shall be Temple property, then the moment he spent the first coin he must bring an *ašam* sacrifice for a possible sin, for the second coin an *ašam* sacrifice for a certain sin, the words of Rebbi Aqiba. But the Sages say, an *ašam* sacrifice for a possible sin is brought only for an offense which if deliberate is punished by being cut off (כרת, cf. J. Milgrom, Leviticus 1-16, New York 1991, pp. 457-460) or, if in error, must be atoned for by a sin-offering."

72 The argument of the Mishnah, that with the first coin he already committed certain larceny, is easier to understand. The difference between possible and certain larceny is in the kind of sacrifice that must be brought for atonement, as stated in the Tosephta. R. Moses Margalit explains the argument of R. Aqiba that the first coin, which was on top of the coins in the wallet, is not really "in" the wallet," but the second coin certainly is "in the wallet."

73 This refers to the Mishnah and the distinction which R. Aqiba makes, that in the second case there is no larceny unless all coins are spent.

74 If he separated the coin after he spent some of the money, the stigma of possible larceny should be removed from the rest he spent earlier.

75 Everybody agrees that *ṭevel* can be removed only by an actual declaration fixing place and modality of heave and tithes.

76 The remaining coins cannot become profane except by either removing the dedicated piece from the wallet or designating it unequivocally as old or new, as in the preceding paragraph. In the Babli (*Meïlah* 34a), this answer is given by R. Joḥanan. But the thrust of the Babli is about retroactive clarification that is excluded here and in the entire discussion of the Yerushalmi, as recognized by *Sefer Nir*.

77 Babli *Meïlah* 13b, in explanation of Mishnah *Meïlah* 3:7: "From water {drawn from the water canal flowing through the Temple courtyard on Friday afternoon of the festival of Tabernacles, to be used next morning for the water libation} in the golden barrel {that was not a sanctified vessel

and in which the water would not become forbidden by standing in a vessel overnight} one may not have any use, but use is no larceny. Once it is poured into the pitcher (the holy vessel in which the water was transported to the altar} its use becomes larceny." R. Simeon ben Laqish holds that there is no larceny from the water of the golden barrel if one uses the excess over the three *log* that are to be filled into the holy pitcher. The interpretation of the Yerushalmi seems to be that if the barrel contained x *log* and somebody drew y *log*, even if $x-y > 3$ one would commit larceny in the amount of the cost of $^{3y}/_{x}$ *log* of water.

78 His statement was a question and not a declaration; he himself gave the same answer later given by R. Jonah.

אָמַר רִבִּי יִצְחָק בַּר אֶלְעָזָר אָדָם עוֹמֵד מֵעֶרֶב שַׁבָּת וְאוֹמֵר הֲרֵי זוּ תְרוּמָה לְמָחָר וְאֵין אָדָם עוֹמֵד בְּשַׁבָּת[79] וְאוֹמֵר הֲרֵי זוּ תְרוּמָה לְמָחָר. אָמַר רִבִּי יוֹסֵי בֵּי רִבִּי בּוּן אֵין אָדָם עוֹמֵד מֵעֶרֶב שַׁבָּת וְאוֹמֵר הֲרֵי זוּ תְרוּמָה לְמָחָר. מַתְנִיתָא פְלִיגָא עַל רִבִּי יוֹסֵי בֵּי רִבִּי בּוּן לָגִין שֶׁהוּא טְבוּל יוֹם וּמִילְאֵהוּ מִן הֶחָבִית מַעֲשֵׂר טֶבֶל אִם אָמַר הֲרֵי זוּ תְּרוּמַת מַעֲשֵׂר לְמָחָר מִשֶּׁתֶּחְשַׁךְ הֲרֵי זֶה תְרוּמָה[80] אִם אָמַר הֲרֵי זֶה עֵירוּב לֹא אָמַר כְּלוּם. פָּתַר לָהּ לְשֶׁעָבַר. וְהָתַנֵּי רִבִּי חִיָּיא אָמַר אִית לָךְ מֵימַר לְשֶׁעָבַר. וְחָזַר בָּהּ רִבִּי יוֹסֵי בֵּי רִבִּי בּוּן מֵהָדָא[81]. מַיי כְדוֹן מִכְּבָר לִכְשֶׁאַפְרִישֶׁנָּה. הַגַּע עַצְמָךְ שֶׁהָיְתָה תְרוּמָה טְהוֹרָה מִכְּבָר לִכְשֶׁאוֹכְלֶנָּה הַגַּע עַצְמָךְ שֶׁהָיְתָה תְרוּמָה טְמֵאָה לִכְשֶׁאֲנִיחֶנָּה בְּזָוִית.

Rebbi Isaac ben Eleazar[82] said, a person can say on Friday, this shall be heave tomorrow[83], but nobody can say on the Sabbath, this shall be heave tomorrow. Rebbi Yose ben Rebbi Abun said, nobody can say on Friday, this shall be heave tomorrow. A Mishnah disagrees with Rebbi Yose ben Rebbi Abun[84]: "If a vessel[85] was immersed that day and somebody filled it from an amphora with *ṭevel* tithe, if he said[86], its contents should be heave of the tithe tomorrow, i. e., after nightfall, then this is heave. If he said, that should be *eruv*[87], he did not say anything." Explain it if he transgressed[88]. But Rebbi Ḥiyya stated: "He says[89]," and you say, if he transgressed? Rebbi Yose ben Rebbi Abun retracted that. What is done[90]? 'From before I shall separate it[91].' Think about it, if it was pure heave, 'from before I shall eat it[92].' Think about it, if it was impure heave, 'from before I shall deposit it in a corner[93].'

79 Reading of the parallel in *Šabbat* 18:1, missing in the texts here.

80 Reading of the Parallel in *Šabbat* 18:1. The reading here is garbled: לגין שהוא טבול יום ומילאהו מן החבית מעשׂר טבל. אם אמר הרי זה תרומת מעשׂר מחלל. אמר הרי זו תרומה מחלל. אם אמר הרי זה עירוב לא אמר כלום.

81 Reading of the parallel in *Šabbat* 18:1, all but the first two words of the sentence are missing here.

82 Probably, this and the following paragraph refer to Mishnah 6. The same text in its main context appears in *Šabbat* 18:1.

83 As explained in the Mishnah below, a person may not be pure for heave on Friday but he may be pure on the Sabbath. If his impurity (or that of his vessel) is derivative he contaminates holy things but not profane food. Hence, he must keep his food in profane state until nightfall. But at nightfall it will be Sabbath and he will not be permitted to change the status of food and separate heave and tithes. He must make a declaration on Friday to separate heave on the Sabbath automatically.

84 *Tevul Yom* 4:4. The exact text of the Mishnah reads: "If a vessel which was immersed that day {and will be pure only after sundown} was filled from an amphora with *ṭevel* tithe, if he said that its contents should be heave of the tithe after nightfall, then this is heave of the tithe. If he said that it should be *eruv*, he did not say anything." Tithe can be *ṭevel* only if the heave of the tithe was not taken; hence, 'heave' in our text should always mean 'heave of the tithe' as in the Mishnah.

85 Latin *lagena, lagaena, lagona, lagoena, -ae, f.* "large earthen vessel with neck and handles; flask, bottle"; same as Greek λάγηνος, perhaps identical with Κνίδιον, τὸ, "a measure of wine."

86 On Friday.

87 Cf. *Peah*, Chapter 7, Note 56. The *eruv* must be deposited on Friday afternoon and be at the right spot at sundown, so that he can acquire the Sabbath rest at that spot. But in our case, at sundown the wine is still *ṭevel*;

since it may not be eaten it is not food, and the *eruv* is invalid.

88 R. Yose ben R. Abun would agree that if someone incorrectly followed R. Isaac ben Eleazar's prescription the declaration was valid.

89 There is a *baraita* in which R. Ḥiyya presents the text of the declaration to be recited in the case considered by R. Isaac ben Eleazar. R. Ḥiyya unconditionally permits the declaration.

90 What is the text of R. Ḥiyya's declaration?

91 When I shall separate it (on the Sabbath), the separation shall be valid from the moment of declaration (on Friday).

92 If a Cohen makes the declaration, he may say so since then he does not have to separate once it was declared to be heave. If another person makes the declaration, he may say: From the moment that a Cohen eats it.

93 Since impure heave must be burned, which is forbidden on the Sabbath, the only thing one can do with impure heave on the Sabbath is putting it away so that it should not be used.

תַּנֵּי מְטַלְטְלָהּ אֶחָד תְּרוּמָה טְהוֹרָה וְאֶחָד תְּרוּמָה טְמֵאָה. אָמַר רִבִּי זְעִירָא הָדָא אָמְרָה טֶבֶל שֶׁיֵּשׁ עָלָיו תְּנַאי מוּתָּר לְטַלְטְלוֹ בְשַׁבָּת. כֵּיצַד הוּא עוֹשֶׂה. נוֹתֵן עֵינָיו בְּמִקְצָתוֹ וְאוֹכֵל אֶת הַשְּׁאָר.

We have stated: "One may move[94] both pure and impure heave." Rebbi Zeïra said, it means that one is permitted to move *ṭevel* that has a condition on it[95] on the Sabbath. What does he do[96]? He thinks about a part of it[97] and eats the rest.

94 On the Sabbath. Since impure heave cannot be used, one would expect that it could not be moved.

95 That heave is taken retroactively on the Sabbath to make the *ṭevel* edible. In that case, the *ṭevel* is food and certainly may be moved on the Sabbath.

96 This refers to the next Mishnah, or to the declaration implied by R. Isaac ben Eleazar, that a person may say on Friday that a certain part of food shall become heave or heave of the tithe on the Sabbath without actually separating heave and profane food on Friday.

97 The part destined to be heave has to be kept in mind all the time while the rest is consumed.

(fol. 26a) **משנה ו-ז**: הָיוּ לוֹ תְּאֵינִים שֶׁל טֶבֶל בְּתוֹךְ בֵּיתוֹ וְהוּא בְּבֵית הַמִּדְרָשׁ אוֹ בַשָּׂדֶה אוֹמֵר שְׁנֵי תְאֵינִים שֶׁאֲנִי עָתִיד לְהַפְרִישׁ הֲרֵי הֵן תְּרוּמָה וַעֲשָׂרָה מַעֲשֵׂר וְתִשְׁעָה מַעֲשֵׂר שֵׁנִי. הָיוּ דְמַאי אוֹמֵר מַה שֶׁאֲנִי עָתִיד לְהַפְרִישׁ לְמָחָר הֲרֵי הוּא מַעֲשֵׂר וּשְׁאָר מַעֲשֵׂר סָמוּךְ לוֹ. זֶה שֶׁעָשִׂיתִי מַעֲשֵׂר עָשׂוּי תְּרוּמַת מַעֲשֵׂר עָלָיו וּמַעֲשֵׂר שֵׁנִי בִּצְפוֹנוֹ אוֹ בִדְרוֹמוֹ וּמְחוּלָּל עַל הַמָּעוֹת.

Mishnah 6-7: If somebody had *ṭevel* figs in his house but was in the House of Study or on the field[98], he says: Two figs that I shall separate in the future shall be heave, ten tithe, and nine heave of the tithe. If they were *demay*, he says: That which I shall separate in the future shall be tithe tomorrow, the rest of tithe near to it. That which I made tithe shall be heave of the tithe for all, and the Second Tithe shall be to the North (or to the South) and be redeemed by coins[99].

98 On Friday afternoon.

99 The *demay* declaration is identical with that of Mishnah 1 and all the rules explained there apply here also.

משנה ח: הָיוּ לְפָנָיו שְׁתֵּי כַלְכָּלוֹת שֶׁל טֶבֶל וְאָמַר מַעְשְׂרוֹת שֶׁל זוֹ בְּזוֹ וְשֶׁל זוֹ בְזוֹ הָרִאשׁוֹנָה מְעוּשֶּׂרֶת. מַעְשְׂרוֹתֵיהֶם מַעְשְׂרוֹת כַּלְכָּלָה בַּחֲבֵירָתָהּ קָרָא לָהּ שֵׁם.

Mishnah 8: If he had before him two baskets of *ṭevel* and he said, the tithes of one are in the other and those of the other in the one, the first one is tithed[100]; (if he said) their tithes are tithes of each basket in the other one, he gave it a name[101].

100 At the moment when he said that the tithes of the first basket are in the second one, the first basket was in order and is fully profane food. Hence, when he comes to tithe the second basket, he cannot use the first one

since profane food never can become tithe. Hence, what he says of the first basket is valid; what he says about the second basket is invalid, it is as if he never said it. He is in trouble with the second basket since he must separate the Second Tithe before he tithes the second basket, which is forbidden. In addition, Second Tithe must be given from tithed produce; hence the tithe of the second basket has to include the produce taken for Second Tithe from that basket. How to compute the amount of tithe to be taken for the first basket is discussed in the Halakhah.

101 In this case, everything is simultaneous. Hence, the designations of tithes are valid and he must separate the tithe of the first basket from the second, those of the second basket from the first, and he may not change his mind.

Most Mishnah codices (including the Rome ms. of the Yerushalmi but excluding the quote of the Mishnah in Babli *Temurah* 25b) have a longer text of the Mishnah which, however, brings nothing new.

(fol. 26b) **הלכה ח**: וְתַנֵּי עֲלָהּ נוֹטֵל מִן הַשְּׁנִייָה שְׁתֵּי תְאֵינִים וּשְׁנֵי עִישּׂוּרִין וְעִישּׂוּר שֶׁל עִישּׂוּר. שְׁמוּאֵל אָמַר לָא מָצֵי תַנֵּיתָהּ. אִין יְסַב חָדָא לְעֶשֶׂר. צָרִיךְ מֵיתַב חָדָא לְמֵאָה. אִין יְסַב חָדָא לְמֵאָה. צָרִיךְ מֵיתַב חָדָא לְאֶלֶף. אִין יְסַב חָדָא לְאֶלֶף. צָרִיךְ מֵיתַב חָדָא לַעֲשָׂרָה אֲלָפִין.

Halakhah 8[102]: We have stated for this[103]: "He takes from the second one two figs and two tenths and a tenth of a tenth[104]." Samuel says, you cannot state that; when he takes one in ten he has to take one in a hundred, when he takes one in a hundred he has to take one in a thousand, when he takes one in a thousand he has to take one in ten thousand.

102 Halakhah 6 in the Venice print.

103 Tosephta, *Demay* 8:15-16 has a similar wording but cannot possibly be the basis of the quote here and either represents a different tradition from that of the Yerushalmi or is hopelessly corrupt. The latter is likely since the second part of 8:16, discussed here in Halakhah 7, is corrupt, as noted by all commentators from R. M. Margalit to R.

S. Lieberman. The relevant part of the Tosephta reads: "If he had before him two baskets of *ṭevel*, in each one a hundred, of which heave was taken. 'The tithes of one are in the other one,' the first one is tithed. 'The tithes of one are in the other, and those of the other in the one' the first one is not tithed. He takes two figs and two tenths and a tenth of a tenth. 'Their tithes are tithes of each basket in the other one,' he gave it a name."

104 How does one tithe the first basket out of the second one? First he takes two figs (assuming 100 figs are there in all) for heave. Then he takes two tenths for the two tithes. But tithe should be taken from the produce itself; after tithe was taken, the profane remainder is nine times the tithe. Hence, ten figs of the second basket free only 90 figs of the first basket; $^1/_{10}$ from above is $^1/_9$ from below. The Tanna then requires one fig to be taken in addition to free the remaining 10 figs. Samuel protests, since $^1/_9 = 0.1111...$, if one includes tenths, the tithing will never end since one always has to add another tenth of the preceding amount.

אָמַר רִבִּי יוֹסֵה[105] בַּר חֲנִינָא עַל הָרִאשׁוֹנָה עוֹבֵר בַּעֲשֵׂה וְעַל הַשְּׁנִייָא בַּעֲשֵׂה וְלֹא תַעֲשֶׂה. עַל הָרִאשׁוֹנָה עוֹבֵר בַּעֲשֵׂה שֶׁקָּבַע שְׁנֵי שֵׁמוֹת כְּאַחַת וְעַל הַשְּׁנִייָא בַּעֲשֵׂה וְלֹא תַעֲשֶׂה שֶׁקָּבַע שְׁנֵי שֵׁמוֹת כְּאַחַת וְשֶׁהִקְדִּים שֵׁנִי שֶׁבָּרִאשׁוֹנָה לָרִאשׁוֹן שֶׁבַּשְּׁנִייָה.

Rebbi Yose bar Ḥanina said, for the first basket he transgresses a commandment, for the second a commandment and a prohibition. For the first basket he transgresses a commandment since he gave both names simultaneously[106], and for the second a commandment and a prohibition since he gave both names simultaneously and he put the Second Tithe of the first basket before the First Tithe of the second basket[107].

105 Reading of the Rome ms. The name is missing in the Venice print; it was correctly supplied from the Babli by R. S. Cirillo and R. E. Fulda.

106 Mishnah *Terumot* 3:7 states that the First Tithe is called "beginning" since it contains heave of the tithe, but the Second Tithe is never called "beginning." Hence, the beginning should precede the non-beginning.

107 In the parallel in Babli *Temurah* 4a/b, both R. Yose bar Ḥanina and R. Eleazar agree that declaring the Second Tithe before the First is a violation. R. Yose bar Ḥanina holds that transgressing a prohibition by words alone is not punishable in criminal law while R. Eleazar declares it punishable.

אָמַר רִבִּי לָעְזָר דְּרִבִּי מֵאִיר הִיא דְּרִבִּי מֵאִיר אָמַר אֵין אַתְּ תּוֹפֵס אֶלָּא רִאשׁוֹן רִאשׁוֹן בִּלְבַד. תַּמָּן תַּנֵּינָן הֲרֵי זוּ תְּמוּרַת עוֹלָה וּתְמוּרַת שְׁלָמִים הֲרֵי זוּ תְּמוּרַת עוֹלָה דִּבְרֵי רִבִּי מֵאִיר. אָמַר רִבִּי יוֹסֵי הֲוִינָן סָבְרִין מֵימַר מַה פְלִיגִין רִבִּי מֵאִיר וְרַבָּנִין לְאַחַר כְּדֵי (fol. 26c) דִיבּוּר אֲבָל בְּתוֹךְ כְּדֵי דִיבּוּר לֹא. מִן מַה דְאָמַר רִבִּי לָעְזָר רִבִּי מֵאִיר הִיא. הָדָא אָמְרָה אֲפִילוּ בְּתוֹךְ כְּדֵי דִיבּוּר אֵינוֹ חוֹזֵר בּוֹ.

Rebbi Eleazar said, this is from Rebbi Meïr since Rebbi Meïr says that you accept only the very first version. There, we have stated[108]: "This one shall be a substitute[109] for a burnt offering and for an offering of well-being, then it is a substitute for a burnt offering, the words of Rebbi Meïr." Rebbi Yose[110] said, we were of the opinion that Rebbi Meïr and the Sages disagree only after the time for speech[111], but not within the time for speech. Since Rebbi Eleazar said, the Mishnah is Rebbi Meïr's, it means that even within the time of speech he cannot retract.

108 Mishnah *Temurah* 5:4: "This one {animal} shall be a substitute for a burnt offering {another animal already dedicated} and a substitute for an offering of well-being, then it is a substitution for a burnt offering, the words of Rebbi Meïr. Rebbi Yose said, if this was his original intention then his words stand since it is impossible to pronounce two names at the same time. But if he changed his mind after he said, this one shall be a substitute for a burnt offering, and said, this one should be a substitute for an offering of well-being, then it is a substitute for a burnt offering." Our Mishnah cannot be R. Yose's since he would accept both the first and second versions if the original intention was the same. In the Babli, *Temurah* 25b/26a, the difference between R. Meïr and R. Yose is reduced to the stylistic nicety whether

there is a difference in meaning between "a substitute for a burnt offering and a substitute for a peace offering" and "a substitute for a burnt offering and an offering of well-being." It is difficult to square that approach with that of the Yerushalmi.

109 While substituting one sacrifice for another is forbidden (*Lev.* 27:9-10), nevertheless once done it is a valid dedication.

110 The Amora. In the Tosephta (*Temurah* 3:5) there are three opinions, that of R. Meïr (who takes only the first statement) and R. Yose (the Tanna, who asks to investigate what was in the mind of the speaker) as in the Mishnah, and that of the Sages who say that the animal should be put out to graze until it develops a bodily defect (and no longer could become a sacrifice) when it should be sold and the money received be split 50-50 to buy burnt and well-being offerings.

111 The measure of "time of speech," the unit for a simple sentence, is defined in *Berakhot* 2:1, fol. 4b (Notes 50-51).

דִּי מַתְנִיתָא מַעְשְׂרוֹתֵיהֶן מַעְשְׂרוֹת כַּלְכָּלָה בַּחֲבֵירָתָהּ קָרָא שֵׁם מִפְּנֵי שֶׁקָּבַע שְׁנֵי שֵׁמוֹת כְּאַחַת. זֶה אַחַר זֶה אֵין אַתְּ תּוֹפֵשׂ אֶלָּא רִאשׁוֹן רִאשׁוֹן בִּלְבַד. אָמַר רִבִּי אָבוּנָא מוֹדִין חֲכָמִים לְרִבִּי מֵאִיר בְּאוֹמֵר תְּרוּמָה זוּ תַּחַת שֵׁנִי חַיָּיב. בְּהֵמָה זוּ תַּחַת זְבָחִים שְׁנֵי חַיָּיב מִפְּנֵי שֶׁקָּבַע בֿ שֵׁמוֹת כְּאַחַת הָא זֶה אַחַר זֶה אֵין אַתְּ תּוֹפֵשׂ אֶלָּא רִאשׁוֹן רִאשׁוֹן בִּלְבַד. לֹא כֵן אָמַר רִבִּי שְׁמוּאֵל בַּר רַב יִצְחָק בְּשֵׁם רַב הוּנָא אָמַר זוּ תְּמוּרַת עוֹלָה חוֹזֵר בּוֹ אֲפִילוּ בְּתוֹךְ כְּדֵי דִיבּוּר. כָּאן בְּמִתְכַּוֵּן לִפְחוֹת. כָּאן בְּמִתְכַּוֵּן לְהוֹסִיף. אָמַר הֲרֵי זוּ תְּרוּמָה אֲפִילוּ בְּתוֹךְ כְּדֵי דִיבּוּר אֵינוֹ חוֹזֵר בּוֹ. אָדָם נִשְׁאַל עַל הֶקְדֵּשׁוֹ וְאֵין אָדָם נִשְׁאַל עַל תְּרוּמָתוֹ.

This is the Mishnah: "Their tithes are tithes for each basket in the other one, he gave it a name," because he declared both names at the same time. One after the other you accept only the very first version. Rebbi Abuna[112] said, the Sages agree with Rebbi Meïr about him who says "this heave substitutes for Second"[113] (that he is guilty). "This animal instead of well-being offerings," he is obligated for two since he declared two names[114] at the same time; hence, one after the other you accept only the very first version. Not so, said Rebbi Samuel bar Rav Isaac who said in the name of Rav Huna: "This one shall be a substitute for a burnt offering," he may retract that within the time for speech. That is, if he wants to retract[115], there if he wants to add. If one said, "this is heave," even within the time of speech he cannot retract. A person can be asked about his dedication[116] but nobody can be asked about his heave.

112 Usually called Rebbi Abun.

113 Since heave cannot become tithe; if he first declares it to be heave and then tithe, the second declaration is void. The words in parenthesis seem to be a scribal error induced by the next clause.

114 By using a plural. An unspecified plural always means two, cf. *Peah*, Chapter 3, Note 78.

115 Rav Huna does not refer to our case but to a person making a substitution and retracting it. In our case, the speaker makes a substitution and then adds to it; he compounds his sin, and the rule of "time for speech" does not apply.

116 All dedications of sacrifices are vows, which are subject to annullment by a court if the circumstances change in which the vow was made. Hence, there is reason to allow a time of reflection. Heave is holy by declaration, not by vow, and no retraction is possible.

[117]כֵּיצַד הוּא עוֹשֶׂה נוֹטֵל עֶשְׂרִים תְּאֵינִים מֵאֵי זוֹ מֵהֶן שֶׁיִּרְצֶה. וְכָל עֶשֶׂר דְּיִסַּב אִית בְּהוֹן תְּרוּמַת מַעֲשֵׂר. עַד כְּדוֹן בְּשָׁווֹת. הָיָה בְזוֹ מֵאָה וּבְזוֹ מָאתַיִם אִם לְשֵׁם מֵאָה נוֹטֵל אַחַת עֶשְׂרֵה. אִם לְשֵׁם מָאתַיִם הוּא נוֹטֵל ששים[118] תְּאֵינִים. בְּזוֹ מֵאָה וּבְזוֹ אֶלֶף אִם לְשֵׁם מֵאָה נוֹטֵל חֲמֵשׁ עֶשְׂרֵה. אִם לְשֵׁם אֶלֶף הוּא נוֹטֵל אֲפִילוּ הוּא נוֹטֵל אֶת כּוּלָּהּ אֵינוֹ מַשְׁלִים.

How does one act[119]? "One takes 20 figs from any basket one chooses[120]." And in any 10 one takes there is one of heave of the tithe[121]. That is, if they were equal. "If in one basket there were 100 and in the other 200, if he takes for the one with a hundred, he takes 11[122]. If for the one with 200 he takes 30[123]. "If in one basket there were 100 and in the other 1000, if he takes for the one with a hundred, he takes 15[124]. If for the one with a thousand, even if he takes the entire basket he does not complete taking."

117 Here starts Halakhah 7 in the Venice print.

118 This is the reading of the Yerushalmi and Tosephta manuscripts (*Demay* 8:16), but it obviously should read שְׁלֹשִׁים.

119 This refers to the last part of Mishnah 8, if he has two baskets and says, "their tithes are tithes of each basket in the other one; he gave it a name." The parallel is in Tosephta *Demay* 8:16, in badly garbled form: "Their tithes are tithes of each basket in the other one, he gave it a name. One takes 20 figs from the one he chooses. In one 100, in one 200, if he takes from the small one, he takes 11, if from the large one, he takes it all and it is not enough. In one 100, in the other 1000, if he takes from the small one he takes 16, if he takes from the large one he takes all of 60. In other cases, by this computation." In the computation, the second number in either case was switched.

120 Since the name of tithe was given for both simultaneously, the tithes have to be taken together. If one took tithes for one of the baskets alone, then the rest of the baskets would be profane and could no longer be used to tithe anything.

121 In all these computations of the preceding Halakhah and the current one, one separates all the tithes but in case of *demay* only heave of the tithe has to be given away; the Second Tithe is redeemed by a coin. In the current *baraita*, only First Tithe is considered.

122 If he takes the tithe of the smaller basket out of the larger basket, he has to take 11 since there remain 100 profane and not 90 as there would be if he tithed the basket for itself. (To be mathematically exact, he should take 11.1111. . . figs, but if at all possible, tithing other than whole fruits is avoided.)

123 In this case, the smaller basket is treated as appendix of the larger one, and the two are tithed together.

124 This is incomprehensible (as is the explanation of R. Moses Margalit.) R. Eliahu Fulda, R. Eliahu Wilna and R. S. Lieberman emend and read 11 instead of 15, as in the previous sentence.

The last case is again clear; he would need 110.

מִי שֶׁיֵּשׁ לוֹ כַלְכָּלָה וְהוּא מְבַקֵּשׁ לְעַשְּׂרָהּ נוֹטֵל שְׁנֵי תִישׁוּעִין וְתִישׁוּעַ שֶׁל תִישׁוּעַ שֶׁהֵן עֶשֶׂר מַעֲשֵׂר וְתֵשַׁע מַעֲשֵׂר שֵׁנִי. וְיֹאמַר תְּשַׁע עֶשְׂרֵה. אָמַר רִבִּי זְעִירָא דִּבְרֵי חֲכָמִים וְחִידוֹתָם. הָרוֹצֶה לְהַכְנִיס מֵאָה תְאֵינִים מְתוּקָּנוֹת לְתוֹךְ בֵּיתוֹ הֲרֵי זֶה נוֹטֵל עַל כָּל־תְּאֵינָה וּתְאֵינָה שְׁנֵי תִישׁוּעִין וְתִישׁוּעַ שֶׁל תִישׁוּעַ שֶׁהֵן עֶשְׂרִים וְשָׁלֹשׁ תְּאֵינִים אַרְבָּעָה אָמַר תִּישׁוּעַ שֶׁל תִישׁוּעַ.

"[125]If someone has a basket and wants to tithe it, he takes two ninths and a ninth of a ninth, corresponding to ten tithe and nine Second Tithe[126]." Why does he not say 19? Rebbi Zeïra said, the words of the Sages and their riddles. He who wants to bring a hundred figs in order into his house takes for ever single fig two ninths and a ninth of a ninth, 23 figs in all, four called ninth of a ninth[127].

125 The text is very close to Tosephta *Demay* 8:17. In all these cases, it is supposed that heave was already taken and only tithe with its heave has to be taken.

126 Since $^2/_9 + {}^1/_{81} = {}^{19}/_{81}$, one takes 19 figs for any 81 remaining. For all other numbers of figs, one has to multiply by this ratio.

127 By the preceding computation, for a remainder of 100 one has to take $19\times100\div81 = 23.4568$ figs. Hence, the interpretation of the final statement must be "23 whole figs, four tenths, and $^4/_{81} = 23.4494$" The word אמר was emended by all commentators but the text is confirmed by the arithmetic.

(fol. 26a) **משנה ט**: מֵאָה טֶבֶל מֵאָה חוּלִין נוֹטֵל מֵאָה וְאַחַת. מֵאָה טֶבֶל מֵאָה מַעֲשֵׂר נוֹטֵל מֵאָה וְאַחַת. מֵאָה חוּלִין מְתוּקָּנִין מֵאָה מַעֲשֵׂר נוֹטֵל מֵאָה וָעֶשֶׂר.

Mishnah 9: A hundred *ṭevel* in a hundred profane, he removes 101[128]. A hundred *ṭevel* in a hundred tithe, he removes 101[129]. A hundred profane fully in order and a hundred tithe, he removes 110[130].

128 The basis of these computations is Mishnah *Ḥallah* 3:9, where it is stated that if tithed and untithed produce are mixed together, it is preferable to tithe the untithed part from other produce, but if that proves impossible the whole turns into titheable produce as far as heaves are concerned, but not for other tithes. Since we are dealing with *demay*, it is always assumed that the first heave was taken and the only problem is heave of the tithe. Hence, in our case, one has to remove the 100 as equivalent of the *ṭevel* to be tithed, and, since the profane returns to the status of untithed as far as heave of the tithe is concerned, another 1% for heave of the tithe.

129 The tithe here is First Tithe, of which heave of the tithe has been taken. First Tithe of which heave has been taken is fully profane in the hands of the Levite. Hence, the rules are the same as for profane produce.

130 Obviously, the tithe here did not have its heave removed, otherwise it would be profane. Hence, the status of the profane now equals that of tithe and heave of the tithe must also be removed from the profane. It turns out that he removes 100 for tithe and another 10 for heave of the tithe, so that the entire heave of the tithe will be 20.

In this Mishnah, "profane" means produce tithed according to the rules of *demay*, and "profane fully in order" is produce of which it is known that both tithes were actually removed according to the rules of certain produce.

(fol. 26c) **הלכה ט**: רִבִּי שִׁמְעוֹן בֶּן לָקִישׁ אָמַר צָרִיךְ לְהַתְנוֹת וְלוֹמַר אִם טֶבֶל עָלָה בְיָדִי הוּא מַעֲשֵׂר. וְאִם מַעֲשֵׂר עָלָה בְיָדִי הֲרֵי הוּא עָשׂוּי תְּרוּמַת מַעֲשֵׂר. אָמַר רִבִּי יוֹנָה צָרִיךְ לִכְפּוֹל תְּנָייו וְלוֹמַר וְאִם לָאו לֹא עָשִׂיתִי כְלוּם. רִבִּי יוֹחָנָן אָמַר אֵינוֹ צָרִיךְ לִכְפּוֹל תְּנָייו. דֵּין כְּדַעְתֵּיהּ וְדֵין כְּדַעְתֵּיהּ. וְאִיתְפַּלְּגוֹן שְׁנֵי כְרָיִים וְאֶחָד מֵהֶן. רִבִּי יוֹחָנָן אָמַר קִדְּשׁוּ מְדוּמָעִין וְרִבִּי שִׁמְעוֹן בֶּן לָקִישׁ אָמַר לֹא קִדְּשׁוּ.

Halakhah 9[131]: Rebbi Simeon ben Laqish said, one has to specify a stipulation and say: If *ṭevel* is in my hands, it shall be tithe, but if tithe is in my hands, it shall be heave of the tithe[132]. Rebbi Jonah said, one has to add the converse stipulation and say, otherwise I did not do anything[133].

Rebbi Johanan said, one does not have to add the converse stipulation[134]. Either one of them follows his own opinion, since they disagreed[135]: Two heaps of grain, in one of them. Rebbi Johanan said, they are both forbidden as *dema'*, but Rebbi Simeon ben Laqish said, they are not forbidden.

131 In the Venice print, Halakhah 8.

132 This refers to the case where *ṭevel* and tithe were mixed together and one takes 101 parts for the *ṭevel* of which the one part in excess is to be addititional heave of the tithe. Rebbi Simeon ben Laqish states that heave can only be taken if it is specified from where it is to be taken. In our case, heave of the tithe can only be taken if the produce was first designated to be tithe. Hence, it is necessary to stipulate that it should be designated tithe if part of the grain originated from what was *ṭevel*.

133 R. Jonah's remark is a technicality. Since the rules of stipulations in Jewish law are derived from the stipulation Moses made with the tribes of Gad and Reuben (*Num.* 32:29-30) in which it was spelled out first what would happen if the conditions were met and second what would happen if they were not, any stipulation in Jewish law is valid only if it is formulated both in the positive and the negative sense. So R. Jonah simply means that the stipulation has to be legally valid.

134 One does not need a stipulation at all; a simple declaration is sufficient.

135 In *Terumot*, Chap. 3. The obligation of heave starts when grain, after threshing, is formed into heaps or put into a silo. If somebody has two heaps and he says, the heave of both heaps should be in one of them, without specifying in which one, then R. Johanan is of the opinion that both heaps are potentially profane mixed with heave, and both of them fall under the strict rules of *dema'* until heave is taken. But R. Simeon ben Laqish holds that heave can only be taken from a designated spot; hence, the declaration is invalid and nothing has changed. It follows that, in our case, R. Simeon ben Laqish must require a declaration which fixes the exact part from which heave of the tithe may be taken, but R. Johanan holds that any produce that is potentially heave may be turned into heave by simple declaration.

אָמַר רִבִּי מָנָא חוֹלְקִין עַל רִבִּי לָעְזָר בֶּן עֲרָךְ דְּתַנֵּי מַעֲשֵׂר טֶבֶל שֶׁנִּתְעָרֵב בְּחוּלִין אִם יֵשׁ לוֹ פַּרְנָסָה מִמָּקוֹם אַחֵר מוֹצִיאוֹ לְפִי חֶשְׁבּוֹן. וְאִם לָאו רִבִּי לָעְזָר בֶּן עֲרָךְ אוֹמֵר יִקְרָא שֵׁם לִתְרוּמַת מַעֲשֵׂר שֶׁבּוֹ וְיַעֲלֶם בְּאֶחָד וּמֵאָה. אָמַר רִבִּי בָּא בַּר מָמָל תִּיפְתָּר בִּדְבָרִים שֶׁאֵין לָהֶן עֲלִיָּה. רִבִּי הִלֵּל בֶּן פָּזִי בְּעֵי וְיִפְצַע. אָמַר רִבִּי יוֹנָה מוּתָּר לְפַצֵּעַ. לֹא כֵן תְּנִינָן נִתְפַּצְּעוּ הָאֱגוֹזִים בְּשֶׁעָבַר. הָא בִתְחִילָּה לֹא.

Rebbi Mana said, they differ with Rebbi Eleazar ben Arakh[136]. As he stated[137]: "*Ṭevel* mixed with profane produce, if it can be provided from another place, one takes it out in proportion. Otherwise, Rebbi Eleazar ben Arakh says, he gives a name to the heave of the tithe and takes it out by 101." Rebbi Abba bar Mamal said, explain it with kinds one cannot take out[138]. Rebbi Hillel ben Pazi[139] asked: Why can he not crack them? Rebbi Jonah said, is one permitted to crack them[140]? Did we not state: "If the nuts were cracked," in the past. That means, not to start out with[141].

136 One of the foremost students of Rabban Johanan ben Zakkai, whose influence on the development of the Mishnah is minimal since after the fall of Jerusalem he did not go to Jabneh but to Emmaus in the foothills of the Judean mountains. The problem here does not come from the position of R. Eleazar but from the *baraita* in which he is mentioned.

137 Tosephta *Terumot* 5:15: "*Ṭevel* mixed with profane produce makes it forbidden even in the tiniest amounts. If it can be provided from another place, one takes it out in proportion. Otherwise, Rebbi Eliezer and Rebbi Eleazar ben Arakh say, he gives a name to the heave of the tithe and takes it out by 101; the same holds if it falls into tithe." The *baraita* in the Yerushalmi expresses the same but from another source. The assertion in the Tosephta that one always tithes in proportion contradicts the Mishnah since no penalty is incurred in form of heave of the tithe of the profane produce, as in the Mishnah.

138 Special kinds of nuts and pomegranates and a few other kinds, enumerated in Mishnah *Orlah* 3:7; they are always sold by the piece and cannot become absorbed by anything

into which they fall. Hence, no substitute can be taken out from any other produce and R. Eleazar ben Arakh himself precribes for them the remedy explained in the Mishnah.

139 A Galilean Amora of the fourth generation, usually quoted in discussions with R. Jonah and R. Yose. His son, R. Simeon ben R. Hillel ben Pazi, is quoted once in the Talmud.

140 Mishnah *Orlah* 3:8: If the nuts were cracked, or the pomegranates split, . . . , they may be taken out (like any other produce.)" In reference to tithes, the same is stated in Tosephta *Terumot* 5:10.

141 If nuts are forbidden because of heave nuts fallen among them, one may not shell all the nuts to reduce them to regular produce.

(fol. 26a) **משנה י**: מֵאָה טֶבֶל וְתִשְׁעִים מַעֲשֵׂר תִּשְׁעִים טֶבֶל וּשְׁמוֹנִים מַעֲשֵׂר לֹא הִפְסִיד כְּלוּם. זֶה הַכְּלָל כָּל־זְמַן שֶׁהַטֶּבֶל מְרוּבֶּה לֹא הִפְסִיד כְּלוּם.

Mishnah 10: A hundred *ṭevel* and ninety tithe, ninety *ṭevel* and eighty tithe, he did not lose anything. That is the rule: Anytime that *ṭevel* is more, he did not lose anything[142].

142 Maimonides explains that the general rule of taking out a replacement for heave from any produce into which it fell needs a minimum of 101 to be taken out. Since here the tithe is less than the *ṭevel*, an application of that rule would make the tithe forever *dema'*.

(fol. 16c) [143]**הלכה י**: אָמַר רִבִּי יוֹנָה כֵּינִי מַתְנִיתָא כָּל־זְמַן שֶׁהַטֶּבֶל מְרוּבֶּה עַל הַמַּעֲשֵׂר מַעֲשֵׂר לֹא הִפְסִיד כְּלוּם.

Halakhah 10: Rebbi Jonah said, so is the Mishnah: Anytime that *ṭevel* is more than the tithe, tithe does not lose anything[144].

143 Halakhah 9 in the Venice print.

144 In contrast to the preceding Mishnah, the rule given here applies only to tithe, not to profane produce.

R. Simson reads: "Whenever the *ṭevel* exceeds the tithe by at least 10, one does not lose anything." Maimonides and R. Abraham ben David clearly read the Yerushalmi as given in the text.

רִבִּי לְוִינְטִי בְּשֵׁם רִבִּי יוֹנָה כָּל־טֶבֶל דַּאֲנָן קַייָמִין הָכָא טֶבֶל לְרִאשׁוֹן וְלַשֵּׁנִי.

Rebbi Levinti[145] in the name of Rebbi Jonah: Any *ṭevel* mentioned here is *ṭevel* for first and second tithes[146].

145 All that is known about him is that he was a fifth generation Amora, student of R. Jonah.

146 All *ṭevel* mentioned in the entire chapter refers to produce of which heave was taken and the question is only about tithes and heave of the tithe.

רִבִּי אַבָּהוּ אָמַר אִיתְפַּלְּגוּן רִבִּי וְרִבִּי דּוֹסְתַּי בֵּי רִבִּי יַנַּאי. חַד אָמַר עוֹשֶׂה אוֹתוֹ שֵׁנִי לְמָקוֹם אַחֵר. וְחָרָנָא אָמַר עוֹשֶׂה כּוּלּוֹ שֵׁנִי לְמָקוֹם אַחֵר וּמַפְרִישׁ עָלָיו רִאשׁוֹן לְמָקוֹם אַחֵר. מַה נָן קַייָמִין מֵאָה טֶבֶל וְתִשְׁעִים מַעֲשֵׂר נוֹטֵל תִּשְׁעִים וּשְׁתַּיִם חָסֵר אִישּׂוּר אֶחָד. מֵאָה טֶבֶל וּשְׁמוֹנִים מַעֲשֵׂר נוֹטֵל שְׁמוֹנִים וְשָׁלֹשׁ חָסֵר שְׁנֵי עֶשְׂרוֹנִים. מִיכָּן וְהֵילָךְ לְפִי חֶשְׁבּוֹן.

Rebbi Abbahu said, Rebbi and Rebbi Dositheos the son of Rebbi Yannai[147] disagree. One says, he takes the second tithe from another place, but the other one says, he makes all of it second tithe and takes the first tithe from another place[148]. What are we talking about? "A hundred *ṭevel* and ninety tithe, he takes 92 minus one tenth[149]. A hundred *ṭevel* and eighty tithe, he takes 83 minus two tenths.[150] Other quantities proportionally."

147 A Tanna of the fifth generation, probably a student of R. Meïr, chiefly prominent as a preacher. It is possible that his father was the Tanna quoted in *Avot* 4:15.

148 This cannot refer to the Mishnah, since there the tithe is reconstituted as it was before. It must refer to the *baraita* quoted in the following sentences, in which the Tanna disagrees with the Tanna of the Mishnah and applies the rule of

Mishnah 9 also to our case. If tithe returns to the state of untithed, then Second Tithe also is due, but it cannot be taken out here without disturbing the entire computation. Hence, it must be taken, and then redeemed, from other sources.

149 If he takes 90 out of the container, it might be that all he takes was originally *ṭevel*. From this, he can legally only take 9 for heave of the tithe. But he has to take in all 10.9 by the rules of the previous Mishnah which the Tanna here also follows in case tithe is less than *ṭevel*. Hence, he has to take another 2-0.1 and then give 10.9 as heave of the tithe. If *ṭevel* is 100 and tithe 80, he has to take 8 + 2.8 as heave of the tithe in order to put tithe and *ṭevel* in order. In general, for 100 *ṭevel* and *n* tithe, he takes n + (1000 - 9n)/100. (Explanation by R. Z. Frankel, the only rational explanation of this paragraph.)

150 A similar text appears in Tosephta *Demay* 5:17-18, which certainly is garbled but might in addition represent a Babylonian tradition opposed to that of the Yerushalmi: "100 tithe and 80 *ṭevel*, he takes 91.9. 100 tithe and 90 *ṭevel*, he takes 92.8. Other quantities proportionally."

(fol. 26a) **משנה יא**: מִי שֶׁהָיוּ לוֹ עֶשָׂרָה שׁוּרוֹת שֶׁל עֶשֶׂר כַּדֵּי יַיִן וְאָמַר שׁוּרָה הַחִיצוֹנָה אַחַת מַעֲשֵׂר וְאֵינוֹ יוֹדֵעַ אֵיזוֹ הִיא נוֹטֵל שְׁתֵּי חָבִיּוֹת לוֹכְסוֹן חֲצִי שׁוּרָה הַחִיצוֹנָה אַחַת מַעֲשֵׂר וְאֵינוֹ יוֹדֵעַ אֵיזוֹ הִיא נוֹטֵל אַרְבַּע חָבִיּוֹת מֵאַרְבַּע זָוִיּוֹת שׁוּרָה אַחַת מַעֲשֵׂר וְאֵינוֹ יוֹדֵעַ אֵיזוֹ הִיא נוֹטֵל שׁוּרָה אַחַת לוֹכְסוֹן. חֲצִי שׁוּרָה אַחַת מַעֲשֵׂר וְאֵינוֹ יוֹדֵעַ אֵיזוֹ הִיא נוֹטֵל שְׁתֵּי שׁוּרוֹת לוֹכְסוֹן. חָבִית אַחַת מַעֲשֵׂר וְאֵינוֹ יוֹדֵעַ אֵיזוֹ הִיא נוֹטֵל מִכָּל חָבִית וְחָבִית.

Mishnah 11: If somebody had ten rows of ten wine jugs[151] each, and he said that one from an outer row was tithe but he does no longer know which one, he takes two diagonally[152] opposite amphoras[153]. One of half an outer row was tithe but he does no longer know which one, then he takes the four amphoras at the four corners[154]. One row was tithe but he does no longer know which one, then he takes one diagonal row[155]. Half a row was tithe but he does no longer know which one, then he takes from the two diagonal rows[156]. One amphora was tithe but he does no longer know which one, then he takes[157] from each amphora.

151 The Babli, *Baba Qama* 27a, notes that the Mishnah starts with "jugs" and continues with "amphoras," to indicate that Biblical כד corresponds to rabbinic חבית.

152 Greek λοξός, ή, όν "slanting, crosswise".

153 Let the rows be numbered by *i* = 1, 2, . . . ,10 and the amphoras in each row by *j* = 1, 2, . . . ,10. Then the position of each amphora is uniquely described by a couple (*i,j*) and the amphoras are filling a square. Also, let * denote any number from 1 to 10. The outer rows are (1,*), (10,*), (*,1), (*,10). Since the problem is not the tithe but the heave of the tithe, if one takes both amphoras (1,1) and (10,10) [or (1,10) and (10,1)] he will have taken one amphora from each boundary row and have valid heave of the tithe. From the last sentence of the Mishnah it becomes clear that in all cases, only one amphora has to be given as heave of the tithe. Hence, the interpretation here is that one takes half of each amphora chosen and pours into a new one, so that the full new amphora will be the heave of the tithe.

154 Since each semi-row ends at a corner, if he takes one quarter of any of the four at the corners, one of them will be the right one.

155 If he takes either (*i,i*) for *i* = 1, . . . , 10 or (10-*i*+1,*i*) for *i* = 1, . . . , 10 then he will have taken one amphora from each row counted in either direction. Here, he takes one tenth out of each amphora chosen.

156 The rows (*i,i*) and (10-*i*+1,*i*) for *i* = 1, . . . , 10. Then one amphora for each half-row starting at the border will have been taken. Here, one takes one twentieth of each amphora chosen.

157 He takes 1% of the volume of each amphora, then he gets the required amphora out of the 100 given and from each amphora some wine is in the new barrel.

(fol. 26c) **הלכה יא**:[158] וְיִטּוֹל שְׁתַּיִם. רִבִּי כֹהֵן בְּשֵׁם רַבָּנִין דְקֵיסָרִין בְּשֶׁהִפְרִישׁ חֲצָיִין מִמָּקוֹם אַחֵר.

Halakhah 11: Why does he not take two[159]? Rebbi Cohen in the name of the rabbis of Caesarea: When he separated half of the heave from another place.

158 In the Venice print, Halakhah 10.

159 This refers to the second sentence in the Mishnah, when he made half a row tithe on 50 of the 100 amphoras. Why can he not declare that the other half is also tithe for the remaining 50 amphoras and reduce this case to the preceding one where he has to take only from two diagonally opposed amphoras? The answer is that the remaining amphoras are already profane, not *ṭevel*, and the method proposed is impossible. (Explanation of R. Eliahu Fulda.)

תַּנֵּי הָיוּ לְפָנָיו שְׁתֵּי חָבִיּוֹת אַחַת שֶׁל מַעֲשֵׂר טֶבֶל טָהוֹר וְאַחַת שֶׁל מַעֲשֵׂר טֶבֶל טָמֵא הֲרֵי זֶה מֵבִיא שְׁנֵי לָגִינִין וְנוֹטֵל מִזּוּ כְּדֵי תְרוּמַת מַעֲשֵׂר מִשְּׁתֵּיהֶן וּמִזּוּ כְּדֵי תְרוּמַת מַעֲשֵׂר מִשְּׁתֵּיהֶן. וְחוֹזֵר וּמַגְבִּיהַּ אֶת הַלָּגִין וְאוֹמֵר. אִם זֶהוּ טָהוֹר הֲרֵי הוּא עֲשִׂיתִיו תְּרוּמַת מַעֲשֵׂר. וְאִם לָאו לֹא עָשִׂיתִי כְלוּם. וְחוֹזֵר וְעוֹשֶׂה כֵן בַּשֵּׁנִי וְטוֹבֵל וְשׁוֹתֶה דִּבְרֵי רִבִּי. רִבִּי לָעְזָר בֵּי רִבִּי שִׁמְעוֹן אוֹמֵר אֵינוֹ נוֹטֵל אֶלָּא בְסוֹף. מַה טַעֲמָא דְרִבִּי אֲנִי אוֹמֵר שֶׁמָּא שָׁתָה מַשְׁקִין טְמֵאִין תְּחִילָּה. וּמַה טַעֲמָא דְרִבִּי אֶלְעָזָר בַּר שִׁמְעוֹן אֲנִי אוֹמֵר שֶׁמָּא שָׁתָה מַשְׁקִין טְמֵאִין בְּסוֹף. הַכֹּל מוֹדִין בְּשׁוֹתֶה מַשְׁקִין טְמֵאִין שֶׁהוּא אָסוּר לוֹכַל אֲפִילוּ סָפֵק תְּרוּמָה. סָפֵק מַשְׁקִין כָּל־עַמָּא מוֹדֵיי שֶׁהוּא מוּתָּר לוֹכַל אֲפִילוּ תְרוּמָה וַדַּאי. אֶלָּא כָא אֲנָן קַיָּימִין כְּהָדָא מַתְנִיתָא. מַה טַעֲמָא דְרִבִּי אֶלְעָזָר בַּר שִׁמְעוֹן מֵאַחַר שֶׁעַל יְדֵי זֶה וְעַל יְדֵי זֶה נִתְבָּרְרָה הַטּוּמְאָה טָעוּן טְבִילָה. מַה טַעֲמָא דְרִבִּי שֶׁלֹּא יָבוֹא לִידֵי רְבִיעִית. לְמַה טַעֲמָא דְרִבִּי לָעְזָר בֵּי רִבִּי שִׁמְעוֹן בְּשׁוֹתֶה פָּחוֹת מֵרְבִיעִית. וְלֵית לֵיהּ לְרִבִּי לָעְזָר בֵּי רִבִּי שִׁמְעוֹן שֶׁלֹּא יָבוֹא לִידֵי רְבִיעִית. אָמַר רִבִּי יוֹסֵי בֶּרִבִּי בוּן אֵין לָךְ אֶלָּא כְהָדֵין פִּיתְרָא קַדְמָיָא. דְּרִבִּי חָשַׁשׁ שֶׁמָּא שָׁתָה מַשְׁקִין טְמֵאִין תְּחִילָּה. וְרִבִּי לָעְזָר בֵּי רִבִּי שִׁמְעוֹן חָשַׁשׁ שֶׁמָּא שָׁתָה מַשְׁקִין טְמֵאִין בְּסוֹף.

It was stated[160]: "If there were two amphoras before him, one of pure tithe which was *ṭevel* and one of impure tithe which was *ṭevel*[161], he brings two vessels and takes from each of them heave of the tithe for both of them. He then turns and lifts one vessel and says: If this one is pure, I am making it heave of the tithe; else I did not do anything. Then he turns, does the same for the second vessel, immerses himself and drinks, the words of Rebbi[162]. Rebbi Simeon ben Eleazar says, he takes it[163] only at the end." What is the reason of Rebbi? I say, maybe he started drinking the impure one first[1624]. And what is the reason of Rebbi Eleazar ben Rebbi Simeon? Maybe he drank the impure one at the end. Everybody agrees that he who drinks impure liquids may not even eat heave that is in doubt[165]. If the liquids were possibly impure, everybody agrees that he may eat what certainly is heave. But here we deal with another Mishnah[166]. What is the reason of Rebbi Eleazar ben Rebbi Simeon? Since according to both the impurity is certain, he needs immersion[167]. What is the reason of Rebbi? That he should not be led into drinking a *reviït*[168]. According to the reason of Rebbi Eleazar ben Rebbi Simeon, he drinks less than a *reviït*[169]. Is Rebbi Eleazar ben Rebbi Simeon not afraid that he would be led into drinking a *reviït*? Rebbi Yose ben Rebbi Abun said, the only explanation you have is our first one. Rebbi is afraid that he drank the impure liquid first and Rebbi Eleazar ben Rebbi Simeon is afraid that he drank the impure liquid at the end[170].

160 There is a similar Tosephta, *Demay* 5:22-23, which first explains how to take two pitchers and the declarations to make, as in the *baraita* here. But then there is no disagreement reported but it is stated that the Cohen who drinks must immerse himself not only before drinking but between the drinks and after them, combining the rules of Rebbi and R. Eleazar ben R. Simeon. That Tosephta explains the practical rule and not the background as does the *baraita* here. Nevertheless, the text of the Tosephta cannot stand as it is in manuscript and print: "The pitchers, one of impure *ṭevel* tithe, the other of pure *ṭevel* tithe. He drinks from one

and immerses himself, and drinks from the other and immerses himself, and drinks from both of them together, and needs an immersion at the end." All commentators of the Tosephta feel compelled to rearrange the Tosephta according to the Yerushalmi.

161 Only pure heave may be consumed; impure heave of oil may be used as fuel but impure heave of wine cannot be used at all. Hence, if the Cohen is the owner of the tithe, he wants to take heave so that he can drink everything.

162 Since no Cohen may eat or drink heave without first immersing himself, it is obvious that here the Cohen did immerse himself first. Hence, the immersion required by Rebbi is between the drinks from both vessels.

163 A scribal error for טובל "he immerses himself."

164 Then he has to purify himself again for the heave since the first pitcher was profane drink.

165 If somebody drinks impure fluids (in a minimum of a *reviït*, about 135 cm^3) then, by rabbinic decree (*Zavim* 5:12), his body becomes impure even if the impurity was only secondary. (Biblical impurity is transferred to a person only by original impurity.) If the impurity is certain, then by rabbinic decree he is impure even if it is in doubt whether the food is heave or not. But if the drink is only suspected of being impure there is no rabbinic decree and impurity is imparted only by original impurity. The discussion here assumes that all impurities discussed are rabbinic in character.

166 *Zavim* 5:12.

167 At the end, the contents of one of the vessels certainly was impure and made his body impure.

168 If he drinks less the immersion is not really necessary; it is a reminder not to make one's body impure by drinking a *reviït* of a questionable liquid.

169 In that case, no immersion at the end would be necessary. Hence, the argument is faulty because otherwise Rebbi and R. Eleazar would not quarrel, one speaking about a person drinking less than a *reviït*, the other about one who drinks more.

170 Hence, the practical rule is the one given in the Tosephta.

Indices

Index of Biographical Notes

Abba Cohen bar Dalaiah 164
Abba Shaul 18
Aquila 590

Bar Pedaiah 178

Cahana 461Ḥananiah ben Samuel 422
Ḥeipha 295
Hilfai 275
Hoshaiah bar Shammai 110

Menaḥem 311
Monobaz 22

Naḥum from Gimzo 343
Neḥemiah from Shiḥin 341

Rav Abba ben Rav Huna 492
Rav Ḥabiba 17
(Rav) Huna bar Ḥiyya 33
Rebbi Abba bar Abba bar Mamal 325
Rebbi Abba ben Zemina 376
Rebbi Abba, father of R. Abba bar Mari 40
Rebbi Abbahu bar Naggara 218
Rebbi Abun bar Cahana 521
Rebbi Aḥa bar Ulla 571
Rebbi Alexander of Ẓedoqa 403
Rebbi Benaiah 21
Rebbi Benjamin ben Levi 4
Rebbi Dosa 21
Rebbi Dositheos ben Rebbi Yannai 634
Rebbi Eleazar ben Arakh 632
Rebbi Eleazar ben Jehudah from Bartota 511
Rebbi Eliezer ben Jacob 344
Rebbi Eliezer from the South 314
Rebbi from Maadiah 413
Rebbi Gamliel ben Ininia 16
Rebbi Gurin, Gurion 154
Rebbi Ḥama bar Bissa 340
Rebbi Ḥama, father of R. Oshaia 340
Rebbi Ḥanan (?) 79
Rebbi Ḥanin 569
Rebbi Hillel ben Pazi 633
Rebbi Ḥiyya from Kefar Teḥumin 39
Rebbi Hoshaia ben Shammai 110
Rebbi Isaac Aṭoshiyya 321
Rebbi Isaac ben Ḥaqolah 73
Rebbi Isaac ben Tevele 422
Rebbi Ismael ben Rebbi Joḥanan ben Beroqa 441
Rebbi Jacob bar Abun 130
Rebbi Jacob bar Aḥa bar Idi 395
Rebbi Jehudah ben Ḥagra 194
Rebbi Jehudah ben Ḥanina 16
Rebbi Jehudah the Great 246
Rebbi Jehudah the Prince 81
Rebbi Joḥanan bar Maria 24
Rebbi Joḥanan ben Nuri 311
Rebbi Joḥanan, son of R. Isaac bar Aḥa 199
Rebbi Joshua ben Bathyra 136
Rebbi Joshua ben Qabusai 472
Rebbi Judah ben Levi 543
Rebbi Levinṭi 634
Rebbi Neḥumai ben Rebbi Ḥiyya bar Abba 371

Rebbi Phineas ben Yaïr 377
Rebbi Redifah 184
Rebbi Samuel, son of R. Yose ben Abun 489
Rebbi Simeon bar Cahana 475
Rebbi Simeon bar Yaqim 266
Rebbi Simeon ben Jehudah 222
Rebbi Simeon ben Rebbi Abba 356
Rebbi Simeon ben Zachariah 413
Rebbi Simeon from Shezur 486
Rebbi Taḥlifa 191
Rebbi Taypha the Red 467
Rebbi Yeshebab 19
Rebbi Yose ben R. Jehudah 296
Rebbi Yose ben Rebbi Jehudah 359
Rebbi Yose of Kefar Dan 413
Rebbi Yose the Great 364
Rebbi Yudan ben R. Simeon 105
Rebbi Yudan, father of Rebbi Mattaniah 526
Rebbi Yudan, son of R. Simeon bar Ioḥai's daughter 35
Rebbi Zachariah, son-in law of Rebbi Levi 340

Samuel bar Abba 294
Samuel bar Shilat 321
Shila 301

Ulla ben Ismael 359

Zavdi ben Levi 603
Zeugos 408

Index of Biblical Quotations

Gen. 4:13 42
15:26 56
18:12,13 45
37:2 43
37:31 43
39:7 43
39:9 42
50:16,17 45

Ex. 15:2 18
20:12 31,34
21:17 32
21:34 461
22:5 261
23:8 337
23:11 219
23:15 11
23:19 220
32:21 42
34:7 57
34:21 11
Ex. 34:27 104

Lev. 11:37 66
19:3 31
19:9 62,66,84
19:10 159,228,251, 301
19:24 290
19:25 297
19:27 67
23:22 84,159,228
24:19 32
25:2 305
25:45 446

Num. 15:31 42
18:26 520,539

Deut. 5:16 36
6:13 31
14:22 461
Deut. 14:23 602
14:25 348
16:11 200
16:20 337
19:14 340
22:9 66
24:10 261
24:19 137,251,253, 254,255,222,223,226
24:20 251
24:21 67,251,300
30:19 25
32:34 226
32:47 41

Jos. 1:8 25
11:15 20

1Sam 2:9 58
17:5 226
23:11 48

1Sam. 24:5 50
26:14 50

2Sam. 2:14 49
3:12 49

1K. 1:14 46
18:13 48
18:22 49

2K. 18:4 410

Is. 3:10 23,52
3:11 52

Jer. 17:7 345,337

Ez. 33:18 54
33:27 543

Hos. 8:12 103

Joel 3:5 614,615,616

Obad. 9-10 53

Micah 3:11-12 564
Micah 7:18 57

Mal. 2:6 20
3:16 53

Ps. 12:4 42
12:5 44
34:15 39
45:9 54
50:16 44
50:20 44
50:22 44
54:1 48
57:6 43
57:9-10 48
62:13 57
66:12 53
85:12 22
103:17 24
105:17 43
107:34 278
132:7 137

Prov. 1:31 52
3:4 58
3:9 16,32,34
3:26 21
Prov. 3:35 58
4:23 36
5:6 35
6:22 41
13:21 58
16:11 43
21:14 340
21:21 38
22:28 218
23:10 218
24:26 156
30:17 36

Job 33:29 58

Ruth 3:3 335

Lament. 1:22 67

Eccl. 1:10 105
4:12 58

Dan. 6:15 53

Ezra 10:8 197

2Chr. 21:3 144

Index of Greek and Latin Words

ἀγορανόμος 405
ἄθυμος 612
ἀργύριον 324
ἄρχων 322,329
ἀτίμητος 41

βολβός 410
βουλευτής 47

δέλφιξ 589
διαθήκη 152
δισάκκιον 371
διφθέρα 104

Ζευγος 407
ζημία 22

ἰδιώτης 62
ἴρινον 392
ἰσάτις 571

καπηλεῖον 332

καυκαλίς 321
κέκρος 143
κέραμα 532
κεφαλωτός 414
κλινικός 413
κόλλιξ 594
κολλύριον 385
κολοκασία 73

λάγηνος 620
λαχανική 413
ληστής 108
λίτρα 277
λοξός 636
λοπάς 279,335

μάλαγμα 385
μηλοπέπων 414
μίνθη 414
μνᾶ 155
μονοπώλιον 526

ξένος 445

ὄγμος 172
ὄχλος 486

πατὴρ βουλῆς 27
περσικόν μῆλον 279
πρατήρ 438,526
πρόνοος 186
προσβολή 139
πρωτογαμία 484
πύλη 415

Ῥωμη 51

σημεῖον 400
σίφων 250
σιτώνης 436
σταφυλῖνος 414

Τέλαμων 408
τιμή 41,285,343
τύπος 523

ὑδρία 532

χαλκίς 321
χάραξ 402
χορδή 27

allium capitatum 418
annona 22,402
argentarius 339
argentum 339
assarius 309

campus 415
castellum 417

delator 49
delatura 49

fibula 499
foliatum 392
follis 41

lagena 620
libellaris 102

mulus 381
muries 384

nummus 436

olentia 384

parum 521

sitona 413

tabula 277

Index of Hebrew and Arabic Words

אגרו, איגרו 101
איפשר 306

בלשי 602
בקר 61

גזירה 369
גלגל 50
גפה 235

די 51

חצב 88

טופח 254

כדו 29
כן 12
כסל 22
כרם 279

נשא 59

סירה 50

עיר 507
עלל 68

פאר 68

צדקה, צדק 23
צמת 47

שחמתית 101
שיתין 359

اريس 215
اكثر 400
الدوم 353
اياس 359

ثمخ 326

جميز 304

حندقوقا 322
حوص 249

خسارة 442
خظب 88
خيل 88

دبس 279

رطب 72
سحم، سخم، شخم 101
سفساف 279

شمرة 362

صلي 285

علل 276

فرس 333
فرفخ 322
فسج 276
فورار 281

قفل، قفلة 322
قلقاس 73

كِدَّة 274

لوف 260

مرج 125
موش 309

وثيق 106

General Index

Acquisition 168,169,224
Afterwine 363
Airspace 566,567
Alienatio 139
Am Haärez̧ 349,366
Appearance 3
Artaban 40
Articles, Religious 18
Assarius, As 309
Avi-Yona, M. 349

Ben Ḥabib, R. Moses 169
Bet Kor 202
Bet Rova' 89
Bet Seah 89
Beth Shean 411
Binyan Ab 68
Biting 581

Caftor Waperaḥ 72,352,419,612,613
Calumny 50
Charity, Administrator 186
  Bowl 324
  Chest 324
  Rate of 17
Cirillo, S. 2,624
Covenant, Nehemiah's 188
Cubit 90

Dama ben Netinah 26
Damages 261
Decimals, infinite 624
Declaration, of Tithes 366
Dema' 388,486,487
Denar, Gold 28
Descendant of Noah 450
Divorce 185
  by Proxy 502
Dough, pure 510
Dowry 298
Dupondius 325

Epicurean 56
Epstein, J. N. 122,270,497,535,536
Eruv, of courtyards 393
  of domains 321
  for food 483
Etrog 320
Extension, legal 261

Fast, Great 282
Fifth 510,635
Find 181
First Born Animal 505,563,574
First Fruits 3,289,495
Fleischer, H. L. 129
Flower Pot 543
Fluids, impure 429
Fourth Year, Yield 288
Frankel, R. Z. 2,120,125,207,635
Fruit Juice 510
Fruit, Sabbatical 282
Fulda, R. Eliahu 2,120,580,591,624,628

Gift, unconditional 204
Gleanings 300
Goodwill 562
Grain, New 199
Greenfield, A. Y. 13
Grünkern 178
Gutturals 291

Hagahot Maimuniot 612
Hair 97
Handbreadth 95
Handle 580
Harvest Baskets 579
Ḥaver 349
Heave, Amounts 17
Hîn 442
Holiday Sacrifice 10

Impurity, by Drinking 639
  Degrees of 430
  Preparation for 431
Inheritance 584
Innkeeper's Wife 475
Iron Cattle 299
Israeli, R. S. 538

Ketubah 147,154,182
  of divorcee 569
Kikkar 165
King's Mountain 540,552
Klein, S. 420,423
Kohut, R. A. 129
Kor 314
Krauss, S. 129

Landowner, Gentile 187
Lease 550
Leper's Bird 10
Levy, J. 125
Lieberman, R. Saul 2,25,207,212, 222,223,256,290,389,392,398,409,418,428, 557,576,624,628
Loans, Availability 82
Log 136,319

Löw, I. 129,352

Maäser 4
Maḥzor Vitry 541
Maimonides 2,60,90,98,123,131, 132,133,149,161,162,171,197,201,203.222, 237,262,265,269,270,271,273,352,361,386, 426,463,488,492,503,517,529,547,562,584, 613
Manumission 185
Margalit, R. Moses 2,120,222,356, 580,628
Marriage 238
Marriage Gift 391
Matthew 547
Milgrom, J. 618
Mina 319
Minor 182
Monopoly 527
Mosaic, from Reḥov 408
Mother-in-Law 477
Mourner, strict 365

Nachmanides 599
Neubauer, A. 349
Nissū'īn 239

Orlah 127,571

Parents, Support of 37
Partnership, with Gentile 586
Peace, intercommunal 500
Plenipotentiary 550
Pliny 352,392
Plural, indeterminate 130
Poverty 165
Practice 474
Produce, Gentile 356
Proselyte 402,587
  Estate of 87
Prozbol 139
Putting in Care 574
Putting in Order 375

Qab 136
Qiddušīn 238,484
Qorbān 547

R. Abraham ben David 98,270,274, 464,488,495,502
R. David ben Zimra 118,209
R. Isaac Simponti 2,269
R. Simson of Sens 36,97,99,101,123,129, 162,211,222,269,270,286,370,389,398,496, 503,529
R. Solomon ben Adrat 598,599
Rabin, I. A. 221
Rashbam 106,141
Rashi 90,141,219,434,465,503
Real Estate 155
  Title 589
Rectangles 115
Red Heifer 10
Redemption 216,291
Rent 550
Restriction, legal 261,580
Retroactive 557,586

Sabbath Markers 99
  Moving Things 608,621
Sachs, M. 612
Sacrifice, simple 391
Samaritan Wine 468
Samaritans, Division of 544
Saracens 379
Seah 136,252
Second Job 612
Second Tithe, alienated 297
Seven Commandments 450
Sharecropper 215,550
Simultaneity 625
Sin, Forgivable 55
Sisera 412
Slaves 150
Sperber, D. 324,532
Spinholz 484
Stipulation, legal 631
Straying Wife 10

Sumac 65
Sycamores, of Jericho 304
Syria 293

Tax Collector 435
Temple Property 306
  Larceny of 618
Temple Staff 328
  Tax 587
  Wine and Oil 263
Terumah 4
Ṭevul Yom 581
Thanksgiving 295
Thief, of Opinions 498
Tithes, of Gentiles 293
  unprepared 277
  voluntary 473
Trader 402
Usha, Decree of 16

Vow of Abstention 484

Washing, of Hands 434
Water, purifying 472
Widow, childless 10
Will, Emergency 151,153
Wilna, R. Eliahu 628
Worker's Contract 182

Yalqûṭ Šim'ônî 21,270
Year, Jewish 199

Zacut, A. 199
Zohar 106

www.ingramcontent.com/pod-product-compliance
Lightning Source LLC
Chambersburg PA
CBHW021412300426
44114CB00010B/467